AF605867

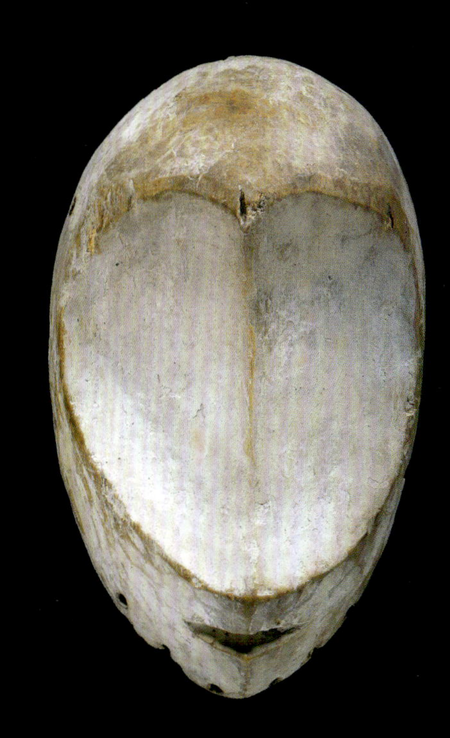

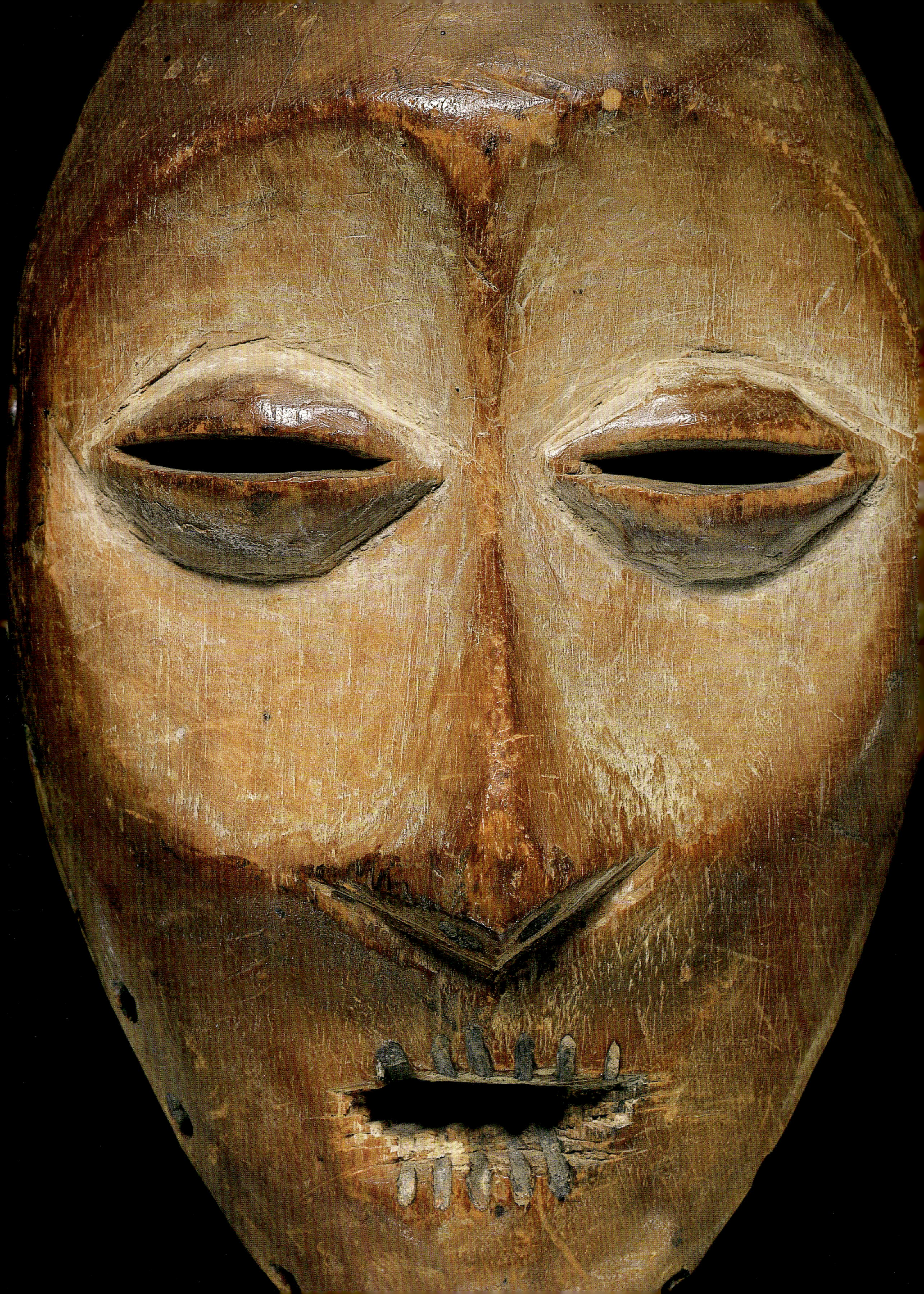

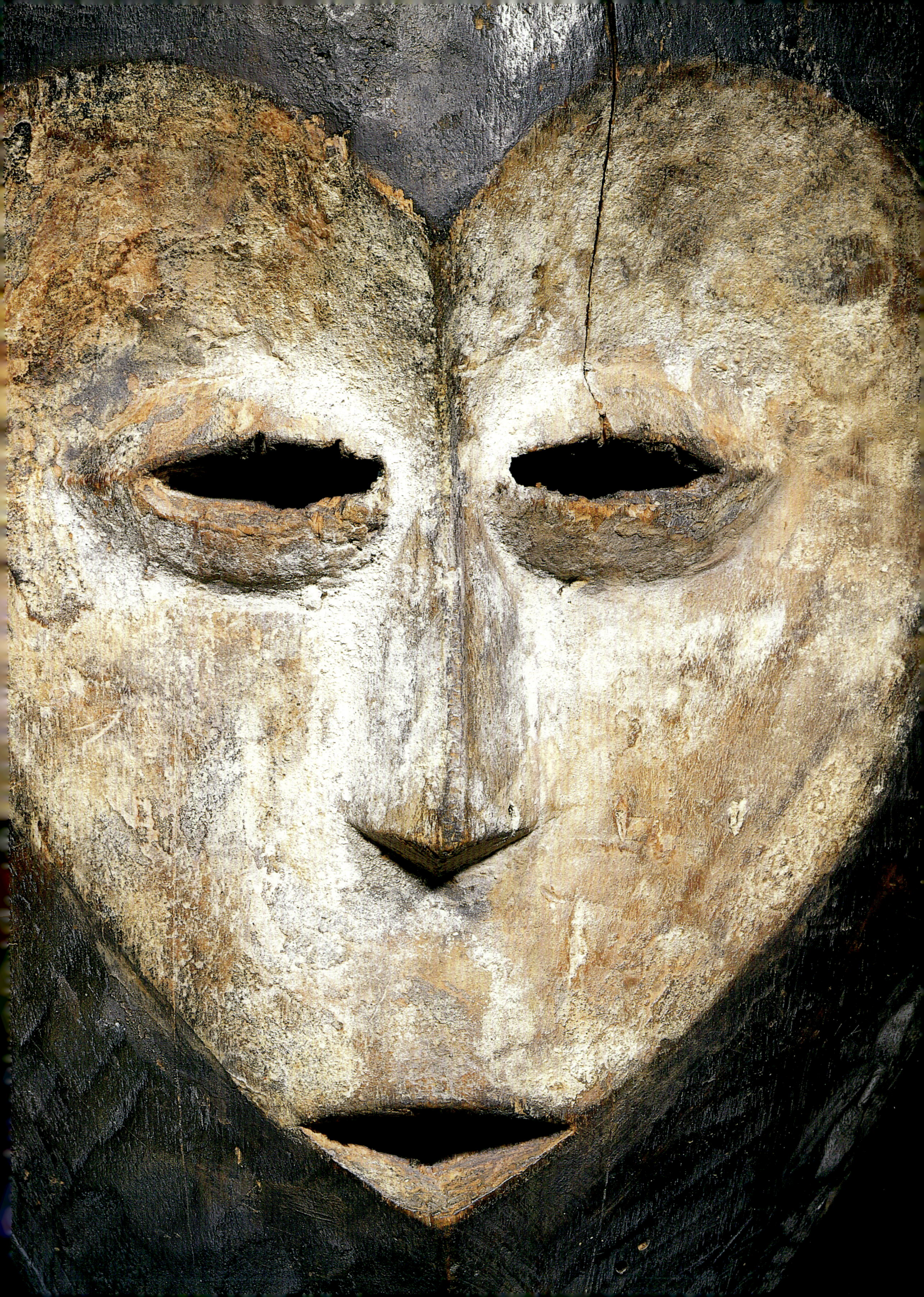

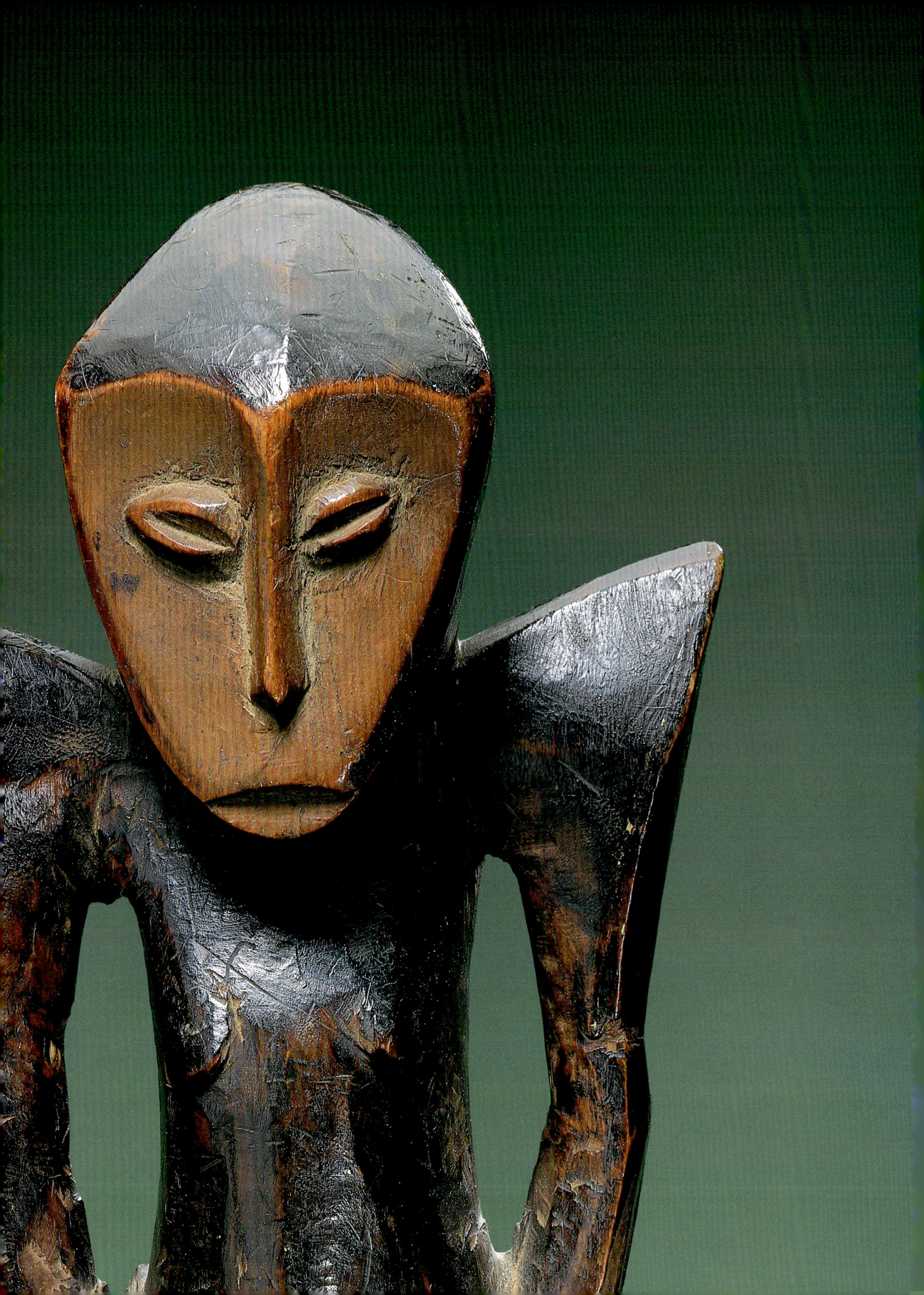

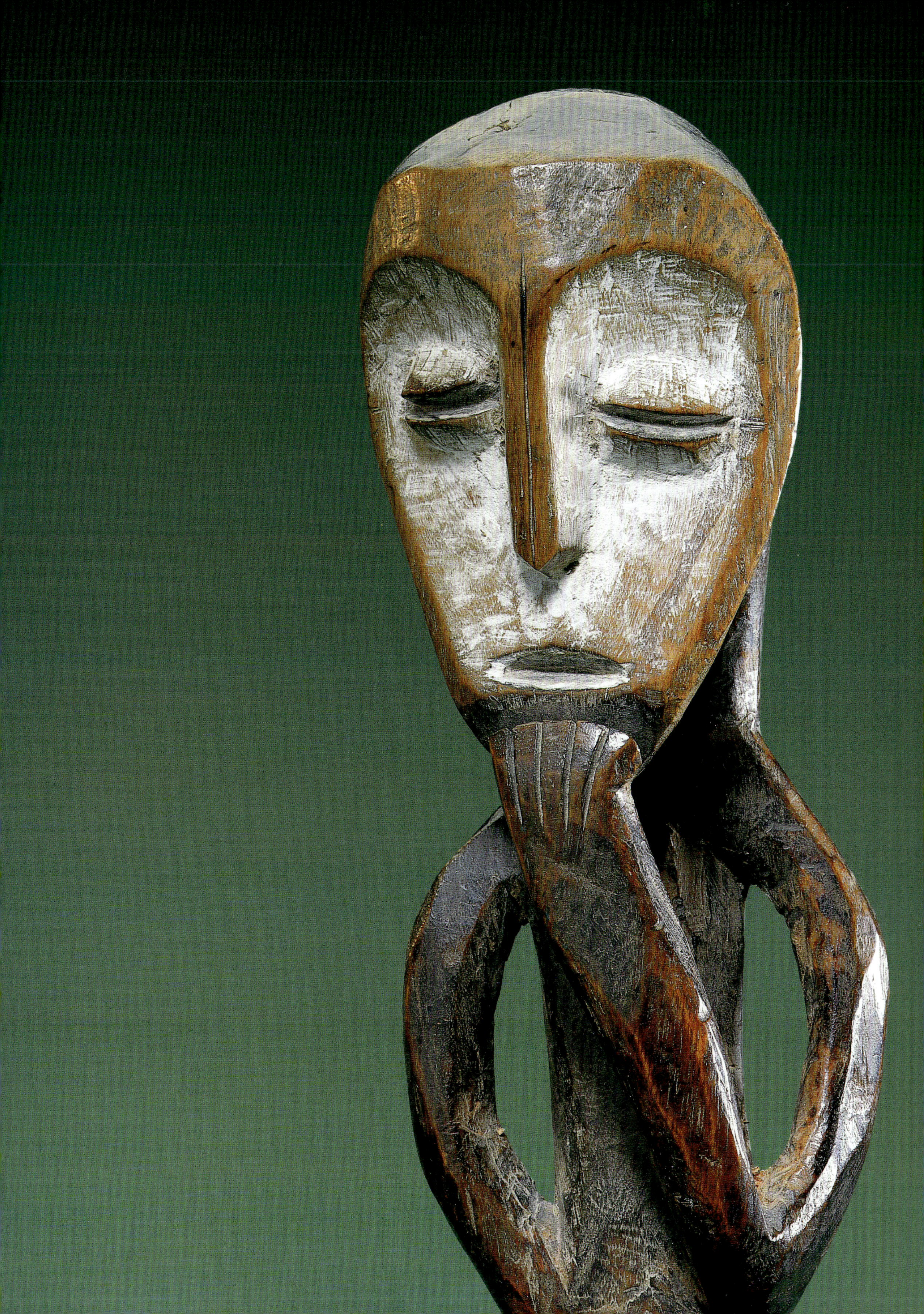

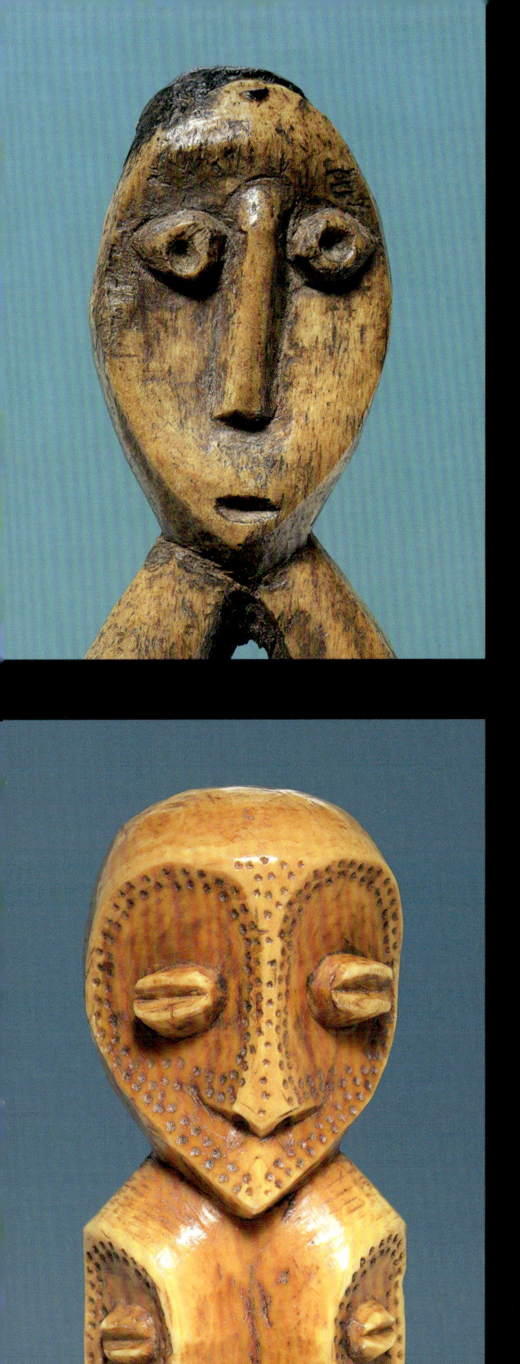
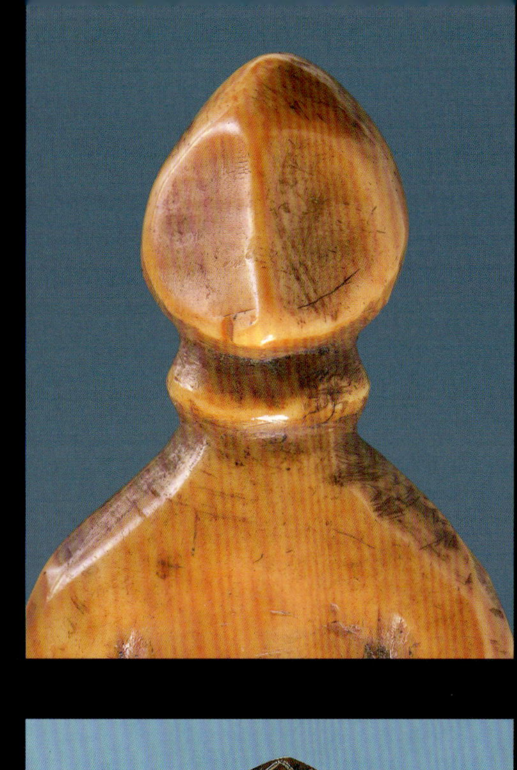
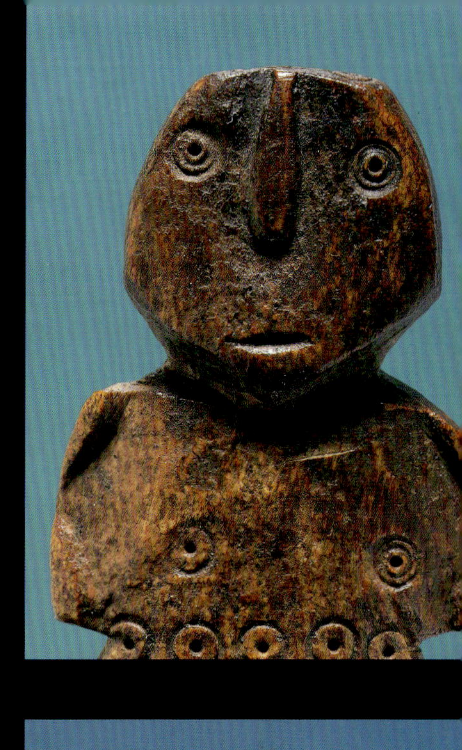
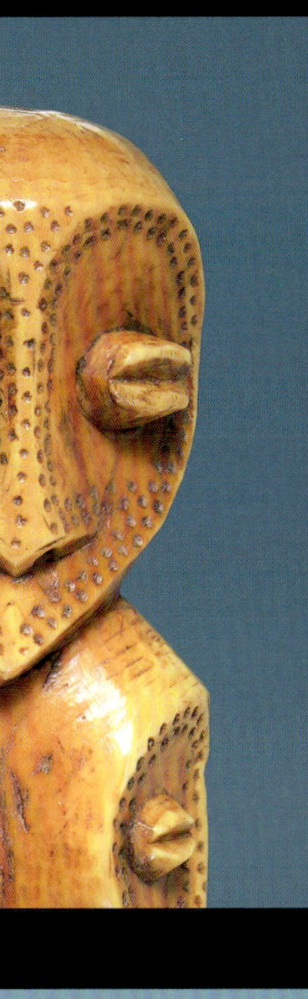
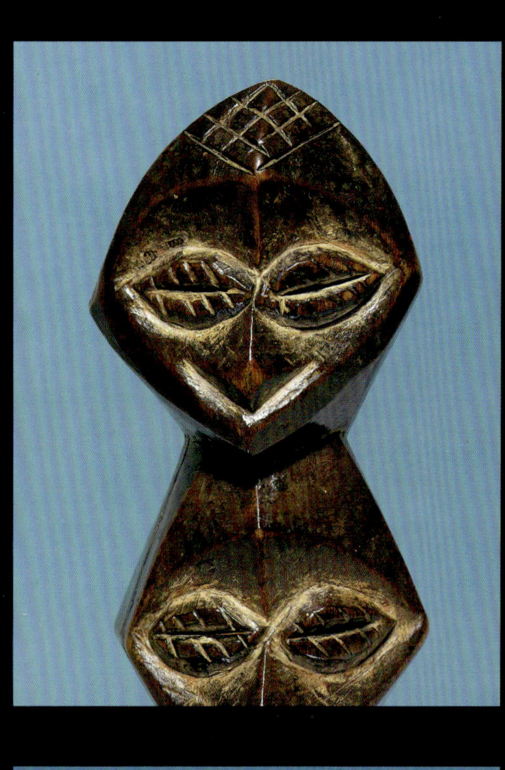
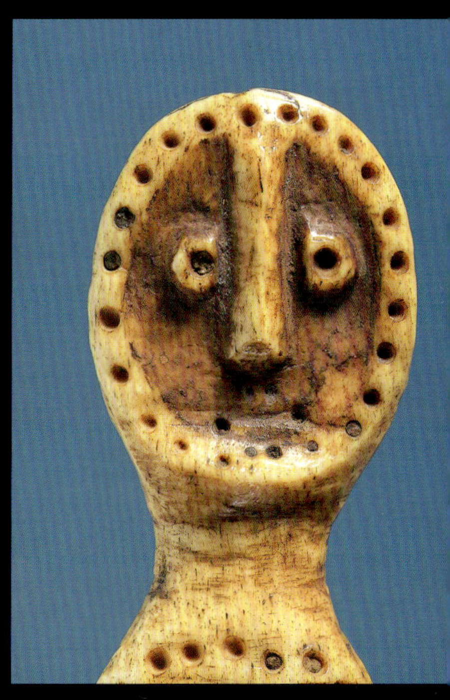
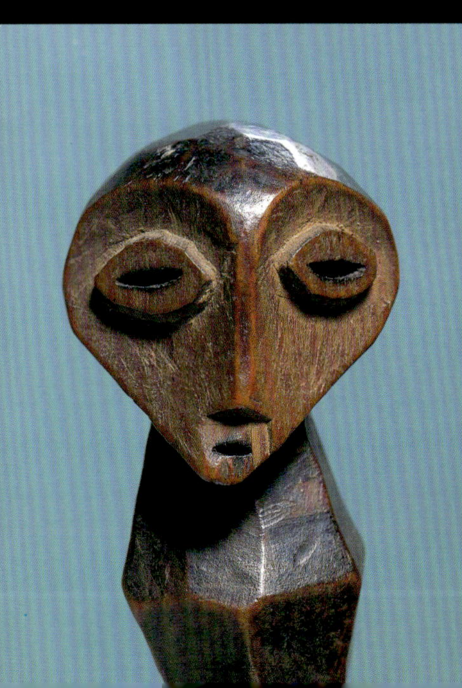
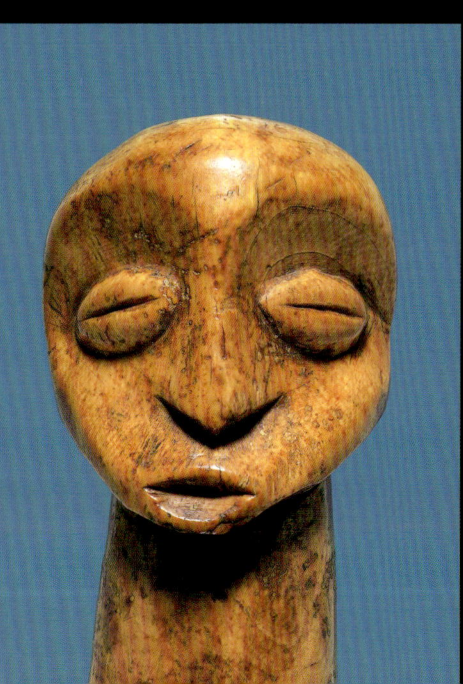
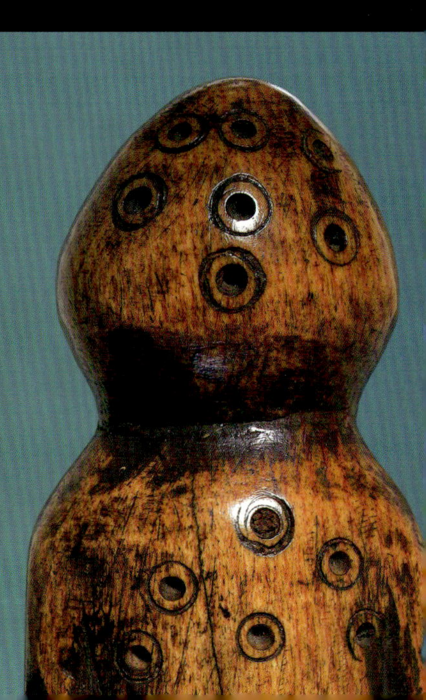

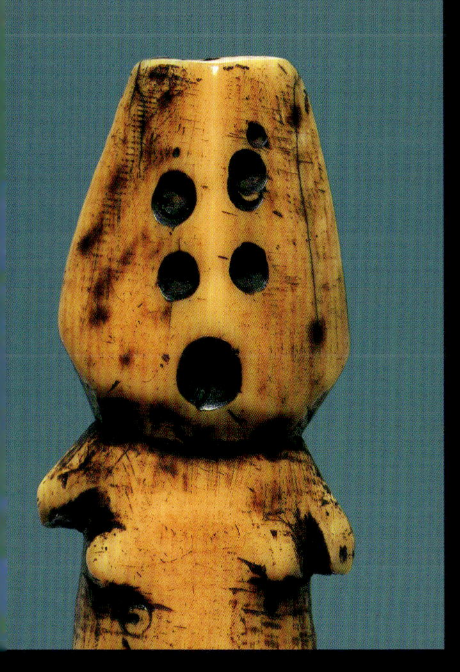
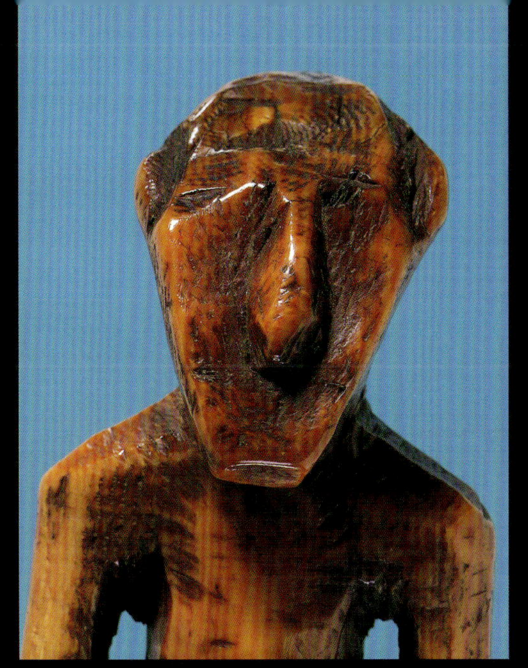
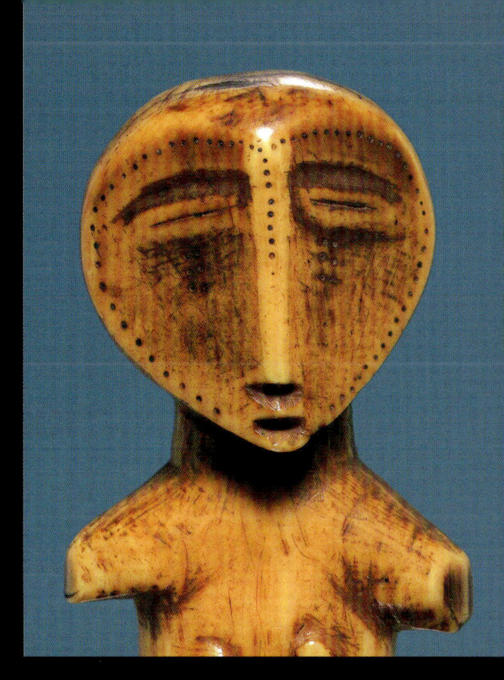

Art of the Lega

ELISABETH L. CAMERON

UCLA Fowler Museum of Cultural History LOS ANGELES

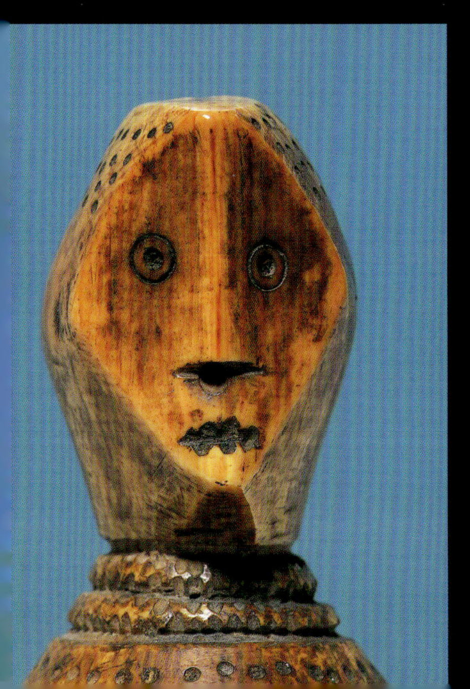
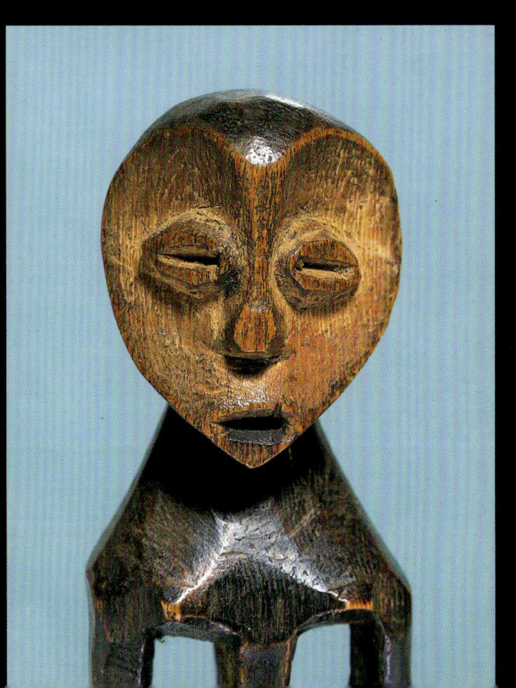
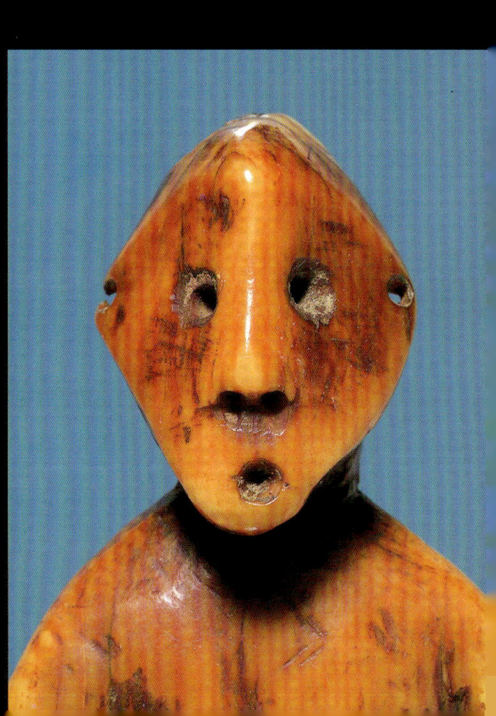

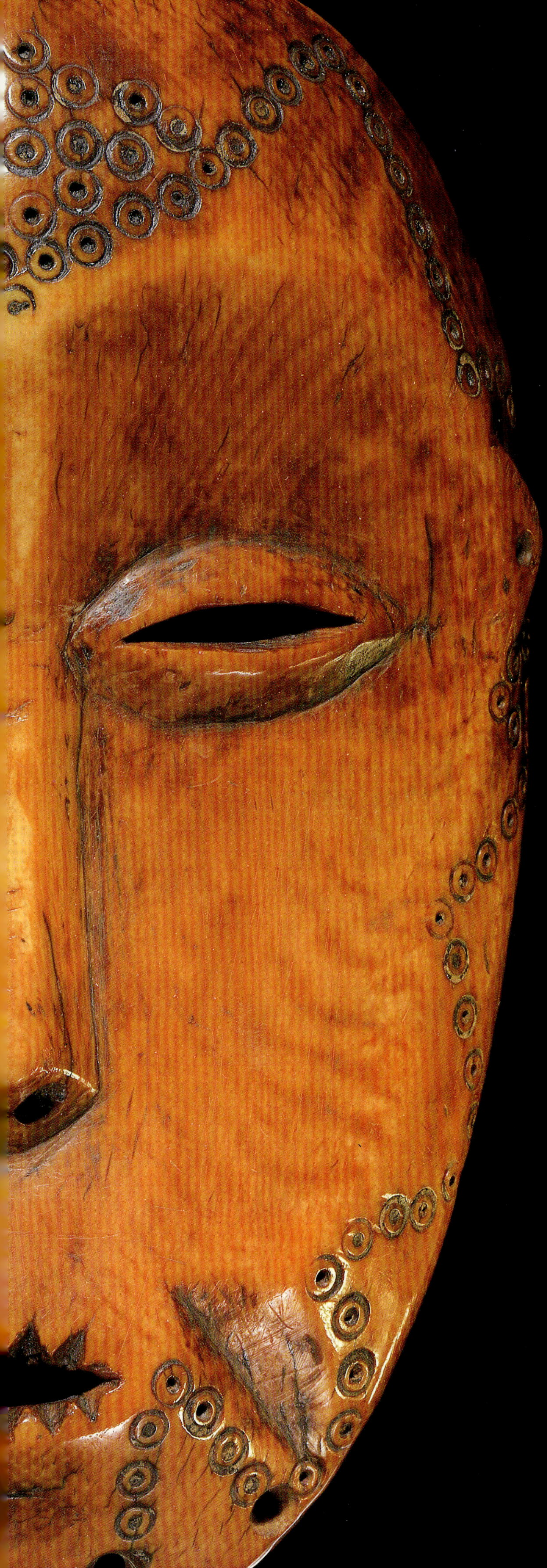

The Fowler Museum is part of
UCLA's School of the Arts and Architecture

Lynne Kostman, *Managing Editor*
Daniel R. Brauer, *Designer and Production Coordinator*
Don Cole, *Principal Photographer*

UCLA Fowler Museum of Cultural History
Box 951549
Los Angeles
California 90095-1549

Requests for permission to reproduce material from this volume should be sent to the UCLA Fowler Museum Publications Department at the above address.

Printed and bound in Hong Kong by South Sea International Press, Ltd.

Cover: Fig. s, p. 24.

Distributed by the University of Washington Press,
P.O. Box 50096, Seattle, Washington 98145.

Library of Congress Cataloging-in-Publication Data

Cameron, Elisabeth Lynn.
Art of the Lega / Elisabeth L. Cameron.
p. cm
Includes bibliographical references.
ISBN 0-930741-87-0 (alk. paper)—ISBN 0-930741-88-9 (pbk. : alk. paper)
1. Lega (African people)—Rites and ceremonies. 2. Lega (African people)—Social life and customs. 3. Art, Lega. I. University of California, Los Angeles. Fowler Museum of Cultural History. II. Title.

DT650.R43 C35 2001
745'.096751—dc21

2001047083

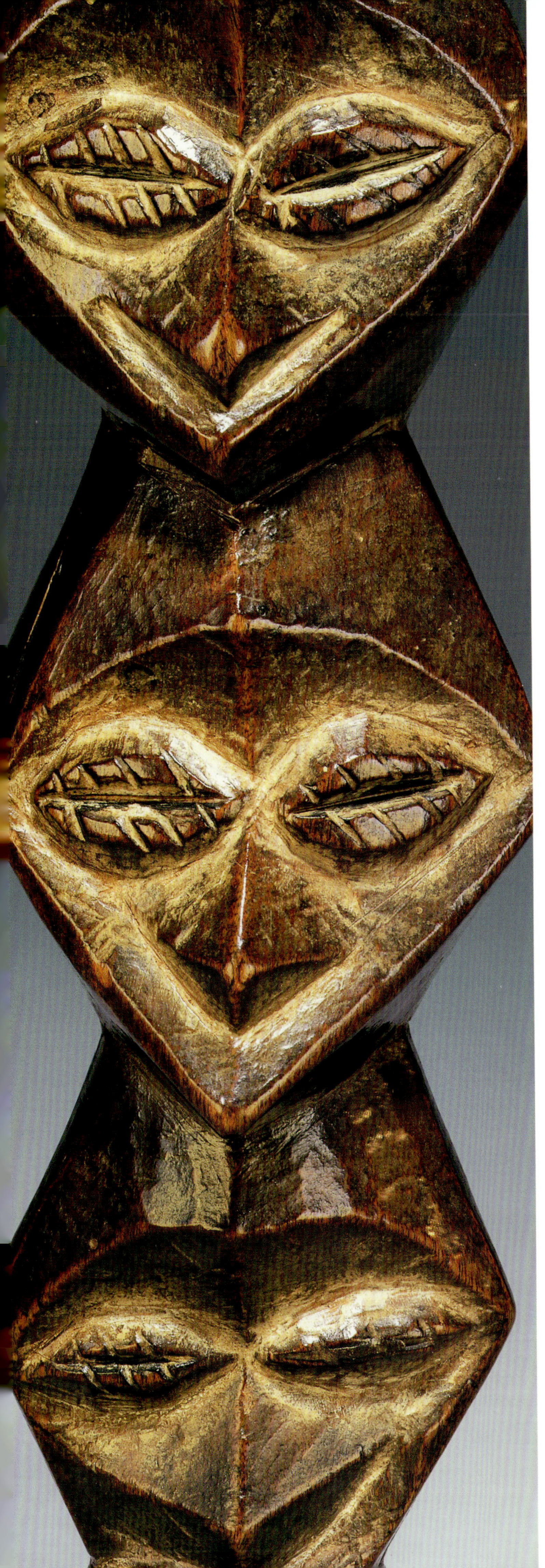

Contents

Forewords

With the present book and its accompanying exhibition, the UCLA Fowler Museum of Cultural History has come full circle. The Museum's initial publication—issued shortly after its founding as the Museum and Laboratories of Ethnic Arts and Technology in 1963—was *Balega and Other Tribal Arts from the Congo* by Ralph Altman, who served as the first curator. Prompting that publication and its attendant exhibition was the acquisition of the Jean-Pierre Hallet collection of central African art by Dr. Franklin D. Murphy, UCLA chancellor from 1960 to 1968 and the founder of the Museum. The endeavor was heavily informed by the impressive research of Dr. Daniel Biebuyck who was in residence at UCLA during part of its development. The compelling abstraction of Lega figures and masks, coupled with the complex and sophisticated societal messages they represent, provided a near ideal visual and intellectual beginning for what was ultimately to become the UCLA Fowler Museum of Cultural History.

It is through the remarkable efforts of Africanist Dr. Elisabeth L. Cameron and collector Dr. Jay T. Last that the present volume on the art and culture of the Lega has reached fruition. Dr. Cameron was born in the Belgian Congo (later known as Zaire and now as the Democratic Republic of the Congo) and lived there until the age of thirteen. She has returned to central Africa many times since, completing her dissertation on female initiation among the Lunda peoples of Zambia. Dr. Cameron has had a distinguished career at the Fowler beginning with her work as a graduate student and research assistant in 1984. Years later she contributed Lega essays to both *Elephant: The Animal and Its Ivory in African Culture* (1992) and *Crowning Achievements: African Arts of Dressing the Head* (1995) and was both curator and author of *Isn't S/He a Doll: Play and Ritual in African Sculpture* (1996). In addition, she has written many essays and reviews for the journal *African Arts,* published by the UCLA James S. Coleman African Studies Center. As a curator at the Los Angeles County Museum of Art (LACMA), Elisabeth collaborated with the Fowler Museum and the California African American Museum on *The Heritage of African Music,* a joint project funded by the National Endowment for the Humanities. As part of this collaboration, she curated the exhibition *Music for the Eyes: The Fine Art of African Musical Instruments* for LACMA and worked with me on the catalog section of the accompanying book, *Turn Up the Volume! A Celebration of African Music* (1999).

Moving on to the Nelson-Atkins Museum in Kansas City in 1999, Elisabeth initiated the collaboration that brought *Art of the Lega* into being. I would like to thank Marc Wilson, director of the Nelson-Atkins, for his ongoing commitment to making this project soar. I would also like to express our gratitude to others on the staff of the Nelson-Atkins Museum who have worked closely with Elisabeth on this project: Joyce Youmans, Amy Rosenfeld, Cindy Cart, and Carol Inge Hockett. Elisabeth's contributions to the Fowler Museum over the past seventeen years, both behind the scenes and at center stage, have been instrumental to the success of many of the Museum's most important African projects, and we are extremely grateful to her for her continued efforts.

Jay Last has been a leading light and a guardian spirit at the Fowler, roles he assumed only shortly after the Museum's inception. Incredibly modest, Jay's name, at his own request, only rarely appears next to his consistently important contributions. Jay and his wife, Deborah, were founding members of Manus, the Fowler Museum's support group, and were major contributors to the capital campaign for the Museum's new building, which opened in September 1992. The Fowler Museum's digital imaging project was inaugurated and initially sustained through the considerable support of the Lasts. Their efforts gained the Fowler a place in the Museum Educational Site Licensing Program (MESL) sponsored by the Getty Trust, which brought museum collections digitally into the classroom in an experimental and highly successful program. This subsequently led to major support from the Getty Grant Program and the National Endowment for the Humanities to complete the digital imaging of virtually all of the Fowler Museum's collections. For the past several years the Lasts have also provided substantial support for the Museum's conservation department, for its visiting scholars program, and for African acquisitions—all key areas of need.

Jay first began collecting Lega art in 1962, and his substantial collection is now a promised gift to the Fowler Museum. Jay's aesthetic and intellectual interests in the arts of the Lega are further evidenced by his support of Dr. Daniel Biebuyck's book *Lega Culture: Art, Initiation, and Moral Philosophy among a Central African People,* published by the University of California Press in 1973. *Art of the Lega* is not the first exhibition we have mounted based upon the Lasts' collections; *California Dreaming: Orange Box Labels 1885–1955,* presented in 1985 turned out to be one of the most successful small exhibitions in the Museum's history. Over the years the Lasts have also lent important pieces to at least ten exhibitions of African art at the Fowler Museum. It should be noted that Deborah Last has matched Jay's enthusiasm for the Fowler. She has been a dedicated volunteer at the Museum, at the journal *African Arts,* and elsewhere at UCLA for many years.

The many visits I have paid to the Last home and the long, enjoyable, and always stimulating conversations I have had with Jay are some of the real joys I have experienced in the course of working at the Fowler Museum in varying capacities since 1974. The Fowler would not be what it is today without Jay and Deborah Last. Daniel Biebuyck has written that Bwami, the principal social and political institution of the Lega, is like the "stampeding of elephants" and that "the place where [they] have passed cannot be forgotten." The same can be said of the Lasts' many enduring contributions to the Fowler Museum.

As I am retiring from the Fowler a few months before this publication will appear in print, I take special pride in thanking both present and past staffs of the Museum for their always remarkable efforts in producing publications, exhibitions, and public programming that have provoked, challenged, and encompassed the many worldviews that represent our audience in Southern California and beyond. It has been a privilege to work with so many people and to have learned so much from them.

Doran H. Ross, Director
UCLA Fowler Museum of Cultural History
June 2001

The secrecy surrounding the Bwami Society—the sole forum for which the Lega peoples of the Democratic Republic of the Congo produce works of art—does not allow for public acknowledgment of an artist's achievement. In fact, the artists who fabricate the wonderful artworks highlighted in this volume and the exhibition accompanying it are required to work in secret. Among the Lega, then, art production is a relatively thankless endeavor, a dubious task to which few might be expected to aspire. Nevertheless, Lega artistic ingenuity has flourished. The simple, elegant forms of masks, spoons, figures, and other artworks describe a minimalist aesthetic that is immensely pleasing to the eye. Lega art is a true testament to the human spirit and its impetus to create visually satisfying works of art and to understand the world through beauty.

It has been an immense pleasure to collaborate with the UCLA Fowler Museum on this important project. Collaborations between institutions allow us to combine our strengths and stimulate new and different approaches to exhibitions. In this case, the focus of the Nelson-Atkins on the aesthetic masterpiece combines with the contextual emphasis of the Fowler to produce a unique exhibition that brings context and artistry together. The *Art of the Lega* is the exciting result of the combination of rich ideas and talented people from these two institutions. Many thanks to Doran Ross and the Fowler Museum staff who carried the primary burden of organizing the traveling exhibition and producing this handsome volume. Elisabeth Cameron curated the exhibition and wrote the text while she was the curator of the Department of African Art at the Nelson-Atkins Museum. Her dedicated efforts were aided by her colleagues: Joyce Youmans, Curatorial Assistant, Department of African Art; Amy Rosenfeld, Departmental Assistant, Department of African Art; Cindy Cart, Curator of Exhibitions Management; and Carol Inge Hockett, who will be coordinating the educational component of the exhibition at the Nelson-Atkins Museum; as well as the many other staff members upon whom we rely for all exhibitions.

Finally, I would like to extend my sincerest appreciation to Jay Last, whose impeccable taste, marvelous collection, and boundless enthusiasm made this project possible.

Marc F. Wilson, Director/CEO
The Nelson-Atkins Museum of Art

Preface: *The Collector's Perspective*

Lega art with its large variety of simple, abstract designs has fascinated me for the past forty years. I have always been interested in simple forms in nature, starting with the rock collection I assembled when I was in grade school in Pennsylvania and continuing through my graduate research work at MIT, where I investigated the effects of temperature decrease on the crystal structure of a class of materials known as ferroelectrics.

During my graduate studies, I gained my first real exposure to abstract art when visiting the Museum of Modern Art while attending meetings of the American Physical Society in New York. Up to this time, I had had no training in art history and little opportunity to see original works; the variety of innovative images at MOMA came as an exciting revelation. On my first MOMA visit I purchased at the bookshop a print of Picasso's *Three Musicians*, which hung on my bedroom wall for years.

I have also had a strong interest in Africa since I was very young. Reading books by African explorers as a schoolboy, I was excited by the mysterious "Dark Continent," as Africa was then often called. I usually had a map of Africa close at hand for ready reference. In 1959 I made the first of many African visits, climbing Mount Kilimanjaro and traveling through Kenya, Uganda, Tanganyika, and Zanzibar. This trip served to heighten my already keen interest in Africa and things African.

During a stop in London on my way back from this first trip, I acquired a copy of Frans Olbrecht's *Les arts plastiques du Congo Belge* (1959), which had just been published, and visited the African collections on display at the British Museum, which at the time consisted mainly of dimly lit Benin bronzes and the Kuba collections assembled by Emile Torday. In 1960 there were few books on African art that were readily available, but I did manage to acquire *The Sculpture of Africa* (1958) by Eliot Elisofon and William Fagg and James Sweeney's catalog of the 1935 Museum of Modern Art exhibition *African Negro Art*. These texts exposed me to the richness and variety of African art. I also studied the survey books by Ladislas Segy, which I found very useful in providing an overview of art throughout the continent.

In 1957 seven of my friends and I founded Fairchild Semiconductor in Palo Alto, California, the first semiconductor company in the area that would later be known as Silicon Valley. I worked on the development of the first commercial diffused silicon transistors and directed the group that made the first integrated circuit chip. In connection with my work I traveled extensively, and on frequent business trips to New York in the late 1950s and early 1960s, I had a chance to see exhibitions at the recently opened Museum of Primitive Art. In addition to viewing the museum's permanent holdings, I saw the 1959 exhibition of the art of the Senufo, the Baga, and the Dogon, and Roy Sieber's exhibition of the art of northern Nigeria. In the early 1960s I was also fortunate to have seen a number of exhibitions of individual collections, including those of Jacques Lipschitz and Raymond Wielgus.

In these early days "primitive art" collecting had not yet become especially compartmentalized. The rich mixture of African, Oceanic, pre-Columbian, and North American art in a single exhibition was often unified by the aesthetic criteria of the collector who had acquired the material. The chance to see this body of comparative material was a very educational experience for me. Seeing these wonderful objects firsthand made me begin to appreciate how a fine patina added to their visual impact, how the continued use and handling of treasured objects enhanced their power.

I realized that I could combine my interest in abstract images and my fascination with things African by acquiring a few objects of my own and began to visit African art galleries on my New York trips. My first visits in 1961 were to the galleries of Ladislas Segy, Julius Carlebach, and John Klejman. Influenced in part by seeing the Kuba material at the British Museum, my first purchase was a Kuba cup, a head on a large foot with tiny arms attached to the side of the neck. I little realized at the time that this acquisition—still one of my favorite pieces—represented the beginning of a lifelong collecting passion that would become one of my principal activities.

Over the next year or so, I acquired about twenty cups, becoming more and more intrigued with the variety of shape and form exhibited by these relatively simple

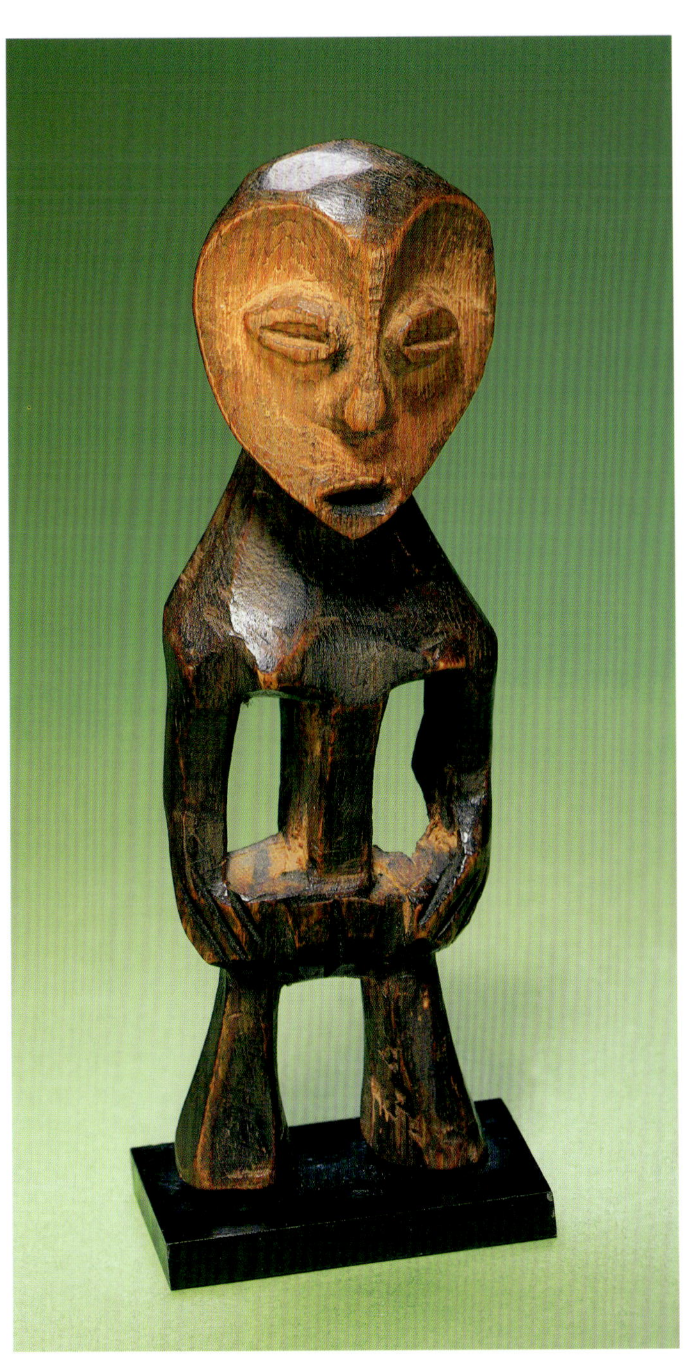

A Human figure. Wood.
H: 14.3 cm (5⅝ in.).

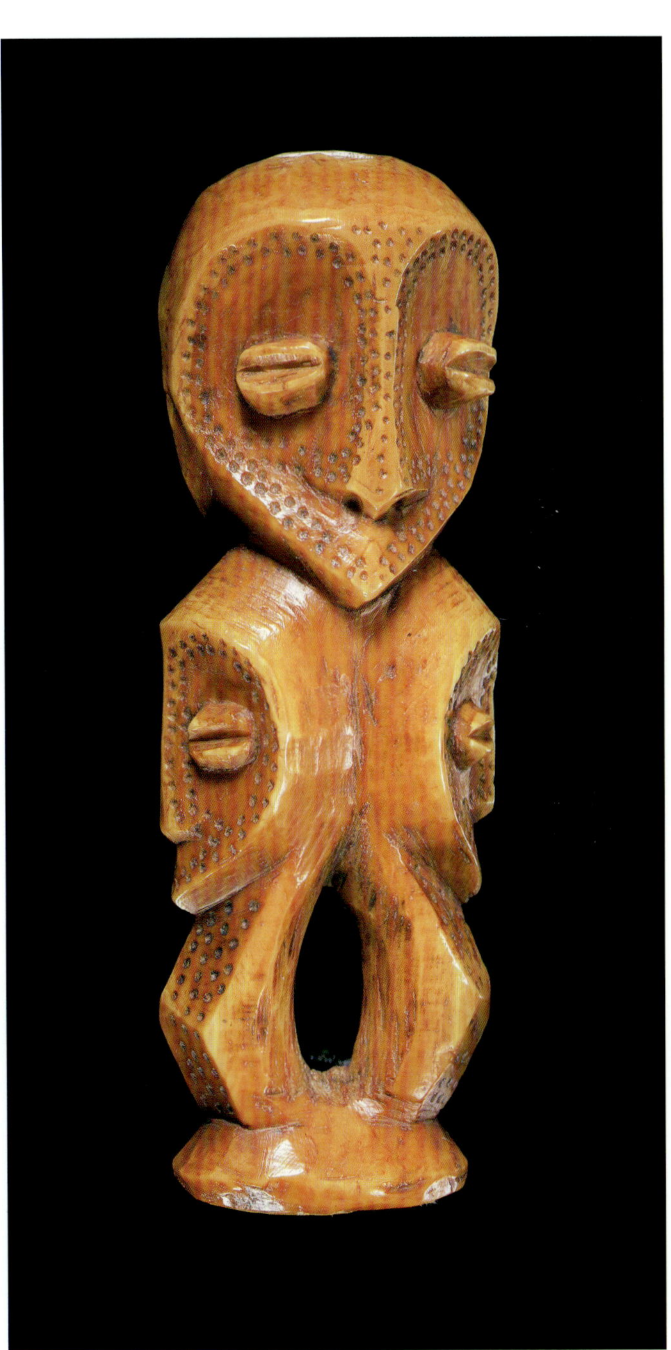

B Bust with multiple heads.
Ivory. H: 14.1 cm (5⅝ in.).

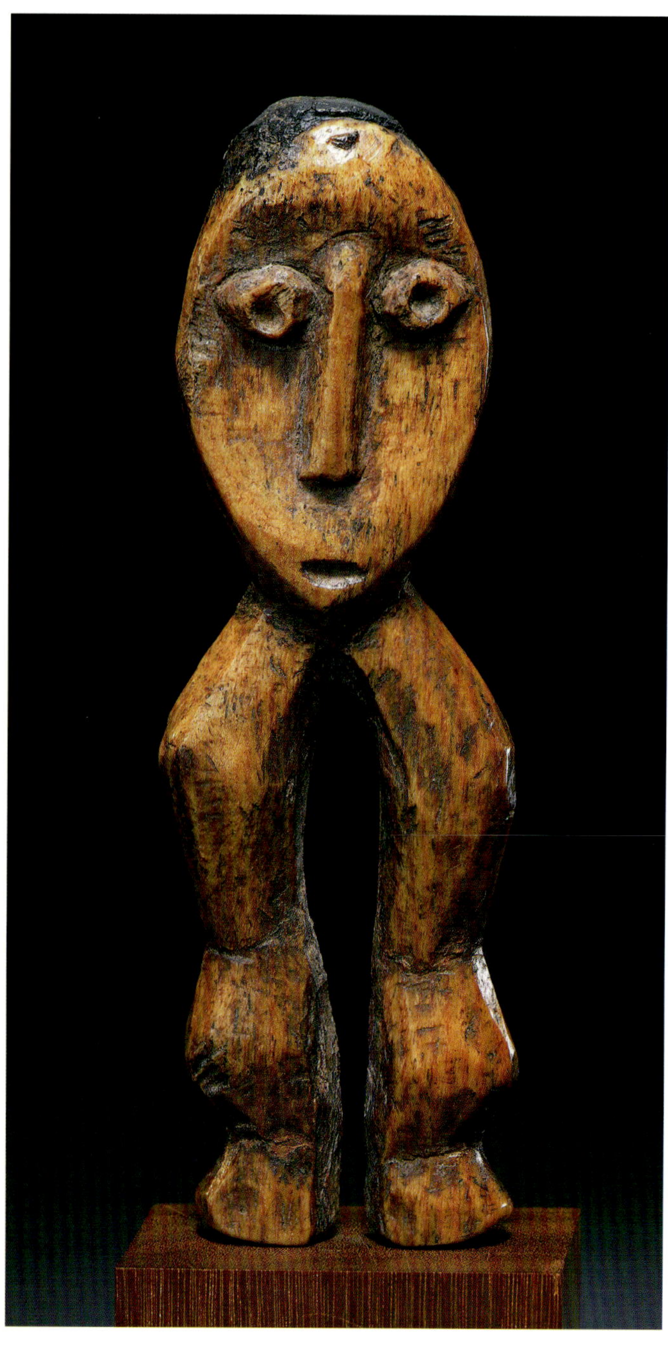

C Multiheaded human figure.
Ivory. H: 17.2 cm (6¾ in.).

vessels. Every cup increased my appreciation of the group as a whole. After this initial " cup collecting" year, I began to expand my interests, acquiring some Dan, Yaka, Asante, Kwele, and Luba material. In mid-1962 I bought my first Lega objects, a one-armed ivory figure, an ivory mask, and a small wooden figure (fig. A), from Aaron Furman.

In pouring over the illustrations in Elisofon and Fagg's *Sculpture of Africa*, I realized that the objects that most intrigued me were the eight Lega busts and figures from the collections of the British Museum, the Musée Royal de l'Afrique Centrale in Tervuren, and the collection of Charles Ratton. I had not seen any comparable material on my visits to the New York dealers and could only dream of owning objects of this caliber. Years later, I would be fortunate to acquire one of these pieces, Ratton's four-headed ivory figure (fig. B).

In 1963 I purchased three or four more bone, ivory, and wood Lega figures, nice objects but far from the masterpieces seen in the literature. One of these, a simple ivory figure consisting only of a head on legs, continues to be one of my favorites (fig. C). I began to develop an appreciation of the influence of African carvings on twentieth-century European art when a museum curator borrowed this piece for an exhibition focused on the relationship between African art and German Expressionism. He illustrated my *Kopffüssler* on the cover of the exhibition brochure, even though I steadily maintained that the relationship between my piece and the German work was remote if not nonexistent. He said that while this might be true, my piece made his points perfectly. Mulling this over, I began to realize the complexity of the interaction between African art and modern Western art, an appreciation that has steadily grown as the years have passed.

In the spring of 1964 I acquired my first great Lega piece, a wood figure with a raised arm incorporated into the neck, cowrie-shaped eyes, and simple bent legs (fig. D). I still consider this one of the very best objects in my collection and feel fortunate to have acquired it so early in my collecting career when I could use it to judge the quality of the Lega objects I would collect in the future. I became aware of the power of this small object when I tried to photograph it and realized that I could not capture the carver's combination of structural elements in a single image; instead, I had to continually move my head as I tried to grasp its artistic complexity.

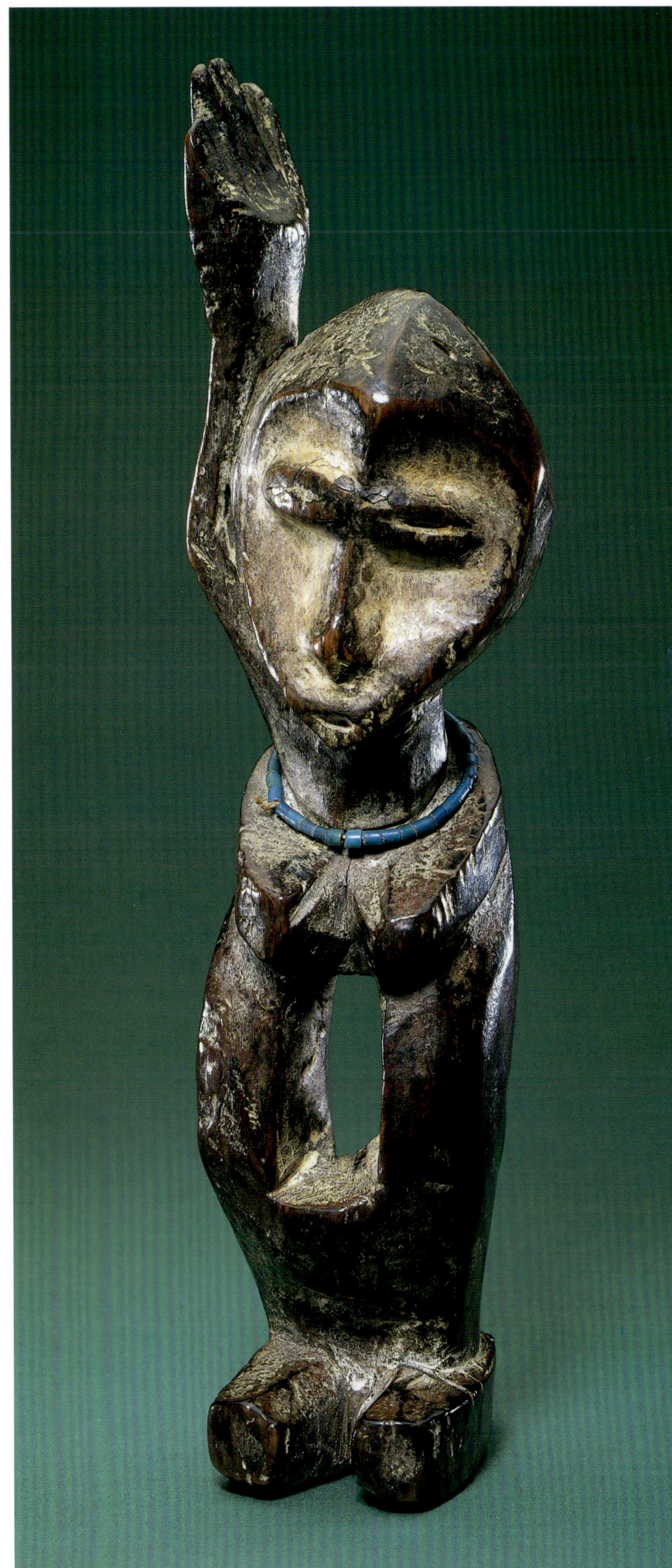

D Human figure with one arm raised. Wood, pigment, and beads. H: 25 cm (9⅞ in.).

At this time I began to have access to more and more fine Lega objects. American dealers in the mid-1960s had begun to make regular trips to Belgium, where a great deal of Lega material was located, and to bring it back to New York. Aaron Furman, Merton Simpson, and John Klejman (who acquired material with the help of Ralph Nash) were my principal sources. I also acquired a number of Lega pieces from French collections that were brought to New York by Henri Kamer and displayed in his galleries in the 1960s and 1970s.

Nicolas de Kun, who became interested in Lega objects while working in Kivu as a mining engineer in the 1950s, proved to be an additional source of material. He sold a number of the objects he had collected to New York dealers and put several up at auction. I was subsequently able to acquire a number of these. As the years passed and my interest in Lega art became known, I was fortunate to have an increasing number of dealers bringing fine Lega objects to my attention. In addition, dealers would provide me with material that they had run across that was not of much interest to most art collectors at the time. These hats, belts, baskets, and simple abstract ivory objects put Lega art in a broader perspective for me and made my overall collection much more comprehensive. Aside from the de Kun material, very few Lega objects of any quality showed up at auctions in the early days of my Lega collecting. A notable exception was the wood mask that had been in the Sweeney MOMA exhibition in 1935, which I acquired at a Parke-Bernet auction in 1970 (fig. E).

As my interest in Lega carvings as artworks increased, I began to wish that I knew more about the culture that led to the creation of these magnificent objects. My very limited knowledge came from the scattered bits of information that I had managed to gather when I acquired pieces from dealers. The great step forward in my Lega education came when I met Daniel Biebuyck at the first African Triennial meeting at Hampton Institute, Virginia, in 1968. I had heard of Daniel's work among the Lega and had unsuccessfully tried to meet him during my trips to Southern California in the mid-1960s while he was teaching at UCLA. When we finally met at Hampton, he realized the degree of my interest in the Lega and began to spend a great deal of time with me discussing their culture and its relationship to their art.

I was fascinated by the concept of the society Daniel described, a society without hereditary or elected rulers,

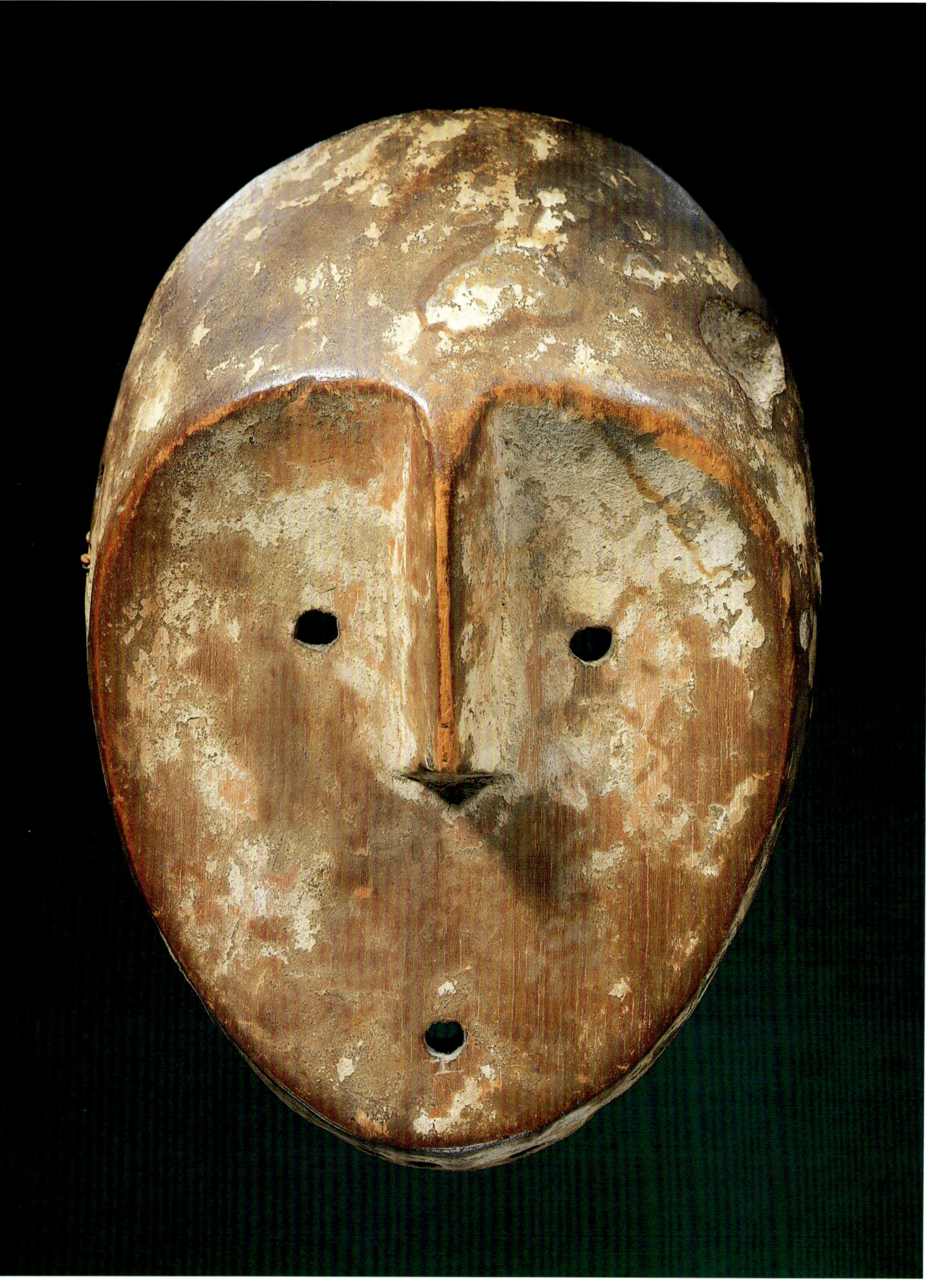

E Mask. Wood and pigment.
H: 21.9 cm (8⅝ in.).

unified by a semisecret group, the Bwami Society, whose members rose in prestige and increasing influence as they practiced a highly moral standard of social behavior. The emphasis, as Daniel outlined it, was on harmony in social relationships, circumspection, filial piety, group spirit, obedience, self-discipline, and tenacity of purpose.

I learned that Lega art was owned exclusively by members of the Bwami Society, either individually or collectively, and served as an emblem of rank. Furthermore, it figured prominently in Bwami initiation ceremonies and rituals wherein members were elevated into higher ranks. It intrigued me that this art form fell outside standard categories of African royal, ancestral, or funerary arts.

After this initial meeting, I visited Daniel a number of times at the University of Delaware, where he was a professor. I encouraged him to finish his book *Lega Culture* and helped him with the photography, maps, and production details as the manuscript wended its way through the University of California Press. The book finally appeared in 1973 and gave a detailed treatment of many aspects of Lega culture that related to the objects I was collecting.

This linking of art with moral culture, the use of art objects to serve as a teaching and inspirational device during Lega ceremonies added a great deal of meaning to my collection. Daniel also pointed out that Lega objects were associated with a lengthy series of aphorisms, although it was usually difficult to make a direct correspondence between a given saying and a specific Lega artwork. I was, nonetheless, touched by the moral power of these aphorisms. One, in particular, dealt with the mark or extra cowrie that sometimes appears above the eye on a Lega figure. This can be seen in figure F, where the face has five holes, abstractly representing the mouth, nose, and eyes, and a small sixth hole over the left eye: "I thought my father was asleep, but he had his third eye open watching over me."

In 1968 I visited *Serial Images* at the Pasadena Art Museum, an exhibition that proved to have more impact on my ideas about art than any I have ever seen. I was very impressed with the serial groupings of Cubist portraits painted by Alexej Jawlensky in the 1920s. Representing the eyes, nose, and mouth by simple lines or curves and working within strict constraints, Jawlensky created a wide spectrum of images conveying a variety of emotions as he reformulated these facial features and experimented with color changes. He greatly multiplied the effect of the basic individual image so that the whole of this body of work was much greater than the sum of its parts.

F Human figure with third eye.
Ivory. H: 11.5 cm (4½ in.).

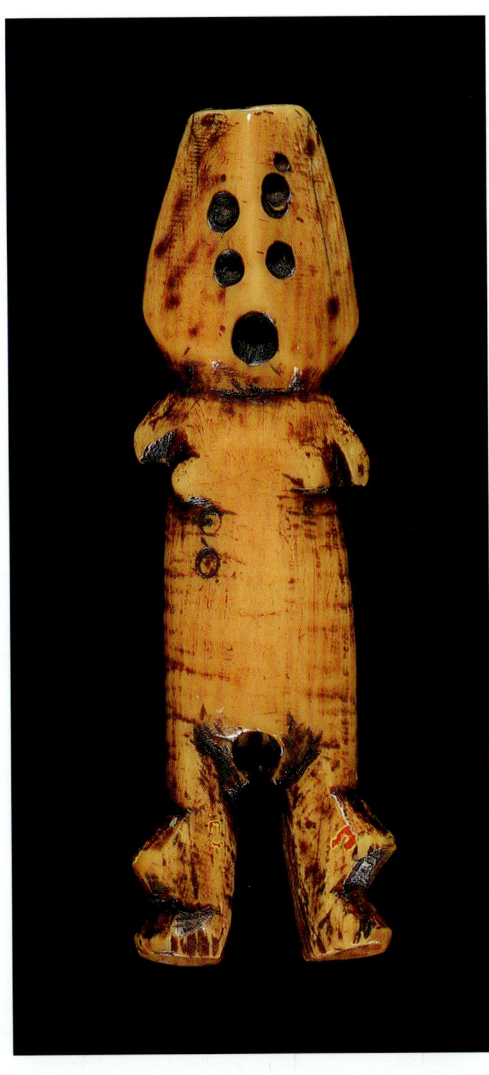

I began to reflect upon appreciation of Lega art, especially masks, in terms of Jawlensky's serial images. Most Lega masks have a heart-shaped face construction with eyes that can be completely blank, horizontal slits, circles, raised cowrie shells, or coffee-bean forms (figs. E, G–M). The nose is usually a vertical line, and the mouth either a simple line or a rectangular or circular hole. Sometimes teeth are denoted with a series of vertical cuts. The masks represent a flat face rather than a fully rounded head and were usually carried or displayed rather than used to cover the Bwami member's face. If they represent a human form rather than an animal, they almost always lack ears.

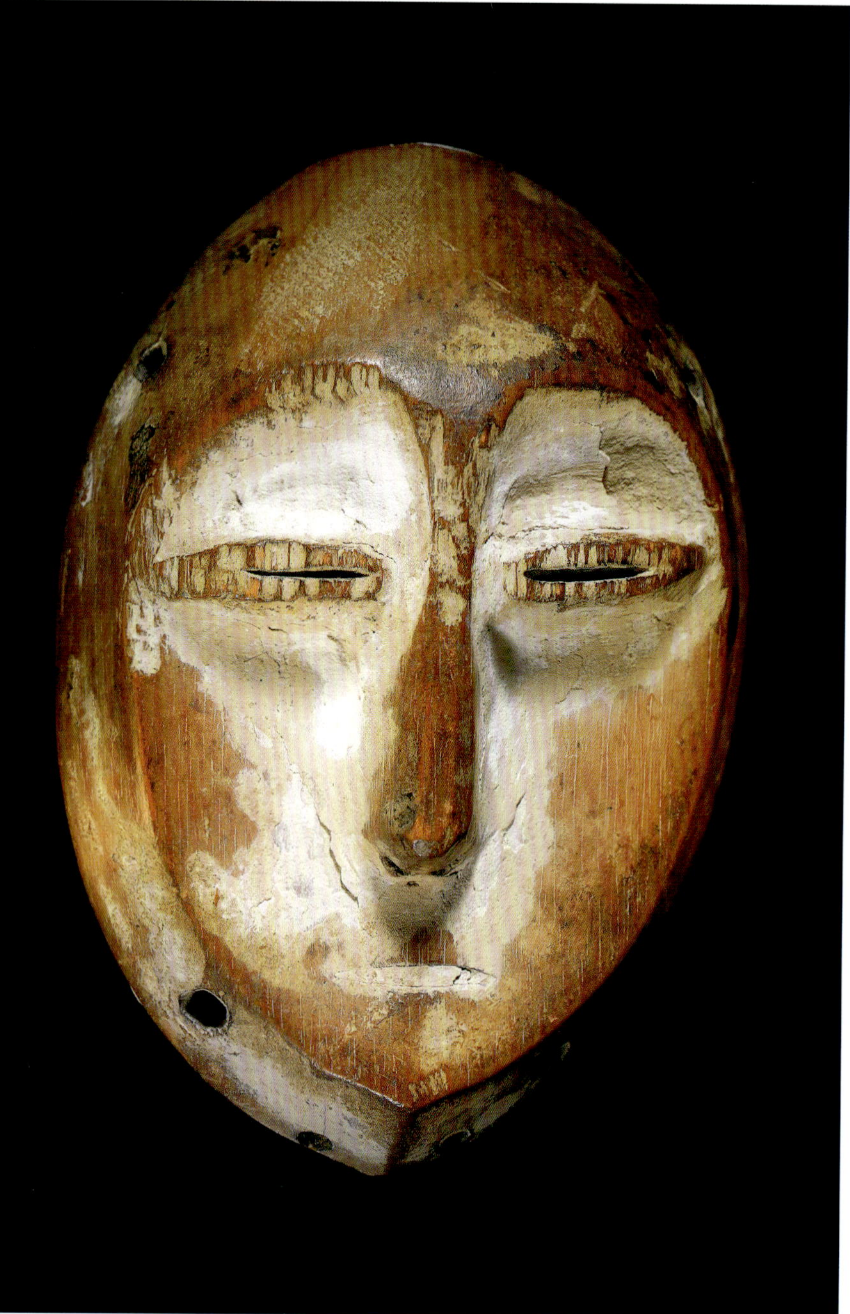

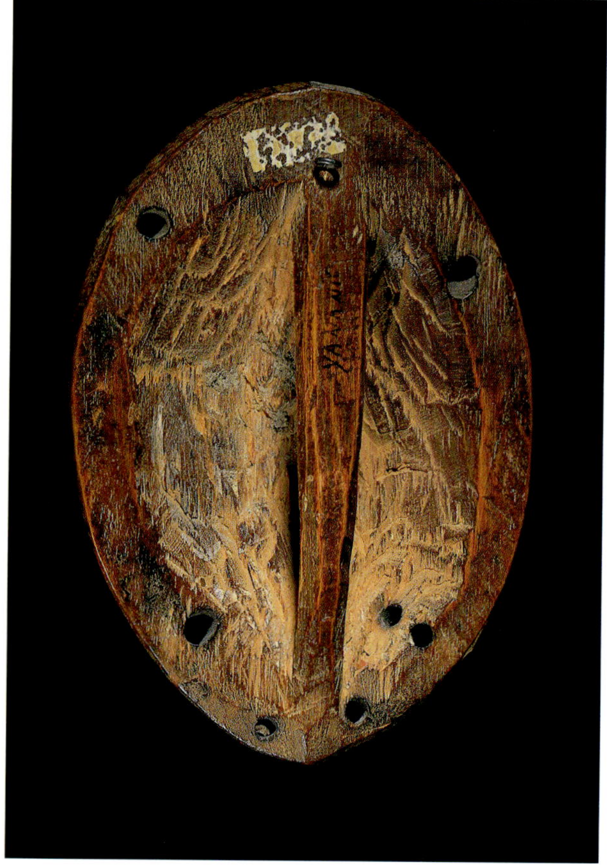

G a,b Front and back views of a mask (*lukwakongo*). Wood and pigment. H: 16.5 cm (6½ in.).

The back view shows the handle with which the mask is held.

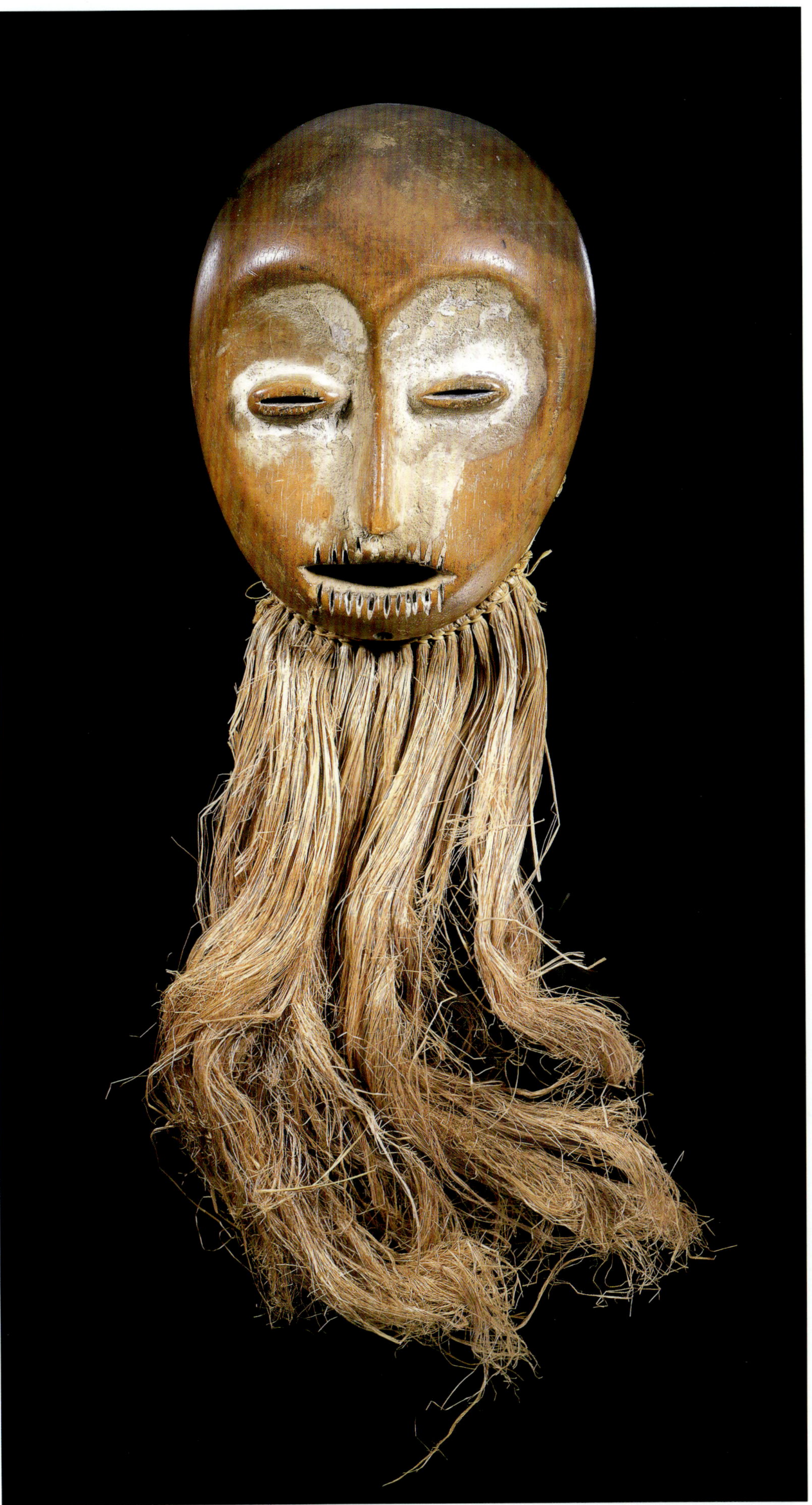

H Mask. Wood and fiber.
H: 51.5 cm (20¼ in.).

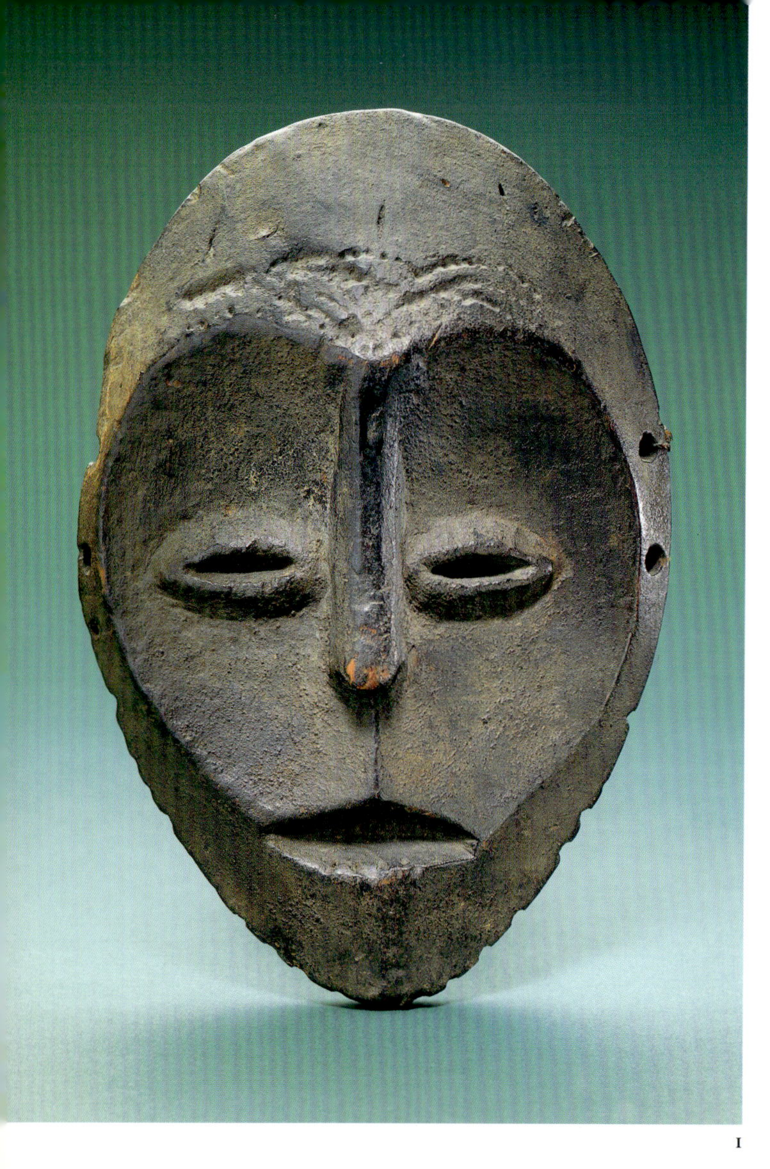

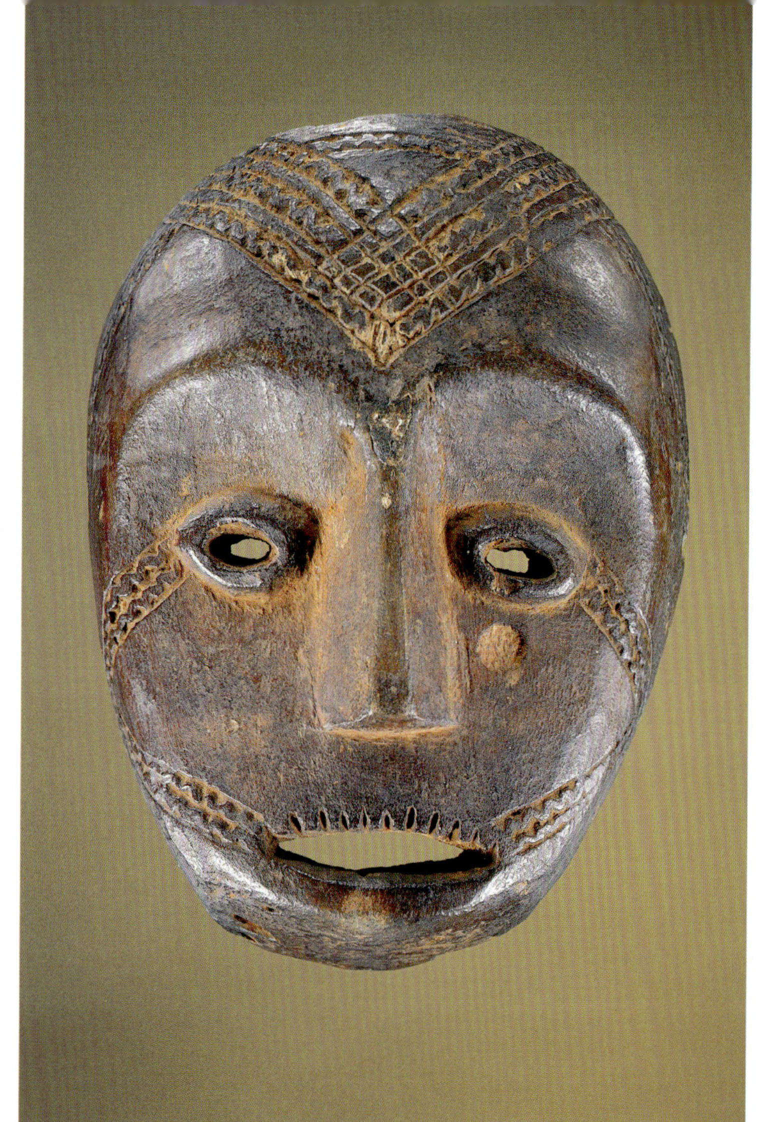

I J

K L

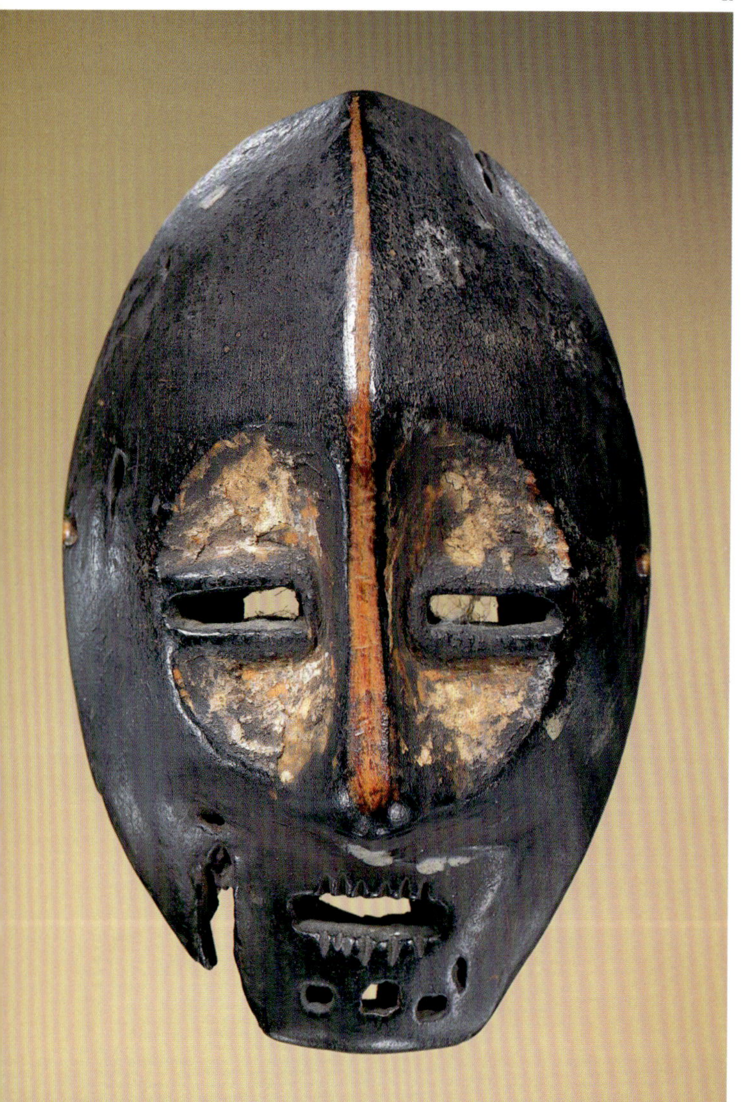

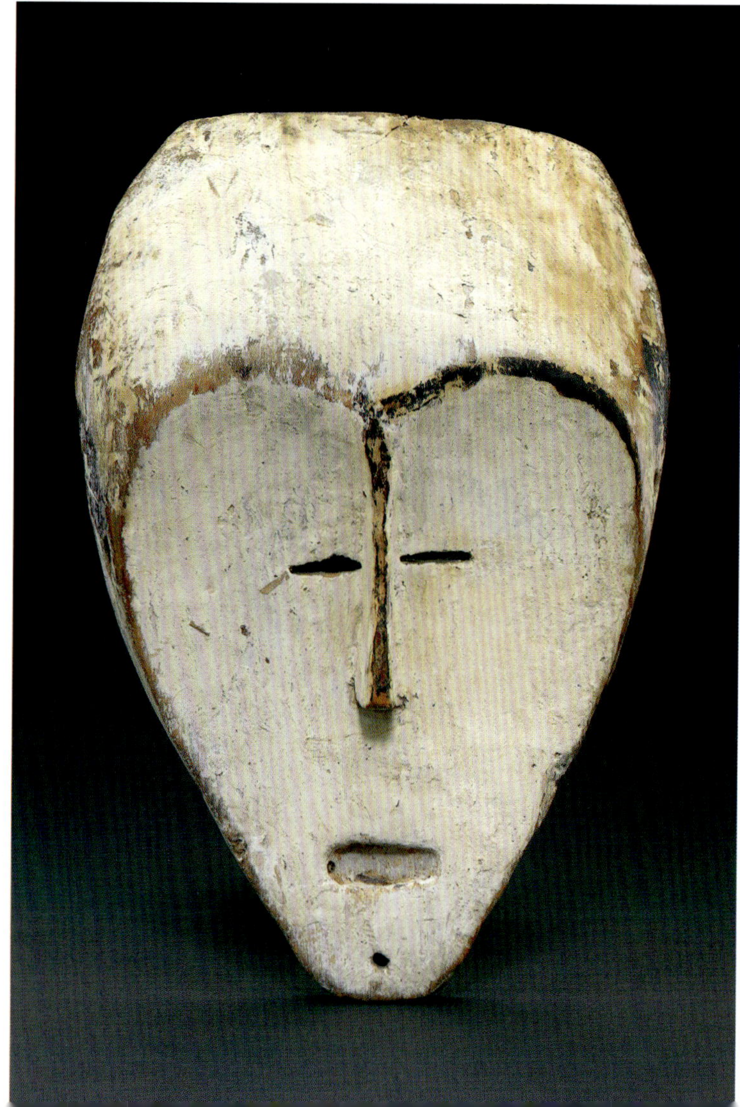

I Mask (*idimu*). Wood. H: 25.5 cm (10 in.).

J Mask (*muminia*). Wood. H: 22.8 cm (9 in.).

K Mask (*lukwakongo*). Wood and pigment. H: 15.3 cm (6 in.).

L Mask (*idimu*). Wood and pigment. H: 29 cm (11⅜ in.).

M Mask (*idimu*). Wood, pigment, and fiber. H: 41.7 cm (16⅜ in.).

The variety of masks created by the Lega within these strict constraints is amazing.

In addition to masks, the Lega produced figures, busts, animal sculptures, and simple abstract objects in a variety of materials—mainly wood, ivory, and bone, but including copal, stone, fiber, ceramic, elephant leather, and gourds. The multiplicity of subjects and materials led to a very rich body of art with the artist's imagination limited only by the technical constraints of carving the material at hand.

These representations of human figures, animals, birds, reptiles, and abstract objects occur in bewildering variety. Animals with human features are sometimes carved (see figs. 7.23, 7.24). Janus or multiheaded figures are common (figs. N, O). One especially interesting design concept renders the legs and body of a figure in zigzag form (figs. P, Q). Analyzing this body of material in terms of the serial image has added to my appreciation of the inventive powers of the Lega carver.

The Lega artist was also proficient in conveying visual puns wherein individual design elements can represent different body parts. For example, the ivory carving illustrated in figure R can be interpreted as a small head with prominent arms, or the arms can be interpreted as ears, leading to a figure with a large head and small torso. Sometimes, this dual interpretation of body elements involves the front and back of the object leading to a complex reading when the piece is handled and turned.

Over the years I have probably seen over two thousand Lega objects in the original or in photographs and have been struck by the fact that I have seldom seen two so similar that they would be confused. Even in the case of the most common Lega form, the *iginga* figure (fig. S and see p. 120), the treatment of the facial features, the neck designs, and the torso result in a body of work where nearly every piece complements the others rather than duplicating them—the serial image in action.

On both wood and ivory objects, an additional dimension is added by the Lega appreciation for patina—ranging from black through red to light blonde. The pieces are polished, oiled, and colored with red *tukula* powder. The aesthetic qualities of the object shown in figure T, for example, are greatly enhanced by the golden brown surface. The rich patina on even utilitarian objects, such as spoons, and on simple abstract carvings heightens their visual appeal. In one of my favorite anecdotes pertaining to the Lega, Biebuyck once recounted having obtained a new

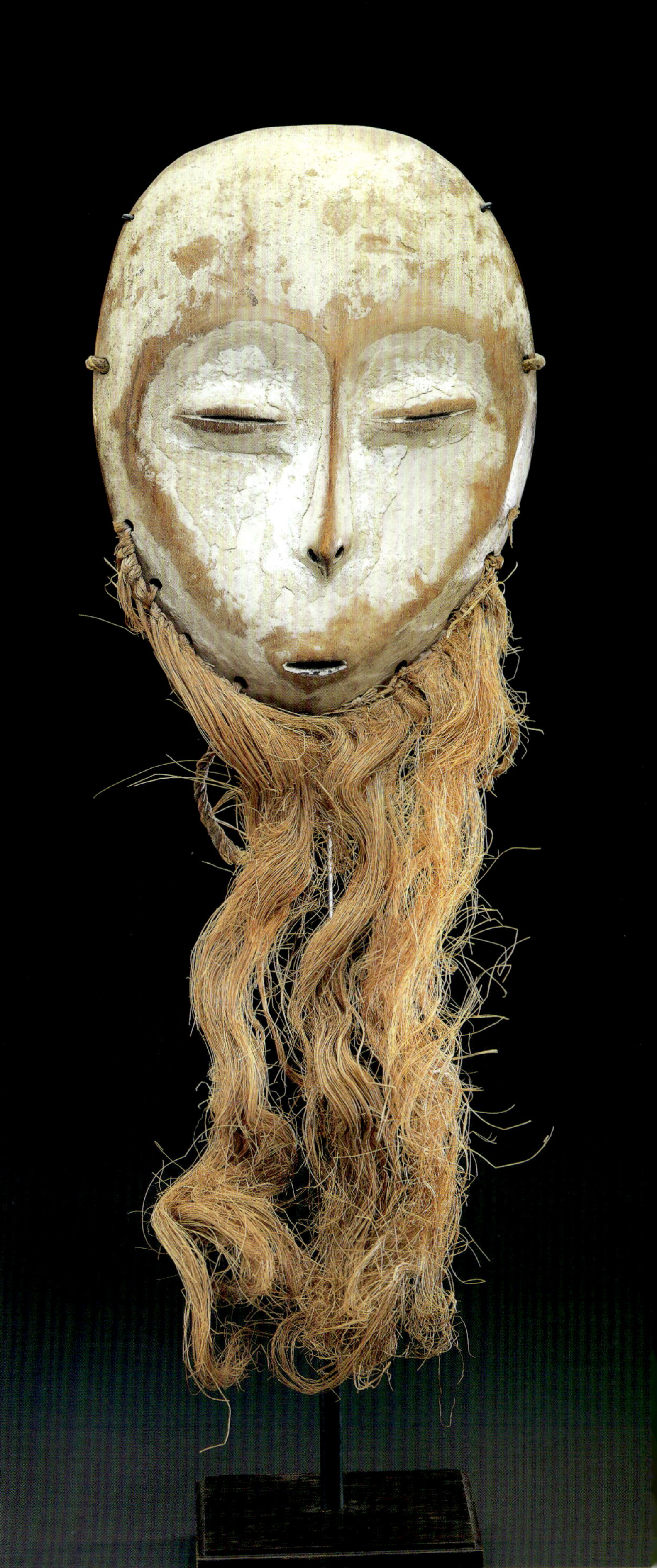

M

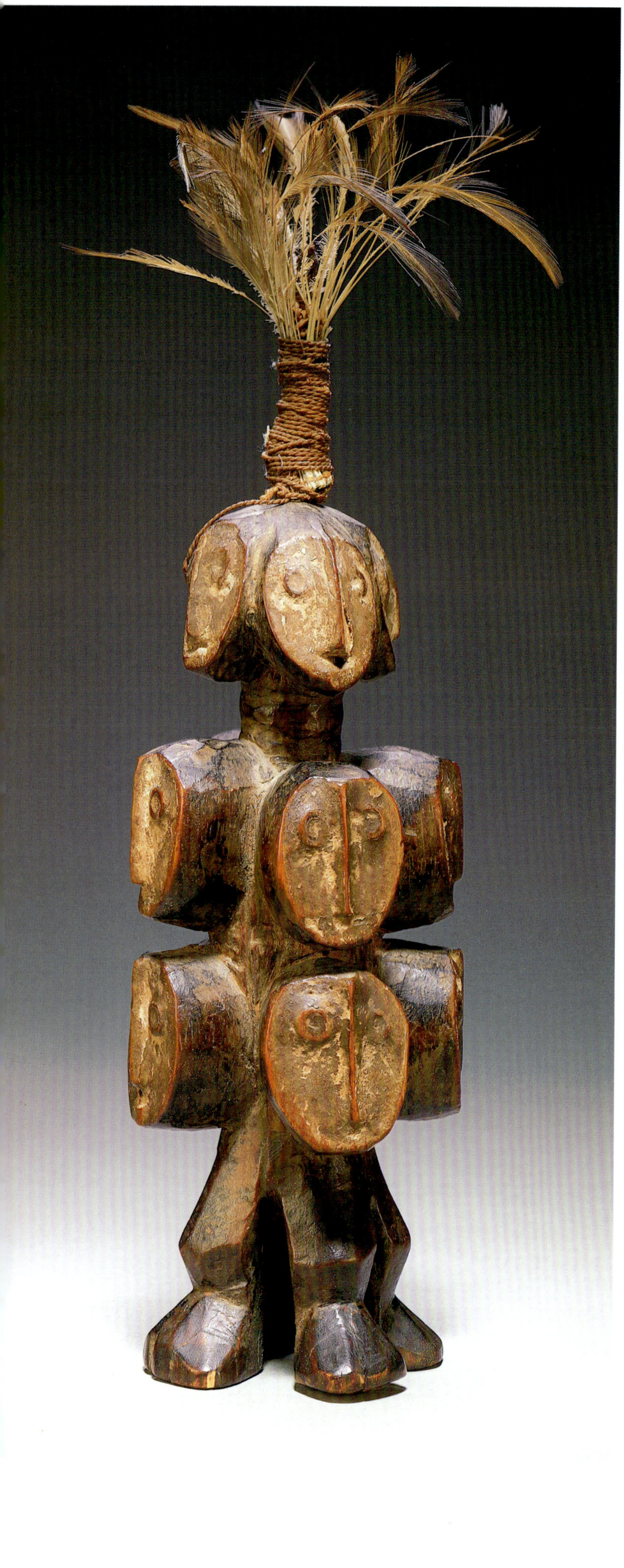

N Multiheaded human figure. Wood, feathers, pigment, and cord. H: 32.3 cm (12¾ in.).

O Multiheaded human figure. Wood and pigment. H: 19.9 cm (7⅞ in.).

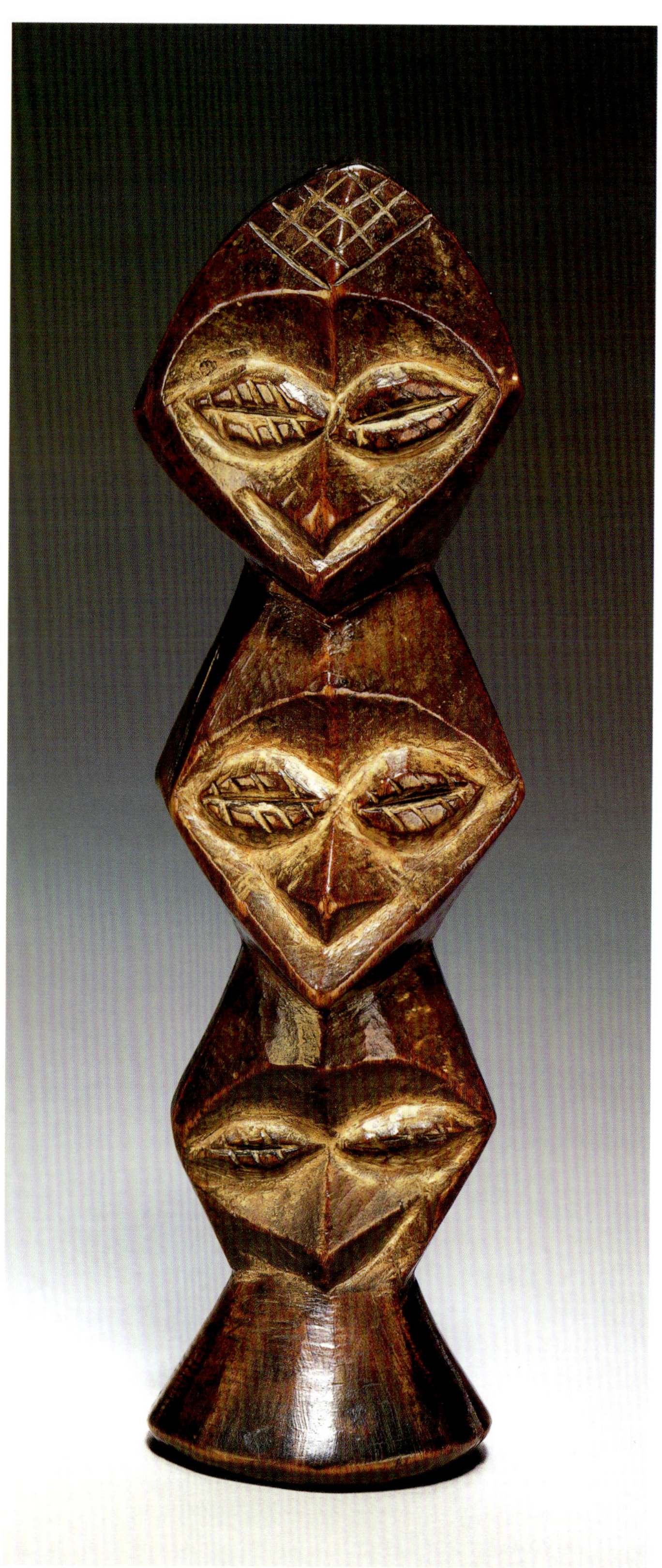

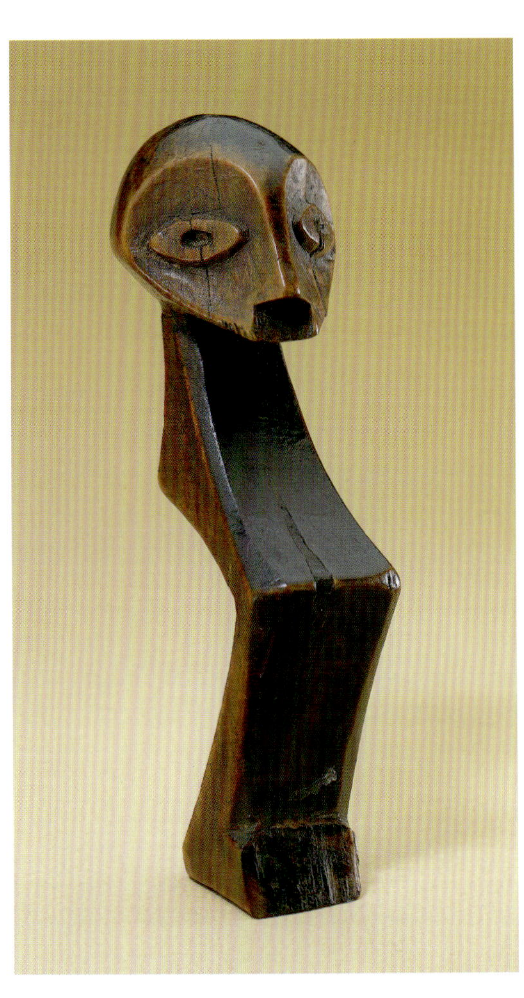

P Human figure (*nkumba* or *mulima*). Ivory. H: 9.8 cm (3⅞ in.).

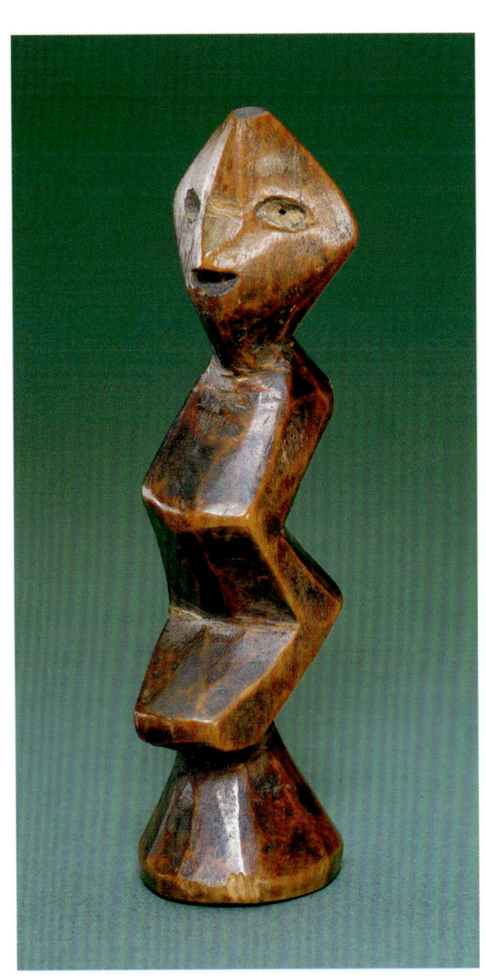

Q Human figure (*nkumba* or *mulima*). Wood. H: 10.1 cm (4 in.).

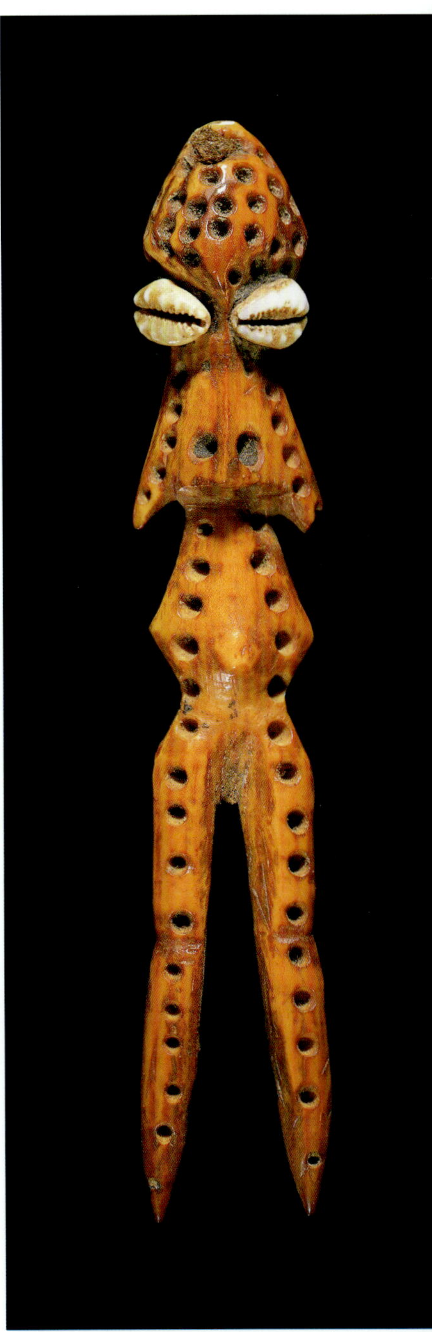

R Human figure. Ivory and cowries. H: 15.5 cm (6⅛ in.).

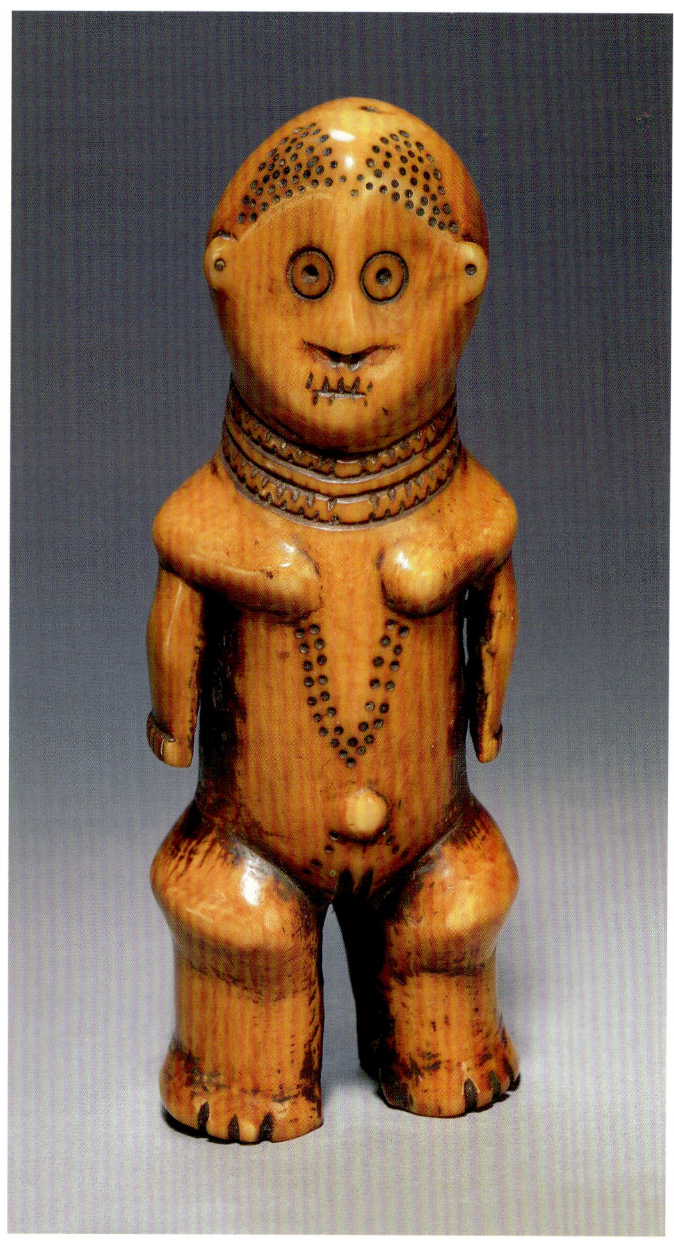

S Human figure. Ivory.
H: 14 cm (5½ in.).

vehicle as part of his research grant and driving it into the Lega country. He thought this European artifact would impress the Lega and was intrigued to see that they restricted their comments to the shiny paint and wood trim and had little interest in the mechanical workings.

In light of the Lega interest in patina, I was struck by a number of pieces where the surface, usually on the back of the figure, was deliberately scraped away. Some pieces were seriously defaced, as is the animal shown in figure U. I was originally told by dealers that this was rodent damage but could not imagine that rodents would be so selective in the areas they destroyed. I then learned from Biebuyck of the practice of ritual scraping, where the dust removed from the object was made into tea to be consumed as a cure for serious ailments.

As I became more and more intrigued with Lega art, I set out to view as many objects as I could. I saw a large number of private collections in the United States and Europe but hardly any had more than a few Lega pieces. In the mid-1960s I visited the Musée Royal de l'Afrique Centrale in Tervuren, Belgium, which has a significant Lega collection, including the large number of pieces that Daniel Biebuyck collected during his fieldwork in the Congo. At Tervuren, I could study masterpieces as well as the collections in their reserves—including the large group of heads on pegs, which I enjoyed looking at from the standpoint of my interest in the serial image. At this same time, I visited Nicolas de Kun in Brussels and saw the Lega objects remaining in his possession. He generously shared details of his experiences in Lega country and made the magnificent gesture of giving me his Lega notes and photographs to be used for my future work in understanding the art.

I also visited the artist Willy Mestach in Brussels who kindly allowed me to make a leisurely inspection of his superb collection of African art, including many Lega masterpieces. Each piece in his collection seemed to form part of an integrated design concept. He and I were struck by the similarity of our tastes, my favorite pieces were usually his as well. During this visit, and many that succeeded it, I sensed that he and I could have exchanged our feelings for evaluating art without making many changes in our individual collections or the way we each collected. This impression was confirmed for me when I saw the selection of objects from his collection in the exhibition *The Intelligence of Forms—An Artist Collects African Art,*

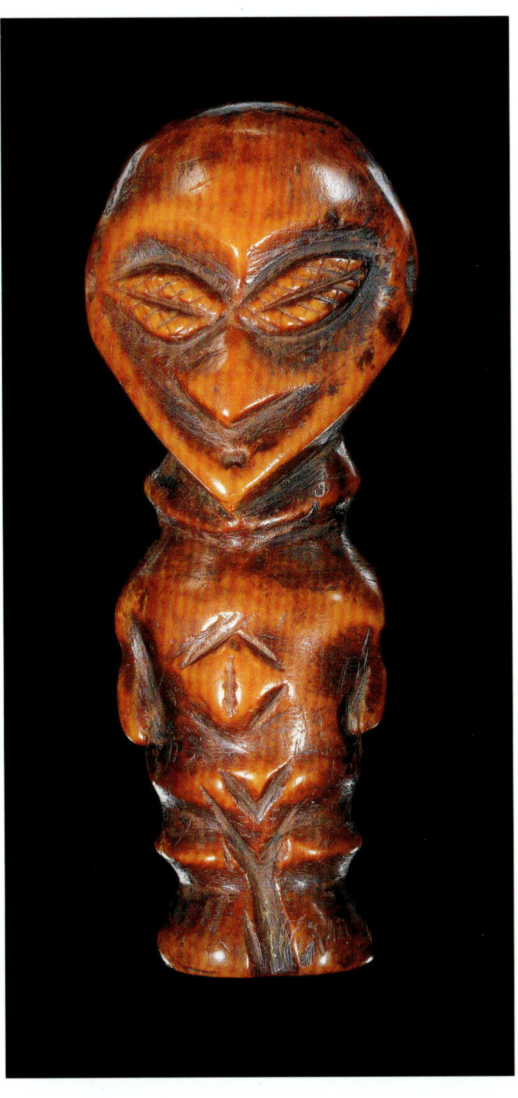

T Human figure. Ivory.
H: 12 cm (4¾ in.).

U Animal figure. Ivory.
L: 18.8 cm (7⅜ in.).

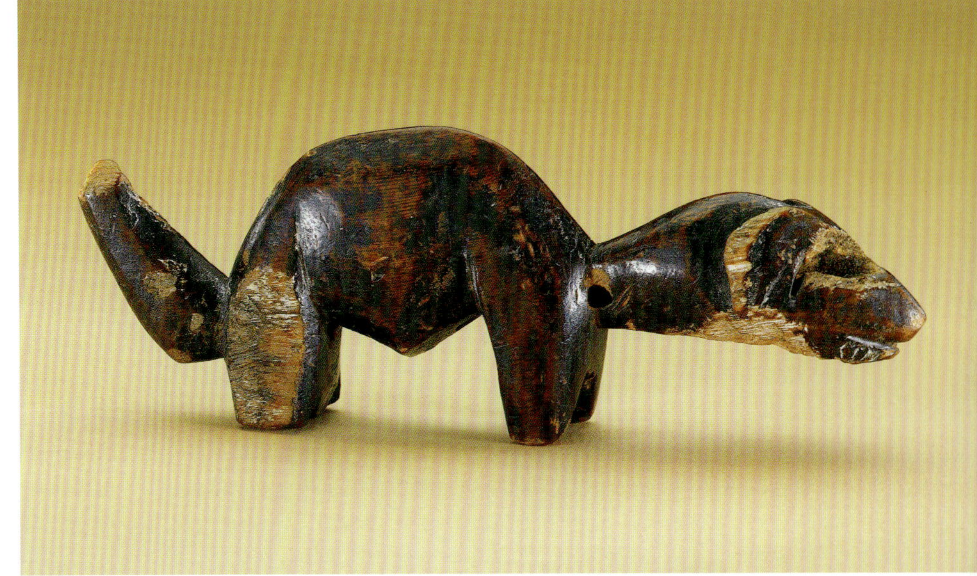

held at the Minneapolis Institute of Art in 1992, where African art was displayed in conjunction with his own paintings and sculpture.

Over the past twenty years, Marc Leo Felix has been of great help to me in my Lega collecting and research. Living in Brussels and traveling widely in Africa, he has been able to find many unusual Lega objects that have added to the breadth of my collection. He has been an invaluable source of information and has been able to put Lega material into a broader context for me with his wide knowledge of the subgroups that surround the Lega.

While I assembled a large general collection of African art during my collecting years—focusing on cultures that produced art tending toward the abstract, such as groups in the Cameroon highlands and in Mali—my main interest remained in material from the Congo in general and with the Lega in particular. After years of reading, viewing objects, and talking to people who have had firsthand experience in the Lega country and surrounding areas, I have developed a great appreciation of the relationship between Lega art and culture. In studying the large number of Lega pieces I have had the fortune to see, I have formulated numerous questions about Lega art and Lega carvers, most of which unfortunately can only be dealt with by speculation.

Little is known about the Lega artists who produced this amazingly varied body of material. The high-quality carving tradition had disappeared by the time Biebuyck did his fieldwork in the 1950s with the last great carvers probably working in the 1920s and 1930s. As Biebuyck discusses in detail in his essay "The Decline of Lega Sculptural Art" in *Ethnic and Tourist Arts* (1976), the variety of external influences to which the Lega were subjected throughout the twentieth century greatly weakened the Bwami Society and led to a decline in the training and teaching process for new artists. For more information on this subject, see chapter 4 of this volume.

Among the questions pertaining to artistic practice that particularly intrigue me are: How was the carver trained, and how were aesthetic concepts passed along? What was the artist's role in Lega society? How was the piece commissioned and acquired by the eventual owner? How important was the artistic quality of the piece to its Lega owner? What went on in the mind of the Lega carver when he was producing these masterpieces? What constraints did he feel he was subject to? While we have only sketchy information relating to many of these points, Elisabeth Cameron does an admirable job of dealing with these matters in the text that follows. Hopefully, more information may yet be discovered in obscure Belgian museum, government, and missionary archives.

Several thousand Lega objects of bewildering diversity remain in existence. As a people, the Lega have never numbered more than about 250,000, and presumably only a small percentage of them were carvers possessing the skill and training to create these beautiful and imaginative objects. How was so much varied material created and preserved? It seems logical to conclude that the body of Lega art existing today was produced over a very long time period and passed down from generation to generation, so that many Lega pieces are very old.

This is consistent with the Lega use of the objects, which were kept hidden away in baskets—unavailable for inspection by those who were not members of the Bwami Society—and were used only during infrequent Bwami ceremonies and funeral rites. Since many objects appear very worn, they must have been used over a long period. Being small, and having been stored away in a protected place, they were not as exposed to the elements and insects that have destroyed so much African material. While a few objects were disposed of in funerary ceremonies, most were handed down to future members of Bwami, forming an increasingly rich body of material as the generations passed.

This lengthy accumulation of art over a very long time period can perhaps explain at least in part the bewildering number of styles in existence. The work of numerous artists over time is certainly represented in the existing body of work, and the extant art can be looked on as a living museum of Lega carving. Lega art may well include some of the oldest surviving African art objects. For example, the massive ivory figure illustrated in figure V appears to be ancient, with its bulky primitive form and weathered aspect.

The fact that there are so many differing styles and variations within styles may have something to do with the fact that Lega art was semisecret, hidden away and used only during ceremonies, many of which occurred at night or with an audience limited to members of Bwami. As opposed to Kuba court carvers, for example, or artists who carved in public among many African groups, the Lega carver would not have had a plethora of examples to consult on a daily basis and copy. Also, as contrasted with much African art, the power of a Lega piece did not depend on it being a duplicate of existing pieces to enable it to fit into a formal Lega iconography. Therefore, if the Lega artist knew in general terms what he was supposed to create and had a good imagination coupled with technical competence, he would be more likely to come up with an innovative design than would have been the case if he were asked to copy an existing work.

It is with wood figures that Lega creativity reaches its highest point. Carving problems, potential breakage, and size limitations involved with producing objects of ivory become less difficult when working in wood. Figures with raised arms, protruding heads, and zigzags can be realized (figs. D, N, P, Q). With the wealth of design treatments possible in wood, it is interesting that wood figures are rare when compared to ivory ones. Wood figures, however, would not have been as likely to survive for generations, being more likely to crack or break and to be subject to insect or rodent damage. Their larger size in general would have contributed to problems of storage and preservation. Ivory objects were certainly more highly valued, so less care may have been given to the preservation of those made of wood. So, even if wood objects had been made in quantities comparable to ivory examples, a smaller number would have been likely to survive. Also of note, ivory objects are in general of more interest to collectors than those made of wood. The colonial officials, missionaries, and mining officials who collected the early Lega material may have focused on acquiring ivory objects rather than wood, and so the body of material existing in Western collections may not be representative of Lega art as a whole.

The number of subgroups in the Lega area, some of which are intermixed with the Lega, further complicates the discussion of Lega art. Most objects coming from the area have for lack of detailed knowledge and for the sake of convenience been grouped together under the designation "Lega." Even if the exact point and circumstances of collection are known, the age of Lega objects and the relatively small distances involved have doubtless resulted in the migration of pieces from one area to another, making a detailed geographical analysis of Lega artistic substyles difficult and not especially enlightening.

I feel fortunate to have been collecting African art during the last four decades of the twentieth century, a time of great change for the world in general and Africa

v Human figure. Ivory.
H: 26 cm (10¼ in.).

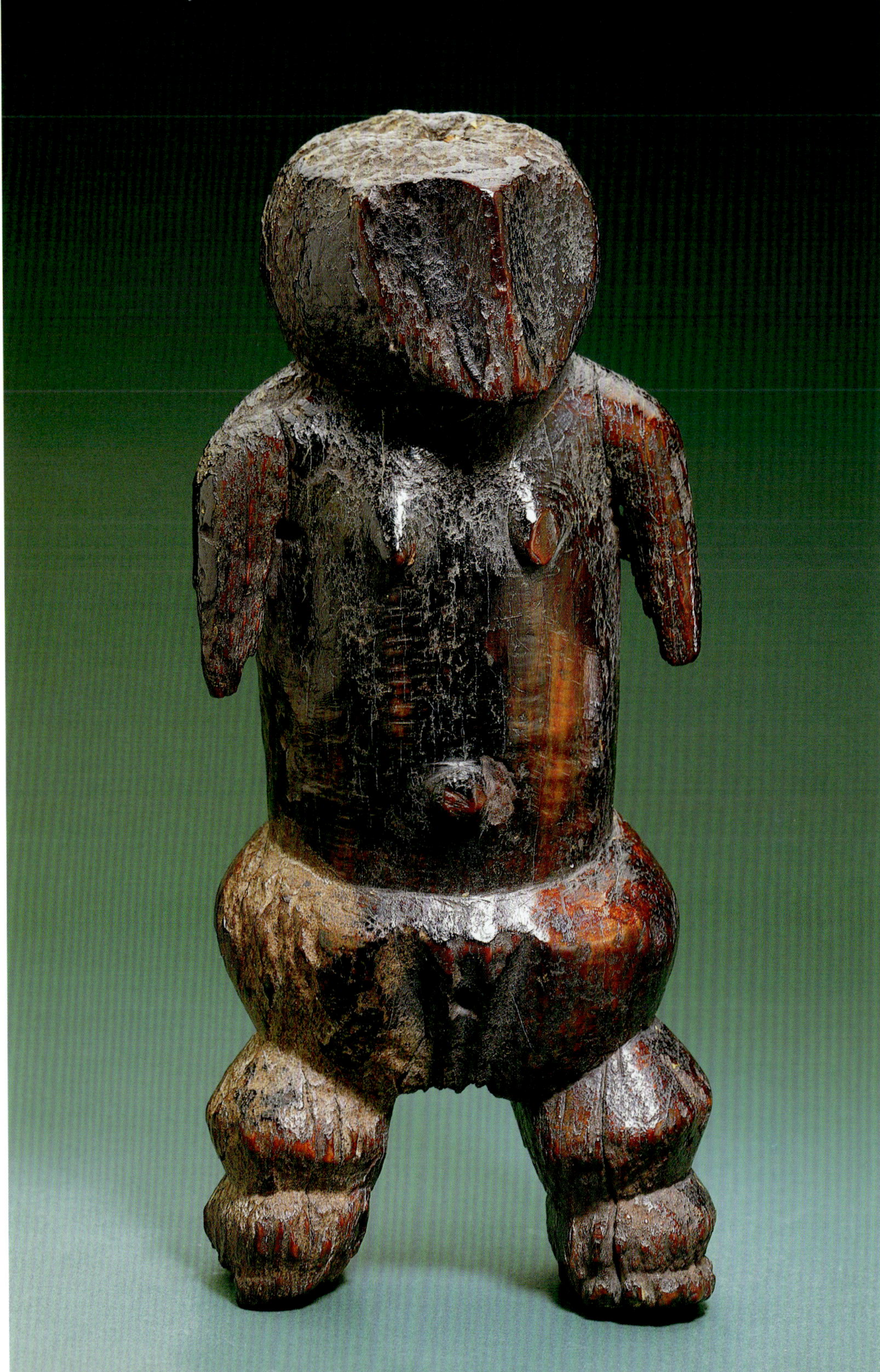

in particular. My voyage among the Lega for these past forty years has been an exciting and rewarding one for me. It is an ongoing voyage, for I continue to increase my appreciation of the Lega and Lega art with every additional piece I see.

I could not have learned about the Lega and built up my collection without the help of the scholars and dealers mentioned here and the numerous collectors and museums who have kindly allowed me to view their treasures. Their cooperation and friendship have been a valuable part of my life, and I extend my heartfelt thanks to them all. I especially want to thank Elisabeth Cameron. I would also like to thank my wife, Deborah, whose companionship, insightful discussions, and astute observations have made collecting a lot more fun and the collection much richer. I am very pleased to have the opportunity to share my interest in the Lega through this book and the accompanying exhibition.

Jay T. Last

Acknowledgments

> Where many have passed, it is there that there are footprints.
>
> Lega Proverb (Defour n.d., 3)

As I have worked on this volume and exhibition, I have indeed walked in the footprints of others. I am pleased now to have an opportunity to acknowledge those who have gone before me in the study and appreciation of the Lega people and their arts. The first who must be acknowledged is Dr. Jay Last. I initially visited Jay's collection in 1987 with my graduate advisor, Arnold Rubin, who was in search of art from the Benue Valley in Nigeria. Little did I know that my path and Jay's would repeatedly cross and converge in regard to topics as diverse as Lega art and nineteenth-century American cigar box labels. I was pleased and honored when Jay and Doran Ross asked me to write this volume and curate the accompanying exhibition. I know that Lega art is the closest to Jay's heart, and I appreciate the trust and freedom he has given me in working with this extraordinary collection. Jay's vast knowledge and deep affection for Lega art make talking to him about his collection stimulating from both an intellectual and an aesthetic perspective. The opportunity to visit with Deborah Last was yet another pleasure derived from frequent trips to study the collection. My apologies to Deborah for removing her favorite Lega mask from her desk for inclusion in the exhibition. Unless otherwise noted in the caption, all artworks reproduced in this catalog are from the collection of Jay T. Last and are promised gifts to the UCLA Fowler Museum of Cultural History.

In my work on the Lega, I have, of necessity, relied heavily on the research of other scholars. One set of footprints that I have constantly walked in belong to Daniel P. Biebuyck. When I first started researching the Lega, I found that Biebuyck's work was the most complete and insightful. In the course of writing my earlier works on the Lega, he shared information and graciously advised, anxious to keep a young scholar on the straight and narrow. Although he was unable to read this manuscript before publication, he has allowed us to reproduce a number of rare photographs. The reader should be aware, therefore, that although the photographs and much of the original research are Biebuyck's, any mistakes or misinterpretations are mine alone.

During the research on this book and the exhibition, I have visited and interviewed individuals in many different places. In Brussels, Boris Wastiau at the Musée Royal de l'Afrique Centrale in Tervuren, Belgium, allowed me access to colonial records, photographs, and the collections, as well as being an excellent colleague who kept pointing me to small caches of seemingly forgotten archival information. Anne-Marie Bouttiaux, also of the Musée Royal, provided an open door, a willing ear, and much assistance. Marc Leo Felix gave me a warm reception, Congolese food, and open access to his incredible library. (I have decided that one version of heaven is to be given carte blanche to examine Marc's library.) Louis de Stryker, with his usual courtly manner, shared several adventures with me while seeking information on the Lega in Belgium. Emile-Alexandre Georges, a Belgian administrator assigned to the Lega area in the late 1950s, and his wife, Jacline, shared with Jay Last and me their large collection of Lega art, valuable information, and extremely rare film footage. Benoit Rousseau, a mining engineer active in the Lega area in the 1960s, showed me his wonderful collection of Lega ivories and has kindly allowed us to use many of his own photographs. The multitalented Charles Henault welcomed us into his home and allowed us free rein with photographs that date from his tenure at the National Museum in Kinshasa. In Washington, D.C., many thanks must go to the staff of the Eliot Elisofon Archives brilliantly led by Christraud Geary.

In Kansas City, Deborah Emmont Scott, chief curator of the Nelson-Atkins Museum of Art, championed this project and was one of the best bosses I have ever had. Director Marc Wilson encouraged the collaboration between the two museums. The staff of the Department of African Art at the Nelson-Atkins deserve more than just appreciation and thanks. Without them, this book and exhibition simply would not have happened. Joyce Youmans, Curatorial Assistant, was a partner in the research and the development of the ideas represented in the catalog. Amy Rosenfeld, Departmental Assistant, organized all the logistics of research trips. More importantly, she proofread the manuscript and told me when I was being too obscure for the non-Africanist reader. Both encouraged me when I most needed it. In other departments at the Nelson-Atkins, Cindy Cart, Curator of Exhibitions Management, worked her magic with contract details. Julie Mattsson will organize the logistics of bringing the exhibition to Kansas City. Carol Inge Hockett and Rebecca Ofiessh will ably organize the community and educational activities for the show's visit to Kansas City. Once the exhibition reaches Kansas City, members of many other departments will exercise their customary professionalism and good humor in its service. My thanks to each and every one of them.

At the UCLA Fowler Museum, the entire staff has again gone above and beyond the call of duty in bringing this project to fruition. My thanks go to Farida Sunada for keeping track of all the information about each artwork and answering frequent requests for information by an off-site curator who needed to know what number was written on the bottom left foot of a piece; to Fran Krystock for keeping track of all the artworks and organizing complicated visits to the collection; Don Cole for bringing out the best side of each piece in his photography; David Mayo for taking my rambling exhibition ideas and giving them dynamic form and shape; Betsy Quick for her ability to interpret the complex ideas surrounding Lega art in ways that are simple and direct; Lyn Avins for once again writing an inspired curriculum that will live beyond the exhibition; Ilana Gatti and Alicia Katano for arranging the details of many visits and events; Karyn Zarubica for organizing the multiple venues; Betsy Escandor for cheerfully answering innumerable logistical questions; Lynne Kostman for making my writing sing, not an easy task; and Danny Brauer for combining the text and images into an elegant and inspired design.

My final deeply felt thanks go to Doran Ross. Doran has shaped my career and scholarship from the time I was a first-year graduate student. If I had to discount everything I have done that Doran had been involved with in some way, my accomplishments would be few indeed. In his many roles at the UCLA Fowler Museum, the last of which was as its director, Doran Ross has helped shape not only my career but the field of African art in the United States. Rather than focusing on his own work and interests, Doran has consistently supported the work of innovative scholars and projects to the benefit of the entire field. Doran is now retiring from the Museum, and I know that I, along with many others, look forward to the success of his own future projects and publications. I count it an honor to consider Doran Ross as a mentor, colleague, and friend.

Elisabeth L. Cameron

Introduction

My introduction to the Lega peoples and their art was abrupt and intense. In 1991, when I was a graduate student, Doran Ross, then deputy director of the UCLA Museum of Cultural History, asked me to write an essay on Lega ivories. Although I had studied the art of the Lega in the course of my graduate work in art history, I was by no means an expert. I felt, however, that this was too good an opportunity to pass up, and as a consequence, I spent countless hours in the library during the next month reading about Lega art, culture, politics, religion, and history. As I immersed myself in the literature, I became especially fascinated by the complex and voluntary society called Bwami that the Lega used to structure much of their lives and their interactions with other communities. My previous research on the Sala Mpasu in the Democratic Republic of the Congo had led me to examine how art could be used as a mechanism of political and economic structure for noncentralized peoples (Cameron 1988, 1991). Studying the Lega, however, convinced me that the political uses of art in noncentralized societies were more varied and, for me at least, more interesting than those observed in centralized chiefdoms or kingdoms.[1] Thus while Jay Last was first attracted to the extraordinary sculpture of the Lega and subsequently became interested in the Lega themselves (see Last, this volume), I was first drawn to Lega culture and then turned with delight to Lega art. I have continued to pursue my research on the Lega and their art over the past decade.

Although only a few scholars have conducted field research among the Lega, the simplicity, strength, and abstract nature of their artistic forms have long attracted the attention of the Western art world. Lega art is first documented as appearing in Arab markets in the nineteenth century and has been known in the West since the beginning of the twentieth century. Early explorers, however, avoided the Lega area because of the defenses the peoples there had developed to fend off Arab incursions. Only after the Belgians took control of the Congo do we begin to see a problematic interest in the Lega and their culture, politics, and art.

Commander Delhaise, the Belgian administrative official who was assigned to the area in 1906 and 1907, wrote the earliest complete report on the Lega, *Les Warega* (1909).[2] Although he took great interest in the peoples around him and was invited to Bwami Society ceremonies, Delhaise did not learn the language; he depended on third parties to tell him what he was seeing and to interpret the experiences for him. After Delhaise left, a string of administrators sent in yearly reports concerning the Lega in accordance with instructions issued by the Belgian government. These reports often addressed such issues as marriage practices (Engels 1939). The length and tone of the reports ranged from an abrupt two pages to longer, more detailed accounts accompanied by careful but amateurish drawings and maps. After Bwami was halfheartedly outlawed in the 1930s, and then more firmly banned in 1947, officials stopped documenting the activities of the Society and describing its arts in their reports. One Belgian who continued to maintain good relationships with Bwami members and to write about Lega culture was François Corbisier. Corbisier lived in the Lega area between 1927 and 1955, spoke the language, and had access to all the territorial archives. In 1968 he wrote a short, unpublished manuscript describing the sculpture used in the Bwami Society.

Government officials were not the only foreigners to visit the region. The Lega area, being rich in minerals, also drew mining engineers. One of these was Nicolas de Kun who worked there in the 1950s. De Kun became interested in Lega art, and in an attempt to gather information, he attached a Lega mask to his windshield. When people asked him why the mask was there, he would ask to see more art and offer to buy it. He also collected information about the Bwami Society and its attendant artworks, checking all his facts with Bwami leaders (Muyololo 1974, 28) and eventually publishing an important article, "L'art Lega" (1966).

Daniel Biebuyck is the most prolific and deservedly the best known of all scholars of Lega art and culture; he is also the author I cite most frequently. After having spent several years among the neighboring Bembe, he arrived in the Lega area in 1952 and worked there until 1954. Because of his patience and the personal relationships he developed, he was allowed to witness the outlawed Bwami ceremonies and to study and collect the art.[3] Biebuyck has written and continues to write nearly all of the primary literature on the Lega and their art. The field of African art owes him a debt of gratitude for his dedication to Lega studies.

Several ethnic Lega scholars, including Mulyumba wa Mamba Itongwa, Muyololo Lutala Amuri, and Yogolelo Tambwe ya Kasimba have provided insiders' perspectives that differ from the accounts of their European colleagues. In the 1970s, they studied at the National University in Lubumbashi and wrote masters theses on Lega art and culture. Some of these were published in *Les cahiers du CEDAF* (Brussels). Mulyumba wa Mamba completed his doctorate at the Université Libre de Bruxelles in 1977 with a dissertation on Lega social structure.

The most recent author to visit the area is Marc Leo Felix, who traveled among the Lega and their neighbors during the 1980s. His book *Maniema* (1989) places masks produced by the various Lega subgroups within the context of the masquerade traditions of the Lega's neighbors. Although my brief discussion of Lega scholars has been limited to those who focus on artistic production, other individuals have studied different aspects of Lega life. Many scholars have researched Lega migrations, history, and oral epics. Others have examined the geographic region inhabited by the Lega peoples. The combination of these resources makes possible a vivid reconstruction of the Lega, their world, and their art.

~

The primary focus of this volume is the art object. The Lega become aware of art in a particular sequence as they proceed through the levels of the Bwami Society. First, they are exposed to natural materials selected because of their particular meaning and their aesthetic form (see figs. 6.1–6.3). The artist might combine these found objects in various ways using assorted materials or techniques, such as wickerwork structures or clay employed to hold multiple objects together (see figs. 6.4, 6.7, 6.9). Only in the highest levels of Bwami will the Lega see those sculptures and masks that are the best known of their artworks in Europe and America. This category includes miniature tools in ivory or bone (see figs. 6.33–6.44); imaginative wood figures in various positions (see figs. 8.1–8.114); zoomorphic figures (see figs. 7.1–7.24); and masks of different sizes and shapes (see figs. 9.1–9.70).

My goal in this volume is to provide enough information about the Lega, their environment, and their social structures for the reader to develop an aesthetic appreciation of the layers of meanings assigned to the objects by the Lega and by the Western world. Since the Lega are keen observers of the world around them and use their environment as a source of symbolic references, I begin part one with a discussion of their physical world. I then move to their social community, focusing on the three structures that provide the framework for Lega life: family, circumcision camp, and the Bwami Society.[4] Once sufficient background has been established, I give an overview of Lega artistic practice and aesthetics. This in turn is followed by an examination of the objects that indicate to the greater Lega public who the Bwami members are and what their status is within the Society.

In part two, I consider the art of the Lega per se. The reader follows the path of the Bwami initiate who moves from simple found objects in the basic levels of the Society to the sculpture and masks of the two highest levels. Reflecting the Lega principle of letting the object be the focus and center around which different meanings radiate, discussions of symbol, meaning, and material are integrated into the analysis of each group of artworks. The Lega as presented in this volume are, to some extent, idealized. In an effort to mitigate this problem, the conclusion traces the history of their contact with outsiders in an attempt to bring the reader up to date.

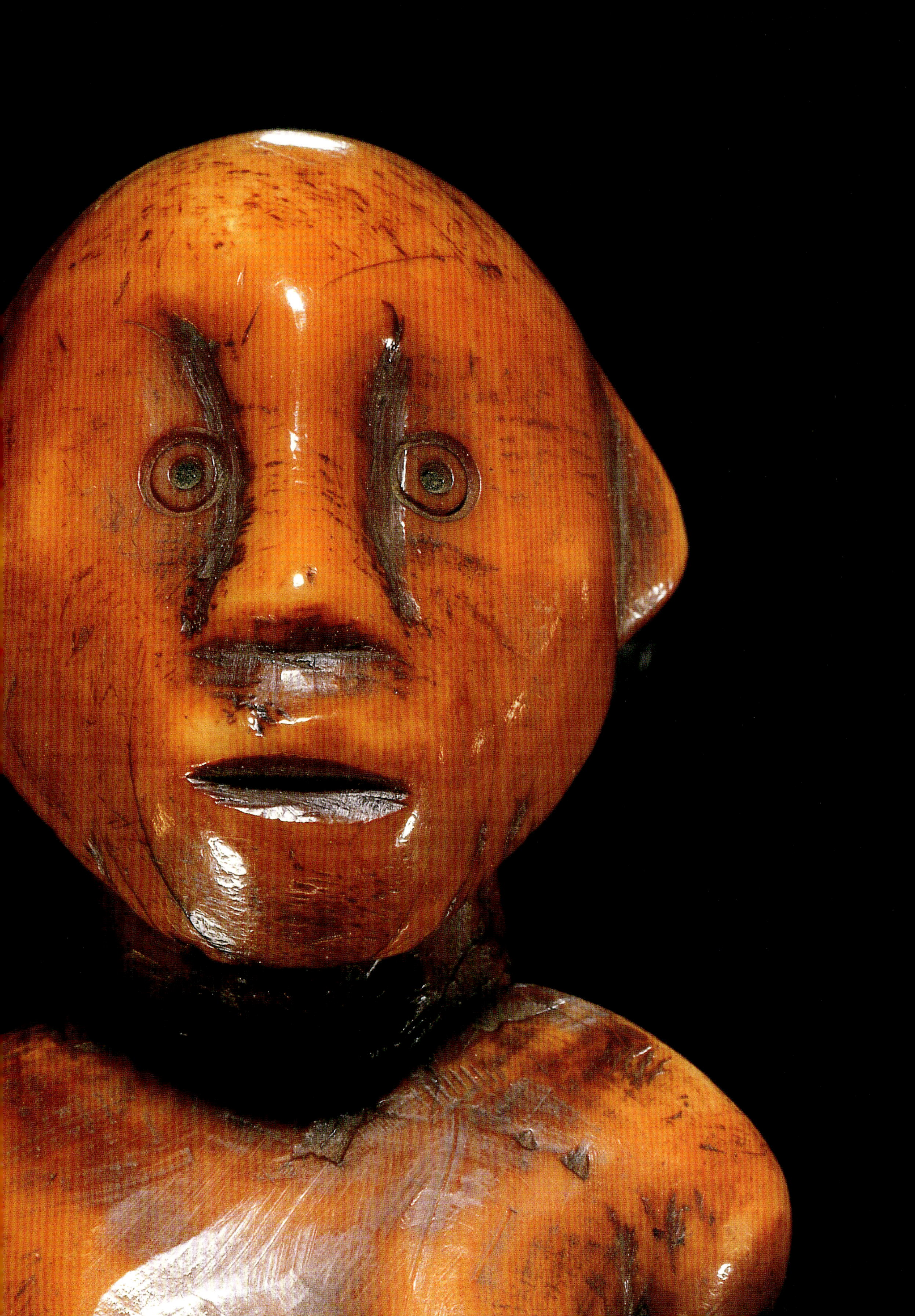

PART 1

Introduction to the Lega and Layered Metaphors

1 The Lega and Their Environment

Nearly all Lega peoples believe themselves to be descended from an original eponymous ancestor. The original Lega's descendants migrated into what is now known as Kivu Province in the Democratic Republic of the Congo (the former Zaire; see map, fig. 1.2).[1] As they moved into the area from the north—a process that may have taken decades or more—they found a varied landscape, ranging from deep tropical rain forests traversed by rock-filled swiftly coursing rivers in the west to a less densely forested region at a higher altitude in the east (figs. 1.1, 1.3–1.5).

As they established themselves in their new surroundings, individual families and settlements retained a sense of group unity based on a common language and value system and a shared past. These traits distinguished them from their neighbors (Mulyumba wa Mamba 1977, 16; Yogolelo 1975, 18; Biebuyck 1973, 3). Nonetheless they identified themselves primarily by their lineage and family and only secondarily as a part of the larger whole (Biebuyck 1966, 507). As a group, however, these peoples did become known among themselves and their neighbors as Balega, or "people of Lega." The Arabs, in the nineteenth century, mispronounced the name as *Warega*, a term that still occasionally appears in the literature.

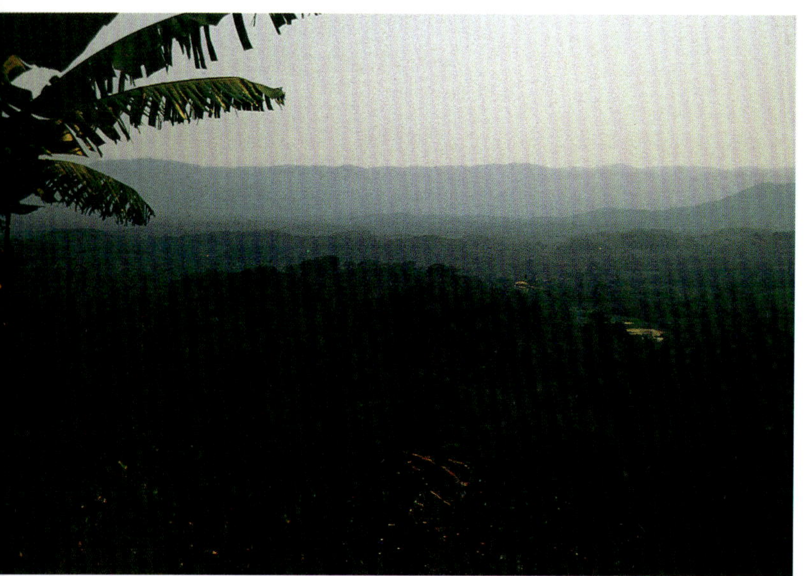

1.1 Lega landscape, mid-1960s. Photograph courtesy of M. Benoit Rousseau.

THE LEGA ENVIRONMENT

Covering a geographical area larger than Belgium, the Lega peoples are found in three administrative districts: Mwenga and Shabunda in Sud Kivu Province and Pangi in Maniema Province (see map, fig. 1.2).[2] Because of the rugged environment, movement throughout the Lega area is difficult. This has resulted in small and fairly isolated communities, especially in the west where the Lega settled amongst the dense rainforest that covers much of the region. There is constant heat and humidity and a two-month dry season (June and July) in contrast to the four- and six-month dry seasons encountered on the savanna. The average rainfall ranges from sixty to eighty inches per year.

The forest is rich with animal and plant resources. These include monkeys and apes, antelopes, large rodents, the tree hyrax, forest elephants, pangolins (fig. 1.6), parrots and other forest birds, and leopards. In addition, the Lega keep domesticated goats, sheep, and chickens. Toward the east, where the land rises away from the Congo River basin and is rocky and less fertile, the climate becomes much cooler, and the resources more limited.

Few of the products of the forest are used as currency for exchange. Game meat can be exchanged for goods with the value defined by how many times a man has carried it on his shoulder; in other words, price is determined by freshness. Other exchange goods are manufactured, such as iron tools, metal arm rings, and small copper or shell discs (fig. 1.7). Domestic animals including goats, sheep, and dogs are also sometimes traded (Biebuyck 1953b, 675). National currency is used within the area but does not replace the exchange of traditional goods necessary in certain ceremonies.

The ecology of the area has contributed to slight and significant differences in all Lega institutions. In the west where the Lega settled in the deep forest (*malinga*), people are able to live well primarily through hunting and gathering

1.2 Map of the area inhabited by the Lega peoples within the Democratic Republic of the Congo.

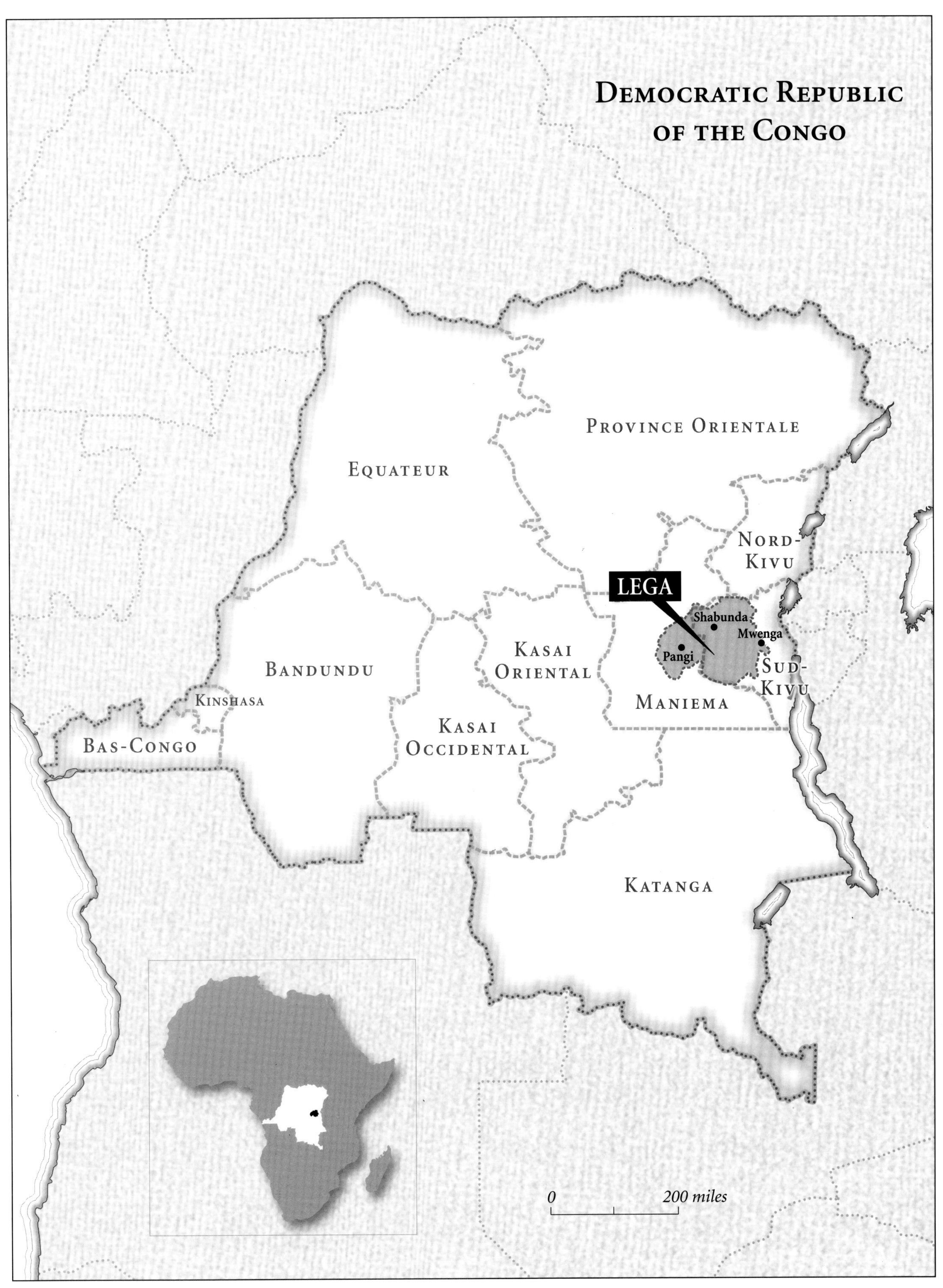
Democratic Republic
of the Congo
Province Orientale
Equateur
Nord-
Kivu
LEGA
Shabunda
Mwenga
Pangi
Kasai
Oriental
Sud-
Kivu
Bandundu
Kinshasa
Maniema
Kasai
Occidental
Bas-Congo
Katanga
0
200 miles

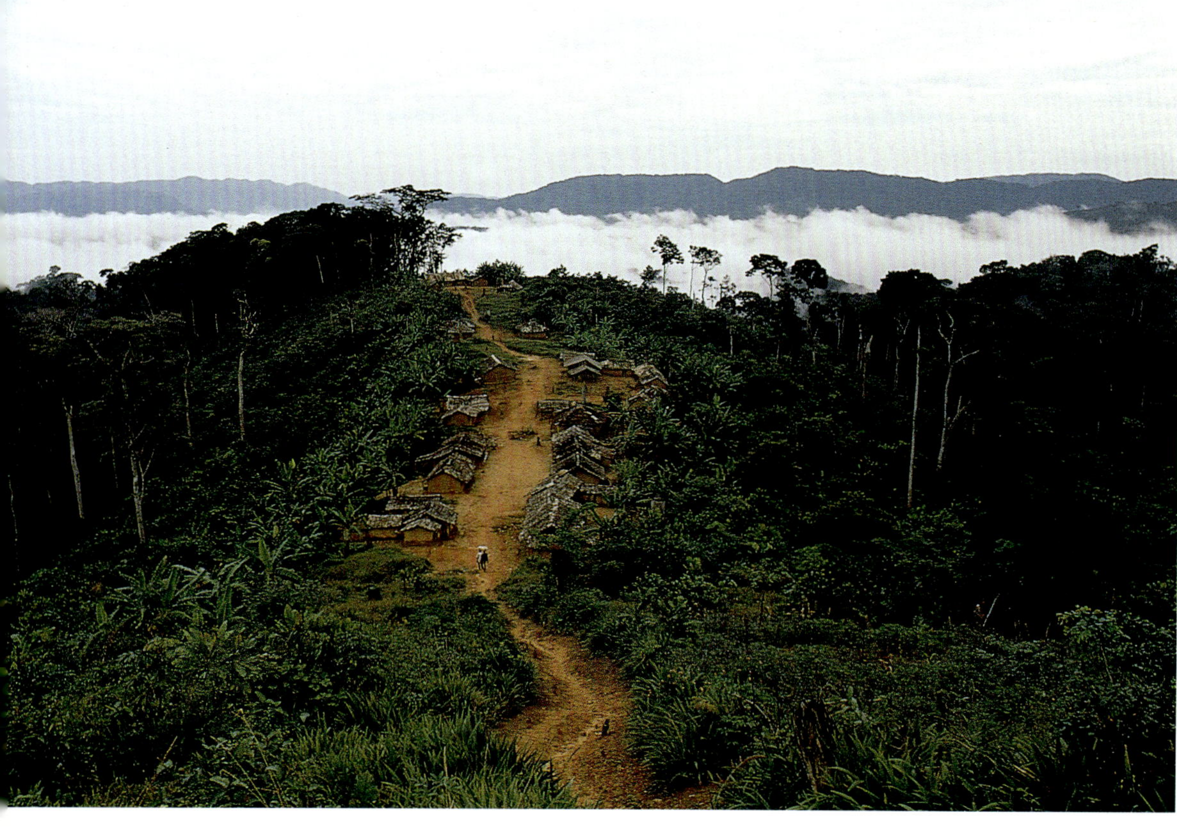

1.3 The Lega village of Bashi within a hillside clearing in deep forest. Photograph by Eliot Elisofon, 1967. Eliot Elisofon Photographic Archives, National Museum of African Art, Smithsonian Institution, no. T 3 LGA 32 EE 67.

the ample wealth offered by their environment. Delhaise, the first Belgian administrator assigned to the Lega area in 1906, noted that the Lega were peaceful hunters (Delhaise 1909, 54). In the east, however, with its higher altitude and poorer soil, people depend less on gathering nature's bounty and rely more on slash-and-burn agriculture. The emphasis changes from man as hunter to woman as farmer, as the overall economic health of the clan comes to depend more heavily on agriculture. Poor farming ability, for example, is ample cause for divorce (Mulyumba wa Mamba 1977, 373). The eastern area is called *ku ntata*, or "to the heights" (Mulyumba wa Mamba 1977, 372).

LEGA SUBGROUPS

The Lega, in spite of natural geographical regions, do not divide neatly into subgroups. In 1966 Biebuyck spoke of five subgroups characterized by cultural differences and regions (Biebuyck 1966, 507). Later in 1986 he listed six major subgroups: northern Lega in Shabunda (Bakisi), western Lega in Pangi (Beia and Babenen), southern Lega (Bababango of Kasamula and Kami of Pangi), southeastern Lega (Bakabango of Moligi in Shabunda), eastern Lega (Bamuzimu of Longangi in Mwenga), and northeastern Lega (Basimwende of Alenga in Mwenga; Biebuyck 1986, 11).

The Basile, a Lega subgroup living in the eastern, or *ku ntata*, area are one of the more divergent groups, and their family structure is slightly different from that of the western Lega (Mulyumba wa Mamba 1977, 380). Perhaps as a result of their less fortunate living situation, they have created a more centralized political and social structure. They are governed by a chief called *mwene-mbuka* and have a more centralized form of Bwami with only three levels as compared to the seven generally found in the west; the chief and the Bwami Society constitute a system of checks and balances. Nonetheless, specific and important families, especially that of the *mwene-mbuka*, control entrance and access to the higher levels (Mulyumba wa Mamba 1978, 9–10).

Biebuyck refers to the situation of the Lega as "unity fostered in diversity" (1973, 23). Each community is independent but bound to others by networks of shared lineage, institutions, and rituals. No matter what subgroup a Lega belongs to, he maintains an awareness of a unity that has its origin in a common past and the superimposed influences of family, circumcision, and Bwami.

LEGA SOCIAL STRUCTURE

In spite of the differences resulting from isolation and ecology, three shared social institutions have helped to distinguish and unify the Lega peoples: family or kinship (*ibuta*), circumcision rituals (*bwali*), and the Bwami Society (Biebuyck 1973, 57). The core social and political structures of the Lega lie within these traditions. Each of them exists independently and in intricate relationship with the others, creating checks and balances within the system. Status achieved within one of these spheres often determines or influences that in another.

IBUTA (KINSHIP)

Among all Lega groups, descent and inheritance pass through the father's family, although the mother's family plays important roles in various ceremonies and institutions. The relationship that one has with the mother's brother, or "male mother," is special. He is someone who can be turned to for financial support and guidance through Bwami and other relationships. Tracing kinship through both the primary patrilineal line (for major family ties and inheritance) and secondary matrilineal line (for ritual support) in areas where most marriages take place within the larger clan creates complicated interlocking relationships (Biebuyck 1973, 37–40; 1994, 26).

While inheritance of material goods and of possibilities for status within Bwami are passed through the father's line, it is important to note that social recognition and authority have to be individually earned (Biebuyck 1973, 37–38). Important clan positions tied to particular families begin with the head of any family unit (*mukota*). The leader of a settlement (called *nene, munzakyumo,* or *ntundu,* depending on the area) is a wise man of the oldest generation. His selection is based not only on age but also on whether he has heart (*mutima*), that is, good character, intelligence, and upstanding comportment. Each clan or lineage also has a leader called *nenekisi* who is ultimately responsible for the physical, moral, and spiritual welfare of his clan. Like the settlement leader, he is chosen from among the family heads based on his character and his record of achievements. He must also have heart and must have a proven record as a diplomat able to deal peacefully with other Lega groups and non-Lega neighbors (Biebuyck 1973, 46–49; Mulyumba 1968, 2). His decisions, made in consultation with a group of senior men often representing secondary lineages in the clan, are binding. The relationship of clan chief and the community of elders provides a system of checks and balances to prevent power from becoming consolidated in one person's hands (Delhaise 1909, 341–42).

To insure success, a clan incorporates both the living and the ancestors within a human-centered belief system. The Lega believe in a trinity of gods: Kinkunga, the creator, who is compared to a potter who has lost his smoothing tool and cannot quite finish his work; Kalaga, the planner, who finishes Kinkunga's work; and Kakinga, a force of chaos, who sometimes assumes a female identity. These gods are not controlling forces; therefore humankind—the living and the dead—is responsible for maintaining

1.4 A calm river crossing within the Lega region, mid-1960s. Photograph courtesy of M. Benoit Rousseau.

1.5 A boat crossing a river in the Lega area, mid-1960s. Photograph courtesy of M. Benoit Rousseau.

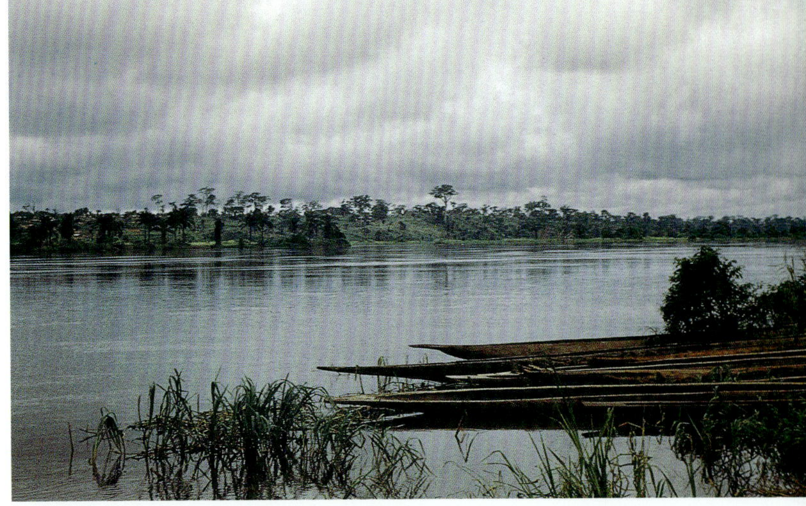

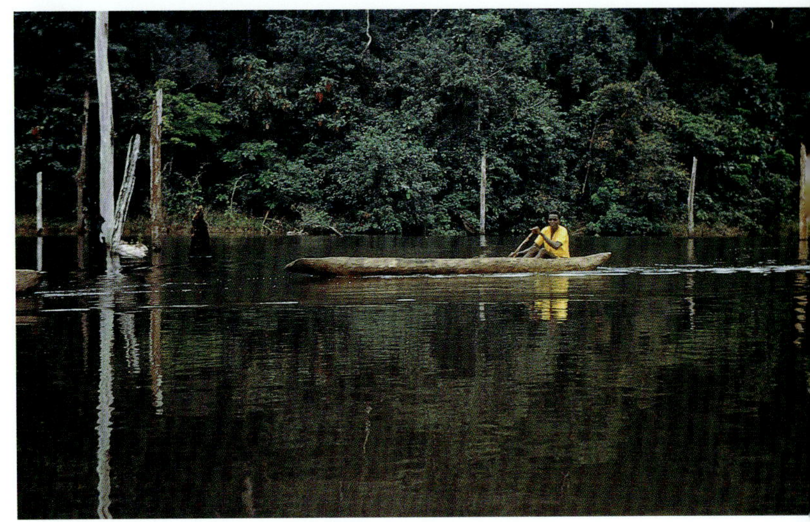

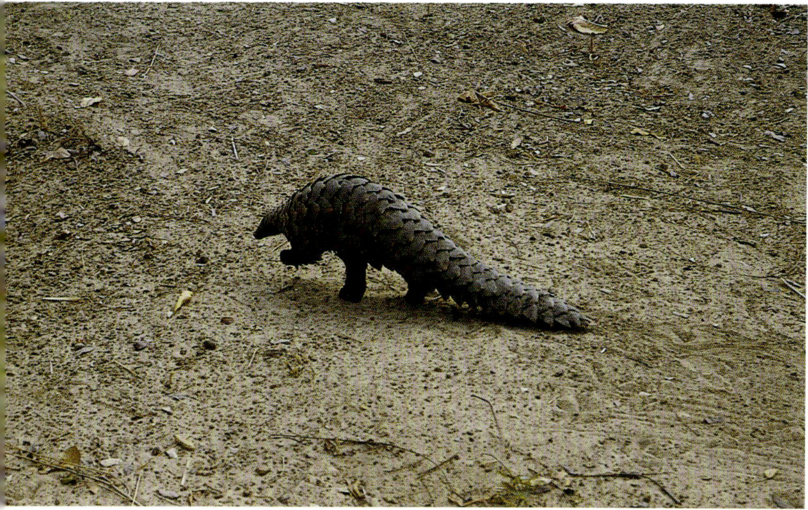

1.6 Pangolin. Photograph by Elisabeth L. Cameron, Chitofu Village, Zambia, 1992.

the moral and social order (Biebuyck 1973, 52–54; Mulyumba 1968). At death, according to information collected by Delhaise, Kalaga takes the body through decomposition and helps the human spirit move to the ancestral world (Delhaise 1909, 217). All people go to this world at death, but those who have not completed the basic rites leading to adult responsibilities—children, adolescents, and the incompetent—do not have the power to associate with the living (Mulyumba 1968, 9).

The Lega conceptualize the realm of their ancestors as a reflection of their own life. At death, one goes to live with the ancestors in Uchimu, a subterranean world divided into clans led by their original founder. A person's status and standing in life continue in the afterlife, so death becomes an extension of the mundane. Living and dead must combine forces to augment the status of the clan in both worlds (Mulyumba 1968, 9–14). While no formalized ancestral cult with priests and devotees exists, attention is always paid to the wishes and needs of the ancestors. The skulls of high-ranking members of Bwami, for example, are preserved by fellow members of equal rank and placed in a special shrine (Felix 1989, 52).

BWALI (CIRCUMCISION RITUALS)

The second important social structure for the Lega is the rite of circumcision (*bwali*). Circumcision is the first rite a boy must go through before he can function as an adult male in Lega society. Once circumcised, he has access to the adult world and the Bwami Society. Women are excluded from circumcision camp and are not allowed to see the boys between the time of the surgery and their return to the village. Although the Lega do not practice female circumcision, oral tradition states that it was formerly engaged in while male circumcision was not. The tradition further relates that because the procedure resulted in a high death rate among women, they passed the responsibility on to men. To counterbalance the exclusive nature of *bwali*, women retain the secrets of childbirth (Biebuyck 1973, 50).

Male circumcision camps (*lutende*) occur every five to ten years. Because of the interval of time between the camps, the boys and men included as initiates can range from as young as twelve to over twenty years of age. The camp moves from village to village and clan to clan in a cycle that lasts up to three years. Only a few lineages hold the *musimbi* right, that is, the authority to institute a camp. They have either held the right in their families or have purchased it from another clan. The person who has *musimbi* is at least a middle-level member of Bwami who has held the communal basket of the first level (see this volume, chapter 2) and has also held the right (*lutala*) to build a separate house (*okanga*) within the initiation camp for the boys of his lineage. Each holder of *musimbi* organizes only two camps before he passes the responsibility on to another (Biebuyck 1973, 51). The *musimbi* holder initiates the proceedings by sending a boy to a camp in a nearby area. The boy, after being circumcised in the neighboring camp, returns with sacred musical instruments, a bull-roarer, and a special piece of wood (*nkola za bwali*) that signifies the transfer of rites to the new location. After the holder of the *musimbi* right has the ritual objects, he establishes the new camp in the forest outside his village, receives a boy from the next village, and the rites begin.

The boys shave their heads and cover themselves with body paint—red with white stripes on the face, trunk, and arms. They wear skirts made of banana leaves. To enter the camp, the initiates must pass wood figures of a male and a female (Corbisier 1968, 10). This is one of the few instances of a non-Bwami use of sculpture among the Lega. Once the circumcisions are completed, the boys live in the small temporary house(s) built for them within the camp. They are taught how to be functioning adults, a process that includes lessons in hunting and fishing, as well as the basics of Lega ritual life (Burk 1956, 376). The older men also begin to impart Lega wisdom, the pursuit of which the boys will engage in for the rest of their lives. After the camp disbands and the boys return to a more normal routine, instruction continues through a process known as "the cord of wisdom" (see this volume, chapter 3; Corbisier 1968, 10–11; Biebuyck 1973, 51–3).

BWAMI SOCIETY

The final Lega institution to be considered is Bwami, a voluntary, noncentralized but highly hierarchical society. The primary purpose of Bwami is to instruct the initiate

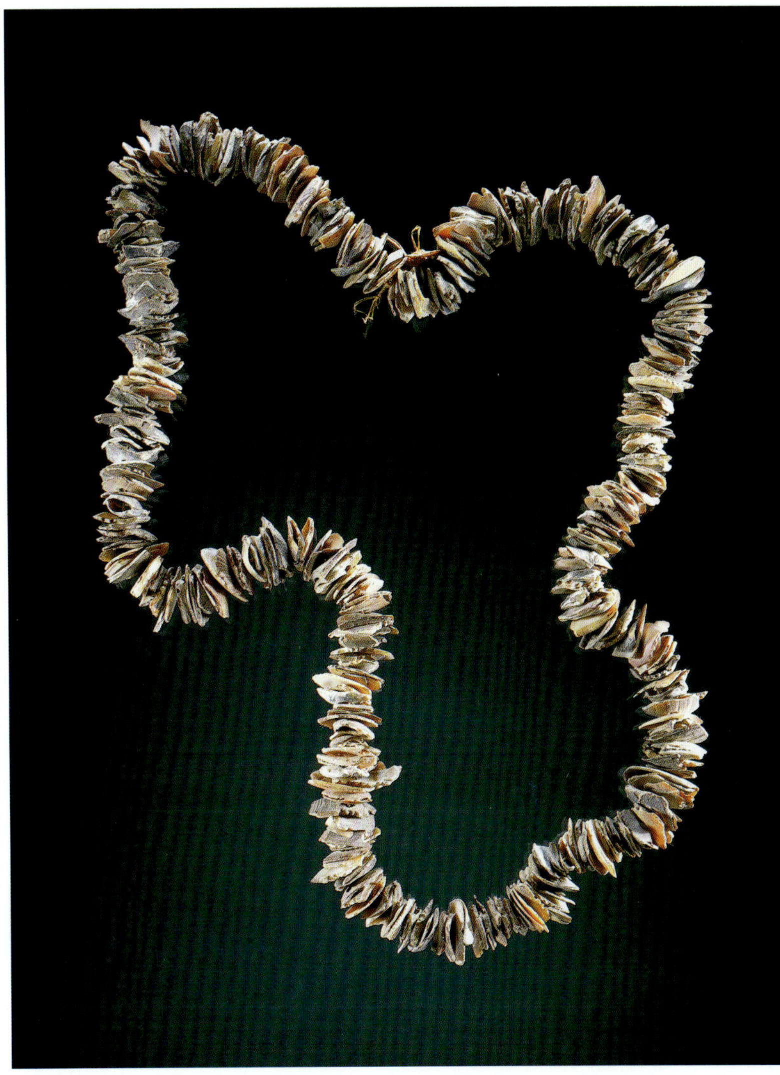

1.7 A Lega form of currency made from the shells of land snails. Land snail shells and vegetable fiber. L: 45.5 cm (18 in.). FMCH X78.644; Museum Purchase.

in "wisdom and moral excellence" (Biebuyck 1973, 91). It also fulfills political, economic, social, artistic, and religious roles in broader Lega society. When Daniel Biebuyck was initiated into the Bwami Society in the 1950s, approximately 95 percent of all adult Lega men were members (Biebuyck 1986, 14; correspondence with the author, 1994).

Marriage is an important factor qualifying men and women to join and move through the ranks of Bwami. A man cannot marry in many Lega areas until he has joined Bwami. A woman can join only if her husband is a member. Once husband and wife are both members, their rise to higher levels must occur in alternate fashion with one spouse moving up a level and not being able to progress further until the other spouse has also risen a level.

Men tend to marry and move to higher levels of Bwami at an older age than women because of the steps they must take in preparation. First, a man must be circumcised, an event which might not occur until he is in his early twenties. Then he has to gather the family and clan support, as well as the financial resources, necessary to participate in the first Bwami initiation, a process that can take several years. Finally he must gather a dowry to be paid to the girl's father.[3] Although distinct from Bwami, family relationships play an important role in accumulating the resources necessary to move up in the hierarchy. Also of note, members of specific lineages or clans must hold some positions in Bwami.

THE LEGA AND THEIR NEIGHBORS

The neighbors of the Lega, including the Bembe, Bangubangu, Zimba or Binja, Songola/Babile, Komo, Babila, Bakwame, Kanu, Konjo, Mitoko, and Nyindu, share Bwami-like institutions and occasionally clans and lineages as well. In addition, the Lega and their neighbors ritualize banana growing and focus on hunting in exchange, ritual, and symbolism (Biebuyck 1973, 17–22). In 1909 Delhaise noted that because of the isolating terrain, the Lega did not have much contact with their neighbors (Biebuyck 1973, 17–22). Nevertheless, high-ranking Bwami members, in spite of the difficulties of travel, participated in Bwami events in neighboring communities. After the arrival of the Belgians, however, most Lega men rarely left their areas except to work for Europeans for short periods of time, staying long enough to accumulate the goods needed for a Bwami event or a dowry and then returning to their homes.

Some groups such as the Mitoko and Bembe are said to have Lega origins but over time have lost their identification with the larger group. The Bembe have Bwami, circumcision, and the same lineage structure as the Lega. Scholars and connoisseurs often confuse the art of the two groups (Biebuyck 1973, 17). The Mitoko are descendants of the ancestor known as Lega through a son who separated at an early point from the Lega peoples. The Mitoko practice circumcision and have Butoka, an institution similar to Bwami (Biebuyck 1973, 17).

Only two Lega subgroups, the Basi-asumba and Bause, do not have Bwami. According to oral tradition, although they are considered to be Lega, these groups are not descendants of the original Lega. They were living on the land when the Lega peoples arrived and were absorbed into the Lega whole. They did not, however, adopt Bwami (Biebuyck 1966, 505).

2 The Bwami Society

Those who suffer from dizziness never get to the top,
They turn back at the intersections of the branches.

Lega Proverb (Biebuyck 1973, 91)

HISTORY, VARIATIONS, AND FUNCTION OF BWAMI
The Bwami Society unifies the Lega peoples, cutting across clans and territories. Ironically, however, the Society itself is not uniform. Because it is neither centralized nor formalized, it adapts to the long-term needs of each Lega community (Biebuyck 1973, 72). Unfortunately, the complete history of the Bwami Society and its variations may never be reconstructed. The Lega say Bwami has no beginning and is not of human origin; it is "something of great age and mysterious origin" and "a fruit that came from above" (Biebuyck 1994, 28). Scholars have tried to use the known variants—especially the differences between the noncentralized form and the more centralized versions to the east and among Lega neighbors—to propose a history of the Society. Some, like Jan Vansina (1990) and Mulyumba wa Mamba (1977), feel Bwami was a noncentralized society moving toward central leadership. Other scholars argue that as the Lega migrated into areas where it became difficult for communities to interact and communicate effectively in support of a single ruler, Bwami became more democratic (Bishikwabo 1979).

In spite of the lore that contends that Bwami had no beginning, some Lega oral traditions attempt to explain the origins of the variations within the Society. One such story recounts that before the Lega migrated to their

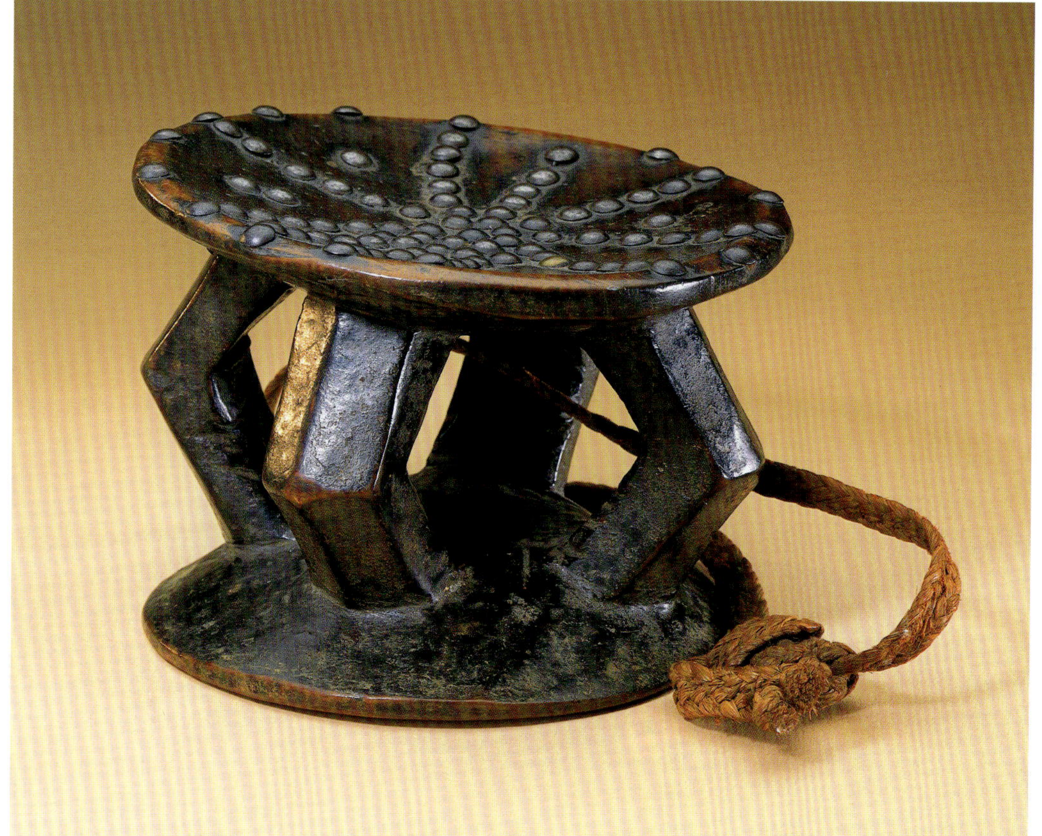

2.1 Lega stool. Wood, plant fiber, and tacks. H: 13.2 cm (5¼ in.); Diam: 17.7 cm (7 in.). FMCH X91.241; The Jerome L. Joss Collection.

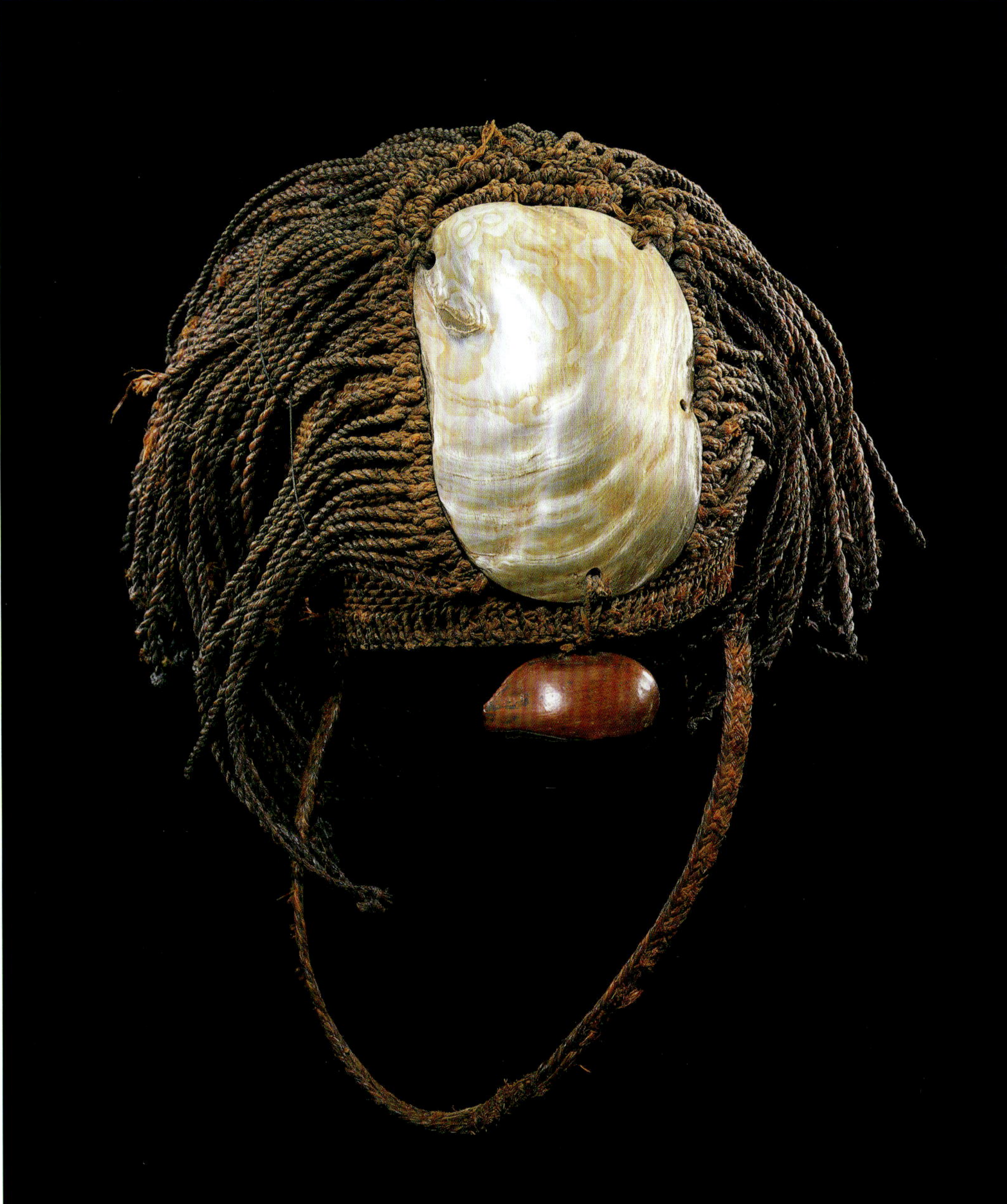

2.2 Hat (*sawamazembe*). Plant fiber, shell, and seedpod. H: 31.5 cm (12⅜ in.); Diam: 27 cm (10⅝ in.). FMCH X99.15.24; Gift of Jay T. Last. Worn by high-ranking Bwami men, this hat with its attached shell ornament resembles the highest-ranking hat among the Bwami bwa Lusembe (Bwami of the shell).

current area, a small group of them met a "man of the bush" who, being very hospitable, stood up to welcome his guests and make sure they were comfortably settled around the fire. The leader of the Lega sat down on the man's personal stool and refused to relinquish it. The stool was a symbol of Bwami (fig. 2.1), and by claiming it and refusing to move, the Lega man assumed the responsibilities and prerogatives of leadership. This type of Bwami, known as Bwami bwa Ishungwe, is characterized by a single paramount chief or king who is called the *mwami*. Although sacred items associated with the *mwami* include a stool and a drum, the primary object identifying him is *ishungwe*, a wickerwork piece filled with power materials and topped with red parrot feathers (Biebuyck 1973, 69).

Bwami bwa Lusembe, or Bwami of the shell, is another variant of the Society found among the eastern Lega. Although it is not characterized by a king, it does have a fairly centralized structure with certain high positions reserved solely for members of specific clans. While several neighbors of the Lega still have a king called *mwami*, the Lega lost their royal figure when Bwami bwa Lusembe absorbed Bwami bwa Ishungwe. The symbol of leadership in Bwami bwa Lusembe is a shell (*lusembe*) attached to the front of the highest-ranking hat (fig. 2.2; Biebuyck 1973, 69–71).

In a story recorded in 1932 by de Villenfagne de Loen and repeated by Biebuyck (1986, 209–10), a Lega man named Nkulu bought a hat called *bwami* from a Luba con artist who told him that it would bring him great wealth and fame if he followed the proper instructions. He must never remove the hat, but he could sell the right to wear a hat of the same type to other people. Nkulu, who was very wise, incorporated a moral code into the price of the hat, and hats remain a primary symbol in Bwami.

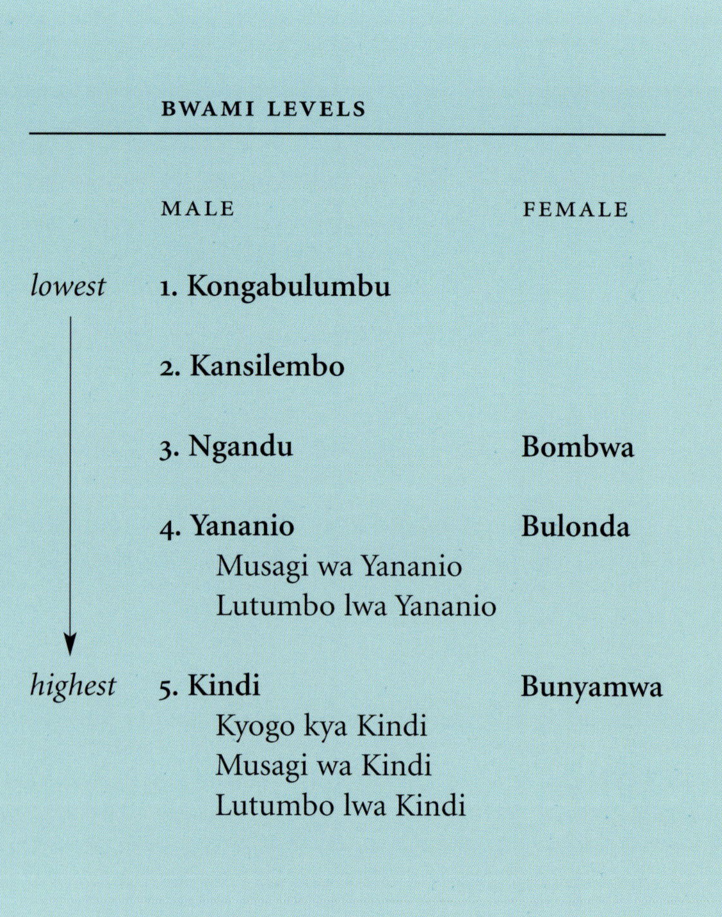

2.3 Male and female Bwami levels and their relationships.

While the oral traditions noted above attempt to explain Bwami's variations, they also illustrate its basic functions across the Lega area. Bwami safeguards the moral and social code necessary for the Lega to live together in harmony. Bwami is also the political power that allows the Lega to live at peace with their neighbors (Biebuyck 1973, 68; Vansina 1990, 183). Finally, it has an economic function, that of controlling distribution of goods among Lega lineages through the large quantities of food and exchange items that are given by the initiate to members.

ORGANIZATION OF THE BWAMI SOCIETY

The Bwami society is made up of different levels or grades (figs. 2.3–2.5). The first three levels for men are fairly constant throughout the Lega area with some areas having fourth and fifth grades as well. The grades are most commonly known as: (1) Kongabulumbu, (2) Kansilembo, (3) Ngandu, (4) Yananio, and (5) Kindi. In Kongabulumbu, the beginning level for men, the initiate becomes *mwami*.[1] A woman may join the grade equivalent to the one in which her husband is a member. Women join when their husbands reach the third level, Ngandu.[2] The women's grades are: Bombwa, tied to Ngandu; Bulonda, tied to Yananio; and Bunyamwa, tied to Kindi.[3] Each grade may also have internal levels. Areas that have Kindi, for example, divide it into Kyogo kya Kindi, Musagi wa Kindi, and the final stage of Lutumbo lwa Kindi (Biebuyck 1973, 78–9).

MEMBERSHIP IN THE BWAMI SOCIETY

While a man cannot choose his family or clan, he can choose in a sense to enter Bwami. In this way it is a "voluntary" association. The clan, however, plays an important part in his position and future in the Society by providing needed wealth and access to clan- or lineage-restricted titles. The high status possible through membership in Bwami and the promise of fame, power, and fortune that it entails prove powerful incentives for men to join and to move up through the ranks. Of note, Bwami rank is believed to be carried into the afterlife and hence ensures a form of immortality (Biebuyck 1973, 136).

Having just indicated that there is an element of choice involved in joining Bwami, it should be emphasized that kinship, personal bearing, character, and control of resources ultimately dictate entry and position. Kinship groups make decisions about membership, and no single person has the final say, regardless of how high his or her rank might be (Biebuyck 1973, 93). In most areas this serves to prevent the centralization of control by a single individual who might potentially become a chief or misuse power. The clan thus acts as a decentralizing force moving decisions away from the individual and into the hands of extended kinship groups.

While any circumcised male can theoretically become a member of Bwami, membership comes about in one of three ways. The most prestigious is through the personal desire and drive of the candidate (*kutunda*). He approaches a member in his kinship group and asks him to sponsor his candidacy. The sponsor must first be satisfied that the membership would not cause problems and tensions within the family. This might occur, for example, if a junior member of a lineage was initiated before a more senior one. The sponsor must also be satisfied that the candidate is of good moral standing and can marshal the material goods required as gifts during the ceremonies (Biebuyck 1973, 86).

Second, a man may be invited to join. A father might invite his son to join (*bungoli*), or a family might request that an individual join to replace someone who has died or moved to a higher grade (*kuingilila*). This is necessary because there are certain artworks that have to be passed down within very specific family relationships.[4] The family

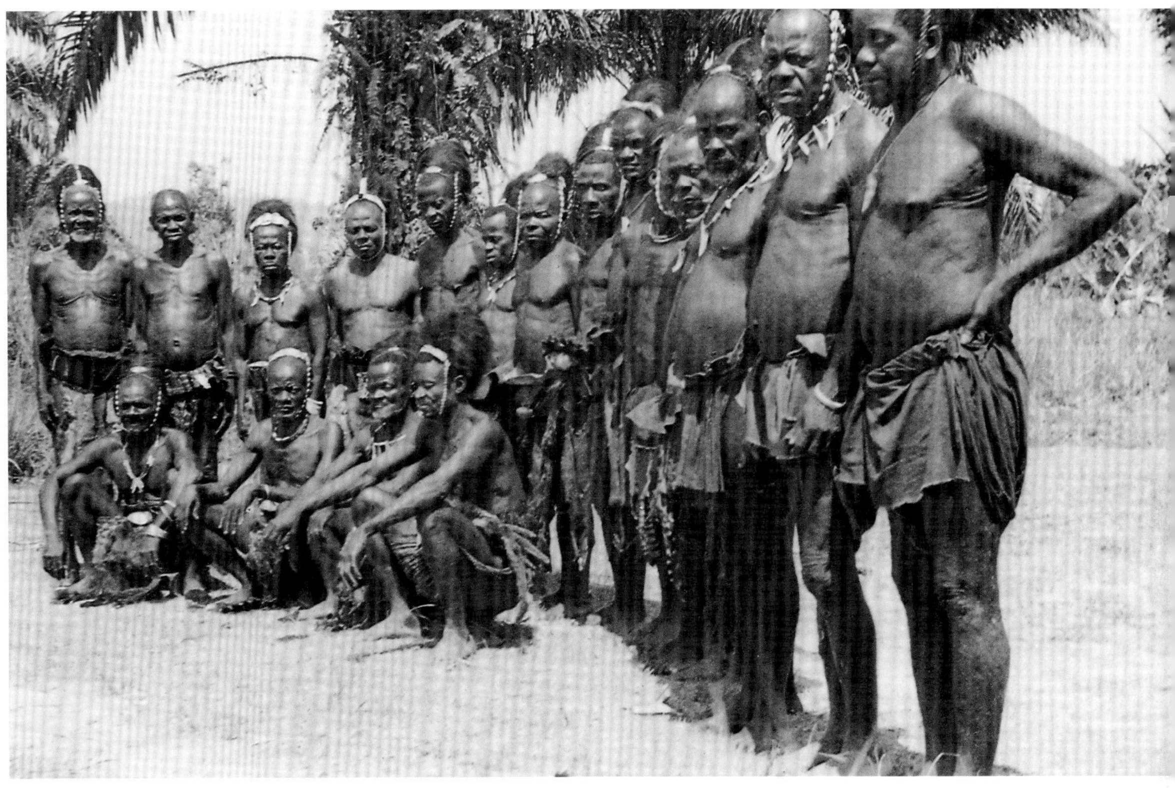

2.4 Bwami members of Lutumbo lwa Yananio and Musagi wa Yananio ranks, circa 1952–1954. Photograph courtesy of Daniel P. Biebuyck.

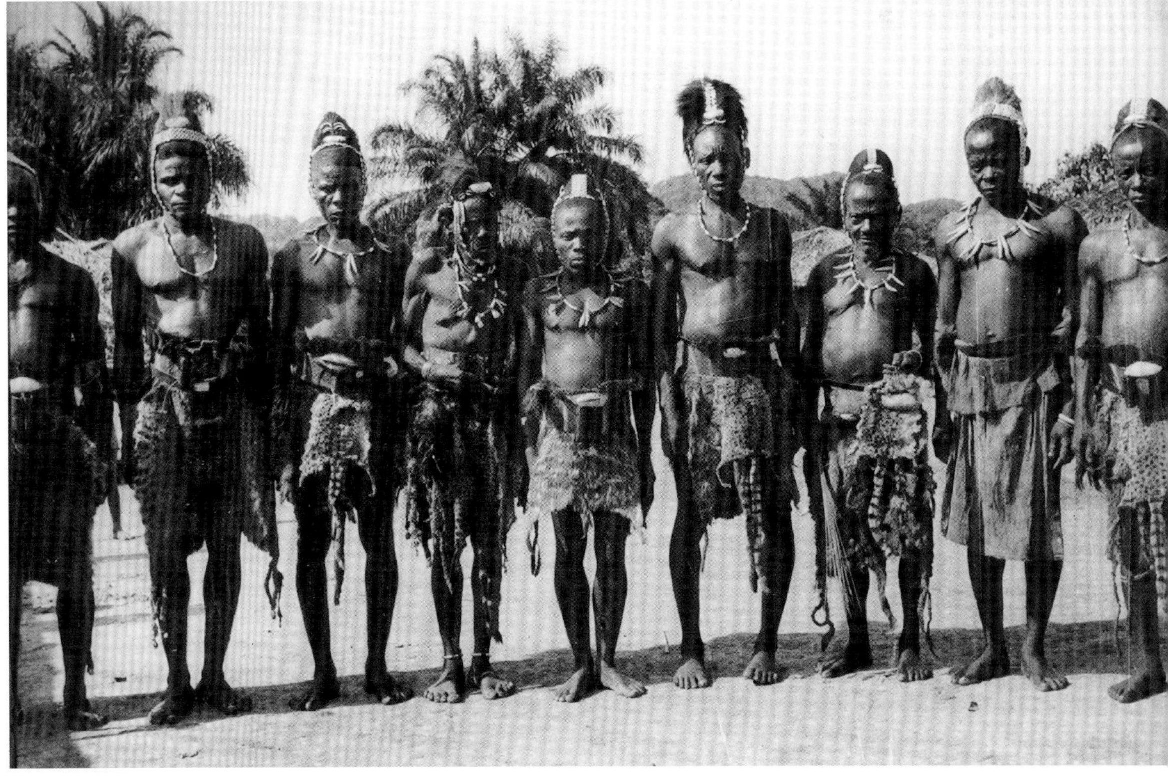

2.5 Members of the lower level of Yananio, 1960s. Photograph by A. or J. Vanden Bossche, courtesy of the Musée Royal de l'Afrique Centrale, Tervuren.

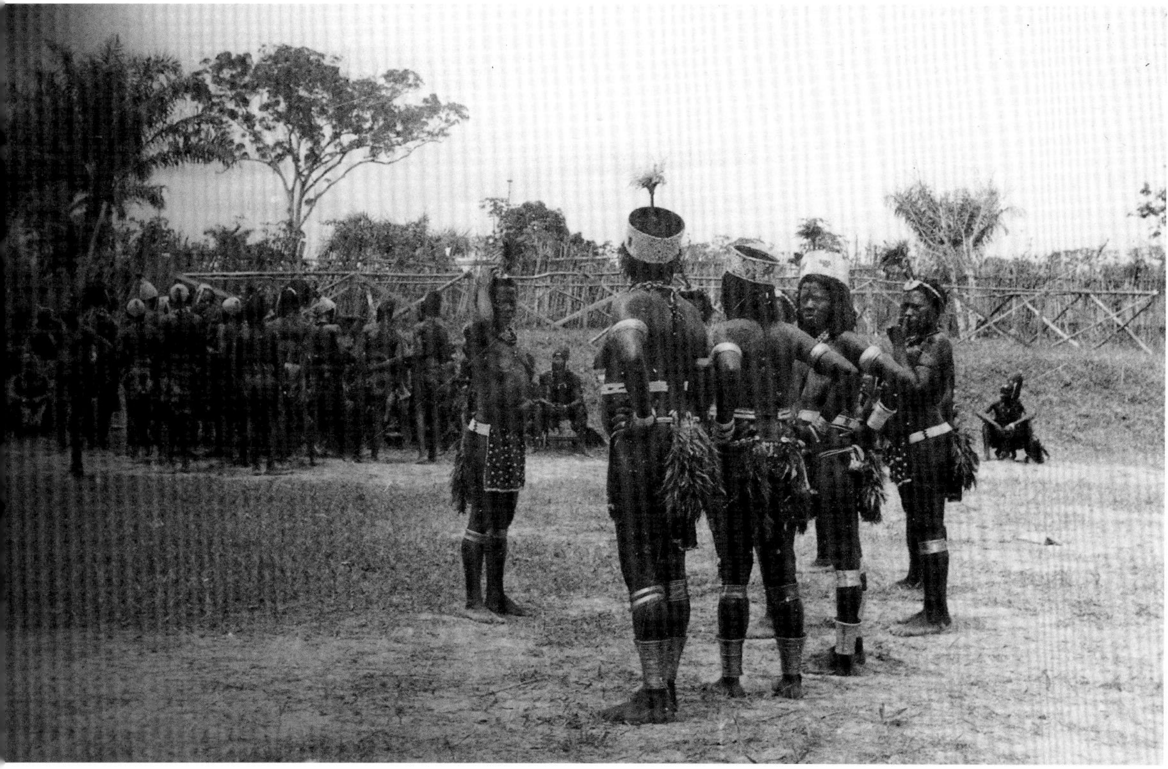

2.6 Members of the highest female level of Bwami wearing their insignia. They are shown preparing for a dance distinctive of their level, 1960s. Photograph by A. or J. Vanden Bossche, courtesy of the Musée Royal de l'Afrique Centrale, Tervuren.

would not make the invitation, however, if the candidate did not qualify morally or financially.

Finally, an individual may be forced to join—at great financial cost to his or her family—if he or she has broken Bwami rules and if membership in Bwami will give the Society control over his or her behavior. An oracle can also prescribe joining as the solution to a problem (*bugila*; Biebuyck 1976, 85–86). All means of joining give families close control of who becomes a member. Families are able to prevent mentally deficient or incapable men from joining the lowest levels as well as to control how representatives from different lineages rise to the top. This demonstrates how lineage and Bwami intersect (Corbisier 1968, 12–13).

A woman's membership and position in Bwami mirror those of her husband (fig. 2.6). She can join only if her husband is a member, and her entry into new levels follows her husband's rise through the men's levels. In turn, a man cannot advance to a higher level until one of his wives has reached the female level corresponding to his position. Thus a man cannot enter the Yananio level, for example, until his wife is initiated into Bombwa. She then must enter Bulonda before he can join Kindi. On his joining Kindi, she rises to the Bunyamwa level. Although a woman has the opportunity to rise through the ranks with her husband, she is not required to do so. If her family cannot afford to sponsor her, or if she does not qualify through her own personal qualities, she may never join. Because a man may have more than one wife, an ambitious man will make sure that at least one of his wives has the ability to rise with him through Bwami (Biebuyck 1973, 55; 1994, 30). The couple that reaches the highest grade together is considered permanently joined with no possibility of divorce (Biebuyck 1973, 43).

Women add an element of danger to Bwami because they are considered able to manipulate natural and metaphysical forces for good or evil. Because no scholars have conducted research on Bwami from the woman's perspective, the literature is unclear as to how this danger is manifested. Mulyumba wa Mamba, a male member of the Sile-Lega subgroup, has related that while all women are potential sorcerers, those in Bwami actively practice sorcery (1977, 327). Another scholar of Lega descent explained that within Bwami women are the instruments used by men to punish or bring retribution (Muyololo

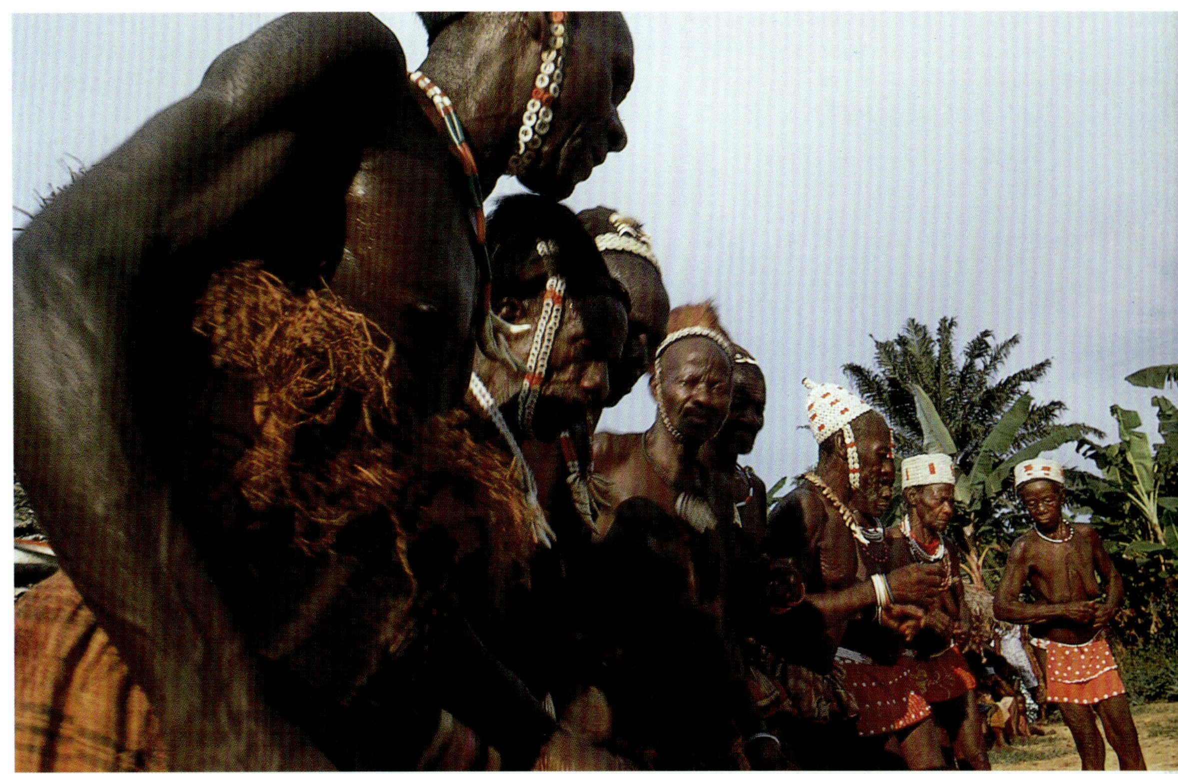

2.7 Bwami members dancing, mid-1960s. Courtesy of M. Benoit Rousseau.

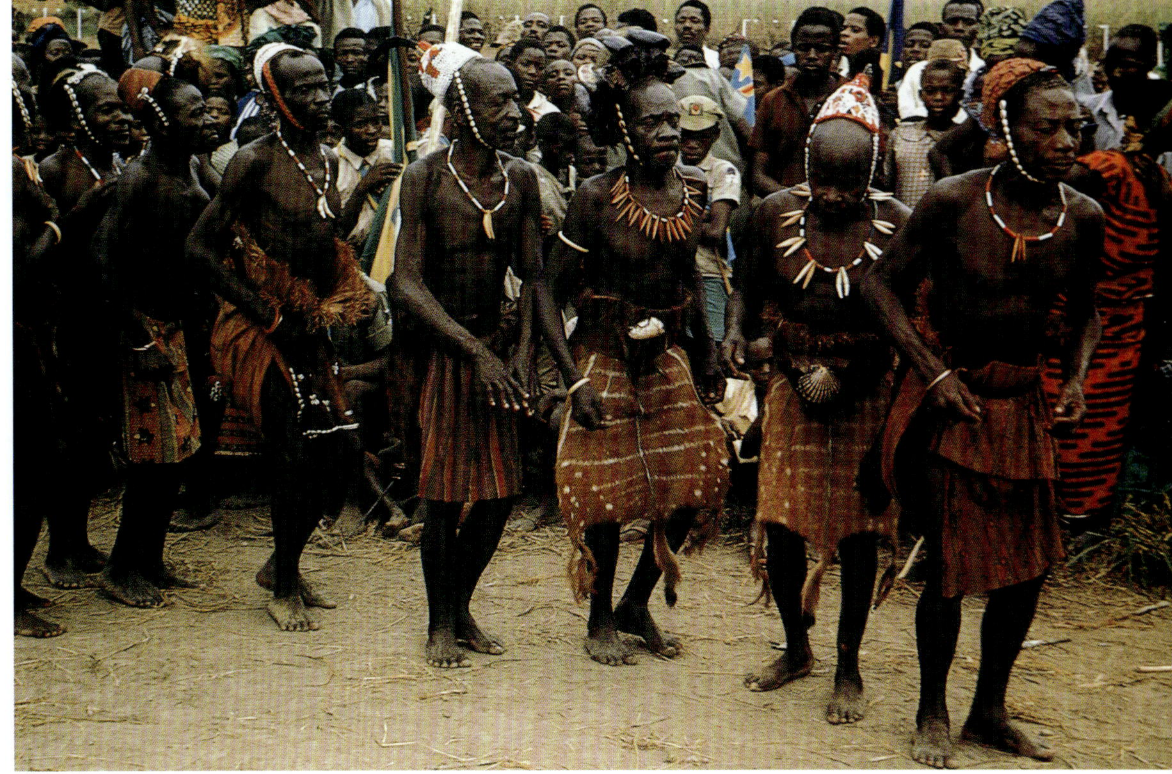

2.8 Bwami members dancing to celebrate an initiate reaching the Yananio level. Photograph by Eliot Elisofon, 1967. Eliot Elisofon Photographic Archives, National Museum of African Art, Smithsonian Institution, no. F 3 LGA 12.1 EE 67.

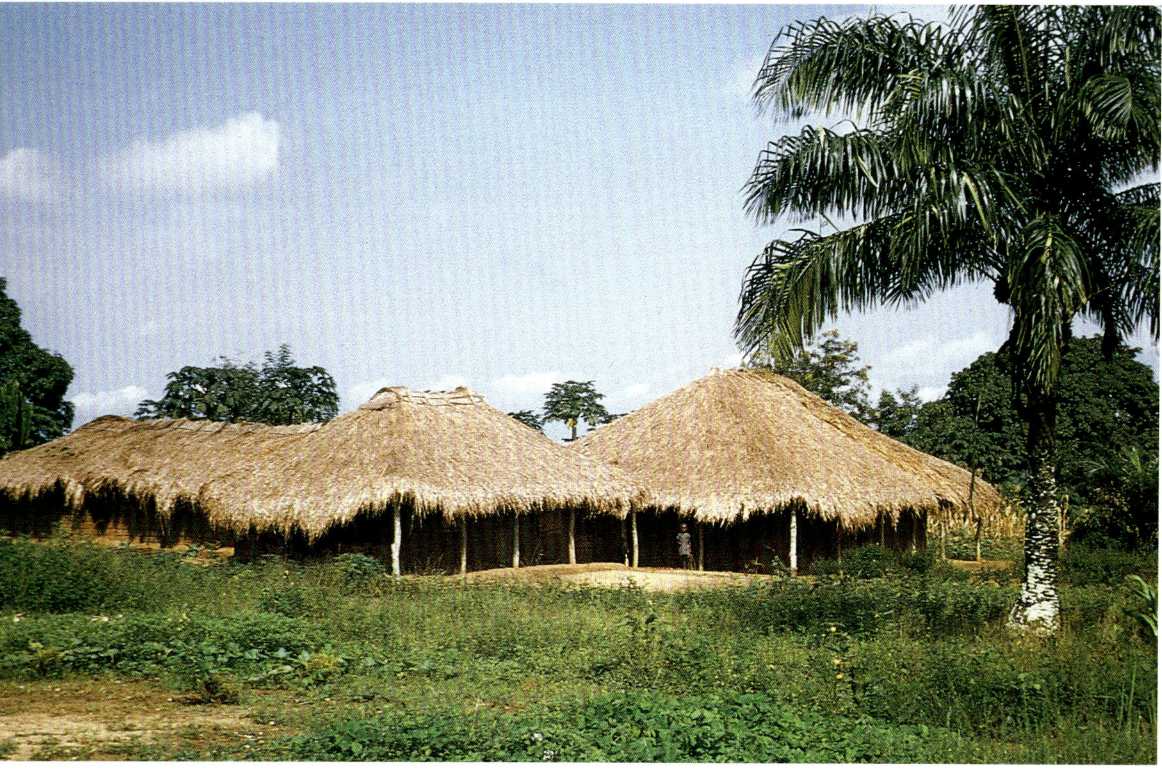

2.9 A house of the type used in Bwami ceremonies, mid-1960s. Courtesy of M. Benoit Rousseau.

1974, 50, 58).[5] In contrast to Lega authors, Corbisier says that the role of women is only honorary (1968, 14). Biebuyck explains that the relationship between the initiated man and his wife is a "fusion of the sexes: a man cannot achieve the highest grades unless one of his wives is co-initiated; the highly initiated husband and wife are bound by indissoluble marriage, the highly initiated wife has male social status" (1982, 65).

MPALA (INITIATION)

Entry into any level of Bwami, male or female, takes place through an intensive initiation that lasts several days and incorporates seven or eight performances (figs. 2.7, 2.8). It is during this time that the owners or guardians of the Bwami artworks bring them out, displaying and manipulating them in combinations of music, drama, dance, and sayings. Through these layered performances, or metaphors, the initiate learns the knowledge for which his or her level is responsible. Once the initiation is complete, the artworks are put away until the next ceremony.

Preparations for the initiation take place when the potential initiate seeks the sponsorship of someone in the desired level. The candidate begins to gather the goods necessary for the ceremonies. He has three ways of obtaining these materials: through his own efforts, through gifts from his family, and through gifts from his wife's family (Biebuyck 1973, 112–14). Most needed are foodstuffs (both game meat and agricultural products), shell money (*musumba*; see fig. 1.7), tools, clothing, and other commodities available on the market (Biebuyck 1973, 109). The candidate and his sponsor invite high-level members of Bwami to examine the collected supplies, a measure aimed at sparing the initiate's family any embarrassment should the goods prove insufficient. The wise candidate hides some of the accumulated goods as insurance. If the assembled commodities are deemed sufficient, the date for the initiation is set. Members from the initiatory rank and above are invited from nearby towns. The higher the initiation the larger the amount of goods that must be gathered (Kjersmeier 1967, 34).

While female members are not allowed to view all the ceremonies in the men's levels, men must bring their wives who are members of Bwami; initiations cannot occur without the women present (Biebuyck 1973, 108).

Since a large percentage of Bwami men are initiates, the lowest-level initiation draws primarily from the candidate's family and local community. In higher-level initiations, however, Bwami Society members come from distant locales to participate.

The initiate, sponsor, and teacher are the key people in the initiation. The initiate watches and learns the wisdom appropriate to the level, the logistics of the initiation, and the ways in which meaning is conveyed. He or she is responsible for feeding all the participants for the duration of the ceremonies and for giving generous gifts. The chief sponsor (*kakusa*) shepherds the candidate through the activities and makes sure that the gifts are appropriately distributed. The teacher (*nsingia*), called "preceptor" by Biebuyck and often called "thinker" (*kalingania*) by the Lega, decides the sequence of the performances and of the presentation of knowledge (Biebuyck 1973, 102). Special training is required to become a teacher, and attainment of that status guarantees the recipient special consideration throughout life (Biebuyck 1986, 15). Additional tutors attend to the logistics of the ceremonies.

Initiations center on a house in the middle of the village that is normally used for public debates and meetings (fig. 2.9). Bwami members prepare it by closing all doors save one with bark. This door is designated the entrance, and a screen of plant fiber is placed over it (Delhaise 1909, 245). The ceremonies are closed to the general public and to Bwami members who have not yet reached the appropriate level of initiation.

As guests and participants in an initiation often come long distances by foot, their arrival occurs over a period of days and is greeted with songs and dances. Once the initiation itself begins, people who do not have the right to witness the ceremonies leave town for the duration of the rites, and the Bwami members ceremonially reenter the village, thus transforming public space into ritual space.

Performances involving art objects take place in cycles or "dances" throughout the following days. These can occur both inside and outside the initiation house. Because the teacher prides himself on the artistry involved in combining different elements in a performance, few of them are repetitive (Biebuyck 1977b, 26). The true meanings that underlie the performances are dependent on lifelong training in the significance of each performative element. As a result, few outsiders have ever completely appreciated their full complexity. Delhaise, for example, witnessed certain Kindi ceremonies and provided the following description:

> Dance of wild pigs: (wild pigs, greatest pest to Lega farms). A Kindi goes into the temple to exit again with an object hidden under an animal skin. Middle of circle of dancers, he finds what he has hidden: it is a fetish in wood representing a woman. It is covered in pemba (white clay). The Kindi takes part in the dance carrying the figure in front of him. He lays it on ground and everyone performs a wild dance. The old one exits circle and cries: you, wild pigs! Why do you always go to other's places and not stay at home? One day you will be caught in our snares! The fetish is returned to the temple. The dance is finished. [Delhaise 1909, 234–35][6]

Delhaise depended on translators to interpret both the sayings and action and was therefore unable to decode many of the deeper layers of meaning behind the performance. At the end of an initiation, art objects appropriate to the level are given to the initiate. The guests take their leave heavily laden with gifts.

3 Rhetoric, Metaphor, and *Mpala*

> Metaphors are much more tenacious than facts.
>
> Paul de Man (1979, 5)

> But the greatest thing by far is to have a command of metaphor. This alone cannot be imparted by another; it is the mark of genius.
>
> Aristotle[1]

Metaphor,[2] one of the most basic figures of speech, is nearly universal. In a metaphor, one thing or idea is conjoined with or replaced by another, forcing the reader or listener to consider the qualities that are shared by elements that might otherwise appear dissimilar if not disparate (Hawkes 1972, 1). When Shakespeare wrote "All the world's a stage,"[3] he did not intend a literal comparison. Rather, by juxtaposing the world and all the life contained within it with a space where scripted performance takes place, he commented on the lack of control each person has over his or her own existence. Metaphors require active participation on the part of the listener or reader who must consider and supply the implied meanings (Hawkes 1972, 72).

While simple literary metaphors combine two verbal images, the Lega peoples routinely create simple and complex metaphors by layering sayings, objects, and often dramatic elements.[4] De Kun describes this metaphorical system as a "closed circle" because each layer, when isolated from the others, becomes meaningless. Lega metaphors explore standards for living—values and morals, accepted comportment, ideal social and familial relationships, and legal, ethical, religious, and political codes. This complex body of wisdom can never be expressed as a whole, but parts of it can be revealed, examined, and redefined through complicated multilayered Lega metaphors.

The Lega attribute metaphoric sayings to the ancestors or to Walukumu, a name representing a mythical wise man who is of the past, always, and of all times (Mulyumba wa Mamba 1973, 4). These sayings focus on mankind, living and dead, and never mention gods or spirits (Biebuyck 1986, 29–36). A simple verbal metaphor is contained in the saying "The one who forgets the bonds of kinsmen, that one should watch how the black ants march" (Defour n.d., 104). As astute observers of their physical environment, most Lega are familiar with the behavior of black ants. The ants march in an organized, almost military, formation with scouts going ahead of the column to find the best route and search for food. When they find food, they carry it back for all to eat. This simple metaphor transfers the cooperation and organization of the ants to human families. The behavior of the ant column is a particularly rich and

3.1 Orchestra made up of Bwami members of the Yananio and Kindi levels shown preparing for an initiation performance, 1960s. Photograph by A. or J. Vanden Bossche, courtesy of the Musée Royal de l'Afrique Centrale, Tervuren.

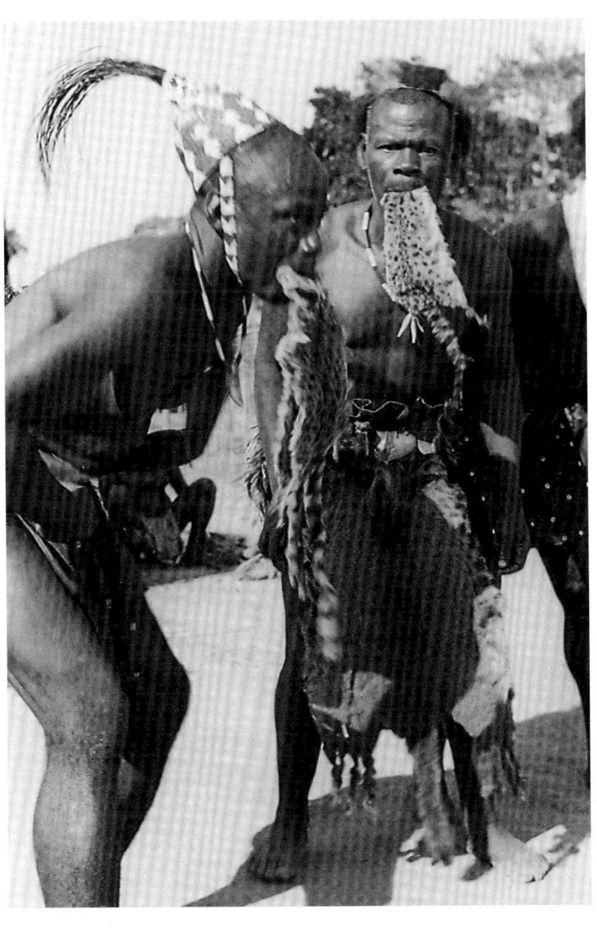

3.2 Two Kindi-level Bwami members dance while holding animal hides in their mouths, circa 1952–1954. The message underlying the performance is respect for older members of Bwami. Photograph courtesy of Daniel P. Biebuyck.

3.3 All Bwami members present at an initiation performance place their shoulder bags in a pile, circa 1952–1954. Photograph courtesy of Daniel P. Biebuyck.

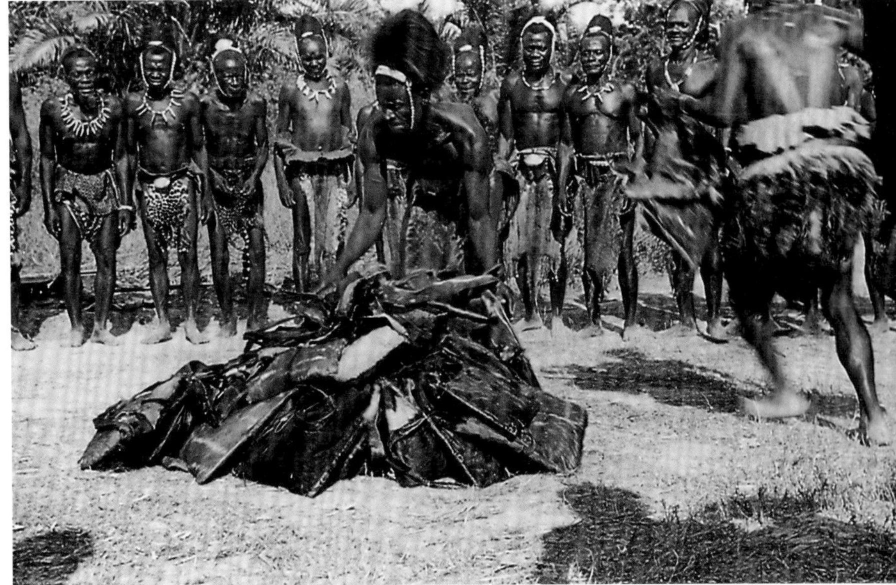

complex source of positive and negative metaphors. The saying "The young girl sometimes resembles a column of ants: she obstinately takes a road where she perishes" refers to the behavior of the column when it approaches a danger such as fire. Even while the ants at the front perish, the column continues to march blindly into the blaze, just as youths anywhere can insist on their own way in spite of proven dangers.

The person citing the metaphor will often hold up a black ant, making reference to all its possible positive and negative metaphorical meanings and ultimately to the whole body of Lega wisdom. The inclusion of a visual element reinforces the verbal component of the saying in the mind of the listener while revealing alternate interpretations as well. While an American or European might organize such information around a topic—sayings about family, for example—the Lega organize and teach ideas around an object, letting all positive and negative metaphors radiate from it (Biebuyck 1973, 124).

The "cord of wisdom" illustrates this point. In the center of a village sits a communal house that most people pass daily. The posts of this house are called "pillars of the universe" (Defour n.d., 6). Older men who are known for their wisdom and are members of Bwami—trained in Lega and Bwami moral code—tie a cord, known as the "cord of wisdom," between the house posts. They suspend an object from this cord and quiz passersby about the different sayings associated with it. The sayings as a whole are called *bitondo bya kisi*, or "words of the land" (Biebuyck 1973, 52). Thus the entire community learns through metaphor what they need to know to live within the Lega community.[5]

If someone who needs to be warned or reminded of the moral code lives at a distance, an appropriate object is wrapped up and sent to that person (Burk et al. 1956, 711; Defour n.d., 6). An individual guilty of ignoring family responsibilities, for example, might receive a black ant. While the gift calls to mind all Lega wisdom, the recipient either immediately understands the implied message because of its relevance to his or her life or is able to infer the meaning through observation of ants.

Although simple metaphors that combine sayings and objects are prevalent throughout the Lega area, the Bwami also deploy more complex metaphors. As initiates move up within Bwami, they are taught the more esoteric wisdom of the Society. Members teach initiates the knowledge appropriate for each level through performances that combine: multiple sayings about positive and negative topics; carved objects, as well as found and constructed objects; and song, movement, and drama (figs. 3.1–3.3).[6] Within the context of the partially revealed Lega wisdom, each initiate must actively consider the meaning implied by the increasingly complex layers. At basic levels, the teachers combine fairly simple, but nevertheless layered, metaphors with sayings, simple found or manufactured objects, and performances. Since this is an extension of the "cord of wisdom" and the "words of the land," most men and women who enter Bwami are familiar with this form of teaching. Even so, in the initiation into Kongabulumbu, the lowest level of Bwami, between one hundred and three hundred metaphors are presented, organized by objects (Biebuyck 1973, 124).

The layers and the wisdom imparted become more complex as one moves further up the Bwami hierarchy. In the top two levels, Yananio and Kindi, the instructors add carved objects to achieve complex metaphors. The final ceremony completes the cycle by incorporating only art objects. The initiate, being a master of Lega wisdom, no longer needs the layering of symbolism and can infer from the art object alone the ultimate meanings.

The uninitiated, therefore, whether Lega or not, cannot understand or correctly interpret the meaning of Lega artwork (Biebuyck 1977a, 59). The Lega say "He who sees the large lusembe-cowrie bare [i.e., for the first time], indeed! he finds it useless" (Biebuyck 1982, 64). As a high school student in Atlanta, for example, I went to see *Art from Zaire: 100 Masterworks from the National Collection* and overheard a young man explain to his companion that a figure with raised arms from the Lengola peoples—neighbors of the Lega who also have a form of Bwami (Cornet 1975, fig. 95)—was searching the skies and calling on the gods who were linked to the stars. I had always assumed that this was a unique, misguided, and fanciful interpretation, but Biebuyck describes a similar Lega figure with one raised arm being interpreted as calling on sky gods (1969, 12).[7] For the uninitiated, the objects maintain a "deliberate vagueness, nebulosity, and ambiguity" (Biebuyck 1969, 12) that helps preserve their power within Bwami (Biebuyck 1981, 120).

For Bwami members, the object itself rarely has a unique message. The teacher, by placing it in various combinations, causes the object to carry a message or meaning (Biebuyck 1969, 11; 1981, 120–21; 1986, 2). Biebuyck describes the teacher thus:

> As a thinker the preceptor wants to excel and to be original. He adds to and subtracts from the common corpus of explanations; he emphasizes certain aspects more than others; he is inspired by methods he has observed elsewhere; he invents or on a particular occasion forgets some points, which he may later add or eliminate. [Biebuyck 1986, 133]

The teacher, in other words, becomes the master of metaphor of whom Aristotle speaks. The best-known and most sought-after teachers are able to create new metaphorical combinations that transform the individual layers into startling, memorable, and specific meanings within the established code.

The teacher combines the initiation objects with the equally rich languages of gesture, drama, song, music, and saying. These objects become a visual vocabulary available in combination with other vocabularies for the teacher to use in different metaphorical structures. Thus each object carries diverse meanings depending on the context in which it is used.

Ignoring the piece as a whole, the teacher may choose to concentrate on one facet or aspect of the artwork to provide meaning in its layered context. Using physical manipulation of the object, along with specific sayings, movements, or sounds, the teacher cues the observer into which part of the object is significant for the creation of a particular meaning (Biebuyck 1973, 185–86).

THE POWER OF THE OBJECT

Although the idea of a "layered metaphor" can aid in understanding how the Lega use initiation objects, these objects are significantly more than a metaphorical vocabulary. For the Lega they contain intrinsic and sacred power because they are exclusively dedicated to use within Bwami. Scholars consistently address this concept. Muyololo, for example, states that "[t]he art of the Lega experiences the sacred" (1974, 50). Biebuyck describes the power inhering in the objects as a "force [that] is not the result of some magical action; rather it is in the very being of the figurines, in the fact that they are what they are: sacred and privileged objects intimately associated with their living and dead owners and symbols of continuity" (1986, 63).

While all things have an undefined force (*magala*; Biebuyck 1973, 53), the Lega consider all objects having a function and context within Bwami to be *masengo*, or "heavy things" (Biebuyck 1976, 338). The decision to move an object out of *magala*, the mundane world of diffuse power, into the concentrated world of Bwami sets the object apart and gives it special meaning. It becomes, as Biebuyck has suggested, "imbued with intrinsic significance"

3.4 Human Figure. Wood.
H: 19 cm (7½ in.).

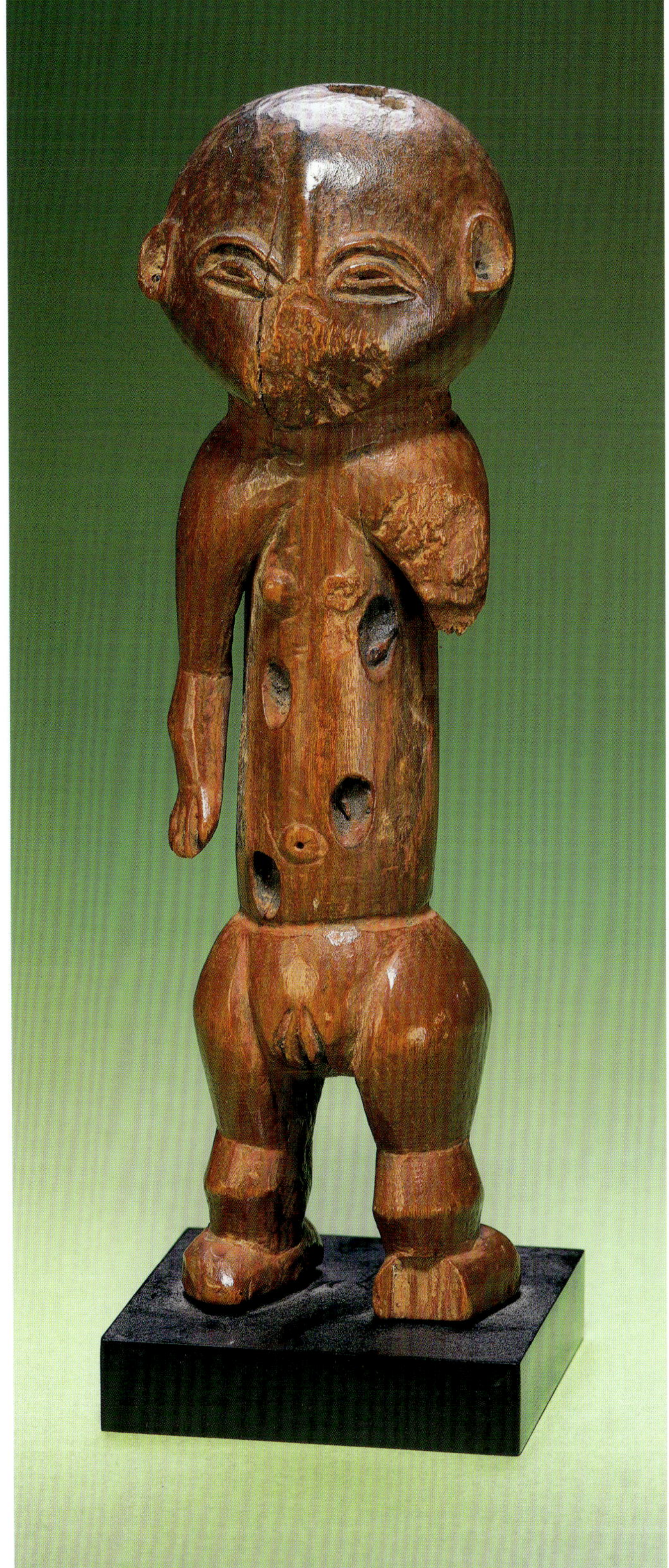

(1973, 158). This move to significance is called *kubonga*. It is the actual act of deciding that the objects will be used in an initiation that makes them *masengo*. Continued use results in history and patina that give pieces their fullest meanings (Biebuyck 1976, 340). The power within the "heavy object" forces the person holding it to commit to abiding by the strict moral code of Bwami (Biebuyck 1973, 158).

An illustration of the intrinsic power of the object can be seen in the Lega belief that a small bit of a "heavy object" has the ability to heal or to punish. When no other medicine has helped a sick person, high-level Bwami officials remove small bits of an initiation object by rubbing it with leaves that are rough and act like sandpaper and then collecting the dust or by scraping the object and making small gouges in it. They mix the particles thus removed into water and give the mixture to the sick person to drink (Biebuyck 1976, 339). Evidence of this practice can be seen on many Lega objects (fig. 3.4).

The intrinsic power of the object and its use within Bwami result in additional functions for it. For example, initiation pieces establish and maintain a connection with the past. At the death of a Bwami member, a "guardian of the tomb" is determined. This individual, who must be a member of the deceased's family and share his or her level of Bwami, places all the deceased's initiation objects on the grave. After a set period, often months, the guardian removes certain pieces and, like the executor of an estate, properly distributes the accumulated wealth. The higher the deceased's achievement, the more pieces specifically made for Bwami he would have accumulated (de Kun 1966, 78). The Bwami member who takes the deceased's position within the Society receives particular pieces that were removed from the grave. Because an appropriate family member must have achieved the proper level of Bwami in order to own the items, the objects may be held in trust by other members of that level until they can be safely passed on. Other pieces are permanently displayed or left on the tomb (Biebuyck 1986, 63). The current owner of an initiation object can recite the list of past owners, sometimes for up to five generations (Biebuyck 1994, 44). The object, therefore, creates a connection to the past in literal ways, through the piece's genealogy, and mystical ways, through the understood transfer of power during the period in which the piece rested on the Bwami grave (Biebuyck 1976, 339).

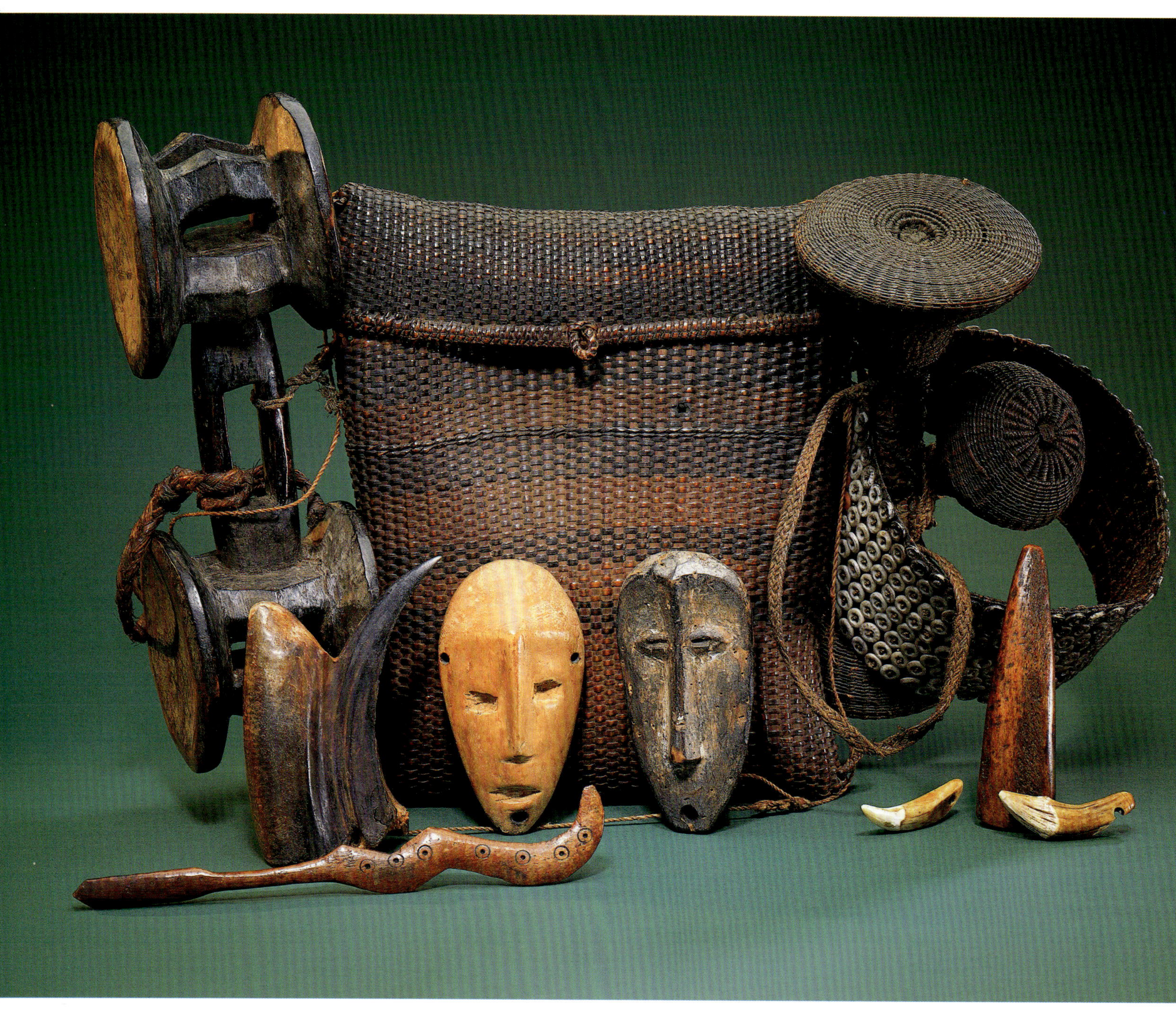

Initiation objects also bring wealth to their owners. In this context, they are sometimes compared to elephant ears: "The ears of the big elephant, it is with the clapping of his ears that he lures them [insects]" (Biebuyck 1986, 27). Just as the elephant uses its ears to trap insects, so possession of initiation objects brings the owner invitations to initiations. At the initiation, a Bwami member receives many gifts. With more important initiation objects, the owner is invited to many initiations and can accumulate a great deal of wealth.

Finally, initiation objects provide protection for their owners. The bearers of the initiation objects on the way to and from *mpala* are immune from fighting and attack. Everyone on the path can recognize the Bwami basket carried by the high-level Bwami member's wife (fig. 3.5). In addition, the male Bwami member carries his stool hung on a string over his shoulder (see fig. 2.1). These clues alert passersby that these Bwami members are on official business and must not be kept from their duties. Biebuyck also gives an example of two Bwami members sitting back-to-back and shaking Bwami rattles to prevent an attack on the community. Because these Bwami members are not to be attacked or bothered while at work, they can prevent a raid (Biebuyck 1986, 27).

Initiation objects, however, also carry an element of danger. The power within the object can help, but it also can harm. People who do not have the right to view certain pieces become ritually polluted if they see them. To

3.5 Initiation basket and contents. Plant fiber, wood, ivory, animal teeth, animal horn, and buttons. H: 34 cm (13⅜ in.).

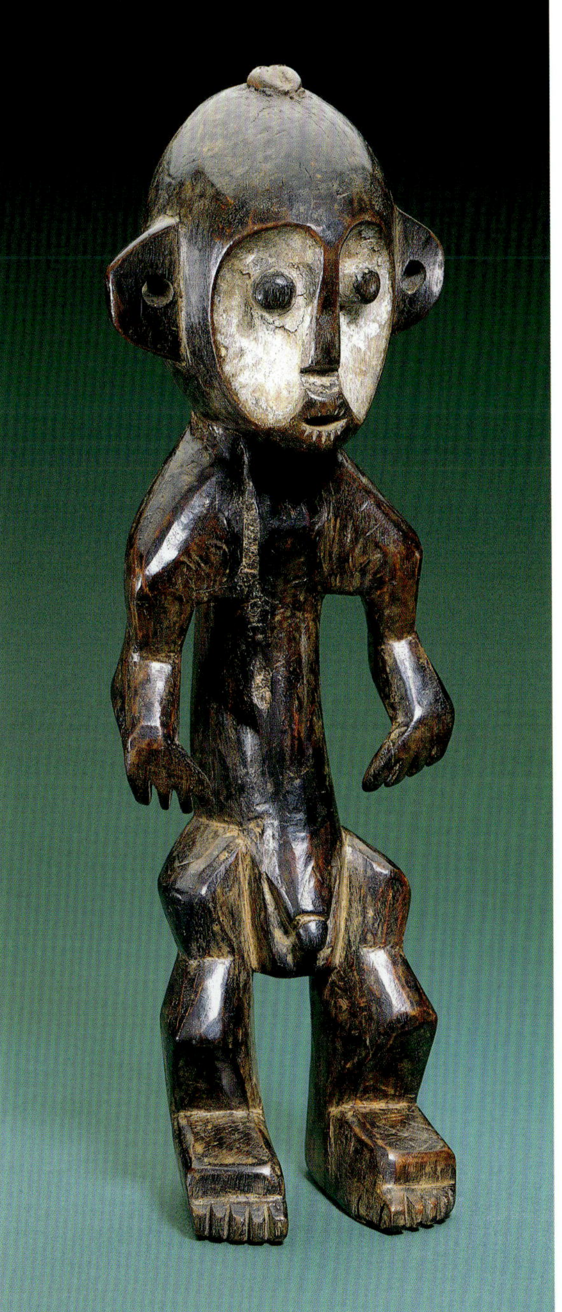

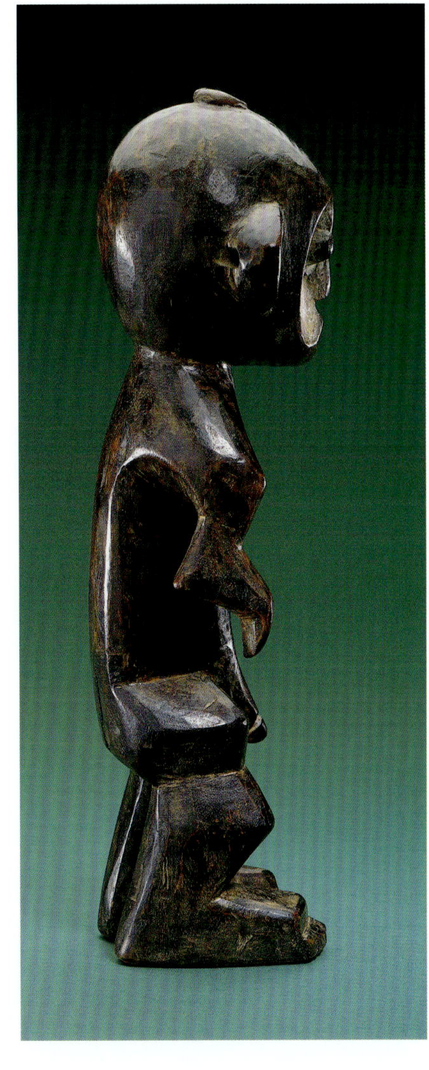

3.6 A, B Front and side views of a human Figure (*iginga*). Wood and pigment. H: 30.5 cm (12 in.).

cleanse themselves, they must undergo costly ceremonies and, in extreme cases where they are not members of Bwami, they must join the lowest level at great expense to their families. People who steal a piece that they have no right to own can be severely punished.[8] Biebuyck gives the example of a guilty person being forced, as punishment, to drink water in which a Bwami skullcap (*bwami*) or ivory bracelet worn by a Bwami member had been soaked (Biebuyck 1986, 27).

TYPES AND OWNERSHIP OF OBJECTS

An object set aside for use in Bwami is called *isengo* (sing. of *masengo*, or "heavy things," see above). Although Bwami divides, categorizes, and ranks objects, all of them—simple or complex, twig or sculpture—contain the power to help or harm depending on how they are treated (Biebuyck 1973, 158). The Lega divide the overarching category of *masengo* in two: found or everyday things lifted from daily life and assigned to Bwami (*mitume*) and objects created specifically for Bwami (*binkungankunga*) with ownership dependent on the position of the person within the Society. Among the pieces specially created for Bwami, there is a distinction made between the category of things seen in public (*binumbi*—including insignia called *bilondo*, or "things that are coveted," and dancewear called *bingonzengonze*, or "things of play"; see chapter 5) and the category of all types of specially created sculptures and assemblages (*bitungwa*). Within *bitungwa* further

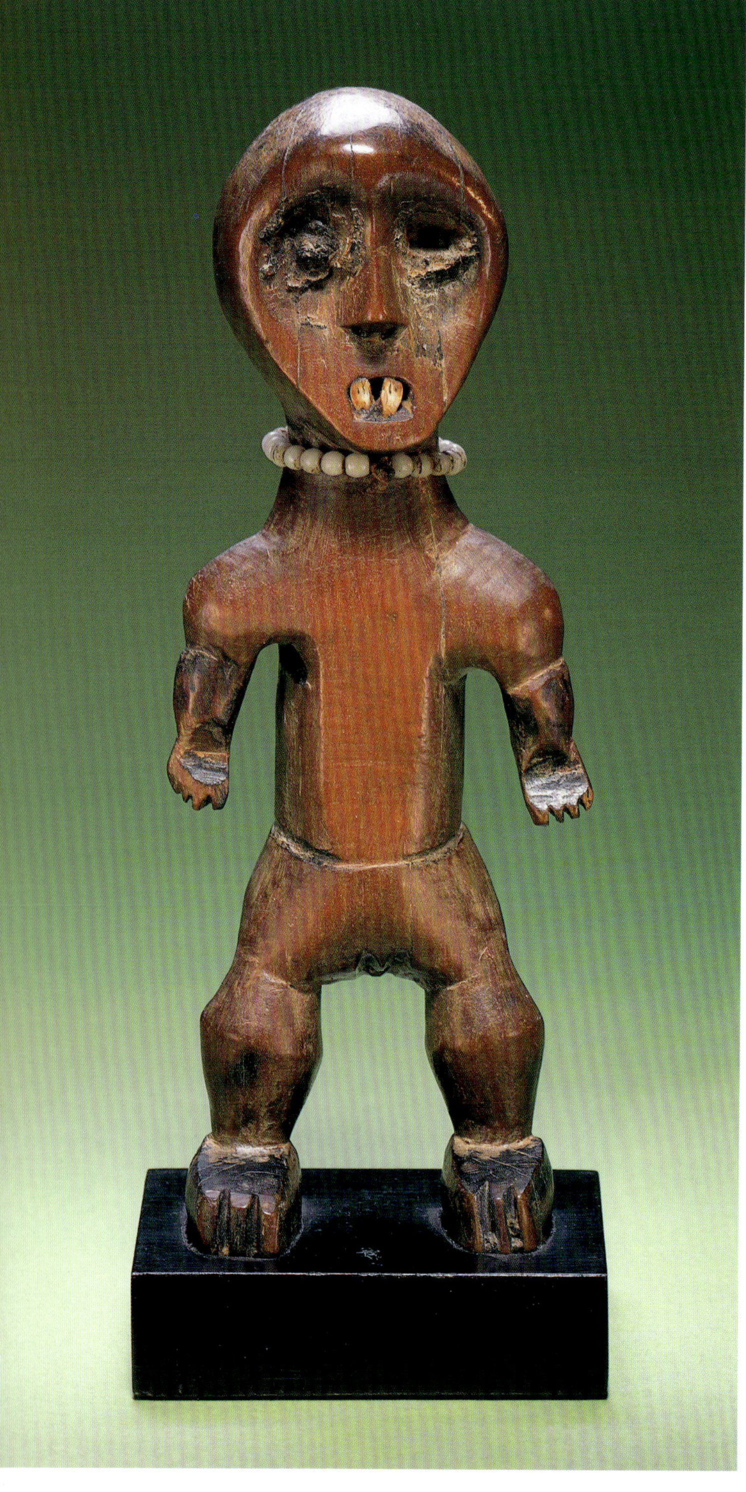

3.7 Human figure (*kalimbangoma*). Wood, beads, and teeth. H: 20.6 cm (8 in.).

3.8 Mask (*lukungu*). Ivory. H: 16.9 cm (6⅝ in.).

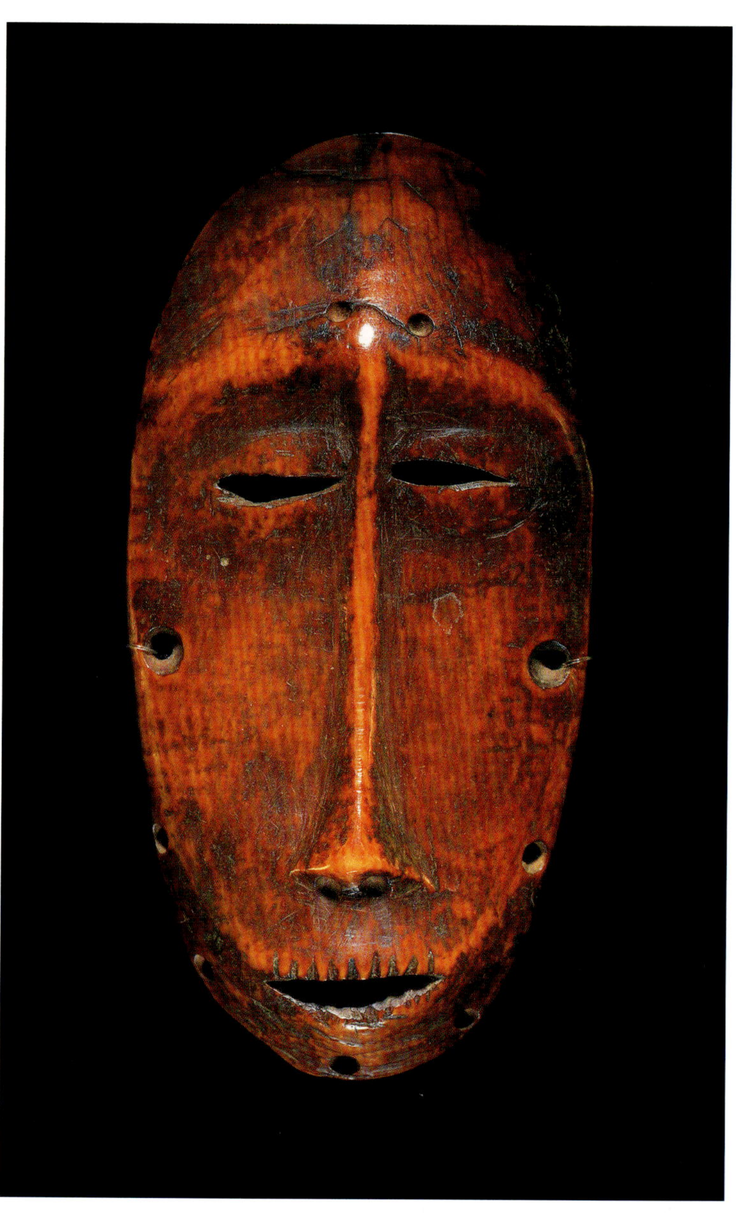

distinctions occur generally along lines of material, size, type, and ownership; for example, masks are divided into five categories: *lukwakongo, idimu, kayamba, muminia,* and *lukungu* (see chapter 9). Small figures of humans and animals, as well as assembled works, are called *kalimbangoma* (fig. 3.7). *Iginga* (pl. *maginga*) refers to both all-human figures and to a smaller category of larger and/or ivory figures (Biebuyck 1973, 157–65; 1994, 34–36).

The objects owned and used during initiations into the different levels of Bwami may be distinguished by material, size, and type. As would be expected, male members of the two highest levels, Kindi and Yananio, own the most sculptures.[9] Female members of Bunyamwa (the highest female level) also use and own a limited group of sculptures (Biebuyck 1976, 339). Ivory is owned primarily by Kindi members (Biebuyck 1953c, 1078). Some objects are individually owned; others are held in trust for the larger community; and yet others are cared for by teachers (Biebuyck 1973, 181–84; 1994, 36). Bwami members keep those objects that they have earned through initiations

3.9 Mask (*lukwakongo*). Wood and pigment. H: 11.9 cm (4¾ in.).

3.10 Mask (*idimu*). Wood and pigment. H: 28.6 cm (11¼ in.).

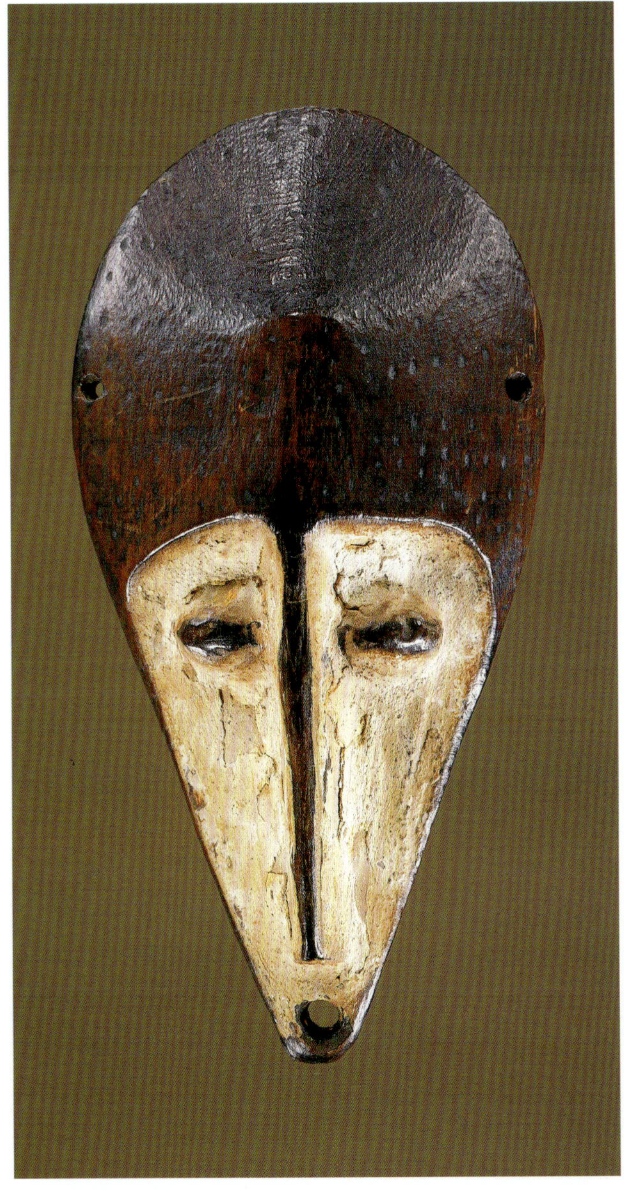

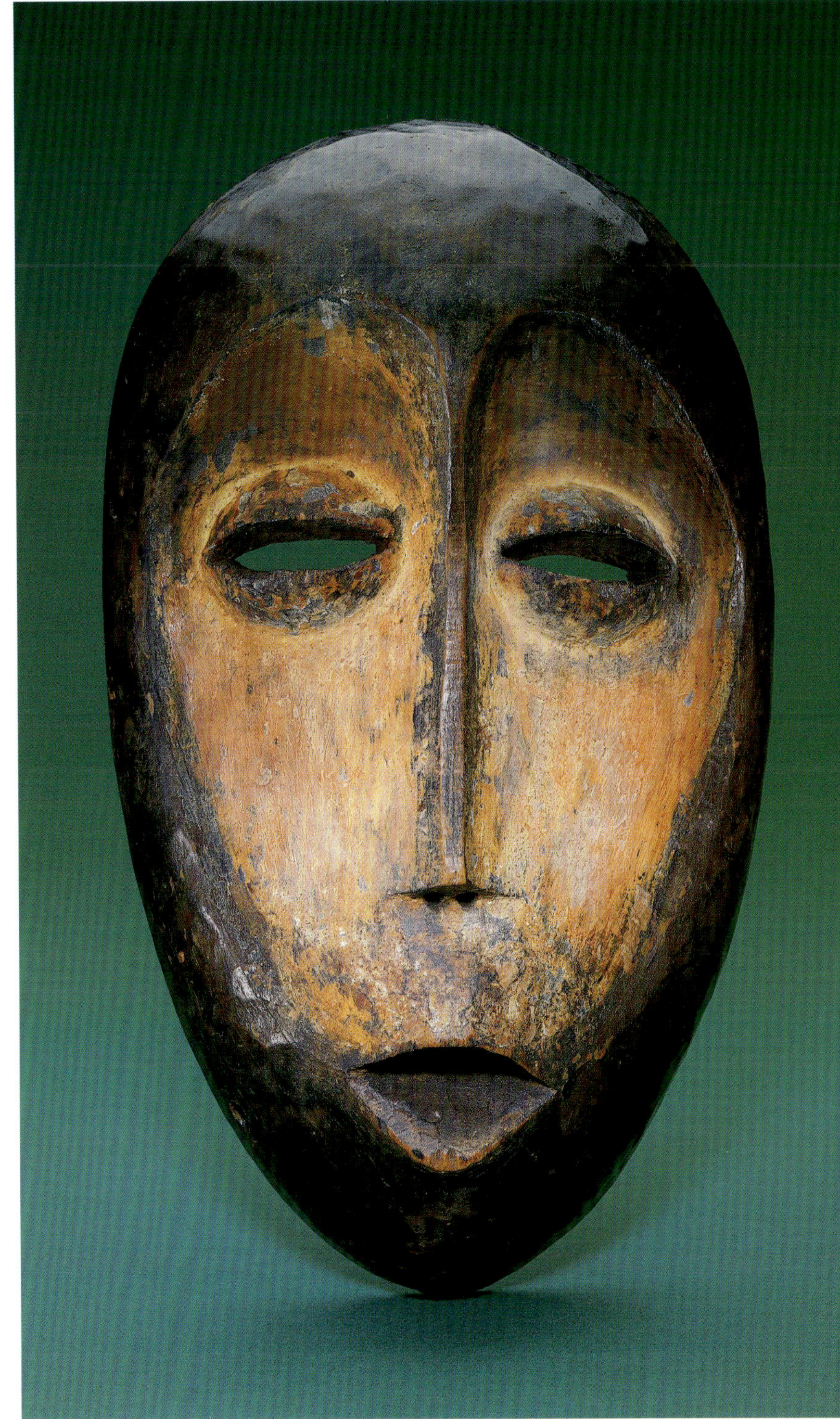

or have received from family members in a woven bag carried over the shoulder. Collectively owned objects are stored in a basket and kept in trust by the most junior member of the grade to which the basket belongs (Biebuyck 1973, 166–69). Advanced members whose wives have also been initiated give their bags and baskets to their wives for safekeeping (Biebuyck 1973, 166–69). Some objects are connected to particular grades and must be relinquished when the person moves to a higher grade (Biebuyck 1994, 38). These objects pass along specific family lines, creating and reinforcing family ties. Through inheritance of objects, clan and Bwami relationships constantly overlap.

SEQUENCE AND ENDING

Teachers in the first initiations into Bwami rely heavily on sayings to create their layered metaphors. They add drama, music, and a few simple objects, usually natural objects such as bird beaks, animal claws, and pieces of wood, which may have been joined together in various ways (see figs. 6.1–6.9). While these found objects are used

3.11 Mask (*idimu*). Wood and pigment. H: 28.8 cm (11⅜ in.).

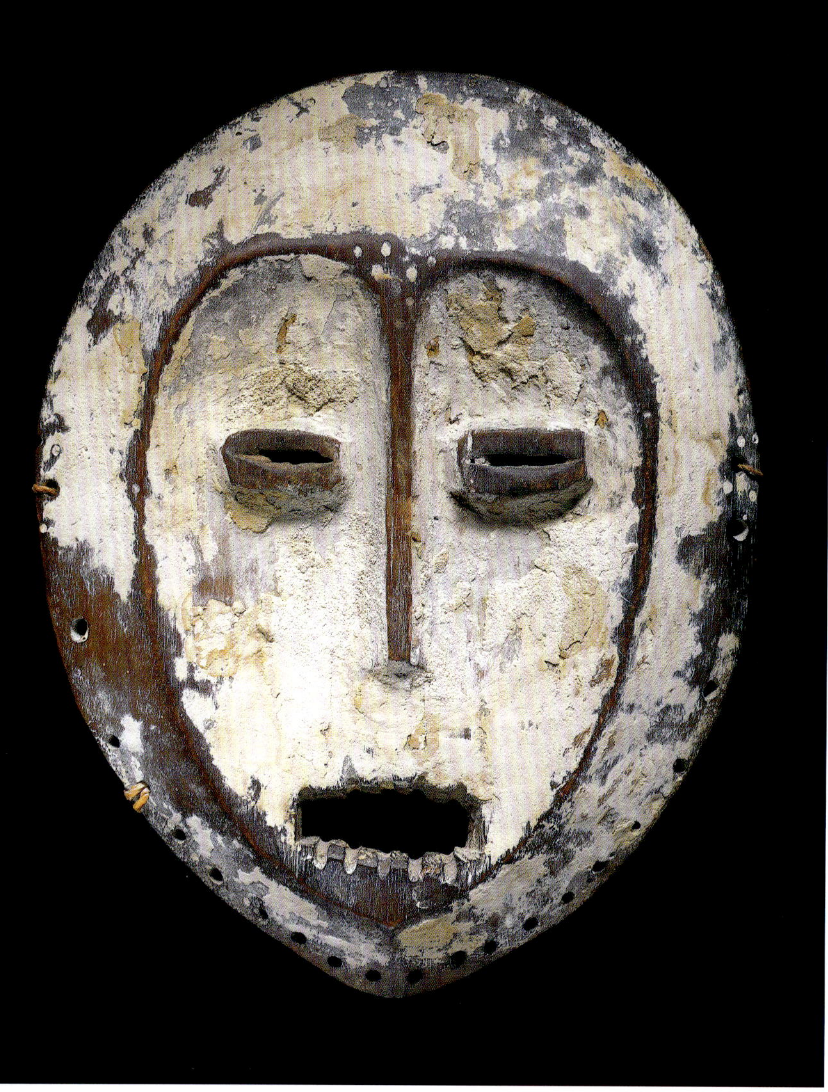

3.12 Mask (*muminia*). Wood. H: 22.8 cm (9 in.).

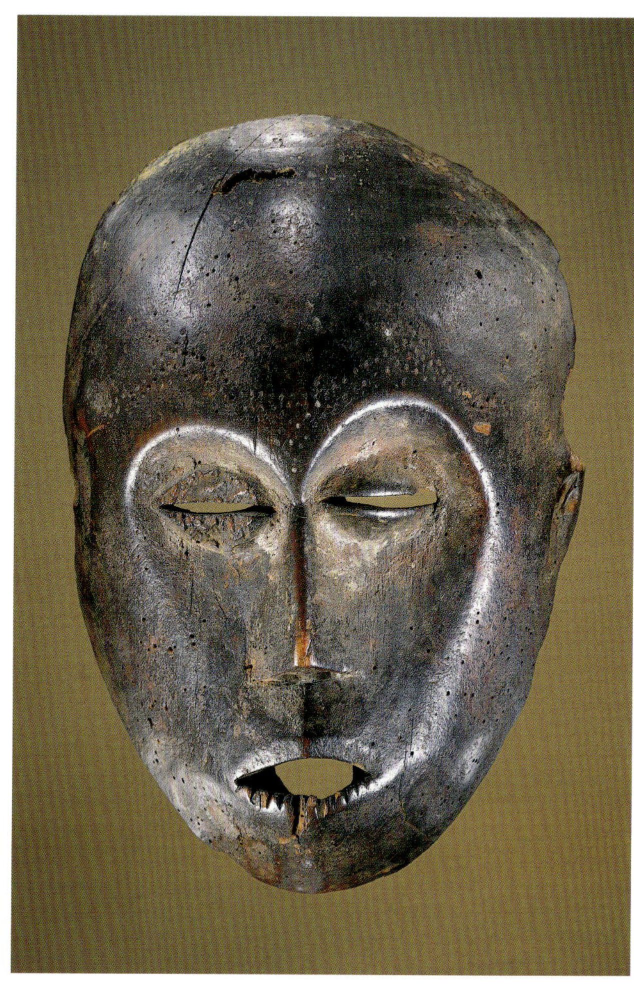

throughout all levels of Bwami, the carefully carved figures (figs. 3.18–3.21, and see figs. 3.6, 3.7) and masks (see fig. 3.8) are reserved for the highest levels. The richness of meaning comes from the possible multiple connotations represented by each initiation object. The objects at the Kindi level, however, hold fewer possible meanings because the initiates who are accomplished and wise men have less to learn.

The final performance in the highest initiation of Bwami strips all metaphorical layers. The teacher escorts the initiate into an area where initiation objects are carefully laid out. No explanations are given and the initiate is left to understand the meaning through contemplation of the exhibition and revelation (Biebuyck 1994, 42).

3.13 Mask (*lukwakongo*).
Wood, plant fiber, and pigment.
H: 31 cm (12¼ in.).

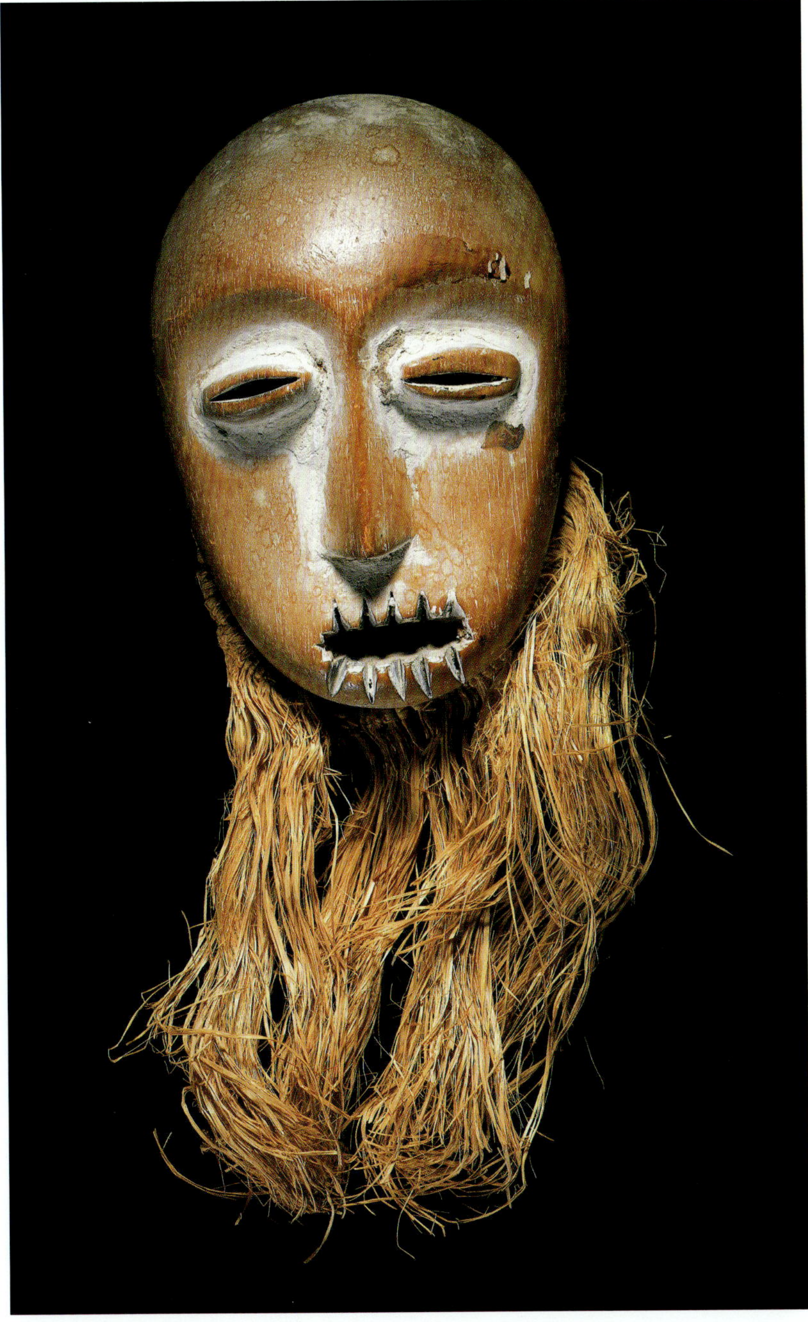

3.14 Mask (*idimu*). Wood and pigment. H: 18.7 cm (7⅜ in.).

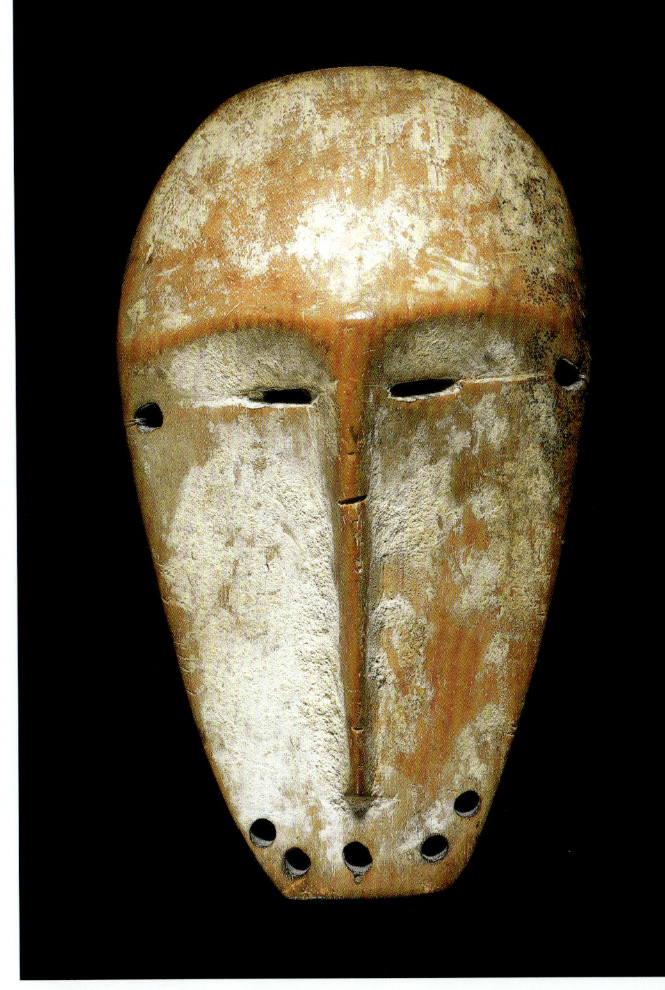

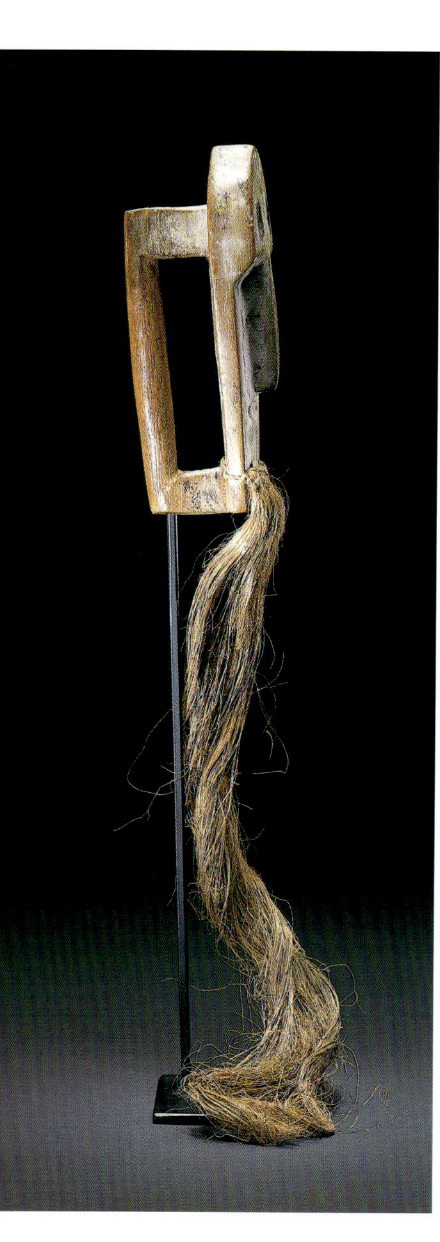

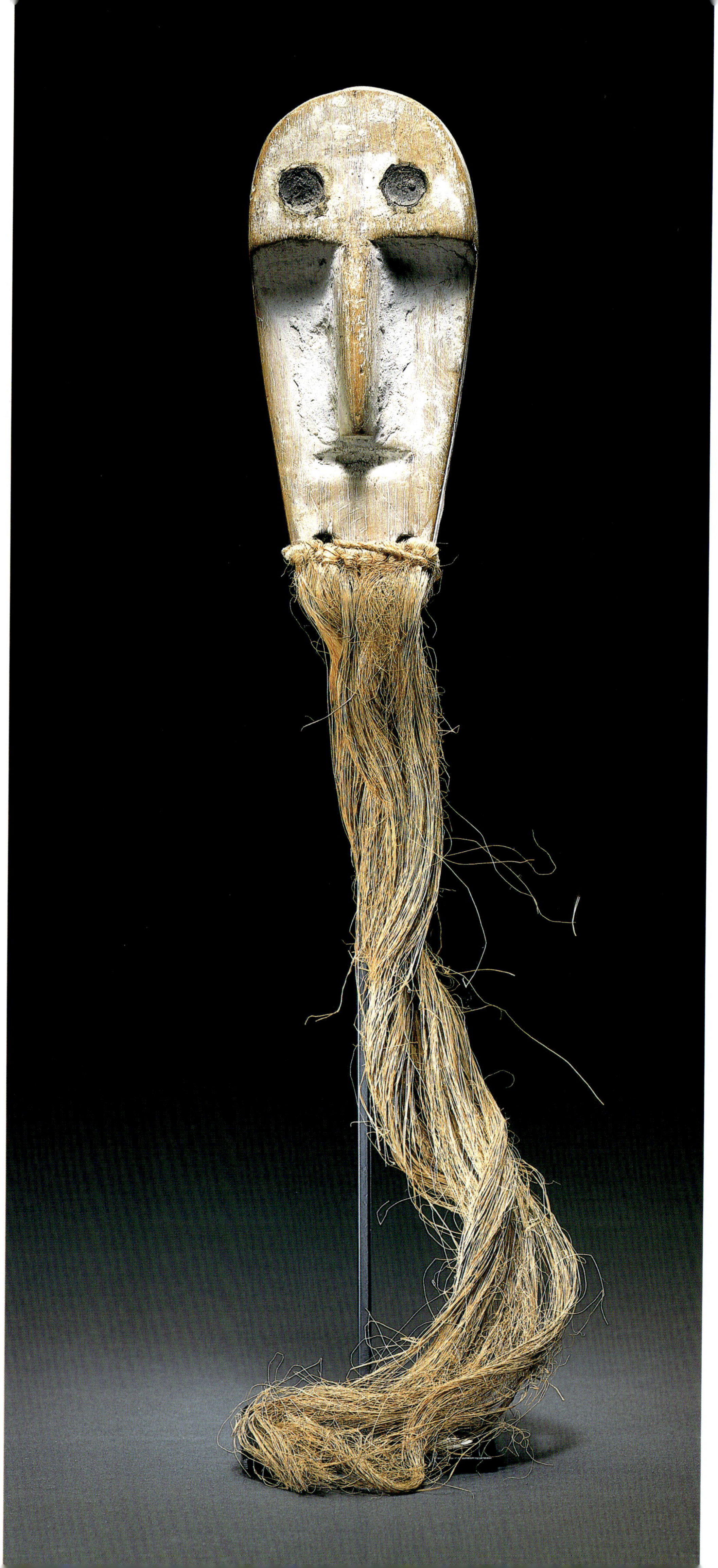

3.15A, B Side and front views of a mask (*lukwakongo*). Wood, plant fiber, and pigment. H: 44.5 cm. (17½ in.).

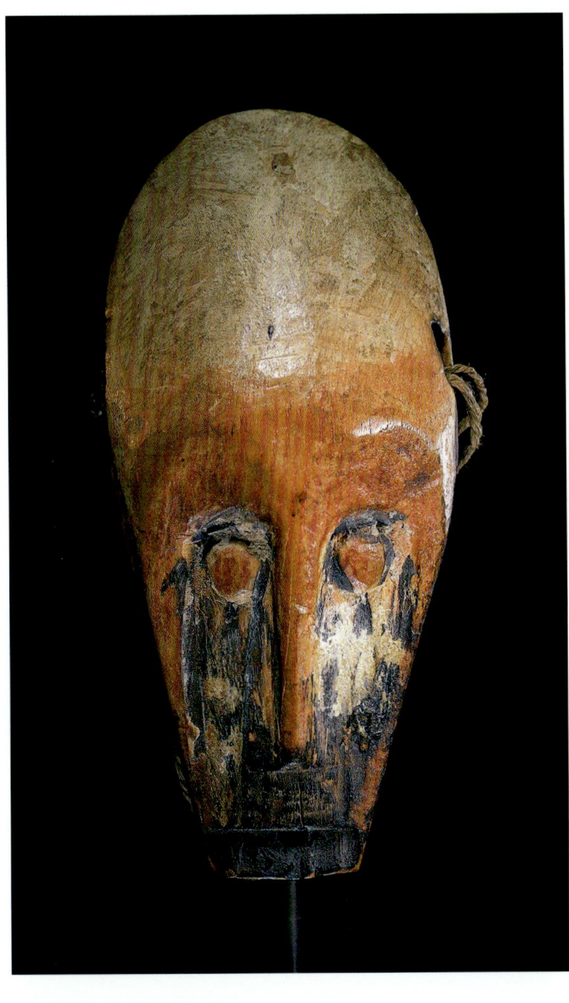

3.16 Mask (*lukwakongo*).
Wood, pigment, and fiber.
H: 13.8 cm (5½ in.).

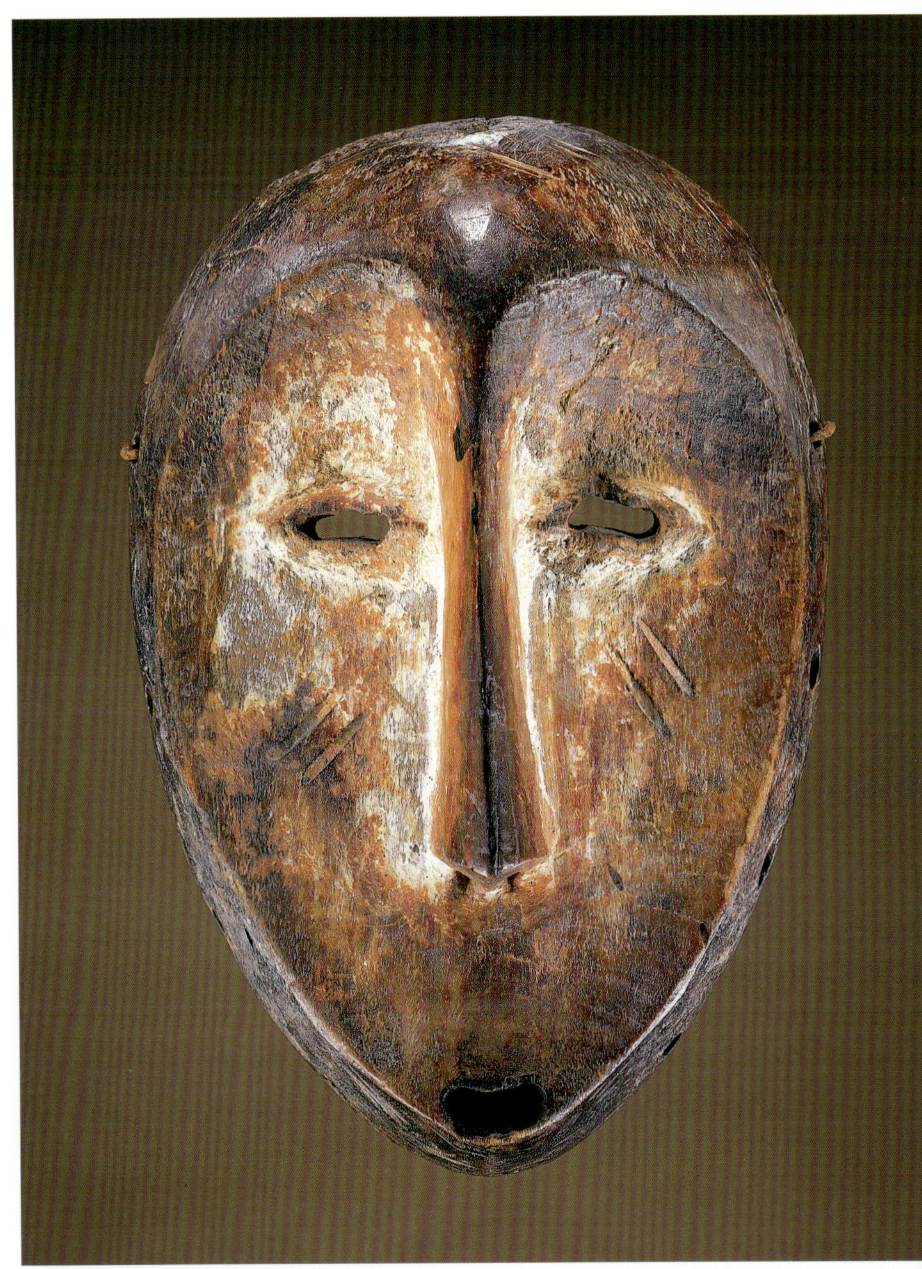

3.17 Mask (*idimu* or *muminia*).
Wood, pigment, and fiber.
H: 25.5 cm. (10 in.).

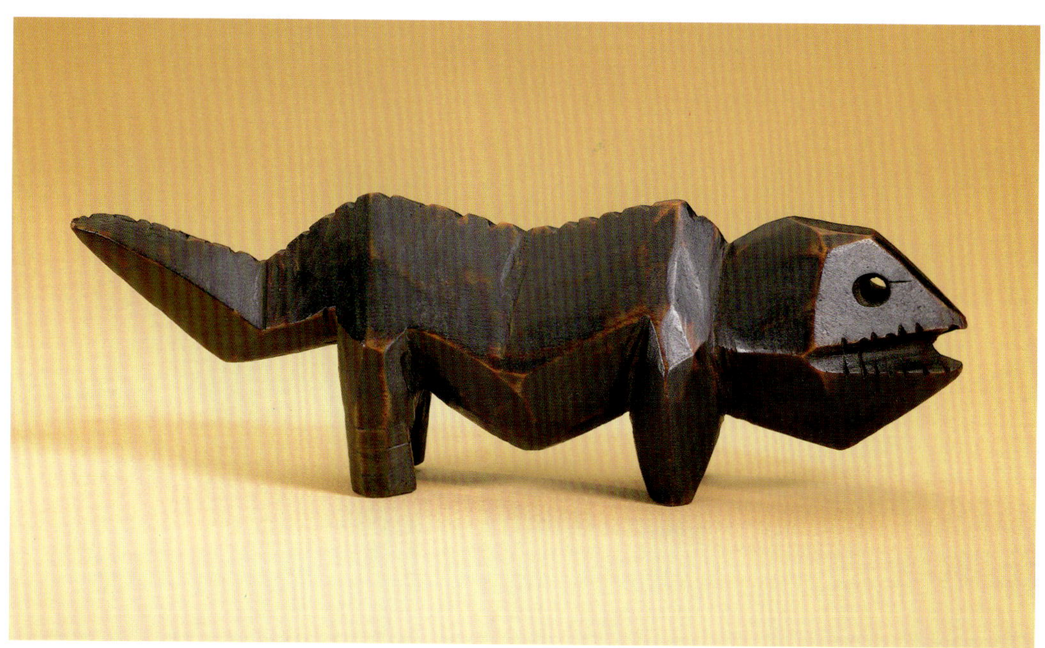

3.18 Generic animal figure. Wood. L: 17.7 cm (7 in.).

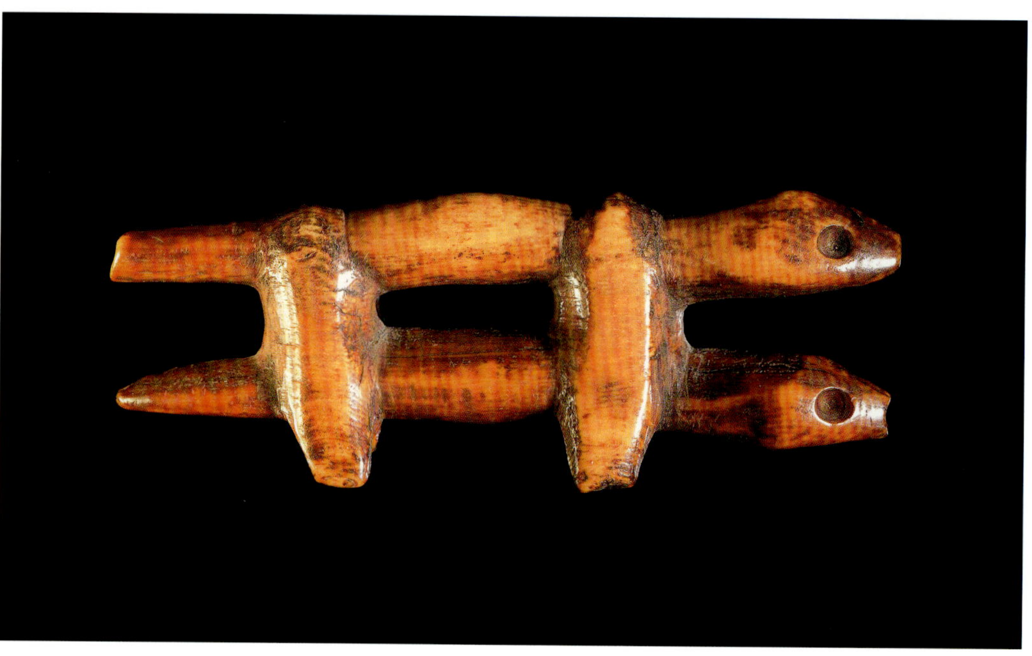

3.19 Generic double-animal figure. Ivory. L: 14 cm (5½ in.).

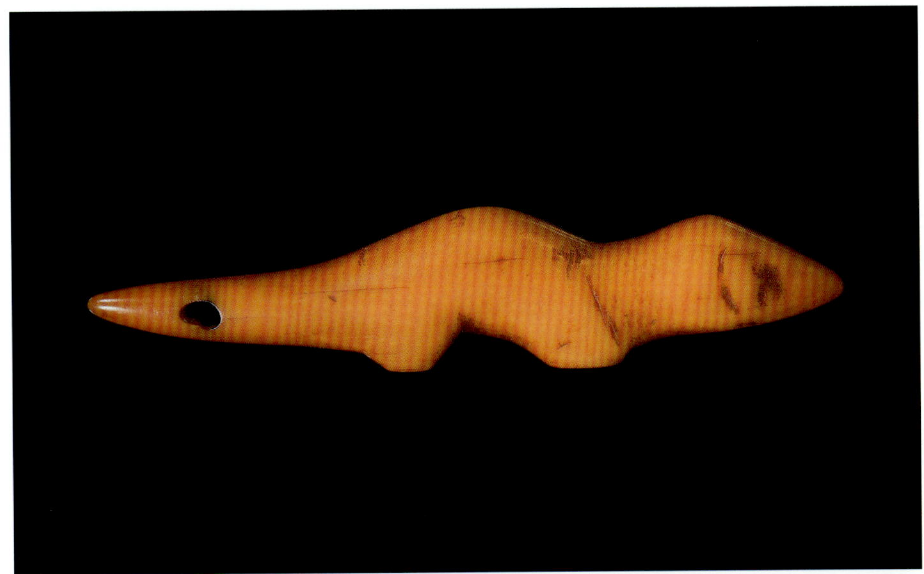

3.20 Generic animal figure. Ivory. L: 12.2 cm (4¾ in.).

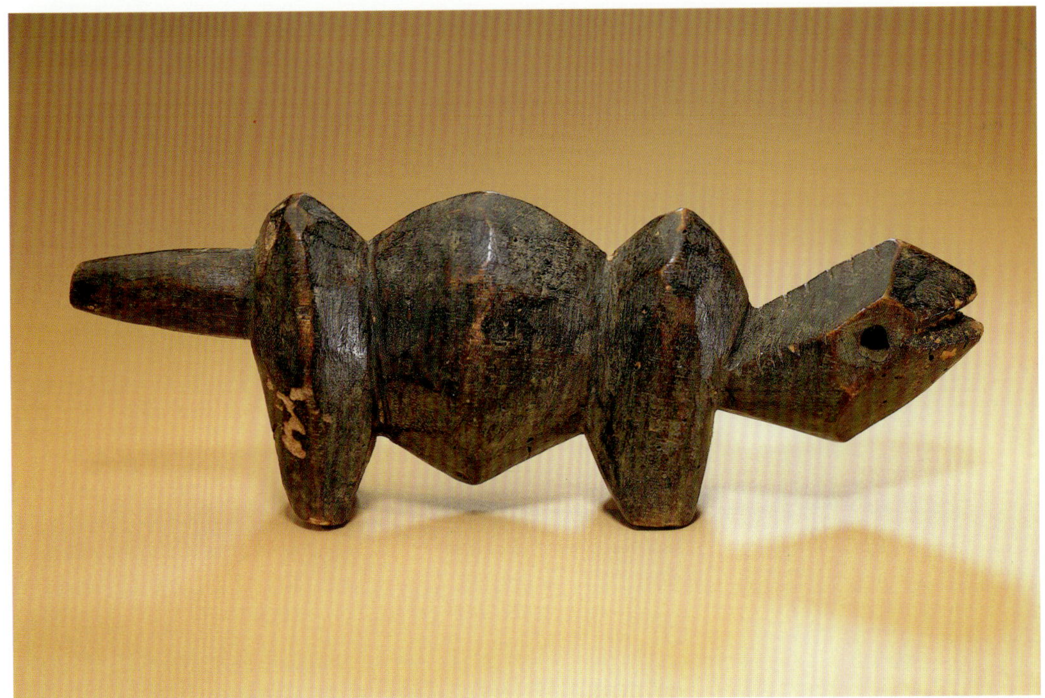

3.21 Generic animal figure. Wood. L: 22.7 cm (9 in.).

4 Artists and Aesthetics

The identities of Lega artists have been lost or concealed. Researchers inquiring about a particular artwork have been met with a standard reply: a list of past owners and their relationship to the present owner. Rarely if ever was an artist mentioned (Biebuyck 1994, 44). At the beginning of the twentieth century, this caused Delhaise to conclude that there were few men who were sculptors because of the lack of associated honor (1909, 275). Biebuyck was able to collect the names of a few well-known artists from the past—Lusungu, Kalimu, Kayonkela, Kilunga, and Itongwa—but found no well-known or long-established artists working in the 1950s (1967, 89; 1973, 226).

Although recent research suggests that Lega artists schooled in the old tradition no longer survive, an idea of their lives can be gleaned from information collected by several researchers, including Biebuyck (1973; 1976; 1994), de Kun (1966), Mulyumba wa Mamba(1977), and Corbisier (1968). A man seeking to become an artist would have apprenticed himself to someone in his mother's family. The best match of master and apprentice was between a young man and his mother's brother (Biebuyck 1976, 340). There are two names for artists in Kilega, the language spoken by the Lega: *mubazi wa nkondo,* or "carver of the adze,"[1] and *mulongo,* or "person who fits things together" (Biebuyck 1973, 106, 228). These terms may reflect a distinction between the carver of sculpture and masks and the maker of objects that are essentially found and bound together. The sculptor worked with a standard group of tools: ax, adze, knife, chisel, simple drill, calipers (used to make the dot-within-a-circle motif known as *bitondi* on ivory), and abrasive leaves used as sandpaper (Corbisier 1968, 20; Biebuyck 1973, 228). Metal tools suggest a connection between the sculptor and the blacksmith, and Biebuyck notes that some blacksmiths were carvers (1973, 228). Delhaise, however, emphatically states that blacksmiths "make no works of art; the objects they fabricate are not ornamented" (1909, 138).

Lega artists used materials they found around them: wood, ivory, bone, occasionally copal or stone, and objects from the environment that had associations within the Bwami metaphorical system (figs. 4.1–4.5). The fact that Bwami members were the principal clientele for any Lega artist resulted in tension between the artist and the Society. The artist did not have to be a member of Bwami but, like all Lega men, was under tremendous societal pressure to join at least the lowest level. The Bwami patron gave the artist a commission, describing the type of object desired, the material (if ivory was specified, the commissioner was responsible for providing it), and the size. Some descriptions were very general, for example, a human figure in wood the length of your hand from the fingertips to the base of the palm (see fig. 3.7). Others, such as an order for a sculpture of Wayinda, the pregnant woman, were fairly precise (fig. 4.6; Biebuyck 1977a, 65). Calling Lega artistic production "constrained diversity" (1973, 179), Biebuyck argues that although artists exercised considerable freedom, the needs of Bwami created an artistic canon (1977a, 63).

The Bwami member would pay the artist with Lega shell money (see fig. 1.7) and, according to Biebuyck,

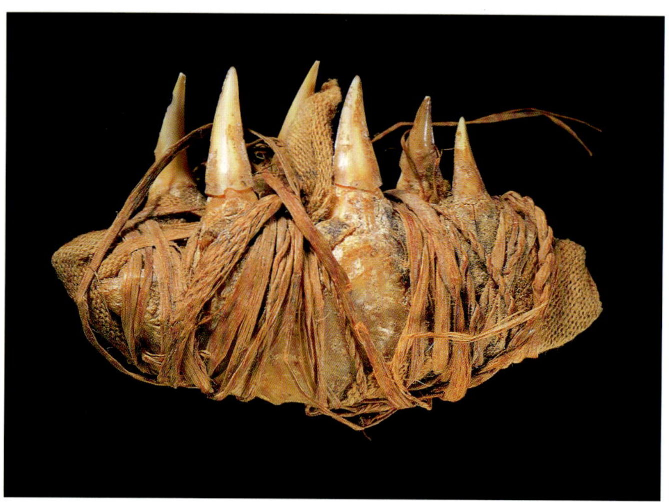

4.1 Assembled initiation object. Jawbone, cotton cloth, and raffia. L: 6.5 cm (2½ in.). FMCH X378.775; Museum Purchase.

4.2 Mask (*lukwakongo* or *idimu*). Wood, pigment, and plant fiber. H: 36.5 cm (14⅜ in.).

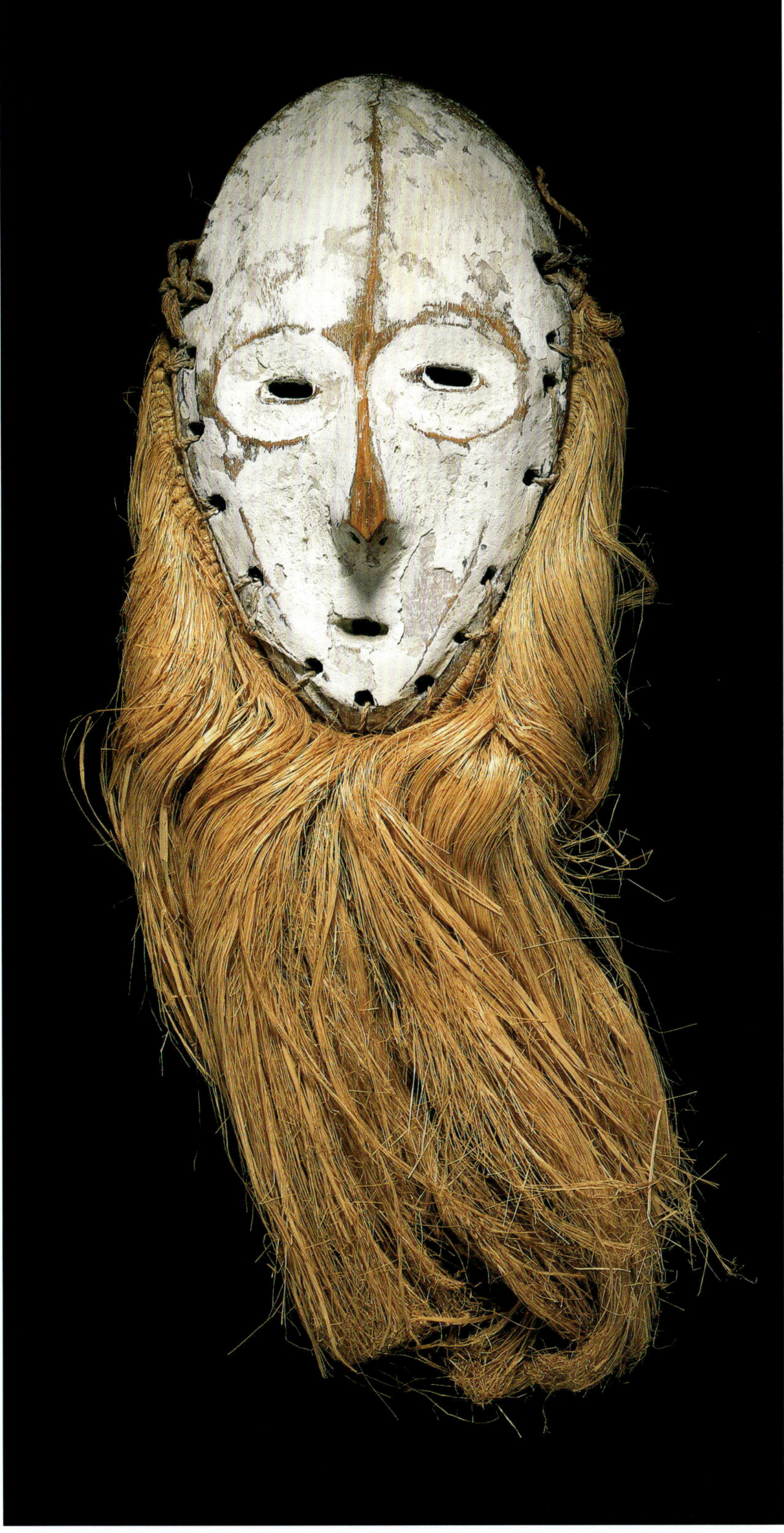

4.3 Sculpture of a human head. Amber or copal (?). H: 9.7 cm (3¾ in.).

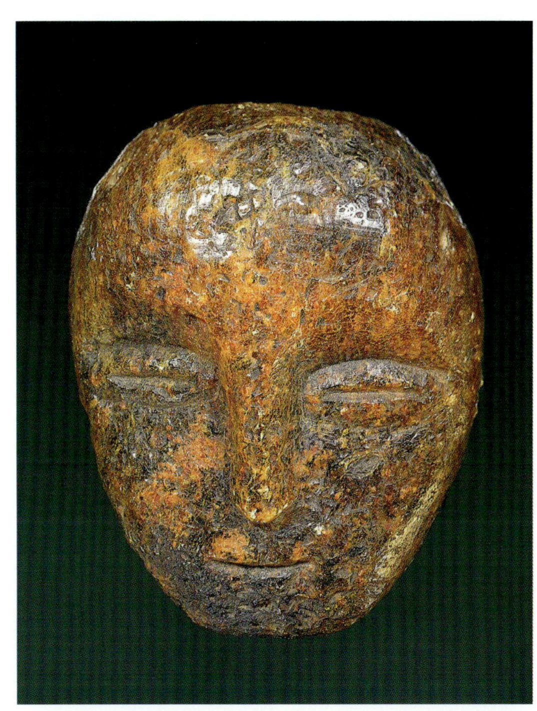

4.4 Human Figure. Ivory. H: 9.6 cm (3¾ in.).

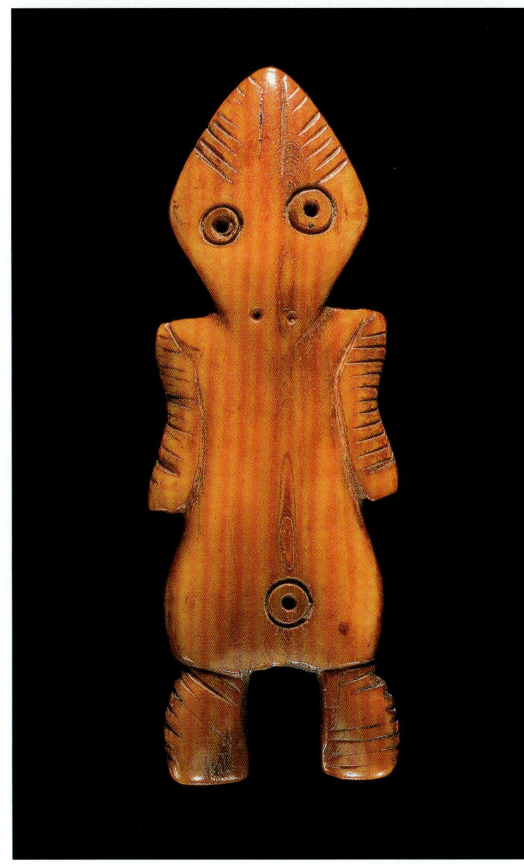

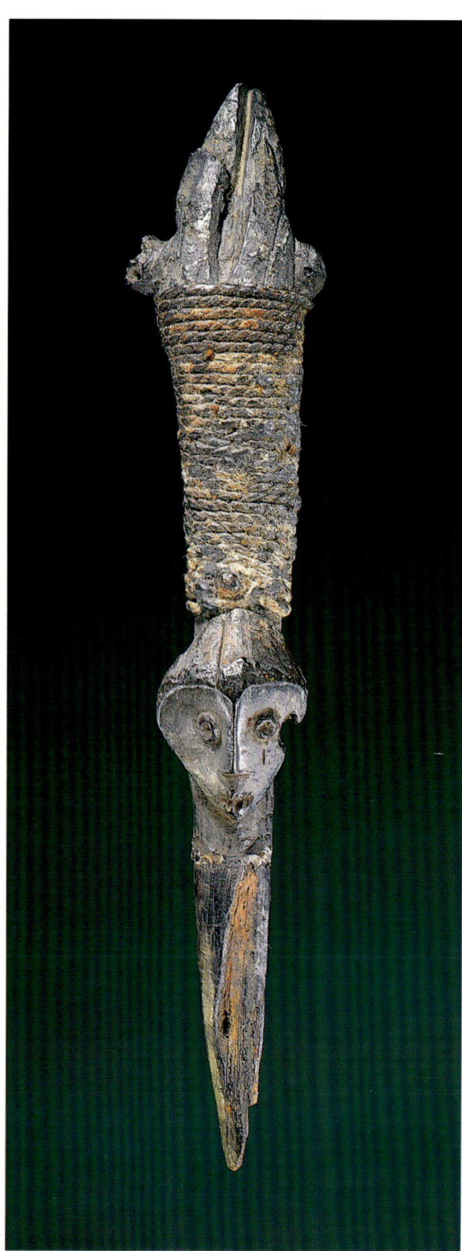

4.5 Assembled initiation object. Wood and plant fiber. H: 25.2 cm (10 in.).

a porcupine. Biebuyck does not state why a porcupine was designated as payment, but it is considered both a source of succulent meat and a potent symbol. A Lega saying states "The meat of the porcupine is savory, but his entrails are very bitter." As with most Lega sayings, this can be interpreted in a variety of ways. One Lega explanation is that the porcupine is ugly on the outside but has good meat on the inside; therefore, the interior should not be judged by the exterior. A converse reading suggests that outside beauty is often paired with inside perversity. A similar English saying would be "Don't judge a book by its cover." The Lega saying also urges discretion in choosing good (i.e., the meat) over bad or evil (i.e., the intestines; de Four n.d., 208). Porcupine quills by virtue of their sharpness (Biebuyck 1973, 190) symbolize the need to stay away from prohibited acts or subjects (Biebuyck 1973, 81–82). All of these meanings could have applied to the artist, who needed to distinguish the good from the bad and, due to Bwami regulations, had to avoid the forbidden.

The apprentice artist learned to carve in the style of his master, who was also a member of his clan. Styles, therefore, were clan specific (Muyololo 1974, 64; Biebuyck 1994, 44). The artist nonetheless had the freedom to interpret the commission within his own personal style (influenced by clan style), as long as it still served its symbolic role and was visually comprehensible (Biebuyck 1969, 10; de Kun 1966, 93). Attempts have been made to use style to localize pieces to their places and clans of origin. The problem is that given the movement of artwork within the systems of Bwami and clan inheritance, it is almost impossible to know where a piece originated.

As most commissions were fairly general in terms of the type of object specified, the artist would not know the intended use of the artwork or its future meaning (Biebuyck 1994, 44). Muyololo suggests that the artist had the right to demand the meaning of the piece and even entry into Bwami (1974, 65), but this is not confirmed in the other literature. Whether the artist understood the meaning or not, the artwork was still intended for Bwami and considered a potent force. The surrounding secrecy and the potential lack of complete understanding on the part of the artist aided in the creation of "cryptic unreadable artwork" (Biebuyck 1994, 44).

To protect the uninitiated community from accidentally seeing a restricted piece while it was being created, artists worked in isolated workshops away from areas where people lived and moved, a situation that according to one argument, helped enforce distinct clan styles (Muyololo 1974, 66). Bwami messengers were responsible for warning people to stay out of the area of the workshop (Muyololo 1974, 66). Although these precautions were taken, the full power of the object did not accumulate until it acquired the patina of use (Biebuyck 1973, 230).

Western scholars and connoisseurs have long critiqued the "aesthetic quality" of Lega and other African artwork on the basis of their own Western art historical framework. Delhaise, for example, reflected a Victorian perspective when he called Lega figures "crude" and "coarsely executed" (1909, 210, 275). Once African art became the model and inspiration for Cubism and subsequent styles, however, Lega art was praised for being strong, schematic, and abstracted. Frans Olbrechts stated that Lega sculpture "shows...virtuosity in the rejection of all realism" (1946,

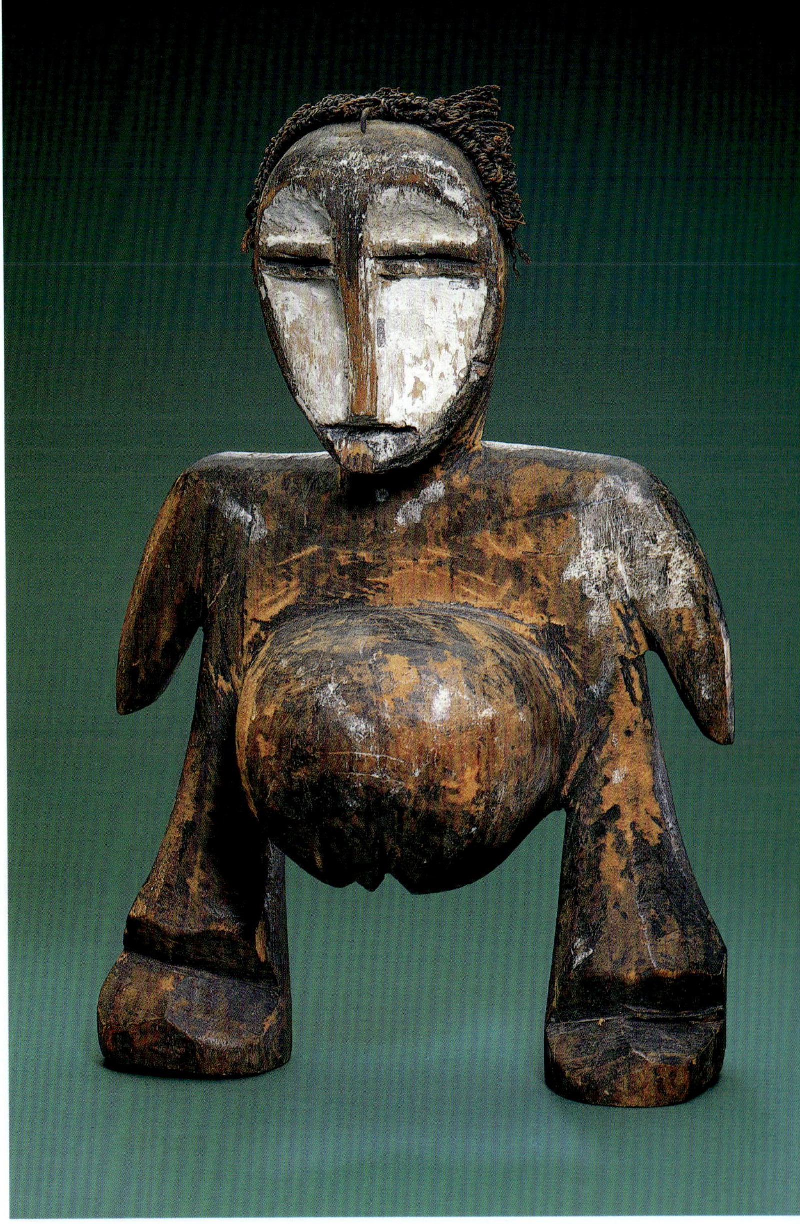

4.6 Figure (Wayinda). Wood, pigment, and plant fiber. H: 31.1 cm (12¼ in.).

82, 91). In 1952 Ladislas Segy described ivory figures as "executed with great simplicity in angular form" (1952, 227). Other writings praise the artworks as "extraordinarily expressive despite their simple, almost classical lines" (Cornet 1971, 261) and as having a "remarkably simplified style which often shows great sensitivity" (Fagg 1965, 108).

Modern Western-trained scholars, however, have turned the tables by asking the Lega to explain their own standards for judging the quality of their art. De Kun, a mining engineer who developed a passion for Lega art, showed a group of Lega figures and masks to an unspecified number of groups of Bwami members of the Yananio and Kindi levels (fig. 4.7a–e). He placed the selection of objects on the ground and watched the order in which the Bwami members picked them up. All the groups examined the pieces in the same order: (1) bust/head, (2) wood or ivory masks, (3) simple abstract figures, (4) expressionistic figures. Based on de Kun's perception of the Lega system of prioritization, the overriding concern seemed to be the permanence of the lineage as expressed through the art of Bwami. This is because the first pieces handled pass down through families and stress continuity. De Kun noted a secondary bias in favor of simplicity of form and diversity of style (1966, 76).

In the early 1970s, Muyololo critiqued de Kun's methods and thesis. Muyololo decided to conduct a similar experiment. He presented a fairly realistic, recent carving to a group of Bwami members. One gentleman picked up the piece and carefully examined it while Muyololo watched with anticipation, sure that the Bwami member would tell him everything about it. What happened next disappointed and mystified the young scholar. Each Bwami member in turn quoted a saying related to the figure. After they had finished, Muyololo asked for the name of the figure. A Bwami member responded, "The one who is not able to think well will not be *mwami*" and advised Muyololo to reconsider the sayings. Muyololo erroneously concluded that the figure had no name (1974, 52–53).

The difference in the responses obtained by de Kun and Muyololo no doubt results from the fact that one scholar was European and the other was obviously a non-initiated Lega. De Kun tried to decode the *actions* of the Lega men who, in turn, did not expect him to understand Lega thought. Muyololo, for whom language and cultural context should not have been a problem, expected the Bwami members to give him a verbal critique of the piece. Instead, they treated him as any other Lega youth, using the objects and sayings to force him to think and consider Lega and Bwami morality.

Biebuyck also attempted, over a period of many years of field research, to understand the Lega criteria for their own art. He found that the Bwami code forbade a member from critiquing the relative quality of an initiation object (1973, 177; 1994, 46). Initiation objects that had been used and thus gained power were judged by Bwami members to be intrinsically good. A simple equation exists: initiation object=*busoga*, "good and beautiful" (Biebuyck 1973, 177). In this mindset, trying to critique an initiation object would be like debating whether the chair you are sitting in is really a chair.

Bwami members do comment, however, on certain aesthetic elements. Size, patina, and medium are important (Biebuyck 1969, 14). It should be noted, however, that

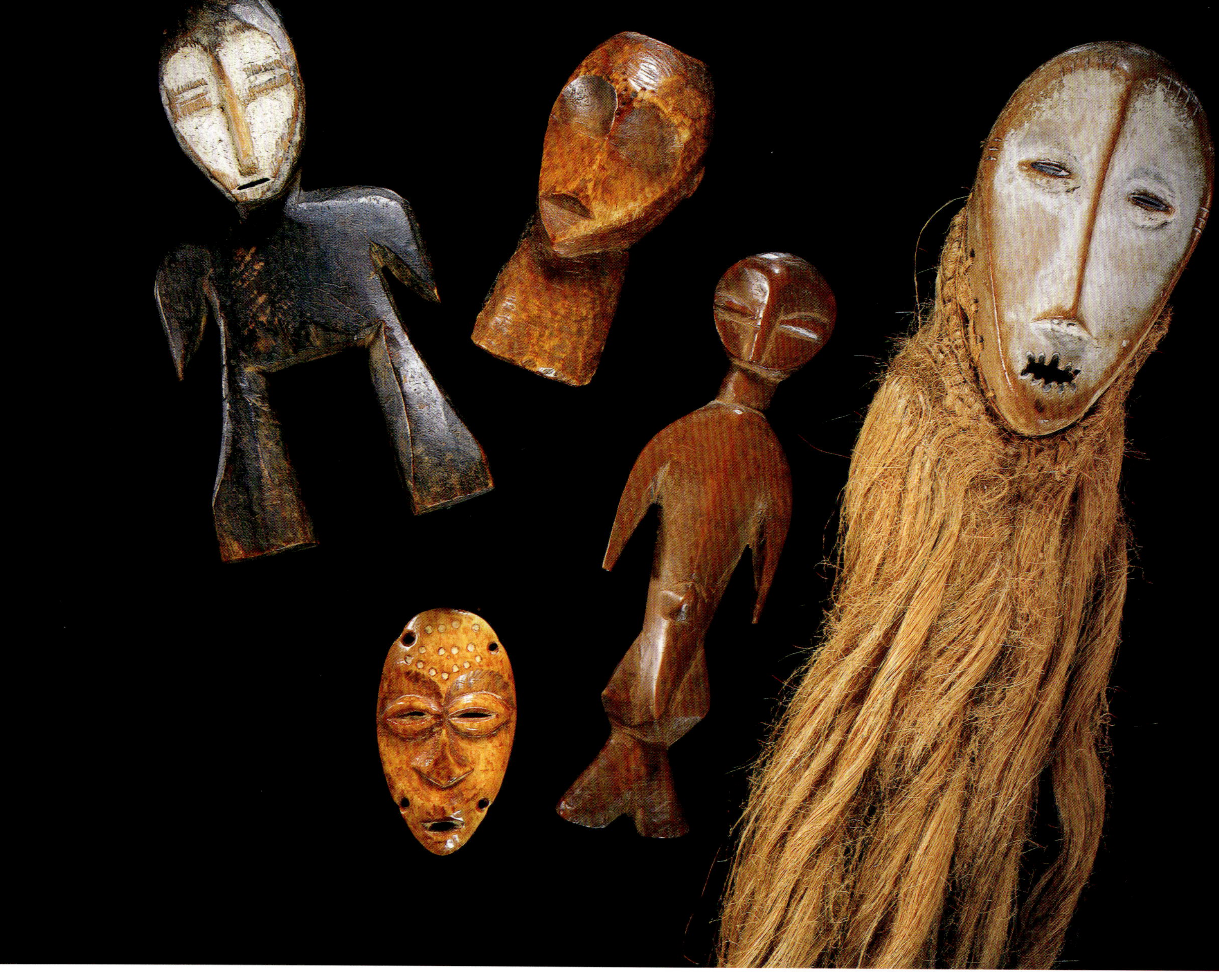

these same criteria are important in determining who may own the object and when it is used, thus aesthetic and contextual considerations are conflated. In addition, certain metaphoric connections give significance to particular characteristics. Thus the smooth glossy surface of a piece is equated with reaching a high level of Bwami (figs. 4.8, 4.9). Just as the piece is rubbed smooth with effort and time, so Bwami members, through many initiations, are made into wise people (Biebuyck 1977b, 18). The patina gained over time represents the buildup of power in a well-used initiation object that has been passed down through generations. Before initiations, members rubbed their pieces with oils that are often prepared with a red powder, resulting in a glossy honey-colored or reddish glow. The handling, rubbing, and oiling of the pieces was designed to prepare the objects for the initiation, "to bring harmony, to produce union" (Biebuyck 1973, 179). It should be noted that Lega art has an intrinsic tactile quality. It is designed to be held, caressed, and even tasted in preparation for and during initiation performances. The small personal size encourages this behavior (de Kun 1966, 78). In the 1950s, the Lega began to replace ancient Bwami pieces that had been destroyed, stolen, or sold with works that were created for the tourist industry. The desired qualities—a glossy surface and a generic form that could be understood in many different ways—facilitated the substitution of such commercialized works for the *isenga,* or initiation object (Biebuyck 1967, 89–90).

As is common in much of Africa, the Lega do not separate visual aesthetics from morality or goodness.[2] The word *busoga* describes them all (Biebuyck 1976, 340–41). Because the Bwami Society is responsible for developing and refining moral character, beauty—of people and of objects—becomes circumscribed by the Society. Goodness and beauty, however, can be described in positive and negative ways. Most Lega portrayals of humans show a composed face that according to Biebuyck, reflects "the extraordinary loftiness of Lega thought" (Biebuyck 1973,

4.7A–E This grouping of objects resembles the one that de Kun assembled. They are described clockwise, beginning with the beardless mask at the lower left: (A) Mask (*lukungu*). Ivory. H: 9.5 cm (3¾ in.); (B) Human Figure. Wood and pigment. H: 21 cm (8¼ in.); (C) Bust. Ivory. H: 13 cm (5⅛ in.); (D) Human Figure. Wood. H: 22.3 cm (8¾ in.); (E) Mask (*idimu*). Wood, plant fiber, and pigment. H: 57 cm (22½ in.).

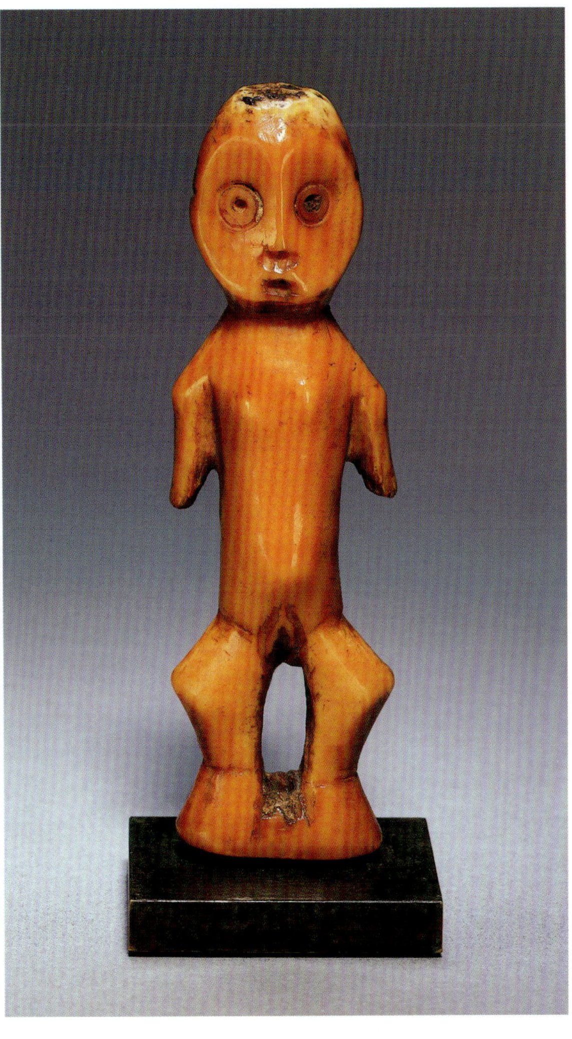

4.8 Human figure. Ivory. H: 11.1 cm (4⅜ in.).

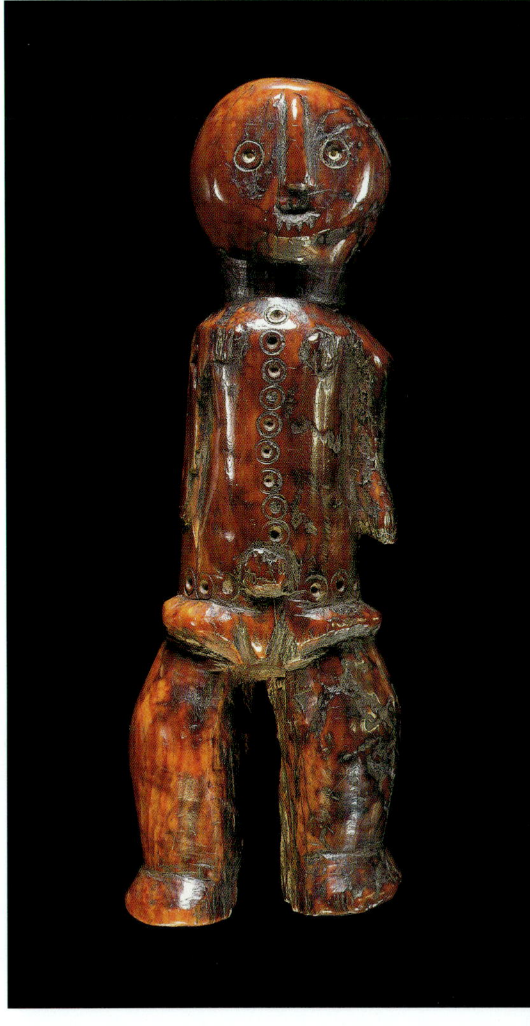

4.9 Human figure. Ivory. H: 13.2 cm (5¼ in.).

234). Some artworks, however, stress the ideal by portraying its opposite, or what Biebuyck has called "the code of the ugly" (1986, 64). Abstraction and realism are also used as tools according to the needs of the initiation context.

The genius of the Lega artist lies in taking the needs of the Bwami patron and producing a unique artwork that fits carefully within the canon. Each mask, for example, is unmistakably Lega in style and carefully fits within the confines of Bwami, but when placed with others, its uniqueness can be seen by the critic from an artistic point of view. When connoisseurs try to define Lega style, however, they find it almost impossible. The forehead bulges, except when it is flat; human faces, especially those depicted as masks, are heart-shaped, except when they are not. As aptly summarized by Ralph Altman, "Balega art...consists mainly of an infinite number of variations of a few motifs and forms of sculpture" (1963, n.p.).

Lega art takes on different layers of meaning as it moves into the Western art world. Western viewers do not see or participate in the performances that feature the artworks. The non-Lega viewer does not share the intense Bwami-centered culture and knowledge of the environment that the Lega viewer brings to the piece, nor will his or her experience include the moral codes so important to the Lega. Westerners rarely have the opportunity to handle Lega pieces with their bare hands and experience the butterlike patina, nor are they able to participate in further enriching the surface by contributing their own hand oils. They experience Lega artworks instead as static form and shape, carefully mounted and dramatically lit behind Plexiglas.

5 The Public and the Secret

> A mwami [is] a Mr. Lusembe [Shell];
> Mubinga [Dendrohyrax] dies because
> of Mbalo [Waxing moon].[1]

The new member of Bwami, after returning from his initiation into the lowest level (Kongabulumbu), drives a wooden stake into the ground by his front door. He adds a stake for each additional level attained so that anyone passing his house knows specifically what he has achieved (Corbisier 1968, 12). While initiations for Bwami levels are held in private, and ceremonies and knowledge are restricted to members of that level and higher, it is important for everyone to know who the members are and what rank they hold. Bwami insignia (*bilondo*), such as the wooden stakes, are public proclamations of rank and status within the Bwami Society and include hats, belts (figs. 5.1–5.4), armbands, girdles, pendants (see figs. 5.22, 5.23), necklaces (figs. 5.5–5.8), rattles, stools (see figs. 6.46–6.51), and staffs (Biebuyck 1973, 182; 1986, 131; 1994, 30). Some insignia, such as hats, necklaces, belts, and girdles, are worn daily (Biebuyck 1973, 91). Bwami members carry other insignia—baskets, stools, rattles, and staffs—while on their way to an initiation, alerting those they pass on the road that they are not to be disturbed.

Symbolic materials used on insignia at the varying levels function as a sort of double entendre: the uninitiated understand only the person's position in Bwami, while members read a deeper meaning. A man who has reached Kyogo wa Yananio, the lowest sublevel within Yananio, for example, attaches a highly polished mussel shell (*lusembe*)

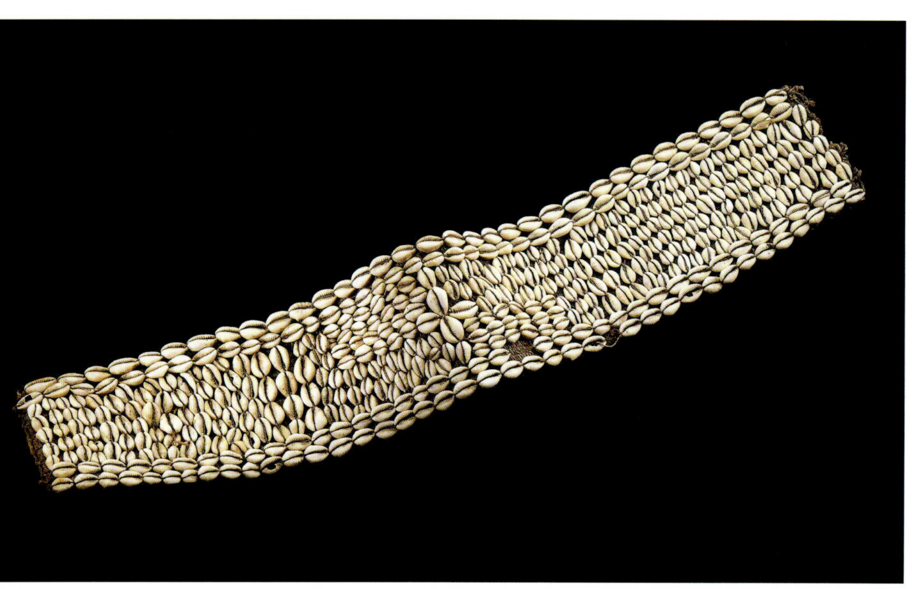

5.1 Belt. Plant fiber and cowrie shells. L: 71.7 cm (28¼ in.). FMCH 378.517; Museum Purchase.

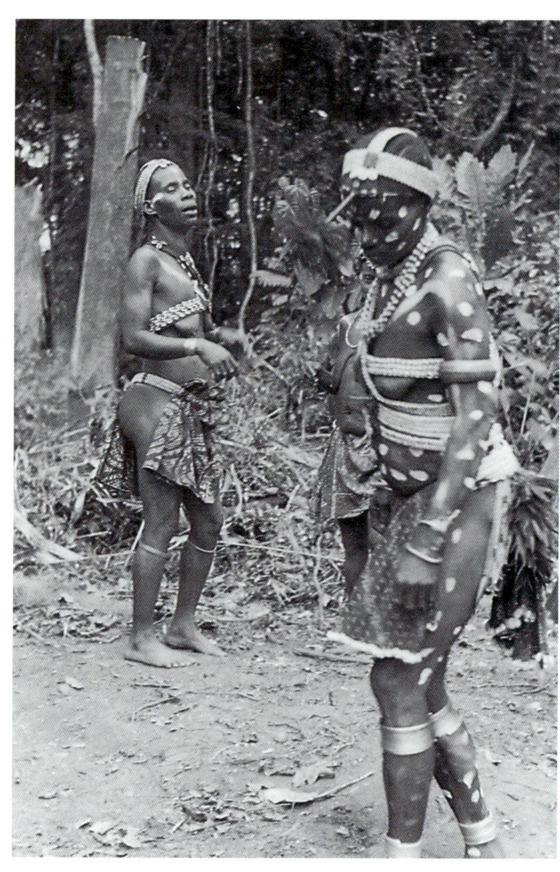

5.2 Two high-ranking female Bwami members dance during an intitiation into Bunyama level. They wear insignia including cowrie-covered belts, necklaces, headwear, and chest straps, circa 1952–1954. Photograph courtesy of Daniel P. Biebuyck.

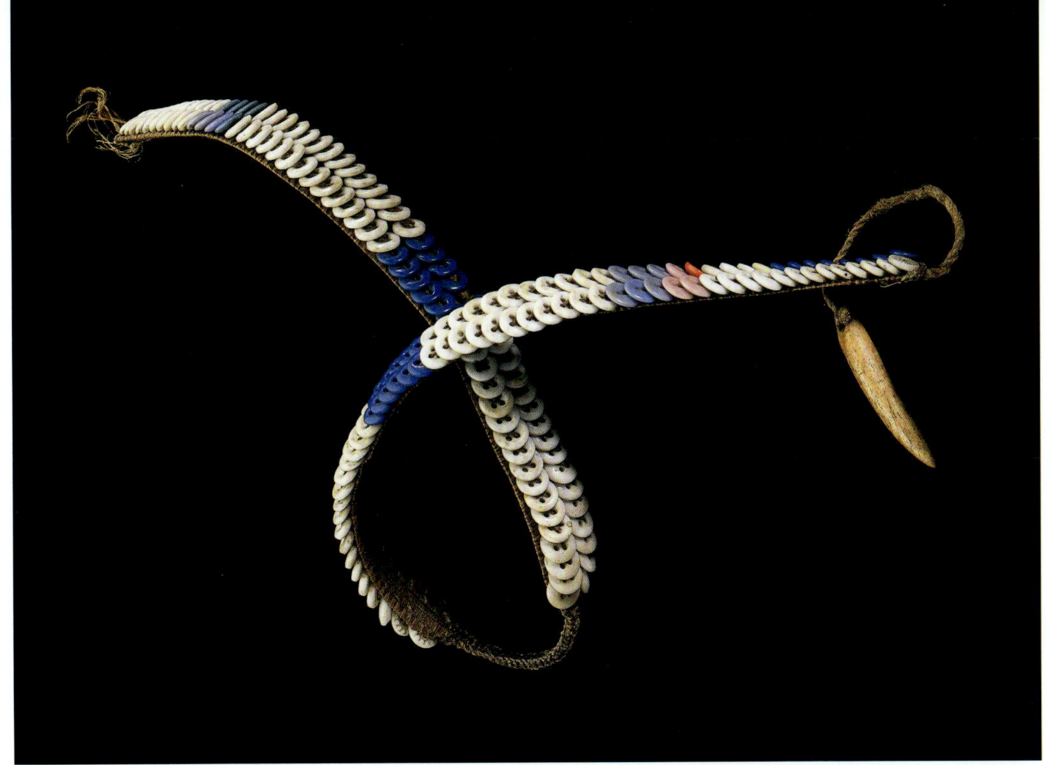

5.3 Belt or chest strap. Plant fiber, buttons, and animal bone. L: 82 cm (32¼ in.). FMCH 378.521; Museum Purchase.

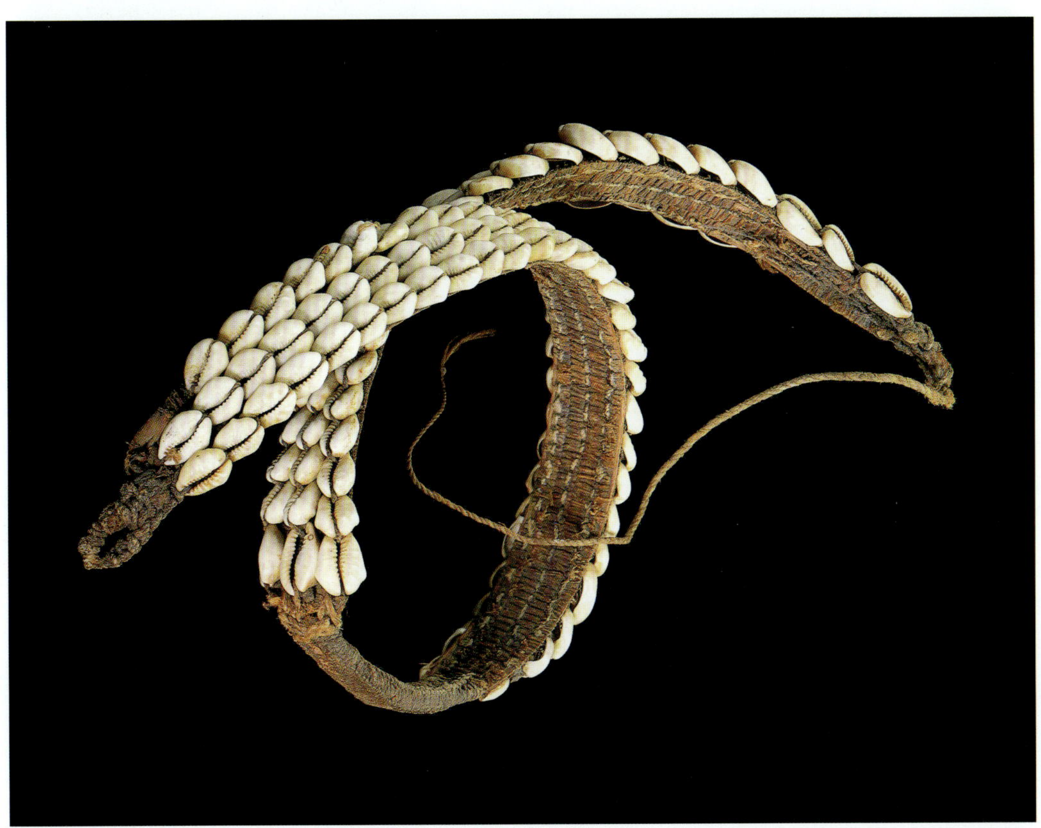

5.4 Belt or chest strap. Plant fiber and cowrie shells. L: 60 cm (23⅝ in.). FMCH X2001.1.1.

to his belt (fig. 5.11; Corbisier 1968, 13). On the most basic level, a young child sees the shell and understands, perhaps after some instruction from an adult, that the person wearing the belt is Kyogo wa Yananio. A fellow member of Kyogo wa Yananio or higher rank sees the shell, understands that it also symbolizes the full moon and recalls various sayings associated with mussel shells such as, "A mwami [is] a Mr. Lusembe [Shell]; Mubinga [Dendrohyrax] dies because of Mbalo [Waxing moon]" (Biebuyck 1986, 31). The initiated understand the implication that the wisdom and presence of a member of Yananio keep a community safe, like the full moon, which provides light, allowing people to walk at night without falling. In contrast to the safety created for the Lega by the full moon, however, is the precarious position of the dendrohyrax, or tree hyrax (*mubinga*), which hunters pursue during the dim light of the waxing moon. The waxing moon and its potential danger are thus also equated with the perils a community would experience without Yananio. When reaching Lutumbo lwa Yananio, the highest Yananio subgrade, the new member places a shell in a more visible location—his hat—as an emblem of his high rank (figs. 5.9, 5.10; Biebuyck 1973, 182).

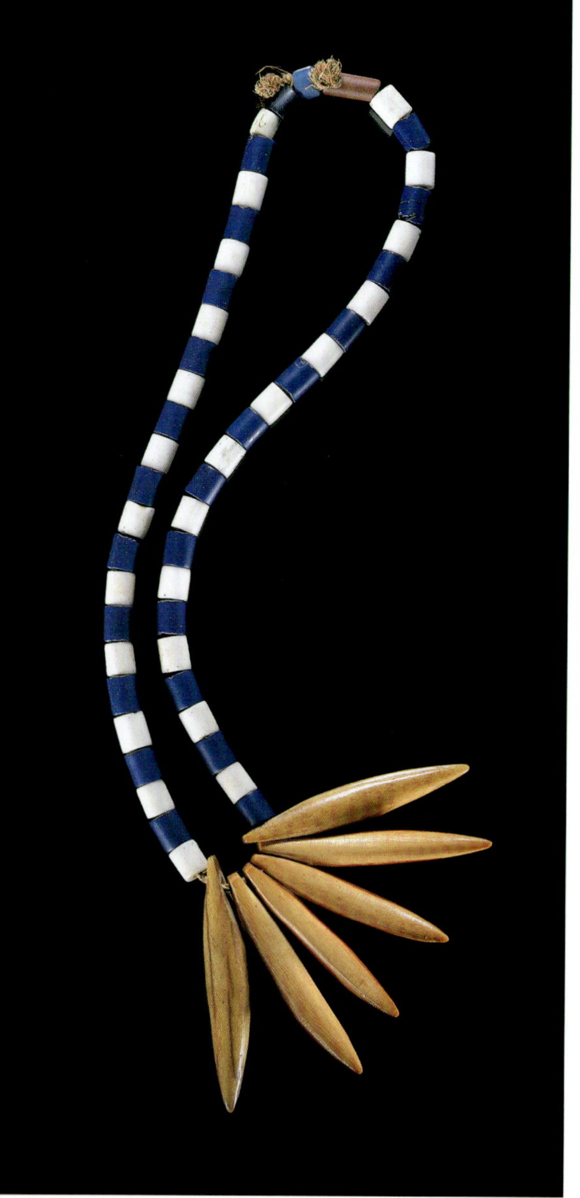

5.5

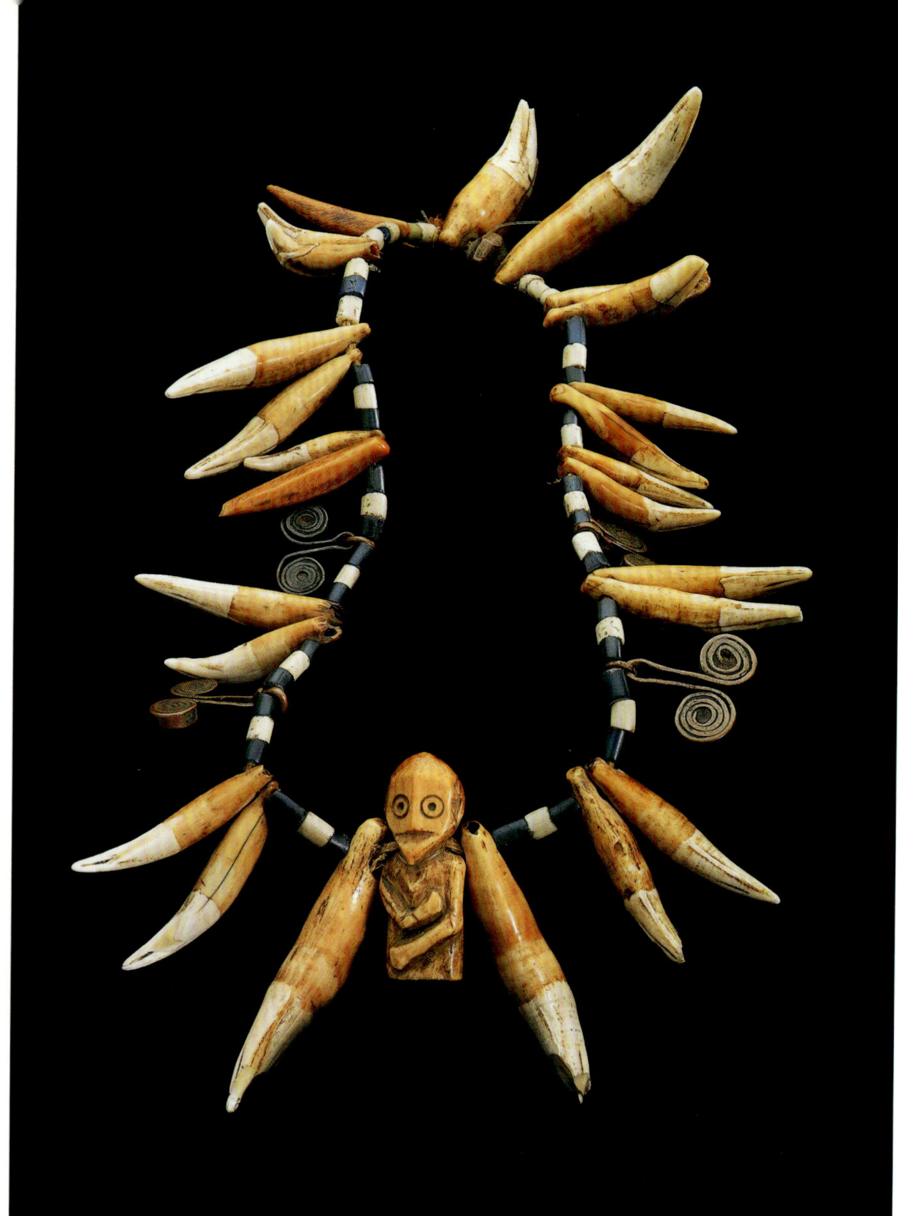

5.6

5.7

5.8

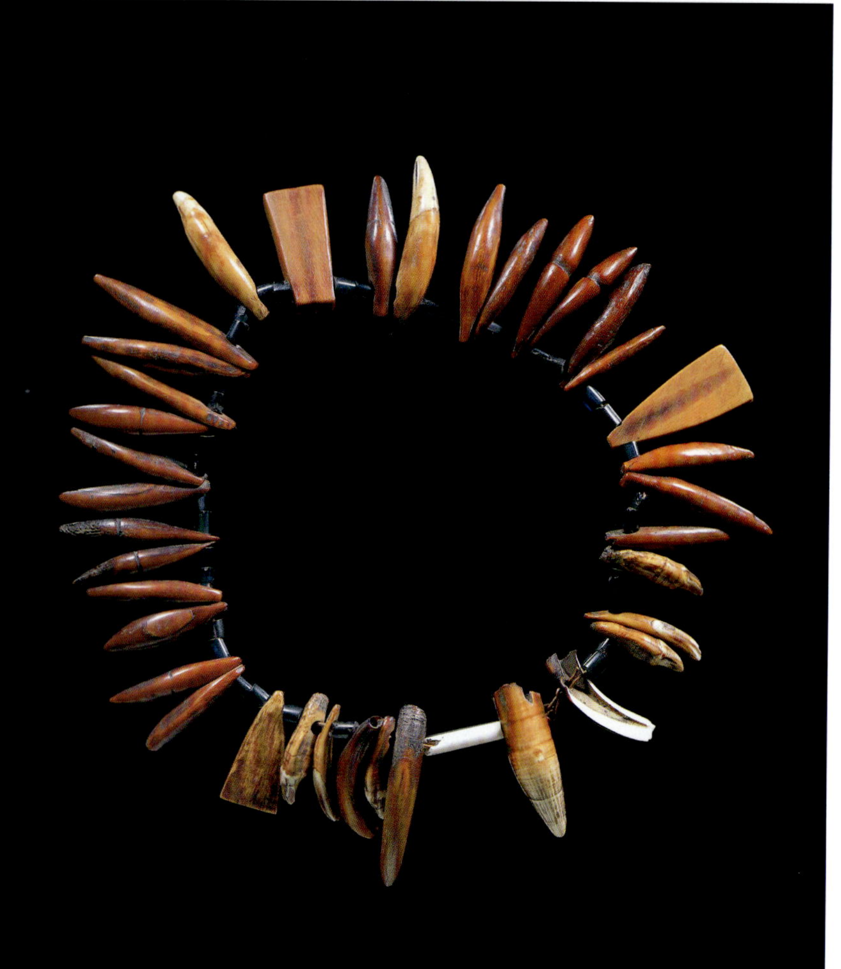

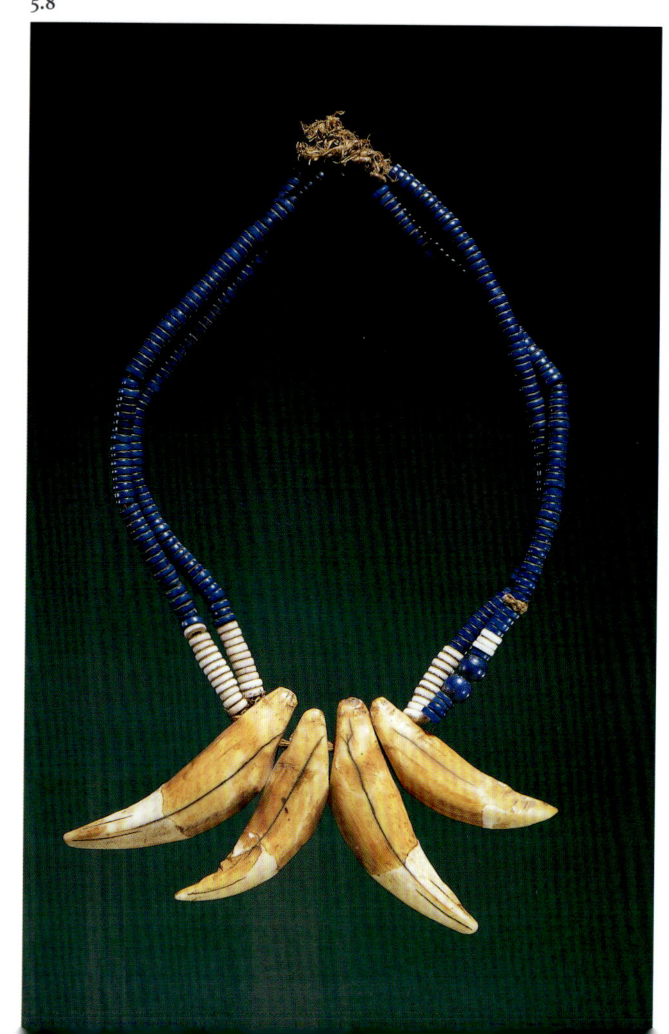

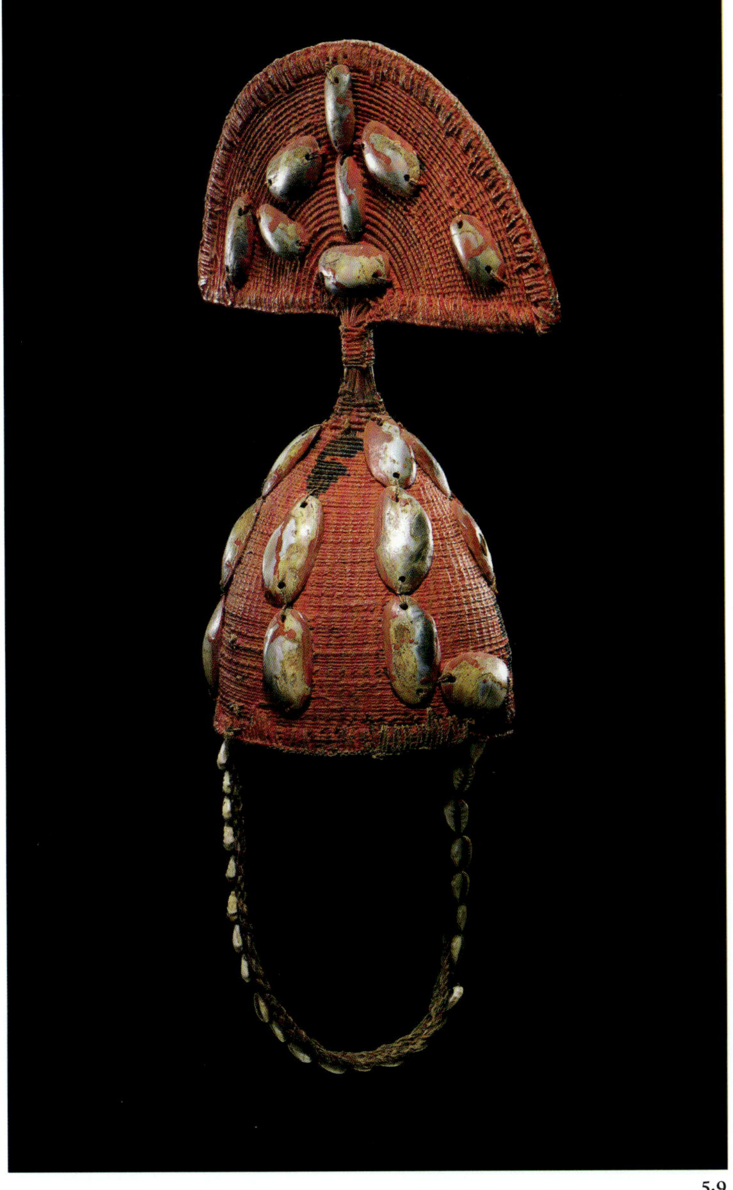

5.9

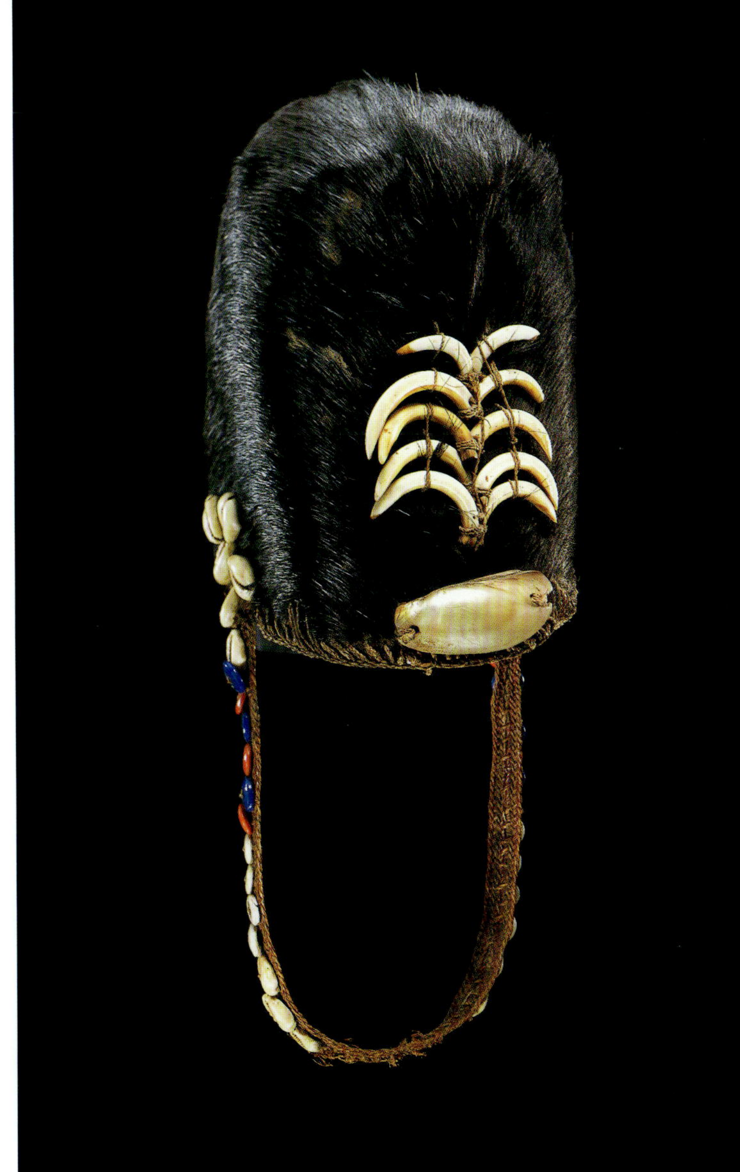

5.10

5.11

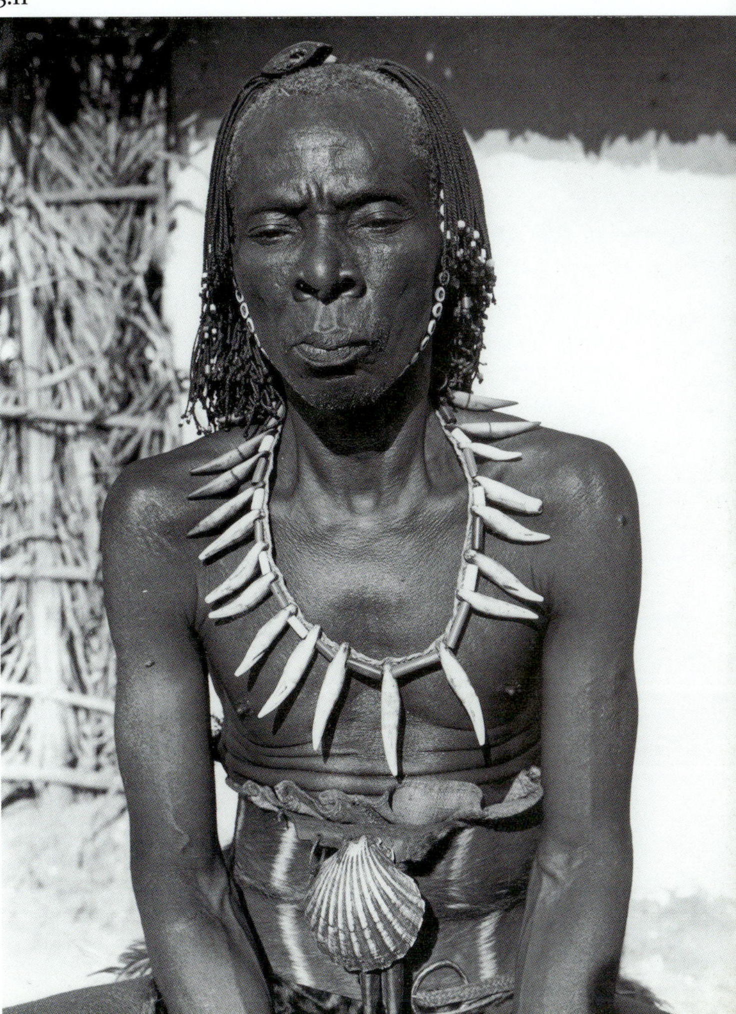

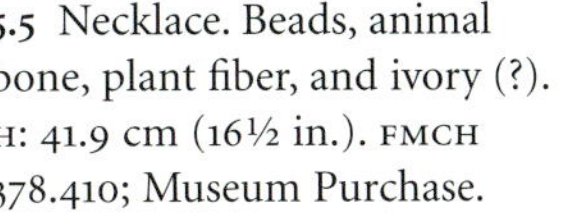

5.5 Necklace. Beads, animal bone, plant fiber, and ivory (?). H: 41.9 cm (16½ in.). FMCH 378.410; Museum Purchase.

5.6 Necklace. Animal teeth, beads, metal, and ivory. H: 40 cm (15¾ in.). FMCH 378.404; Museum Purchase.

5.7 Necklace. Ivory, animal teeth, and beads. H: 30 cm (11¾ in.).

5.8 Necklace. Animal teeth and beads. H: 27 cm (10⅝ in.).

5.9 Hat. Plant fiber, shells, pigment, and cowrie shells. H: 51.5 cm cm (20¼ in.). FMCH X99.15.7; Gift of Jay T. Last.

5.10 Hat. Goat hide, cowrie shells, teeth, fiber, buttons, and shell. H: 33 cm (13 in.). FMCH 378.395; Museum Purchase.

5.11 A Kyogo wa Yananio member has substituted an imported scallop shell for the usual mussel shell. Photograph by Congopresse, No. 31.544/2, courtesy of the Musée Royal de l'Afrique Centrale, Tervuren, no. E. PH. 13782.

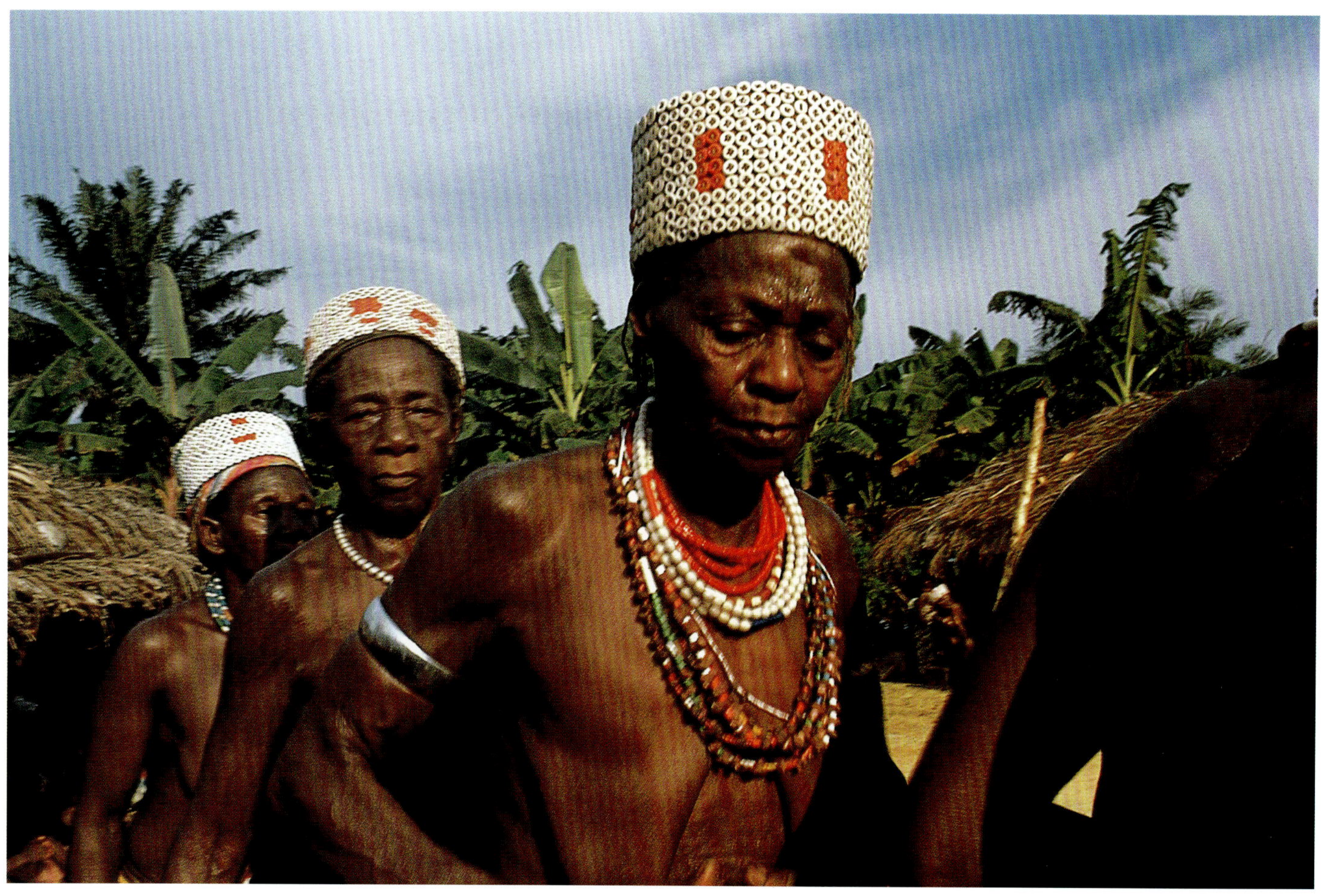

A public symbol of Bwami rank, the shell carries many levels of meaning, but, as noted above, it refers especially to the moon which is visible to all (Biebuyck 1986, 24), just as Bwami rank is known because of insignia. Knowledge, wisdom, and performances belong only to members. The stability of the Lega society, however, depends on the power of Bwami; therefore the identity of its members and their ability to mediate problems must be common knowledge.

FIRST IDENTIFYING INSIGNIA

The first hat given to a man after joining Bwami exemplifies both the public and secret nature of insignia. It is a skullcap made of woven fibers, covered with a red powder, and adorned with an attached seedpod (Cameron 1995, fig. 8.1a,b). Like the larger Society, it is referred to as *bwami.* It is presented to the initiate at the end of the initiation into Kongabulumbu, the basic level of Bwami. In the past, Bwami members wore this skullcap at all times, although in the privacy of his house, a man was allowed to remove his hat to shave his head.[2] When shaving, the Bwami member always left a small tuft of hair on the back of his head. Using a string, he attached the hat to the hair. The Bwami member wore this hat until his death—exchanging it for another when it became worn—but he never allowed it to be seen in public. He covered it with another larger hat that showed his current Bwami rank (Biebuyck, personal communication, 1994; 1986, 210). When a member reaches Yananio, he adds four cowrie shells in an X shape and a nutshell to the skullcap to mark his new rank. Only the owner of the *bwami* and perhaps his wife see it and know if it has the extra cowrie shells. Although conspicuously covered, the greater Lega public knows it is there and understands its significance.

The shared name (*Bwami* referring to the greater Society, *bwami* denoting the skullcap) demonstrates the conceptual link between the group and the resourcefulness of the individual. In initiatory settings, the skullcap can also be called *kilembo*, or "the thing being sought" (Biebuyck, personal communication, 1994), because the initiate seeks both entry into the Society and the skullcap that signifies his initial acceptance. The skullcap in turn symbolizes the power of Bwami and the success of the new member (Biebuyck 1973, 160). Just as Bwami, the Society, must be treated respectfully, so must *bwami,* the skullcap. It cannot be allowed to touch the ground, which would result in ritual impurity, and it must be treated with honor (Biebuyck 1973, 69; 1986, 26). When the skullcap becomes extremely worn, it is burned, the ashes are distributed among the Bwami members, and the Bwami member who owned the burned skullcap receives a new *bwami* to wear. At the death of the owner, the skullcap is buried with him (Biebuyck, personal communication, 1994). If a Bwami member

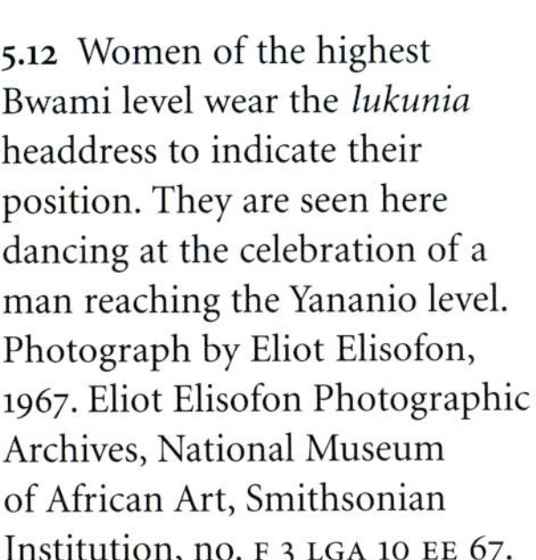

5.12 Women of the highest Bwami level wear the *lukunia* headdress to indicate their position. They are seen here dancing at the celebration of a man reaching the Yananio level. Photograph by Eliot Elisofon, 1967. Eliot Elisofon Photographic Archives, National Museum of African Art, Smithsonian Institution, no. F 3 LGA 10 EE 67.

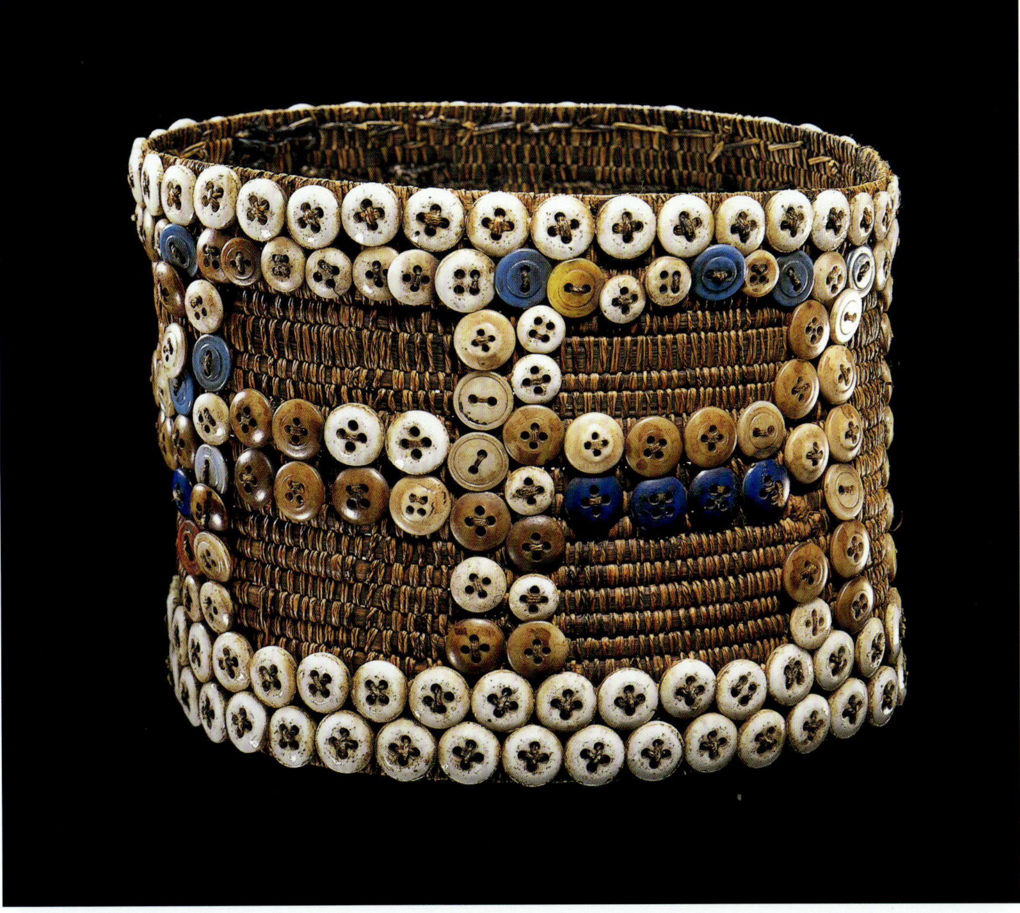

5.13 Hat (*lukunia*). Plant fiber and buttons. H: 14 cm (5½ in.). FMCH X99.15.5; Gift of Jay T. Last.

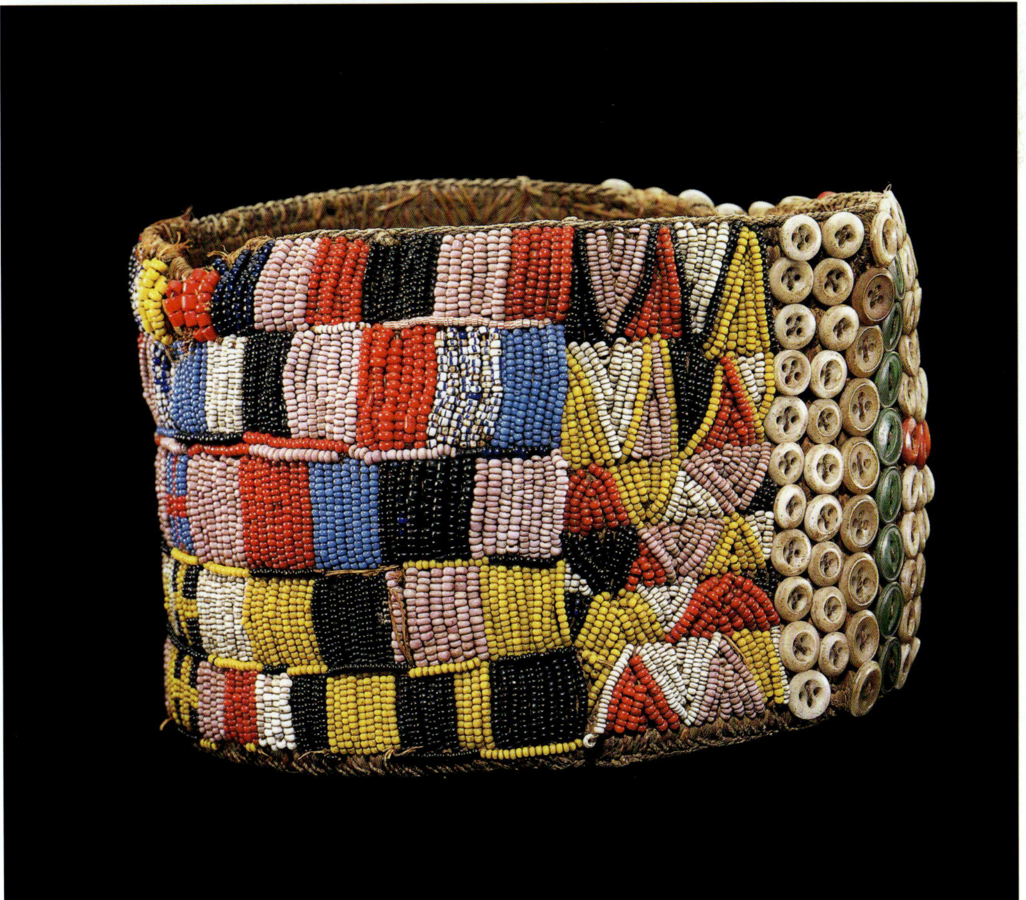

5.14 Hat (*lukunia*). Plant fiber, beads, and buttons. H: 12 cm (4¾ in.). FMCH X99.15.6; Gift of Jay T. Last.

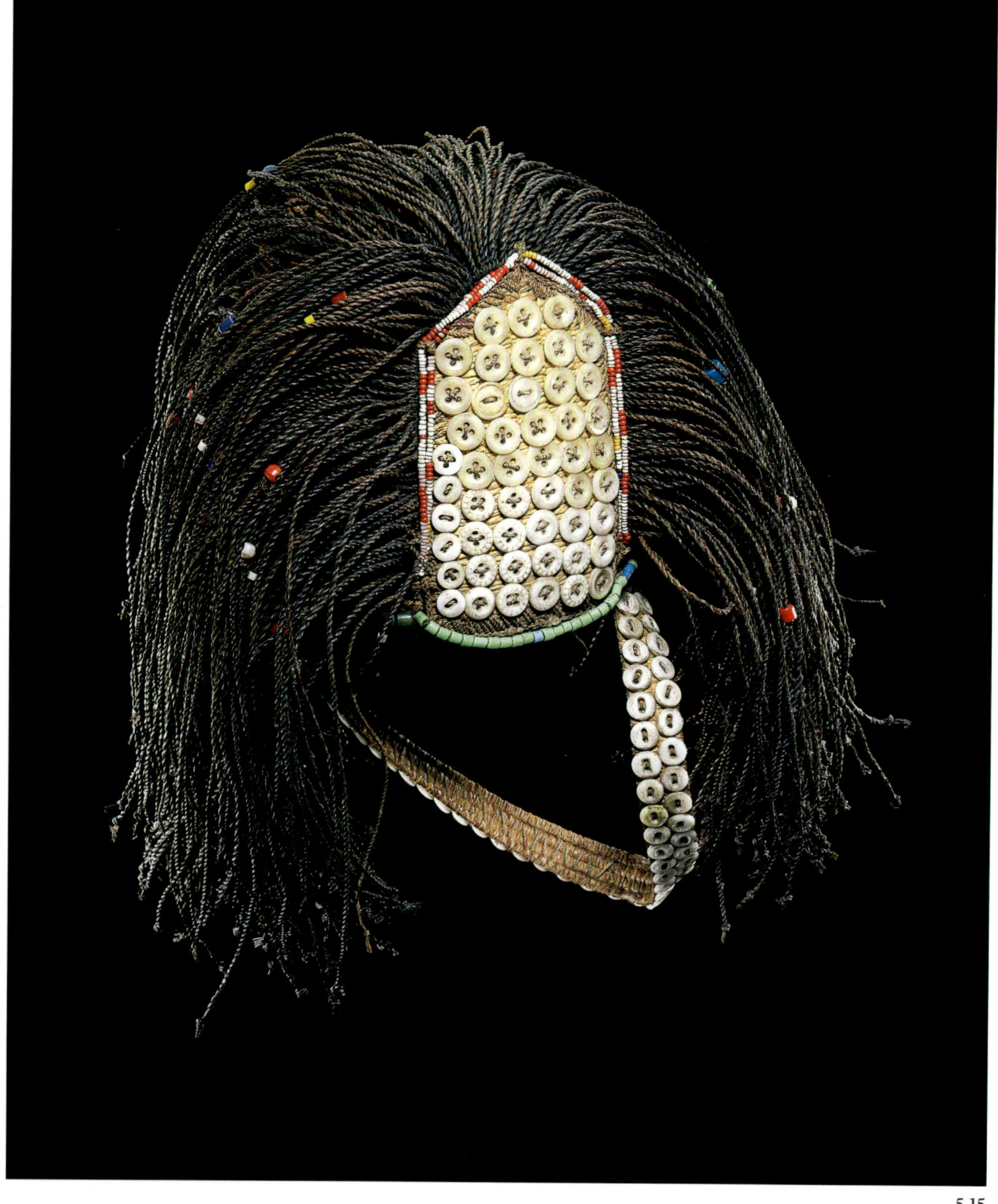

5.15

5.15 Hat (*sawamazembe*). Plant fiber, buttons, and beads. H: 30 cm (11¾ in.). FMCH X99.15.9; Gift of Jay T. Last.

In this instance the mussel shell that usually identifies the wearer's high rank has been replaced with buttons.

5.16 A man wearing the hat known as *sawamazembe*. Photograph by Eliot Elisofon, 1967. Eliot Elisofon Photographic Archives, National Museum of African Art, Smithsonian Institution, no. C 3 LGA 1.1 EE 67.

5.17 The woman on the right and the one on the left wear the headdress known as *muzombolo*. Photograph by A. or J. Vanden Bossche, courtesy of the Musée Royal de l'Afrique Centrale, Tervuren, no. E. PH. 11689.

5.18 Hat (*muzombolo*). Plant fiber, wood, feathers, buttons, cowrie shells. H: 25.5 cm (10 in.). FMCH X99.15.4; Gift of Jay T. Last.

5.16

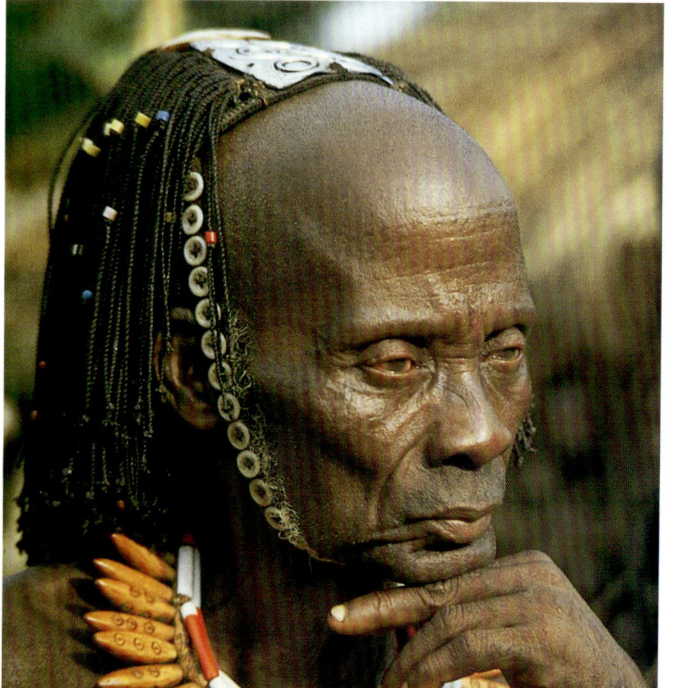

should die away from home, the *bwami* will be returned and buried in place of the body (Biebuyck 1986, 170).

Women do not have a symbol that identifies them as Bwami members in the same way that the skullcap identifies a male member. Only when a woman reaches the highest Bwami level (Bunyamwa) does she receive a headdress called *lukunia* (figs. 5.12–5.14; Biebuyck personal communication, 1994). This consists of a wide band encircling the head, which is made of fiber and covered with beads, cowries, buttons, and occasionally other materials. Like the skullcap, it is worn on a daily basis and during ceremonies, but it is not hidden under other headgear (Biebuyck 1986,63).

PUBLIC REMINDERS OF BLENDED GENDER

Insignia in the form of hats refer to a secret/public dichotomy that is an essential component of the Bwami Society. They also publicly reveal the blending of gender

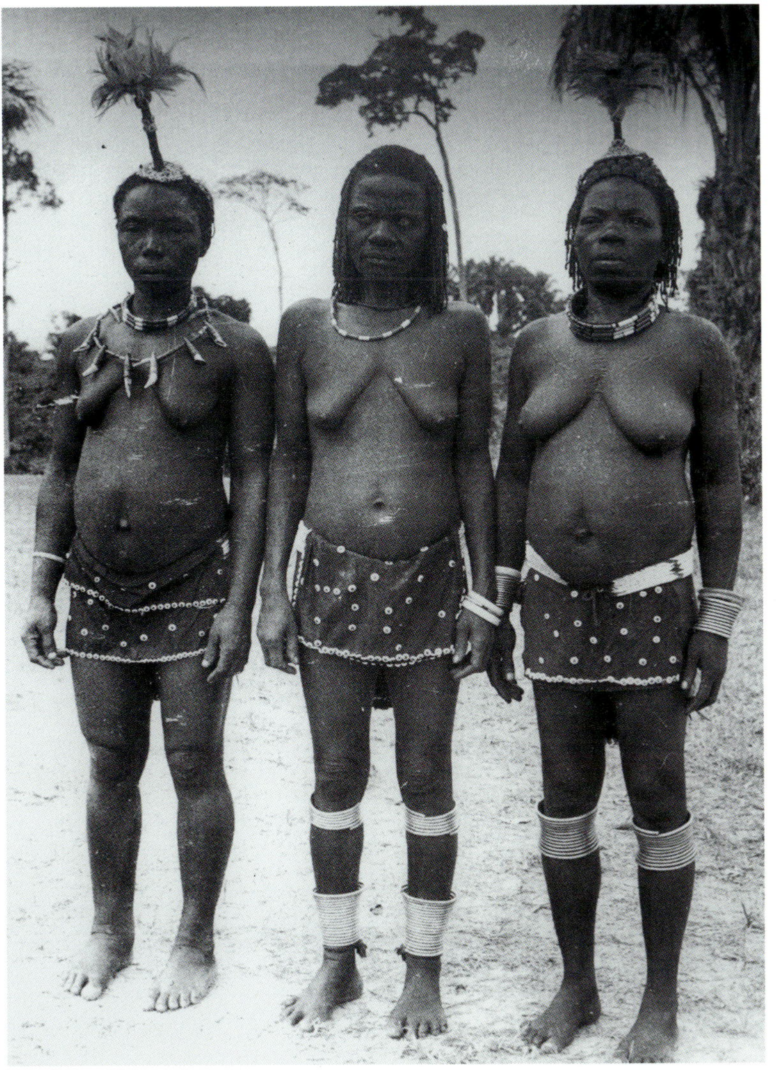

5.17

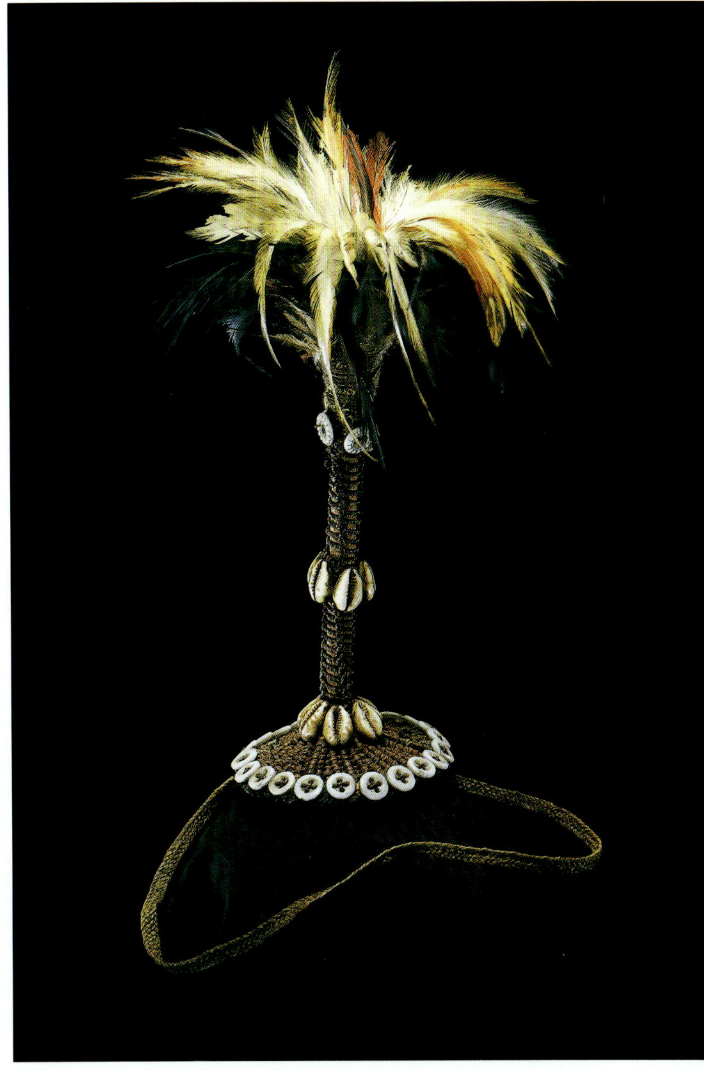

5.18

in the higher ranks as the male takes on female characteristics and the female takes on those of the male. With the respect that is automatically given to a Kindi-level man, the acknowledgement of his acquiring some female characteristics may not greatly enhance his public standing. A public statement, however, of a woman's almost-male status is especially important because the rights and responsibilities of a high-level female Bwami member are significantly different from those of noninitiated or lower-ranking women. The hat known as *sawamazembe* worn by men at the Kindi level duplicates a woman's *mazembe* hairstyle (figs. 5.15, 5.16, and see fig. 2.2; Biebuyck 1986, 84). Attached to the front are mussel shells that publicly proclaim the status of the wearer (see figs. 5.9, 5.10). The hat referred to as *muzombolo* worn by women of Bunyamwa level, the highest female grade, is composed of a long shaft of wicker surmounted by feathers and worn on top of the head (figs. 5.17, 5.18). The hat has a phallic shape (Biebuyck and Van den Abbeele 1984, 82) that when paired with the *sawamazembe* stresses the interdependency of the Kindi initiate and his Bunyamwa-level wife.

In one Kindi rite, women wear their husbands' *mukuba*, another type of hat, to emphasize their own high status (Biebuyck 1984, 84). This hat is made of canvas, covered with shells, cowries, and more recently buttons, and surmounted by an elephant tail (figs. 5.19–5.21; Biebuyck 1973, fig. 10). The attached elephant tail refers to the association between Bwami, especially the highest grade of Lutumbo lwa Kindi, and the quiet, yet destructive, strength of the elephant. Kindi members wear this hat daily (Biebuyck and Van den Abbeele 1984, 84). While the women wear their husbands' *mukuba* hats in performance, they hold their own hats, moving them back and forth in their hands. This rite signifies the danger of fighting and the peacekeeping role of Bwami (Biebuyck 1986, 156).

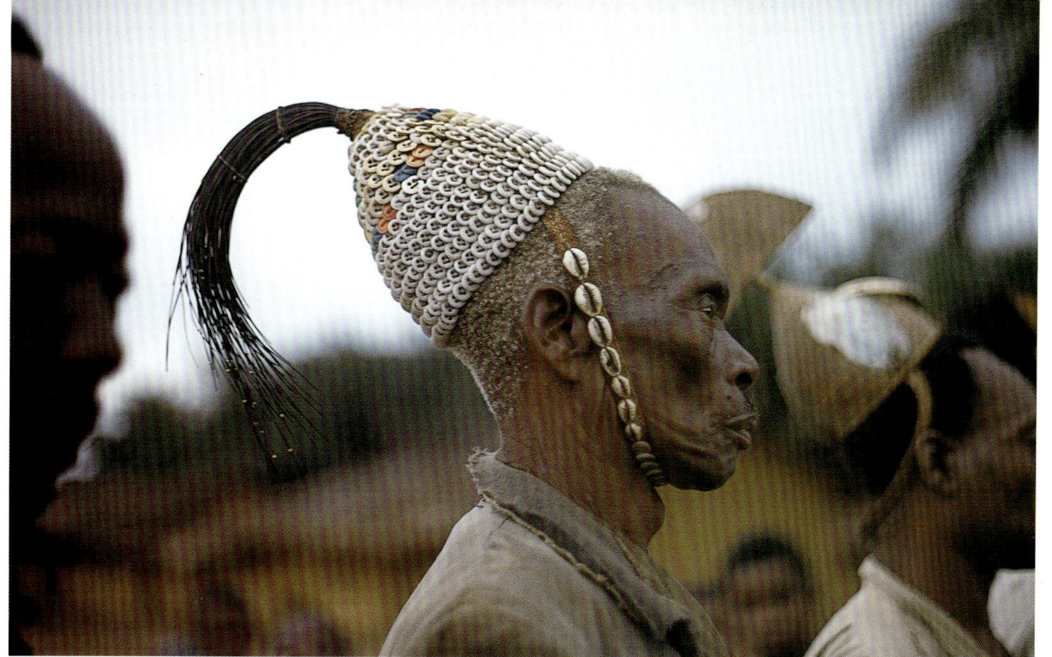

5.19 Man wearing a *mukuba* hat. Courtesy of Charles Henault.

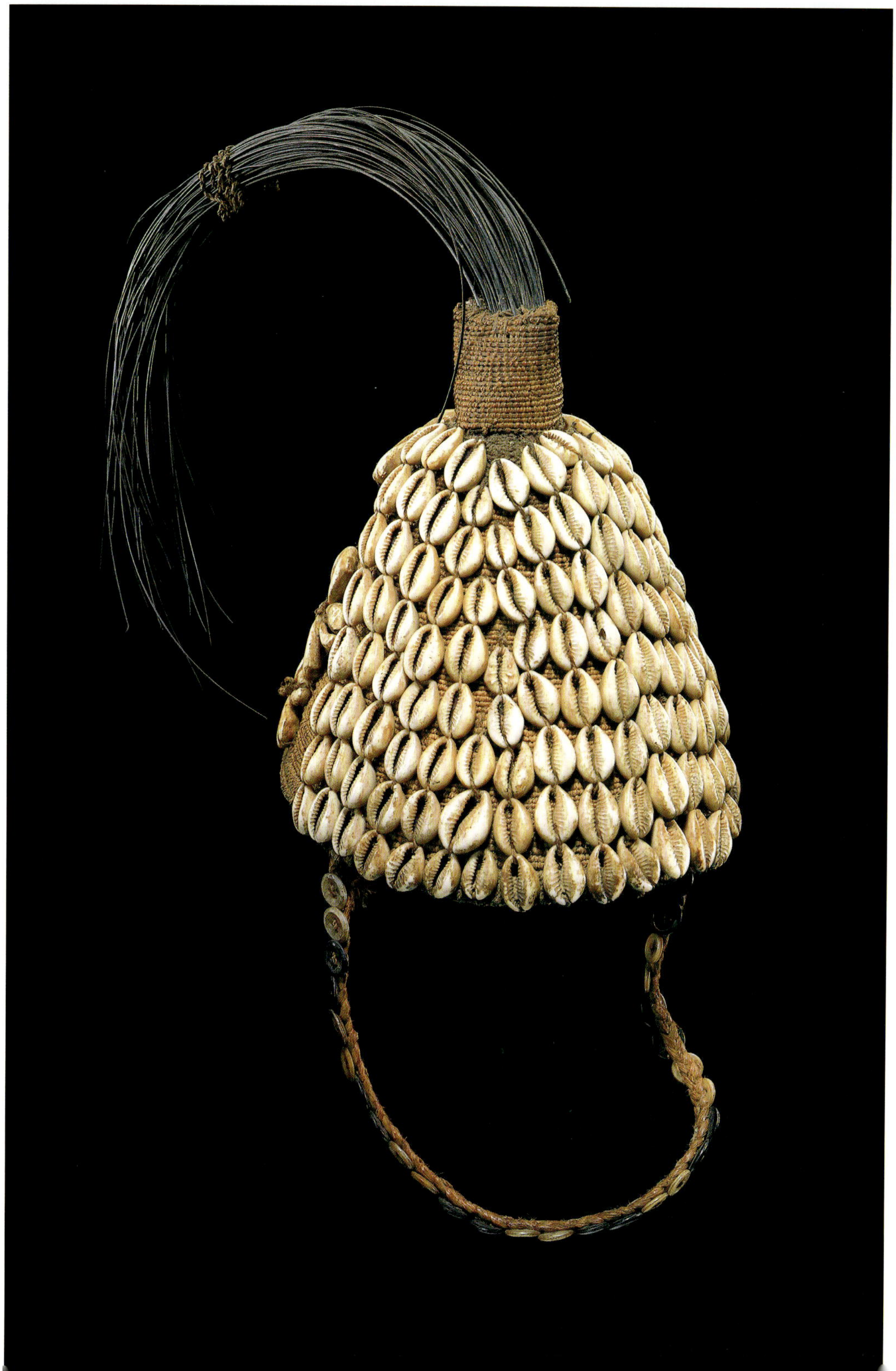

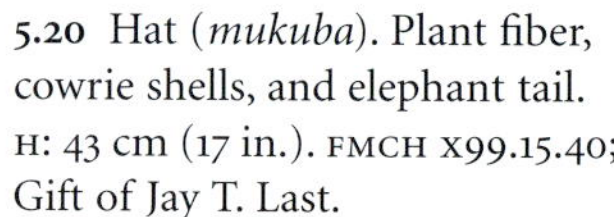

5.20 Hat (*mukuba*). Plant fiber, cowrie shells, and elephant tail. H: 43 cm (17 in.). FMCH X99.15.40; Gift of Jay T. Last.

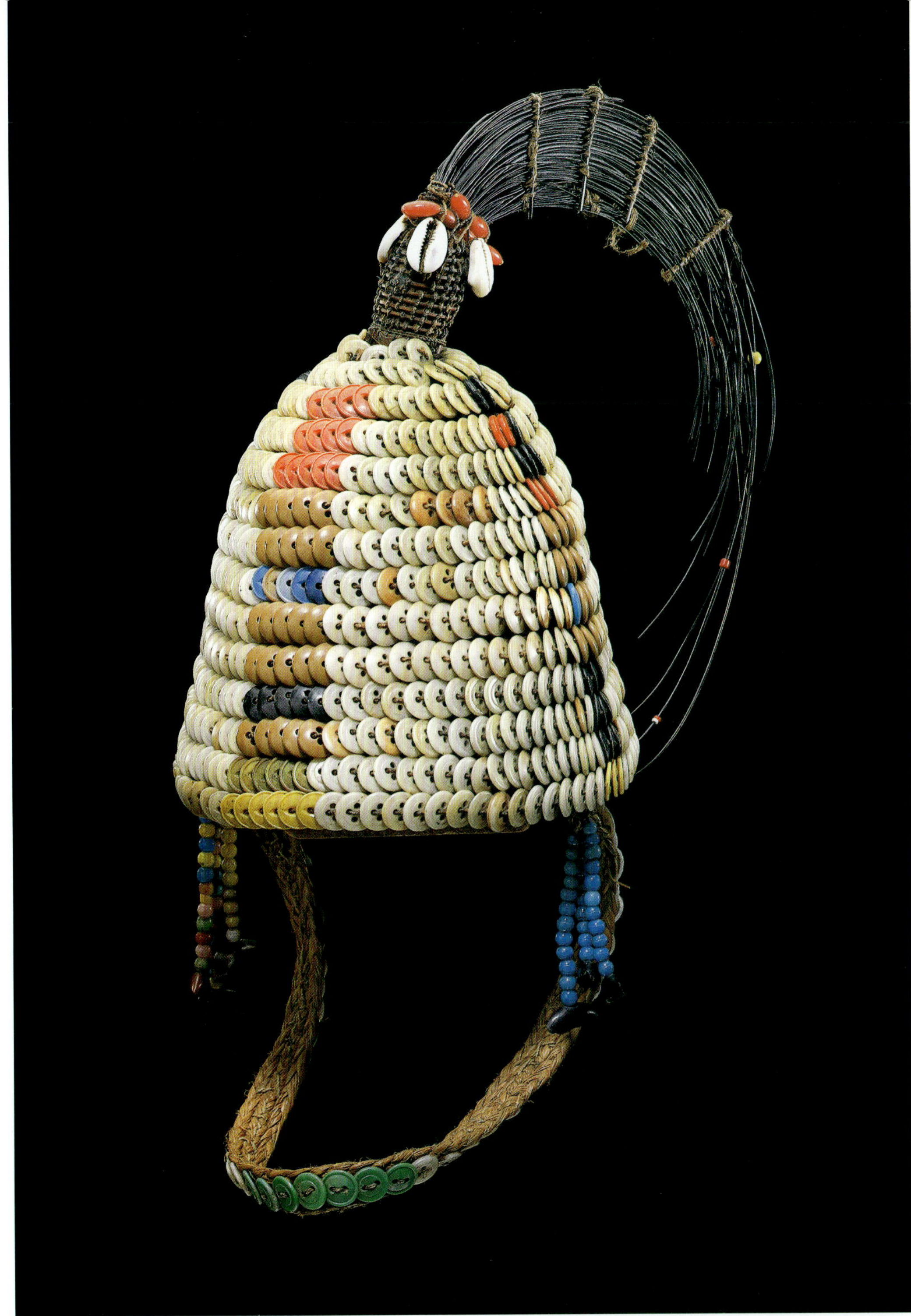

5.21 Hat (*mukuba*). Plant fiber, buttons, elephant tail, beads, cowrie shells, and seedpods. H: 44 cm (17⅜ in.). FMCH X99.15.35; Gift of Jay T. Last.

CARVED IVORY PENDANTS

Small ivory pegs, carved in phallic shapes or so that they appear topped with a human head, are attached with a fiber threaded through a hole in the end to anything dedicated to the sole use of Bwami. Any material resource—animal or foodstuff—set aside as part of the goods necessary for an initiation, for example, is identified publicly with an attached pendant (figs. 5.22, 5.23; Biebuyck 1973, 163; 1986, 63).

High-level female Bwami members wear a ring of these pendants tucked into their belt and hidden from sight. Like secret insignia, the pendants identify these women as Bwami members who should be respected. The phallic-shaped pendants, called *katimbitimbi*, or "what shivers passionately" (Biebuyck 1986, 63), again reflect the blending of gender in the higher ranks of Bwami. The pendant also identifies women who, as Bwami wives of high-level Society members, are in unbreakable marriages. The ancient penalty for seducing one of these women was death by poisoning (Biebuyck 1986, 63). Unless the woman were to reveal the pendant to the potential seducer as a warning, however, he would not encounter it until she began to undress.

As is true of most insignia, ivory pendants are also initiation objects. The phallic pendant becomes a metaphorical symbol of male sexuality. The saying "Katimbitimbi, the little penis that has not seen [undergone] circumcision," when used in conjunction with a pendant representing an uncircumcised penis, implies that women do not find uncircumcised men to be attractive sexual partners (Biebuyck 1973, 155).

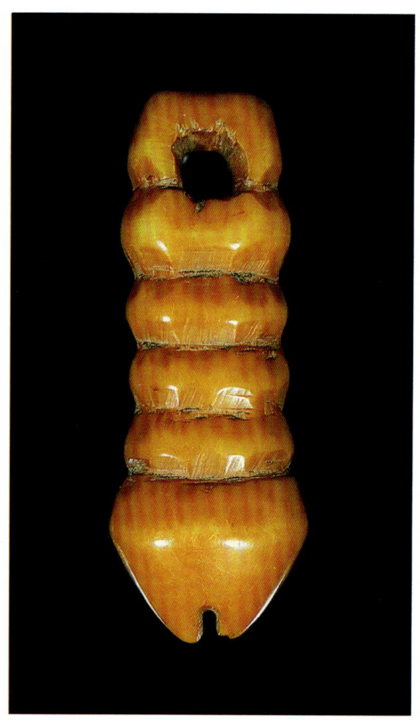

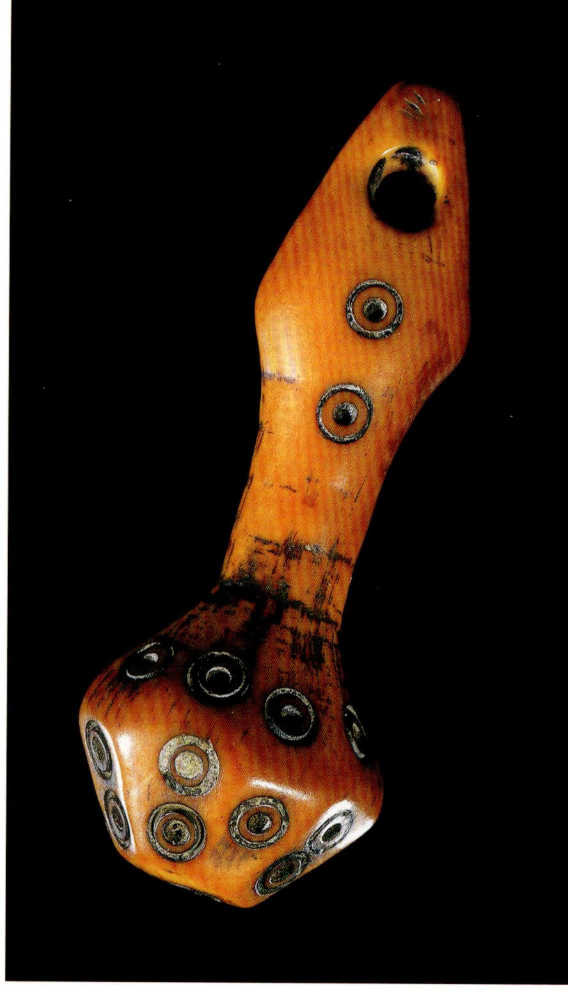

5.22 Woman's pendant. Ivory. H: 4.2 cm (1⅝ in.).

5.23 Woman's pendant. Ivory. H: 6.5 cm (2½ in.).

Men or women manipulate the phallic pendant in initiation performances to represent a man seeking sexual contact. A shell with a hole in it or a small carved canoe might represent the receptive woman (Biebuyck 1986, 192). In one performance that is designed to remind the gathered community of the virtue of female Bwami members, a male member of the Society unsuccessfully maneuvers the pendant with the goal of touching a woman's hat, which represents the high-level female, and the saying "The wife of a Big-One may be alone in the glen; she does not call you" is recited (Biebuyck 1986, 192).

INSIGNIA USED IN INITIATIONS

Bwami teachers use insignia during initiations as part of the layered metaphors they construct. As initiation objects, the insignia become *masengo*, or "heavy objects," and acquire a meaning understood by Bwami members of the appropriate level (Biebuyck 1976, 338). The meaning of the insignia is understood through the symbolism of its materials, its form, the activities or theater involving it, and the sayings related to it (Biebuyck 1973, 146).

The small feather hat (*idumbi*), for example, is used in all levels of male and female initiations (fig. 5.24; Biebuyck, personal communication, 1994). Feather hats rich with use and meaning are insignia that appear primarily in Bwami performances but are not always worn (fig. 5.25; Biebuyck 1994, personal correspondence). "These are not the feather hats of war but the feather hats of dance" is a saying attached to the hats (Biebuyck and Van den Abbeele 1984, 82), stressing one of the original and most basic functions of Bwami, the keeping of peace (Biebuyck 1973, 67). During the initiation into Kongabulumbu, a young woman related to the initiate appears wearing a feather hat, standing on a stool, and surrounded by shoulder bags filled with initiation objects. Here the purpose of the hat is to give the initiate and the woman a hint of future greatness (Biebuyck personal communication, 1994; 1977b, 14–15). In an initiation into Bombwa observed by Biebuyck, a character representing Kingungungu, a poor beggar, wore a feather hat (1986, 149). In the woman's grade Bulonda, a woman wearing a feather hat represents Kiluku, a female character who seems to have the material goods for initiation but does not have the moral requirements (Biebuyck 1977b, 15). During one Kindi rite, two initiates appear with feather hats in their mouths (Biebuyck 1986, 156–57).

Men's hats and women's headdresses are also used in combination with and display of other initiation objects. During one episode in Kindi initiation, ivory and wood

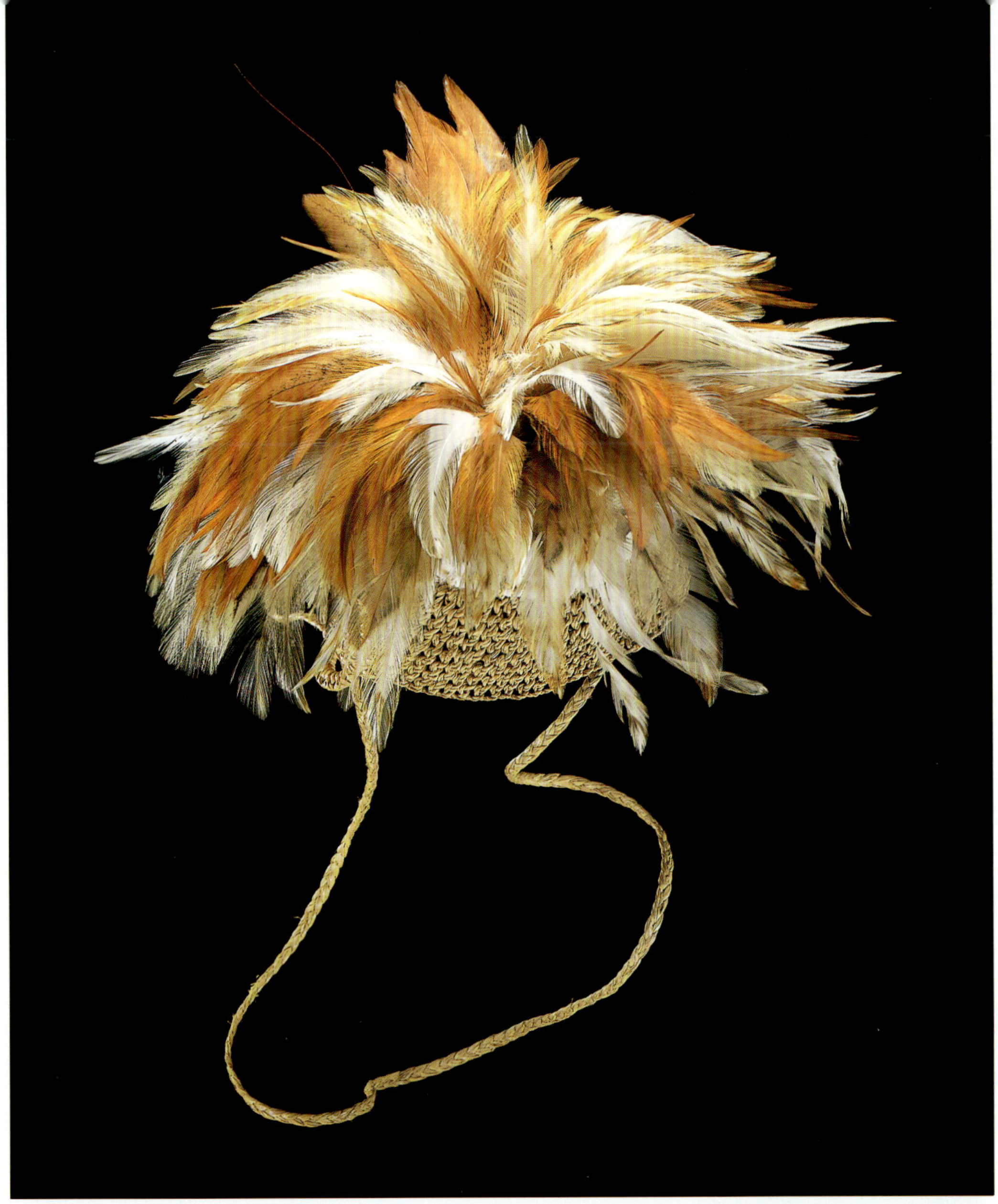

5.24 Hat (*idumbi*). Fiber and feathers. H: 30 cm (11¾ in.). FMCH 378.371; Museum Purchase.

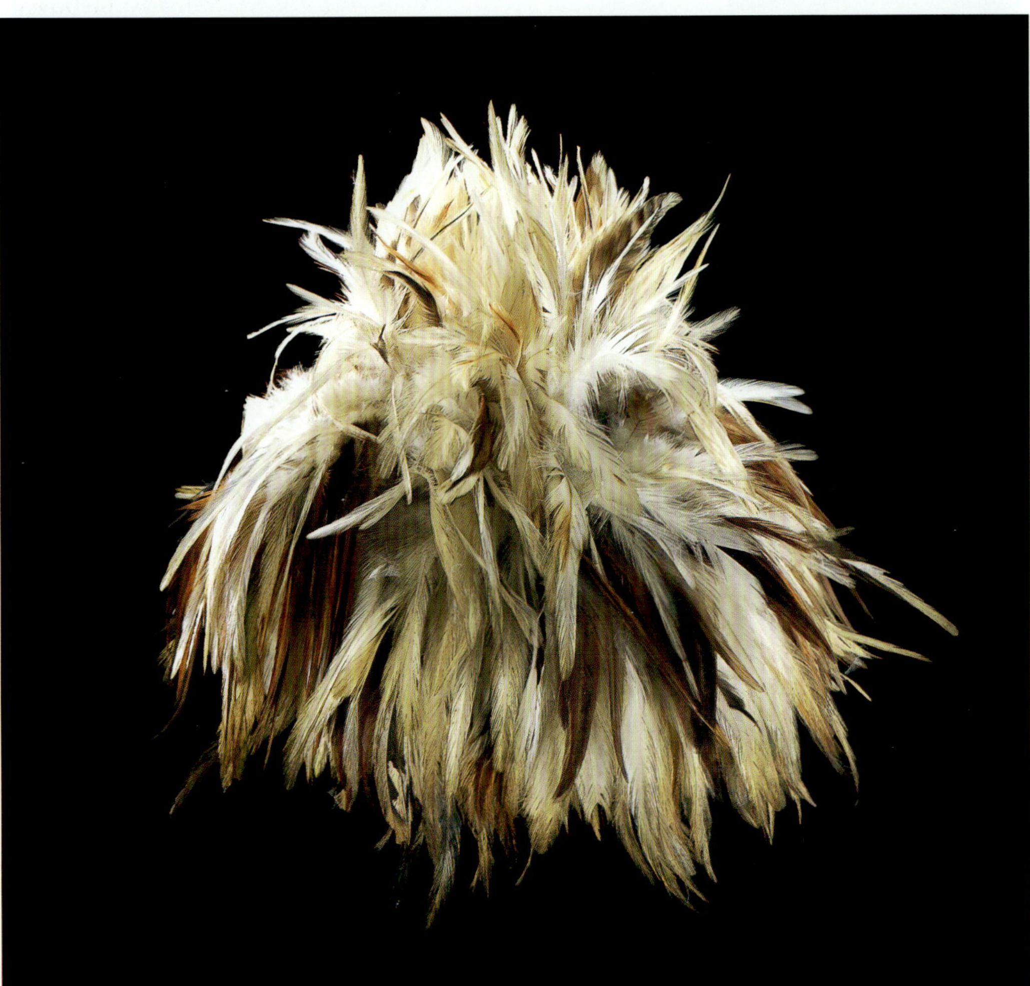

5.25 Hat (*isala*). Fiber and feathers. H: 20 cm (7⅞ in.). FMCH 78.372; Museum Purchase.

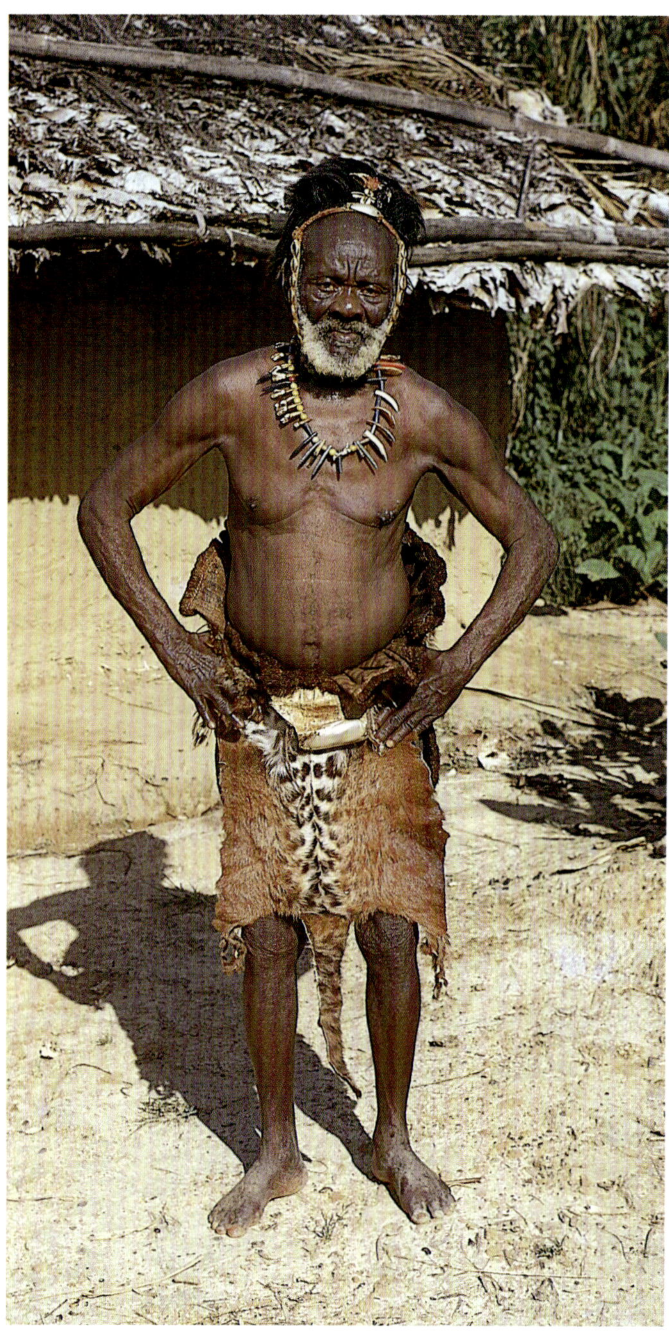

5.26 Mr. Wambale wears hyrax teeth on his goatskin cap to indicate that he is a Bwami member of the Yananio level. Photograph courtesy of Charles Henault.

figures are rested against hats that symbolize their owners (Biebuyck 1986, 58). Women's headdresses are used to support small ivory figures during a rite of female Kanyamwa-level initiation. This display of women's insignia reminds the initiate of the status she will attain if she is successful (Biebuyck 1973, 57, 203). Finally, in some initiations, teachers use anthropomorphic figures that represent Bwami members wearing hats and occasionally employ masks representing noninitiates who have bare heads (Biebuyck 1986, 39).

INSIGNIA, RANK, AND MEANING

Insignia revealing status and serving as initiation objects draw much of their meaning from symbolically potent animals that are also specific to rank. The use of these objects in initiations reinforces their meaning for members of Bwami. The public placement of the symbolic elements reminds these same members of specific aspects of the Bwami moral code and their responsibility to uphold it.

Animals are especially important in Bwami symbolism and insignia. Initiates refer to themselves publicly as specific animals. Members of Yananio, for example, call themselves Bamibinga, or "People of the hyrax," because of the hyrax teeth they wear on their hats (fig. 5.26 and see fig. 5.9; Biebuyck 1986, 101). Parts of initiation ceremonies themselves can be named after an animal that has symbolic significance within the performances (Biebuyck 1979, 77). Finally, many animals are sacred and must be treated according to strict guidelines and distributed carefully according to Bwami status (Biebuyck 1953b, 907).

The bill of the hornbill, which is occasionally attached to hats, identifies membership in Bwami (figs. 5.27, 5.28). While not symbolic of specific rank, the hornbill symbolizes the man who has high ambitions but is unaware of the cost of attaining them. It also stands for a woman with the habit of wandering from home so that her husband must go and fetch her (Biebuyck 1973b, 189). This latter meaning derives from the hornbill's habit of trapping the female and her chicks in a nest with a wall of mud (Biebuyck 1986, 93).

The pangolin is associated with the Ngandu, Yananio, and lower level of Kindi (fig. 5.29; Biebuyck 1953b, 910). The scales of the small pangolin (*kabanga*) attached to hats symbolize piety and respect and call to mind Isamukulu, the "Great Old One" (Biebuyck 1973, 190; personal communication, 1994). Pangolins are rich in meaning, symbolizing power, family, and knowledge (Biebuyck 1953b, 909–10).

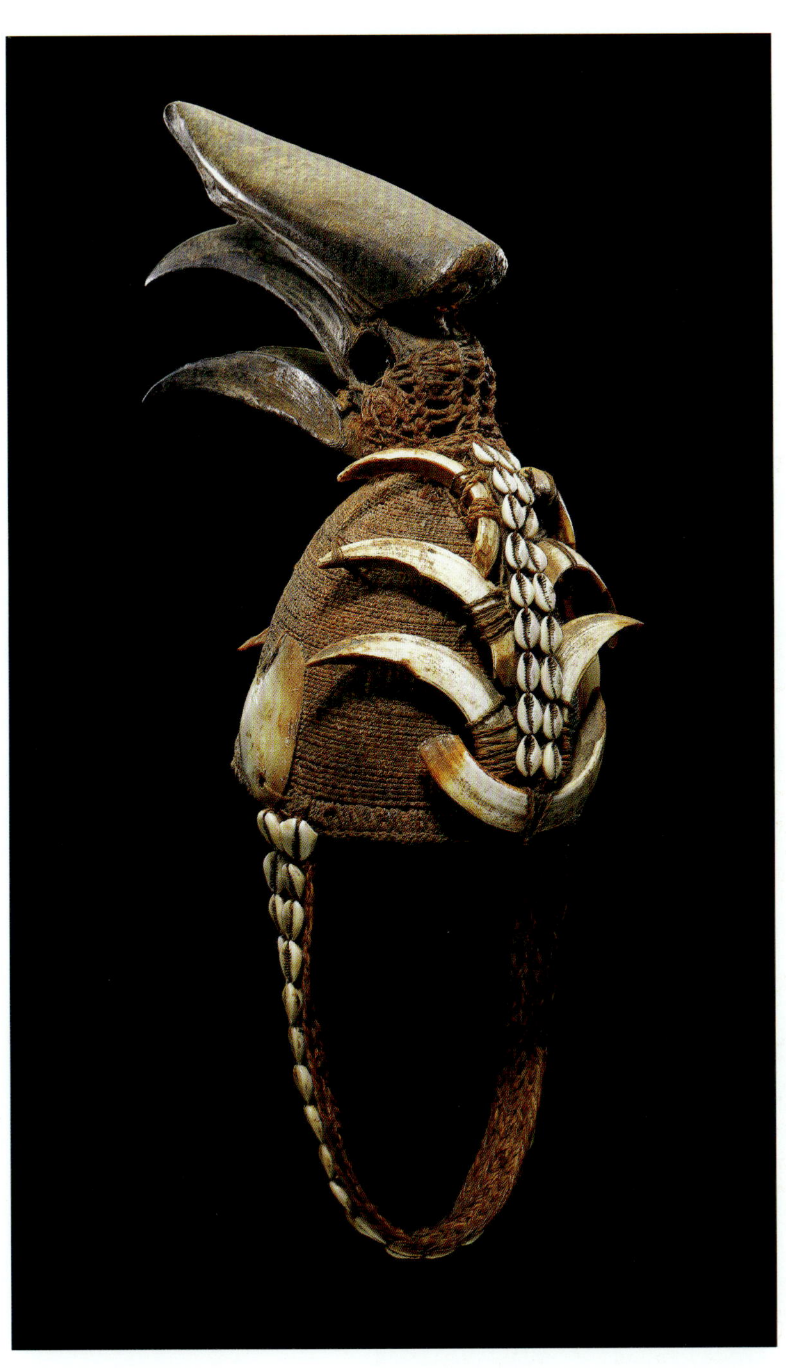

5.27 Hat. Plant fiber, hornbill, shells, tusks, and cowrie shells. H: 55 cm (21¾ in.). FMCH X99.15.8; Gift of Jay T. Last.

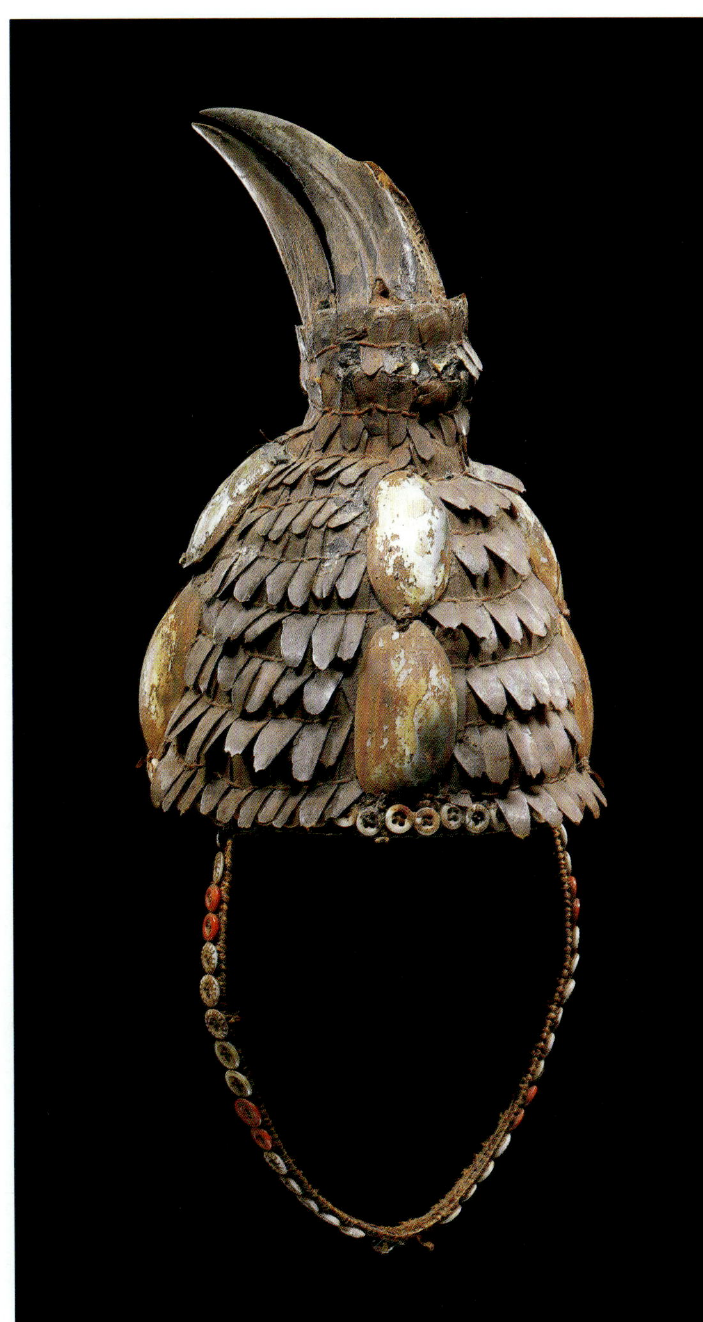

5.28 Hat. Plant fiber, pangolin scales, hornbill, shells, and buttons. H: 45 cm (17¾ in.). FMCH X99.15.11; Gift of Jay T. Last.

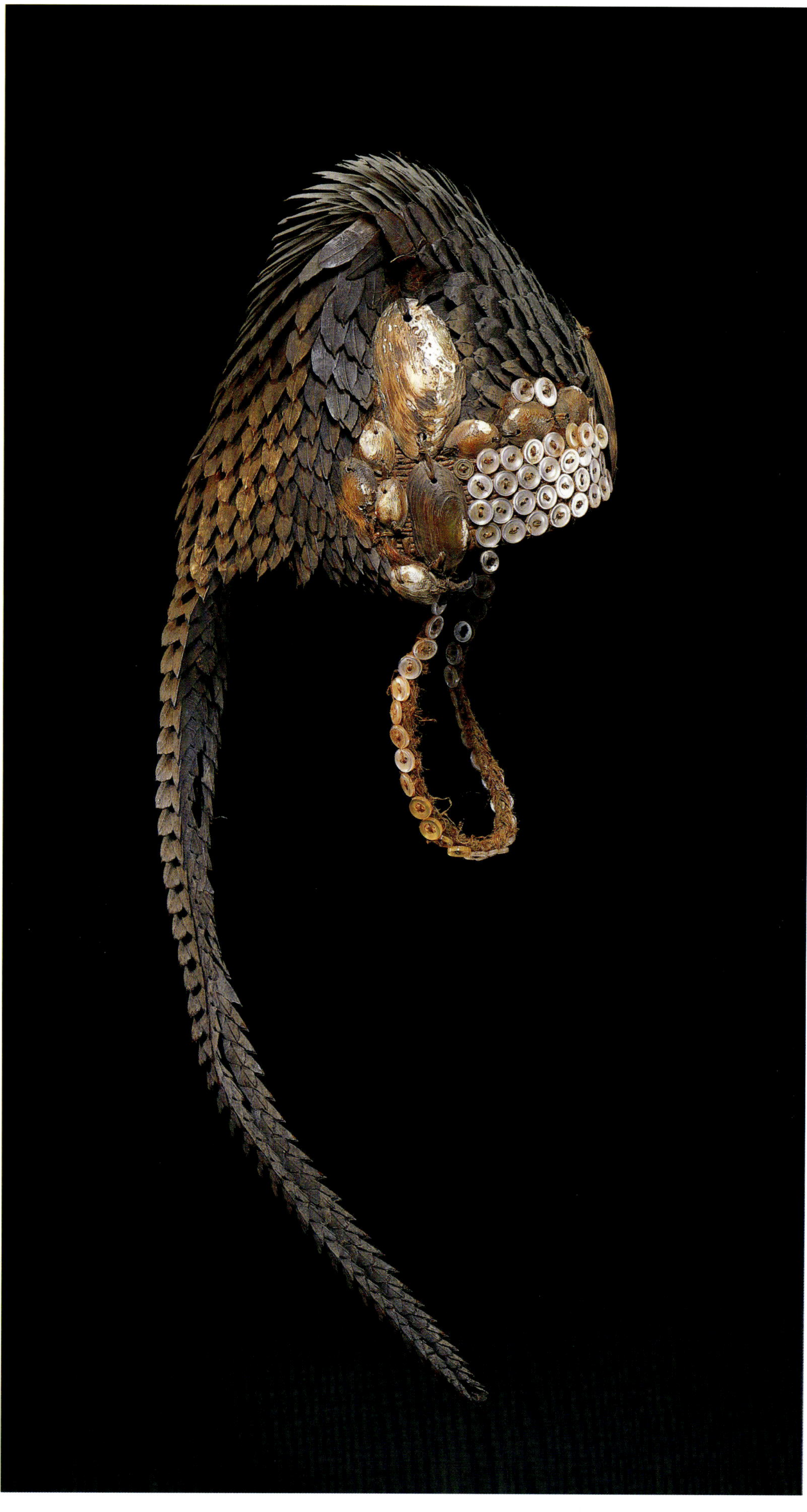

5.29 Hat. Pangolin scales, plant fiber, buttons, and shells. H: 56.5 cm (22¼ in.). FMCH X9.15.18; Gift of Jay T. Last.

5.30 Men and women dance to celebrate a man reaching the fourth level of Bwami. Photograph by Eliot Elisofon, 1967. Eliot Elisofon Photographic Archives, National Museum of African Art, Smithsonian Institution, no. K 3 LGA 14.2 EE 67.

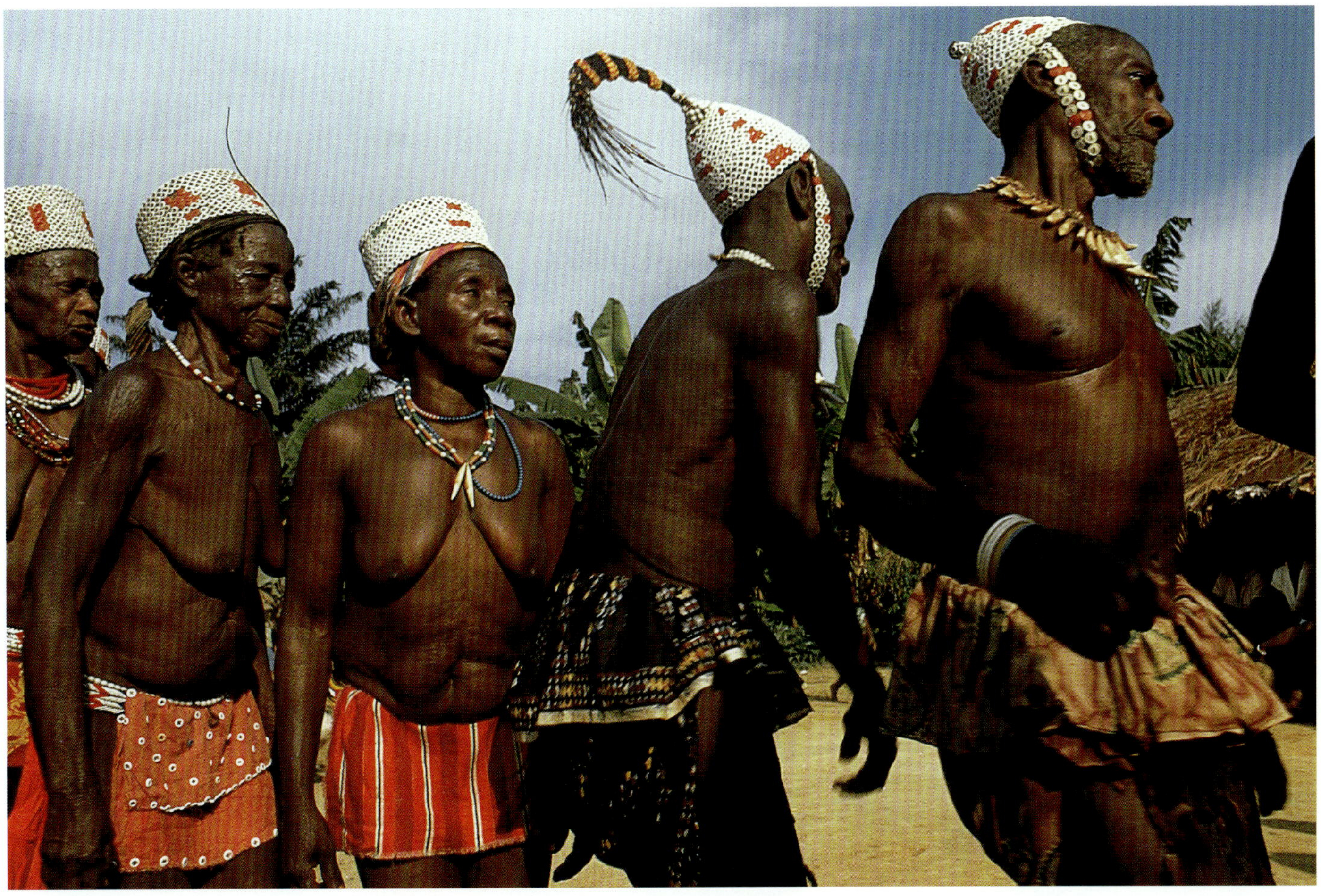

The Bwami Society has strict guidelines about how the pangolin, a sacred animal, is to be treated. Anyone who does not follow these guidelines is sanctioned and often forced to leave the clan and village. Pangolins are never hunted, but if a hunter finds a trapped pangolin or one already dead in the forest, he is obligated to take the pangolin to a Bwami member who has the "right of the pangolin knife."

Elephants simultaneously represent all of Bwami and its highest level, Kindi. Elephant products, however, are reserved for members of Kindi. Hats worn by Kindi members can be made of elephant ears and adorned with elephant tails (fig. 5.30, see also figs. 5.20, 5.21; Cameron 1992). Members of Kindi refer to themselves as "People of the elephant tail" (Biebuyck 1986, 101). Sayings exist, furthermore, that compare all Bwami members to elephants: "Bwami, the stampeding of elephants; The place where it has passed cannot be forgotten" (Biebuyck 1973, 127).

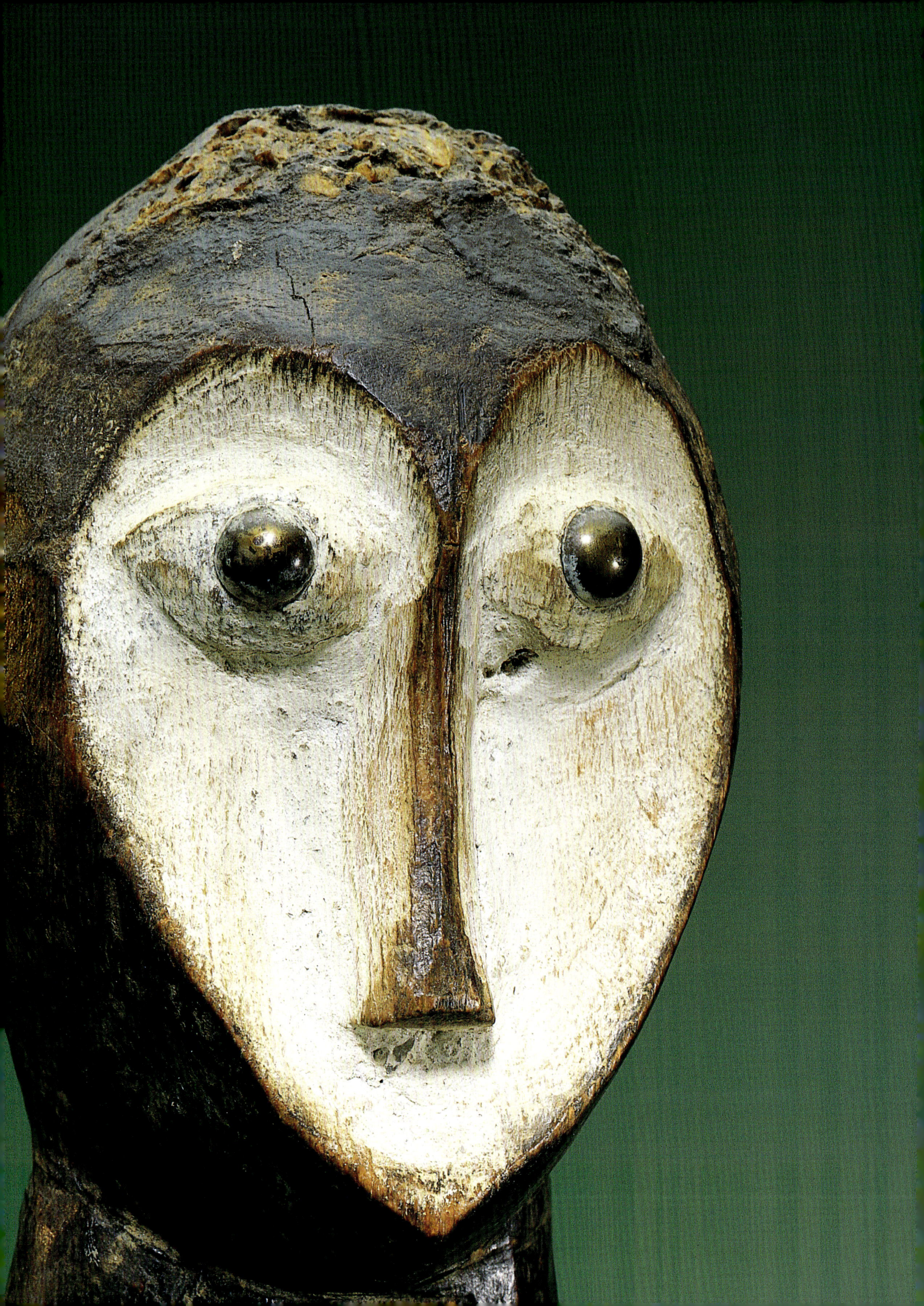

PART 2

Visual Vocabulary

6 Found, Assembled, and Utilitarian Objects

FOUND AND ASSEMBLED OBJECTS

Use of ordinary found objects to form layered metaphors in conjunction with Lega sayings occurs in Bwami as well as in everyday life. As previously described, older men hang many types of objects—found, assembled, and roughly carved—from the "cord of wisdom" and quiz passersby about their multiple meanings. Familiar objects such as a snail shell or a piece of wood reveal truths to the broader community (figs. 6.1–6.10). On becoming Bwami members, however, the Lega discover new levels of meaning attached to objects they may have previously thought they completely understood.

A piece of dead wood combined with the saying "The chimney stack of an abandoned village often receives the visit of elephants" teaches young girls and boys to seek the counsel of senior citizens (Defour n.d., 26). As these

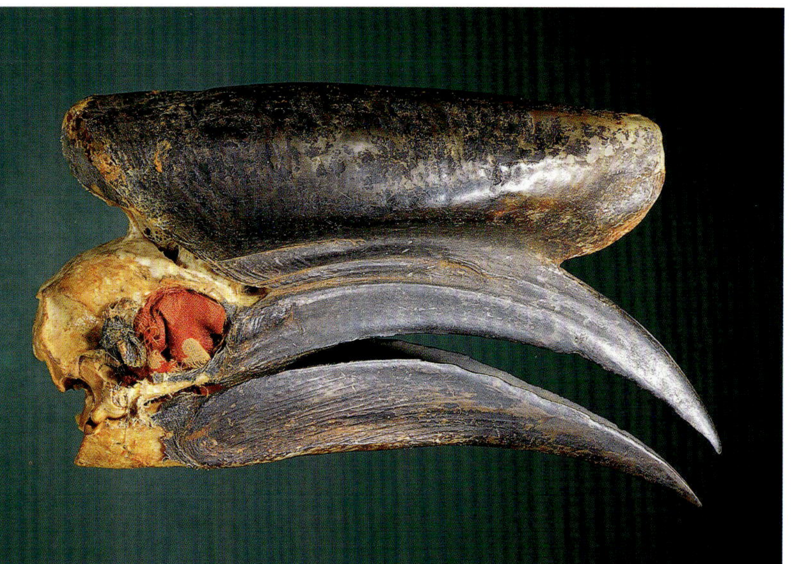

6.1

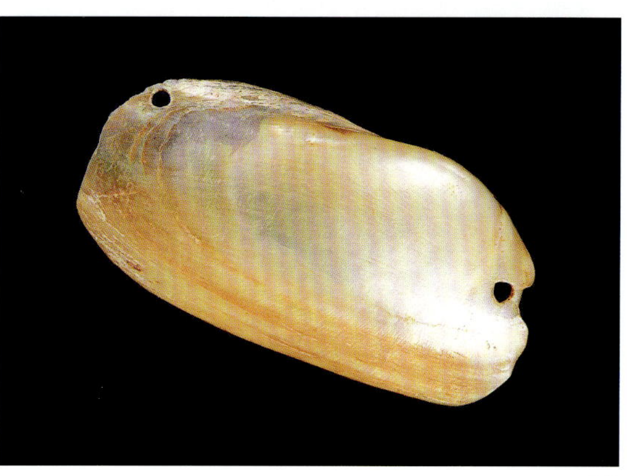

6.3

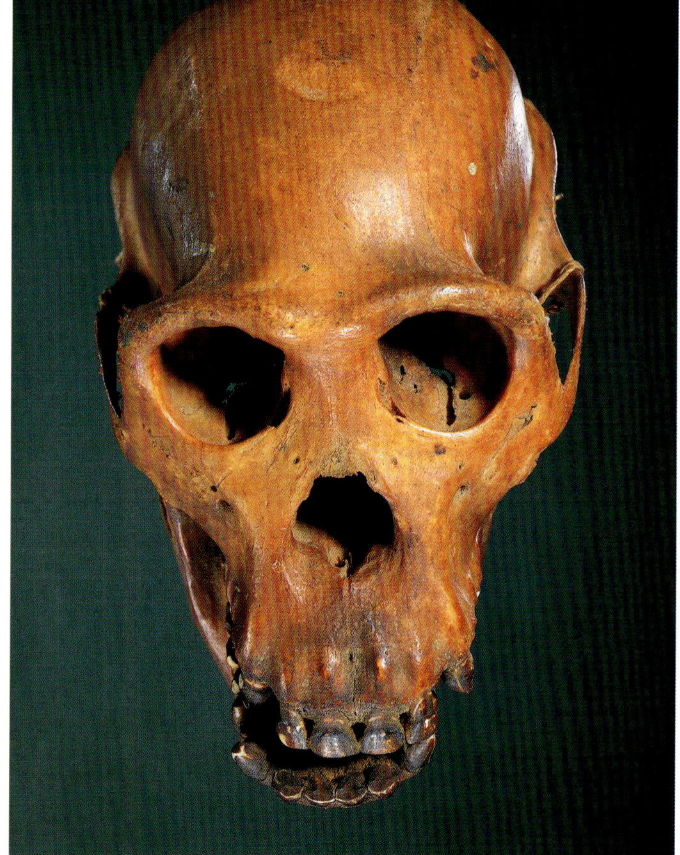

6.2

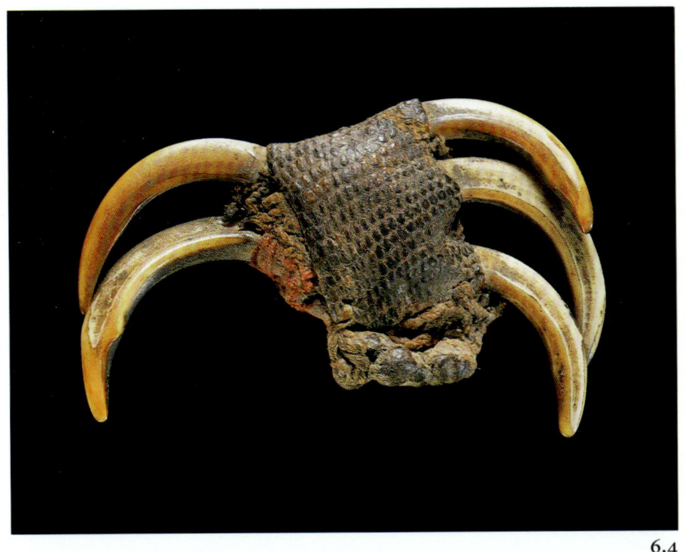

6.4

youths enter and progress through the levels of Bwami, they discover new meanings associated with this ordinary object. Thus the saying "A walking stick of the crippled is what he used to defend himself," in conjunction with the visual layer constituted by a simple stick, reminds members that while the symbol of Bwami is a walking stick rather than a spear, one must protect oneself with whatever means are available. More simply put: a person must use the available resources to achieve his or her goals (Biebuyck 1973, 155). As noted earlier, while found objects and assemblages of found materials appear throughout every level of Bwami, they dominate initiations into the lower levels. Masks and figures are reserved predominantly for the top two ranks (Biebuyck 1973, pl. 110; 1986, 28).

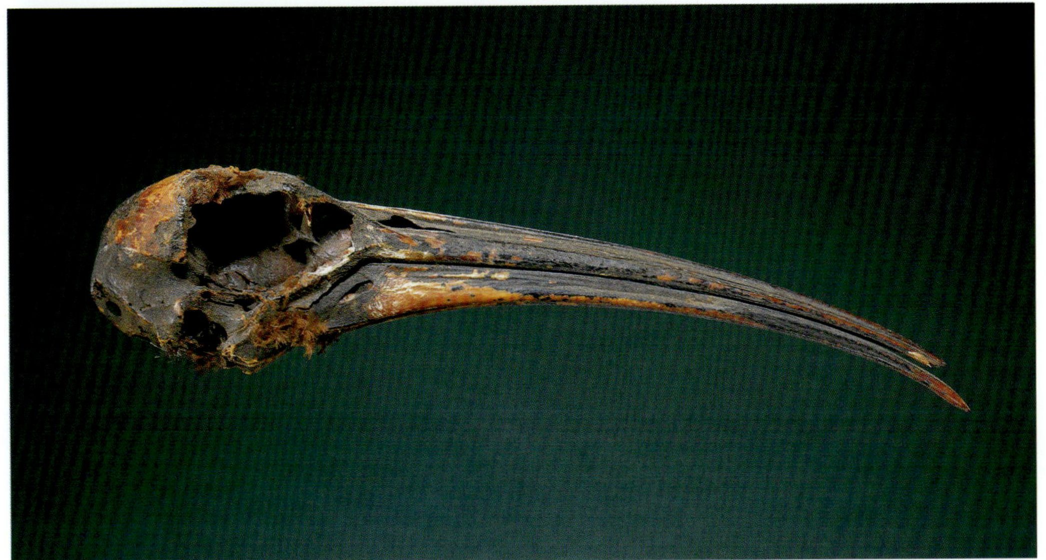

6.5

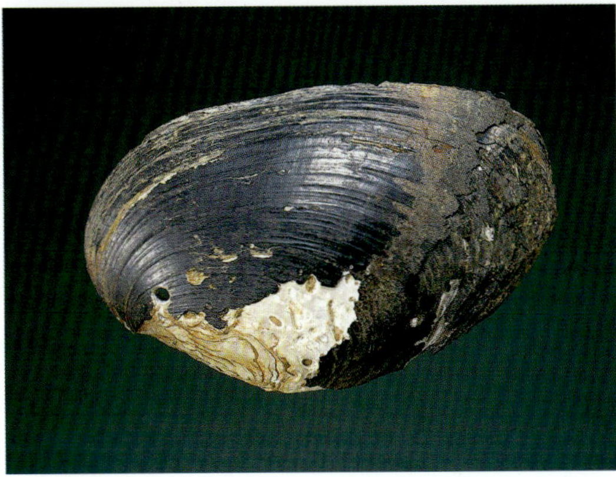

6.6

6.7

6.1 Hornbill skull. H: 20.32 cm (8 in.). FMCH 378.359; Museum Purchase.

6.2 Chimpanzee skull. H: 20.32 cm (8 in.). FMCH 378.300; Museum Purchase.

6.3 Shell. L: 9.9 cm (3⅞ in.). FMCH 378.765; Museum Purchase.

6.4 Assembled initiation object. Animal teeth, animal skin, textile, and plant fiber. L: 7.62 cm (3 in.). FMCH 378.628; Museum Purchase.

6.5 Ibis beak. H: 3.5 cm (1⅜ in.). FMCH 378.619; Museum Purchase.

6.6 Mussel shell. L: 10.6 cm (4 in.). FMCH 378.624; Museum Purchase.

6.7 Snail shells attached with clay. H: 2.54 cm (1 in.). FMCH 378.631; Museum Purchase.

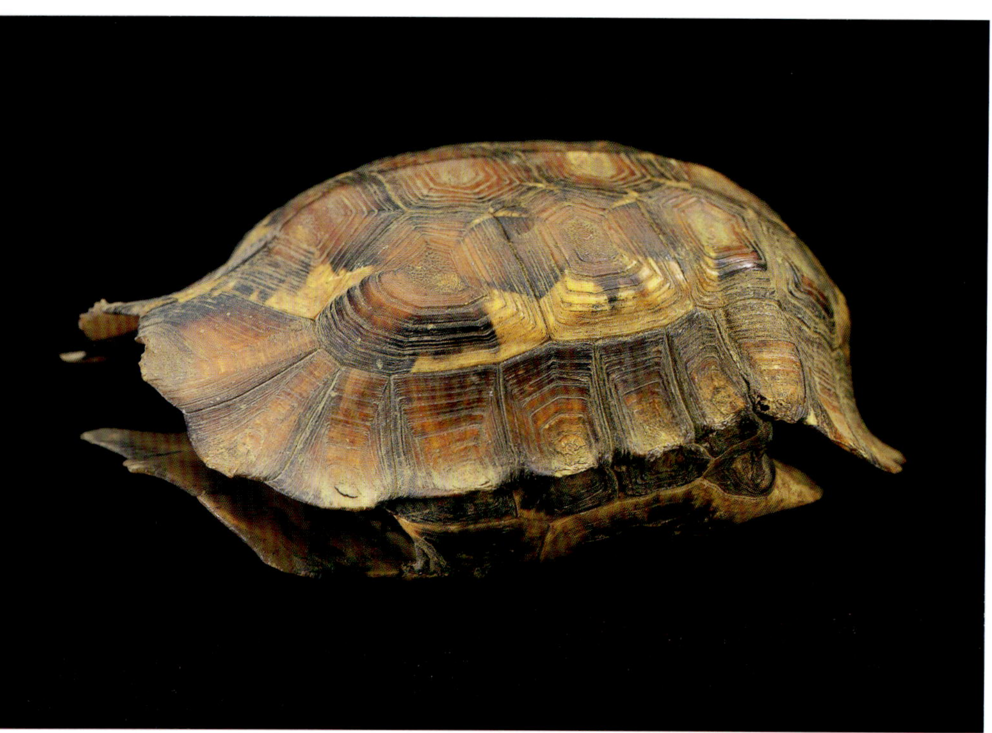

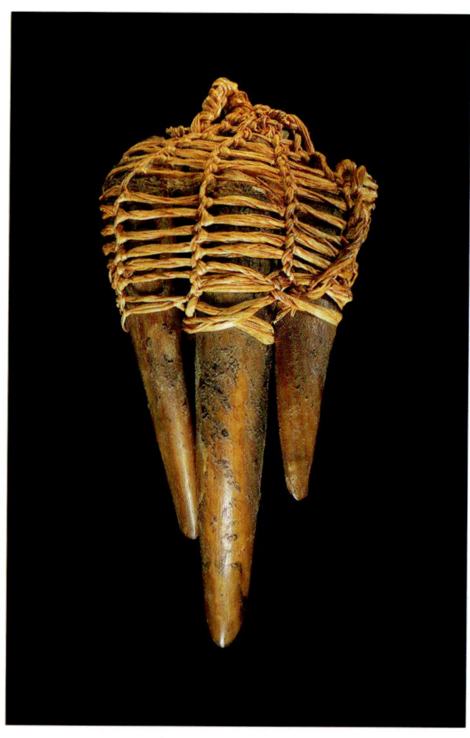

6.8 Tortoise shell. H: 15.24 cm (6 in.). FMCH 378.645; Museum Purchase.

6.9 Pangolin claw in fiber network. Pangolin claw and fiber. L: 10.2 cm (4 in.). FMCH 378.625; Museum Purchase.

6.10 Twisted vine (*muzigi*). L: 38.1 cm (15 in.). FMCH 378.609; Museum Purchase.

A vine, carefully shaped and allowed to dry so that it vaguely resembles a human form, represents a man in lower-level initiations and can be used to replace a wooden figure in higher-level events. Many sayings used in conjunction with this figure refer directly to a member of Bwami. Occasionally it may also be used to refer to a woman as in "Muzigi, who does not close itself [hold on], will fall down with crown and root." This combination of object and saying describes a woman who will not take the advice of her husband (Biebuyck 1973, 153–54).

TOOLS AND UTENSILS

Given their heavily forested environment, metal tools such as axes, billhooks, knives, and spears are essential to the survival and proliferation of the Lega. As in most Bantu cultures, metal tools serve as a medium of exchange among neighbors and as a portion of dowry payments (Biebuyck 1986, 181–83). The tools also provide an important visual vocabulary for use in Bwami metaphors, although they cannot be employed during initiations. Because Bwami consistently teaches pacifism, anything that can also serve as a weapon is banned from ceremonies and performances (Biebuyck 1983, 56). Miniature and nonfunctional tools fashioned from ivory, wood, and bone—including knives, spoons, hammers, and billhooks—take their place as Bwami initiation objects (Biebuyck 1986, 22).

Except for ivory spoons, which are used at all levels of Bwami, objects made of ivory are reserved for the top ranks. While all Bwami members conceive of themselves as elephants (*nzogu*), Kindi members call themselves "owners of ivory" (*nenemulamba*) and claim the use of ivory, elephant bone, and other elephant parts in sculpture and dress as their prerogative (Biebuyck 1986, 40). In Bwami rites, the meanings assigned to elephants are dramatically enacted through pantomime and referenced through the presence of ivory. In one ceremony, for example, male and female Bwami members sit on the roof of a house waving banana leaves in imitation of elephant trunks (Biebuyck 1986, 101). The initiation house itself is conceptualized as an elephant. Initiation into the highest level of Kindi (Lutumbo lwa Kindi) ends with the ceremony called "skinning the elephant" (*ibago wa nzogu*) (Biebuyck 1973, 117). Bwami members "skin" the initiation house/elephant by recklessly removing

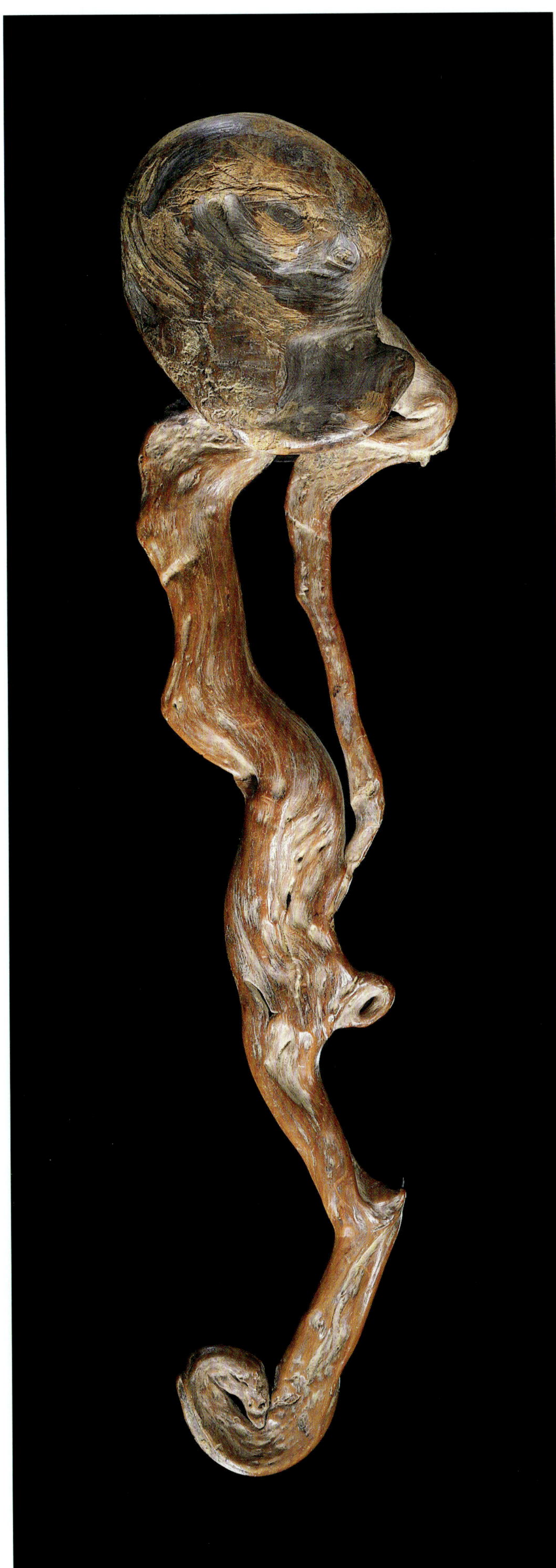

the roof and other parts of the house with small ivory utensils (Biebuyck 1986, 17, 59, 116, 190), leaving only its frame or skeleton.

Careless handling of ivory knives and spoons recalls the proverb "The *banamulua* skinned the elephant in a confused way," referring to the necessity of leadership and presumably stressing the community's need for Kindi as the means through which stability is preserved (Biebuyck 1986, 190). In the same vein, a ceremony known as *ndinde* refers to this carelessness as a warning against a person taking something he or she has not earned, an action that could result in tension within the group.

SPOONS

Ivory spoons, known as *kalukili* or *kakili*, seem to emphasize continuity (Biebuyck 1973, 226), perhaps through reference to feeding and growth (figs. 6.11–6.23). The word *kalukili* is also used to mean an heir (Biebuyck 1983, 59). Older men who are high-level members of Bwami eat their porridge with an ivory spoon, reminding all those watching of their status and value to the community. Bwami members symbolically feed performers wearing masks (Biebuyck 1973, 180), who then chew slowly and painfully. The saying "Old-Turtle is eating pounded bananas" (Biebuyck 1983, 58) compares the masked figure's chewing to the elderly Bwami member who must eat soft food due to the poor state of his teeth. Spoons also are used in circumcision rites. The man who has the authority to organize the rite owns an ivory or bone spoon. In addition, men place an ivory spoon in the mouth of a young boy for him to bite on during his circumcision (Biebuyck 1983, 59).

Many spoons have an anthropomorphic shape (see fig. 6.11), and all spoons are used as symbols for humans: the concave side of the bowl can refer to the front of a woman's body and the convex side to her back. With this in mind, the saying "Kalukili, you used to give me *idago* (the concave part, the lap, the vulva); you now give me the back" (Biebuyck 1983, 55) takes on tones of sexual rejection. By layering the saying "The buttocks are small and flat! Nzogu (Elephant) does not listen to the words of people" with the fondling of a spoon and with dancing, the teacher refers to a man who commits adultery within his own clan (Biebuyck 1983, 55).

6.11 Anthropomorphic spoon.
Ivory (?). L: 22.23 cm (8¾ in.).
FMCH 78.106; Museum Purchase.

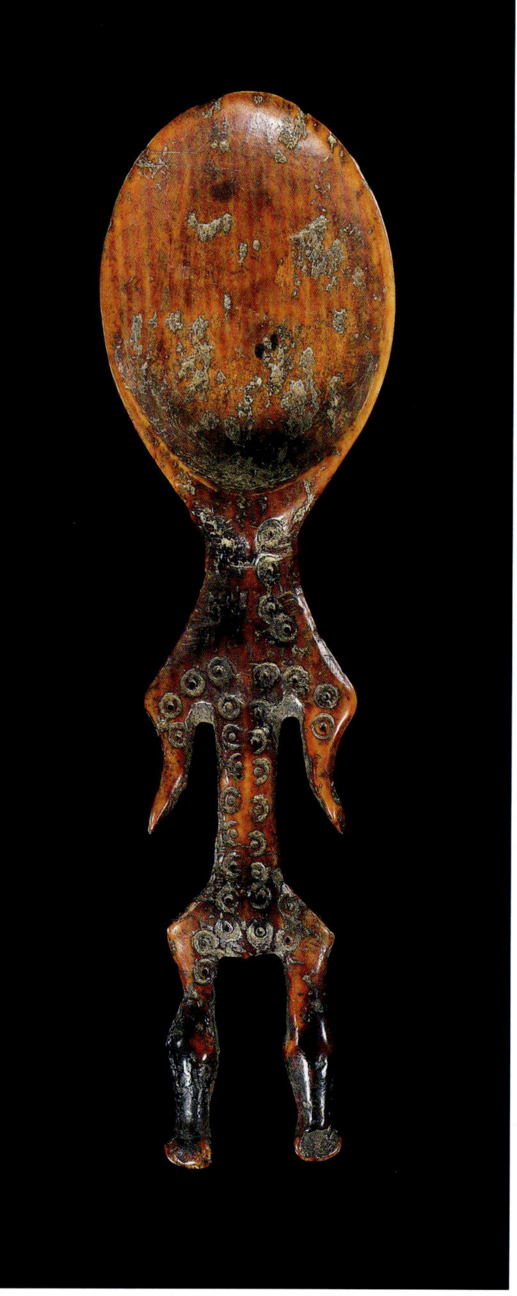

6.12 Double spoon.
Animal horn or ivory (?).
L: 27.2 cm (10¾ in.).

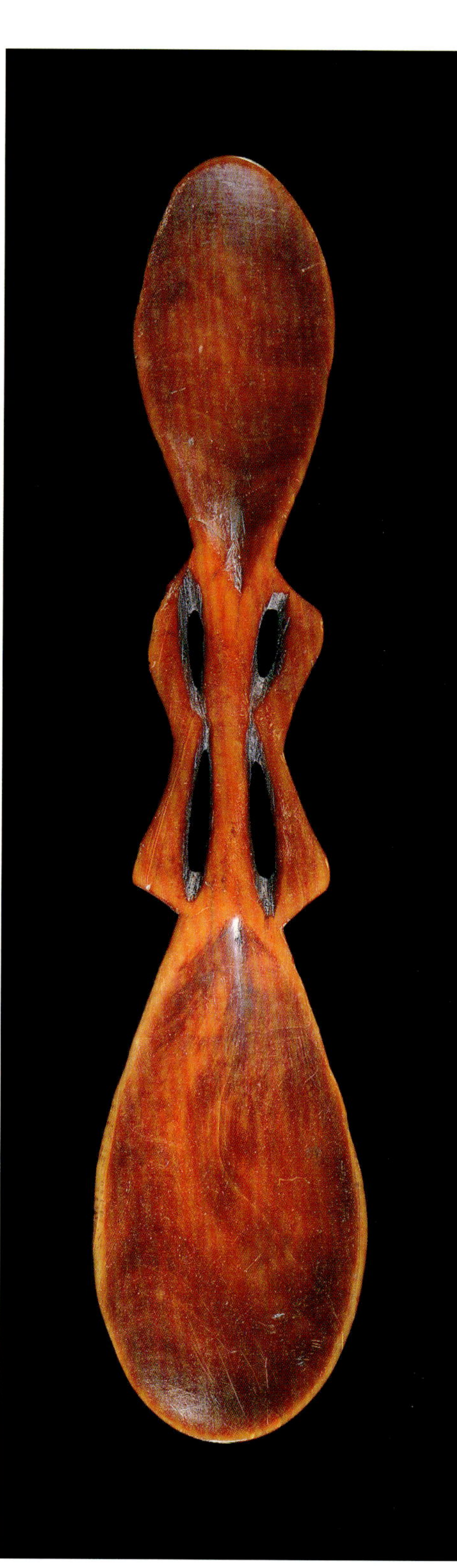

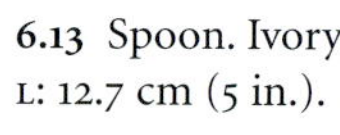

6.13 Spoon. Ivory.
L: 12.7 cm (5 in.).

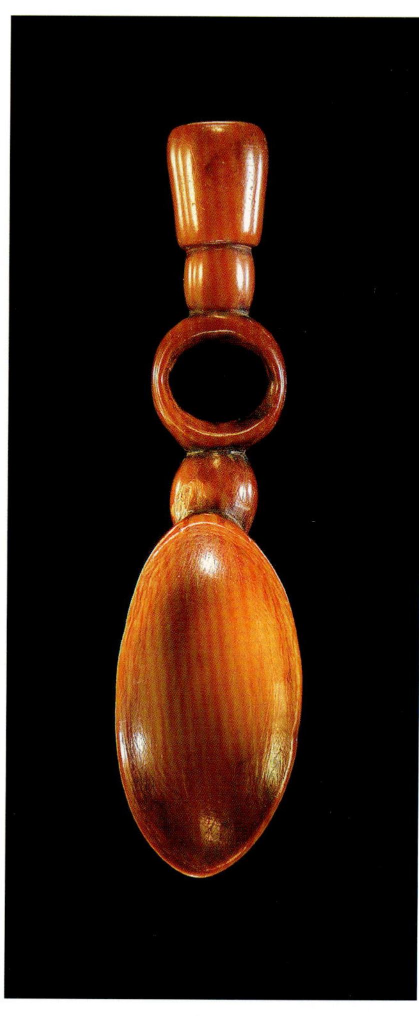

6.14 Spoon. Ivory.
L: 20 cm (7⅞ in.).

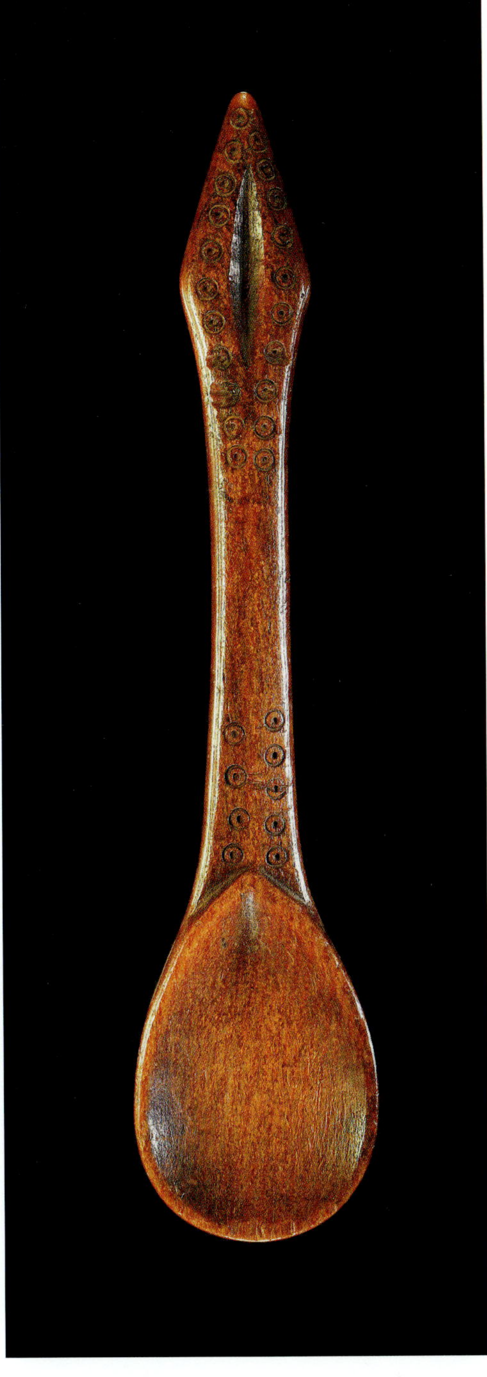

6.15 Spoon. Ivory.
L: 17.5 cm (6⅞ in.).

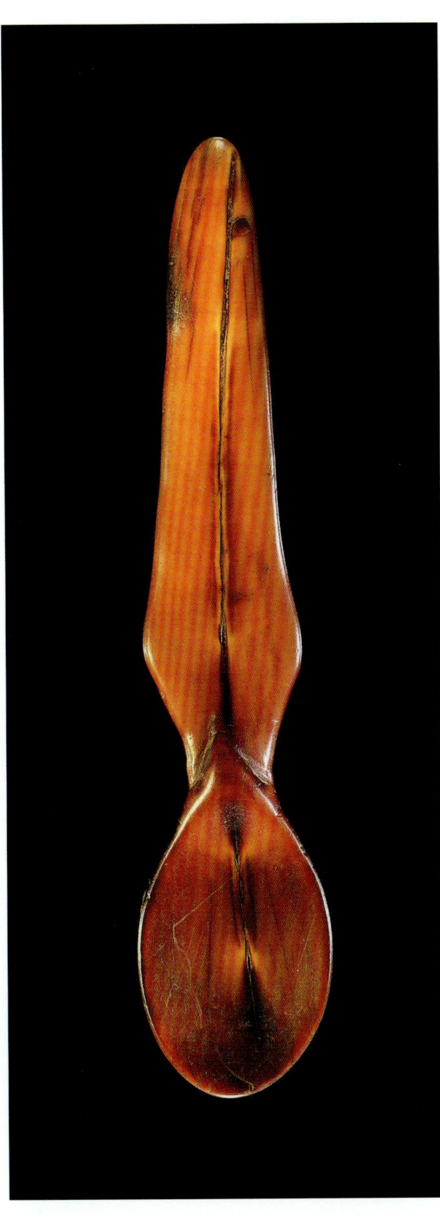

6.16 Spoon. Ivory.
L: 23.8 cm (9⅜ in.).

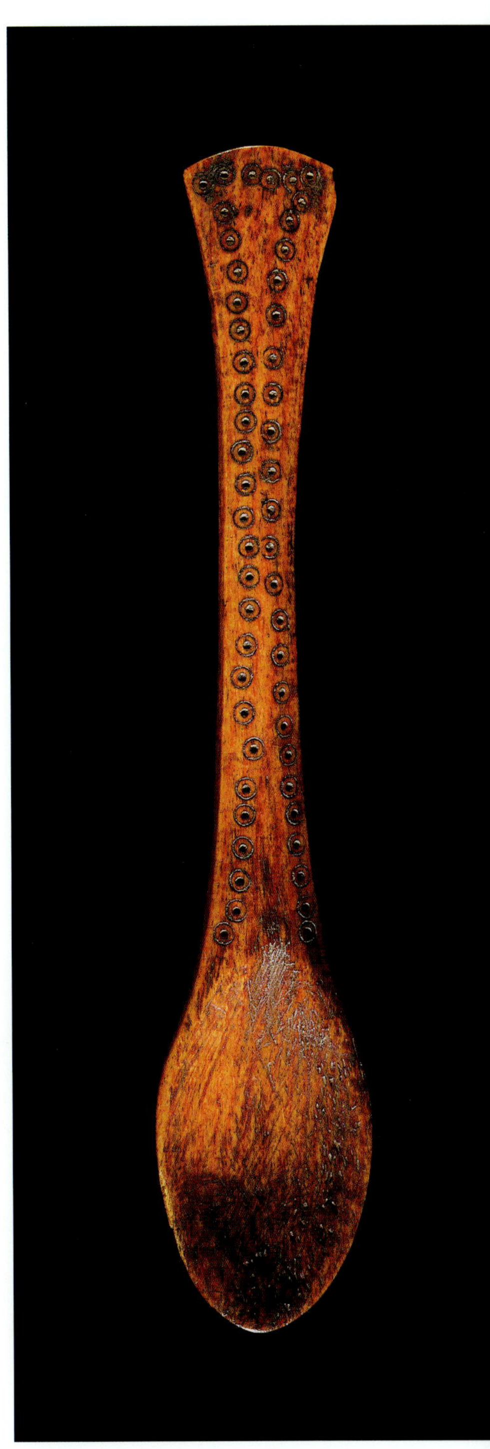

6.17 Spoon. Ivory.
L: 15.6 cm (6⅛ in.).

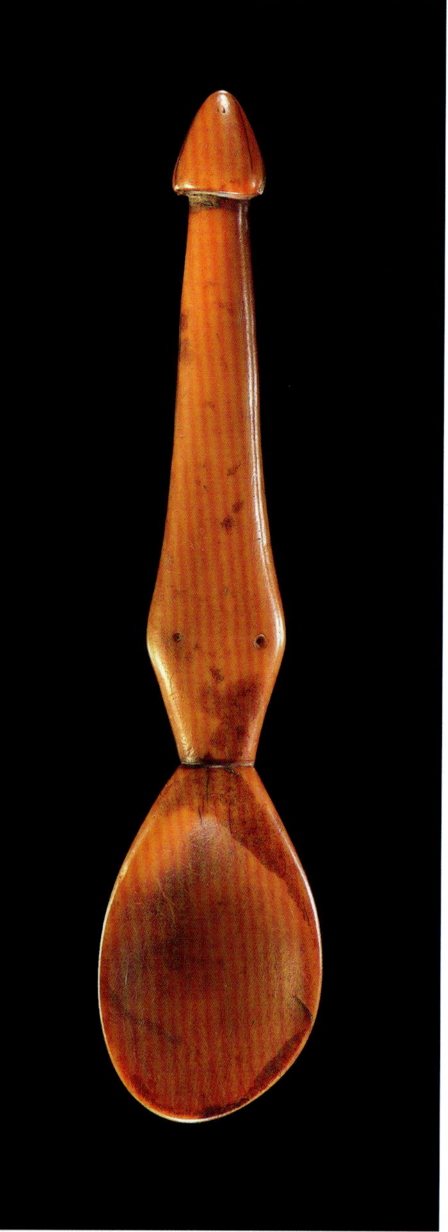

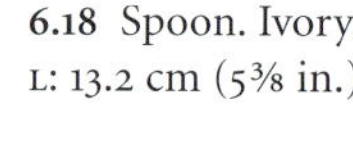

6.18 Spoon. Ivory.
L: 13.2 cm (5⅜ in.).

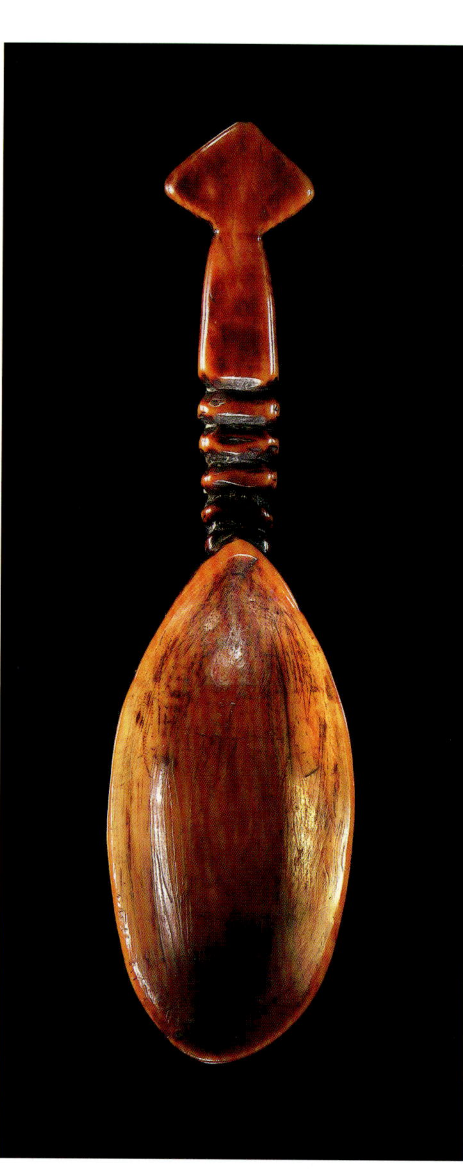

6.19 Spoon. Ivory.
L: 15.3 cm (6 in.).

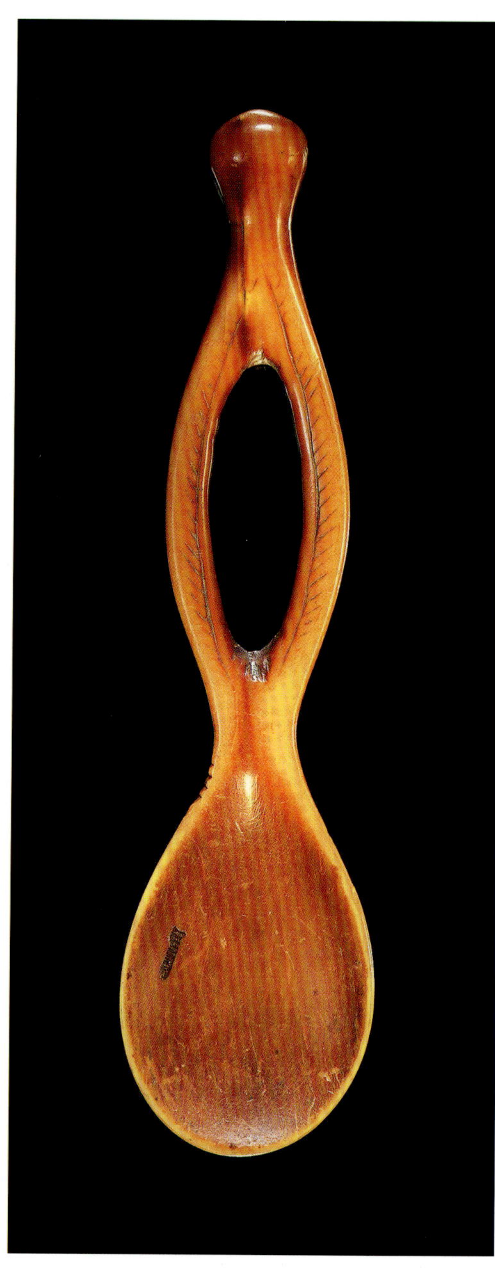

6.20 Spoon. Ivory.
L: 17.9 cm (7 in.).

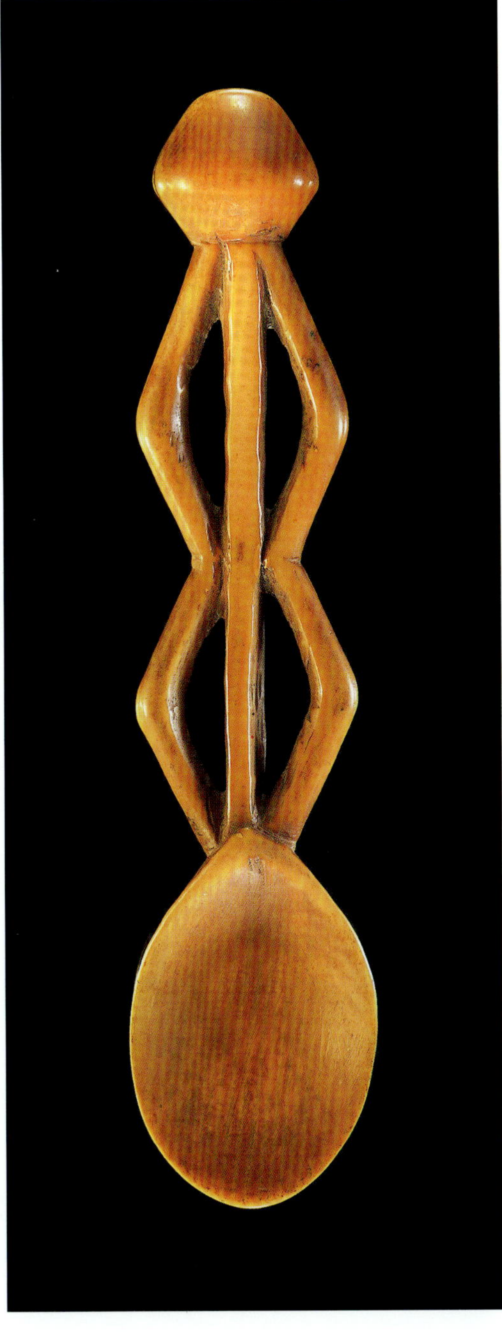

6.21 Spoon. Ivory.
L: 11.7 cm (4⅝ in.).

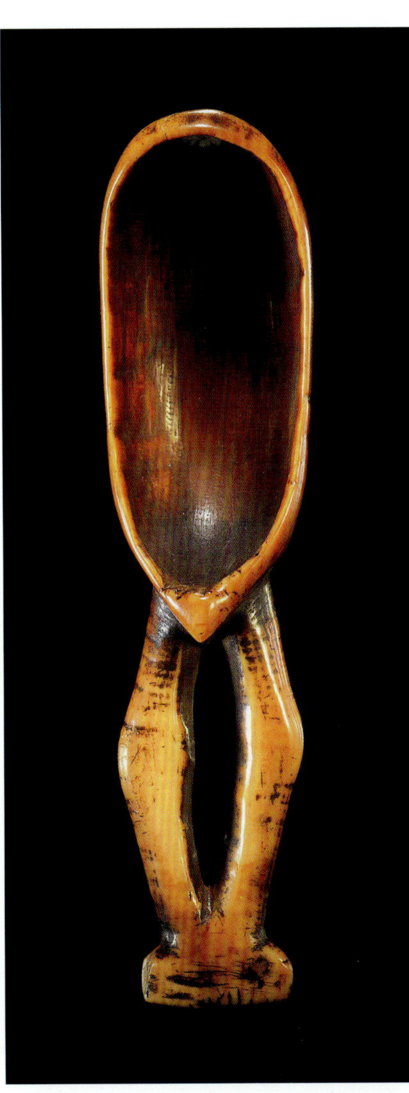

6.22 Spoon. Ivory.
L: 20.6 cm (8⅛ in.).

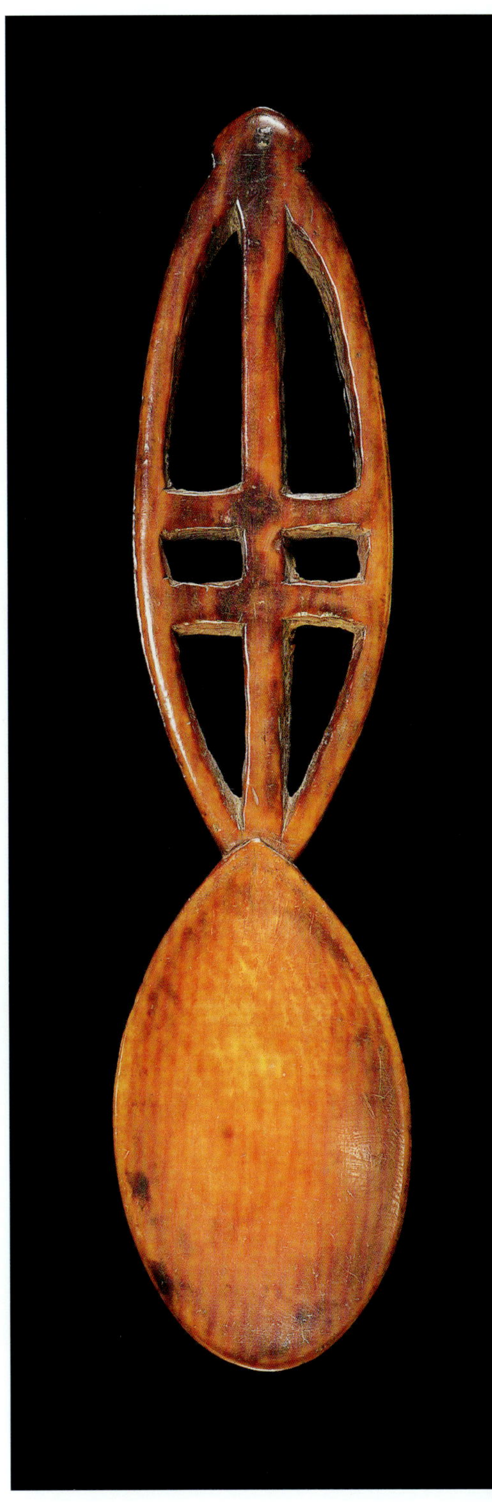

6.23A,B Front and back views of a spoon. Ivory. L: 17 cm (6¾ in.). FMCH X67.830; Gift of the Wellcome Trust.

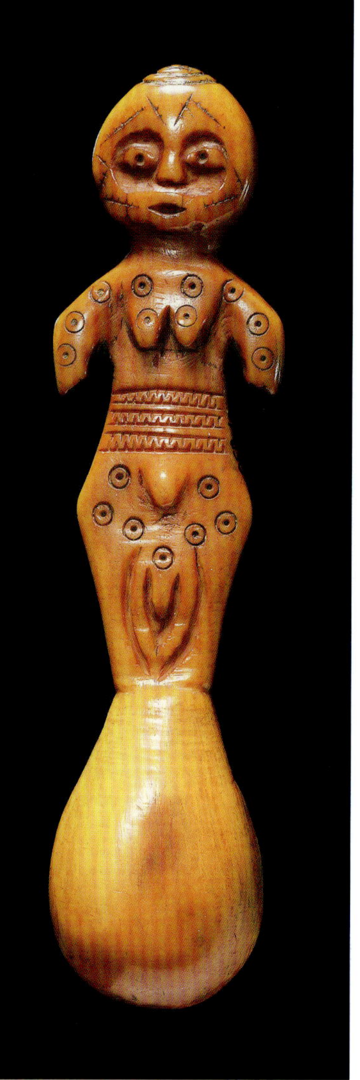

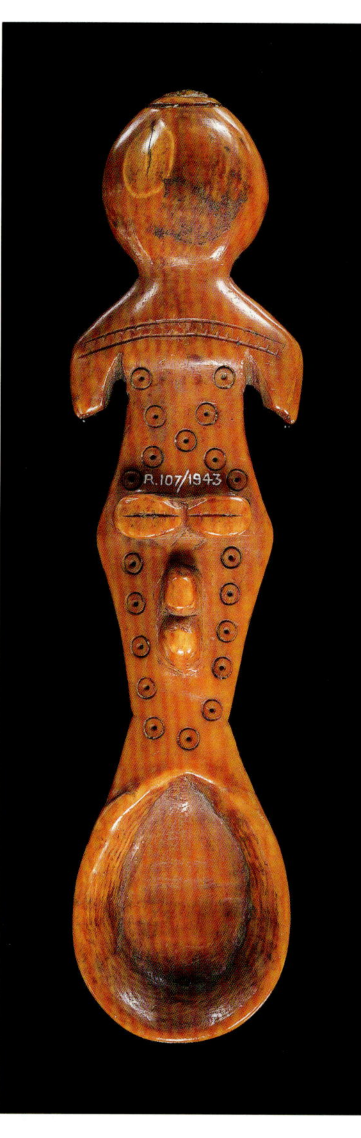

KNIVES

> Give me my little knife, I am spending the night
> at the place of skinning of the elephant.
>
> Lega Proverb (Biebuyck 1983, 57)

In addition to being used, along with other utensils, in the skinning of the elephant ceremony, small ivory knives (fig. 6.24) are owned by people who have special rights, such as the authority to distribute sacred animals or to organize circumcision camps. Teachers may also be recognized with a gift of a small ivory knife (Biebuyck 1973, 180; 1986, 190).

PEGS

Pegs made of elephant bone represent the elephant's ribs, and they also remind the viewer of the multiple meanings that Bwami assigns to the elephant (figs. 6.25–6.32). The image of the dead elephant, decomposed so that its ribs are exposed, is evoked in the saying "Where elephant rots, there are many ribs." The saying, combined with the pegs, refers to the material possessions of a high-level Bwami member that are distributed at death (Biebuyck 1986, 191).

AXE BLADES

The ivory blade (*isaga*) refers to the tool used by the Lega to clear living space out of the deep forest (figs. 6.33–6.36). It also reminds the viewer of tasks undertaken within Lega culture, such as cutting the honeycomb from its hive or circumcision (Biebuyck 1973, pl. 105). A blade and its handle (*kamima*) refer to the indissoluble marriage of a husband and wife who are both Bwami members. The blade represents the penis nestled deep in the vulva or handle (Biebuyck 1986, 183).

BILLHOOKS

Large iron billhooks are used to clear away the brush on the forest floor. Small ivory billhooks (figs. 6.37, 6.38) symbolize diligence and cooperation between many people: "He who has not many [people] cannot clear the tangle of lianas" (Biebuyck 1973, pl. 103; 1986, 183).

6.24 Miniature Knife.
Ivory. L: 12.6 cm (5 in.).

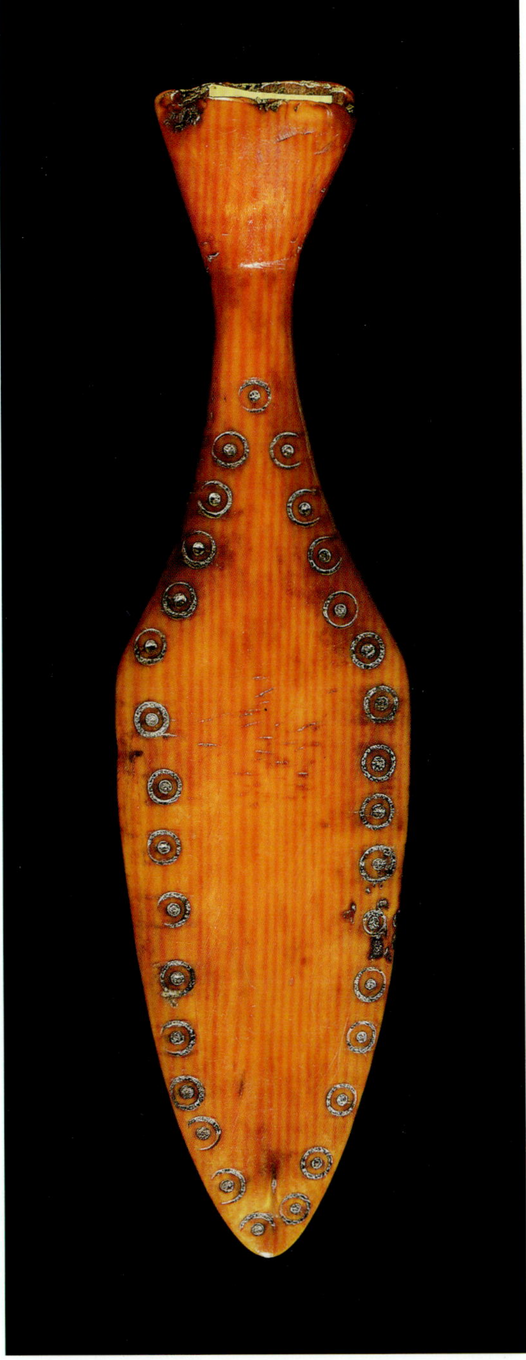

6.25 Peg. Ivory.
H: 20.9 cm (8¼ in.).

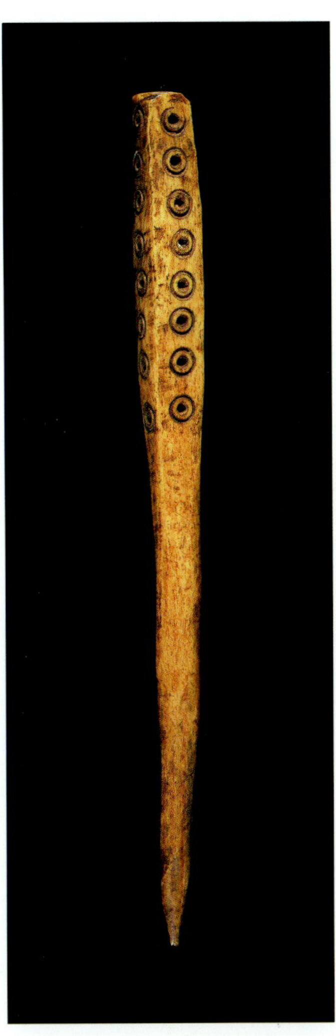

6.26 Anthropomorphic peg.
Ivory and wood.
H: 32 cm (12½ in.).

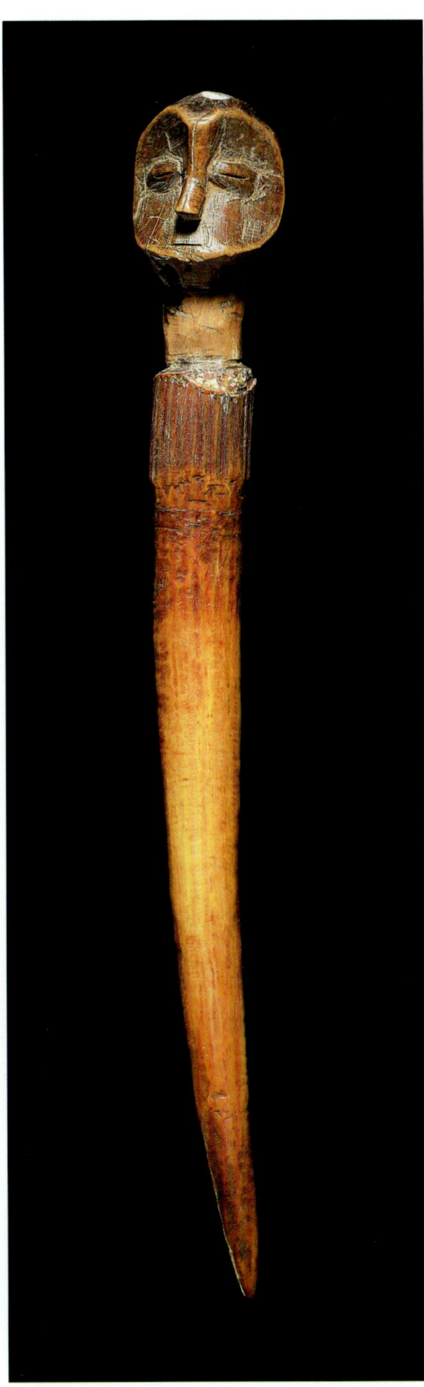

6.29 Anthropomorphic peg.
Ivory. H: 17.6 cm (7 in.).

6.28 Anthropomorphic peg.
Ivory and cowrie shells.
H: 19.5 cm (7¾ in.).

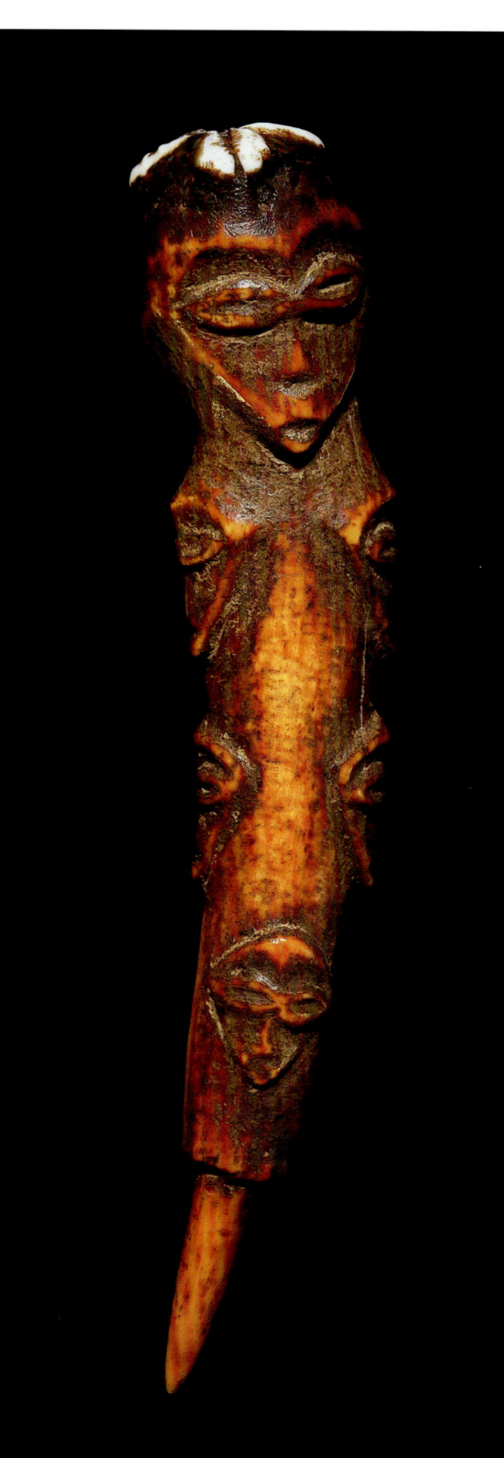

6.29 Anthropomorphic peg.
Ivory. H: 17.6 cm (7 in.).

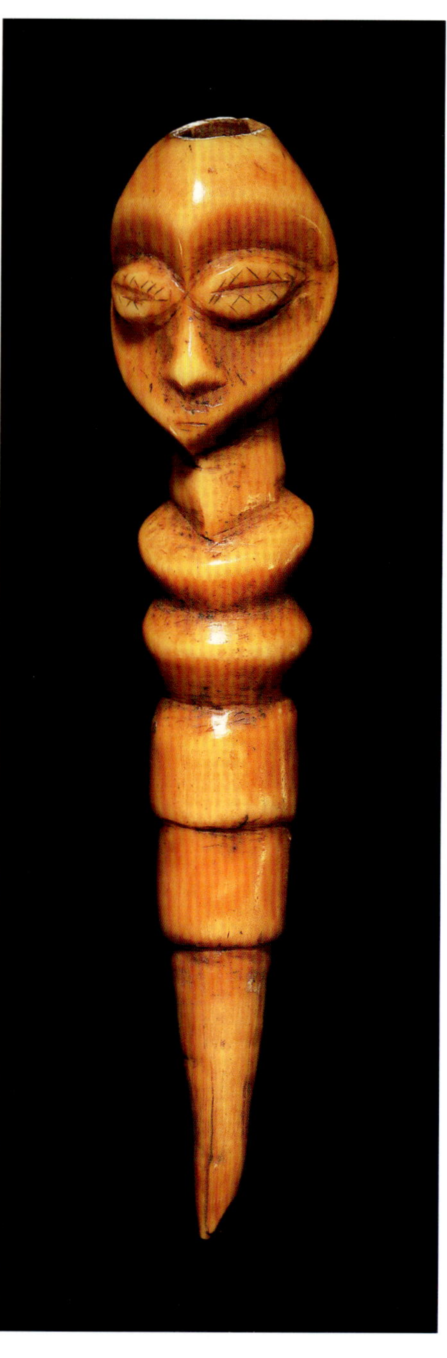

6.30 Anthropomorphic peg.
Ivory. H: 9.6 cm (3¾ in.).

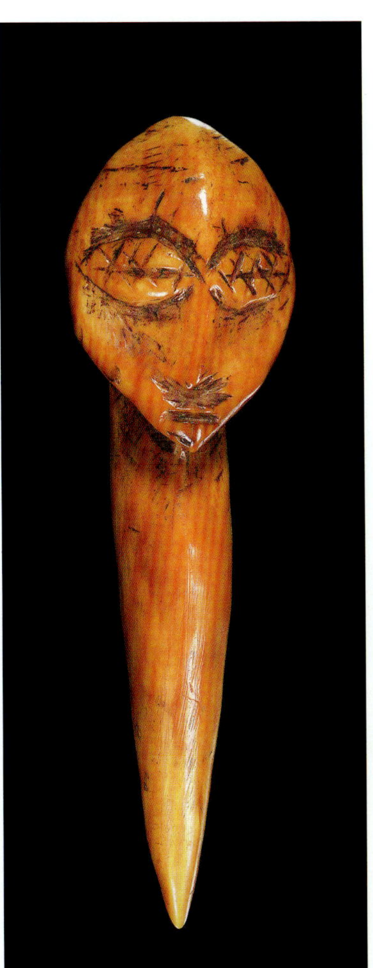

6.31 Anthropomorphic peg.
Ivory. H: 12.3 cm (4⅞ in.).

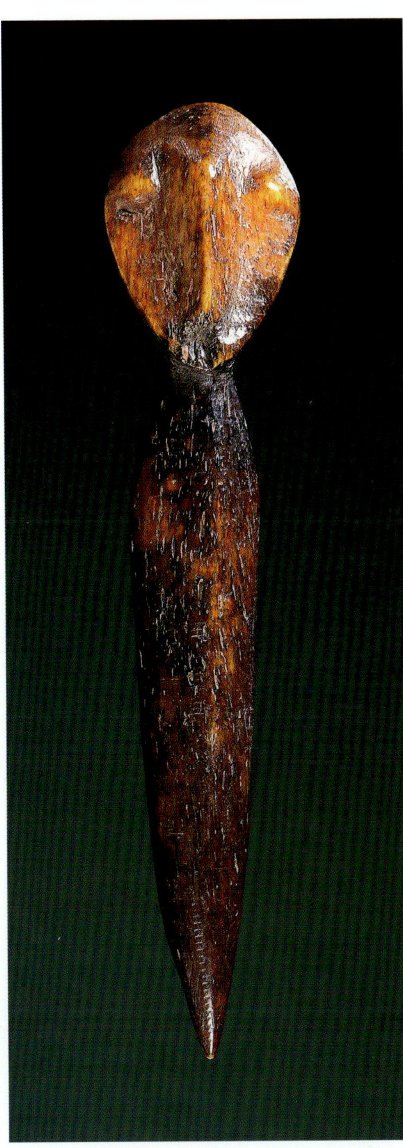

6.32 Anthropomorphic peg.
Ivory and feathers. H: 19.2 cm (7⅝ in.).

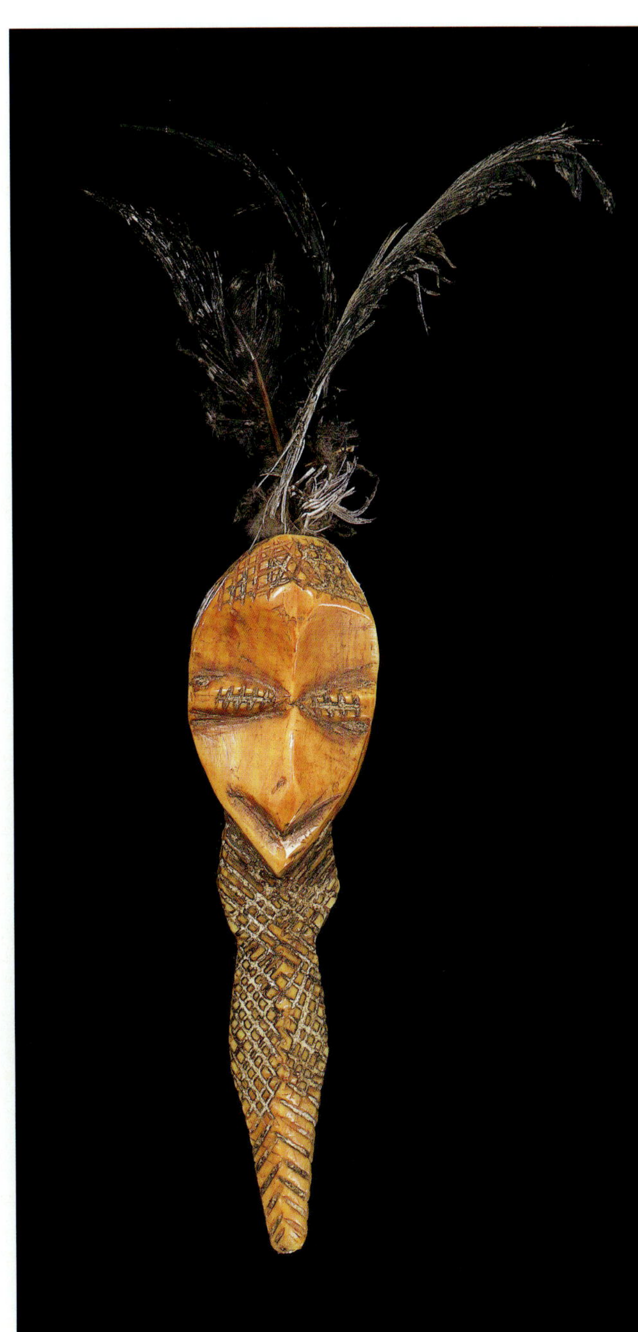

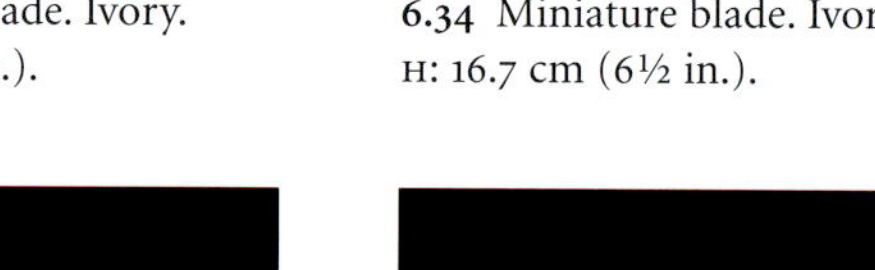

6.33 Miniature blade. Ivory.
H: 16.2 cm (6⅜ in.).

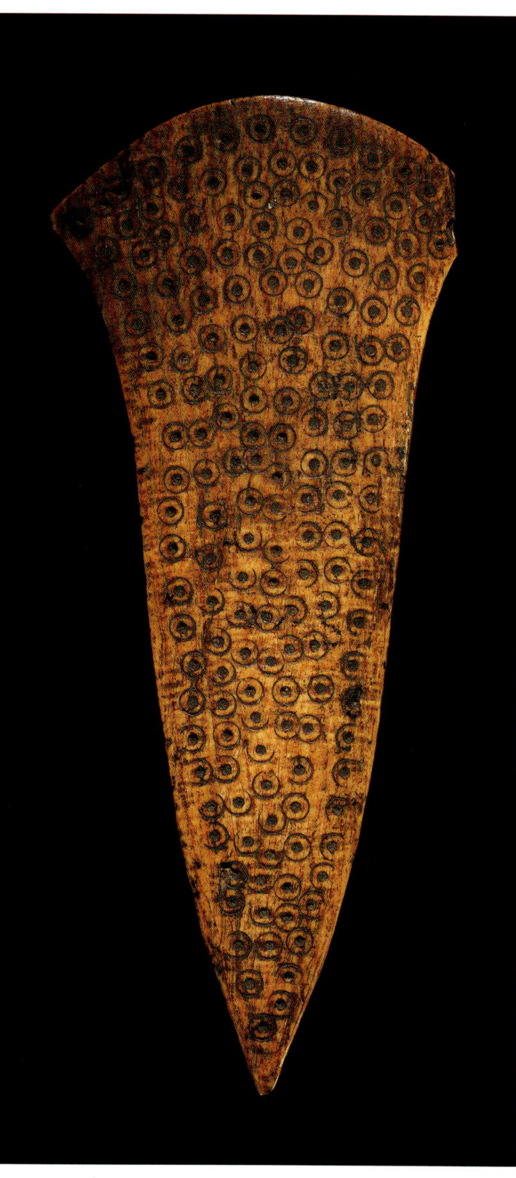

6.34 Miniature blade. Ivory.
H: 16.7 cm (6½ in.).

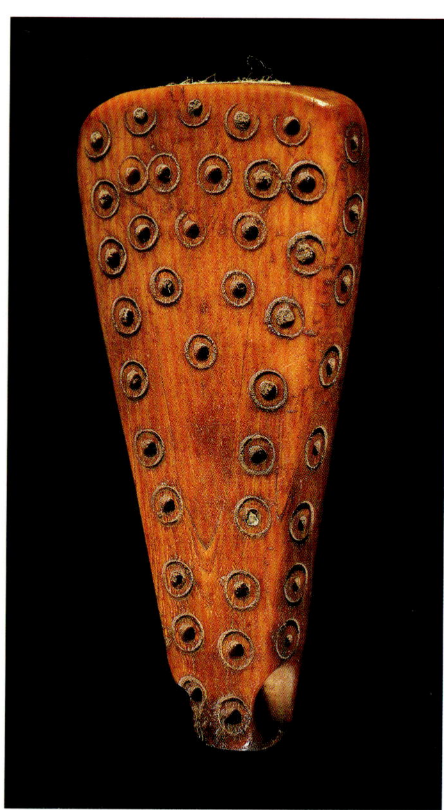

6.35 Miniature blade or pendant.
Ivory. H: 6.7 cm (2⅝ in.).

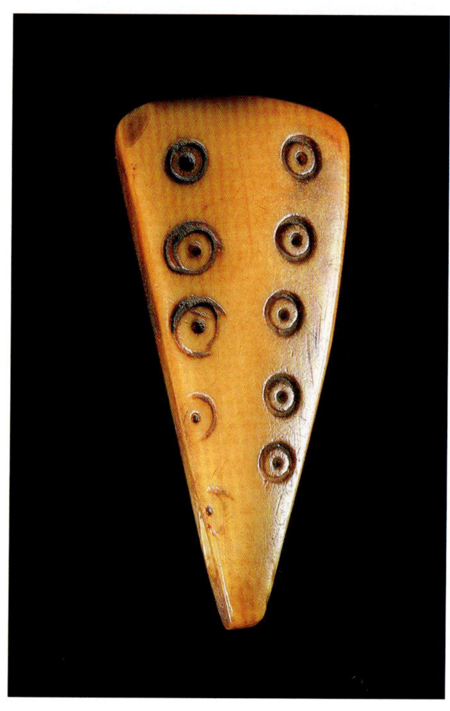

6.36 Miniature blade or pendant.
Ivory. H: 5.2 cm (2 in.).

6.37 Miniature billhook. Ivory.
H: 29.2 cm (11½ in.).

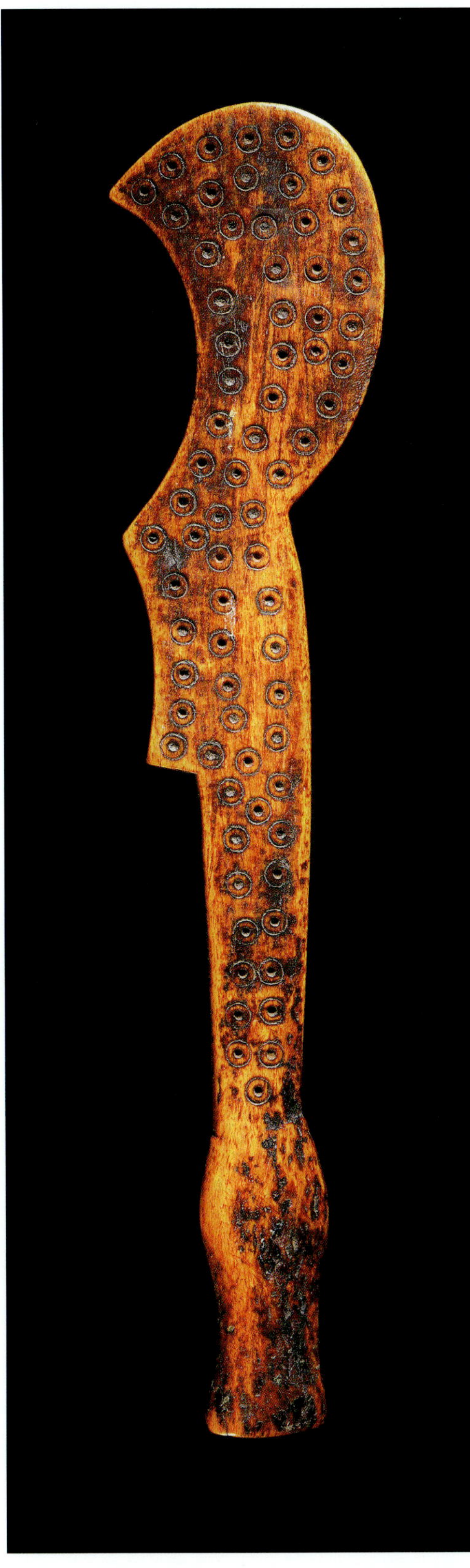

6.38 Miniature billhook. Ivory.
H: 20.6 cm (8⅛ in.).

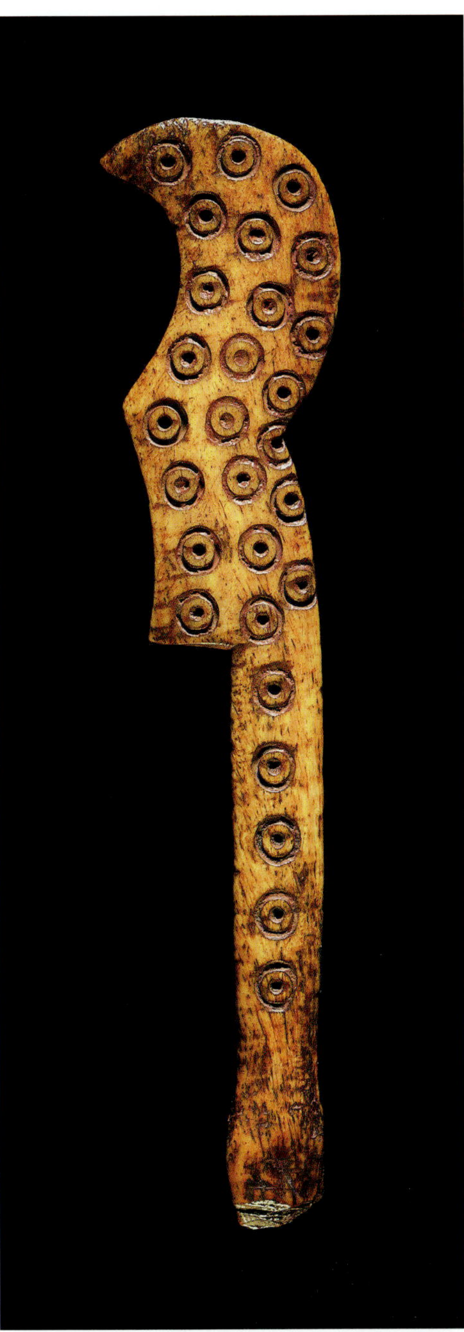

6.39 Miniature hammer. Ivory.
H: 16.5 cm (6½ in.).

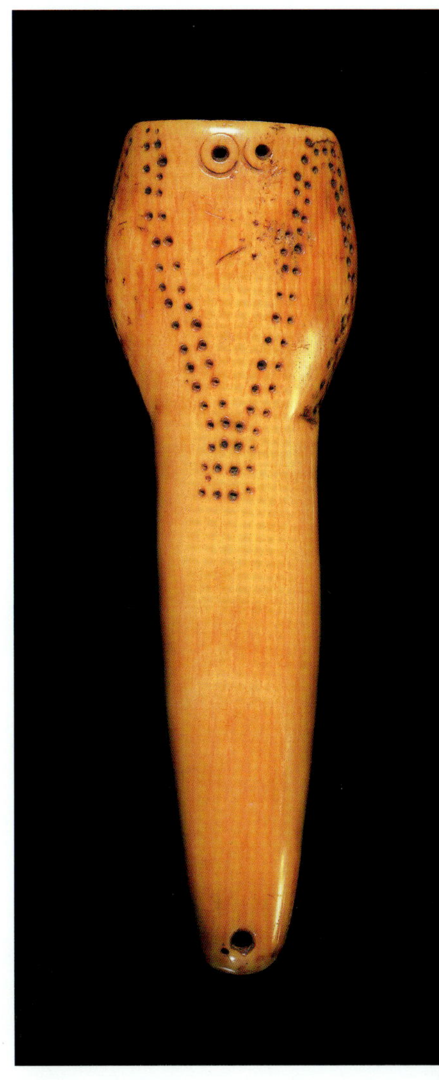

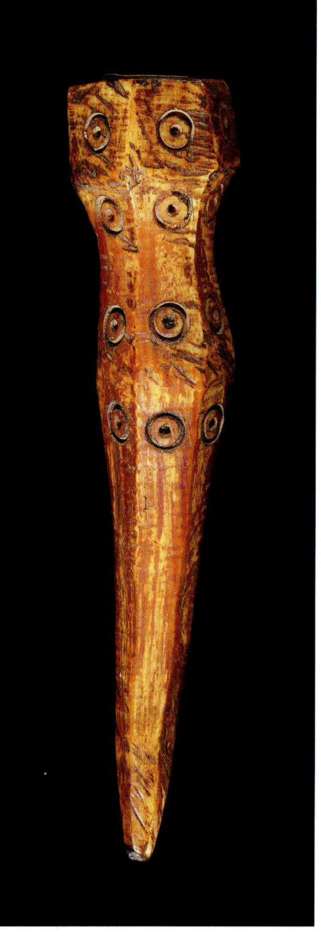

6.40 Peg. Ivory.
H: 12.5 cm (5 in.).

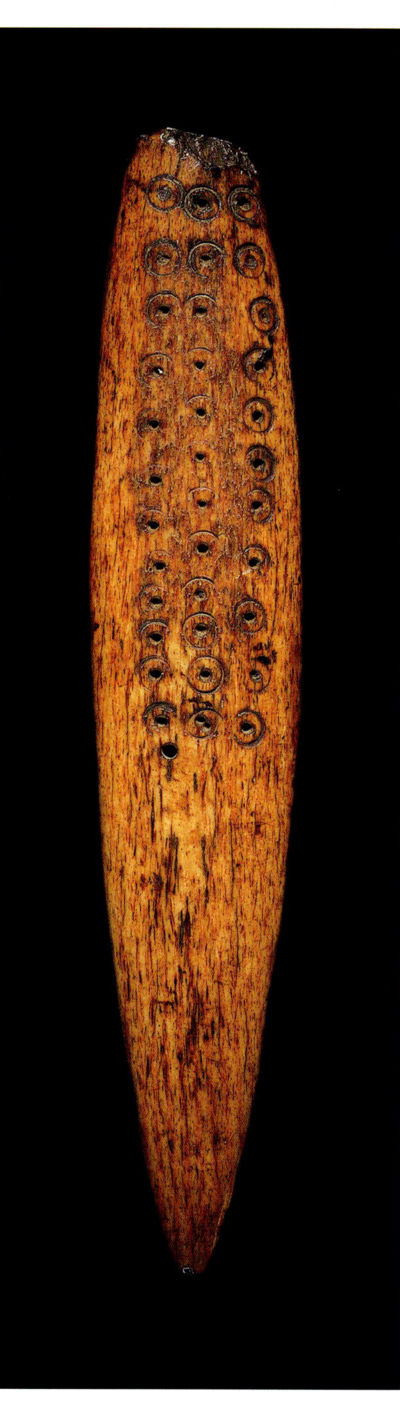

6.41 Peg. Ivory.
H: 22.5 cm (8⅞ in.).

HAMMERS AND POUNDERS

> When the blacksmith is absent, his child risks being hit with a hammer.
>
> Lega Proverb (Defour n.d., 157)

Among the Lega, hammers usually bring a blacksmith to mind (fig. 6.39). Sayings about hammers remind blacksmiths and members of Bwami that they deal with dangerous powers. Both are responsible for protecting the family and community from unwitting harm (Defour n.d., 157).

6.42 Knife handle (?). Ivory. H: 11.1 cm (4⅜ in.).

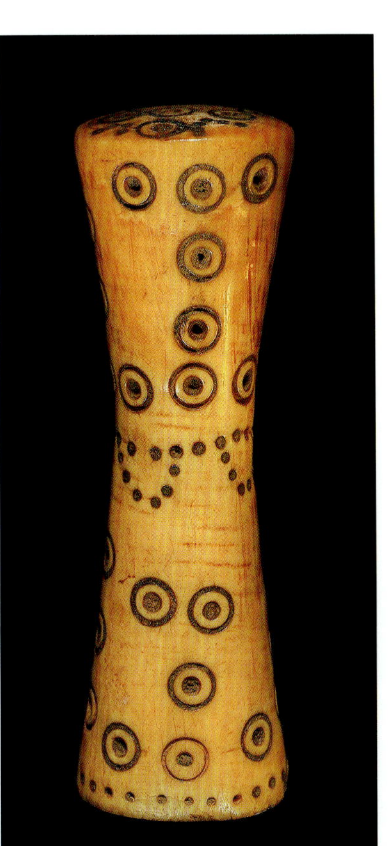

6.43 Unidentified miniature tool. Ivory. H: 15 cm (6 in.).

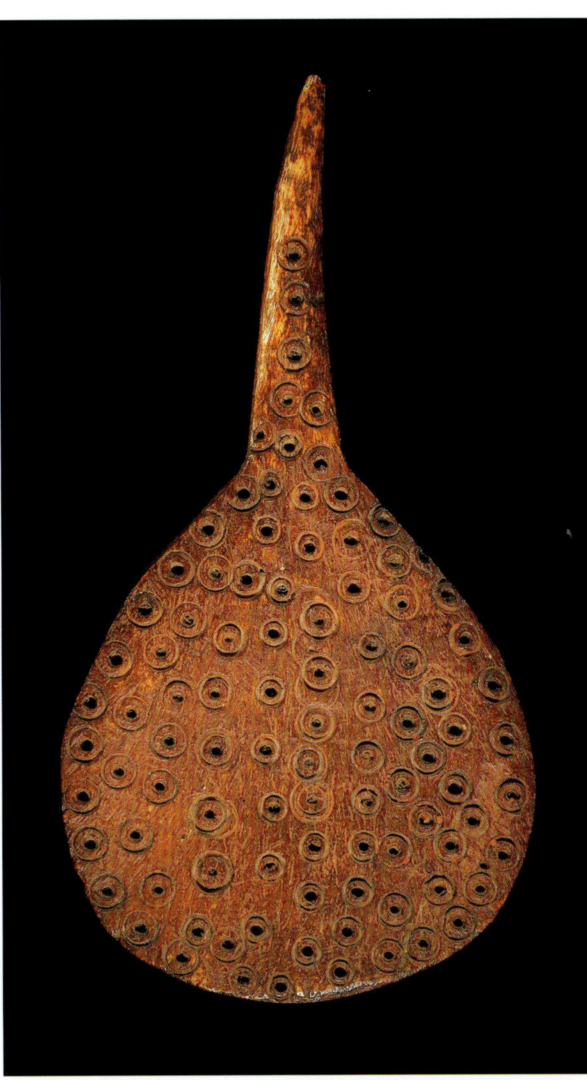

6.44 Unidentified miniature tool. Ivory. H: 9.7 cm (3⅞ in.).

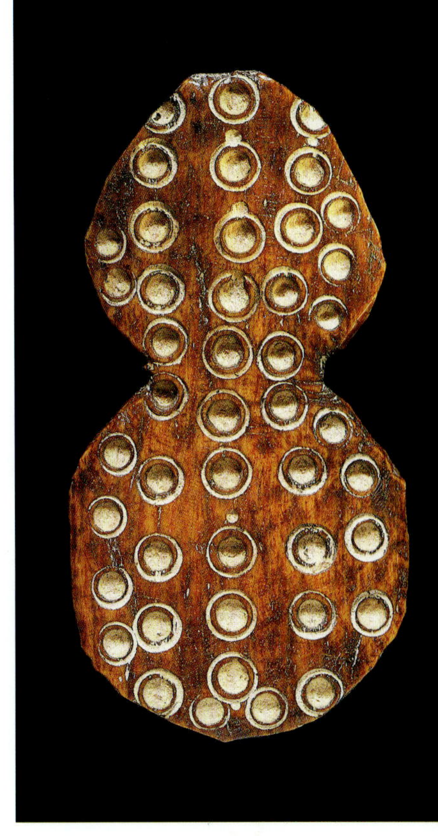

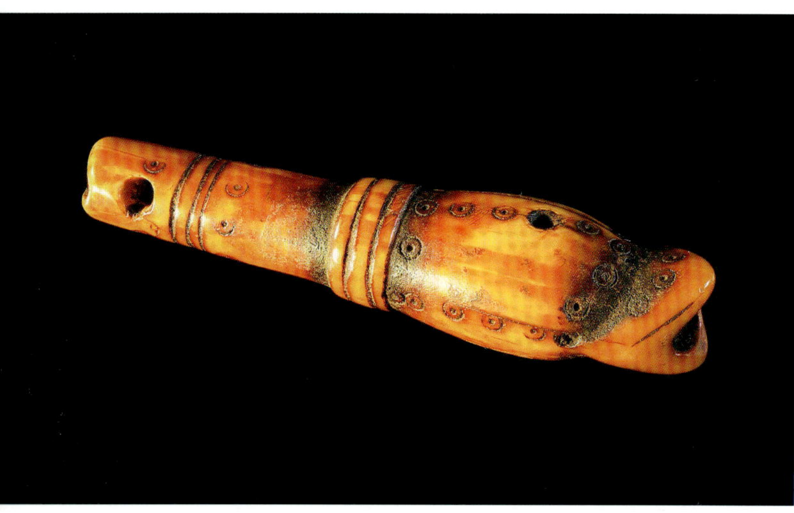

6.45 Whistle. Ivory.
L: 9.7 cm (3⅞ in.).

WHISTLES

> He who will die because of *mwale* [lit., "an ambush;" here, "the whistle"]; the parrots tell him where to go.
>
> Lega Proverb (Biebuyck 1986, 20)

Whistles are used in many arenas, including Bwami ceremonies, circumcision rites, and divination (fig. 6.45). In the proverb above, the whistle refers to the instrument's parrotlike sound. The thinking seems to be that many people will be attracted by a parrot's call, perhaps seeking the bird's feathers. Others who wish to do them harm thus imitate the bird's sound to lure their victims into an ambush (Biebuyck 1986, 201). The proverb warns that even attractive things should be carefully investigated if one wishes to avoid falling into a trap.

STOOLS[1]

In a world of shifting metaphors, the symbolism of the Lega stool remains fairly consistent (figs. 6.46–6.49). The Lega make and use a variety of stools and backrests, but symbolism centers around a single type called *kisumbi.* This stool has a concave circular top and a mirroring convex bottom with four connecting supports, each bending outward to form an angle. All Yananio-level members own a stool as an emblem of their high rank. They keep it until death, at which time it is given to their replacement in Bwami. Since movement through the ranks of Bwami cannot be delayed, if there is not an appropriate stool available when a man moves into Yananio, his teacher will commission a stool for him.

Older men do not use the *kisumbi* stool on a cord to teach youths who are not yet Bwami members. Use of the stool as a seat or for metaphoric purposes is restricted to Bwami members and their ceremonies. Outsiders might view the stool of a high-level Bwami member as designating status in the same way that a hat or a belt might. As a metaphor, the Bwami stool represents the individual member and the complete moral code. The seat and base of the stool represent human faces, causing stools to recall two-faced figures (see fig. 8.72). The conceptual link between the stool and Janus figures reminds Bwami members that, as leaders, they should be aware of everything that happens in the community. The permanent connection of the top and bottom symbolize the unbreakable

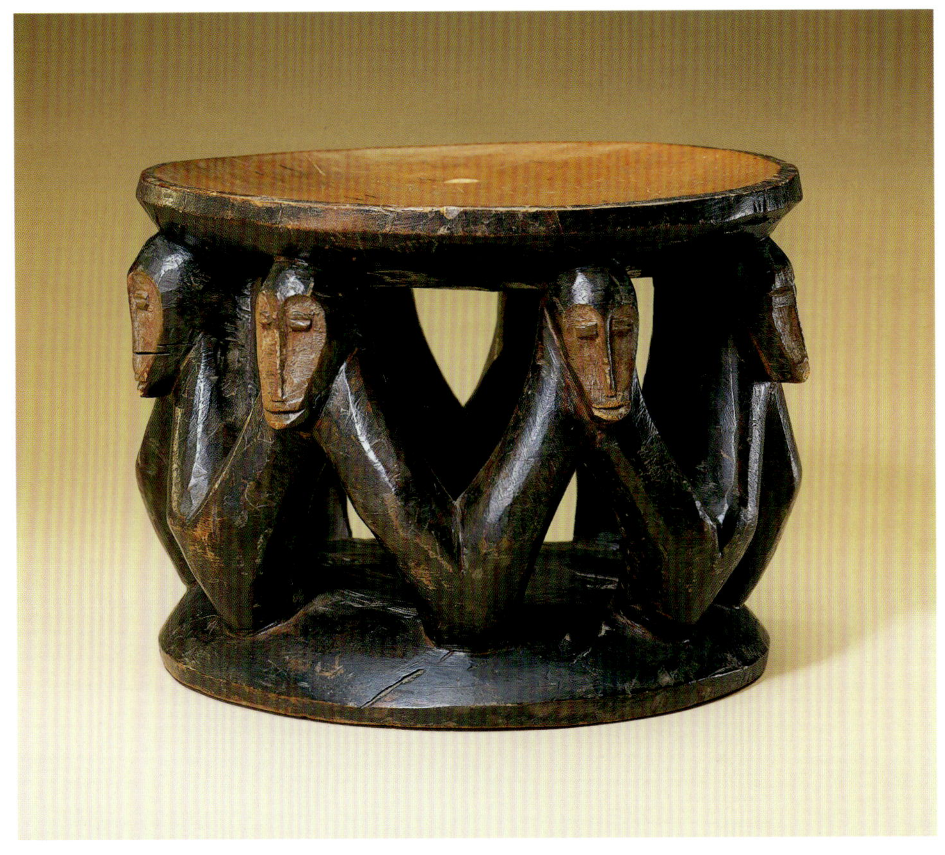

6.46 Stool. Wood.
w: 26.9 cm (10½ in.).

6.47 Double stool. Wood.
w: 31.5 cm (12⅜ in.).

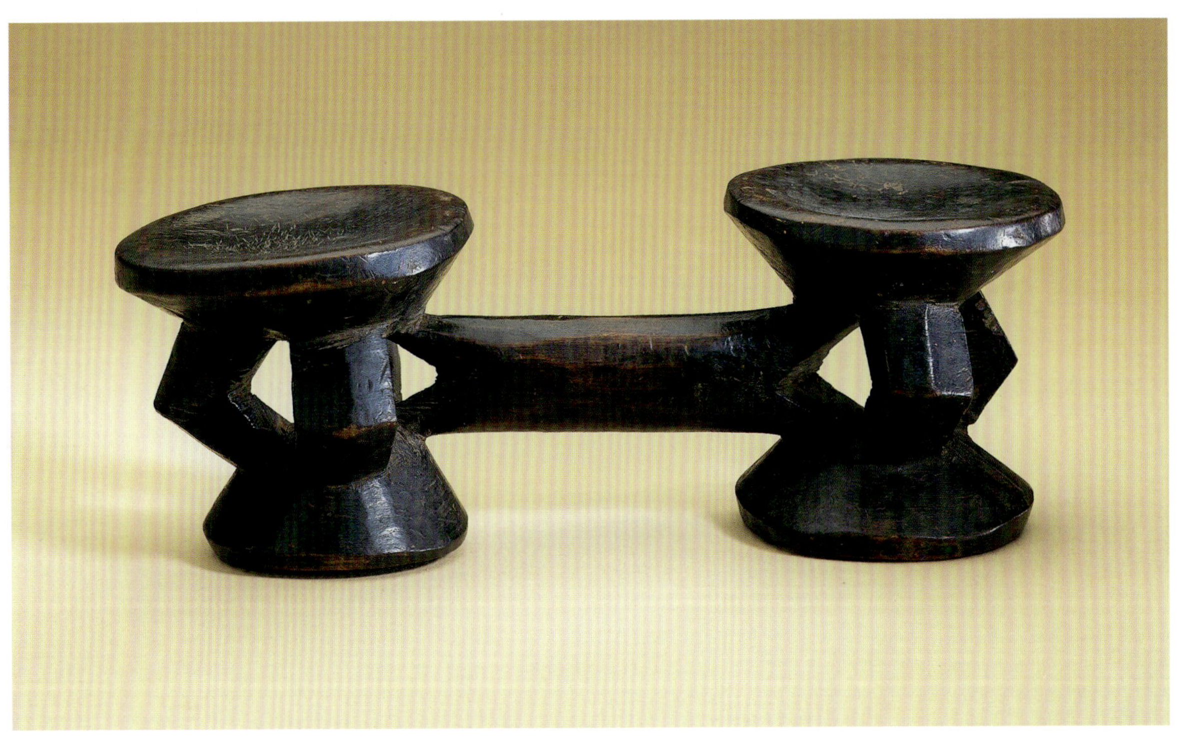

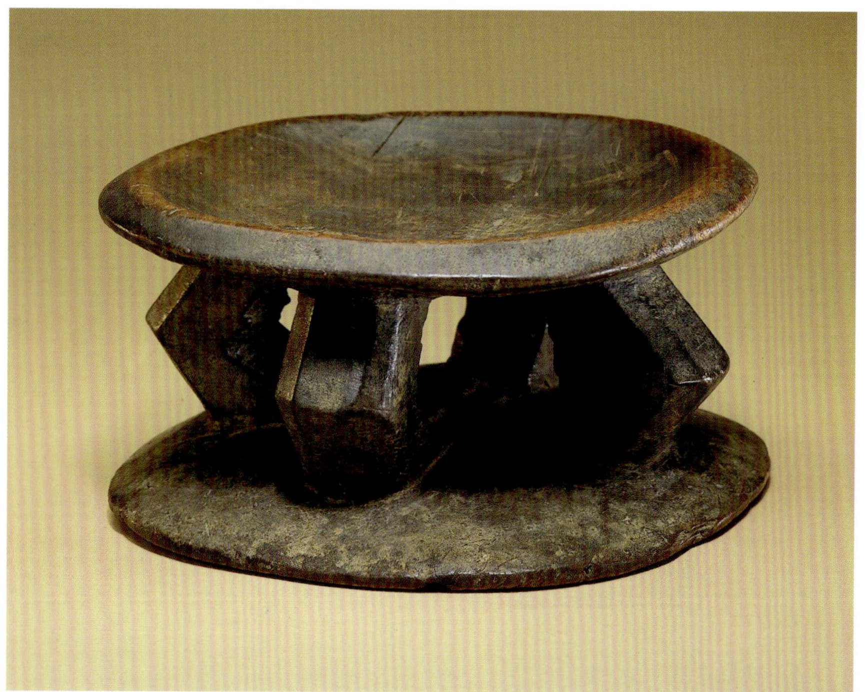

6.48 Stool. Wood.
w: 19 cm (7½ in.).

6.49 Stool. Wood.
w: 30.3 cm (12 in.).

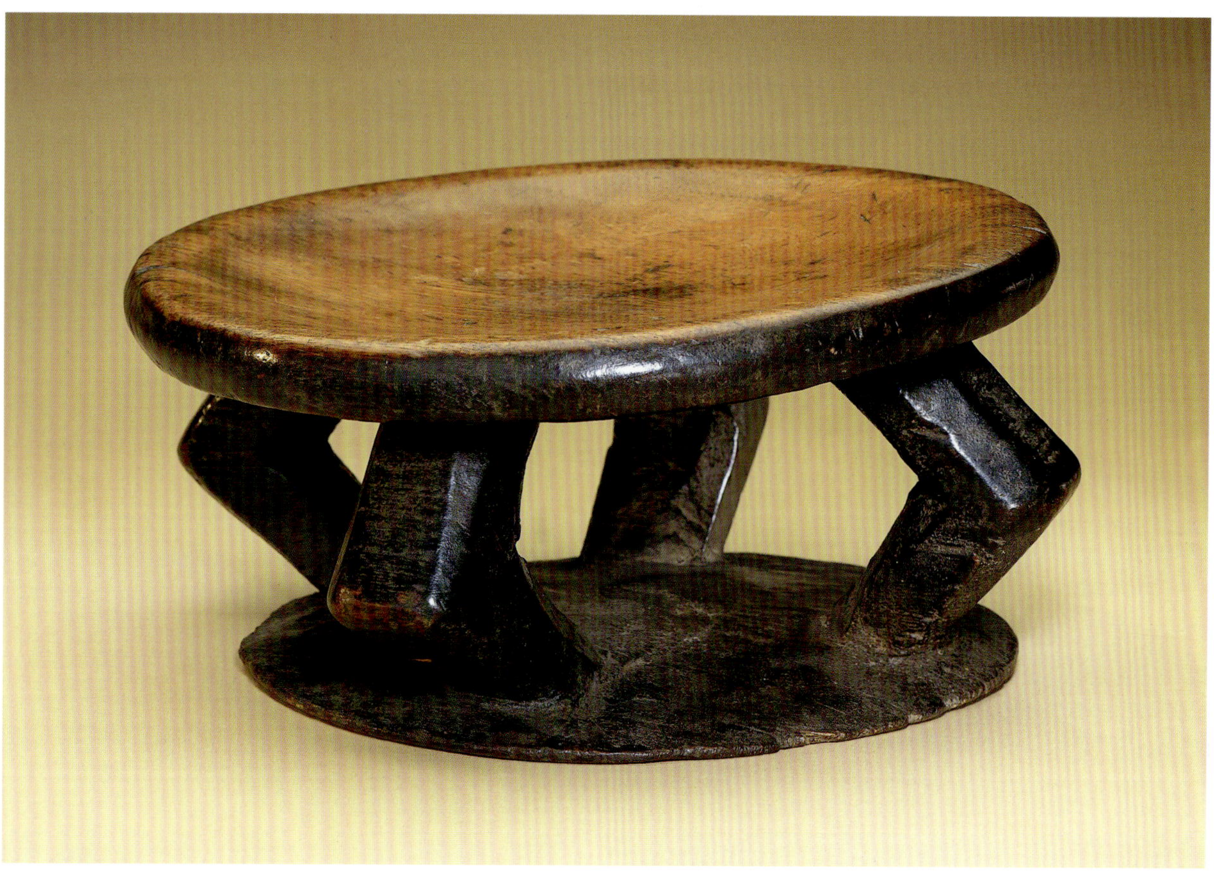

bond between the Bwami member and his initiated wife, the initiate and his teacher, a man and his clan, and Bwami itself. The four supports represent the ideal family or clan separated into four branches.

The stools themselves take on different meanings in initiation performances. Members carry them, sit on them, and use them as a center stage for the display of a group of objects. Lower-level initiates might stand on the stool as a promise of things to come. The final initiation into the highest level of Yananio is known as "stool" (*kisumbi*). Stools appear in all performances, either held in the hand or hanging on a string. During these performances, the initiate learns the complete symbolism of the stool.

MINIATURE STOOLS

Miniature stools carry the same symbolism as the larger versions but are used in more limited ways (figs. 6.50, 6.51). When carved of ivory, a miniature *kisumbi* is part of a basket, known as *lutala,* that holds circumcision-related objects. The stool becomes a marker of the man with the authority to organize and conduct the circumcision rites. Miniature stools also appear in initiation ceremonies for women's Bwami levels.

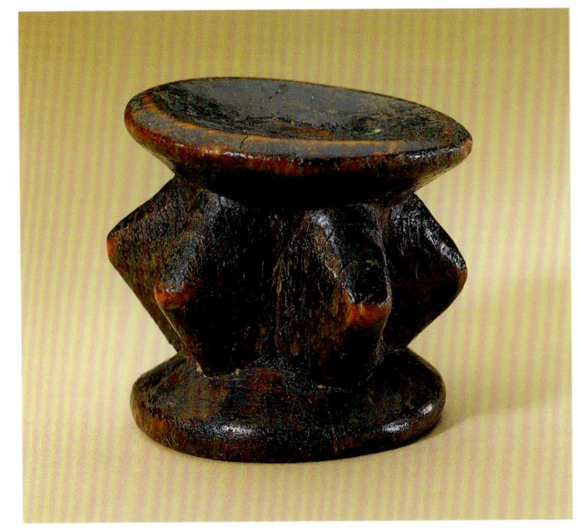

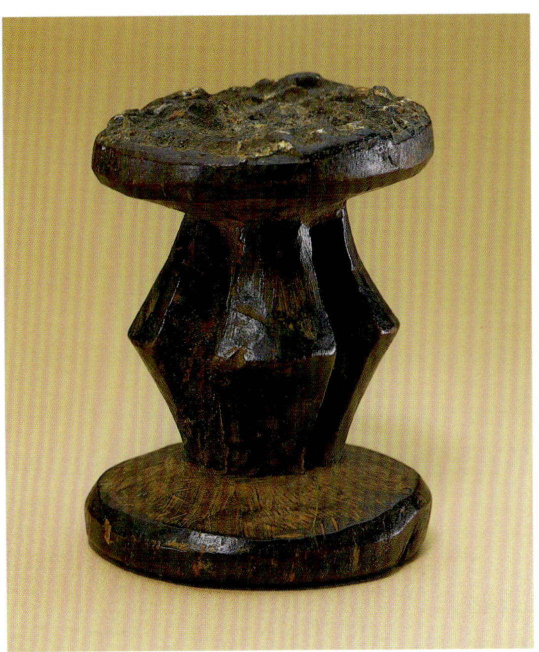

6.50 Miniature stool. Ivory. H: 6.4 cm (2½ in.).

6.51 Miniature stool. Wood. H: 8 cm (3⅛ in.).

7 Animal Figures

Close observation has led the Lega to become extremely familiar with the animals who share their environment. As a result they have extensive knowledge of the physical attributes and behavior patterns common to many species. As noted earlier, Kindi-level initiates refer to themselves as Bakinsamba (People of the elephant tail),[1] and members of other Bwami levels often take the names of various animals, attempting to attribute to themselves the creature's desirable traits (Biebuyck 1979, 77; 1986, 101). The Lega use animals when teaching with "the cord of wisdom" and with layered Bwami metaphors. Animals can be represented by people imitating them in various ways: by a portion of the animal's anatomy, such as a beak, claw, or tooth (see figs. 6.1–6.9); by simple assemblages of sticks; or by an artist's carving in wood or ivory (Biebuyck 1986, 101–102).

TYPES OF ANIMAL FIGURES

There are two types of sculpted zoomorphic figures: generic four-legged animals (*mugugundu*) and figures of specific animals. Both types are owned solely by high-level Bwami members (figs. 7.1–7.10). Yananio members own the generic figures made of wood and consider them a symbol of continuity through the generations of Bwami (Biebuyck 1973, pl. 25, 88). In performance, members of the Society use the generic figures in groups to represent mainly dogs, pangolins, and antelopes.[2] Occasionally an object is attached or several objects are combined in performance to clarify the figure's identity. A dog bell, for example, might be attached to a generic animal figure to suggest a dog. One figure might chase another, imitating various scenarios, such as a dog chasing an antelope (Biebuyck 1973, 222–23; 1994, 54). Members of Lutumbo lwa Kindi individually own generic animal figures in ivory (Biebuyck 1994, 54) that often appear alone rather than in combinations (Biebuyck 1973, 222). Members of Lutumbo lwa Kindi who carry out specific responsibilities, such as teaching or acting as a sponsor of initiations, also own figures carved to portray specific animals (Biebuyck 1994, 54). These can include turtles, birds, elephants, and snakes.

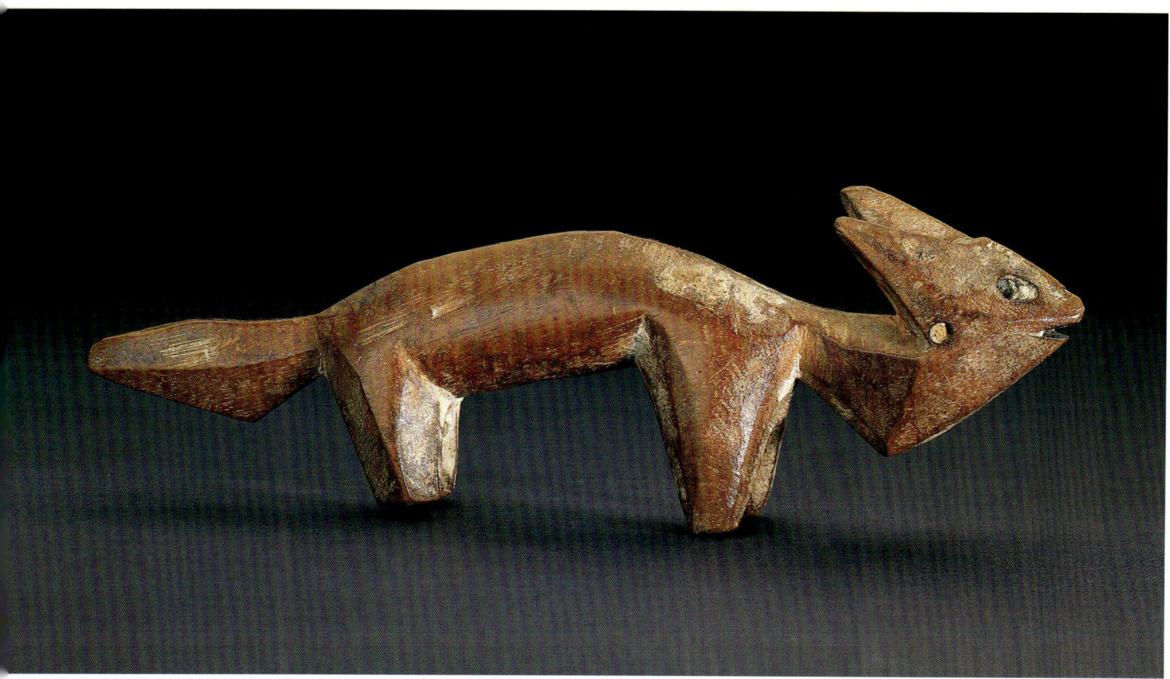

7.1 Generic animal figure. Wood and pigment. L: 24 cm (9⅝ in.).

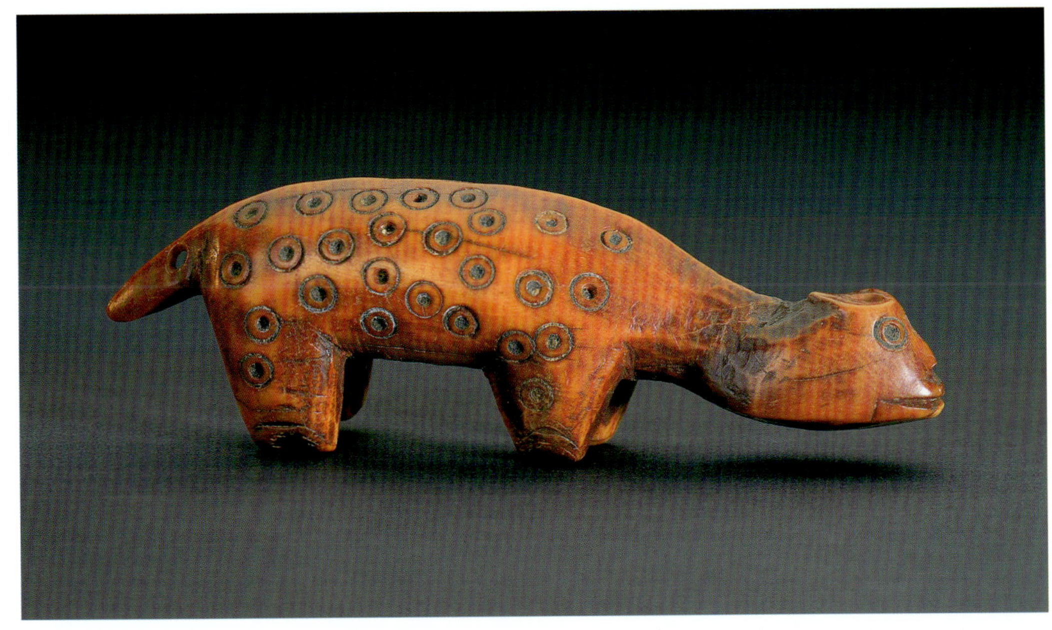

7.2 Generic animal figure. Ivory.
L: 12.4 cm (4⅞ in.).

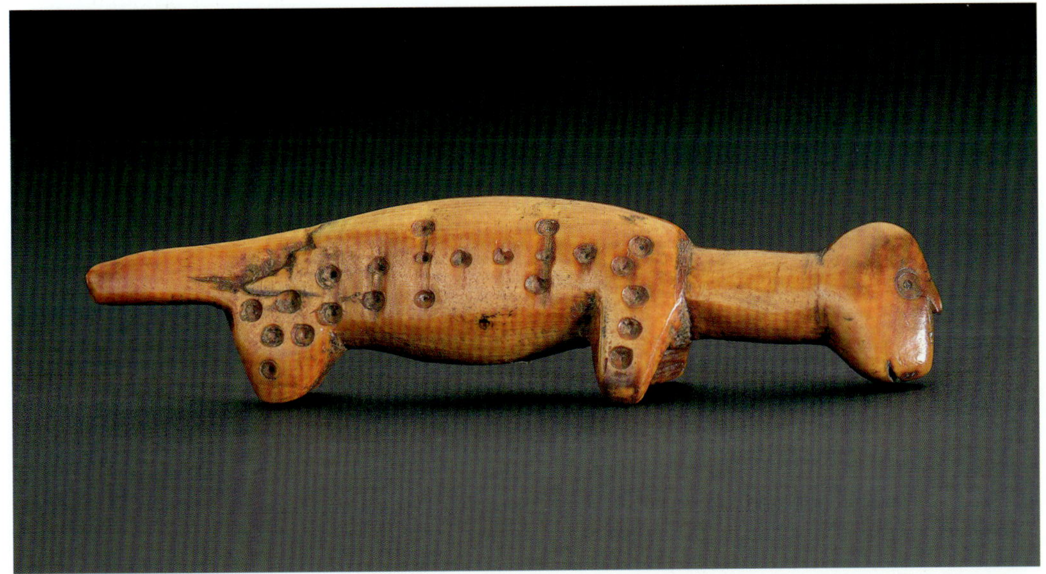

7.3 Generic animal figure. Ivory.
L: 13.5 cm (5⅜ in.).

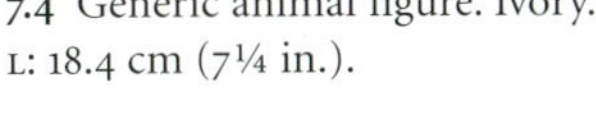

7.4 Generic animal figure. Ivory.
L: 18.4 cm (7¼ in.).

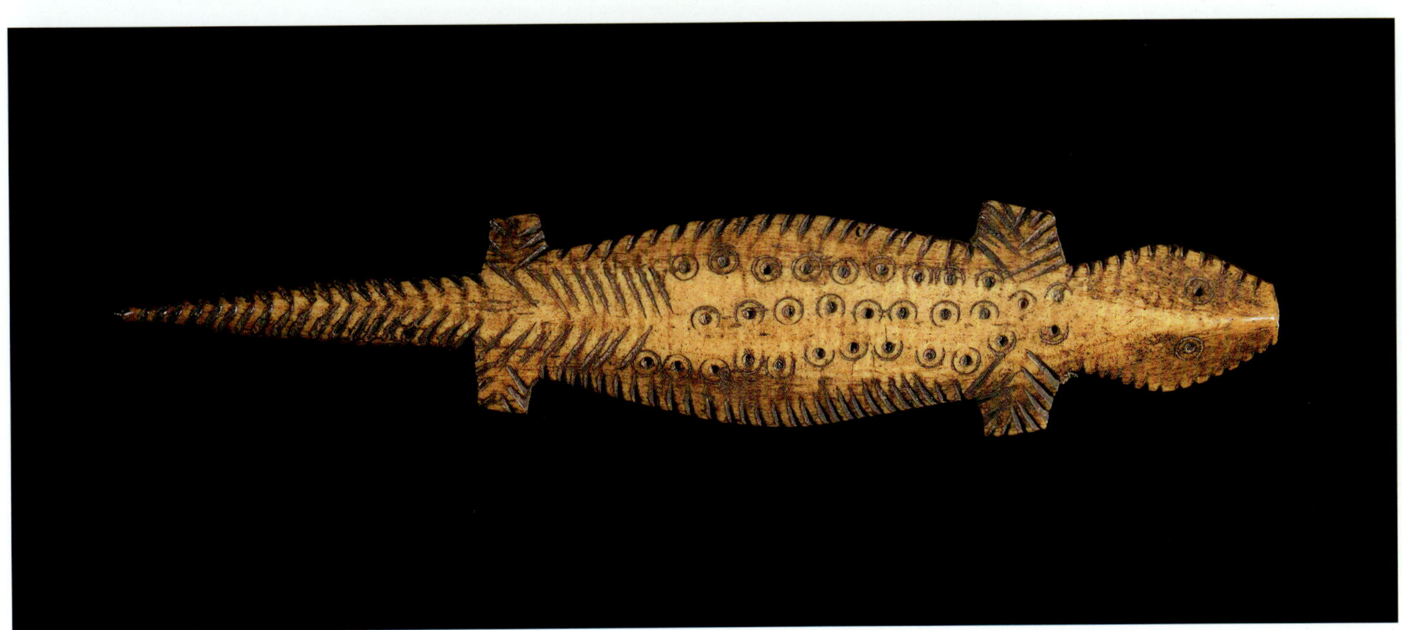

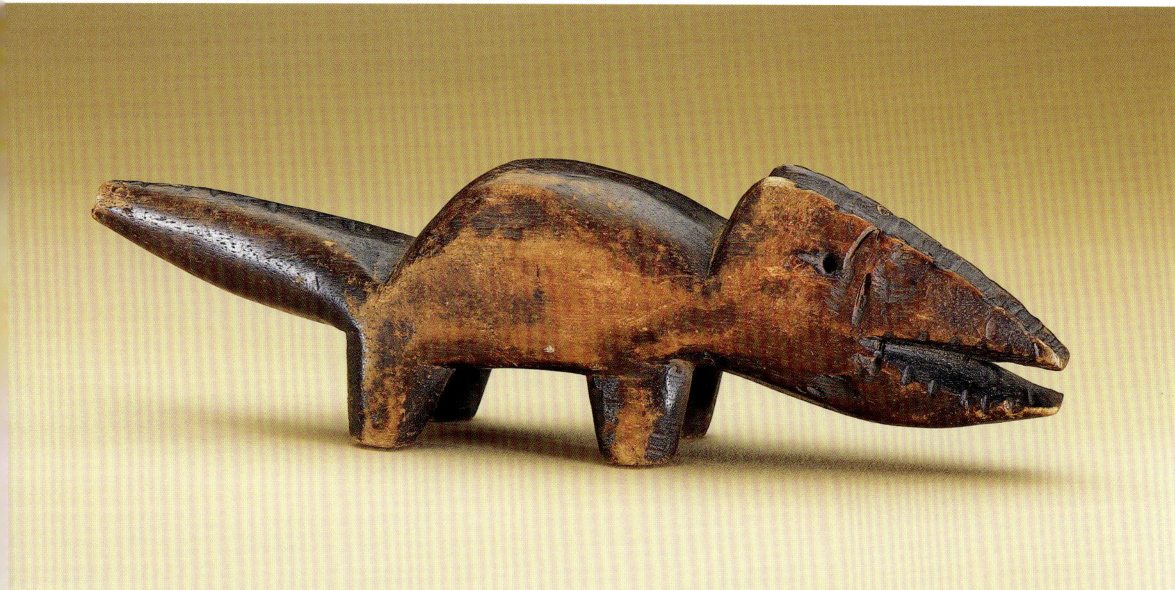

7.5 Generic animal figure. Wood. L: 26.2 cm (10¼ in.).

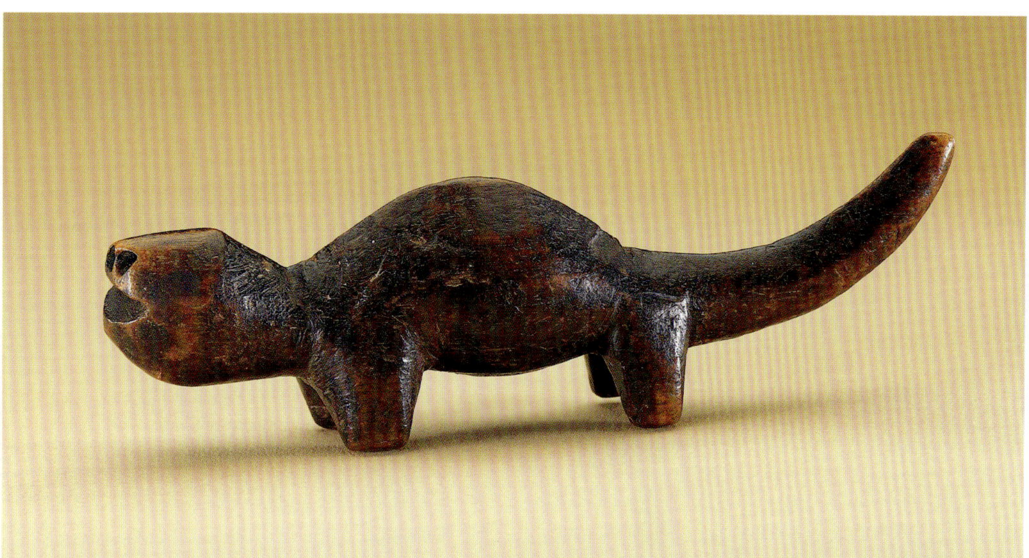

7.6 Generic animal figure. Wood. L: 17 cm (6¾ in.).

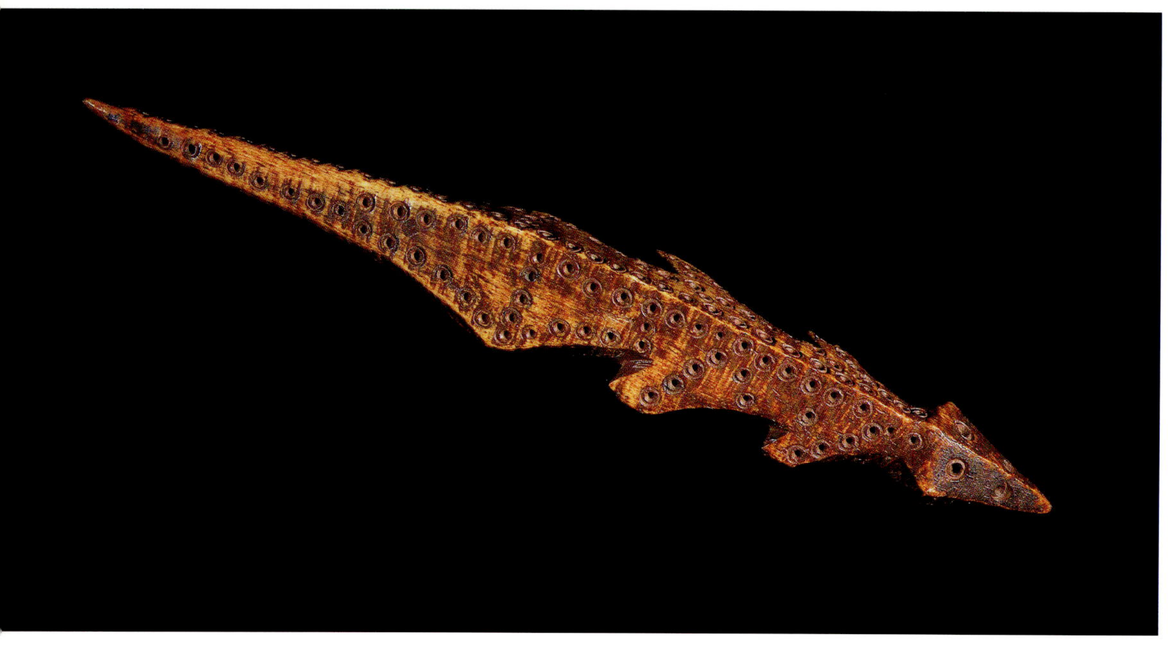

7.7 Generic animal figure. Ivory. L: 27.7 cm (10⅞ in.).

7.8 Generic animal figure. Ivory.
L: 11.2 cm (4⅜ in.).

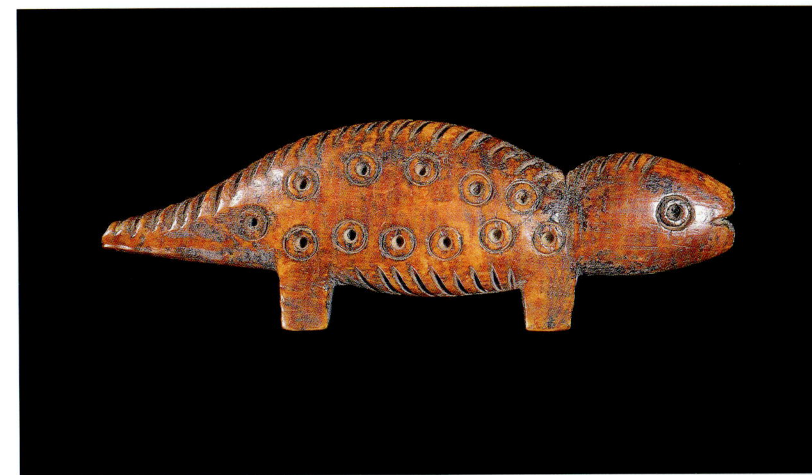

7.9 Generic animal figure. Wood.
L: 33.3 cm (13⅛ in.).

7.10 Generic animal figure. Wood.
L: 35.3 cm (13⅞ in.).

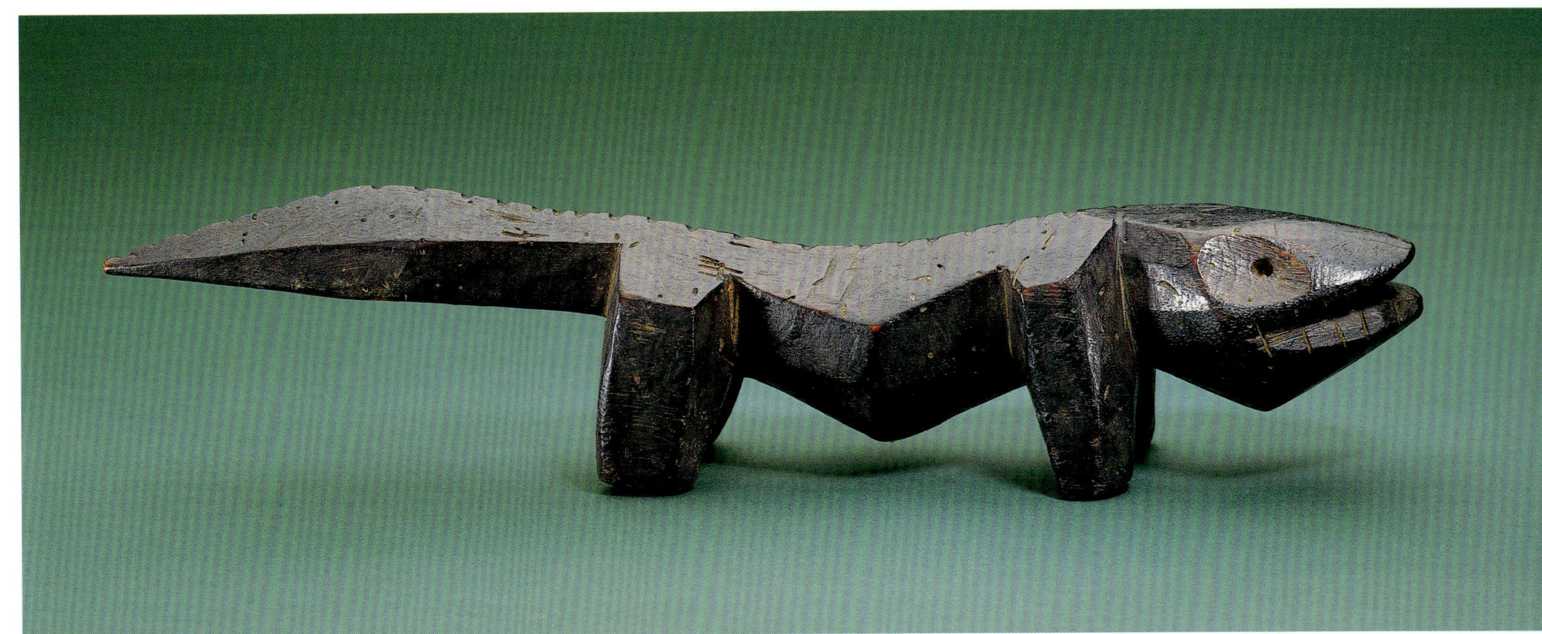

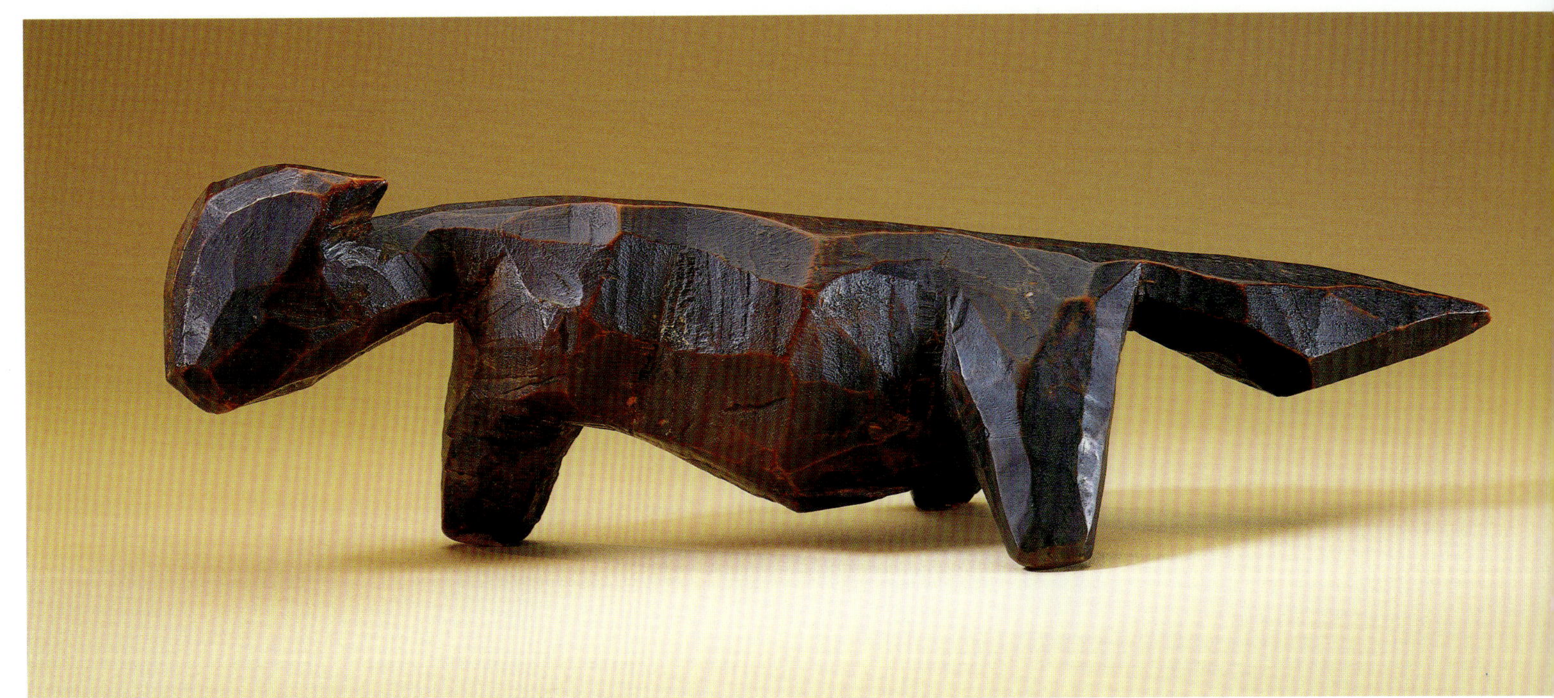

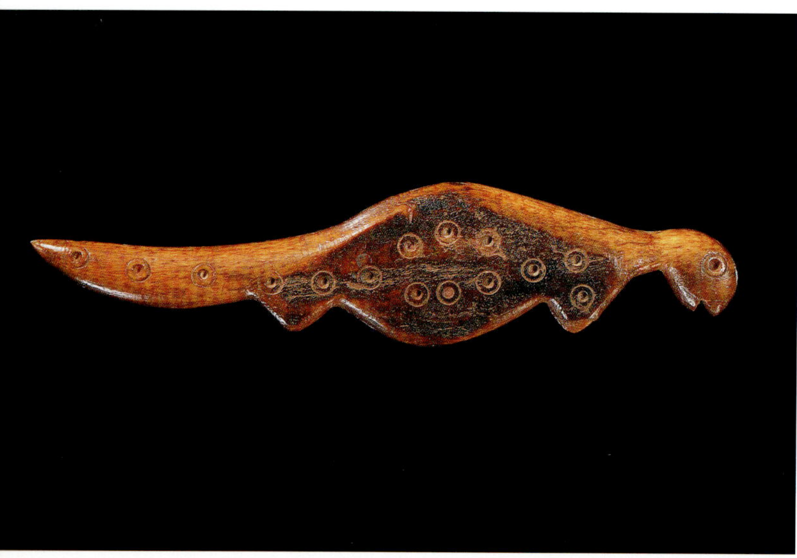

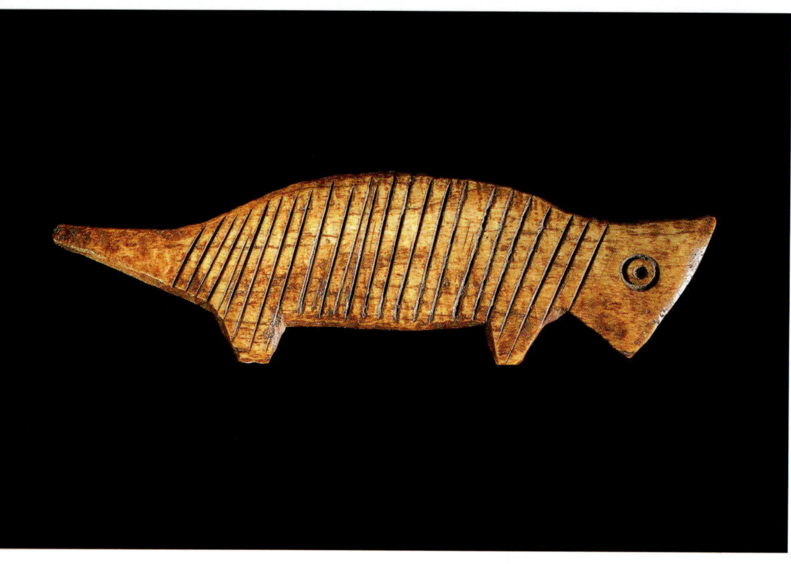

7.11 Animal figure representing a pangolin. Ivory. L: 16 cm (6¼ in.).

7.12 Animal figure representing an aardvark. Ivory. L: 14.3 cm (5⅝ in.).

GIANT PANGOLINS

Daniel Biebuyck identified figure 7.11 as a giant pangolin, or *ikaga* (Biebuyck 1973, pl. 91). The dot-and-circle motif represents the pangolin's scales. According to Lega oral traditions, the pangolin taught the Lega how to put roofs on their houses and is therefore considered a culture hero (Biebuyck 1973, pl. 91). Pangolins are connected with members of Lutumbo lwa Kindi who act as teachers (Biebuyck 1986, 104). Because the Lega consider the pangolin to be sacred, it is not hunted. If a hunter finds a dead pangolin or accidentally kills one, the carcass must be delivered to a member of Kindi who then conducts elaborate purification ceremonies (Biebuyck 1986, 105).

AARDVARKS

This figure (fig. 7.12) has been identified by Biebuyck as the aardvark, or *ntumba* (1973, pl. 93). Pangolins and aardvarks are often used interchangeably in Bwami rites because of their similar tongues and eating habits (Biebuyck 1986, 105). When the sculptures of these animals appear together in layered metaphors, the pangolin is viewed as the the senior animal and the aardvark as its junior (Biebuyck 1973, pl. 93).

SNAKES

> The little child in the wading place, *ngimbi* is death.
>
> Lega Proverb (Biebuyck 1986, 112)

When they appear in Bwami, carvings of snakes (*ngimbi*) warn everyone to remember the potency and danger of initiation objects (figs. 7.13, 7.14). Notice the artist's imaginative use of a dot-and-circle motif to suggest a face on the snake in figure 7.13.

TORTOISES

The Lega admire tortoises (*nkulu* or *kikulu*) because of their slow, careful movements and also consider them to be intelligent (fig. 7.15). In performance tortoises are represented by a carved figure, as seen here, or by a tortoise shell (see fig. 6.8). They symbolize wise, old high-level members of Bwami (Biebuyck 1986, 117).

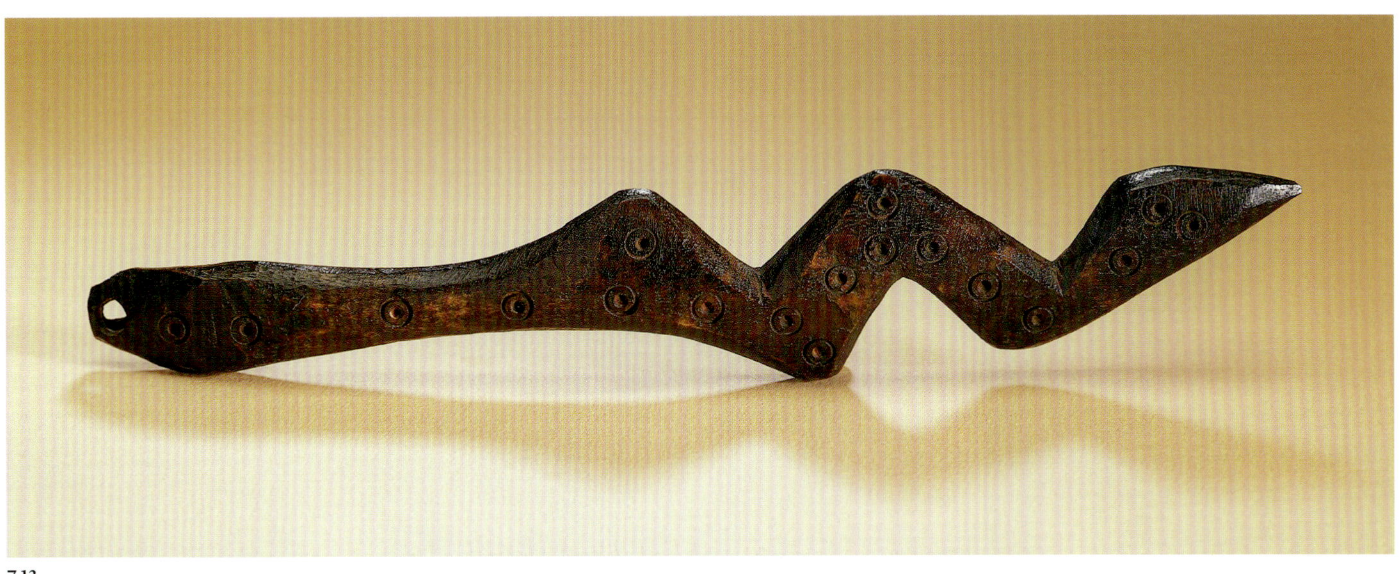

7.13

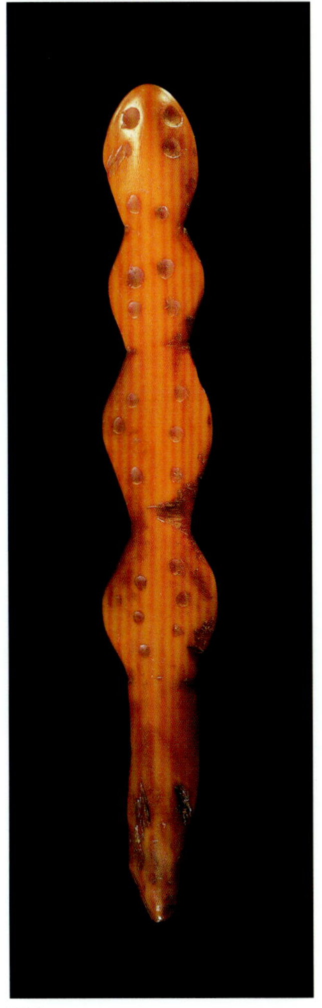

7.14

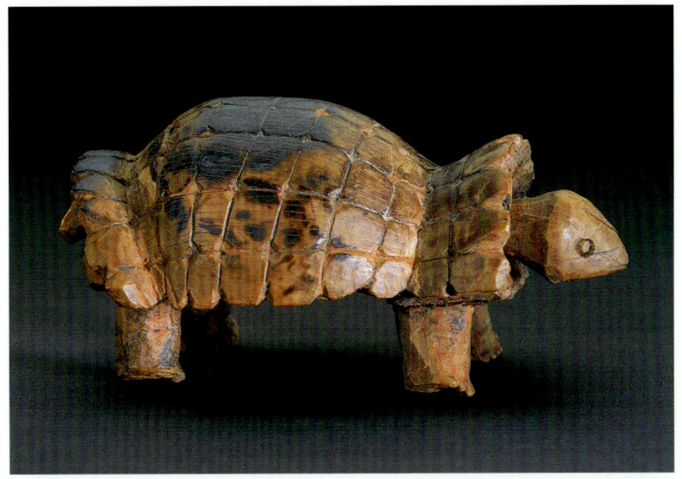

7.15

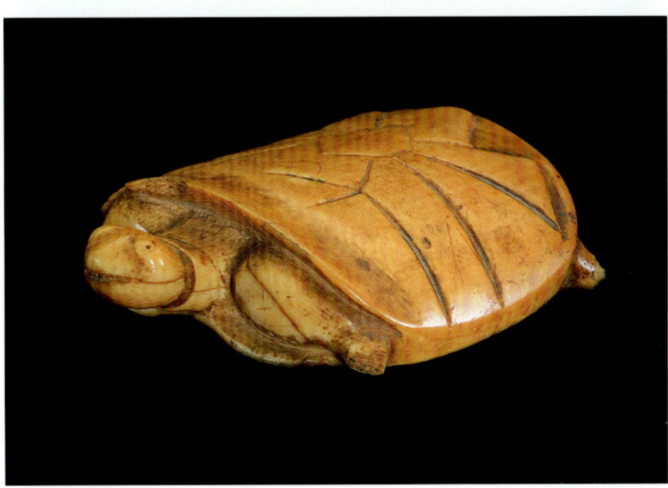

7.16

7.13 Animal figure representing a snake. Ivory. L: 20.4 cm (8 in.).

7.14 Animal figure representing a snake. Ivory. L: 12.3 cm (4⅞ in.).

7.15 Animal figure representing a tortoise. Wood. L: 14.7 cm (5¾ in.).

7.16 Animal figure representing a turtle. Ivory. L: 11 cm (4⅜ in.).

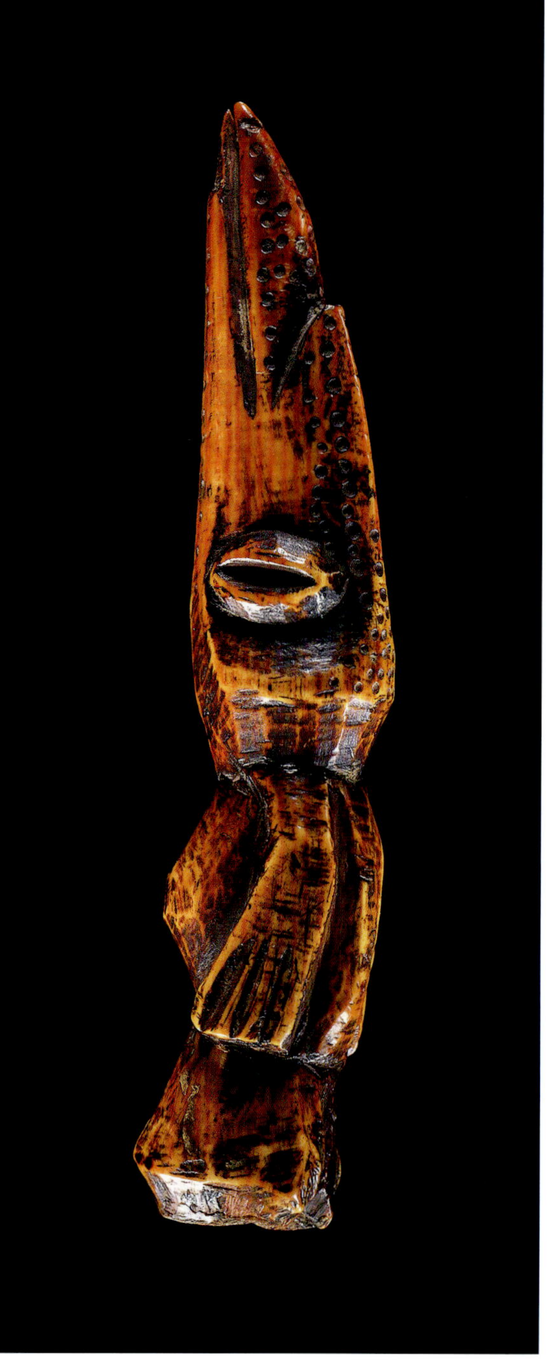

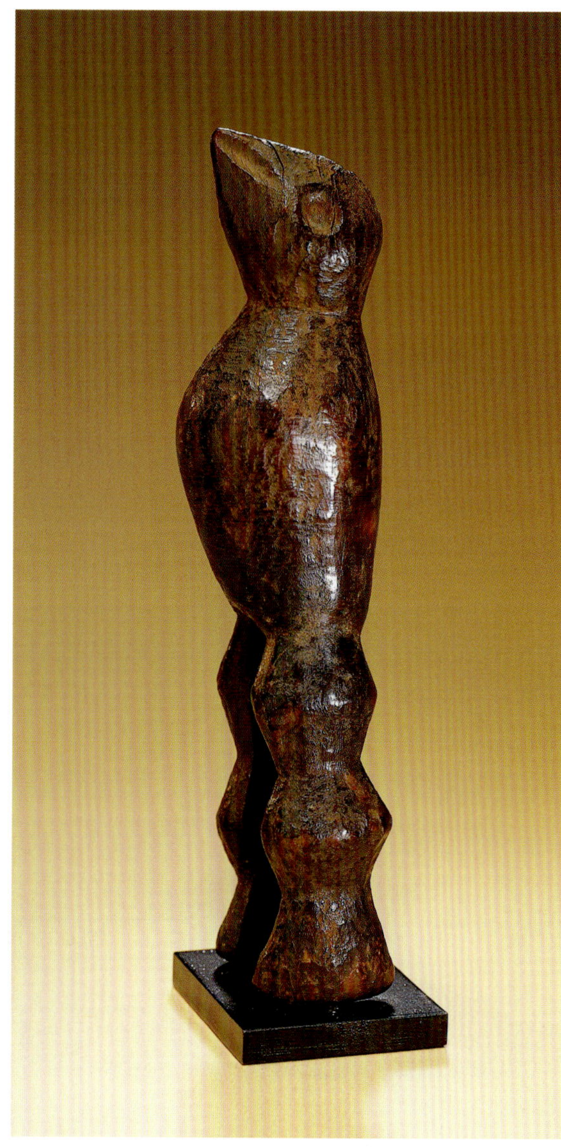

7.17 Animal figure representing a bird. Ivory. H: 18.9 cm (7⅜ in.).

7.18 Animal figure representing a bird. Ivory. H: 14.5 cm (5⅜ in.).

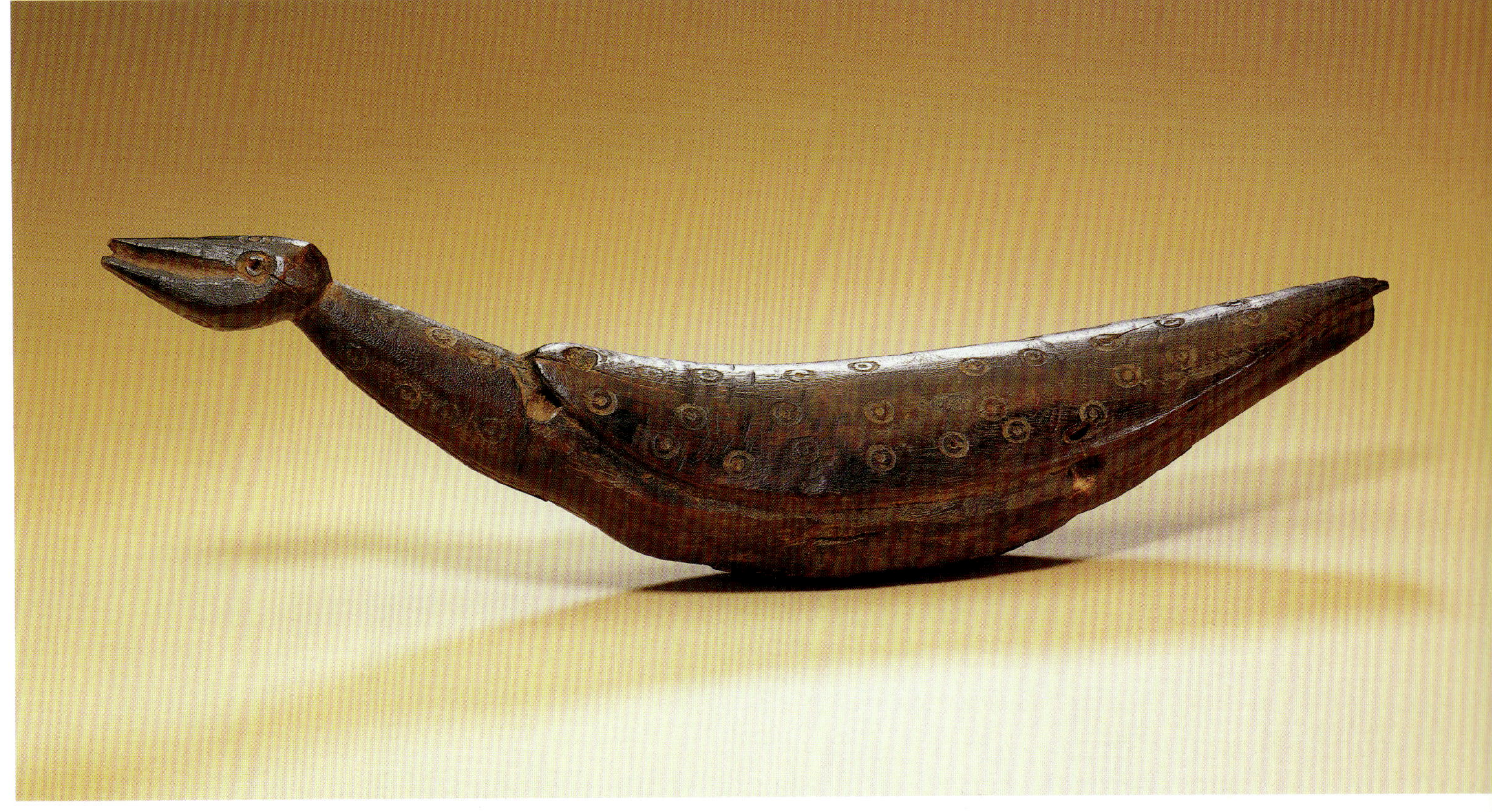

7.19 Animal figure representing a bird. Wood. L: 25.7 cm (10⅛ in.).

BIRDS

Birds can refer to success or failure within Bwami (figs. 7.17–7.19). The most senior member of Kindi may be called the "bird that sings for termites." The arrogant candidate who will not succeed is called the "bird that talked too much" (Biebuyck 1986, 118–20).

ANIMAL FIGURES COVERED WITH SKIN

The Lega sometimes attach an identifying feature from one animal to a generic four-legged figure in order to make a specific reference. The animals shown in figures 7.20–7.22 are covered with reptile skin, perhaps referring to iguanas or crocodiles.

ANIMAL FIGURES WITH A HUMAN FACE OR MASK

Rarely do the Lega combine human and animal features (figs. 7.23, 7.24). When they do occur, these combination figures belong to members of Yananio or Kindi (Biebuyck 1986, 104).

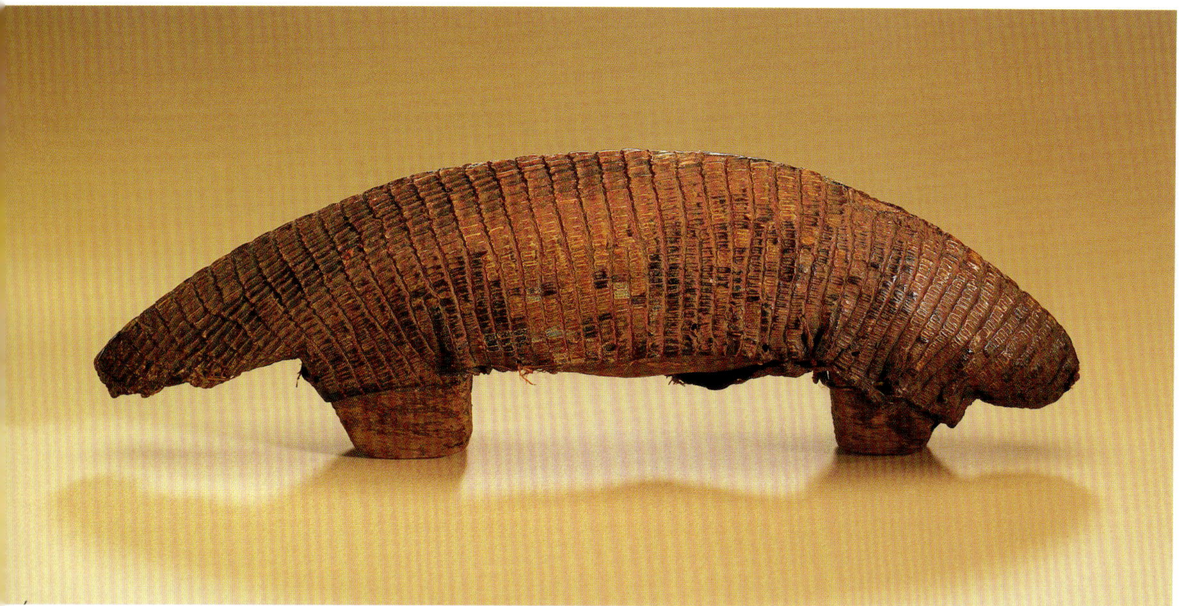

7.20 Animal figure.
Wood, animal skin, and fiber.
L: 19.2 cm (7⅝ in.).

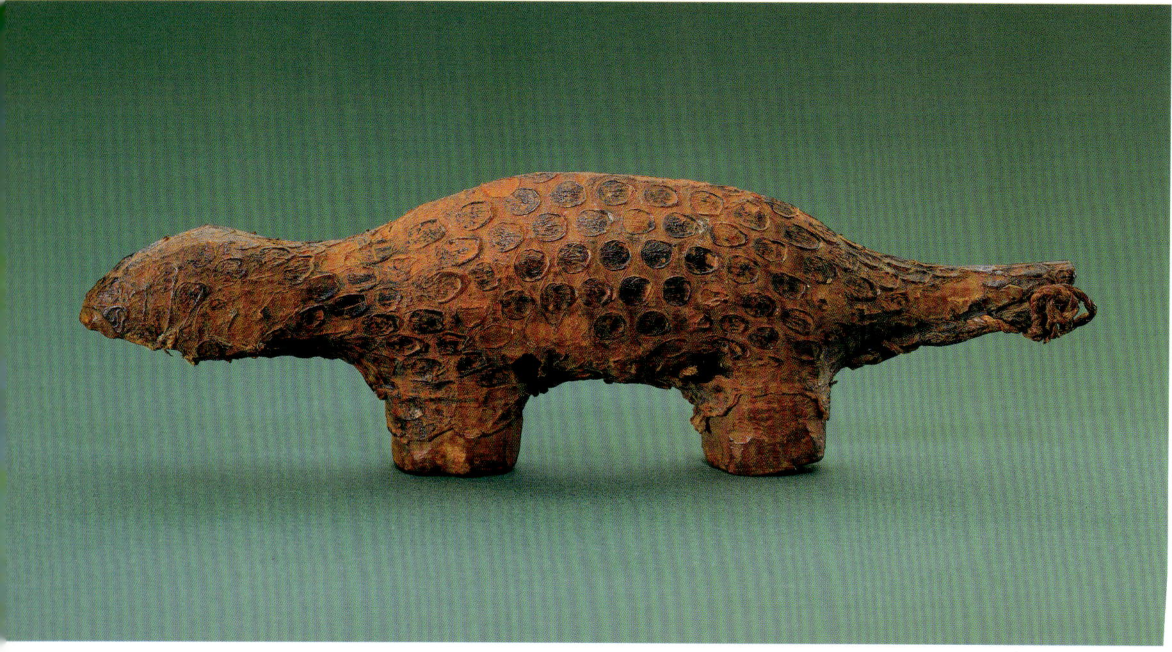

7.21 Animal figure.
Wood, animal skin, and fiber.
L: 17.5 cm (6⅞ in.).

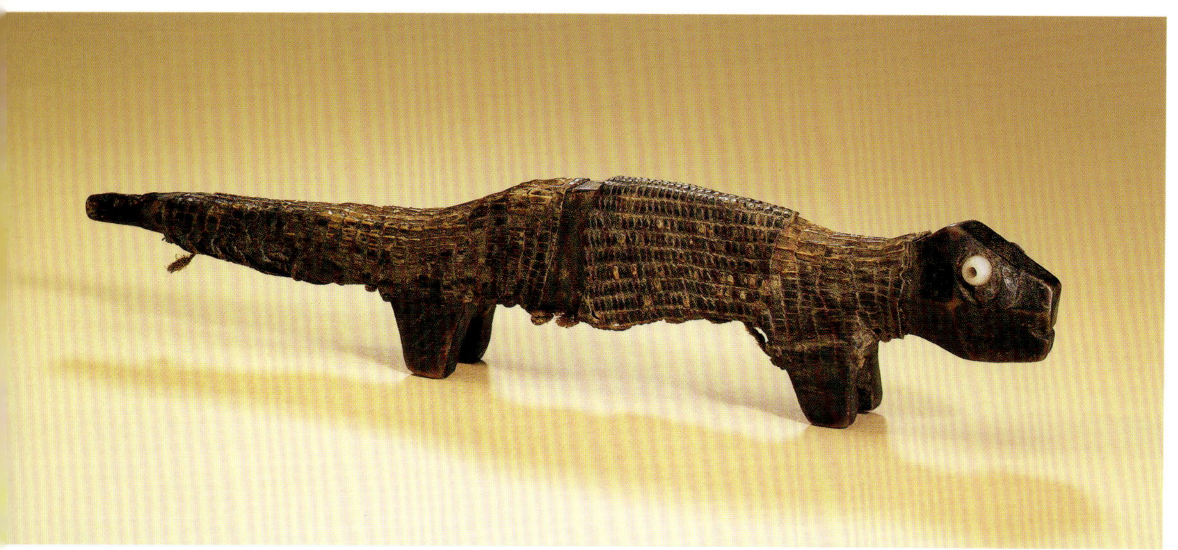

7.22 Animal figure.
Wood, animal skin, fiber, and beads. L: 17.5 cm (6⅞ in.).

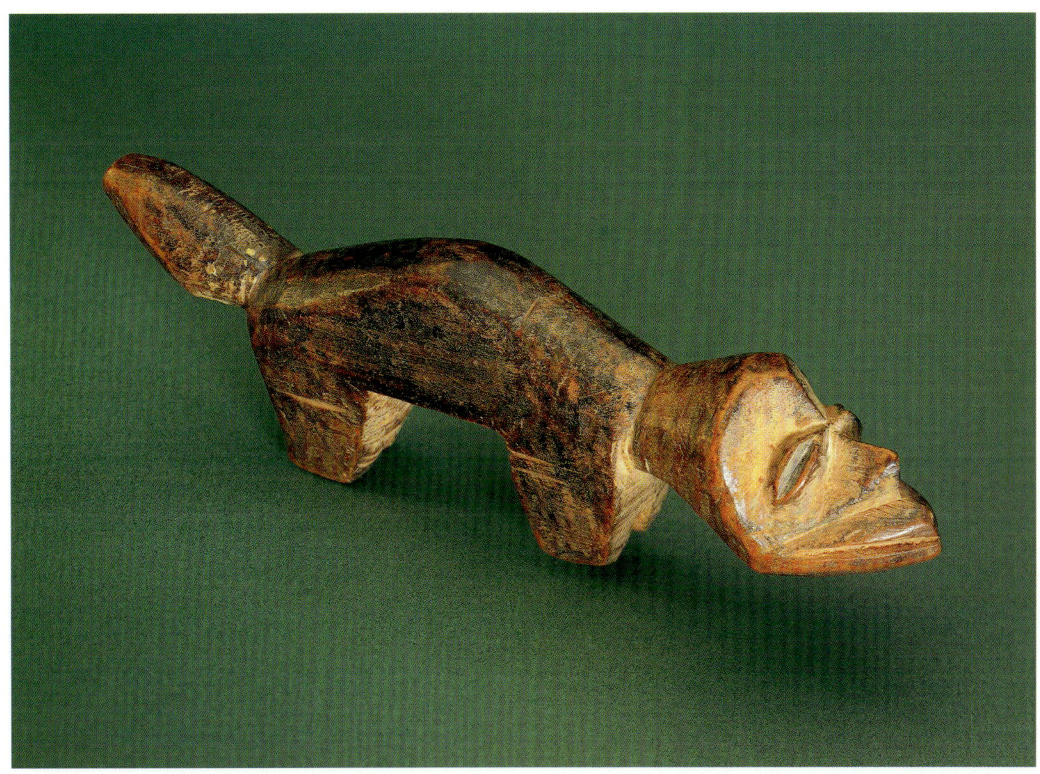

7.23 Animal figure with human face or mask. Wood. L: 13.3 cm (5¼ in.).

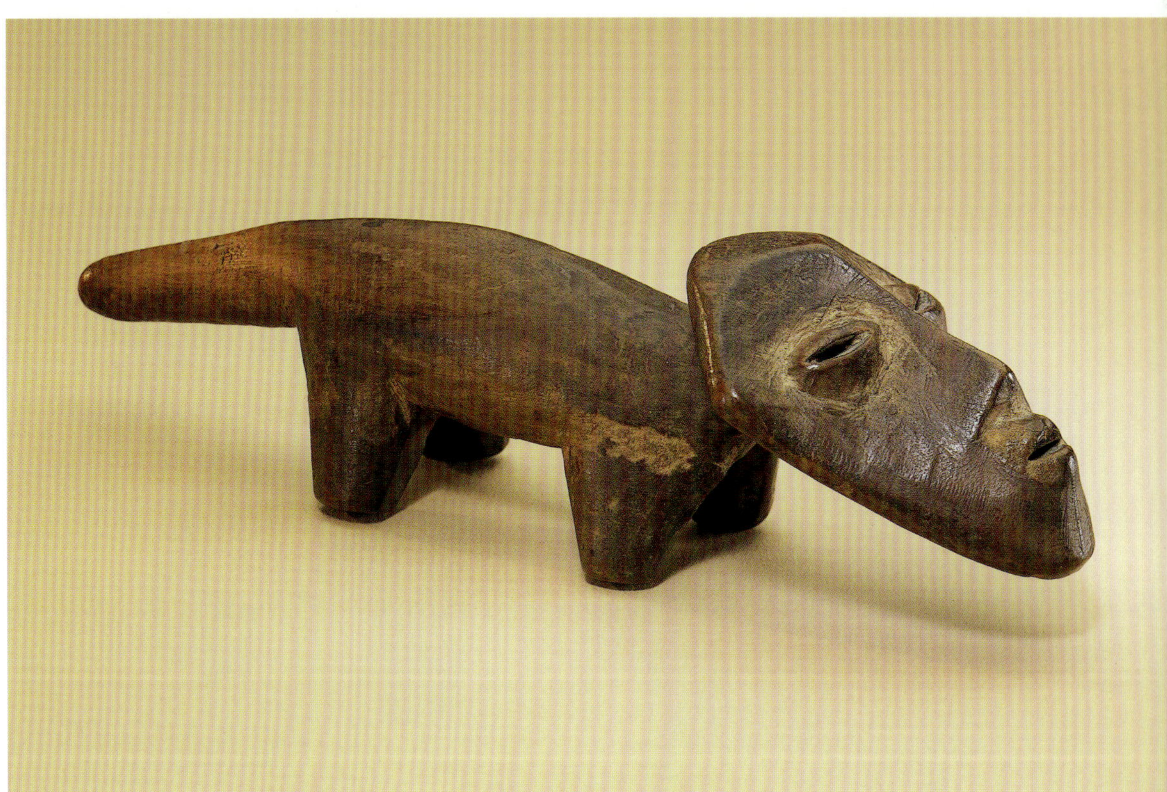

7.24 Animal figure with human face or mask. Wood. L: 19.5 cm (7⅝ in.).

8 Human Figures

CATEGORIZATION OF HUMAN FIGURES
Lacking a knowledge of Bwami, art historians specializing in African subject matter and collectors from Europe and the Americas took the rich visual vocabulary of Lega art and reduced it to categories based simply on form and material. The anthropomorphic figure was thus subdivided into works in wood and ivory. Works within this category were also classed as full figures, heads, figures with raised arms, figures with one arm raised, and so forth.

The Lega, however, use completely different criteria to categorize their art. They do not conflate all anthropomorphic figures and thus lack a single word to describe them (Biebuyck 1986, 51–52). Furthermore, they use full figures and heads interchangeably. Some individual figures can be given specific, often unique, names and meanings. If a piece is taken out of the Lega context without the name and meaning being recorded, it is impossible to recover that information. The small wooden figures (figs. 8.1–8.13), busts (figs. 8.14–8.24), and ivory figures (figs 8.25–8.55)

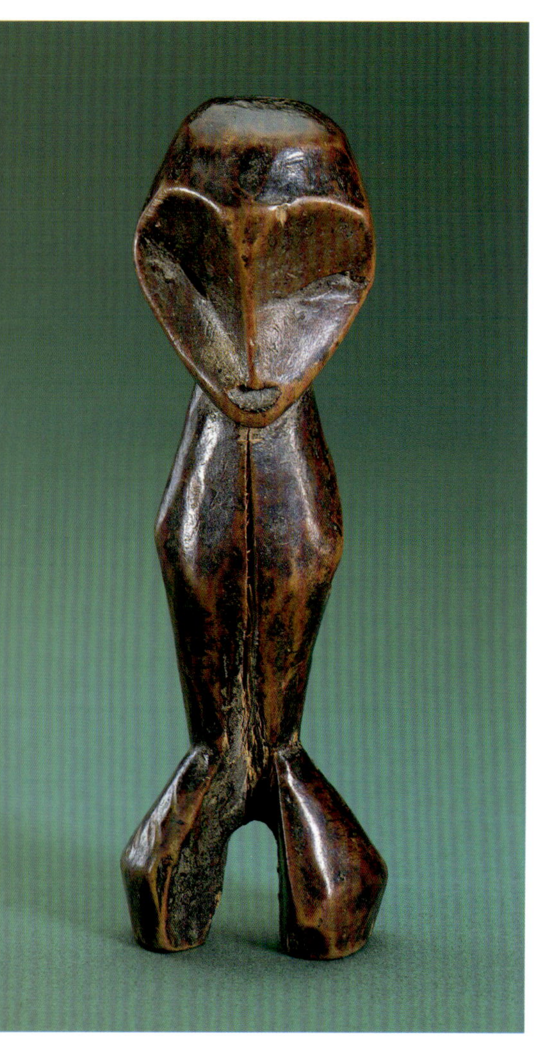

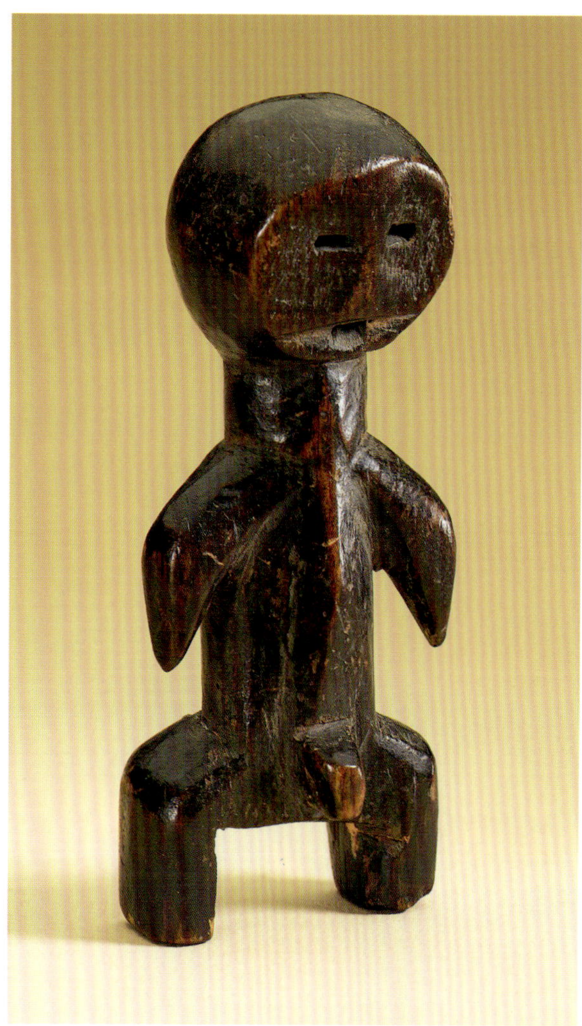

8.1 Human figure.
Wood. H: 12.7 cm (5 in.).

8.2 Human figure.
Wood. H: 12.1 cm (4¾ in.).

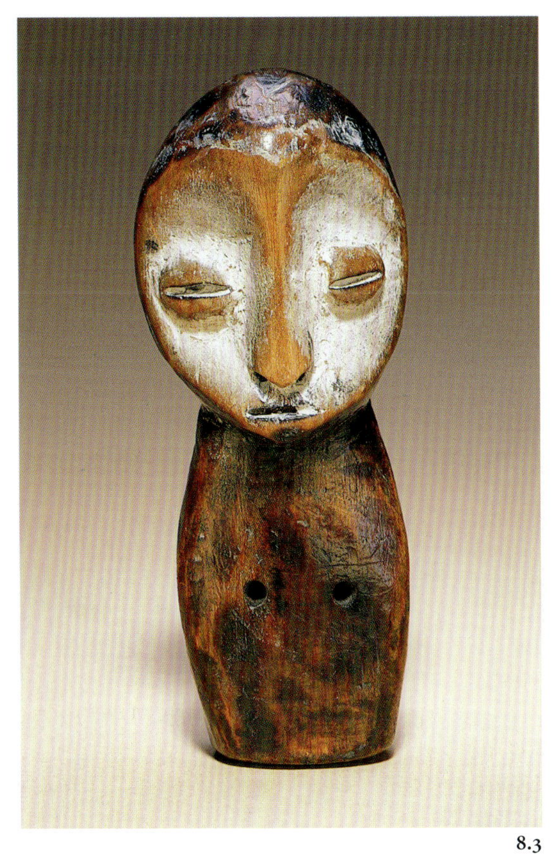

8.3

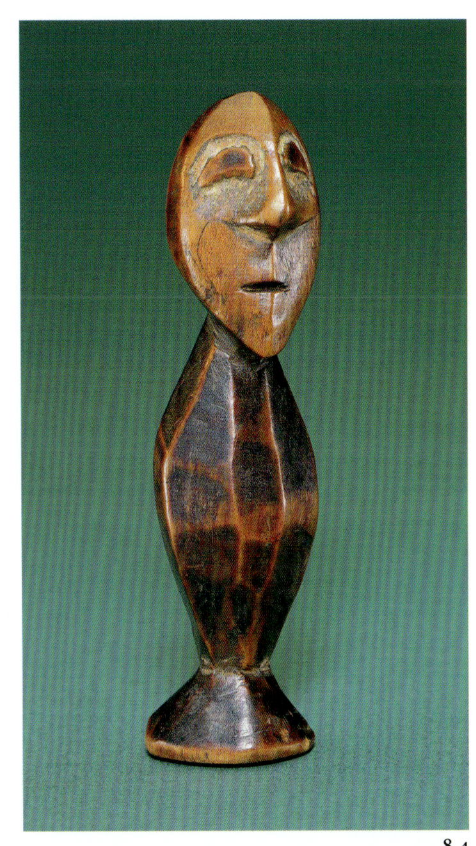

8.4

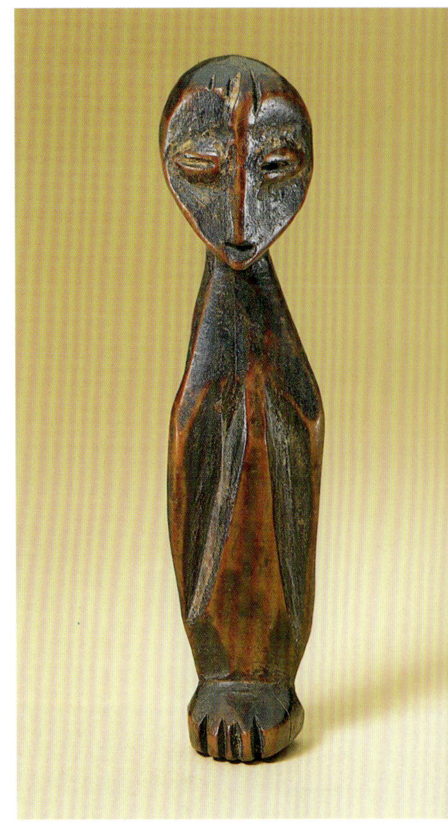

8.5

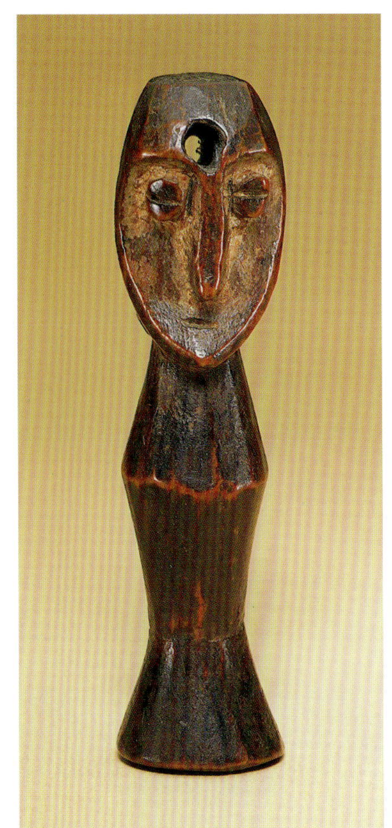

8.6

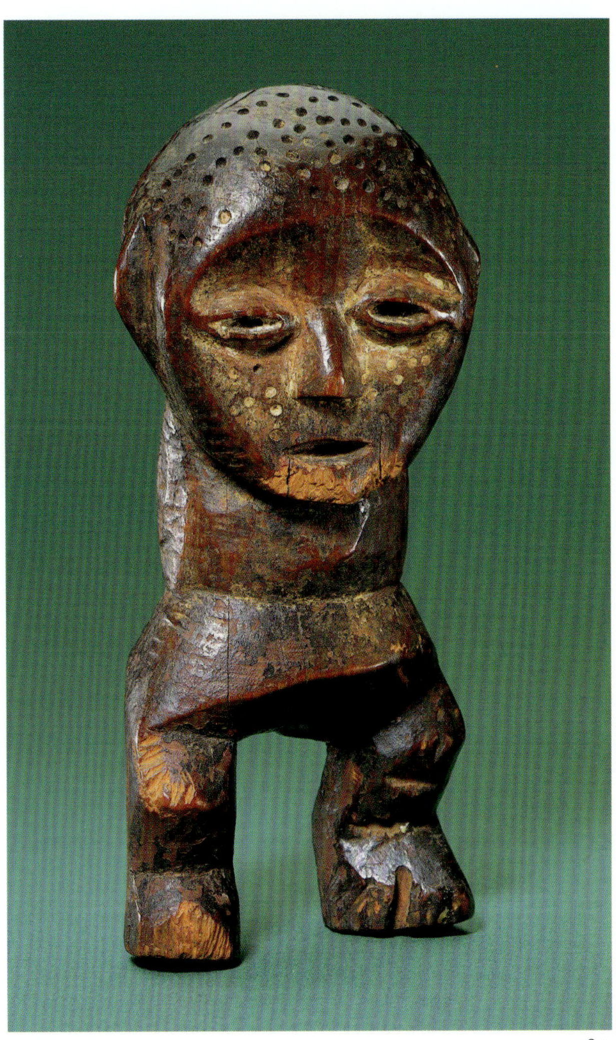

8.7

8.3 Human figure. Wood and pigment. H: 9.6 cm (3¾ in.).

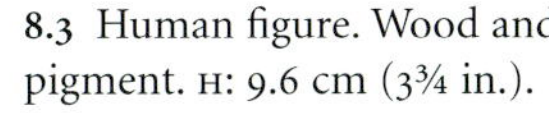

8.4 Human figure. Wood. H: 8.3 cm (3¼ in.).

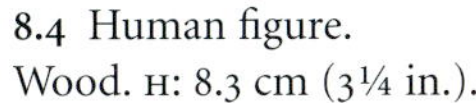

8.5 Human figure. Wood. H: 9.9 cm (3⅞ in.).

8.6 Human figure. Wood. H: 10.1 cm (3⅞ in.).

8.7 Human figure. Wood. H: 16.9 cm (6⅝ in.).

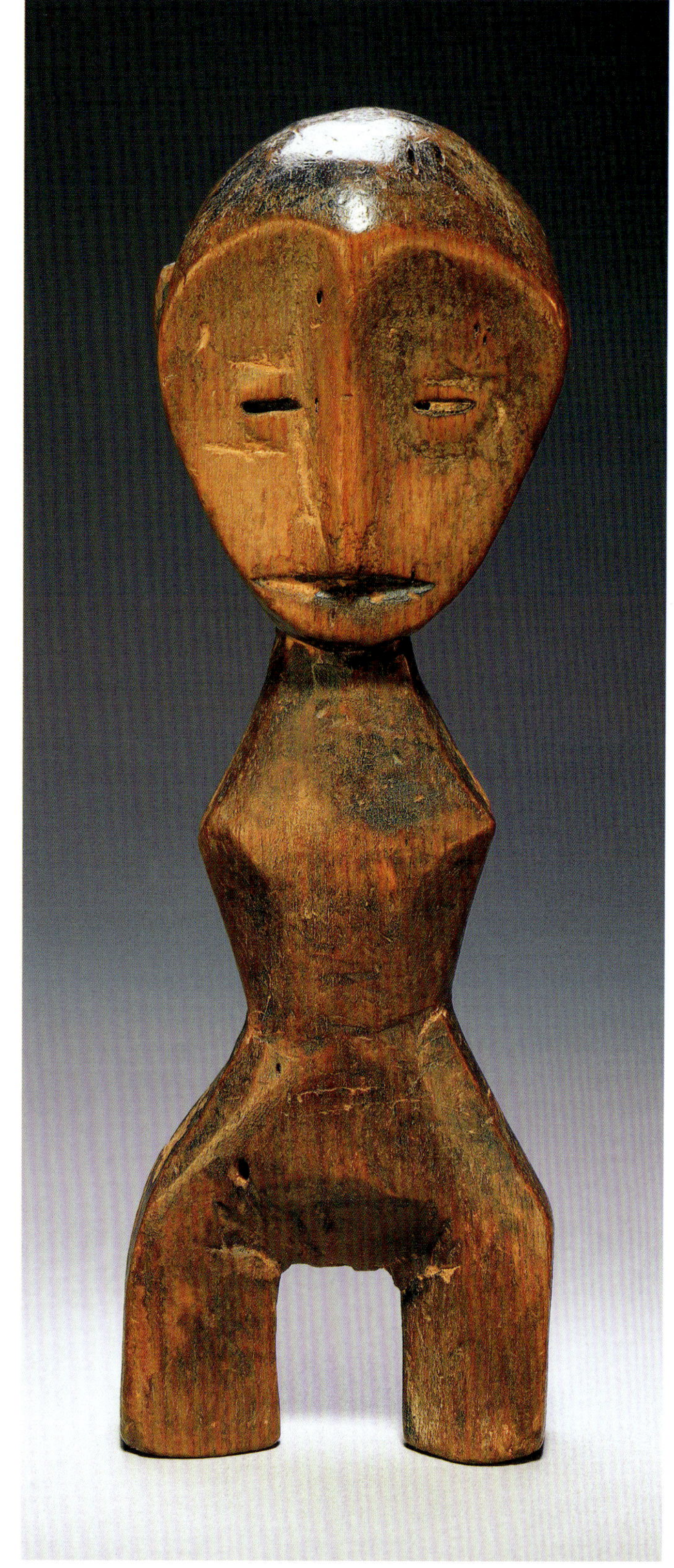

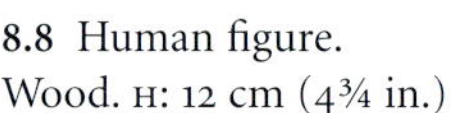

8.8 Human figure.
Wood. H: 12 cm (4¾ in.).

8.9 Human figure.
Wood. H: 23.4 cm (9⅜ in.).

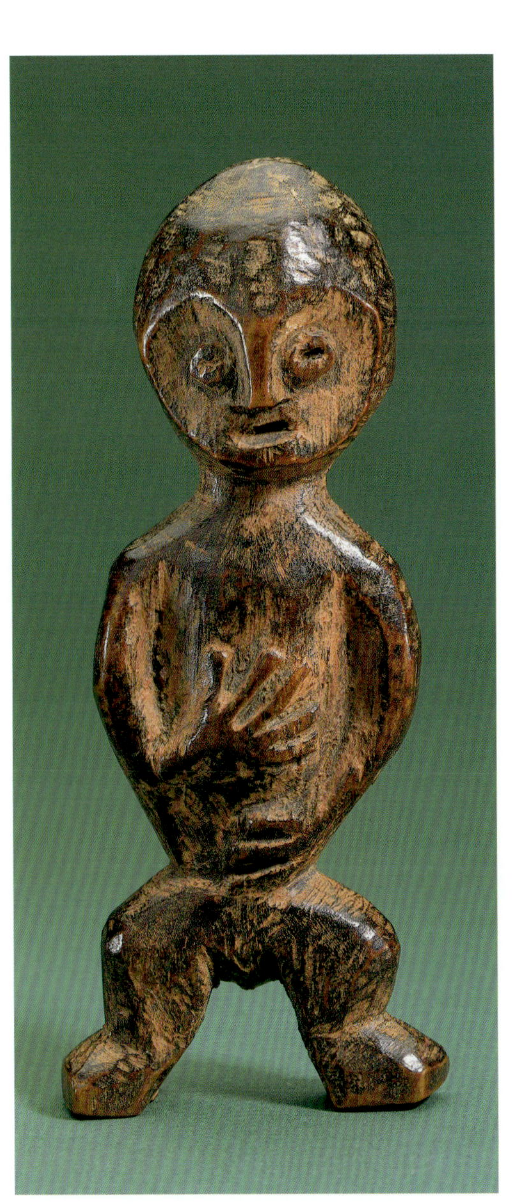

8.10 Human figure.
Wood. H: 14.8 cm (5⅞ in.).

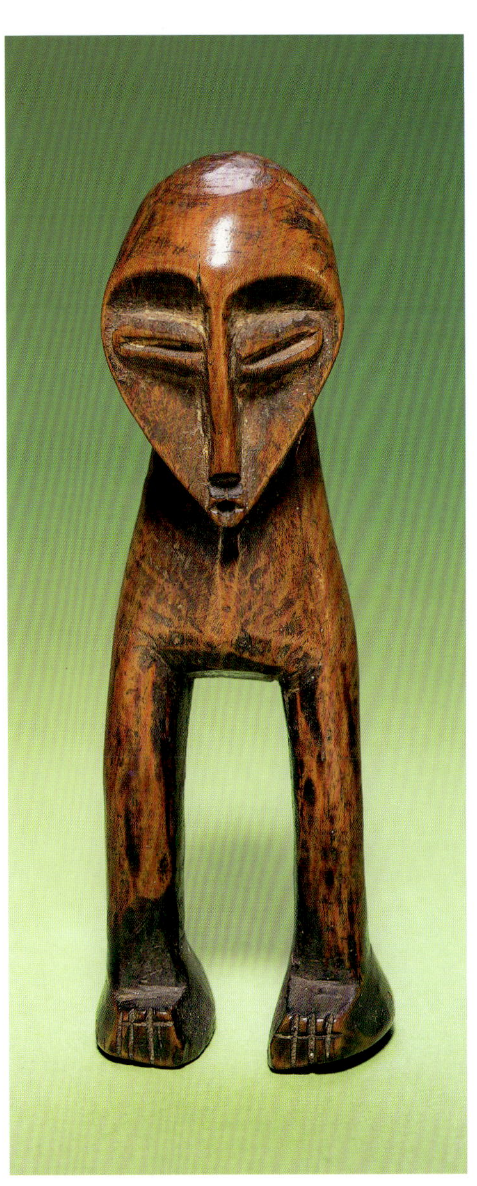

8.11 Human figure.
Wood. H: 13.8 cm (5⅝ in.).

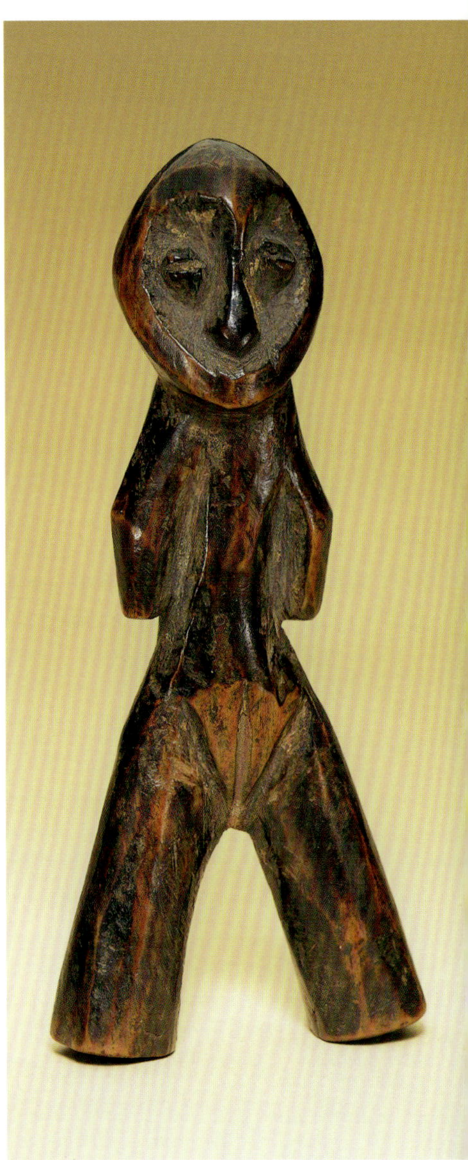

8.12 Human figure.
Wood. H: 13.7 cm (5⅜ in.).

8.13 Human bust. Wood and pigment. H: 21.5 cm (8½ in.).

8.14 Human bust. Ivory. H: 13.9 cm (5½ in.).

8.15 Human bust. Ivory. H: 10 cm (3⅞ in.).

8.16 Human bust. Ivory. H: 10.2 cm (4 in.).

8.17 Human bust. Ivory. H: 11 cm (4⅞ in.).

illustrated in this chapter are thus impossible to identify precisely because their original context is unknown. Exceptions to this rule occur with anthropomorphic figures that have a common meaning expressed through specific poses or physical characteristics, for example, a figure with one or both arms raised (see figs. 8.90–8.92) or a pregnant woman (see figs. 8.81, 8.82).

Daniel Biebuyck acquired the only figures that I am aware of in Western collections for which identifying information was gathered firsthand from their Lega owners.[1] He illustrates the pieces and gives their names and meanings in *Lega Culture* (1973, pls. 64–65, 70, 72, 75). Some scholars have compared similar artworks and used Biebuyck's illustrations and detailed collection information to conclude that the pieces they were examining have the same name and meaning. While attractive, this method is implausible because each piece described by Biebuyck is unique in terms of its nomenclature and significance.

Wood and ivory figures show the greatest range of form in Lega art. One explanation for this might be found in the process by which a figure was commissioned.[2] A Bwami member in need of a figure approached an artist, specifying minimal requirements: material (wood, bone, or ivory) and a brief description (male, female, size, and general position, e.g., both arms raised). As a result the artist had great freedom in carving the work while rarely knowing its intended use. The Bwami member collected the piece, and, as it was dedicated by use, it took its place within defined categories and was often given a specific name and meaning (Biebuyck 1994, 56). Teachers owned some figures as signs of their reputation, or they may also have inherited pieces that demonstrated a link with the past. As these works have no distinguishing attributes, we cannot identify them (Biebuyck 1994, 58).

The finished anthropomorphic figure within the Bwami context is likened to the initiate's body—washed, shining, and proud (Biebuyck 1986, 96–97). Most figures exhibit the desired physical qualities of the Lega man: large forehead, shaved head with a cap (*bwami*) marking membership in Bwami, and straight posture (Biebuyck 1986, 64). To strengthen this comparison, a piece is removed from the Bwami basket and cleaned, oiled, and, where appropriate, rubbed with white or red powder before it is used. These actions duplicate those of the initiate preparing him or herself for the ceremonies. Figures might also display the "aesthetic of the ugly" to illustrate negative traits or what is to be avoided. An example of a cautionary figure is Wayinda, a woman who, while she is pregnant, commits adultery and brings ruin to her family (see figs. 8.81, 8.82). She is usually crudely carved with prominent genitalia and a distended stomach (Biebuyck 1973, pl. 67, 68).

Bwami members of Yananio or Kindi levels can individually or collectively own anthropomorphic figures, depending on the identity of the piece. All figures, however, are initiation objects and share certain characteristics: they appear in layered metaphors; they present positive and negative role models within the Bwami ethical system (Biebuyck 1986, 61); they are only viewed during Bwami initiations. Therefore, noninitiates or Bwami members of lower ranks do not see or theoretically know about the existence of the pieces (Biebuyck 1986, 58–60).

The Lega divide figures into several categories that might contain other art forms. Some anthropomorphic figures are *kalimbangoma*, a category that includes small zoomorphic figures, miniature sculptures, and assemblages of other objects (Biebuyck 1986, 52). Larger anthropomorphic pieces in this category tend to be owned by members of higher ranks. Each member of Musagi wa Kindi, a lower sublevel of the highest Bwami rank, owns a bone or ivory human figure from the *kalimbangoma* category as a sign of his status. This figure is placed in the care of its owner's high-level Bwami wife. She is responsible for bringing it to initiations and sometimes for preparing it with oil (Biebuyck 1986, 98). With the object comes the saying "Nyaminia [Mrs. Black] my good and beautiful one, every man has his good and beautiful one," which refers to the function of this figure as an insignia but also implies that a person must rely on other people and cannot live alone (Biebuyck 1973, pl. 79).

Bwami members in the higher ranks of Yananio or the lower ranks of Kindi own ivory *kalimbangoma* figures. They also may belong to women of the highest ranks (Biebuyck 1994, 82). These items are occasionally displayed at the center of an assemblage of other initiation objects to show that no one reaches these levels of Bwami alone. Everyone has a teacher, wife, sponsor, or kinsman who plays an active role in his or her ascension to Yananio and Kindi (Biebuyck 1994, 82).

A second category of anthropomorphic figures, carved mainly in ivory, is called *iginga* (pl. *maginga*).[3] These figures are individually owned by the highest-ranking members of Bwami and are the most coveted of all initiation objects

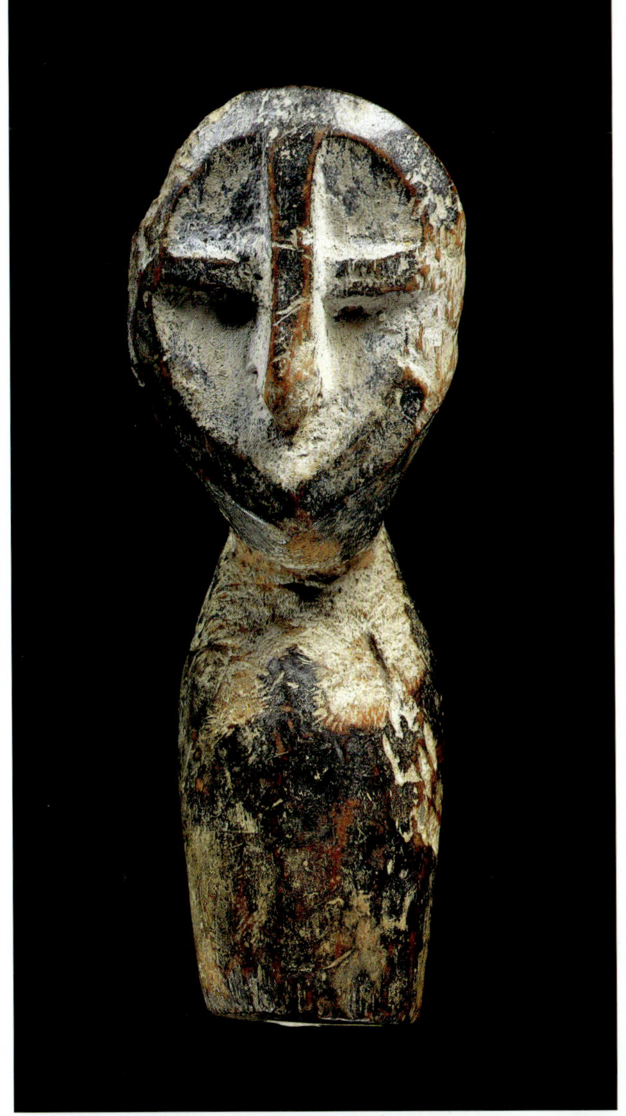

8.13

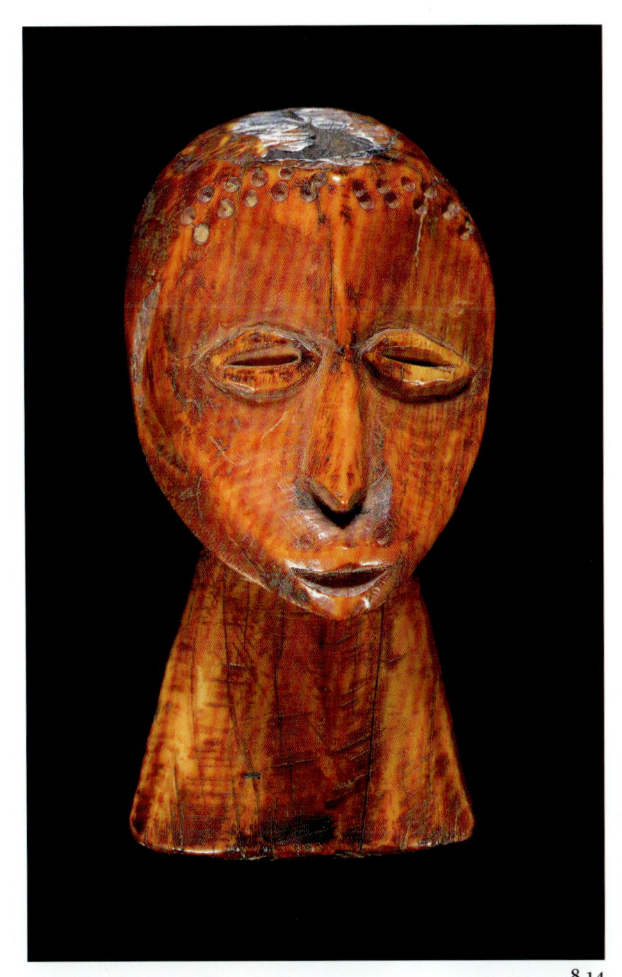

8.14

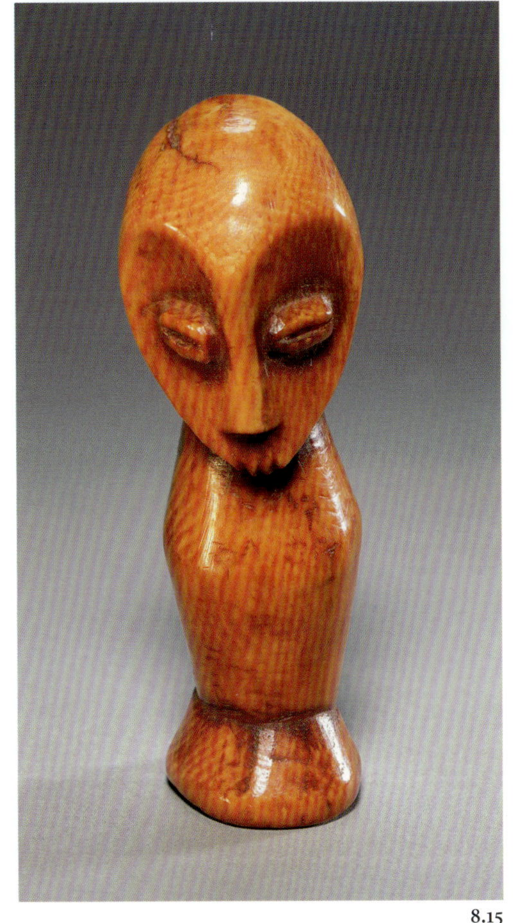

8.15

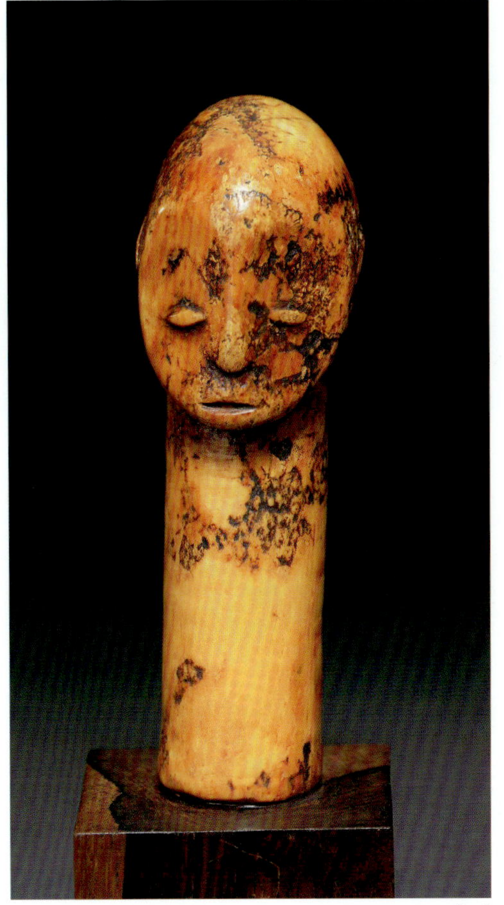

8.16

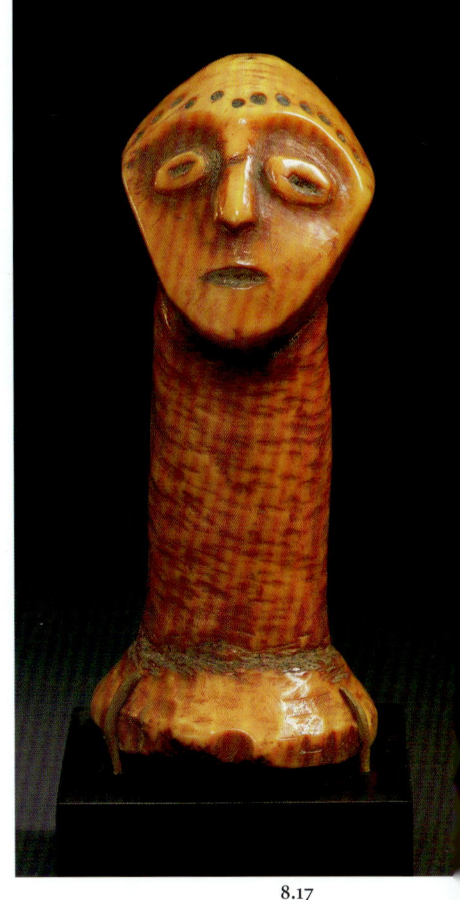

8.17

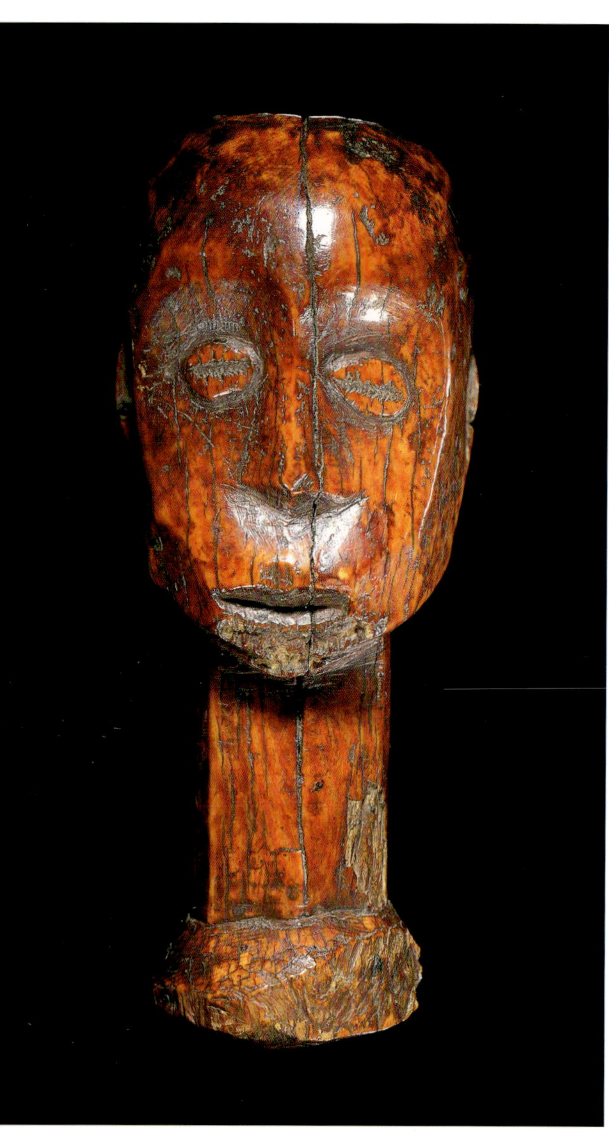

8.18 Human bust.
Ivory. H: 17.5 cm (6⅞ in.).

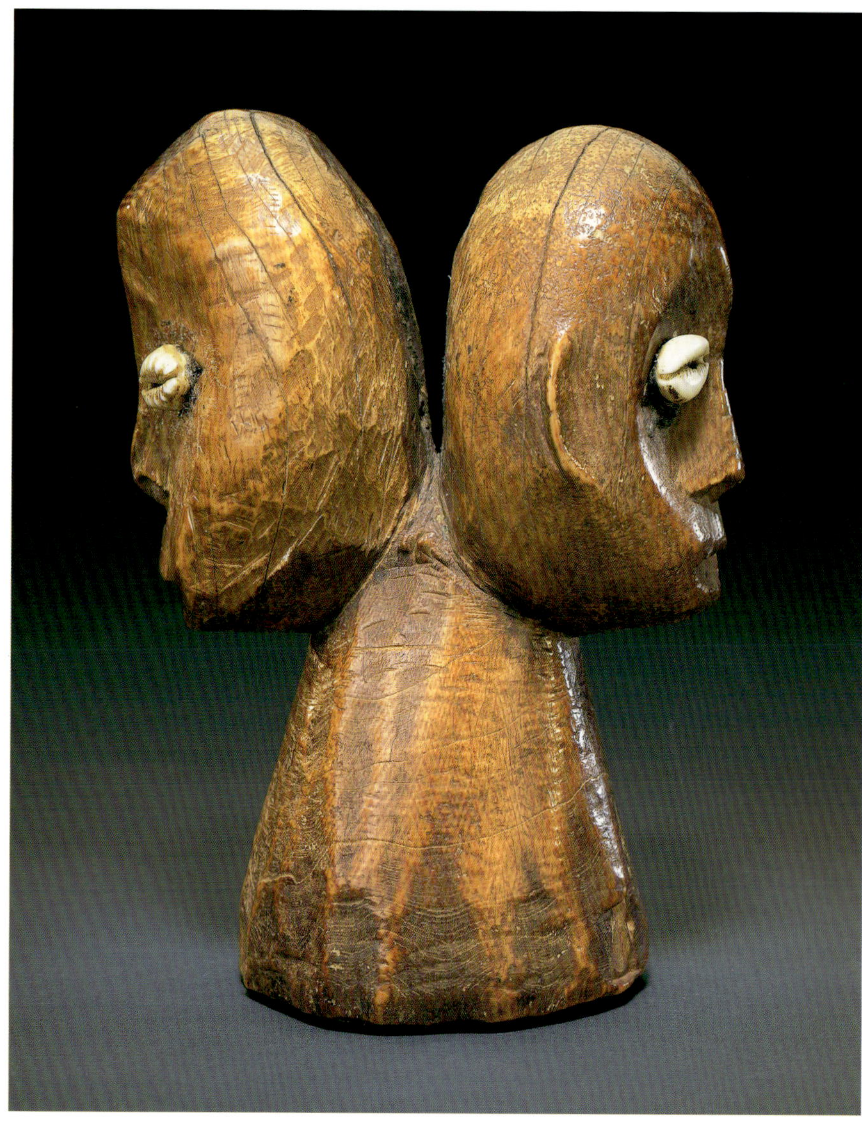

8.19 Human bust. Ivory and cowrie shells. H: 16.6 cm (6½ in.).

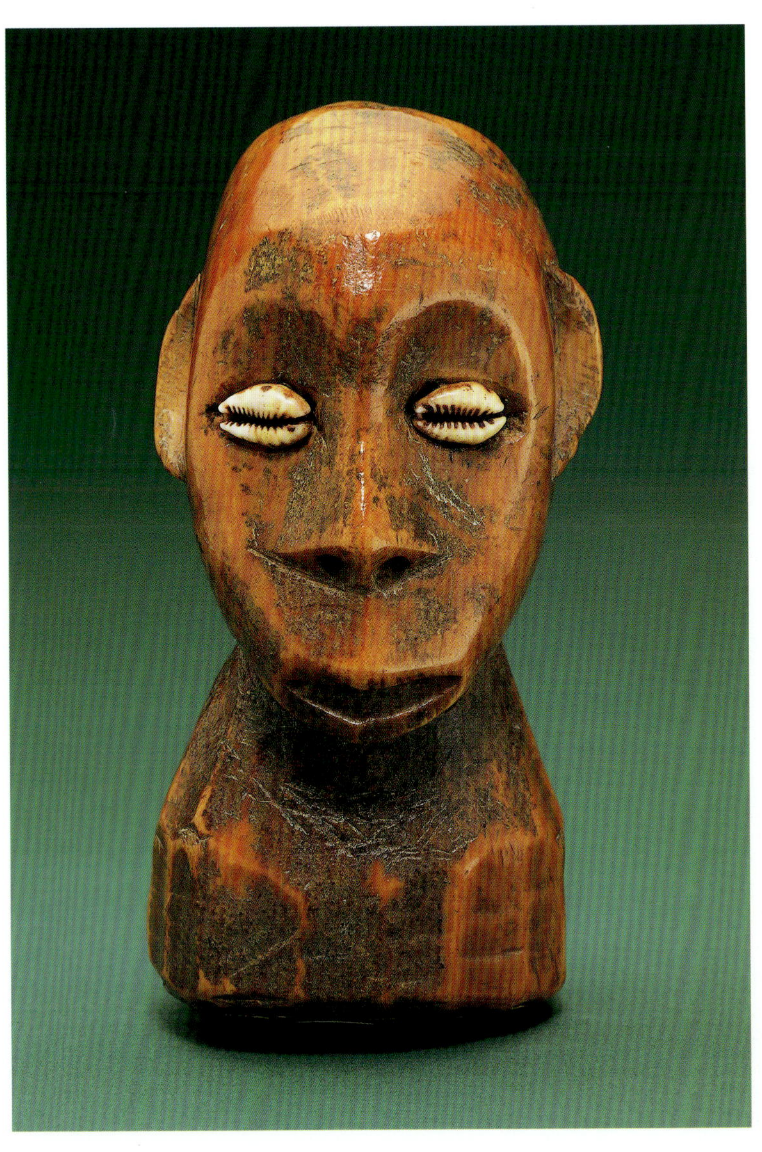

8.20 Human bust. Ivory and cowrie shells. H: 15.2 cm (6 in.).

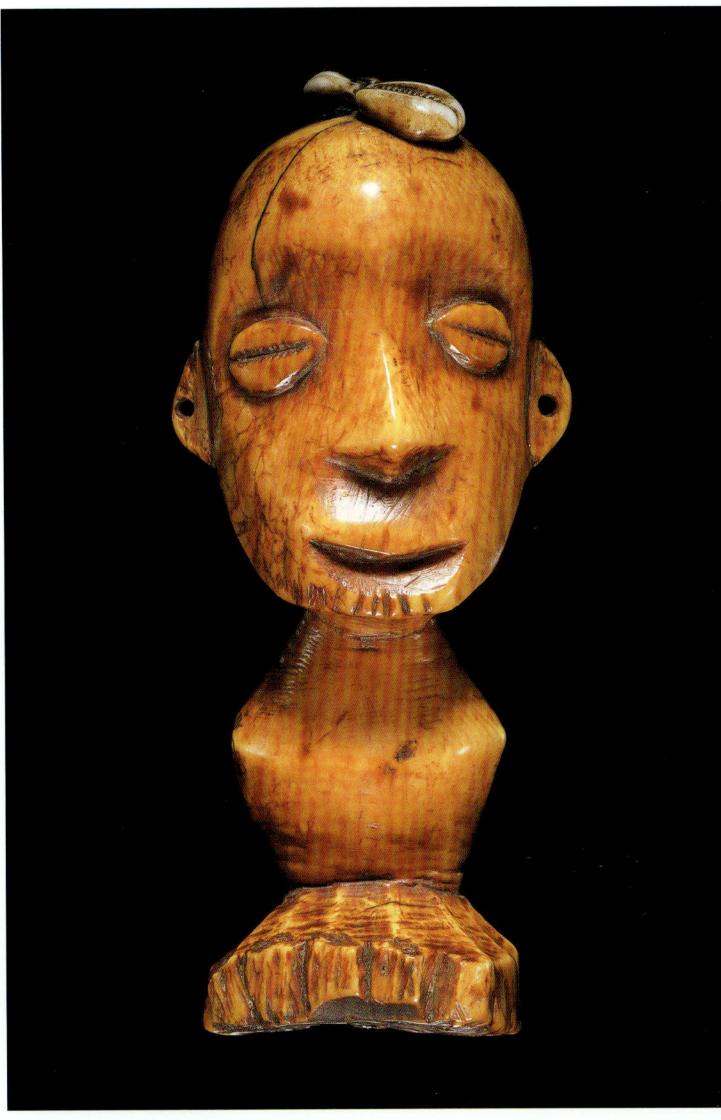

8.21 Human bust. Ivory and cowrie shells. H: 15 cm (5⅞ in.).

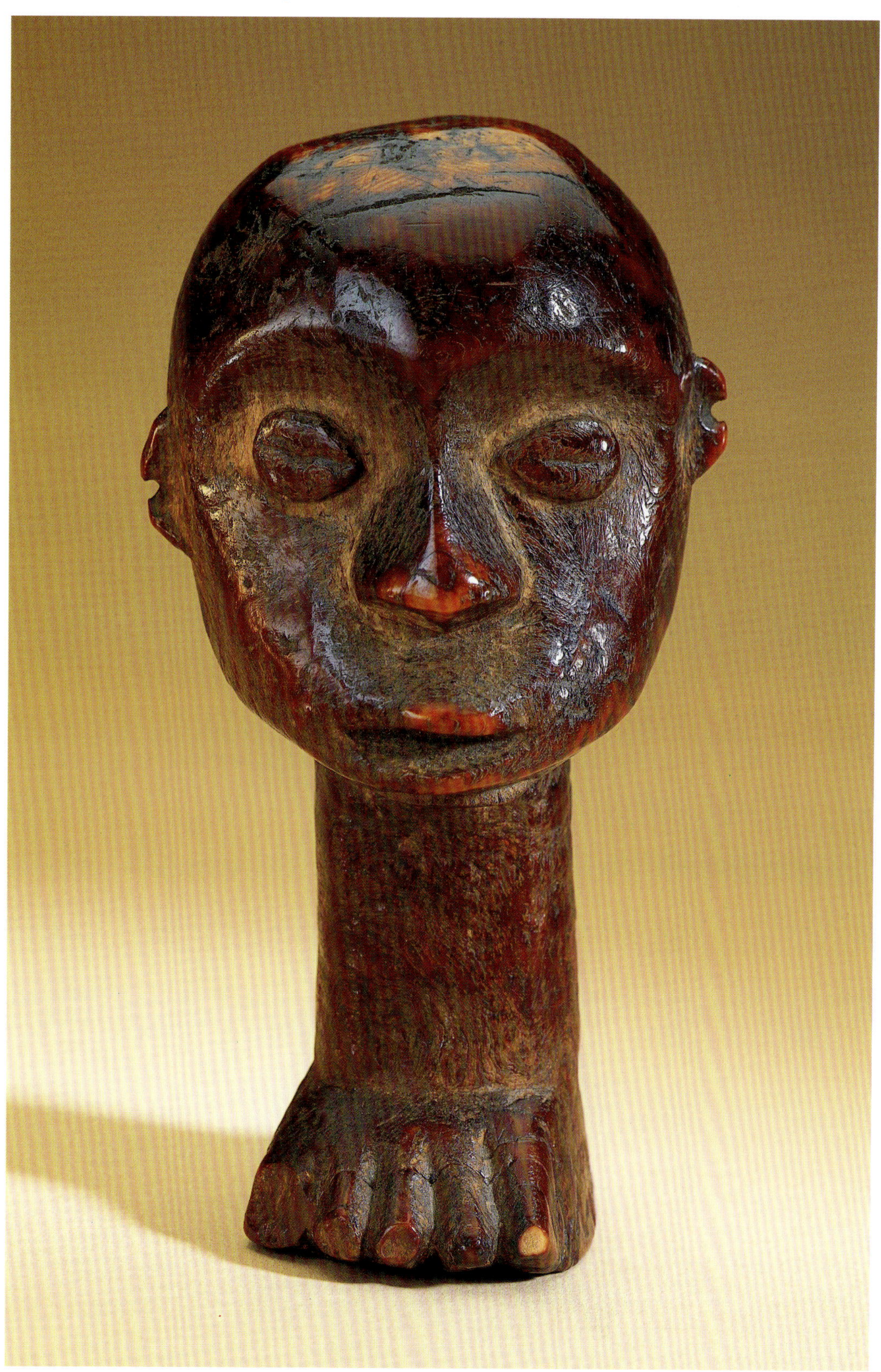

8.22 Human bust.
Ivory. H: 16.8 cm (6⅝ in.).

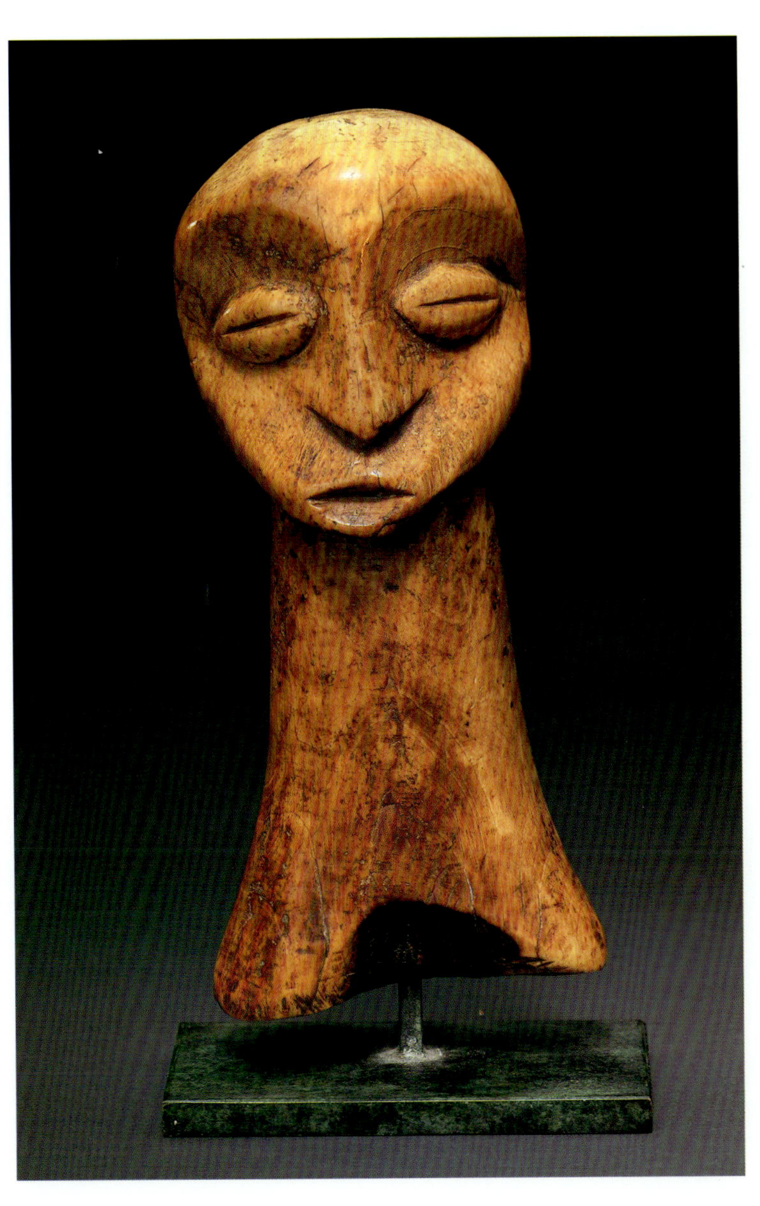

8.23 Human bust.
Ivory. H: 15.5 cm (6 in.).

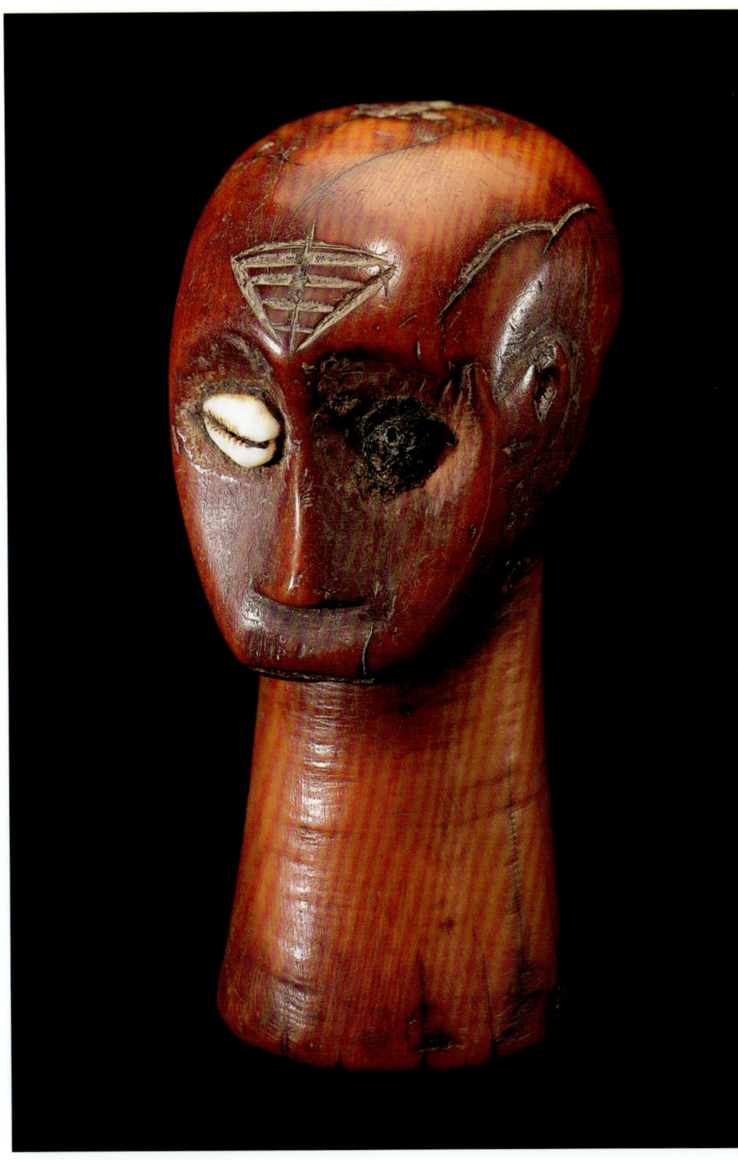

8.24 Human bust. Ivory and cowrie shells. H: 12.8 cm (5 in.).
FMCH X76.889; Gift of Jay T. Last.

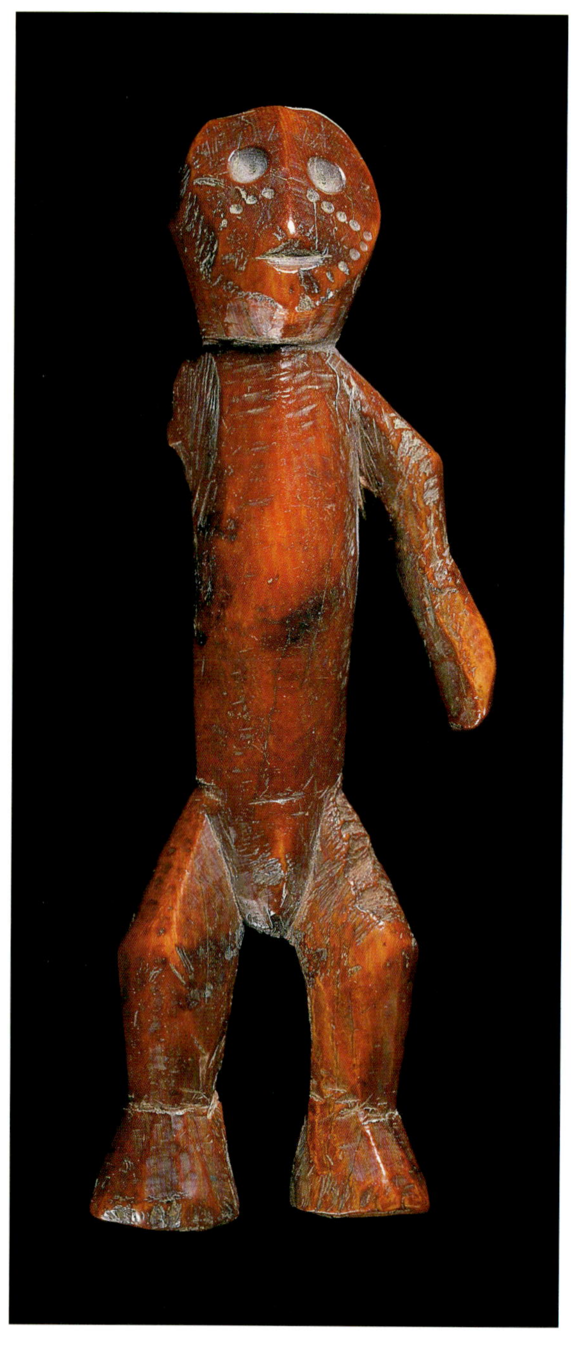

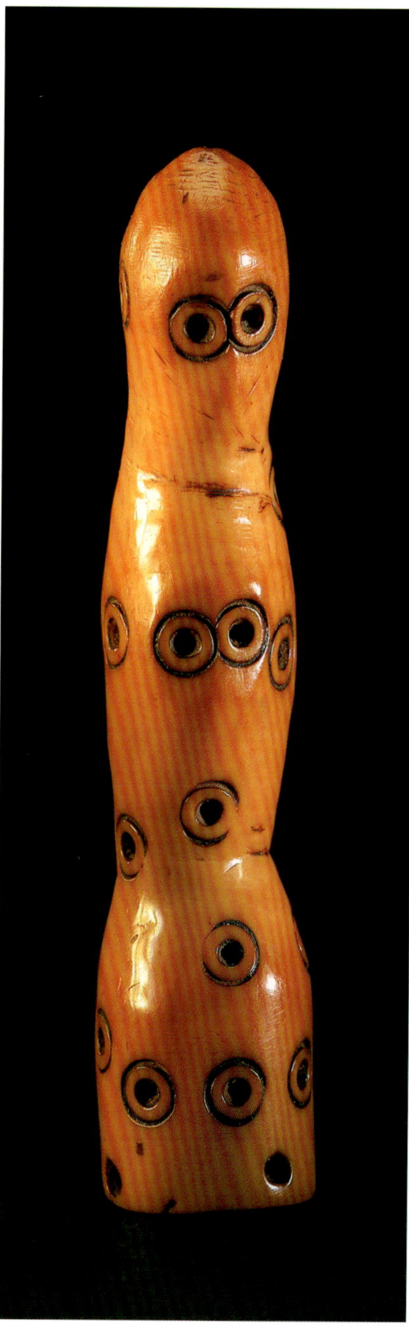

8.25 Human figure.
Ivory. H: 16.5 cm (6½ in.).

8.26 Human figure.
Ivory. H: 12.8 cm (5 in.).

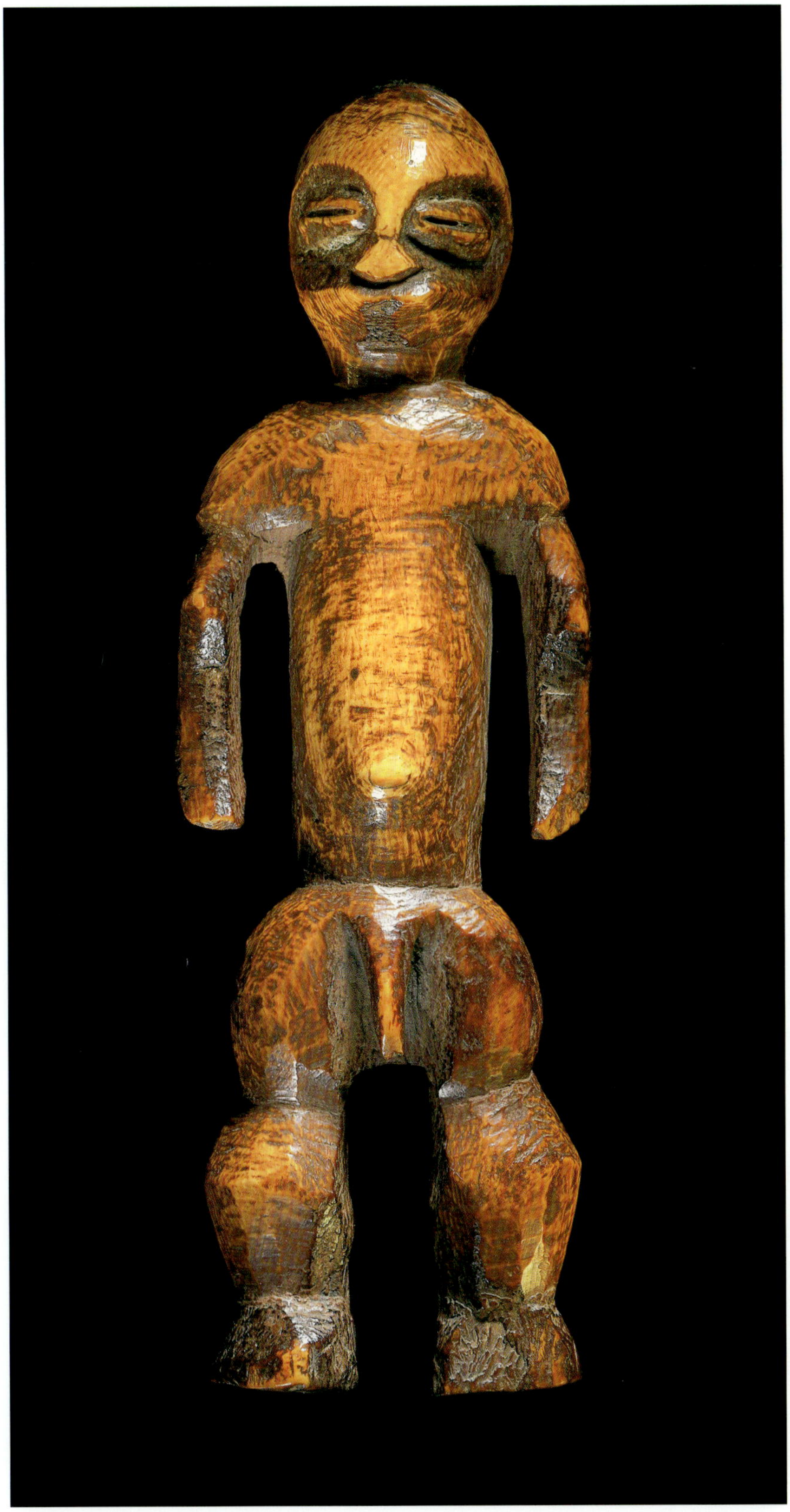

8.27 Human figure.
Ivory. H: 26 cm (10¼ in.).

8.28 Human figure.
Ivory. H: 7.9 cm (3⅛ in.).

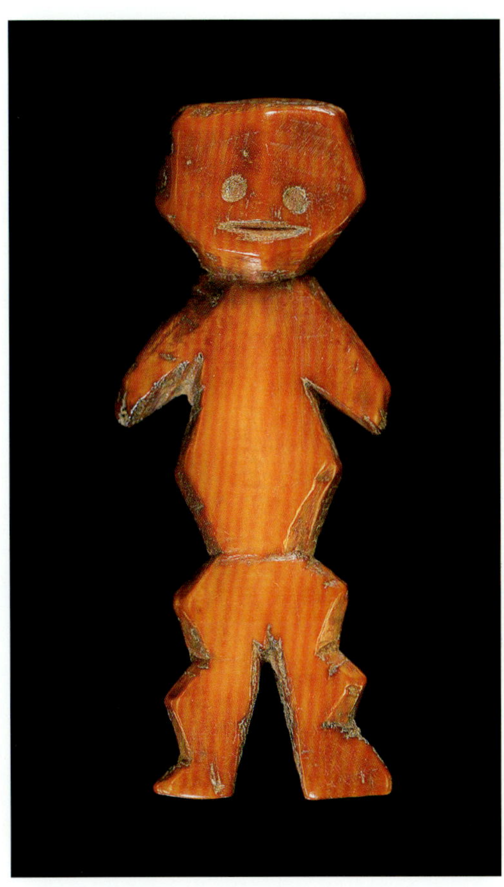

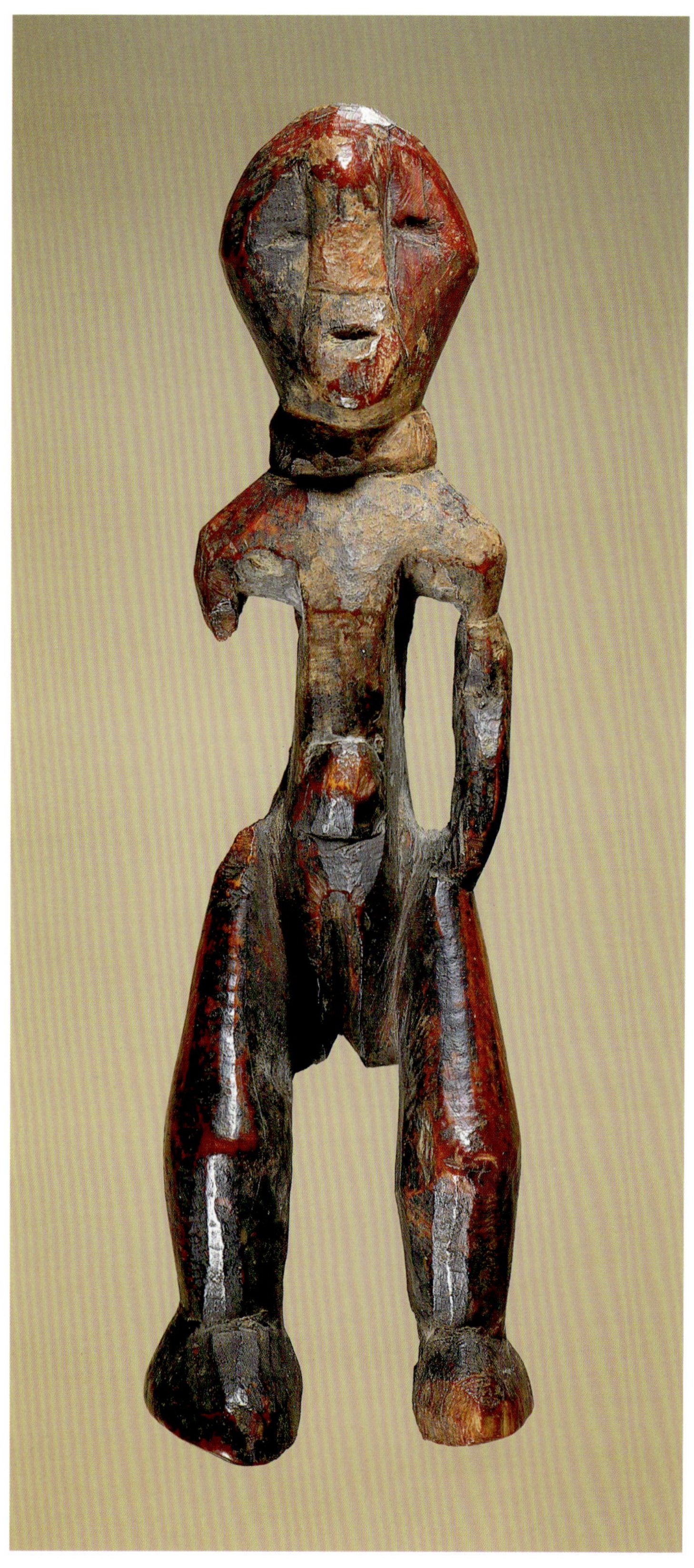

8.29 Human figure.
Ivory. H: 21.7 cm (8½ in.).

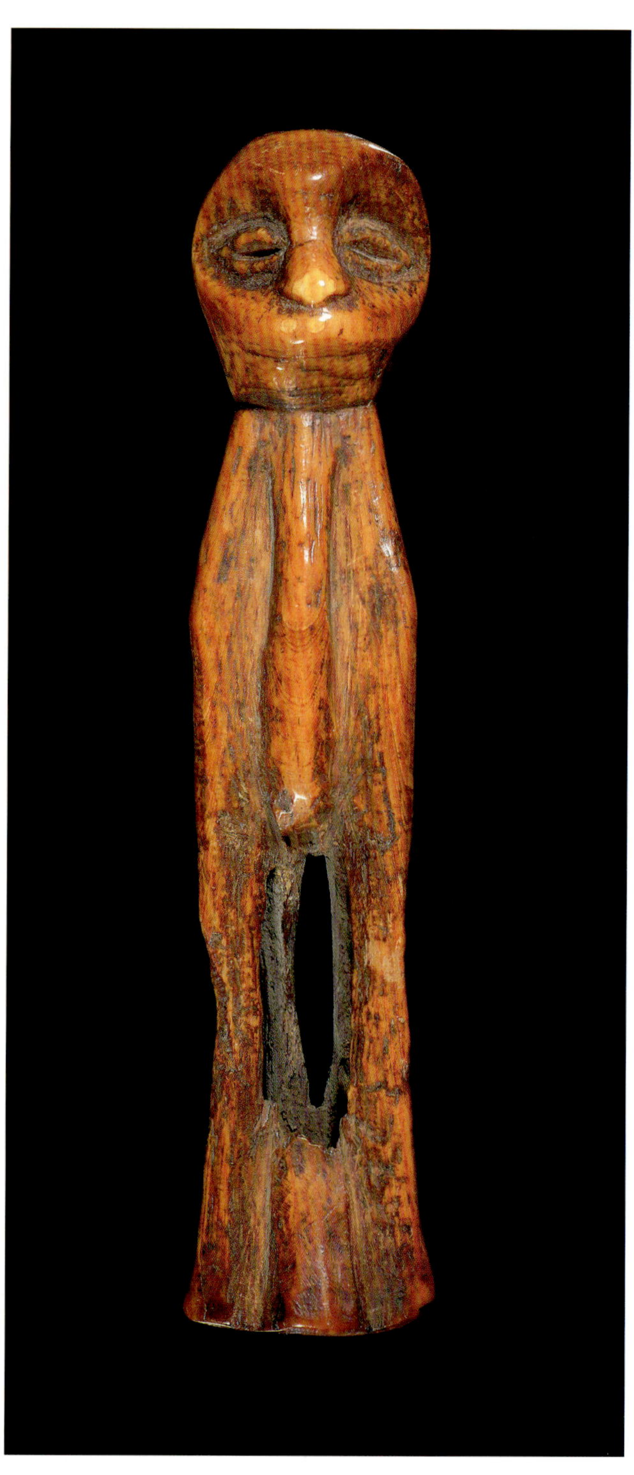

8.30 Human figure.
Ivory. H: 17.5 cm (6⅞ in.).

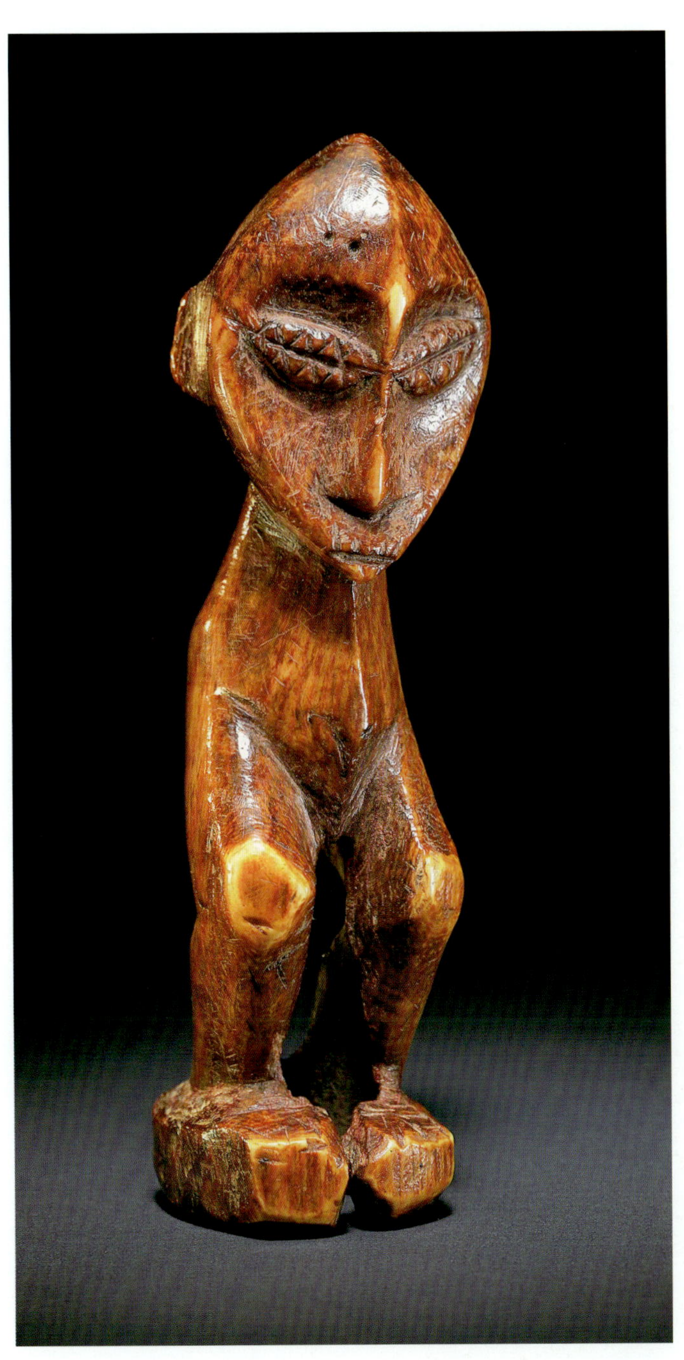

8.31 Human figure.
Ivory. H: 15.2 cm (6 in.).

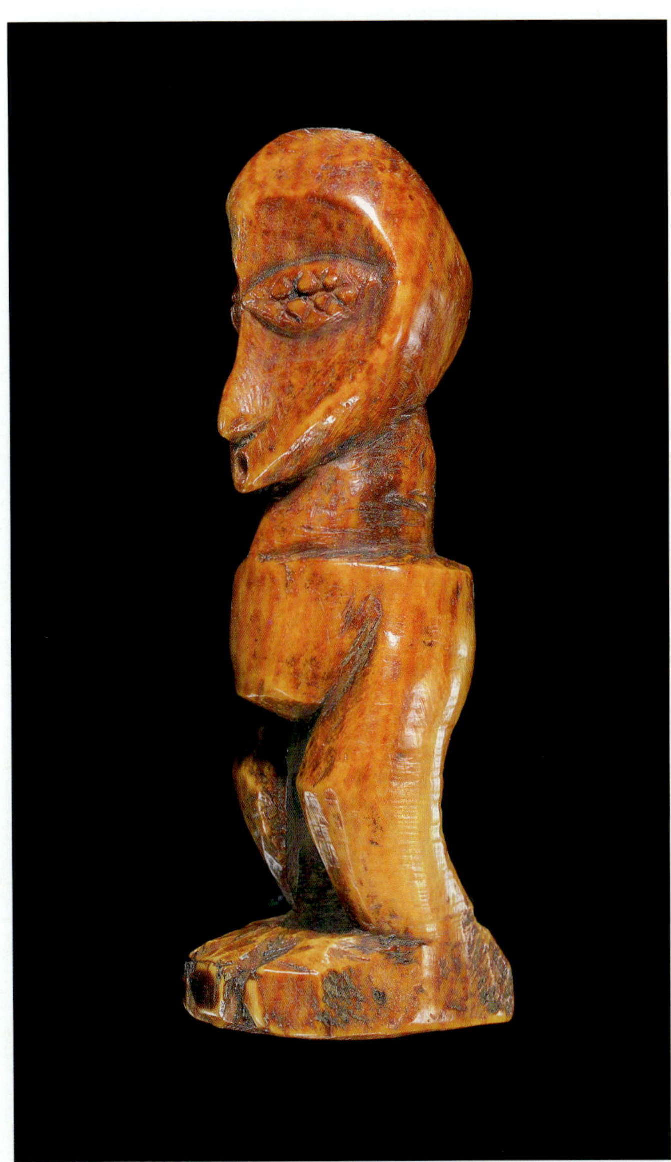

8.32 Human figure.
Ivory. H: 13.3 cm (5¼ in.).

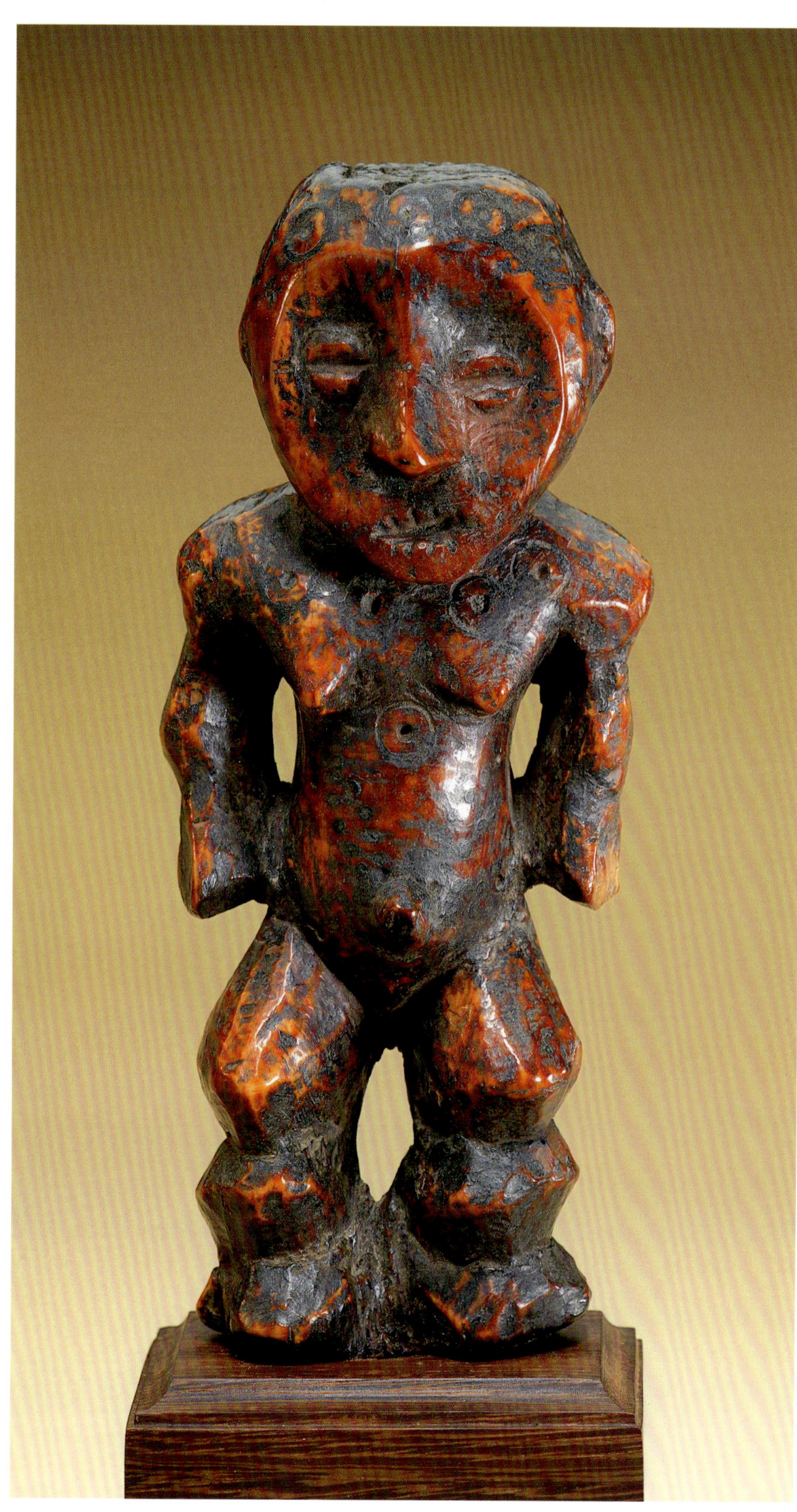

8.33 Human figure.
Ivory. H: 15.5 cm (6⅛ in.).

(Biebuyck 1986, 54; 1994, 92). Occasionally women of Kanyamwa rank own small versions of these pieces. The works can either be inherited through the mother's family or can be commissioned by a teacher to give to an initiate (Biebuyck 1986, 54). Of all the initiation objects, the Lega consider *maginga* to have the strongest innate power, and they often use bits of the ivory scraped from these figures to mix in a drink intended for medicinal purposes (Biebuyck 1973, 174).

At the death of a Bwami member, certain of his initiation objects are exposed on his grave. For a member of Yananio or Kindi, the anthropomorphic figures are placed on the grave, and when the others are removed to be distributed to the appropriate Bwami members, one figure is abandoned there (Biebuyck 1986, 54). The graves of Yananio or Kindi members are inside the houses of their initiated wives and are not open to public view, so inappropriate eyes do not see the figures. Because of the figures' link with the grave, they mark relationships between the living and the ancestors, or, in the words of Biebuyck, "It is as if possession of the figurines ensures the permanent presence of the deceased Big-Ones and serves as storage of their power" (Biebuyck 1986, 95).

Finally, large wood and ivory pieces mark the right of a particular Bwami community to hold specific initiations (figs. 8.56–8.69). When a community wants, for the first time, to begin initiating into a higher level of Bwami, they ask another community who has members at that level to come and initiate a member of their Society into the secrets of the higher level. As a sign of this transfer, the new high-level member is given a large wood or ivory figure that he keeps in trust for his own community. No initiations can take place without the presence of this figure, reminding everyone of the legitimacy of the ceremonies (Biebuyck 1986, 55; 1994, 38), but it is publicly displayed only at initiations into Lutumbo lwa Kindi, the highest level in Bwami (Biebuyck 1986, 96–97).

Stylistically, it should be noted, that whether large or small, wood or ivory, Lega figures may appear monumental. When looking at photographs of these pieces, it is often impossible to tell whether they are six inches or six feet in height. The artist may fully articulate the piece or may place a head on a cone-shaped body. The piece may also appear as a bust. Body positions vary, allowing the figures not only to mark rank but also to illustrate sayings and enrich meanings.

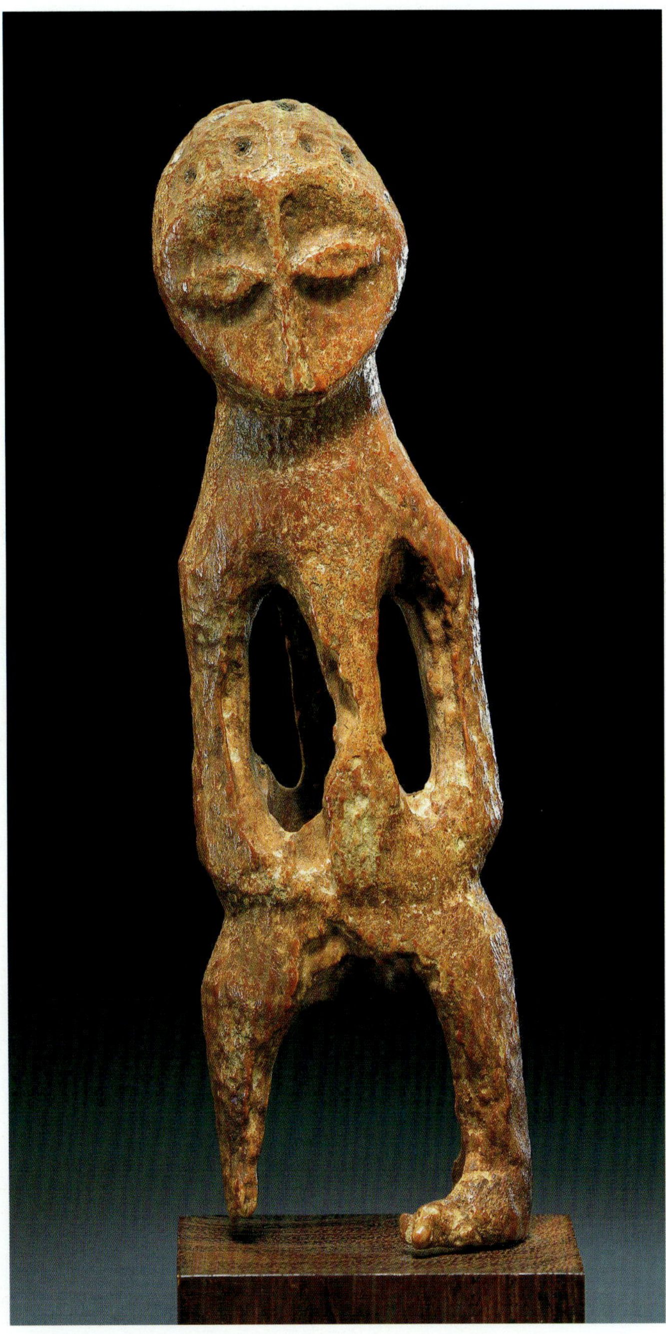

8.34 Human figure.
Ivory. H: 15 cm (5⅞ in.).

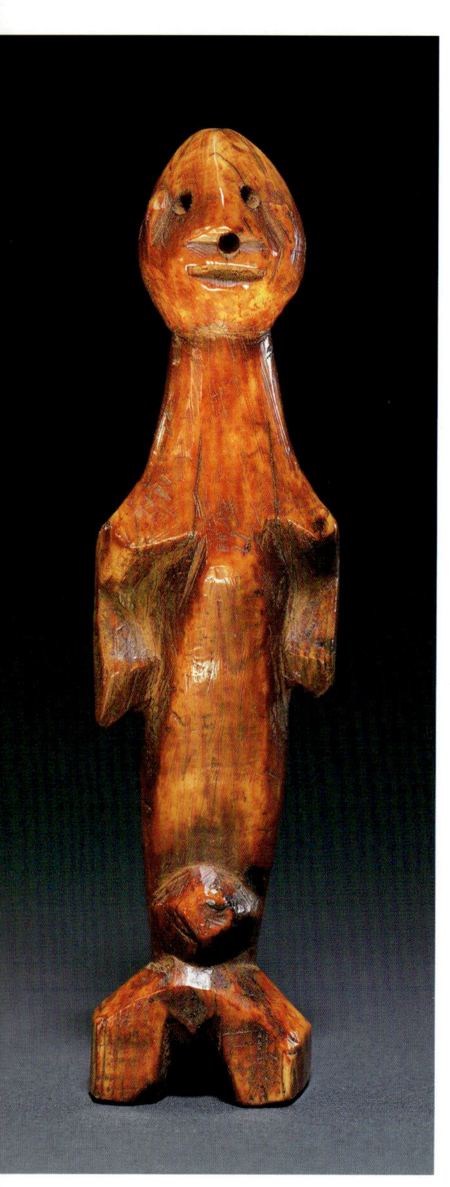

8.35 Human figure.
Ivory. H: 11.9 cm (4⅝ in.).

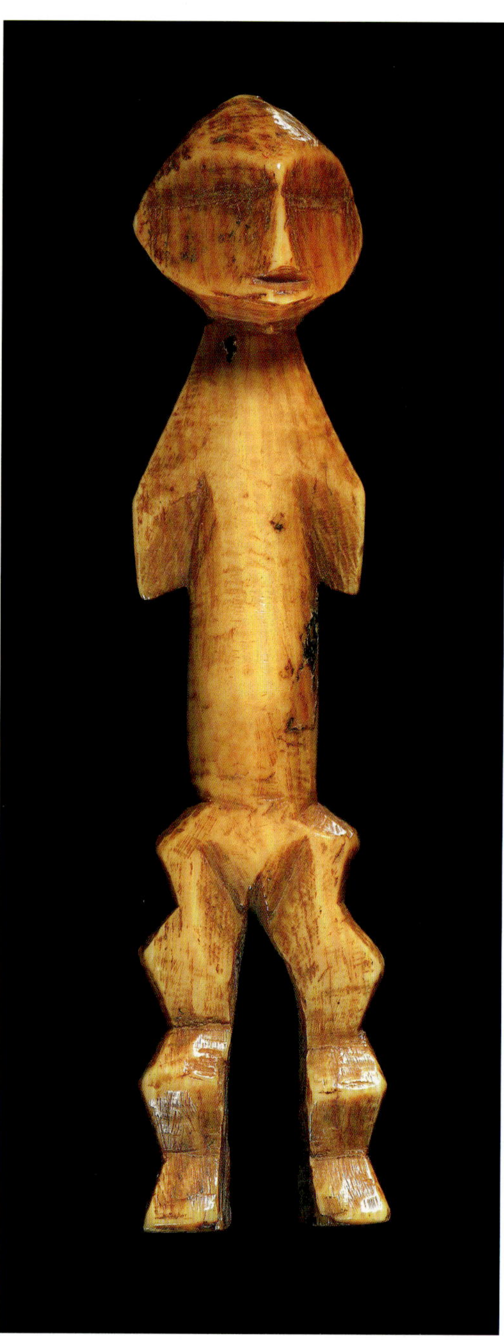

8.36 Human figure.
Ivory. H: 15.6 cm (6⅛ in.).

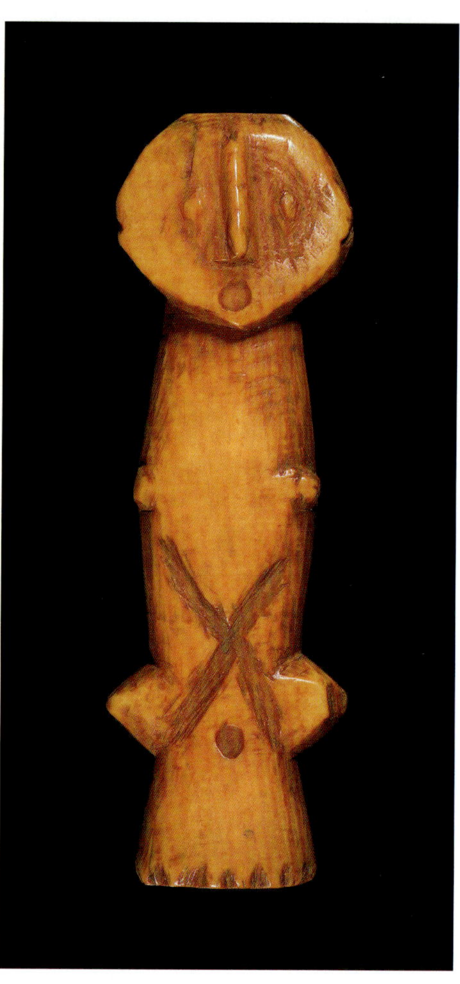

8.37 Human figure.
Ivory. H: 9.9 cm (3⅞ in.).

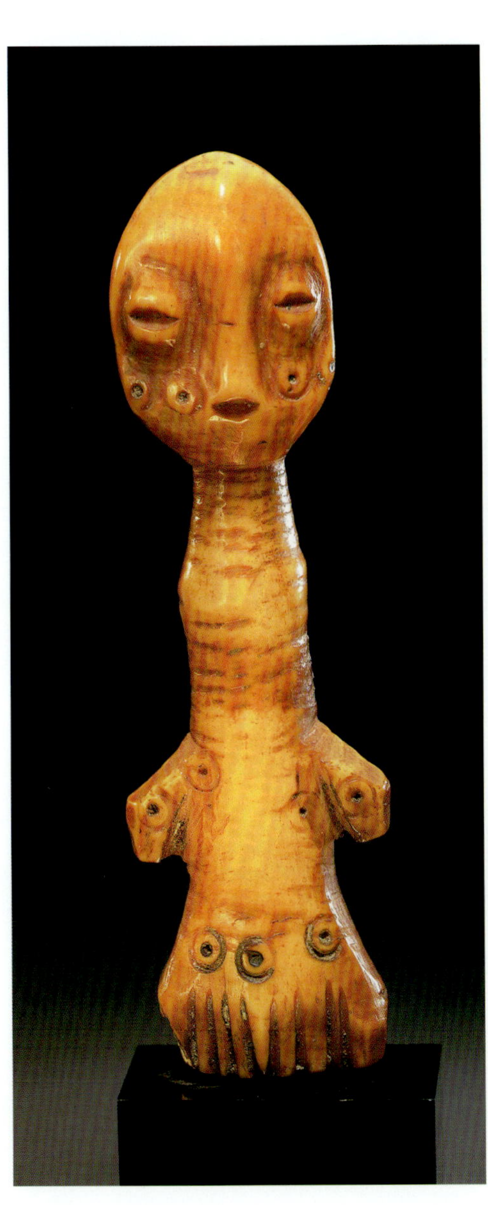

8.38 Human figure.
Ivory. H: 12.3 cm (4⅞ in.).

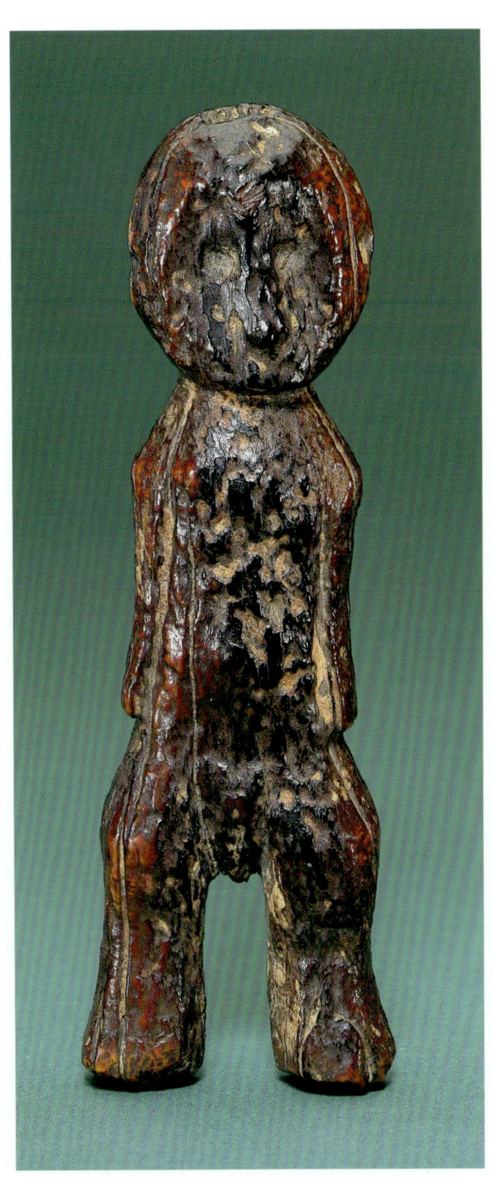

8.39 Human figure.
Ivory. H: 13.2 cm (5⅛ in.).

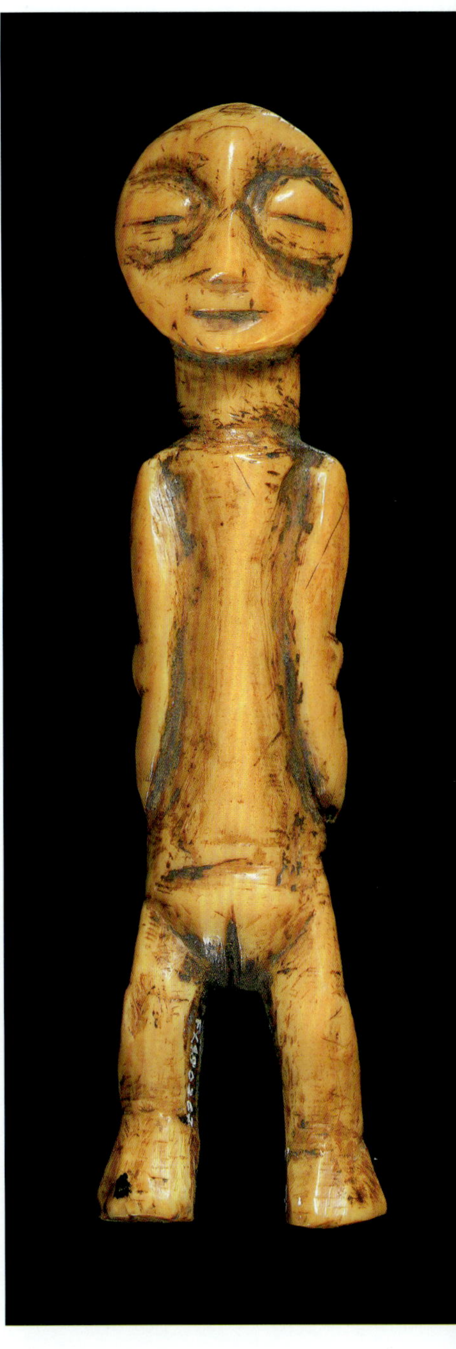

8.40 Human figure.
Ivory. H: 14.5 cm (5¾ in.).

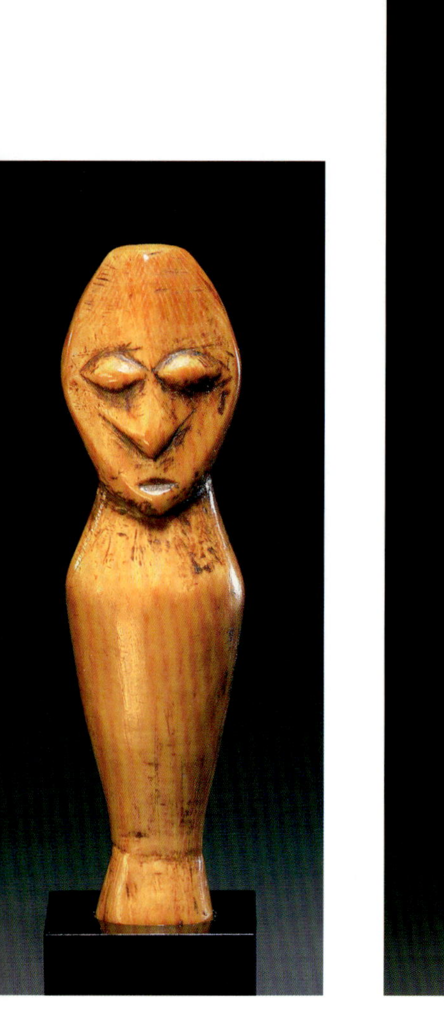

8.41 Human figure.
Ivory. H: 9.7 cm
(3⅞ in.).

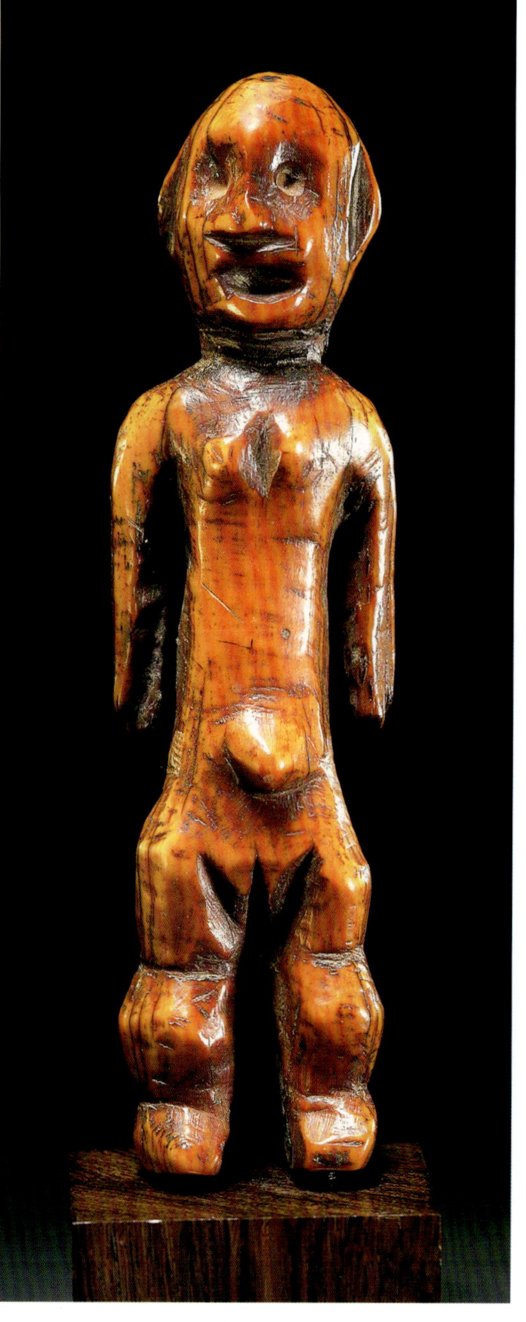

8.42 Human figure.
Ivory. H: 15.1 cm (5⅞ in.).

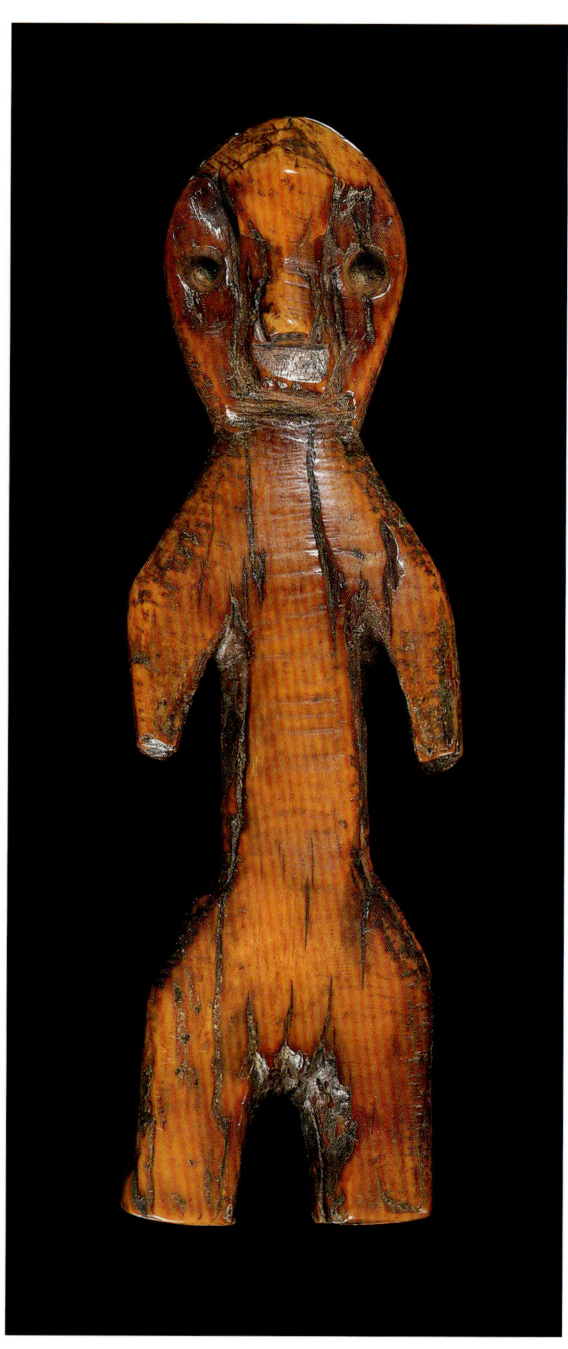

8.43 Human figure.
Ivory. H: 15.9 cm (6¼ in.).

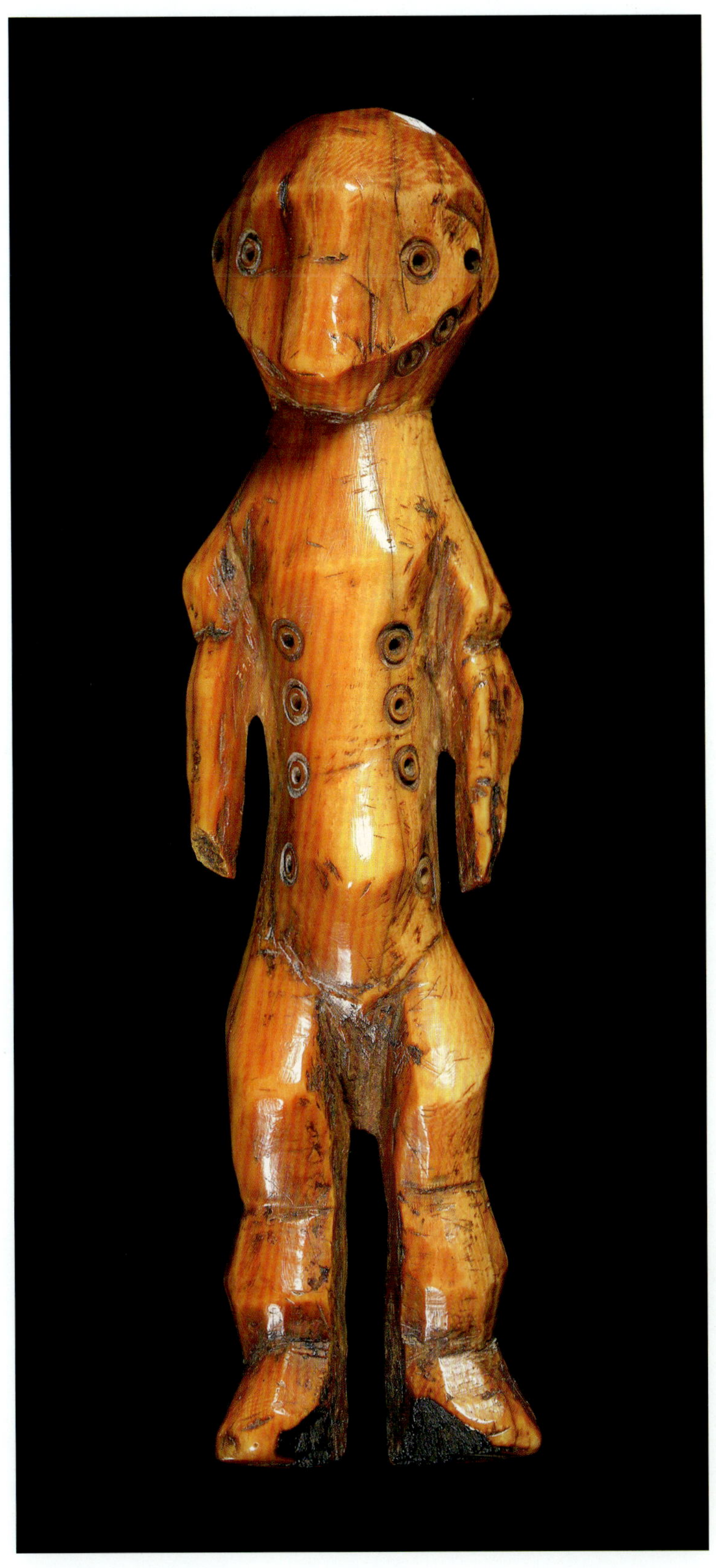

8.44 Human figure.
Ivory. H: 19.9 cm (7¾ in.).

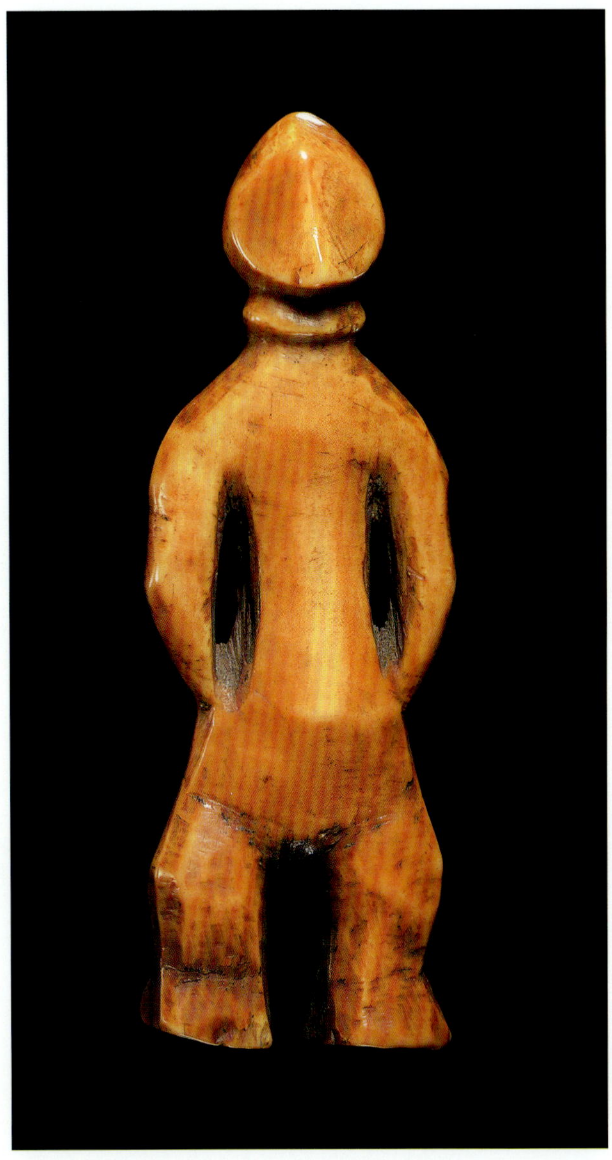

8.45 Human figure.
Ivory. H: 13 cm (5⅛ in.).

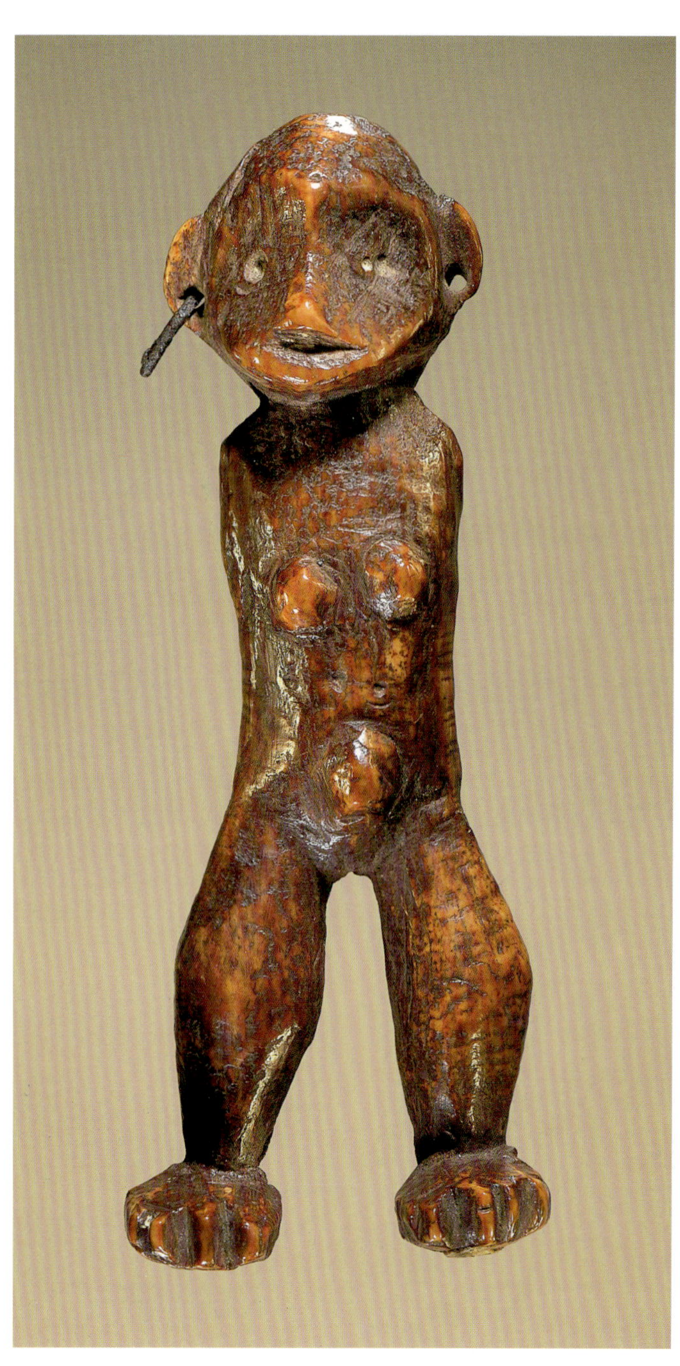

8.46 Human figure. Ivory and metal. H: 15.6 cm (6⅛ in.).

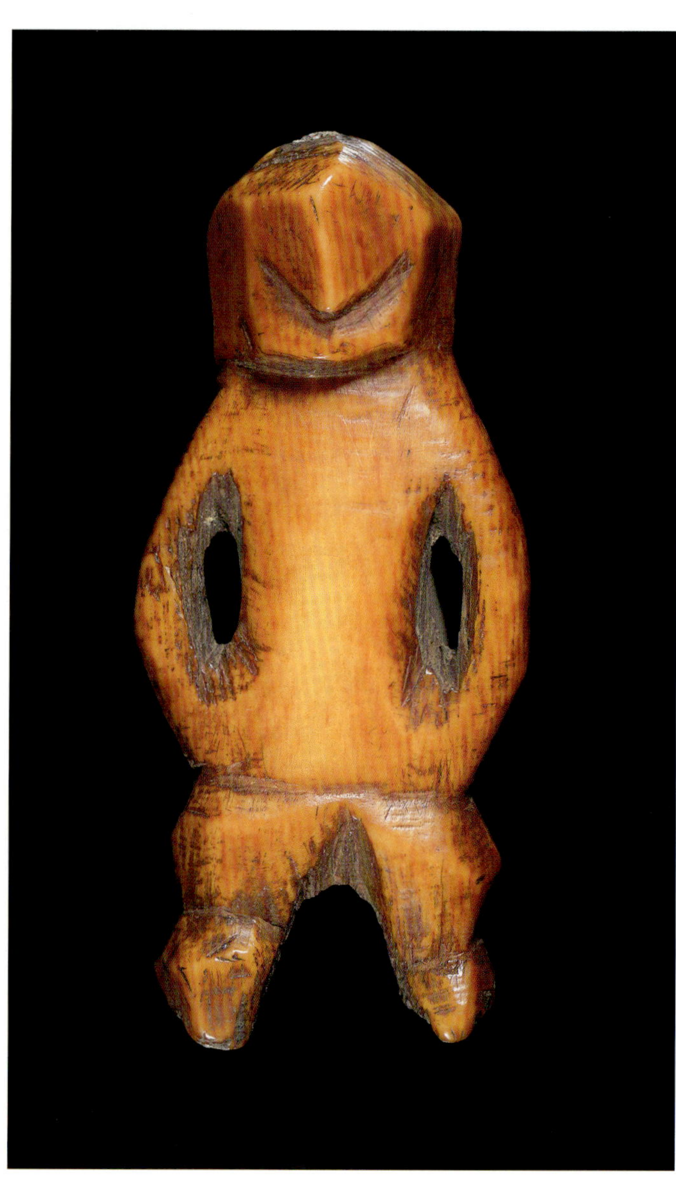

8.47 Human figure. Ivory. H: 11 cm (4⅜ in.).

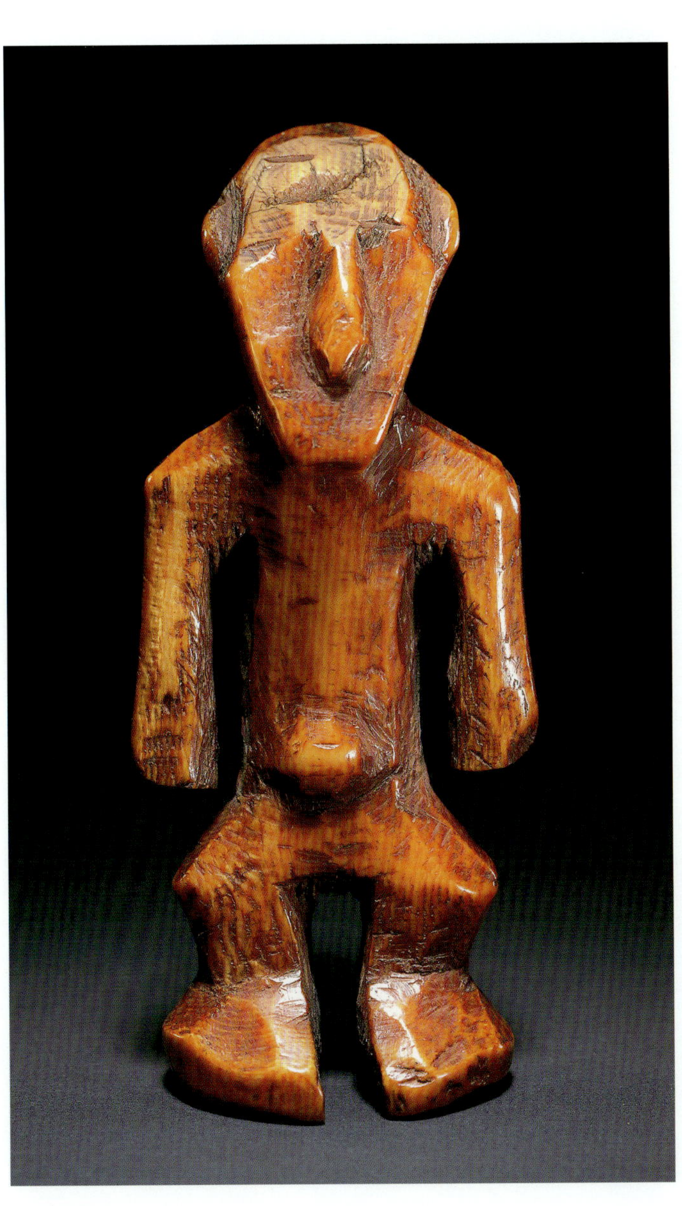

8.48 Human figure.
Ivory. H: 13.3 cm (5¼ in.).

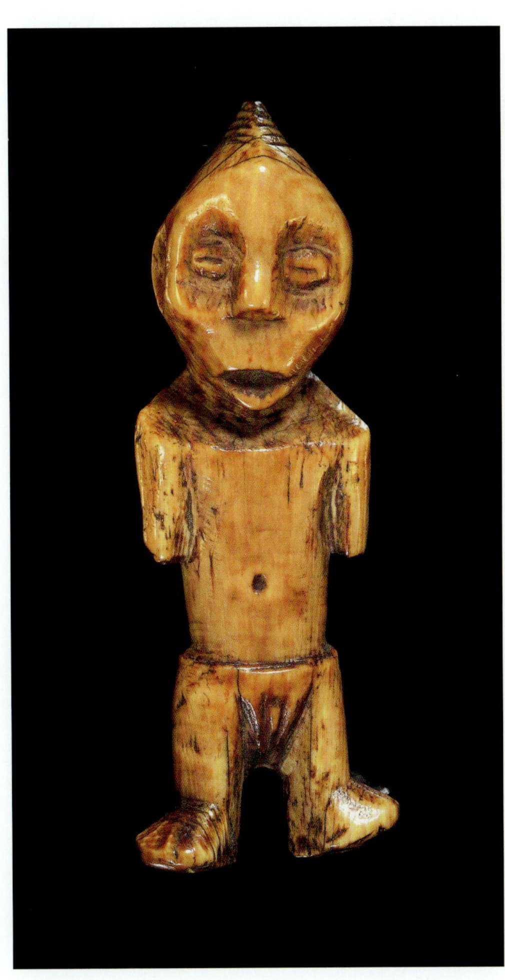

8.49 Human figure.
Ivory. H: 10.2 cm (4 in.).

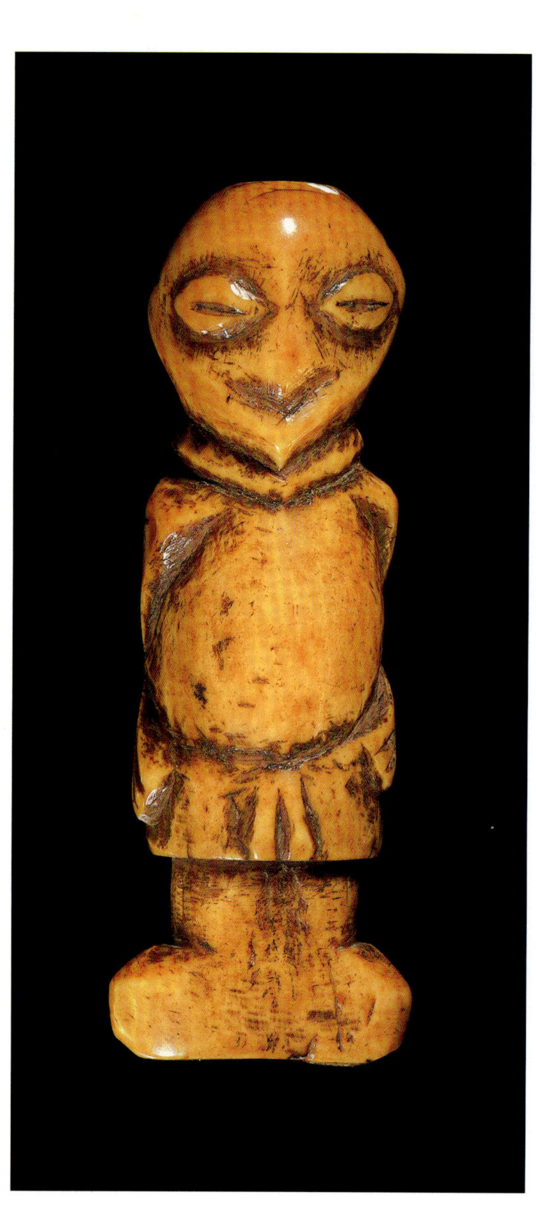

8.50 Human figure.
Ivory. H: 11.5 cm (4½ in.).

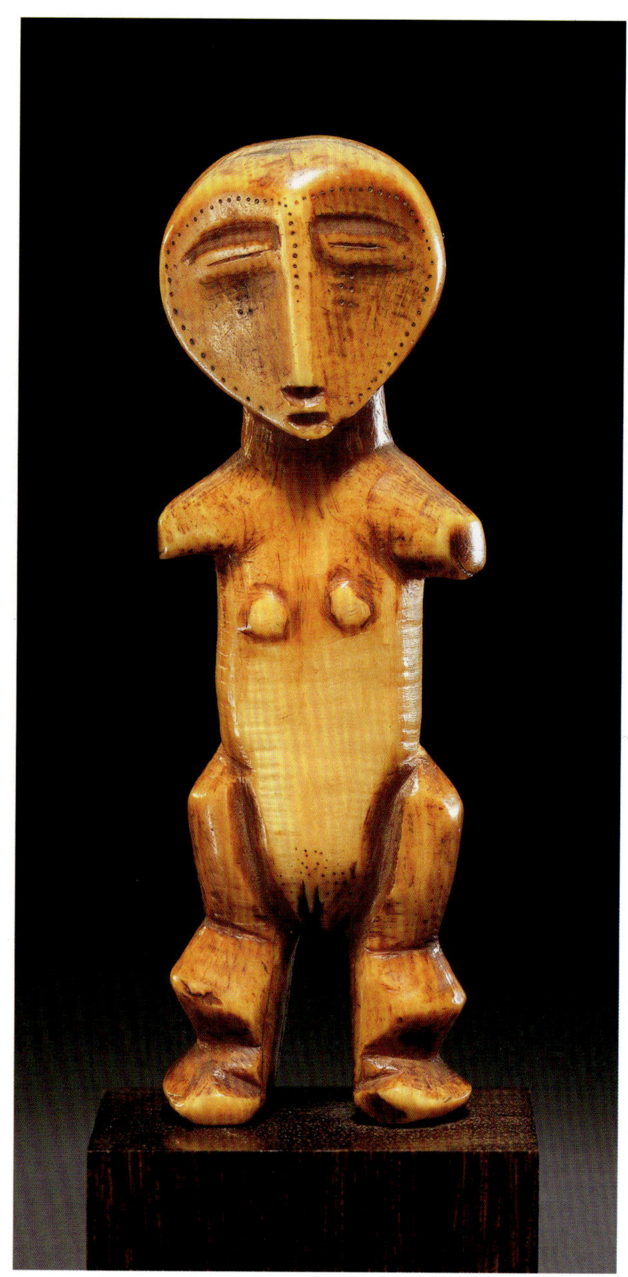

8.51 Human figure.
Ivory. H: 13.1 cm (5⅛ in.).

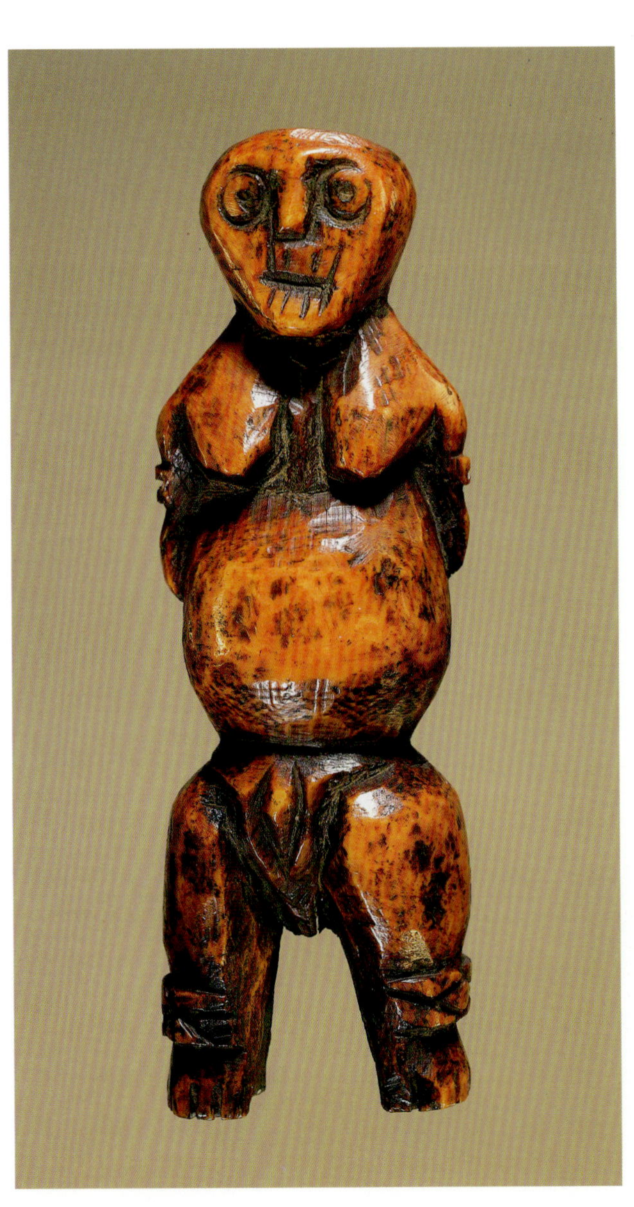

8.52 Human figure.
Ivory. H: 13 cm (5⅛ in.).

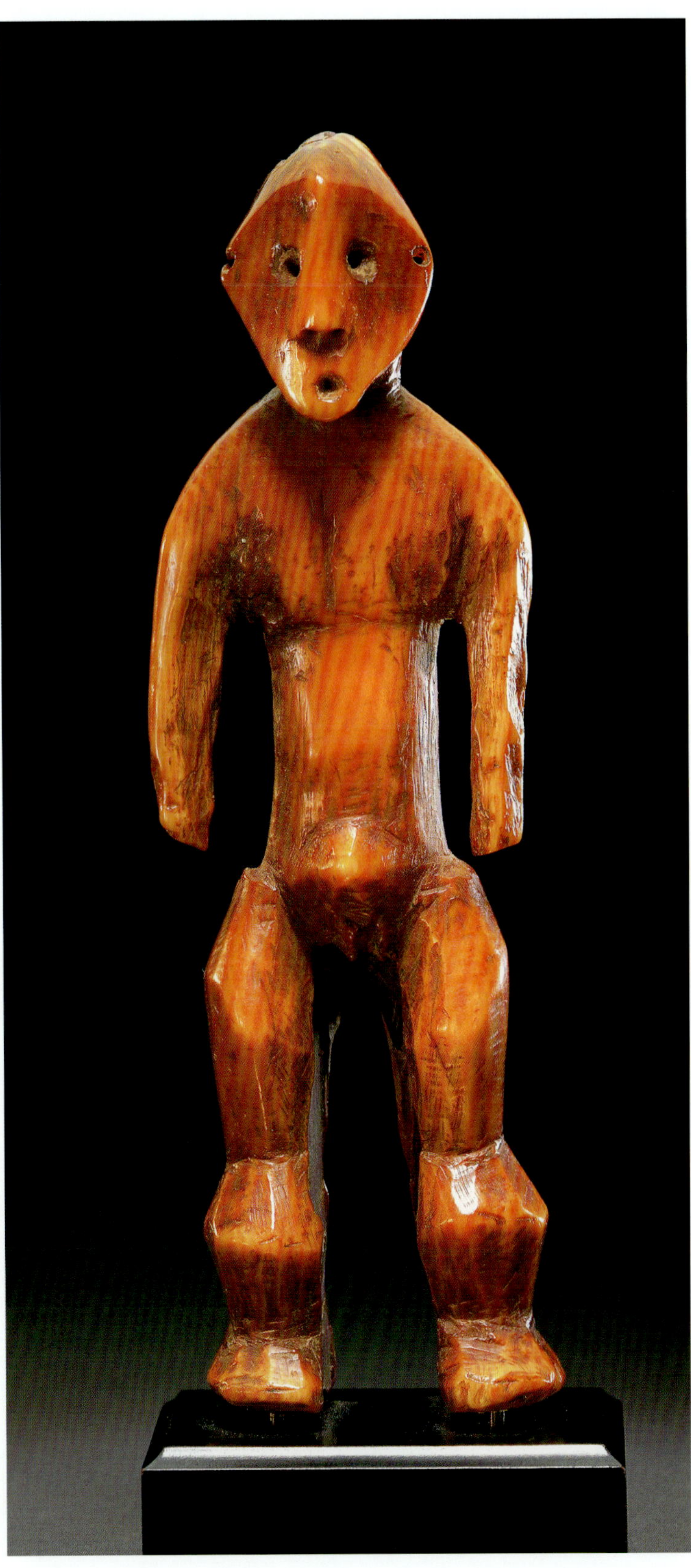

8.53 Human figure.
Ivory. H: 18 cm (7 in.).

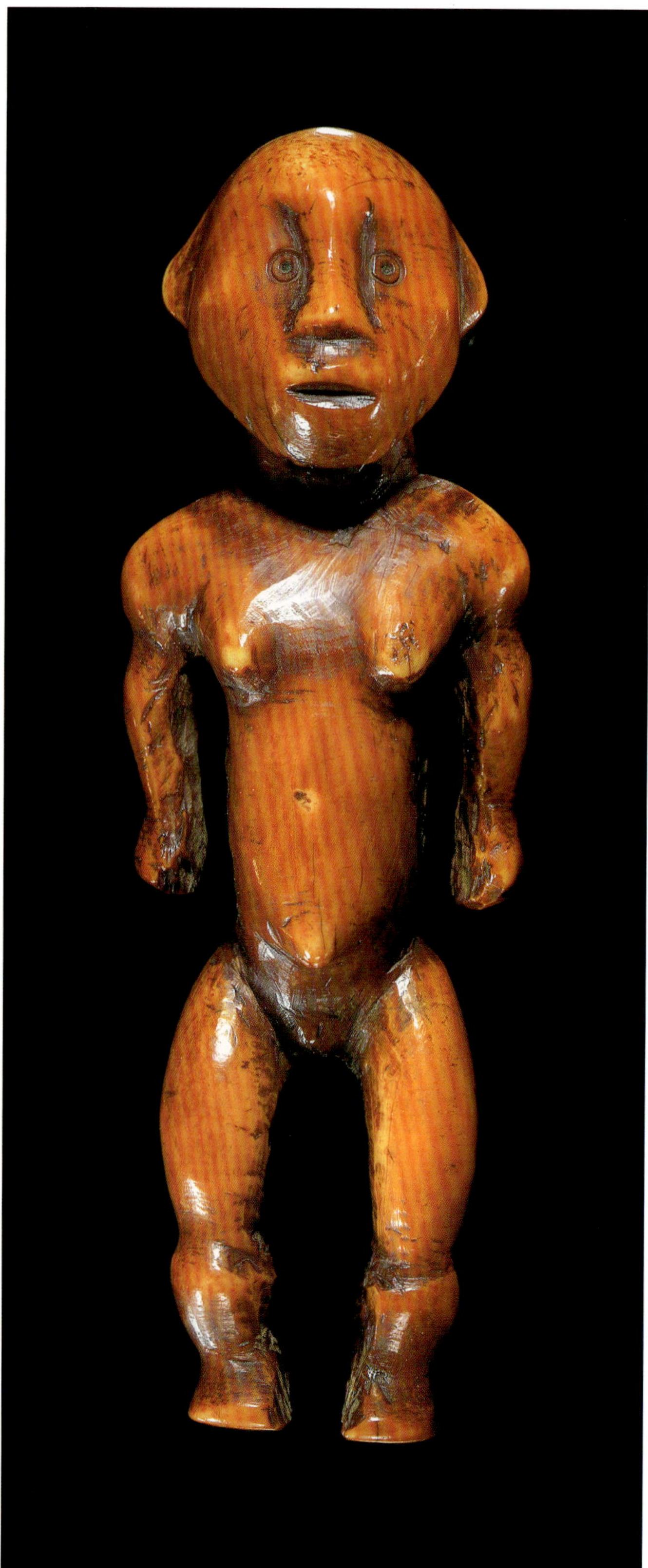

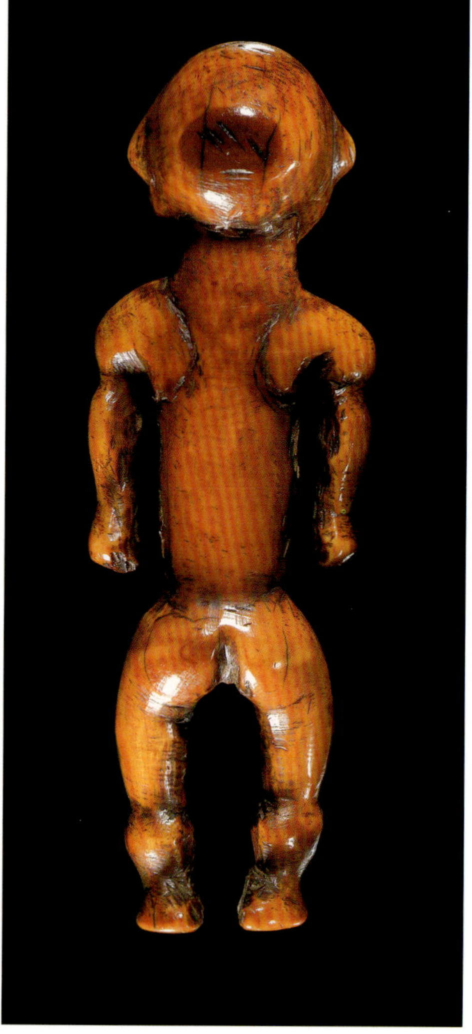

8.54A,B Front and back views of a human figure. Ivory. H: 17.3 cm (6¾ in.).

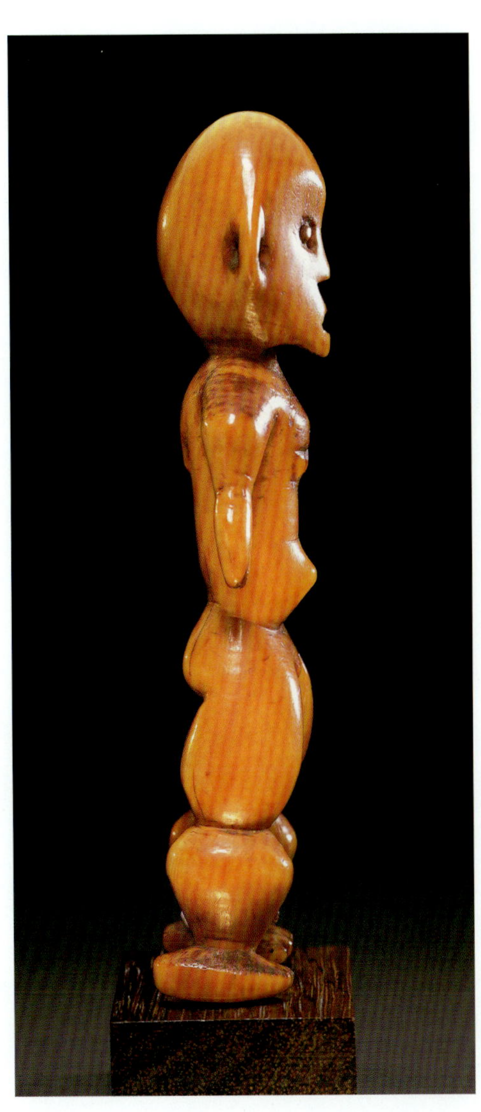

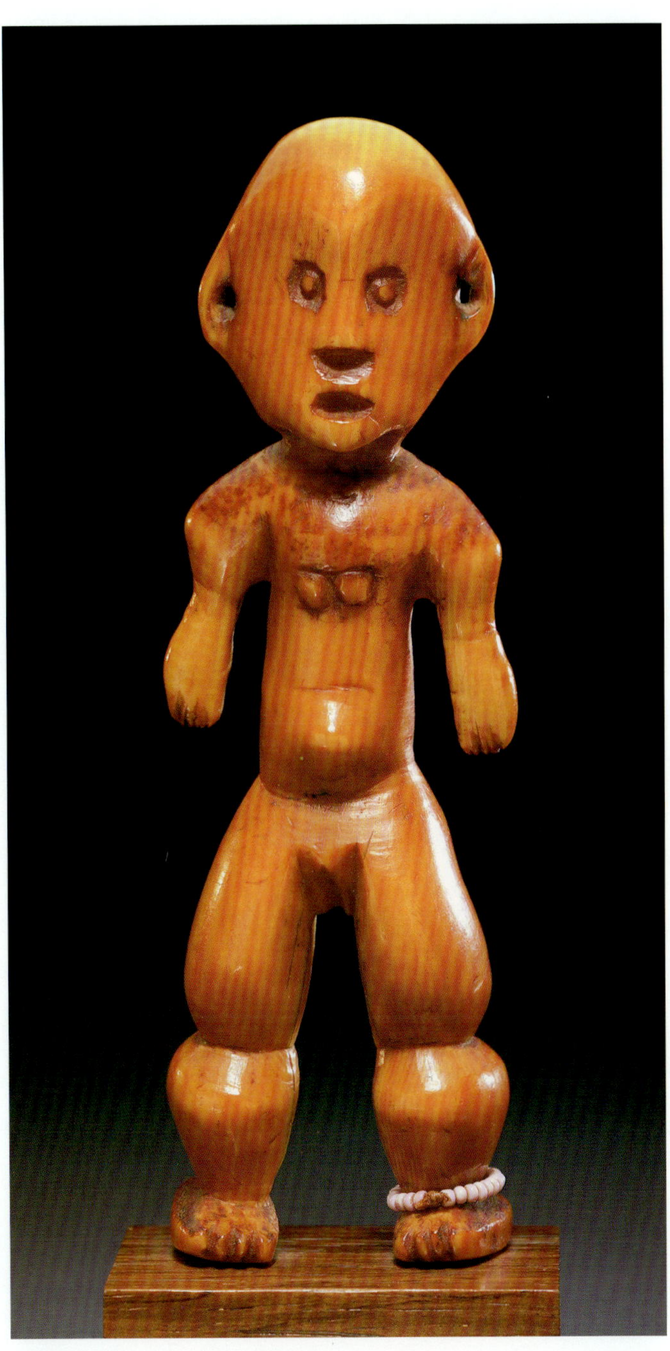

8.55A, B Side and front views of a human figure. Ivory and beads. H: 15.2 cm (6 in.).

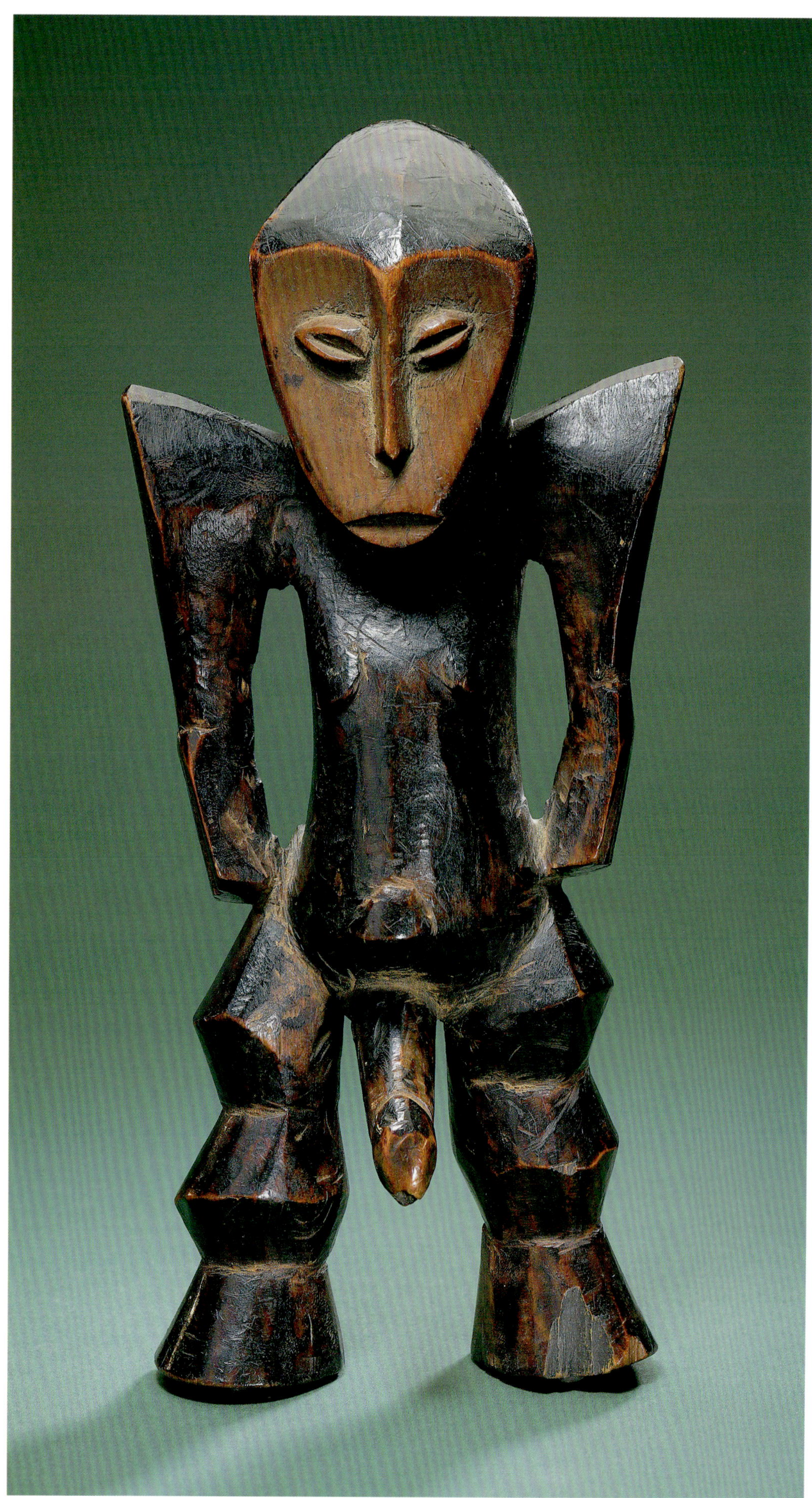

8.56 Human figure.
Wood. H: 30 cm (11¾ in.).

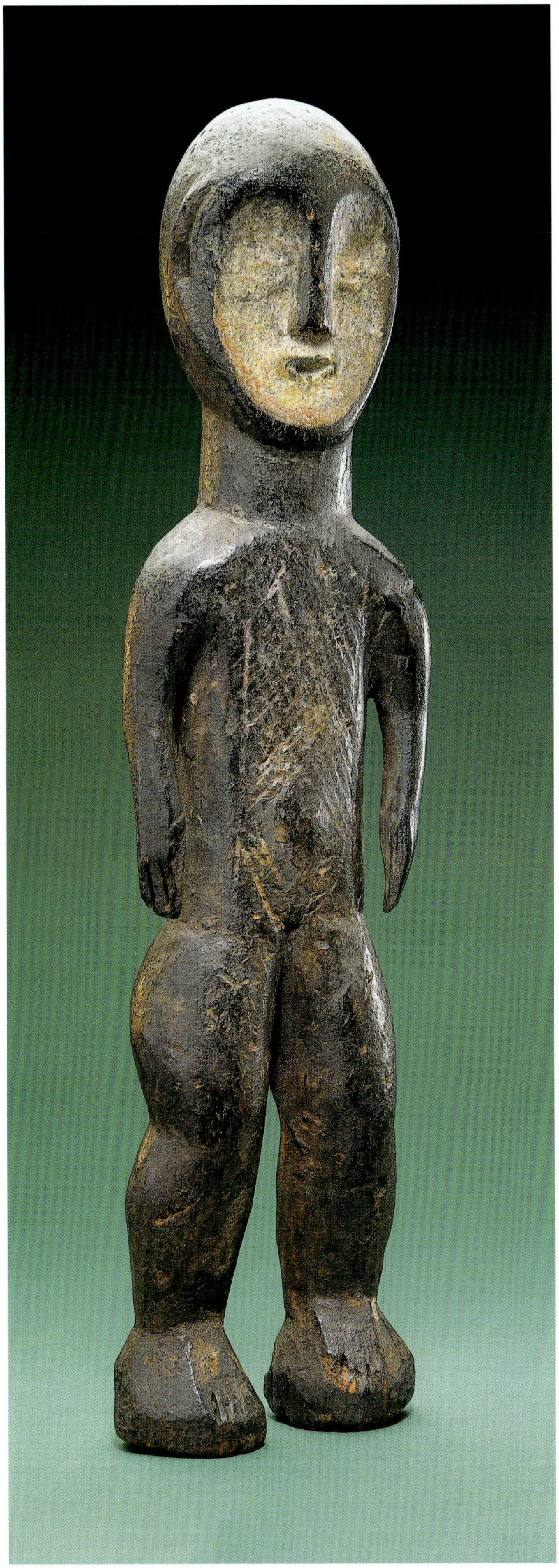

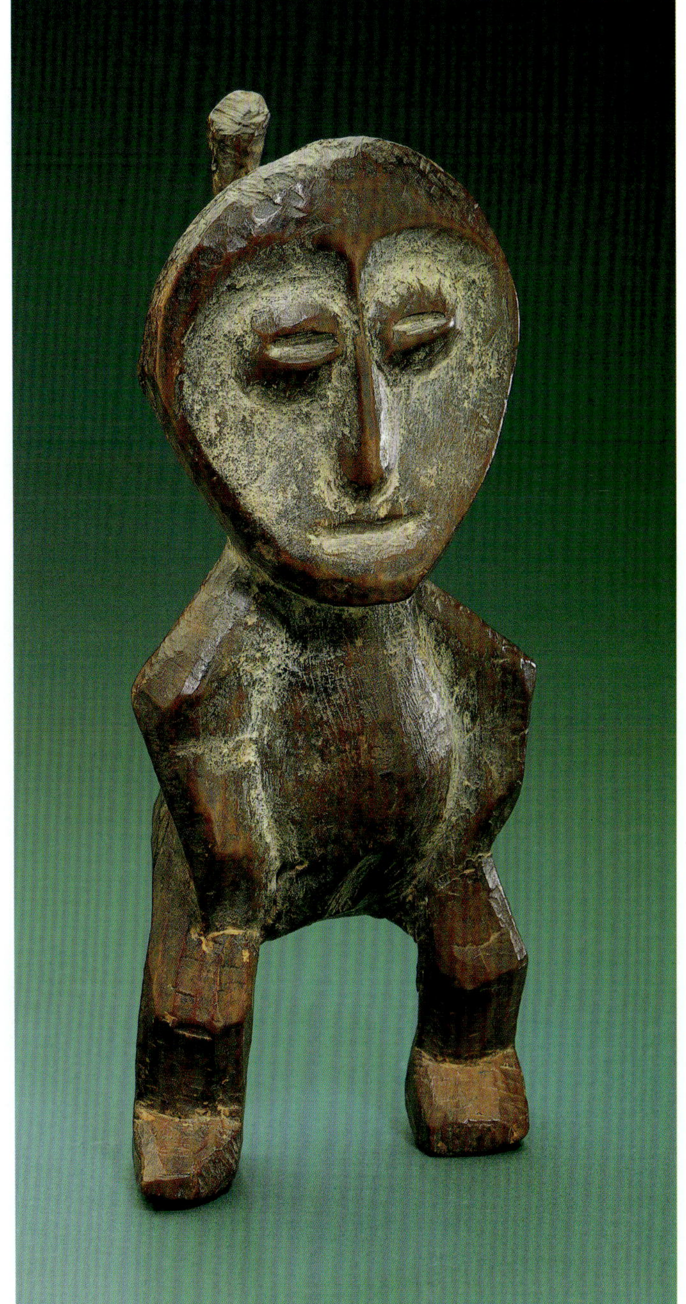

8.57 Human figure. Wood. H: 38 cm (15 in.).

8.58 Human figure. Wood and pigment. H: 24 cm (9½ in.).

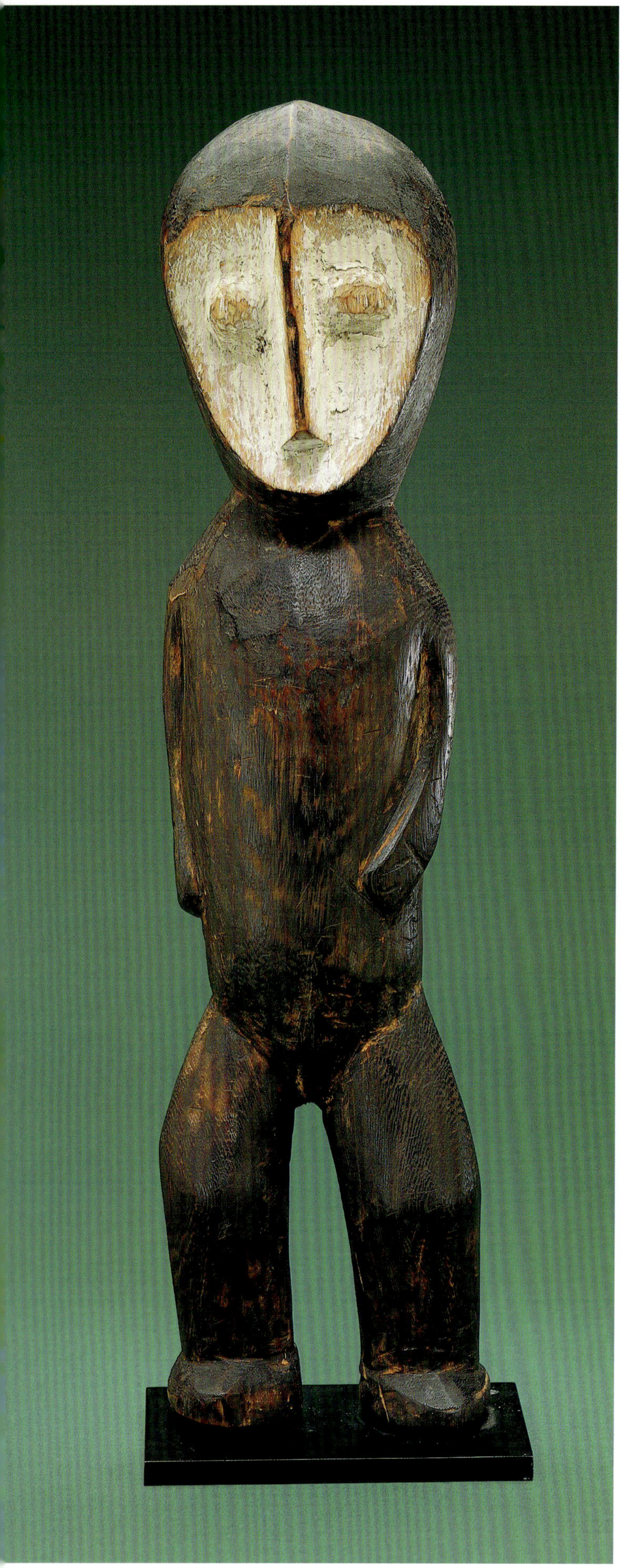

8.59

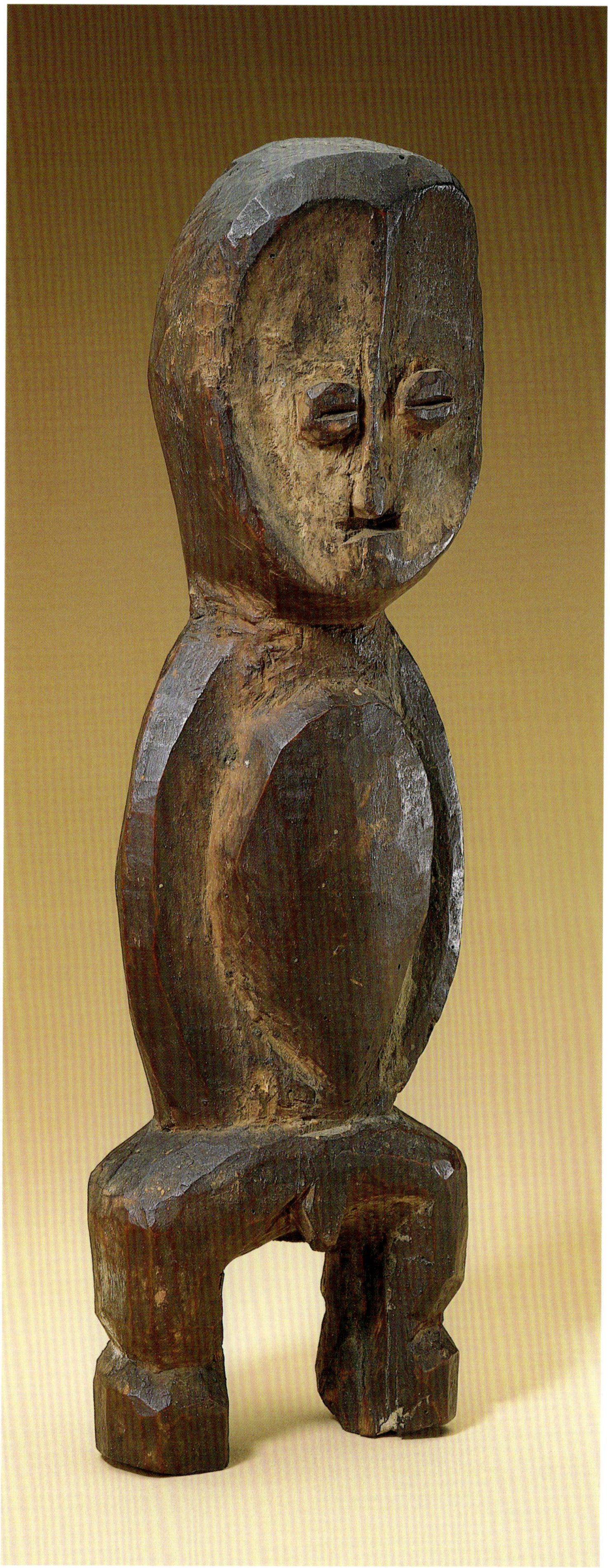

8.60

8.59 Human figure. Wood and pigment. H: 34.3 cm (13½ in.).

8.60 Human figure. Wood. H: 33 cm (13 in.).

8.61 Human figure. Wood and pigment. H: 29 cm (11⅜ in.).

8.62 Human figure. Wood. H: 33.4 cm (13⅛ in.).

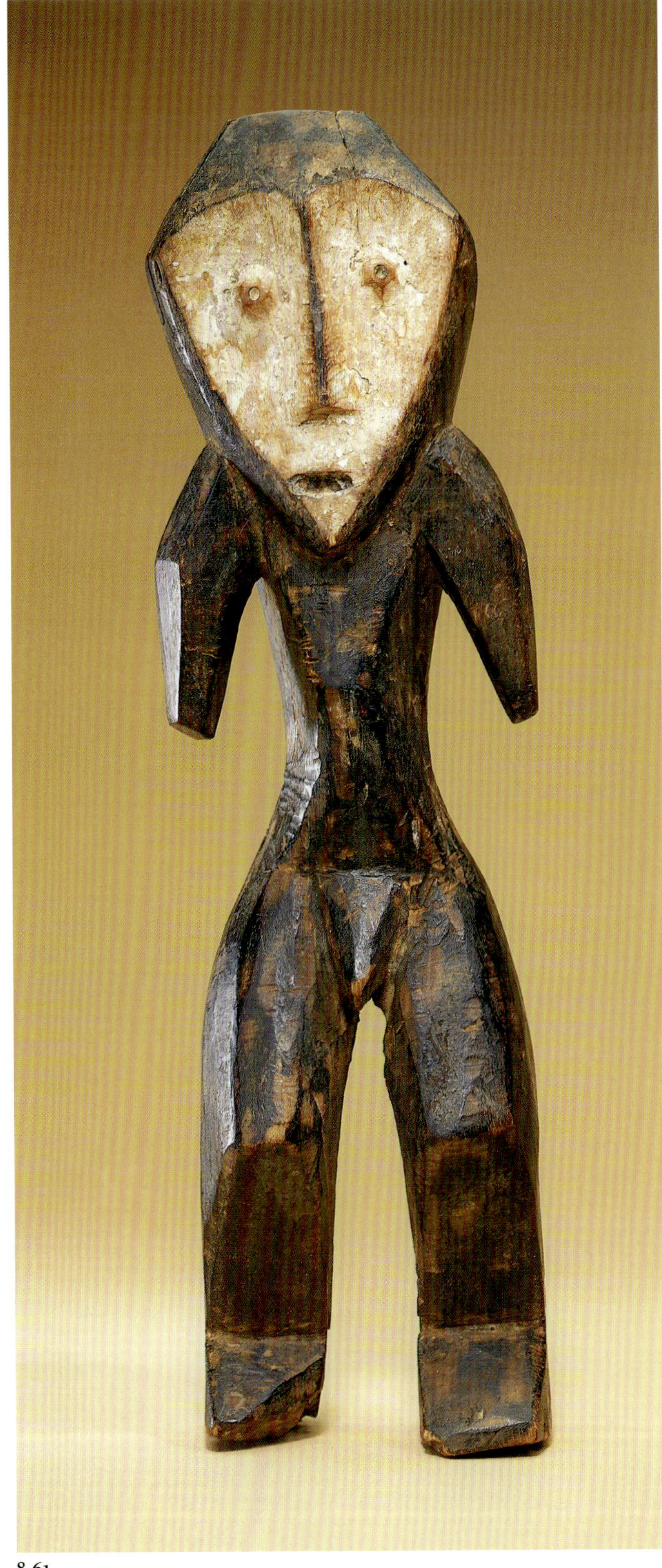

8.61

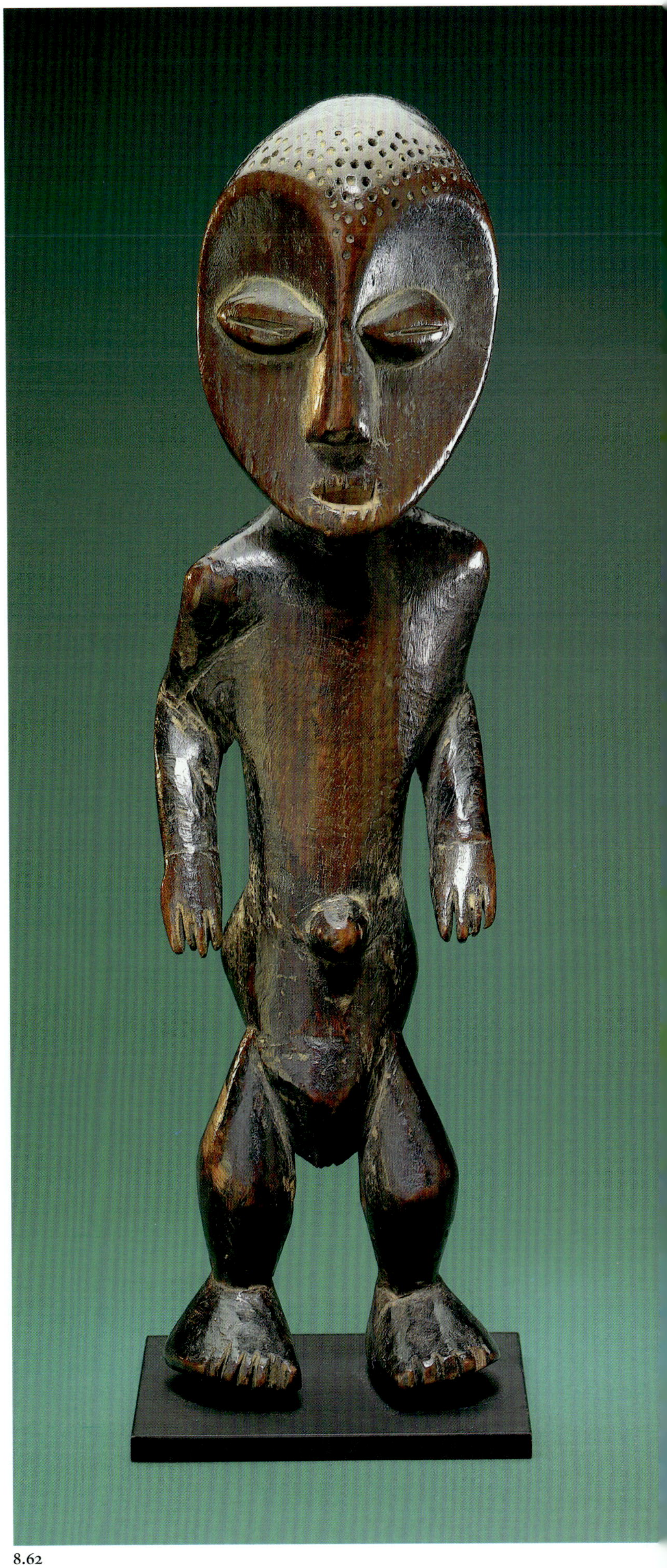

8.62

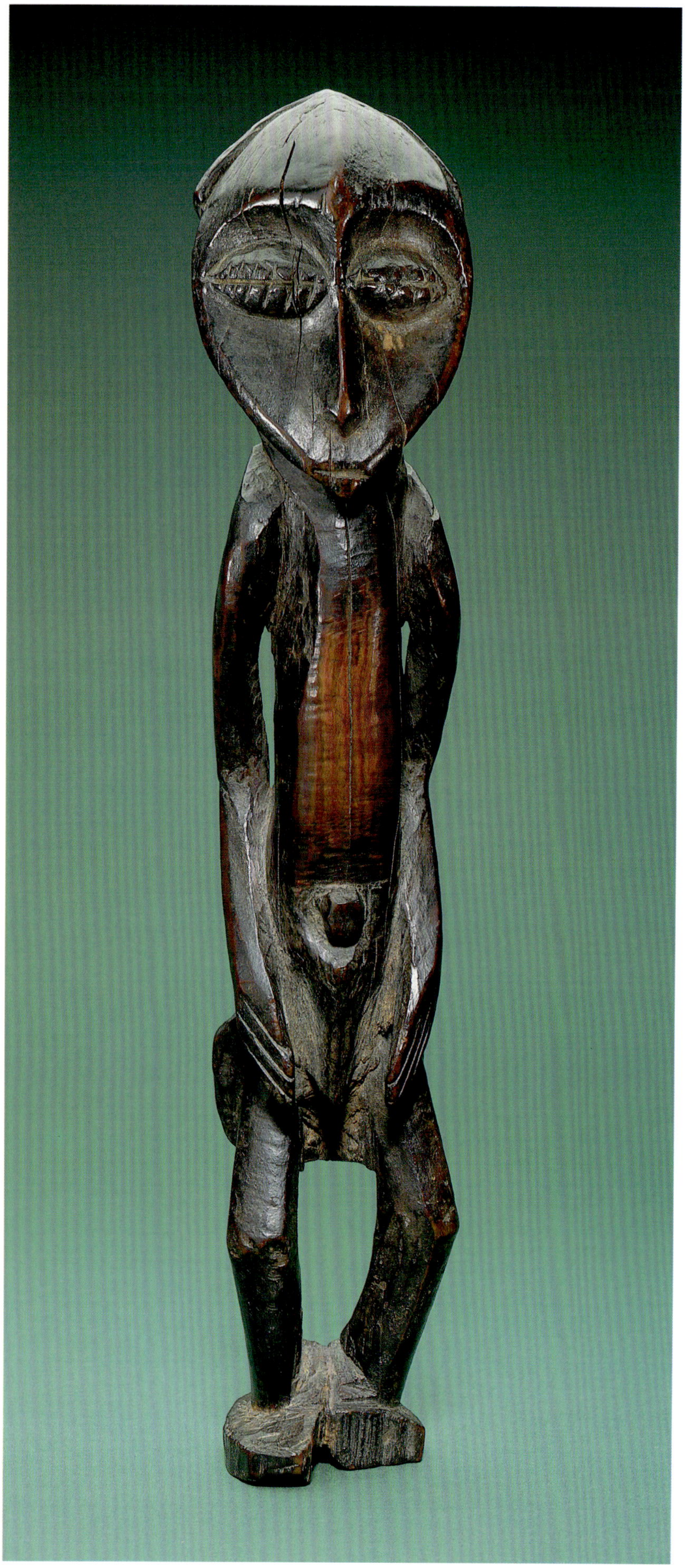

8.63A, B Front and side views of a human figure. Wood. H: 35.4 cm (14 in.).

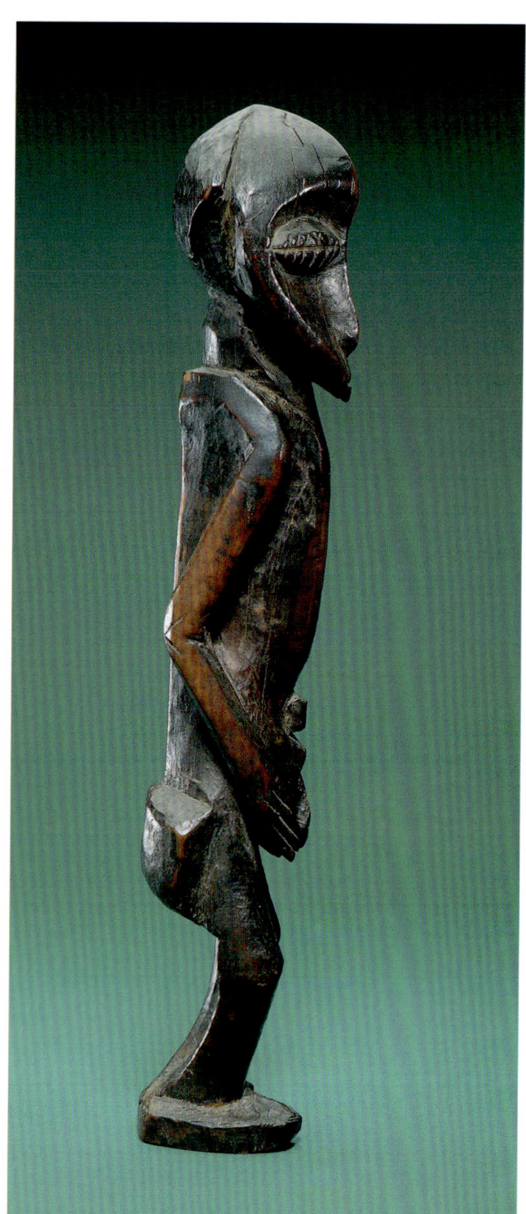

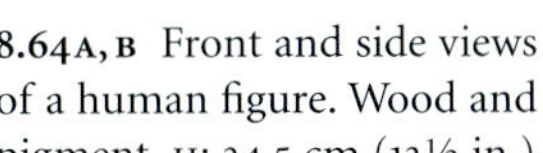

8.64A, B Front and side views of a human figure. Wood and pigment. H: 34.5 cm (13½ in.).

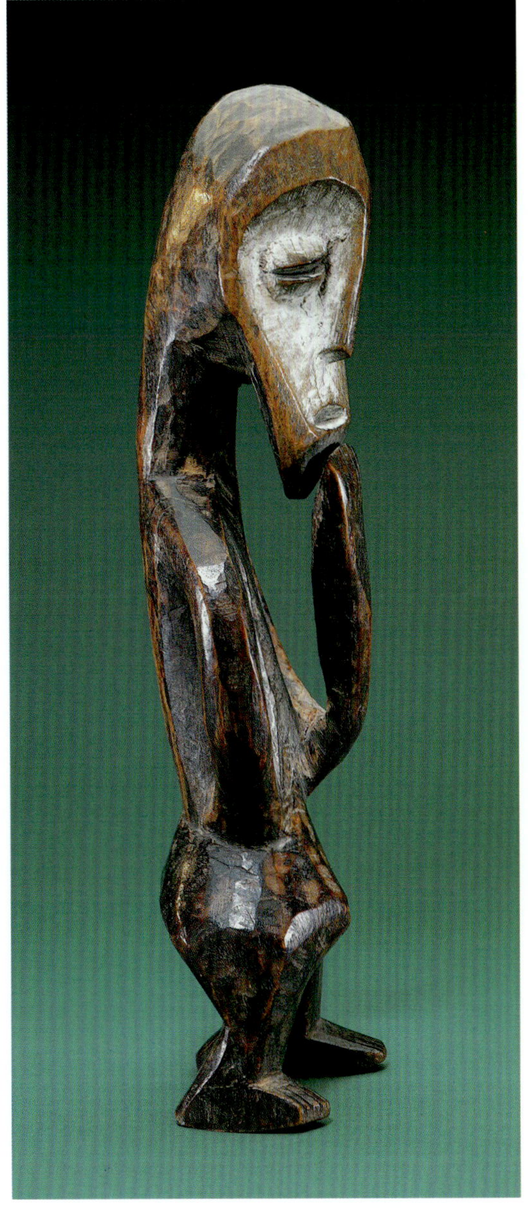

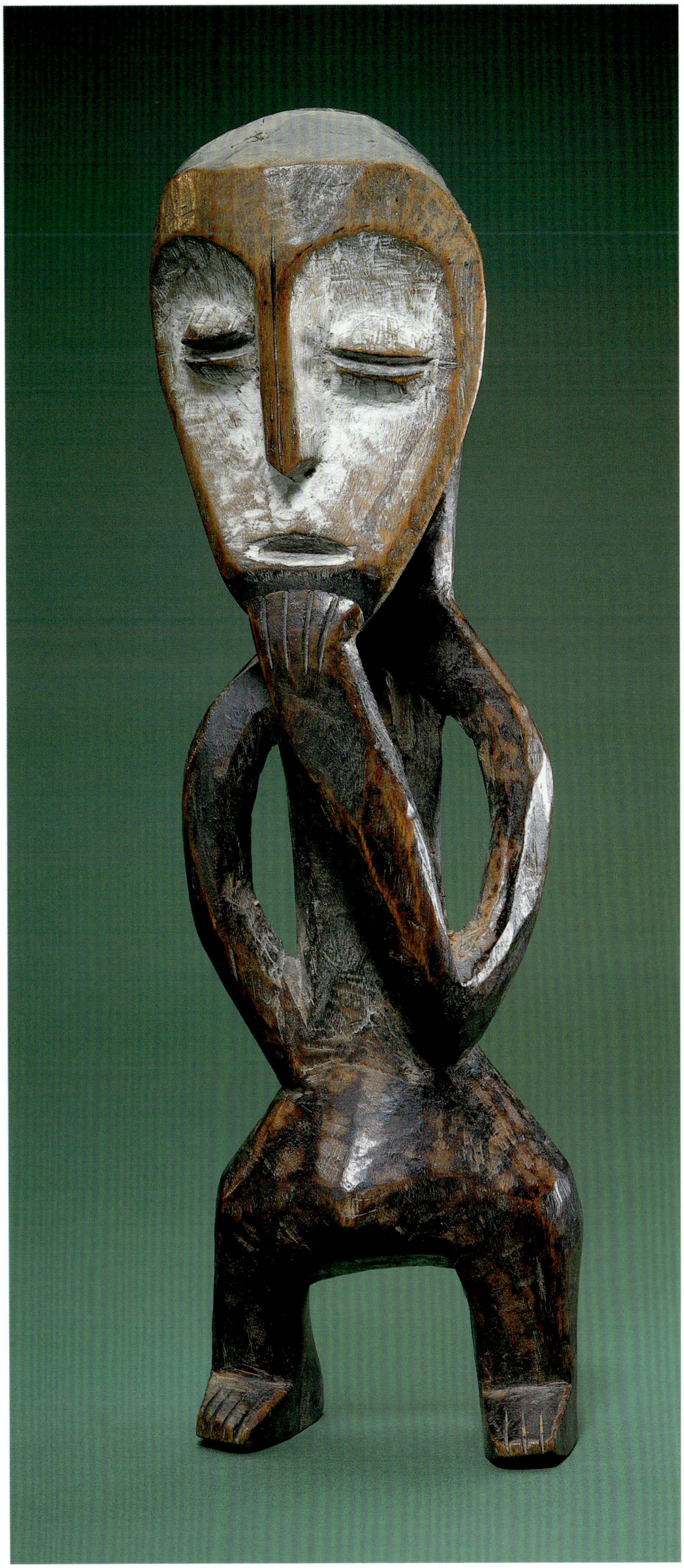

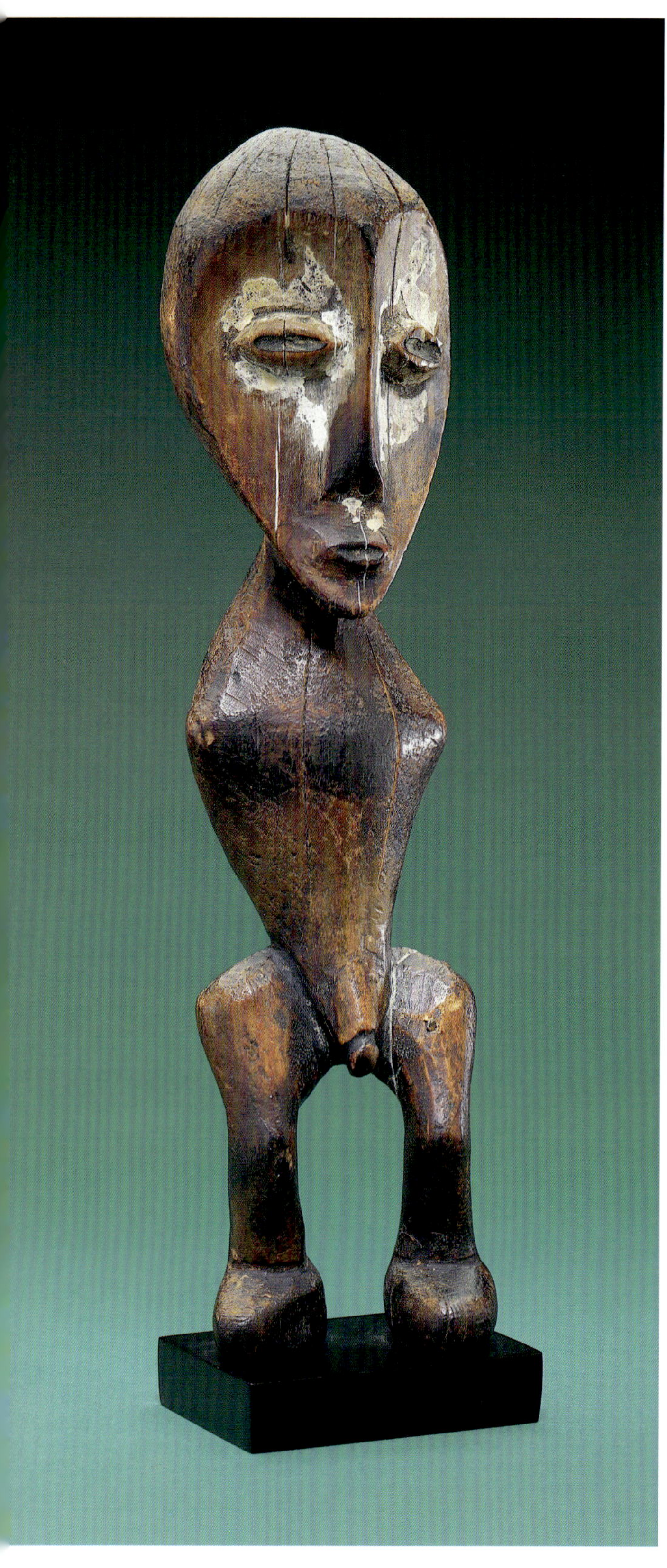

8.65 Human figure. Wood and pigment. H: 34.2 cm (13½ in.).

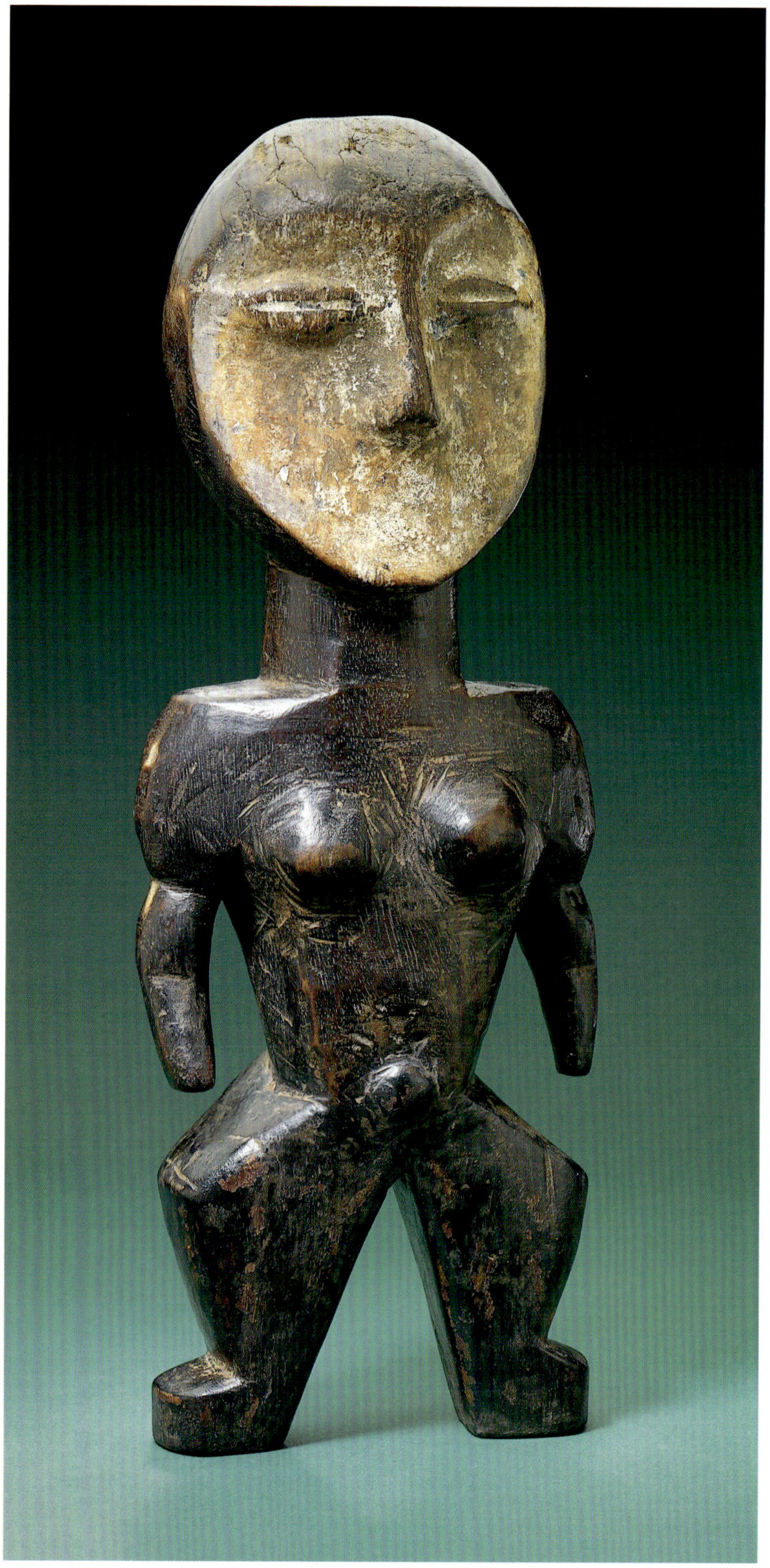

8.66 Human figure. Wood and pigment. H: 35 cm (13¾ in.).

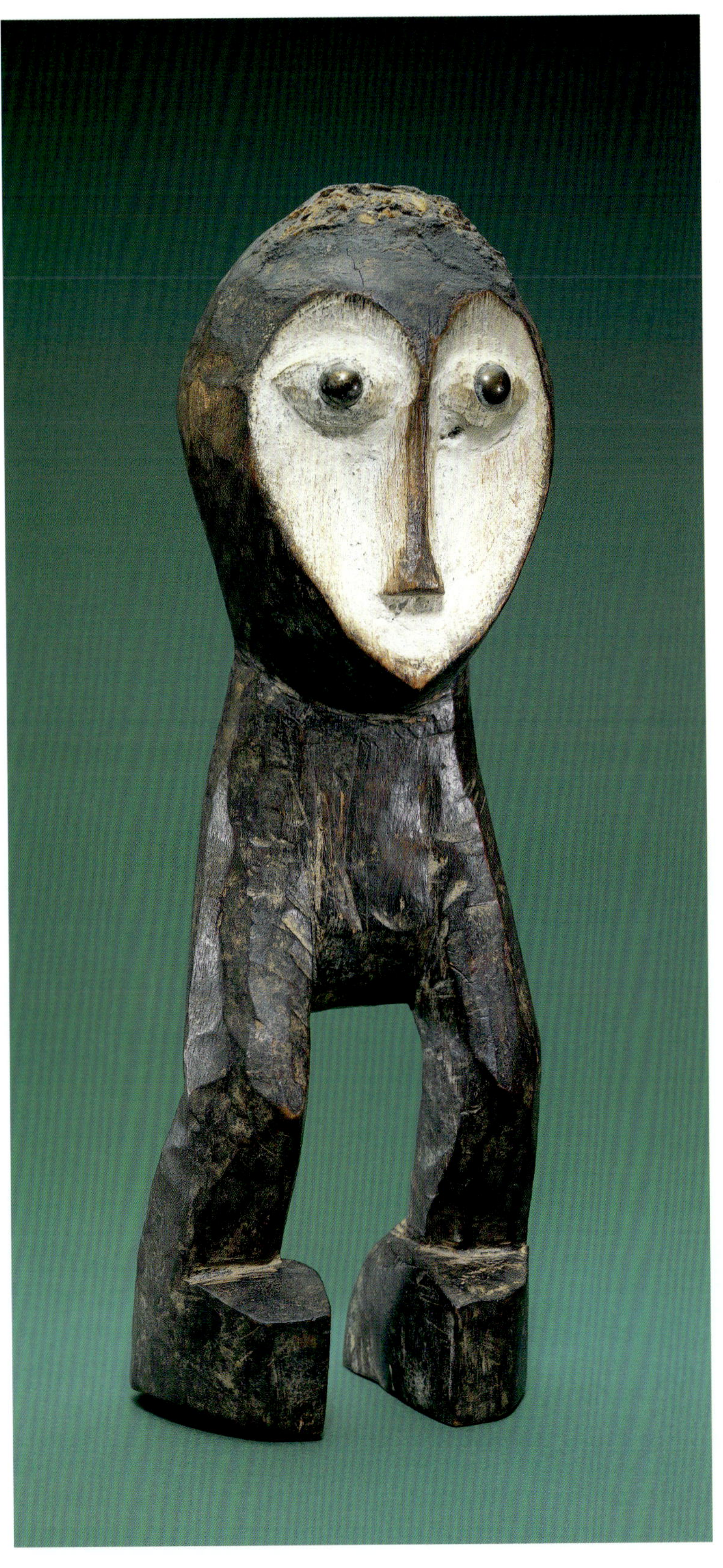

8.67 Human figure. Wood and pigment. H: 30.7 cm (12 in.).

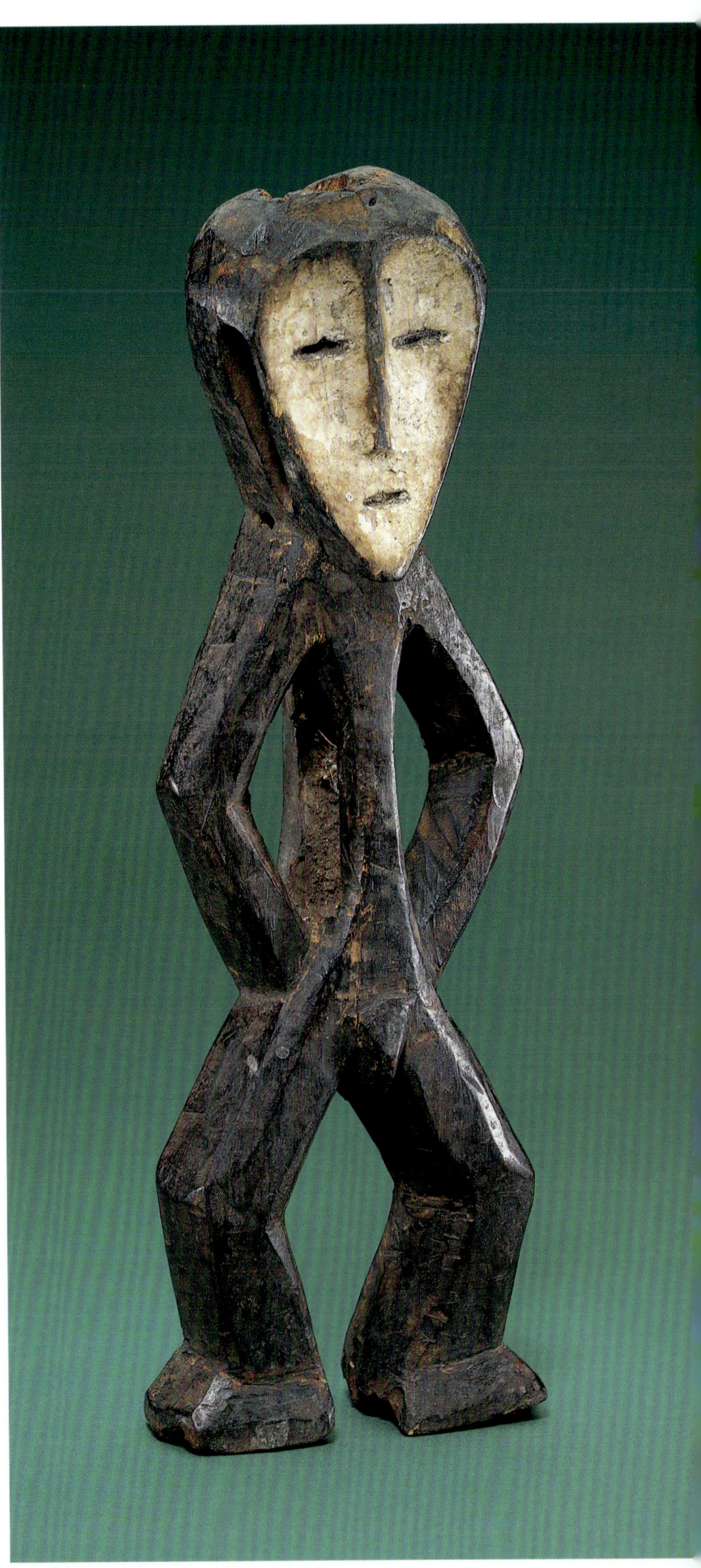

8.68 Human figure. Wood and pigment. H: 27.5 cm (10¾ in.).

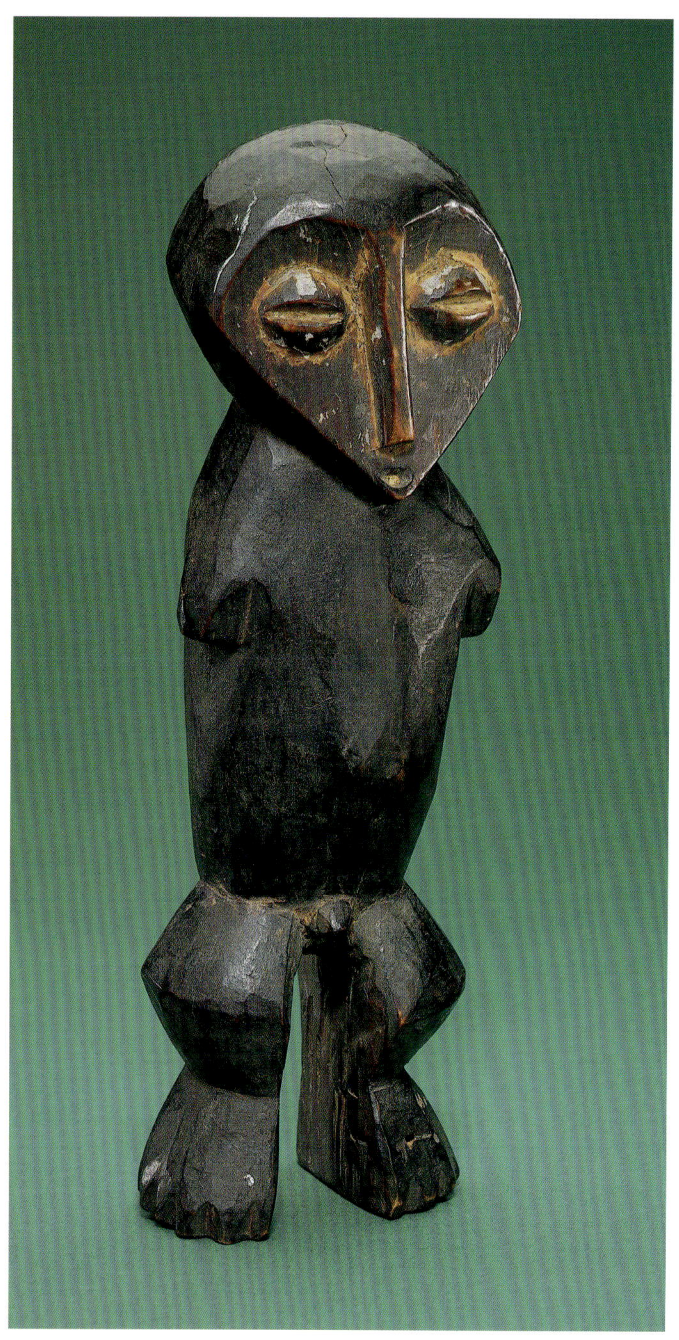

8.69 Human figure.
Wood. H: 24 cm (9½ in.).

MULTIHEADED FIGURES

The teacher uses initiation objects in layered metaphors to communicate many different things. Only rarely and primarily in the higher-level initiations does form contribute a single meaning to such a piece. An example of this is the multiheaded figure called Sakimatwematwe (Many-Heads). There is an interesting variety of ways in which the artist can render the multiple heads when creating this figure (figs. 8.70–8.80). But whether it has two heads or twelve, has a body or not, the multiheaded figure has the same meaning and function (Biebuyck 1981, 120).

The saying most often connected to these figures is "Many-Heads who has seen an elephant on the other side of the river" (Biebuyck 1973, 220–21). De Kun explains the saying this way: "A hunter goes across a great river, sees an elephant on the other bank, returns to look for other hunters to help but when he returns he finds that the others have already killed the elephant" (1966, 88). Biebuyck suggests that the saying stresses the ability of the high-level Bwami members, as a result of the initiation process, to see in many different directions and to be wise and fair minded (Biebuyck 1973, 220–21; 1981, 121).

The multiheaded figure also points to the inability of anyone to act alone. To move up in Bwami, a man needs his wife, a wife needs her husband, and a person needs a sponsor and teacher. Completeness and accomplishment only come when the links between people are acknowledged and utilized (Biebuyck 1981, 122). Biebuyck also suggests that the lack of sexual characteristics on these figures reflects the merging of genders that occurs in the higher levels of Bwami (1981, 119, 125). Occasionally multiheaded figures will have only one arm. This serves as an illustration of the downfall of a high-level Bwami member and a reminder to other members that attaining a high grade does not guarantee future success (Biebuyck 1981, 123).

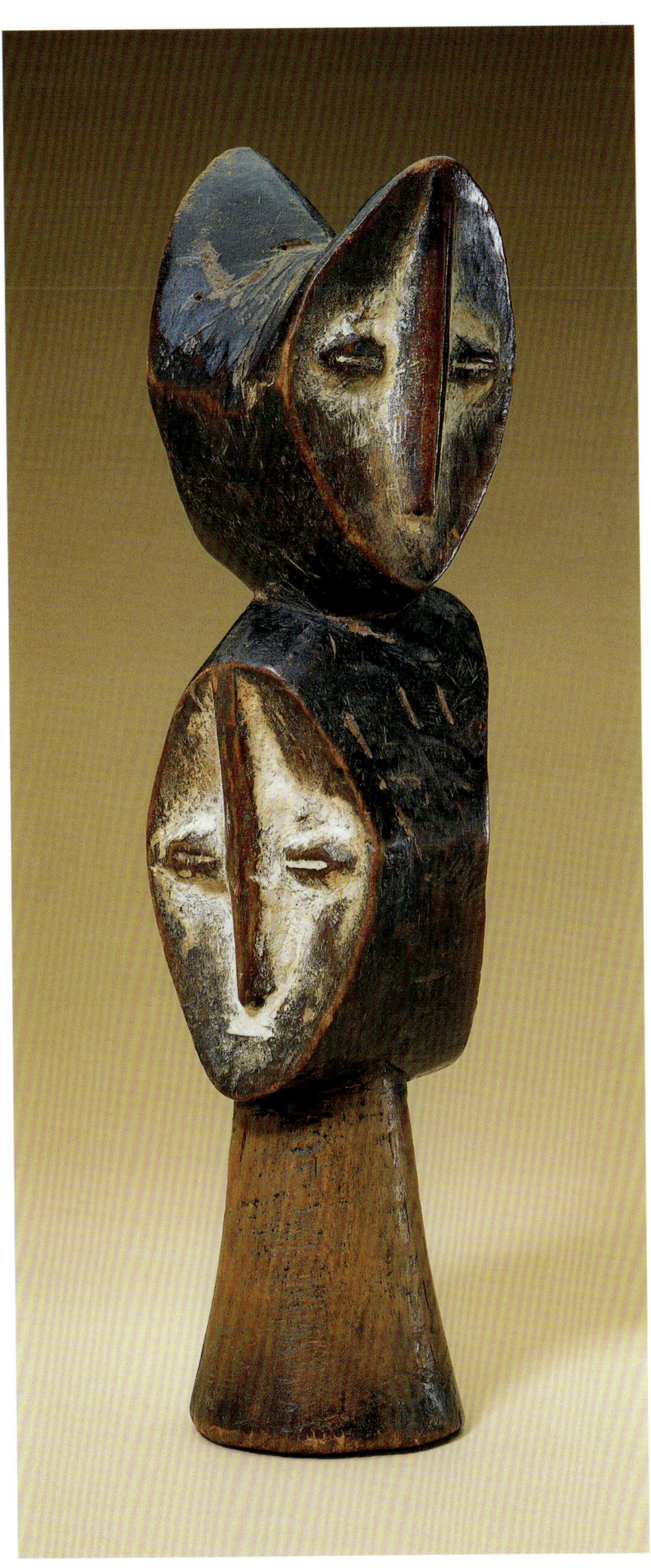

8.70 Human bust with multiple heads. Wood and pigment. H: 31.6 cm (12½ in.).

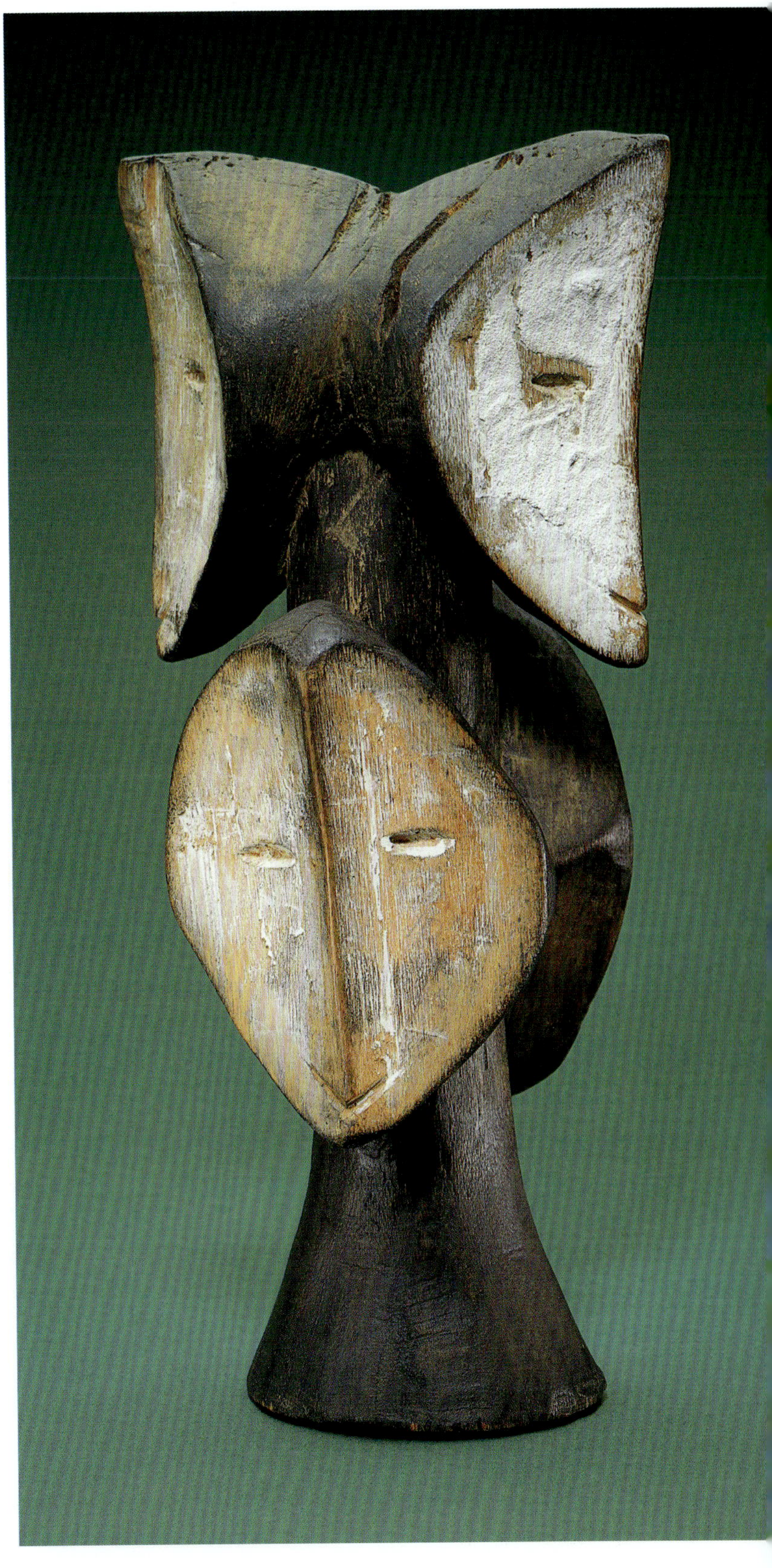

8.71 Human bust with multiple heads. Wood and pigment. H: 31.5 cm (12⅜ in.).

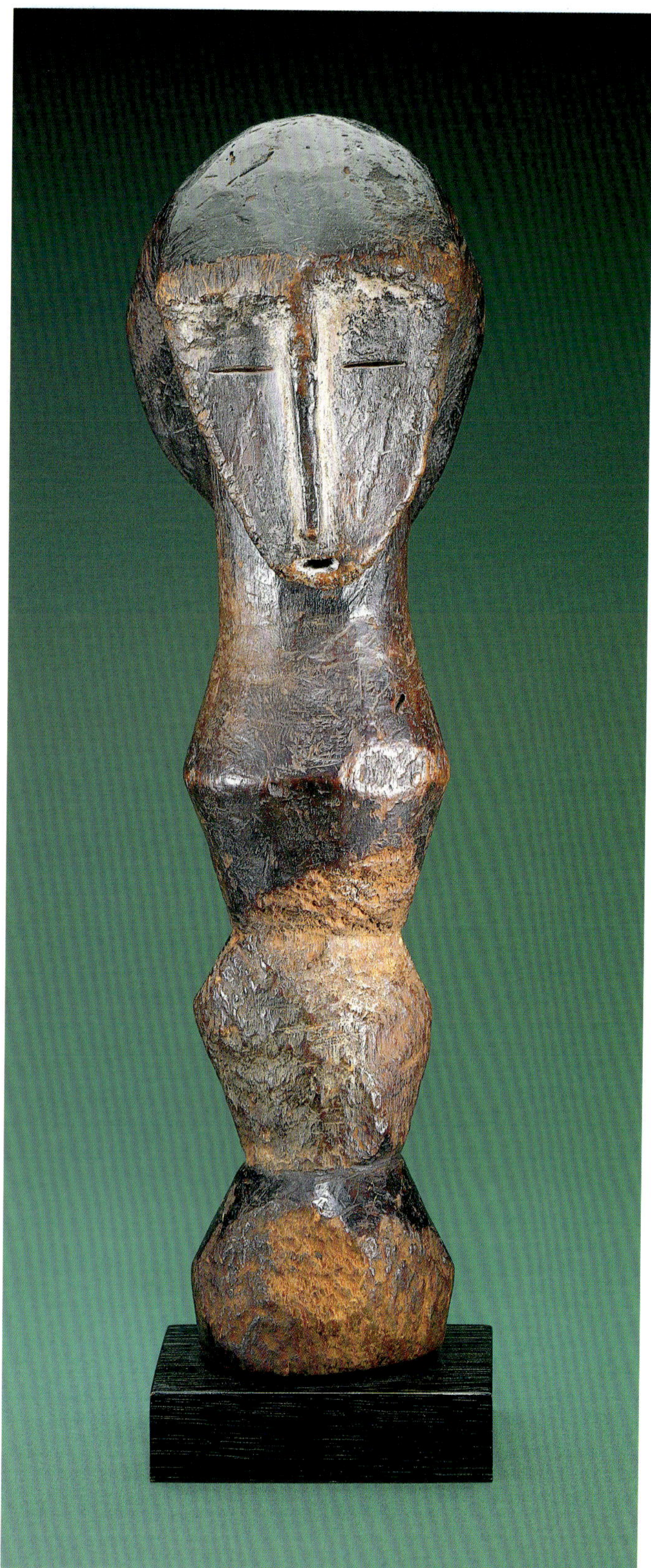

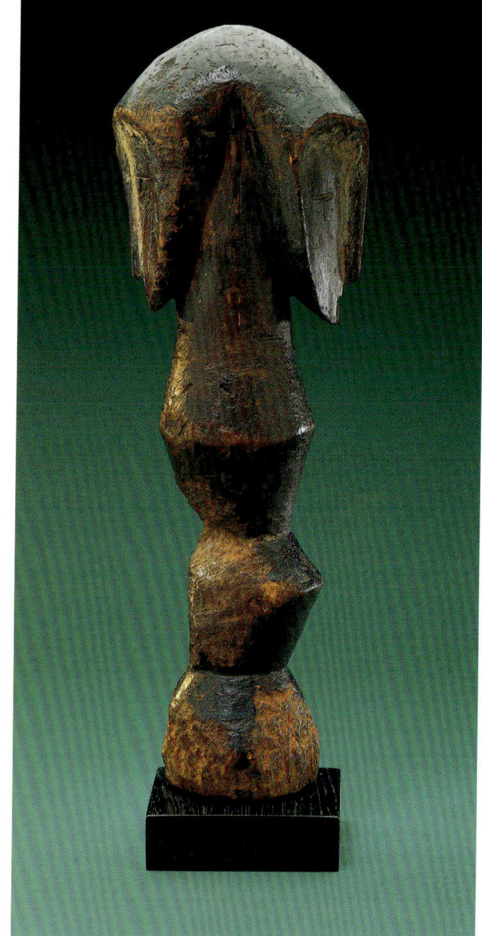

8.72A, B Front and side views of a human figure with multiple heads. Wood. H: 29 cm (11⅜ in.).

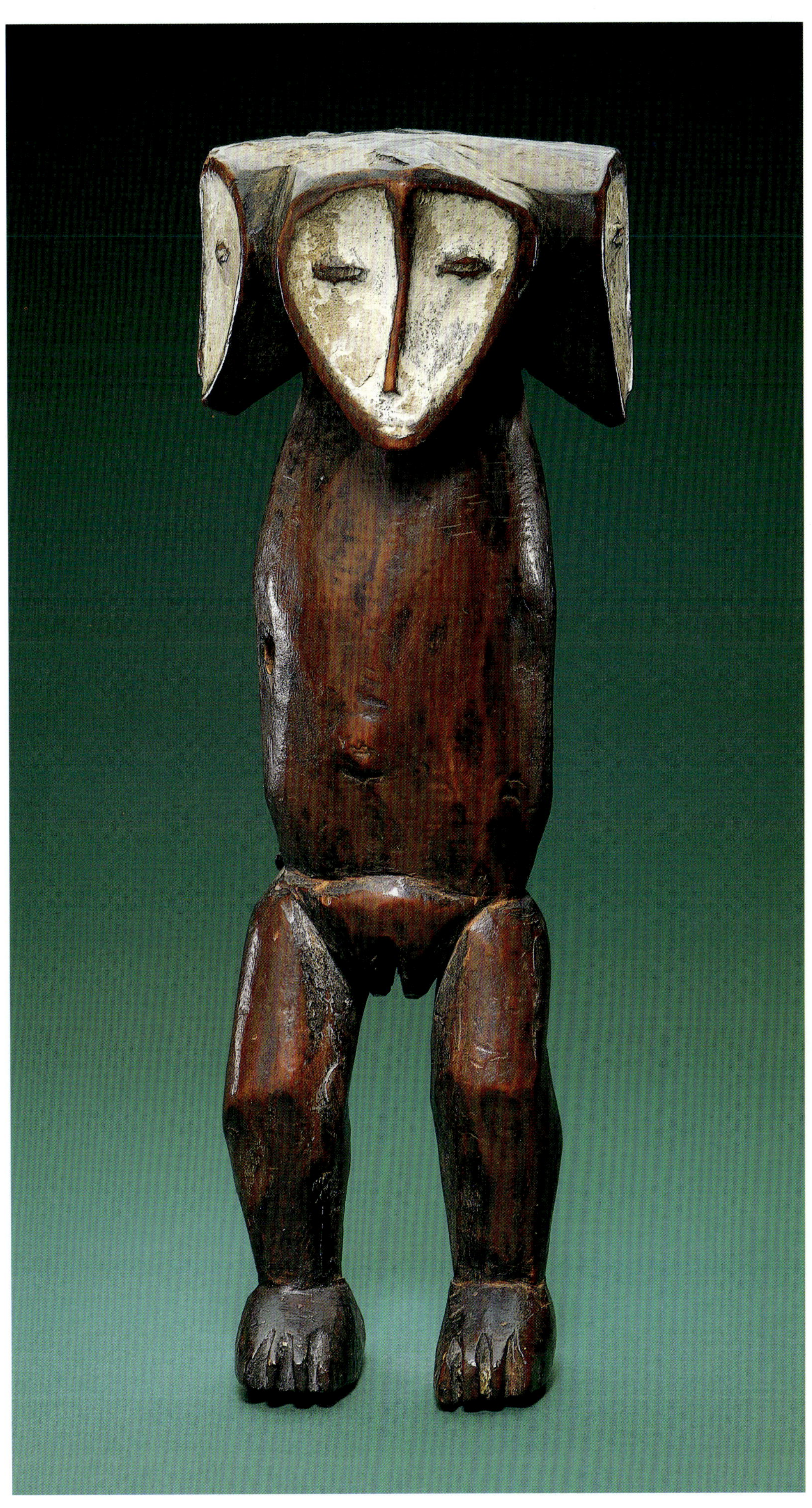

8.73 Human figure with multiple heads. Wood and pigment.
H: 28.5 cm (11¼ in.).

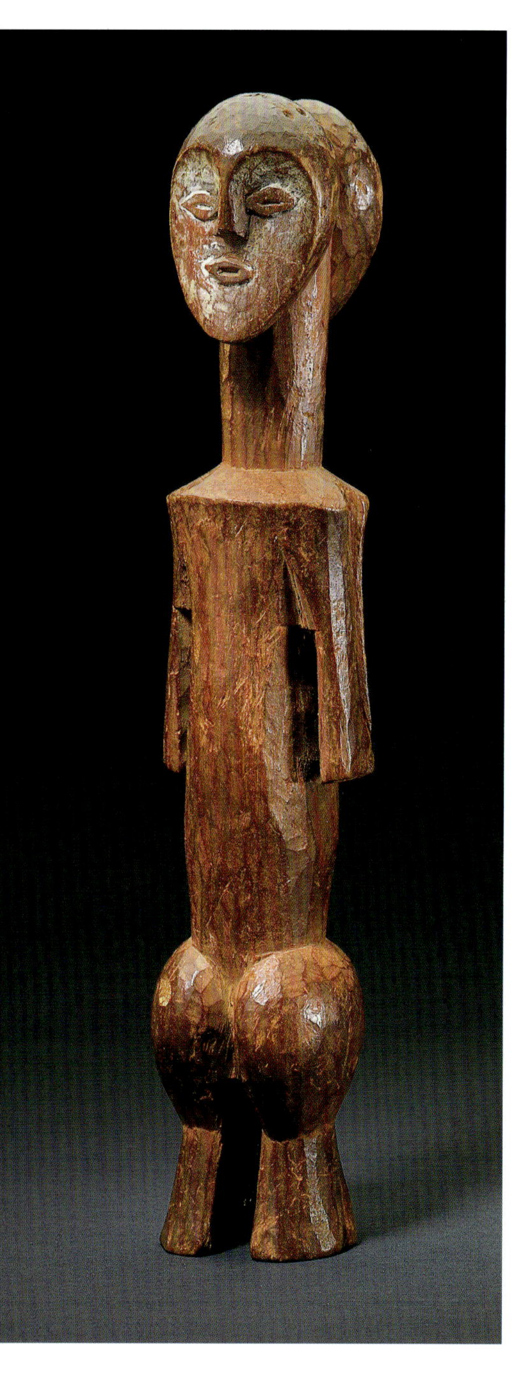

8.74 Human figure with multiple heads. Wood and pigment. H: 35 cm (13¾ in.).

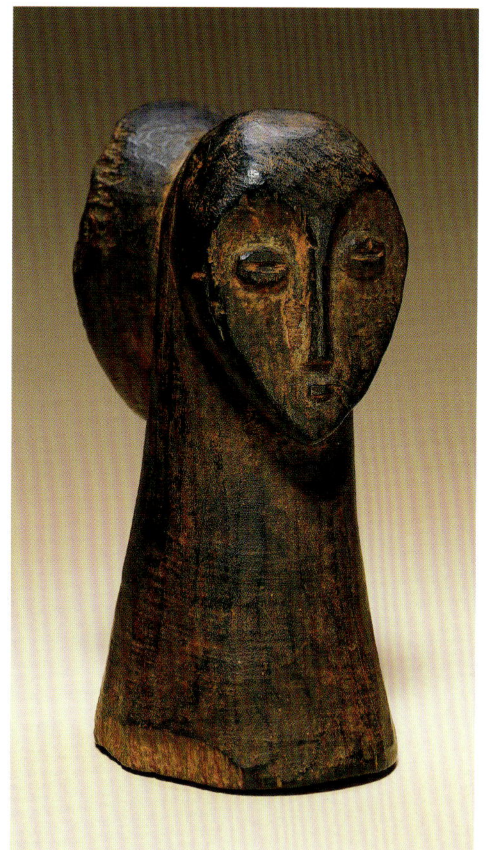

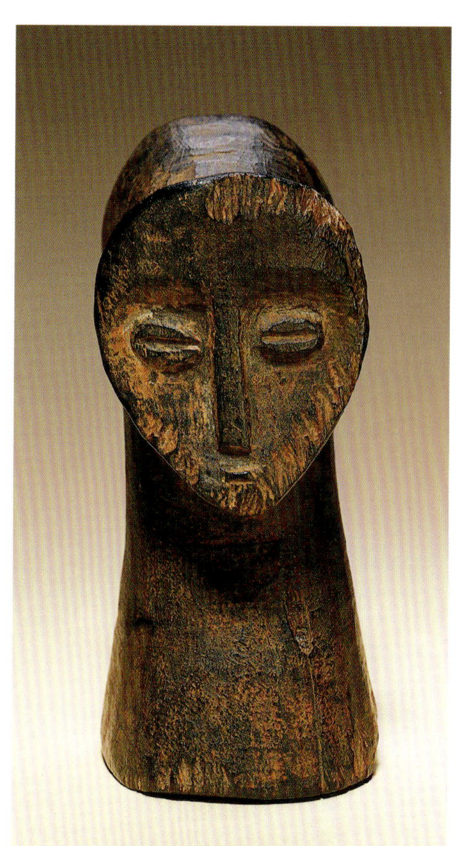

8.75A,B Two views of a bust with two heads. Wood. H: 10.6 cm (4¼ in.).

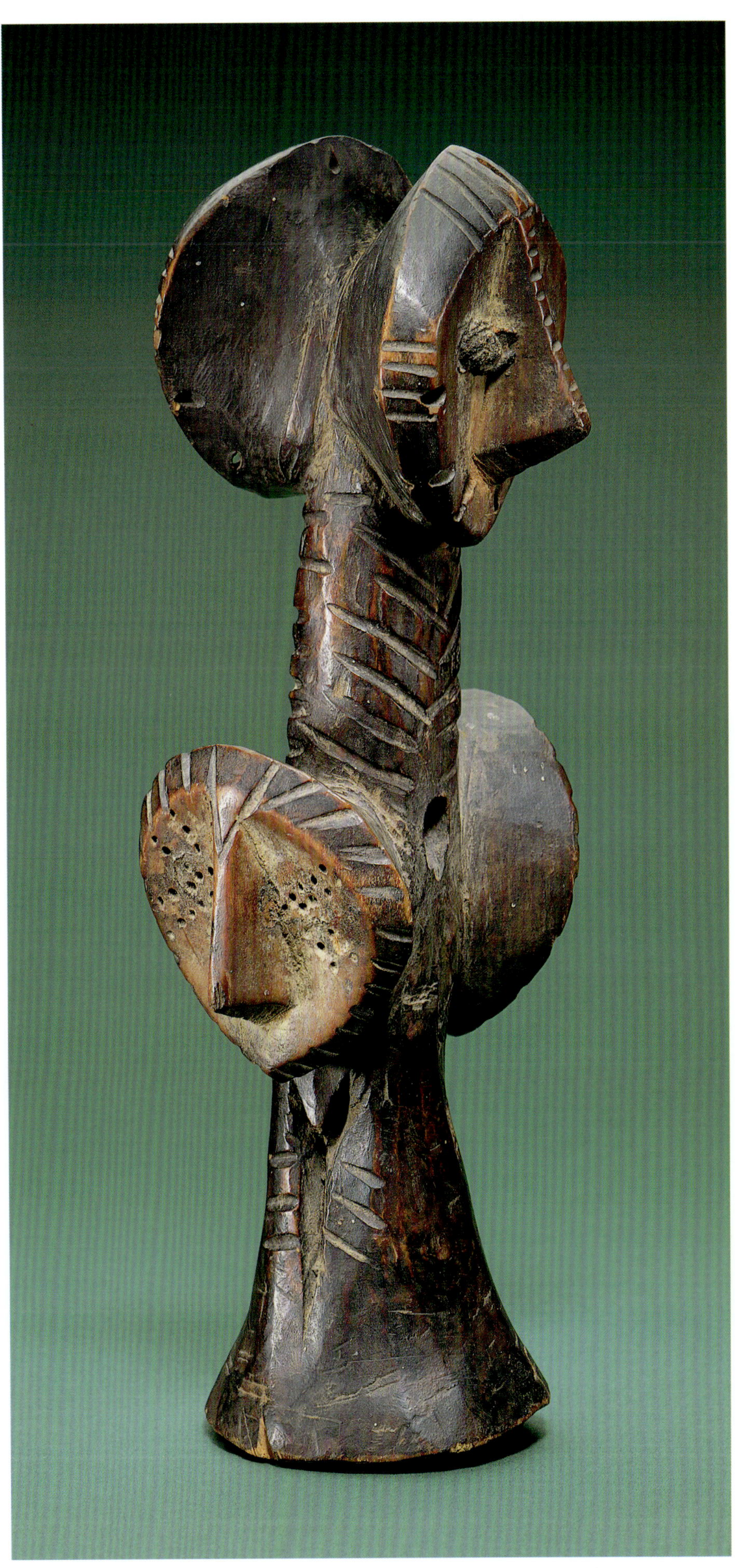

8.76 Human figure with multiple heads. Wood. H: 31 cm (12¼ in.).

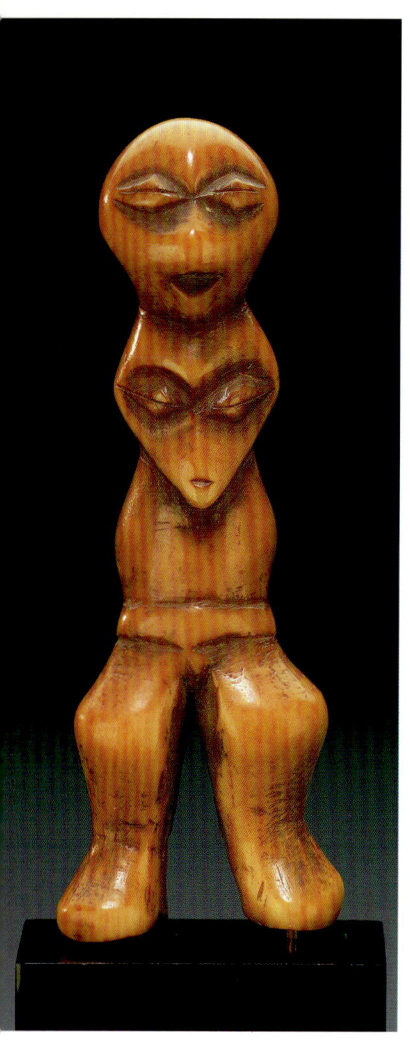

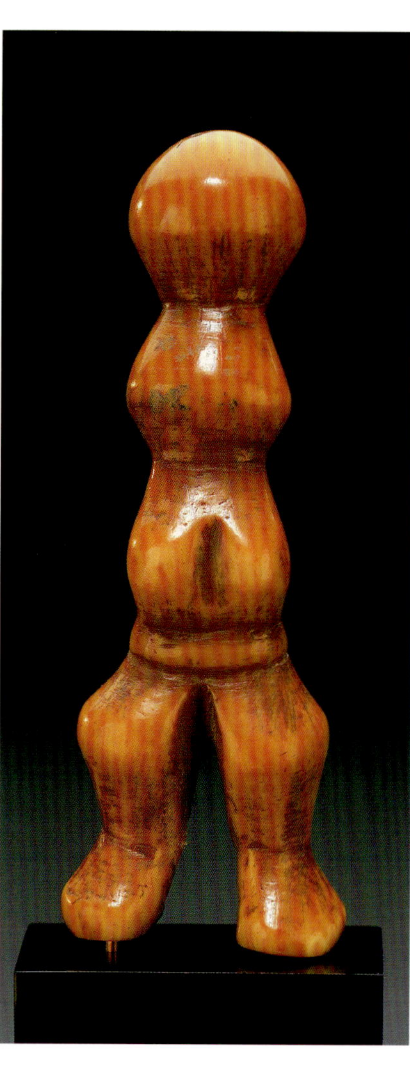

8.77A, B Front and back views of a human figure with multiple heads. Ivory. H: 10.8 cm (4¼ in.).

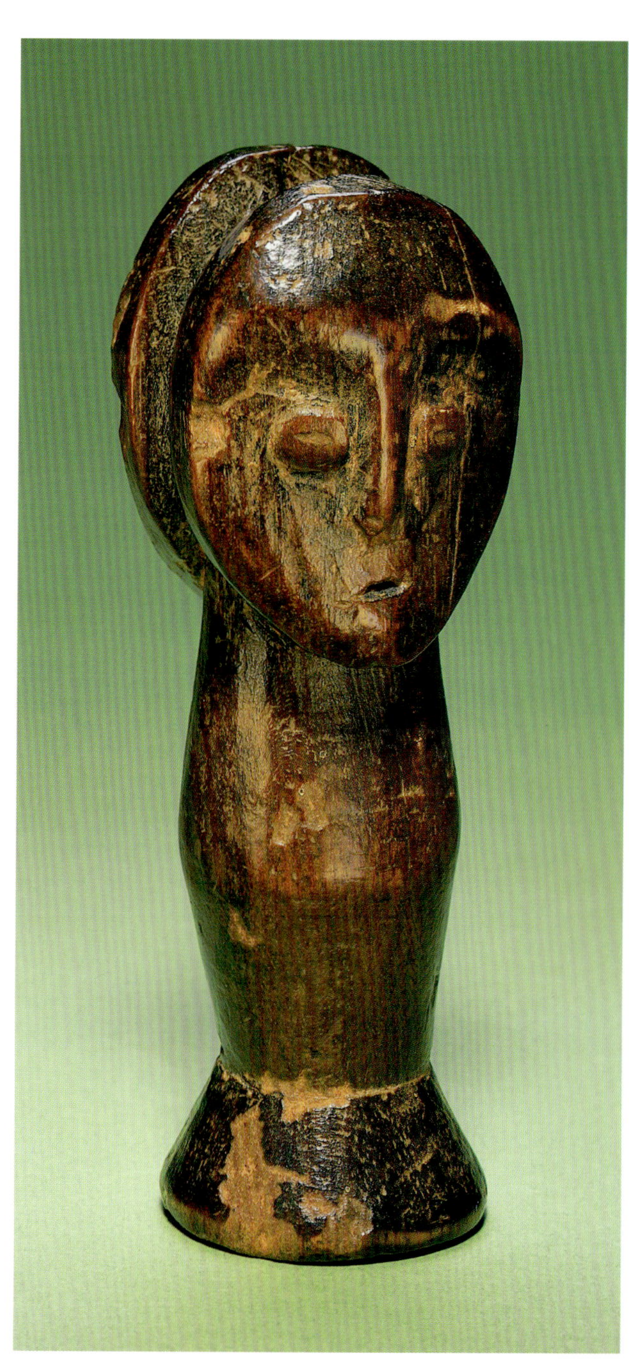

8.78 Bust with two heads. Wood. H: 15 cm (5⅞ in.).

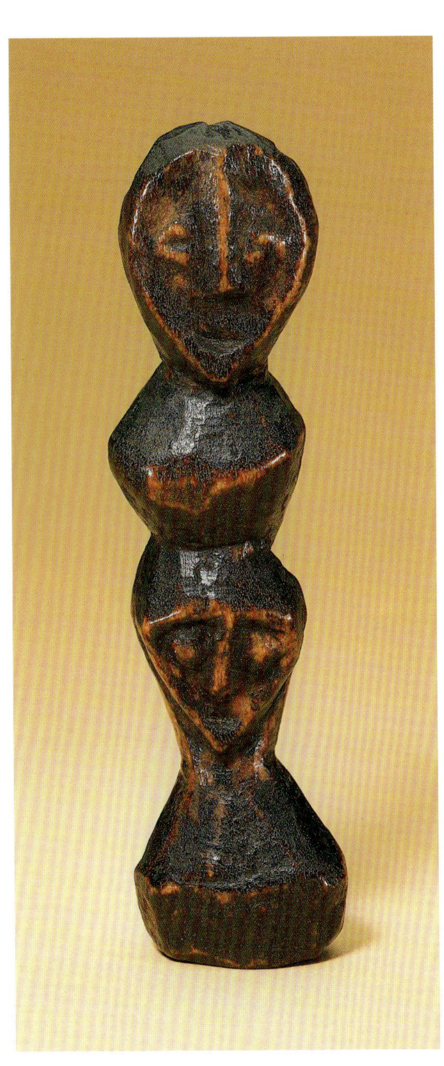

8.79 Human figure with multiple heads. Ivory. H: 11.5 cm (4½ in.).

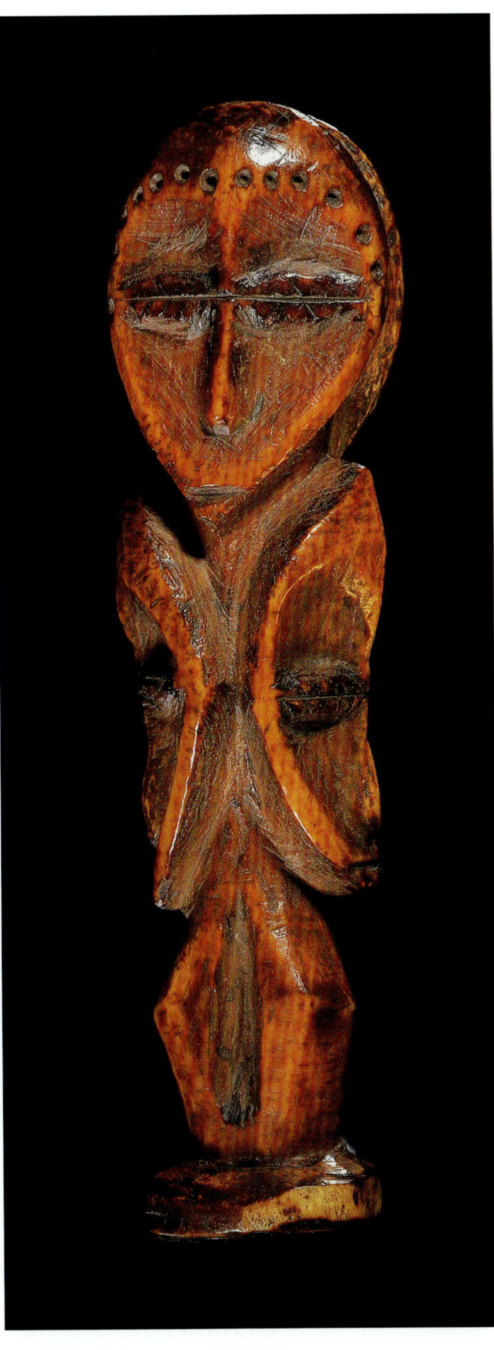

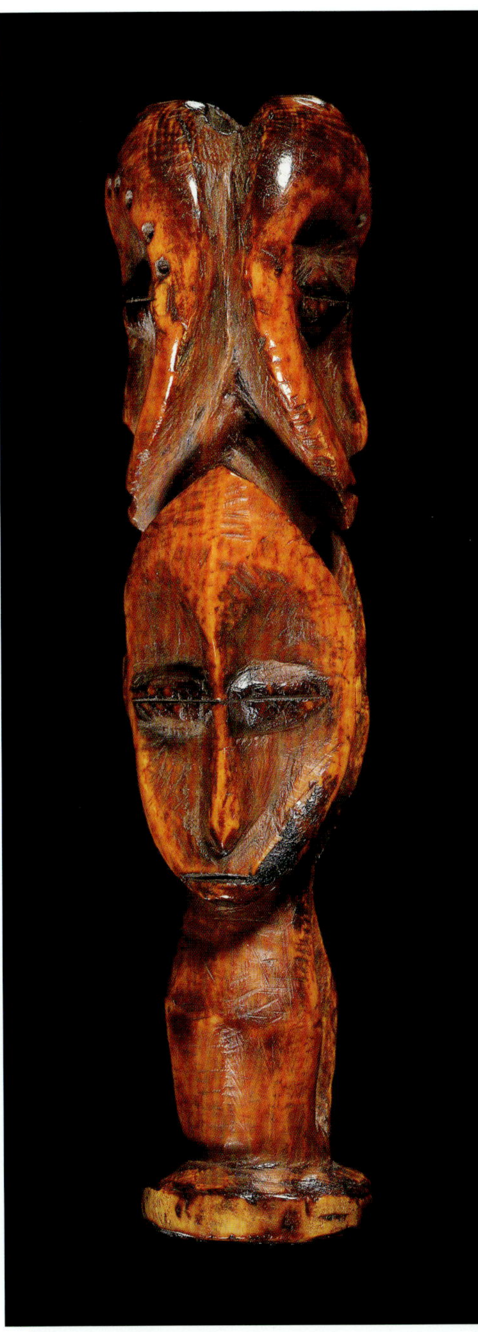

8.80A,B Two views of a human figure with multiple heads. Ivory. H: 15.4 cm (6 in.).

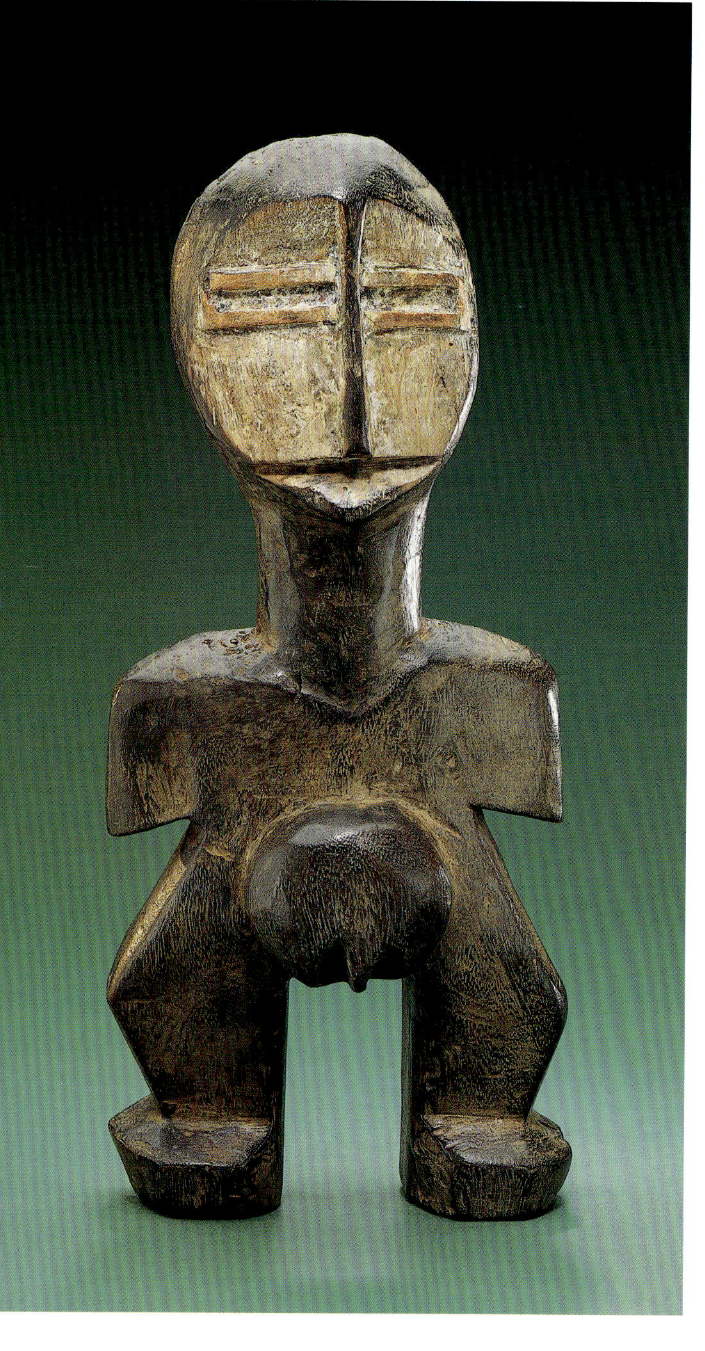

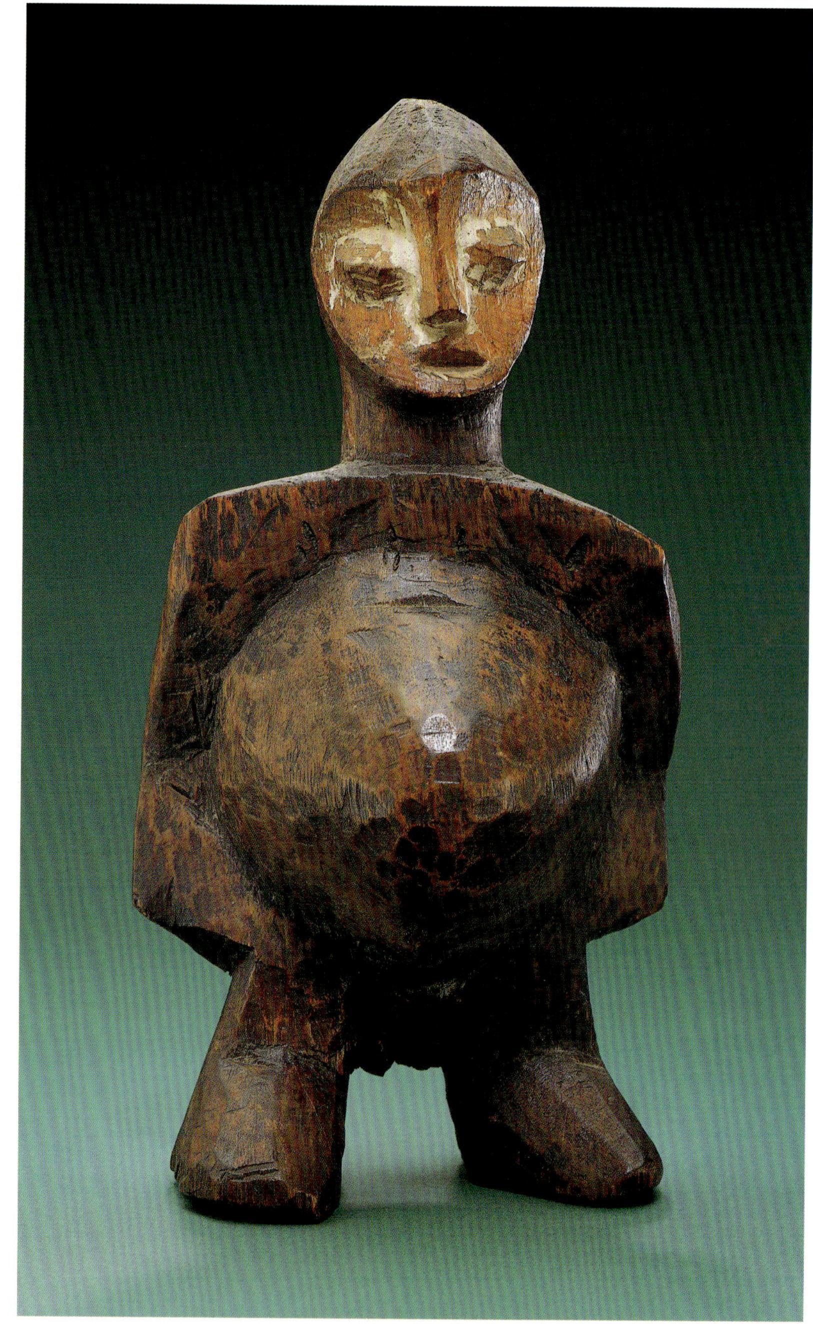

8.81 Figure (Wayinda). Wood and pigment. H: 27 cm (10⅝ in.).

8.82 Figure (Wayinda). Wood and pigment. H: 28.7 cm (11¼ in.).

WAYINDA AND KAKULU KA MPITO

Wayinda is the pregnant, adulterous woman who brings shame to her entire family (figs. 8.81, 8.82). Kakulu ka Mpito (figs. 8.83, 8.84), portrayed as an armless figure with goat hair circling his face, is her husband who suffers the consequences of his wife's actions. Occasionally this male

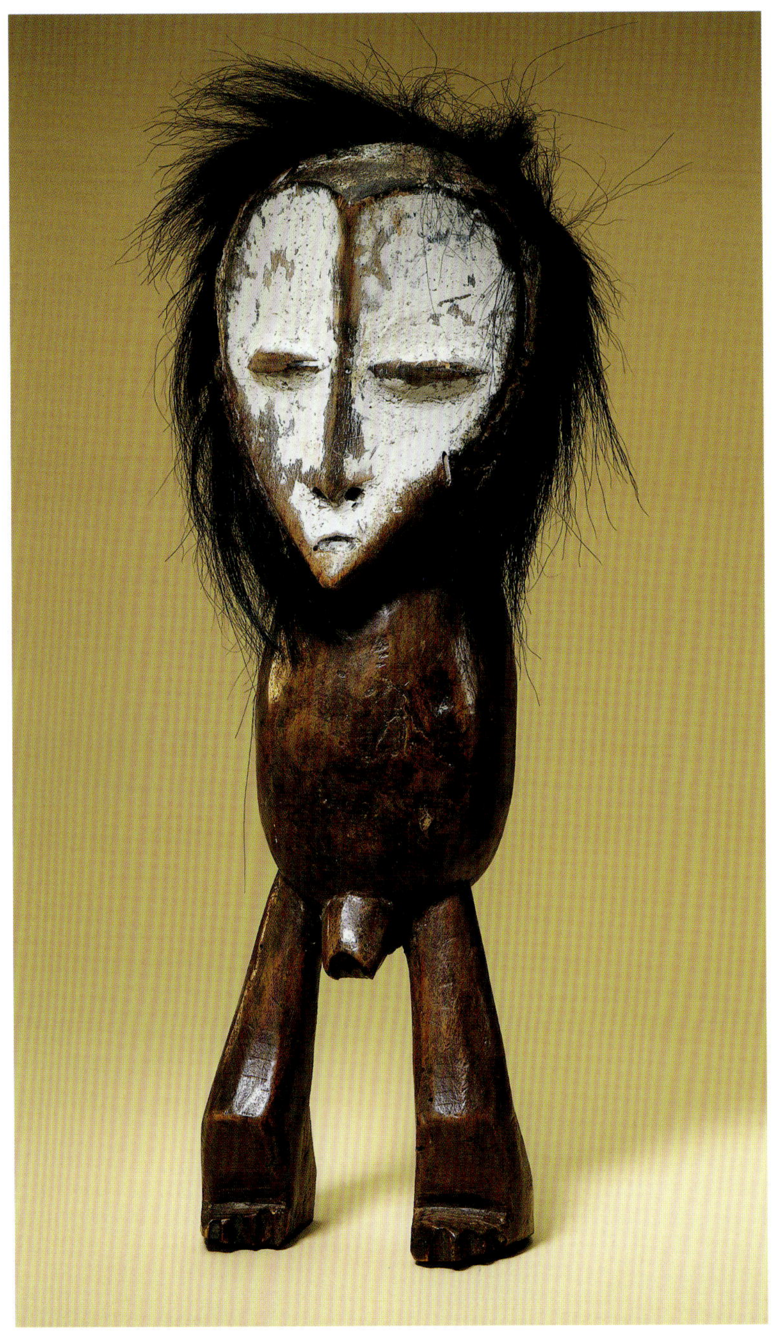

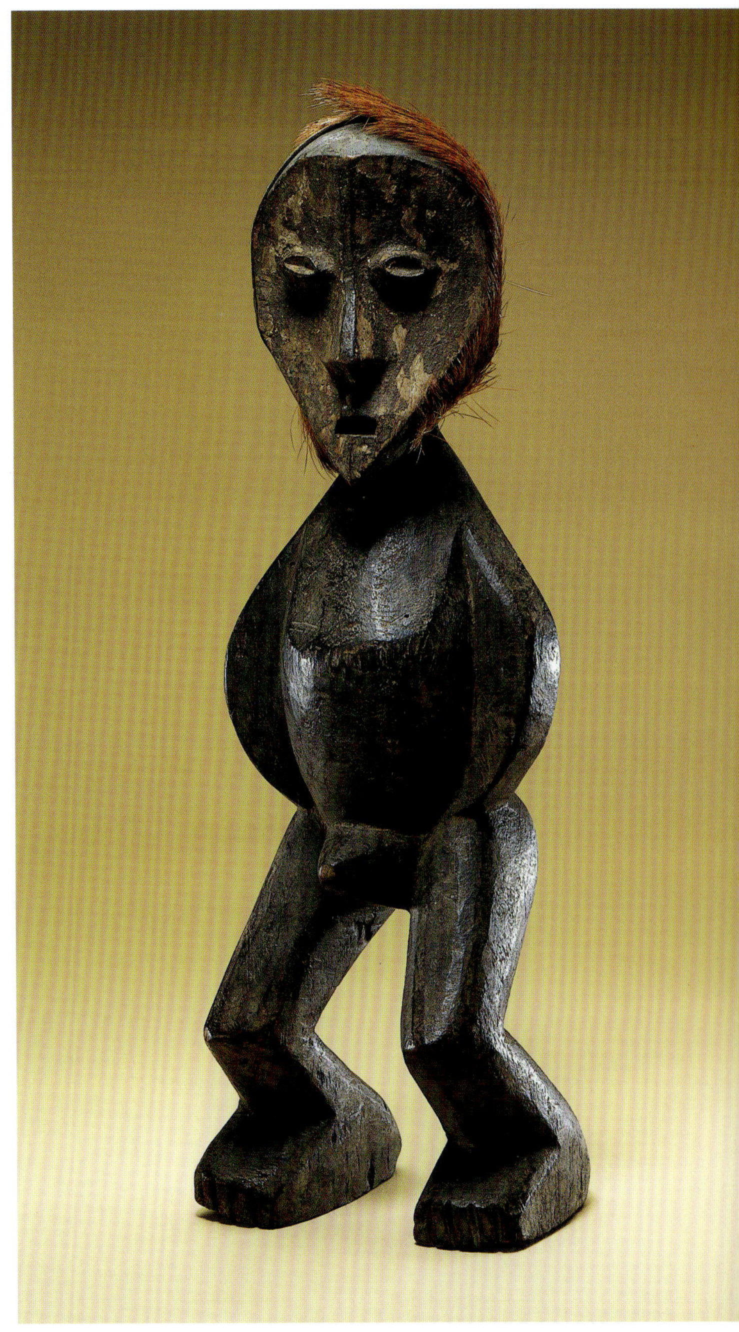

figure is also called Mukobania, a young man who courts disaster by throwing a party and inviting a group of strangers who cause trouble. Both the male and female figures are kept by members of Lutumbo lwa Kindi and are often paired during performances (Biebuyck 1973, pl. 69; 1994, 122).

8.83 Human figure (Kakulu ka Mpito). Wood, hair, and pigment. H: 31.9 cm (12½ in.).

8.84 Human figure (Kakulu ka Mpito). Wood and fur. H: 35.5 cm (14 in.).

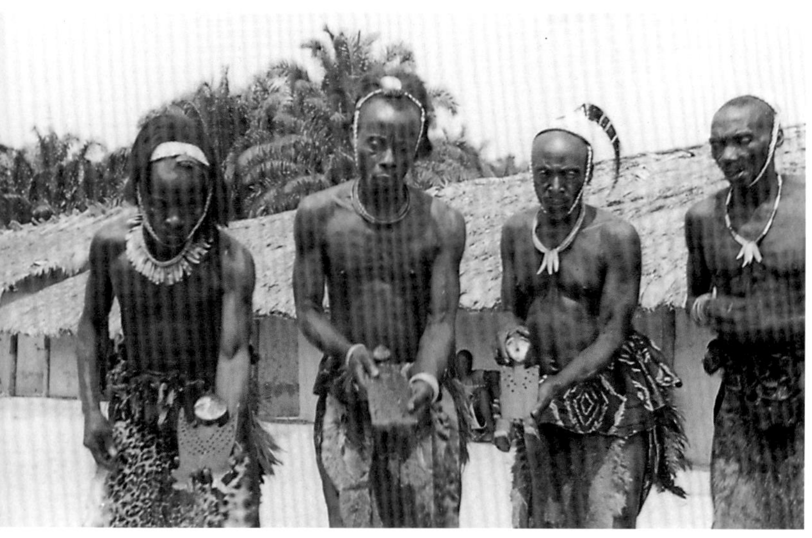

8.85 Four high-level Bwami members dance and display the sculpture called *katanda*, or "mat," circa 1952–1954. Photograph courtesy of Daniel P. Biebuyck.

MR. SLEEPING MAT

In Lega thought, sleeping mats (*katanda*) imply laziness and sexual laxity. An often-used Lega metaphor compares a swarm of red ants (*katanda ke ibazi*) to a mat. Further, a sexually promiscuous person (also understood metaphorically as a mat) spreads disorder in a community in the same way that red ants can beseige a town (Defour n.d., 169). The figure shown to the right (figs. 8.86a,b) is an anthropomorphized mat filled with holes, as if it had been destroyed by ants. The holes are also interpreted as the ants in the "mat of ants" (Biebuyck 1973, pl. 63). The saying most often used with the mat is: "I used to love you; fondling destroys good ones; it has destroyed Katanda" (Biebuyck 1973, pl. 63).

WOMAN'S HAT

Zigzag figures (figs. 8.87–8.89) are called *nkumba* or *mulima*. *Nkumba* is also the name of the phallic-shaped hat worn by high-level Bwami women (see fig. 5.17). In performances, the figure represents such a woman. When it is hung head-down by a string and coupled with the saying "Bat hangs with the head downward because of the bad word spoken by Sun," the figure is called *mulima*, meaning "bat" (Biebuyck 1973, pl. 72).

FIGURES WITH RAISED ARMS

Figures with one or both arms raised, usually called *kasangala*, remind the audience of Kindi's prerogative to arbitrate community problems (figs. 8.90–8.92). The figure points to the sky as a reminder of the size of the problems solved in the past: "What shoots up straight; I have arbitrated Igulu [lit., the sky]; I have arbitrated something big" (Biebuyck 1973, pl. 66).

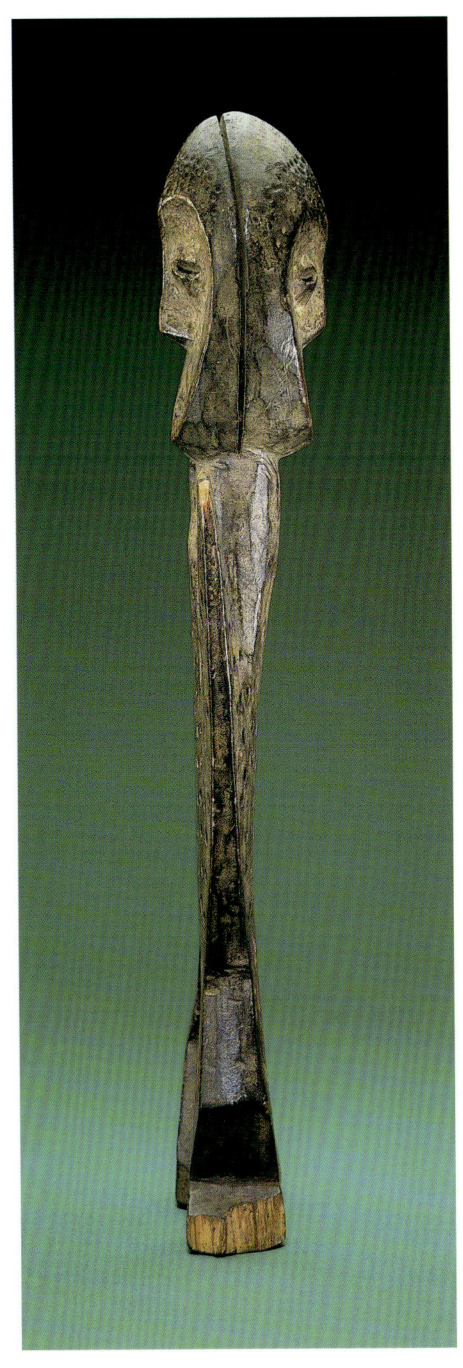

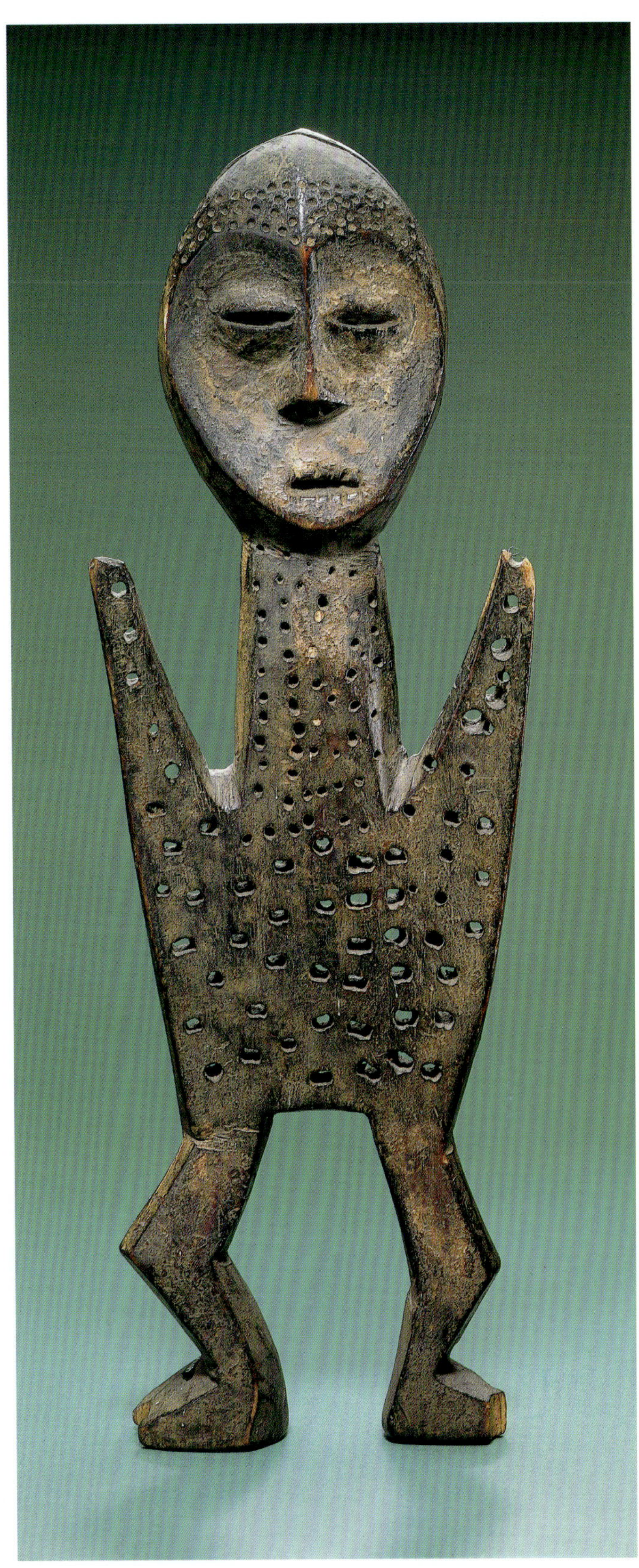

8.86 A, B Side and front views of an anthropomorphic sleeping mat (*katanda*). Wood. H: 35.7 cm (14 in.).

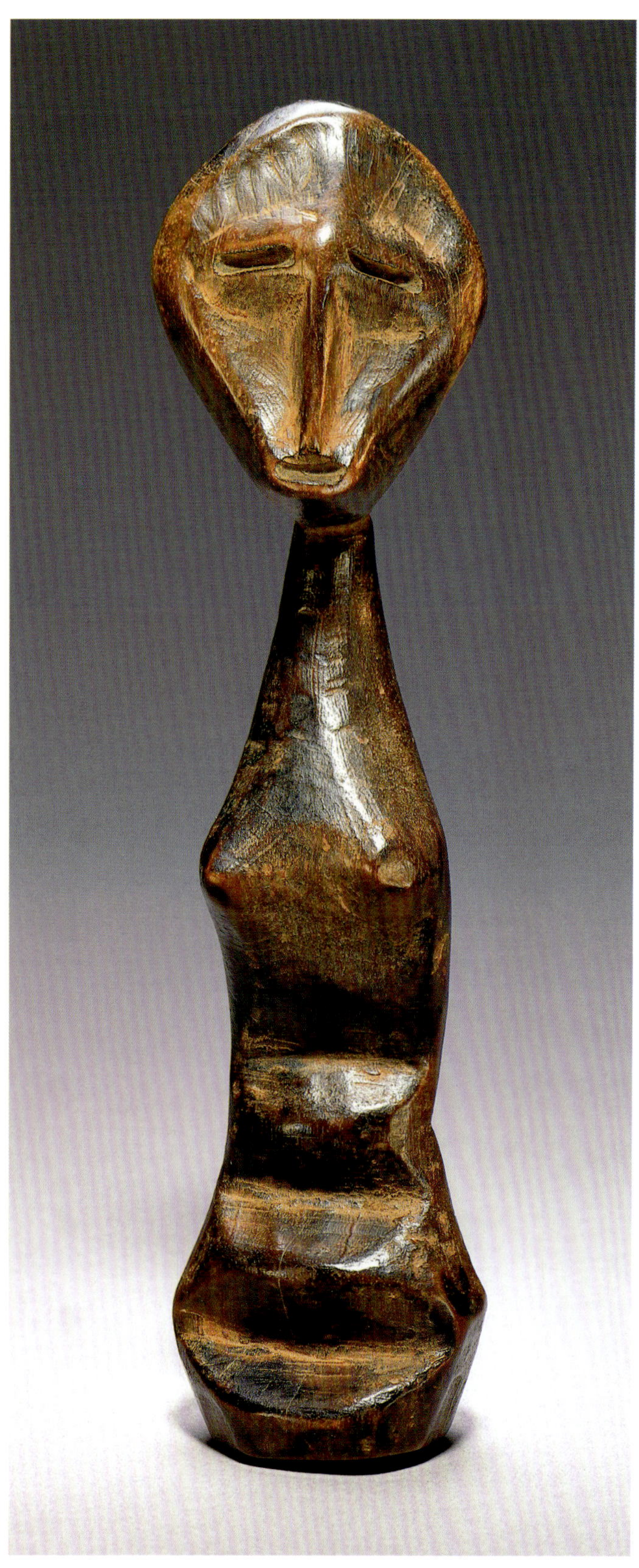

8.87 Figure (*nkumba* or *mulima*).
Wood. H: 20 cm (7⅞ in.).

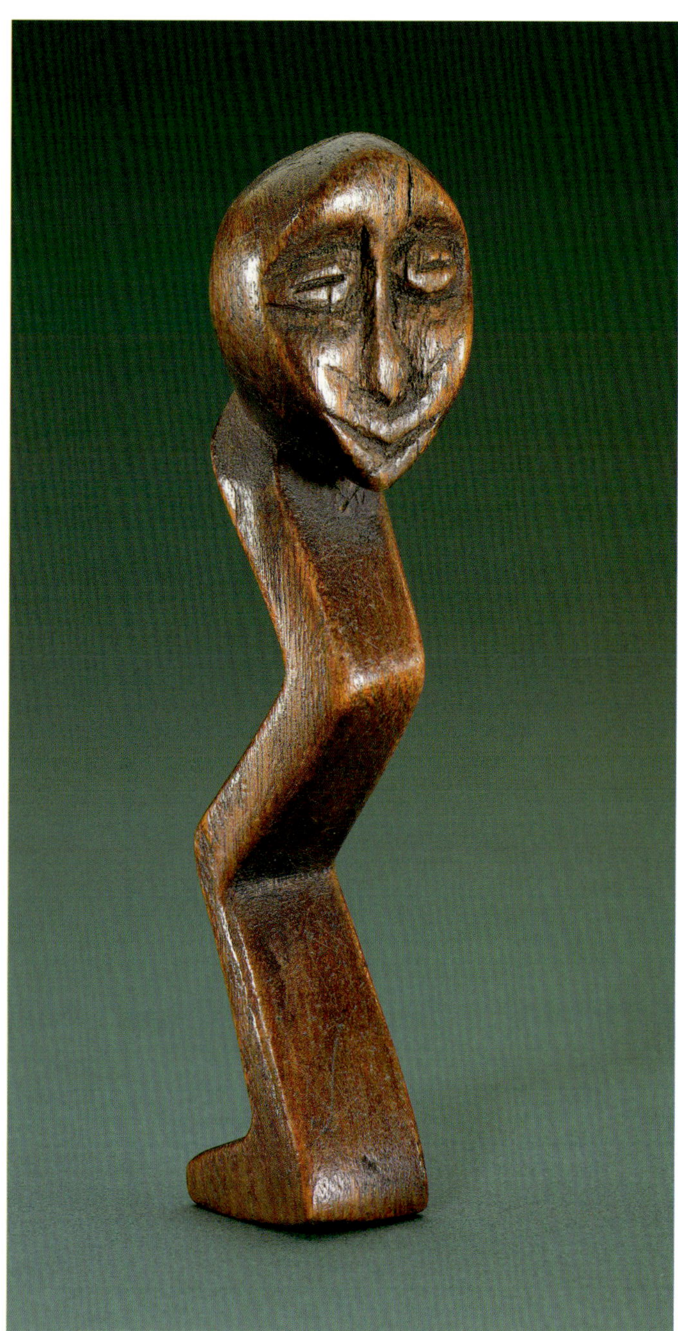

8.88 Figure (*nkumba* or *mulima*).
Wood. H: 13.5 cm (5¼ in.).

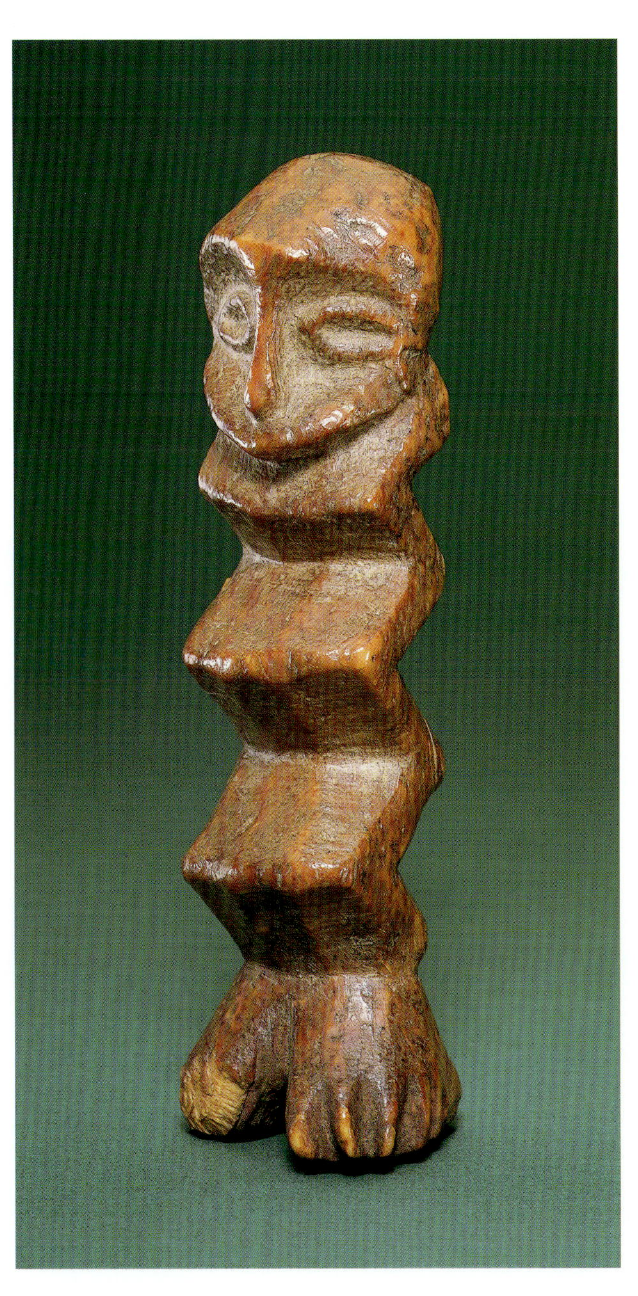

8.89 Human figure. Ivory. H: 13.3 cm (5¼ in.).

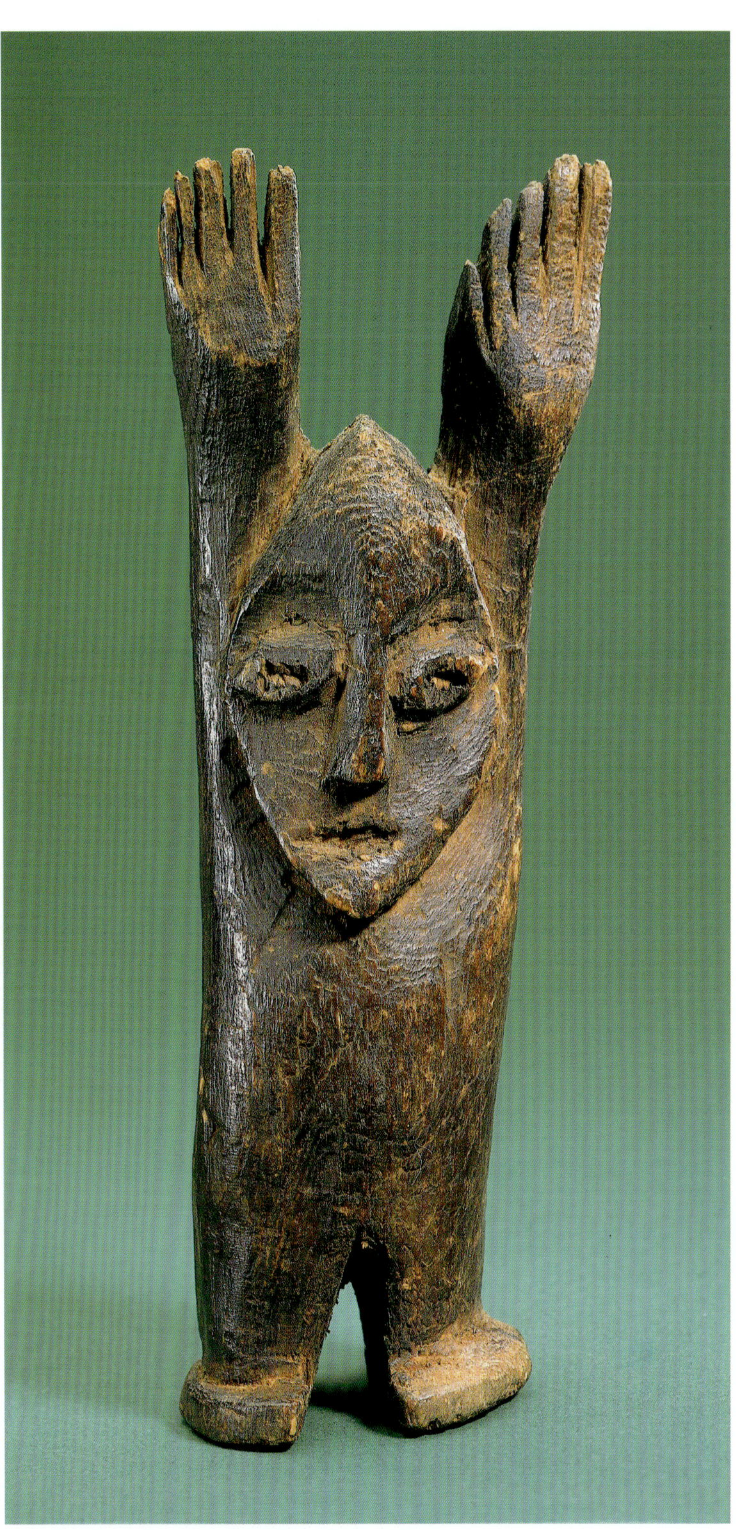

8.90 Human figure with raised arms. Wood. H: 17.5 cm (6⅞ in.).

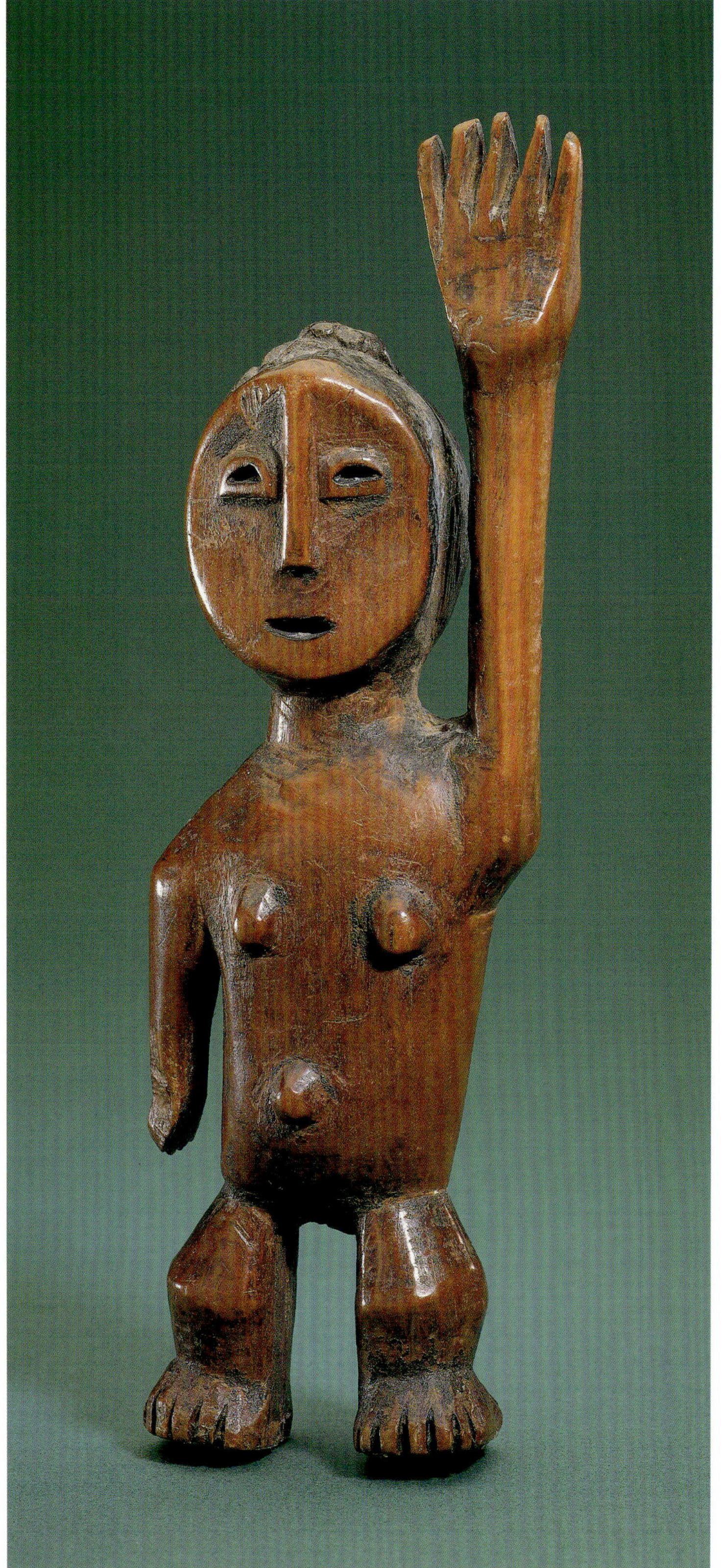

8.91 Human figure with raised arm. Wood. H: 17.8 cm (7 in.).

8.92 Human figure with raised arm. Wood. H: 10.3 cm (4 in.).

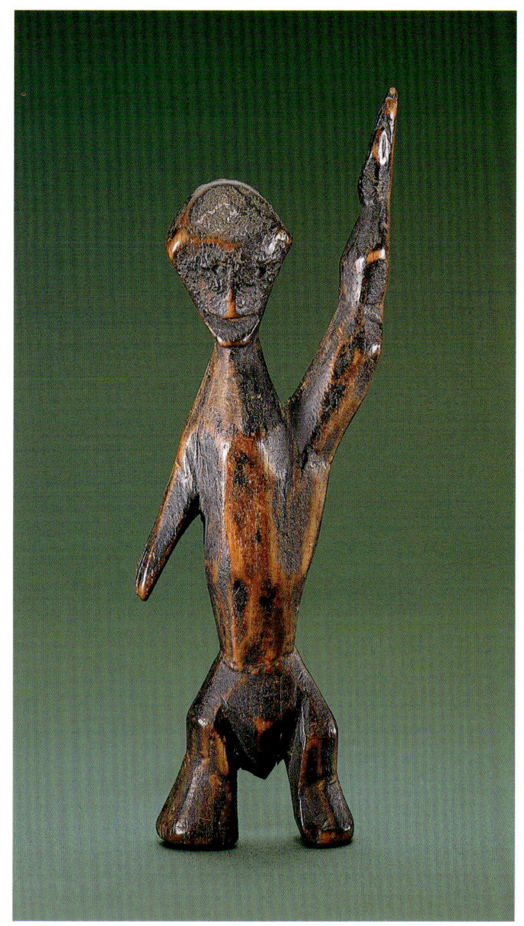

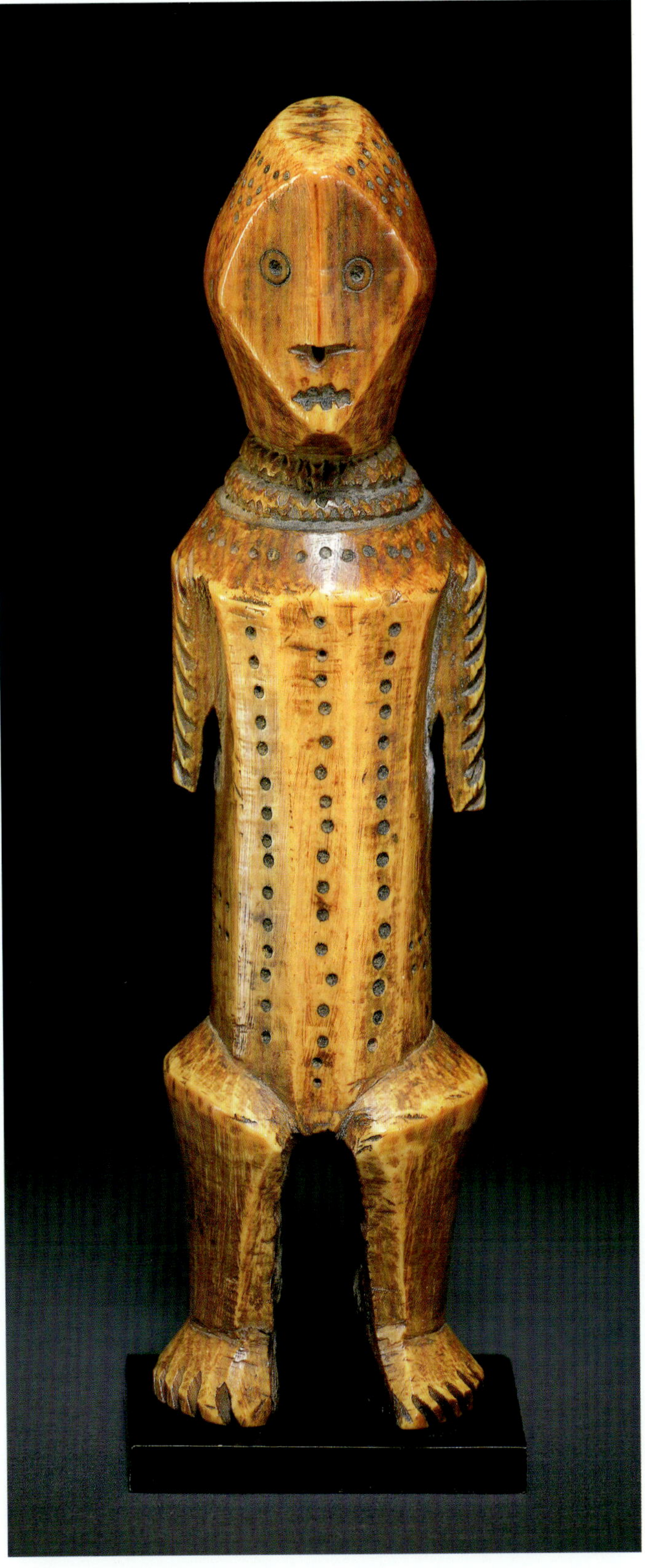

8.93 Human figure. Ivory.
H: 17 cm (6¾ in.).

ARTISTS' WORKSHOPS

Whether from the same workshop, clan, or hand, many figures are stylistically very similar, if not identical. Placing them side-by-side, as in these photographs of ivory figures (figs. 8.93–8.99), clearly illustrates the striking consistencies. The fact that artists were given only rudimentary directions by the patron and that only a few high-level Bwami members could see the pieces strengthens the argument that they come from a single workshop.

CONSISTENT SCRATCHES

Striking coincidences in style can occasionally be noted. All figures of one type documented in Western collections, for example, have a vertical scratch below the eyes (figs. 8.100–8.102).[4] The consistency of the scratches suggests that they are intentional rather than the work of a clumsy artist.

AREA STYLES

Four figures shown here (figs. 8.103–8.106) share stylistic elements but are not consistent in appearance, suggesting that they come from a general area or clan but not from the same hand or workshop.

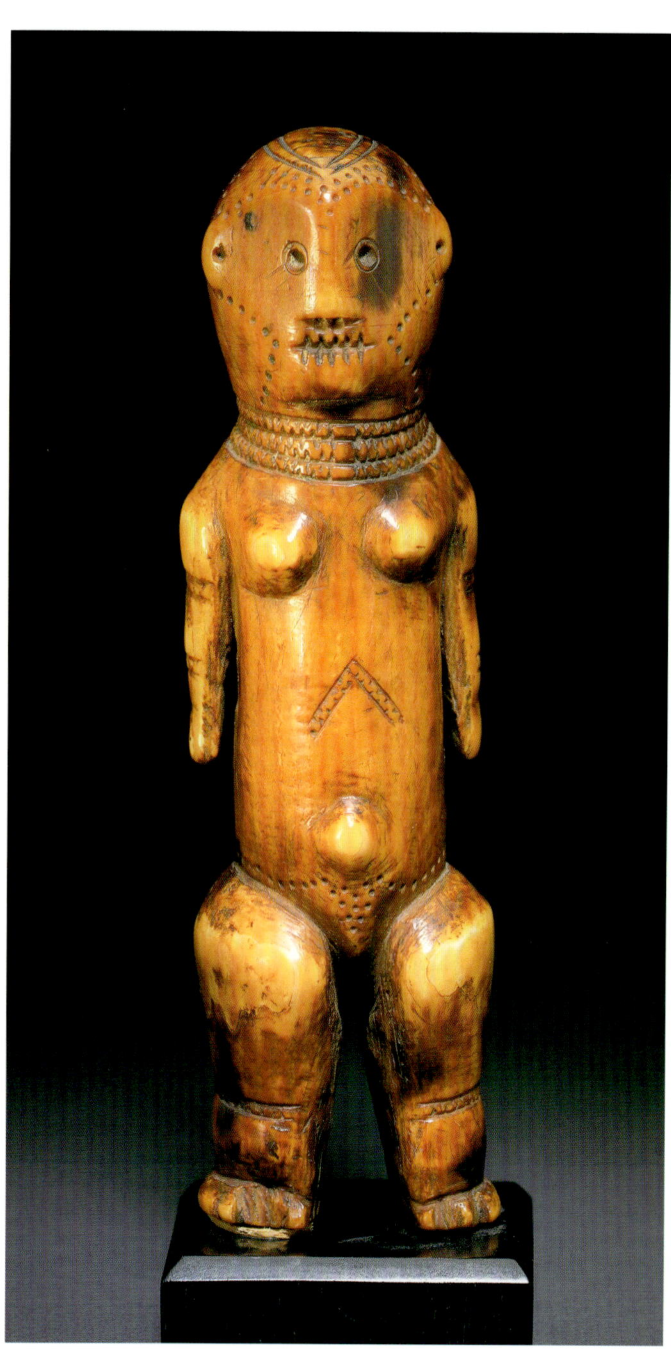

8.94 Human figure. Ivory.
H: 16.3 cm (6½ in.).

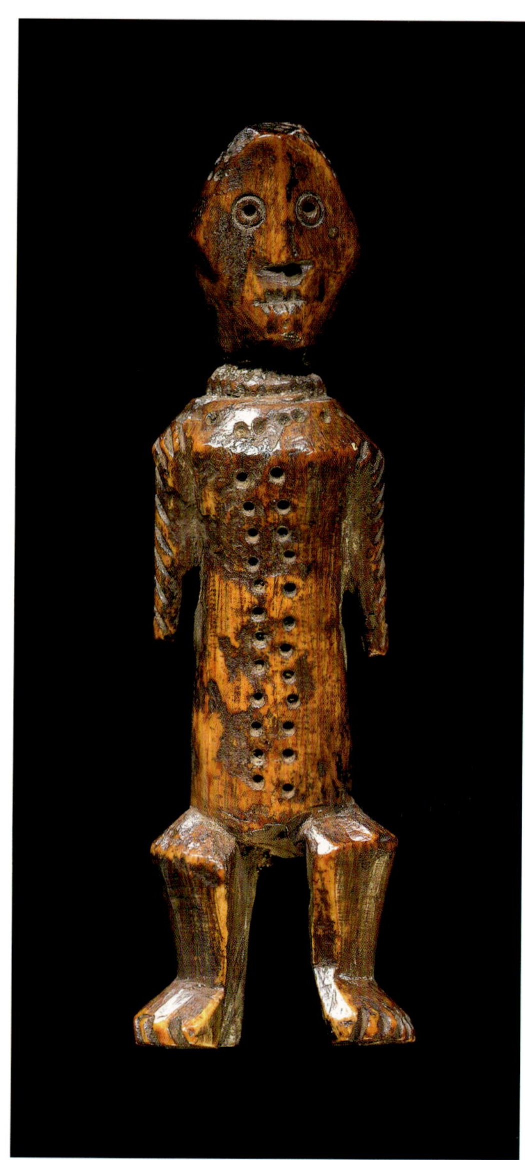

8.95 Human figure. Ivory.
H: 12.2 cm (4¾ in.).

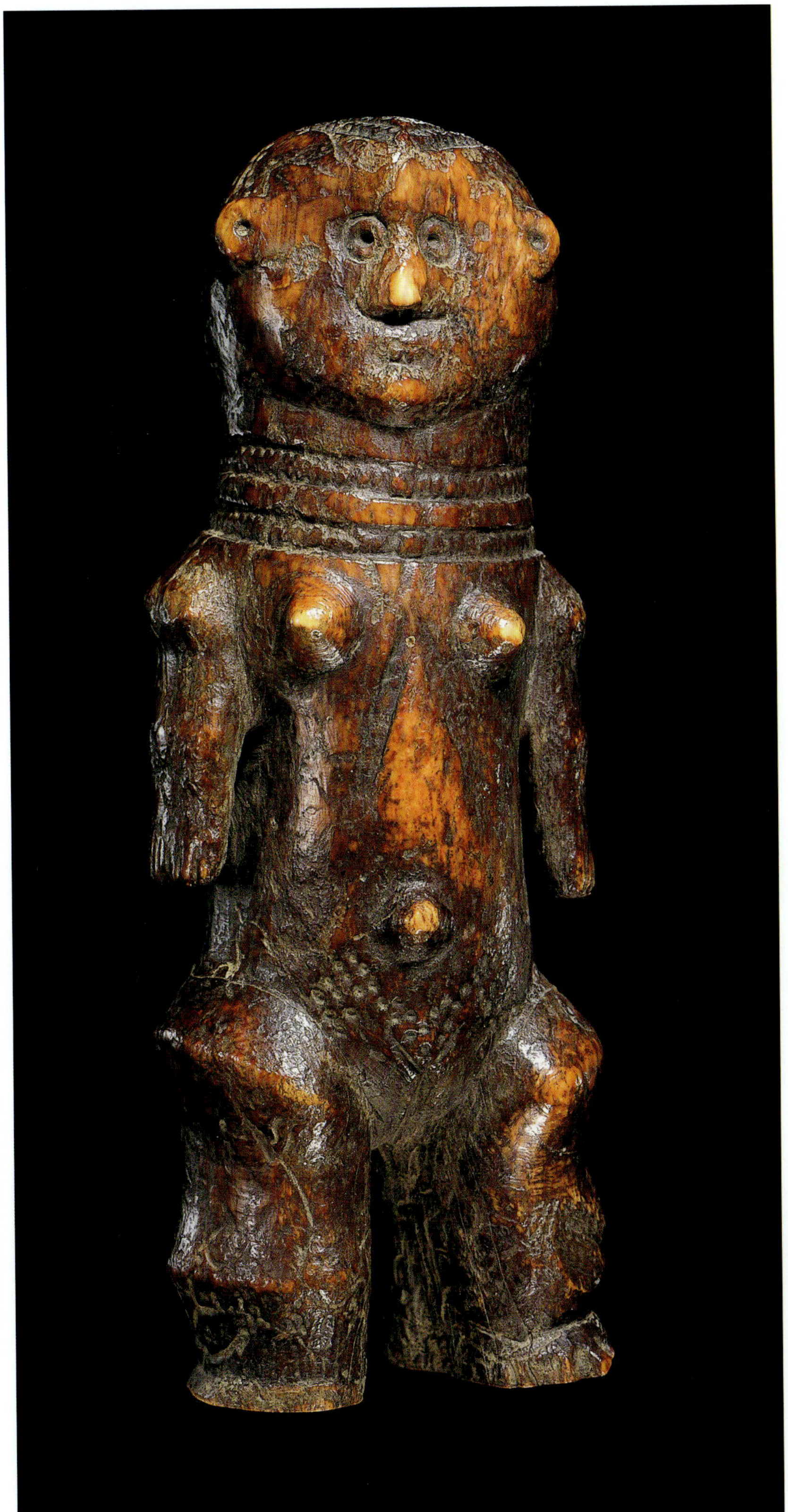

8.96 Human figure. Ivory.
H: 18.6 cm (7½ in.).

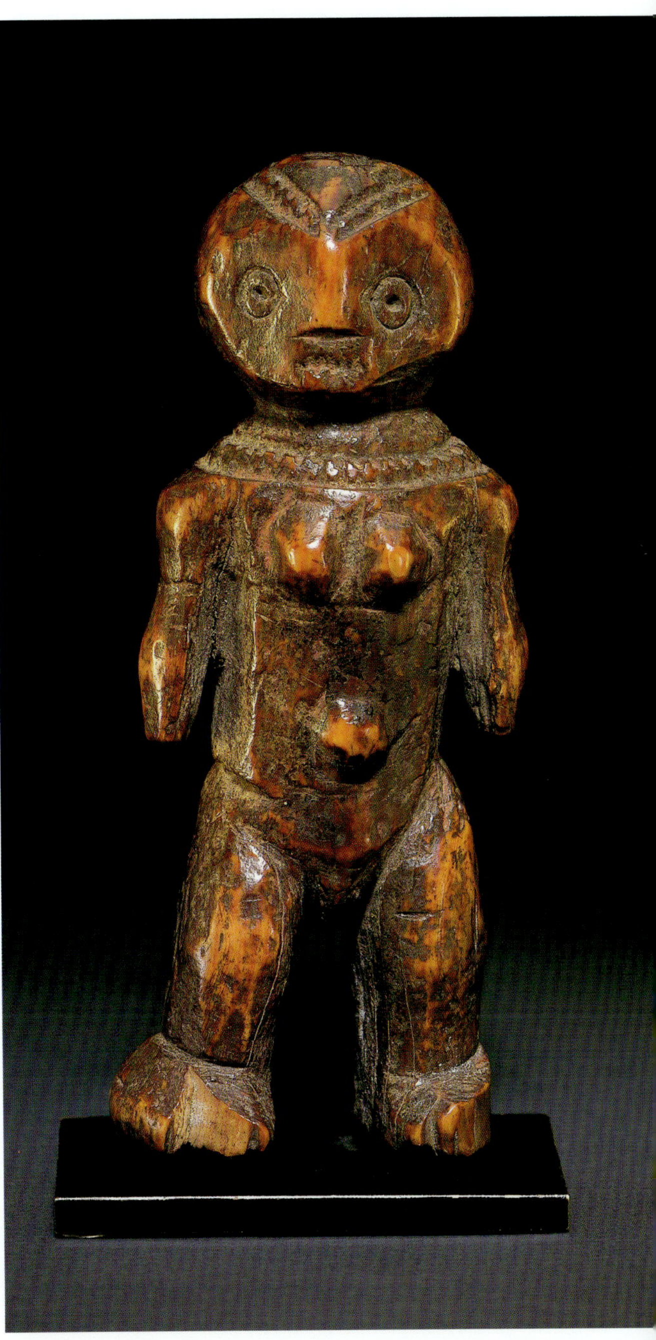

8.97 Human figure. Ivory.
H: 13.2 cm (5¼ in.).

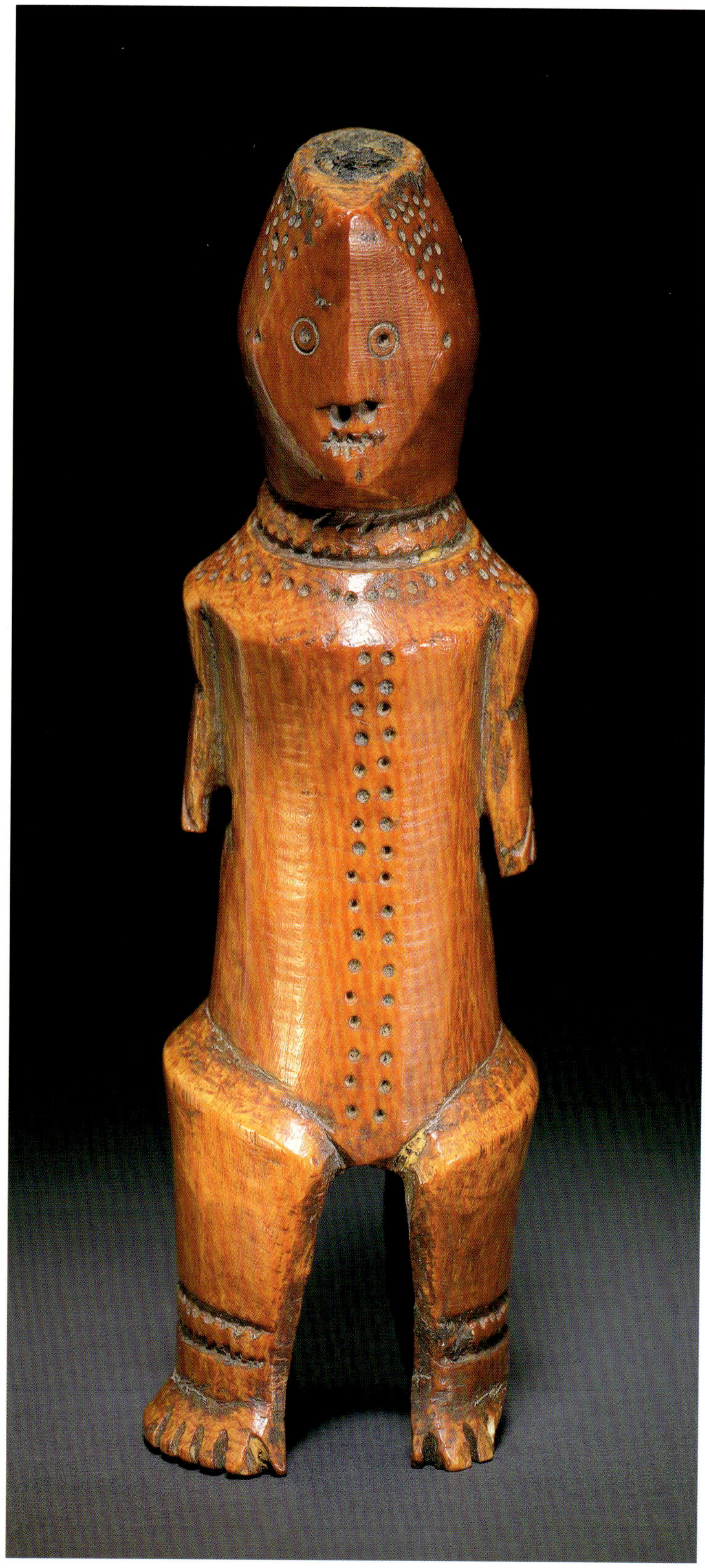

8.98 Human figure.
Ivory. H: 18 cm (7 in.).

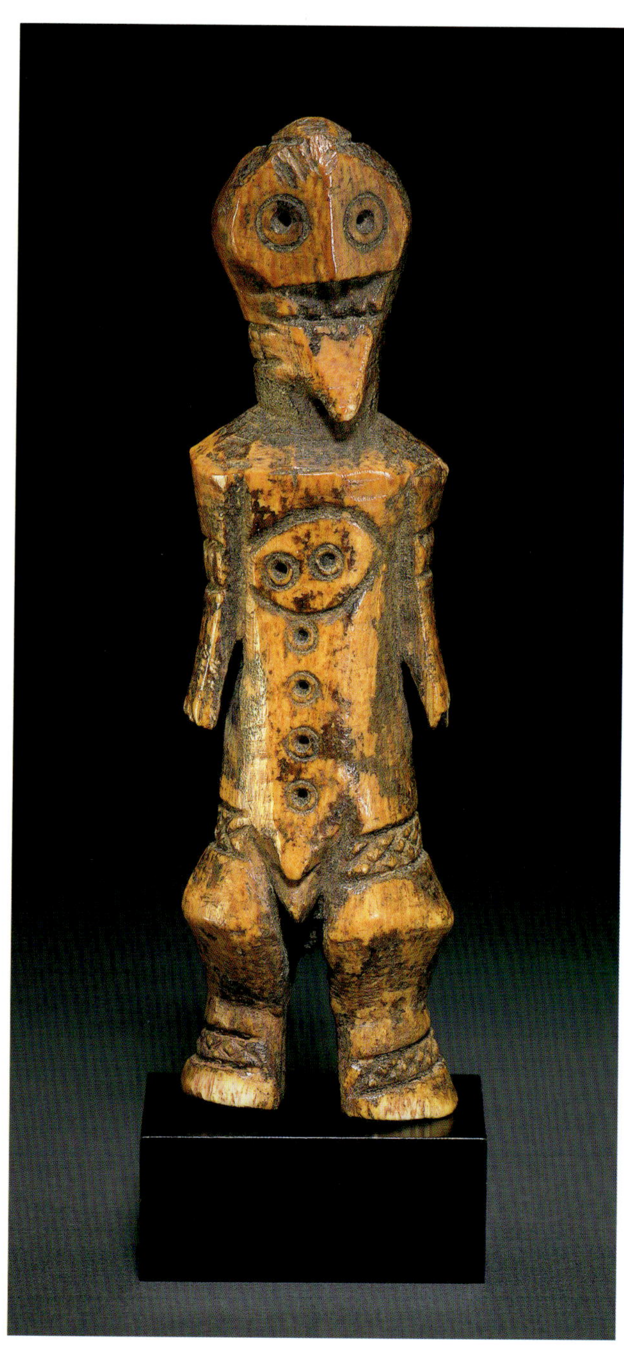

8.99 Human figure.
Ivory. H: 13.1 cm (5¼ in.).

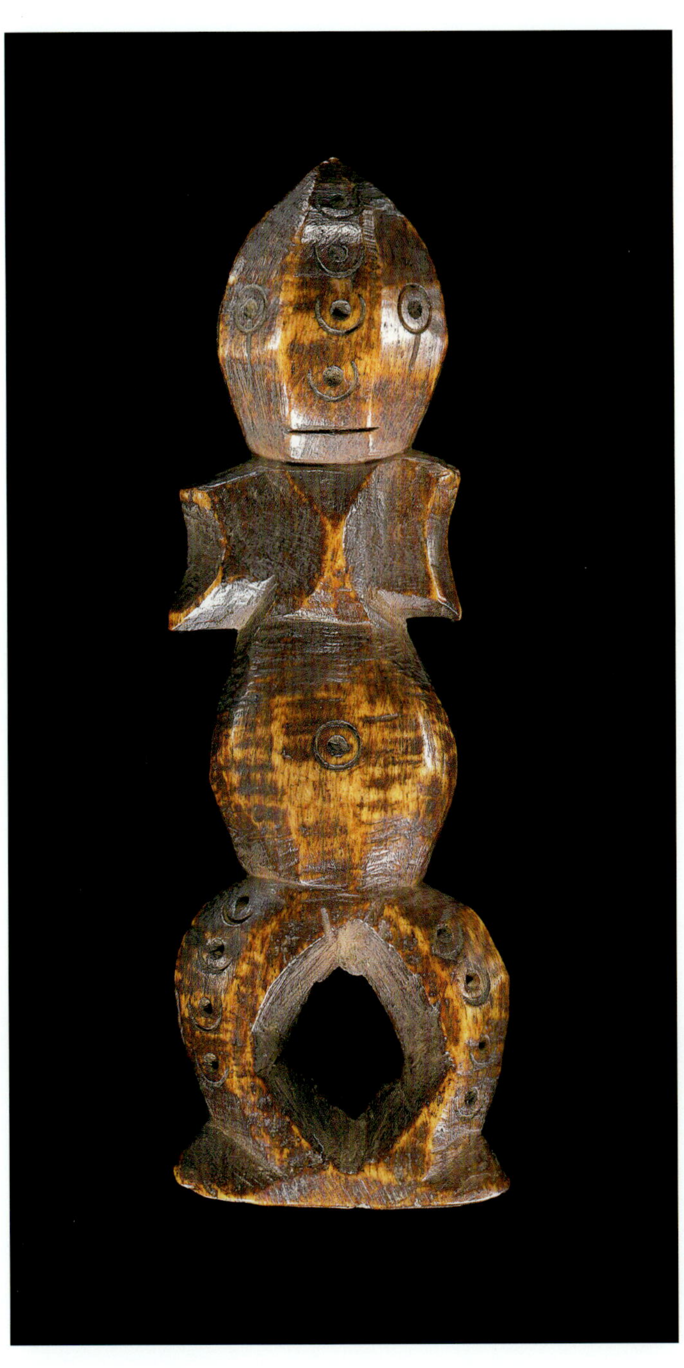

8.100 Human figure.
Ivory. H: 13.7 cm (5⅜ in.).

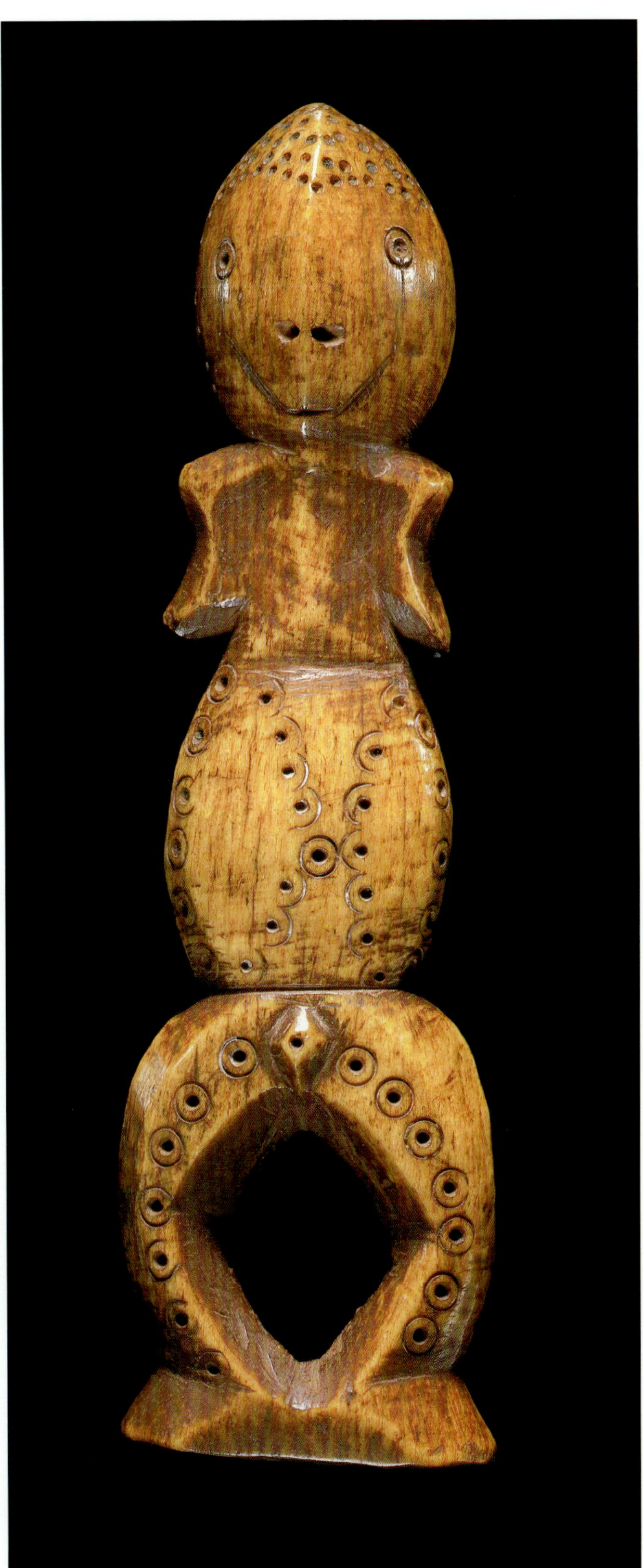

8.101 Human figure.
Ivory. H: 20.2 cm (8 in.).

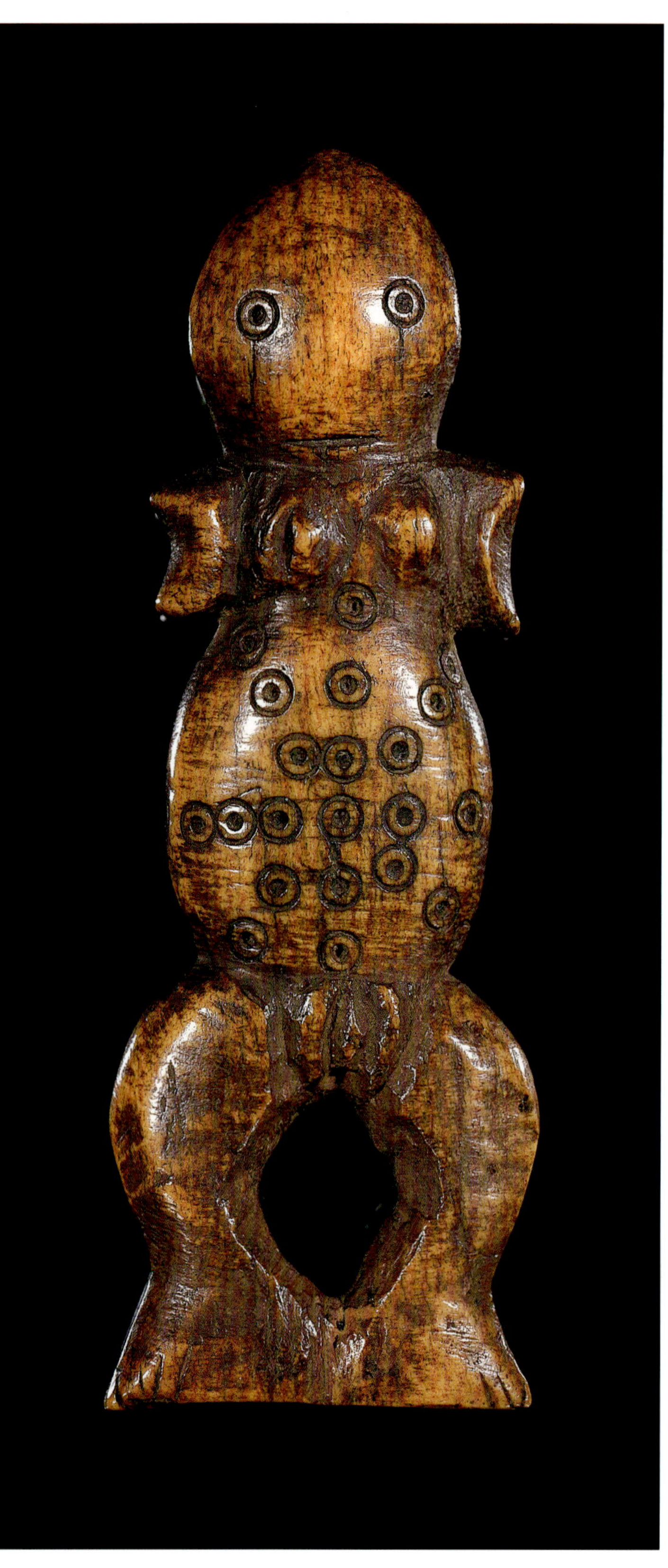

8.102 Human figure. Ivory. H: 16 cm (7 in.). FMCH X87.1323; The Jerome L. Joss Collection.

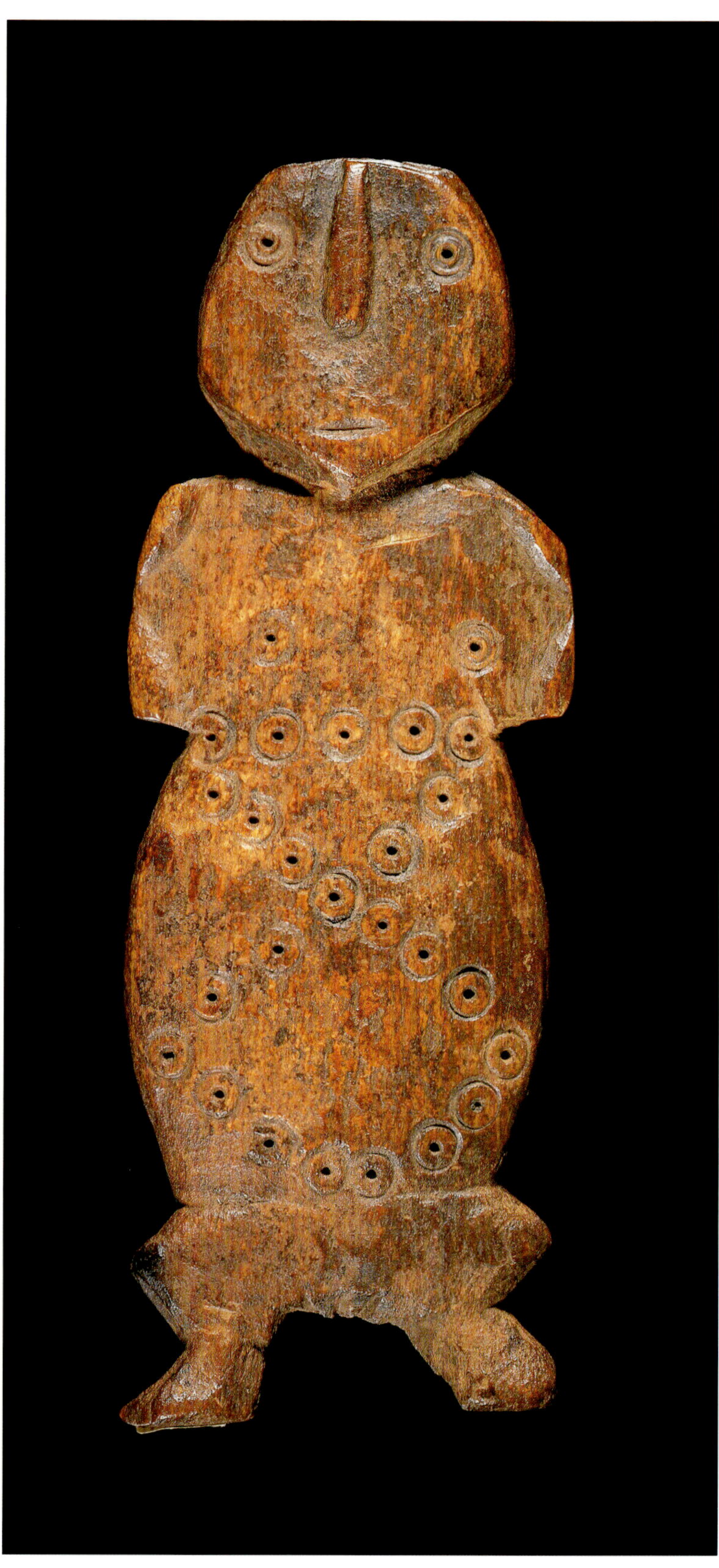

8.103 Human figure. Ivory. H: 18.5 cm (7¼ in.).

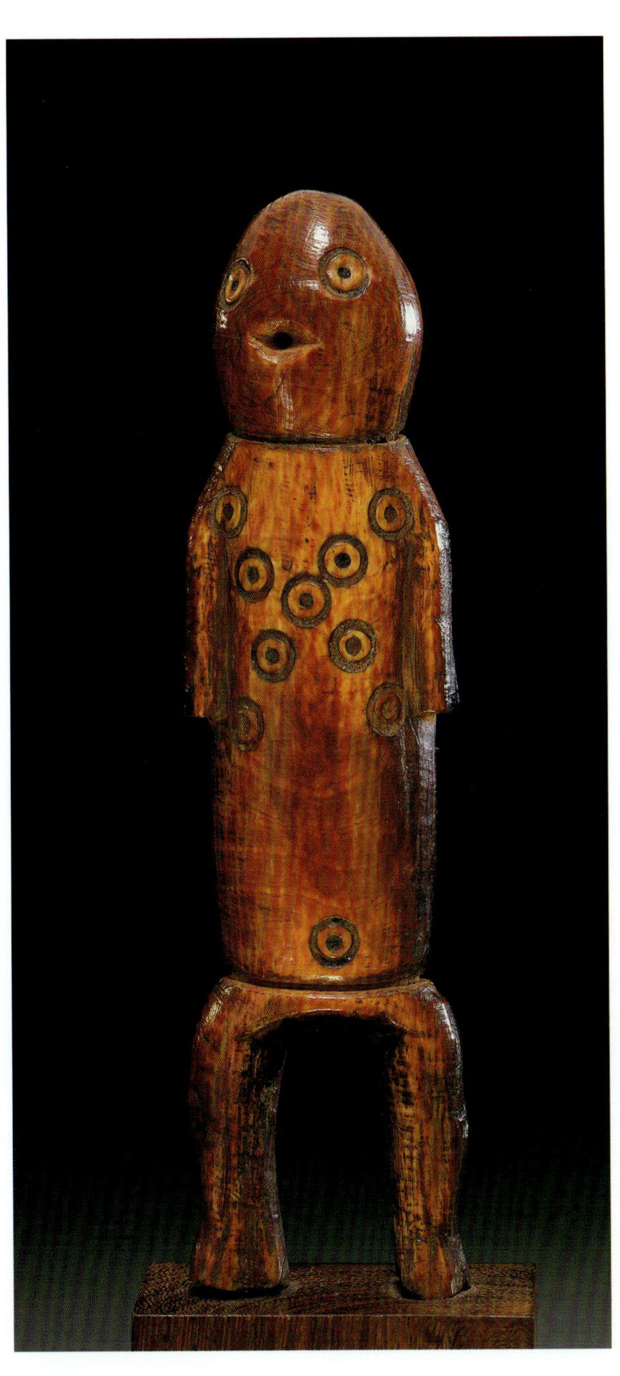

8.104 Human figure.
Ivory. H: 14.5 cm (5¾ in.).

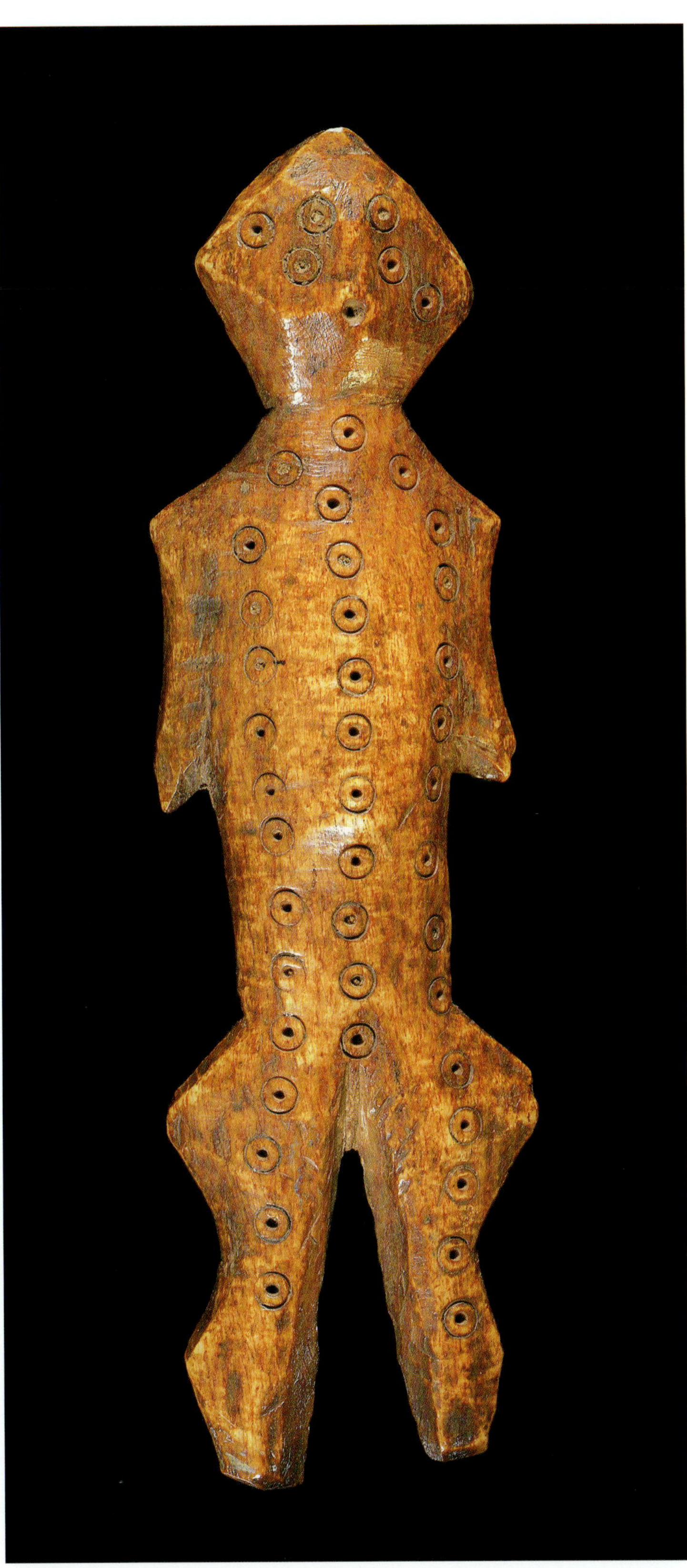

8.105 Human figure.
Ivory. H: 20.1 cm (8 in.).

8.107 Woman with scarification patterns on her forehead and temples. Such patterns are frequently reproduced on anthropomorphic sculpture. Photograph courtesy of Charles Henault.

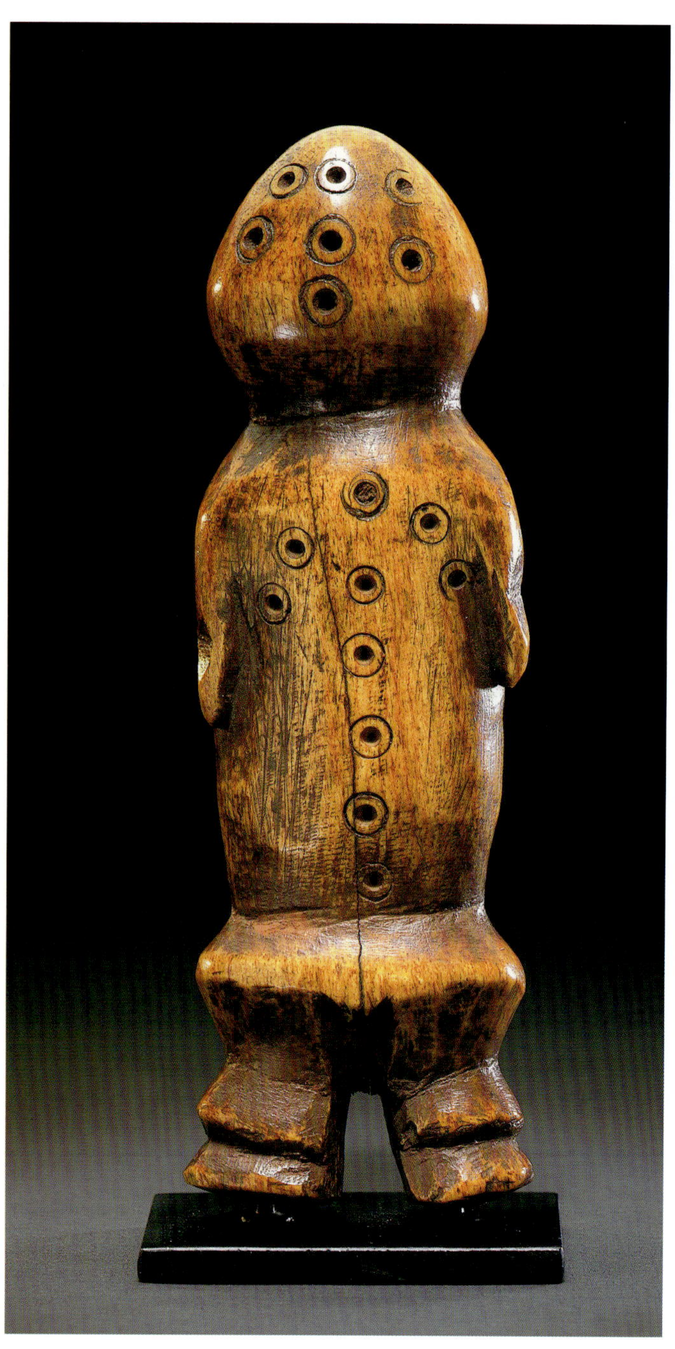

8.106 Human figure.
Ivory. H: 17.8 cm (7 in.).

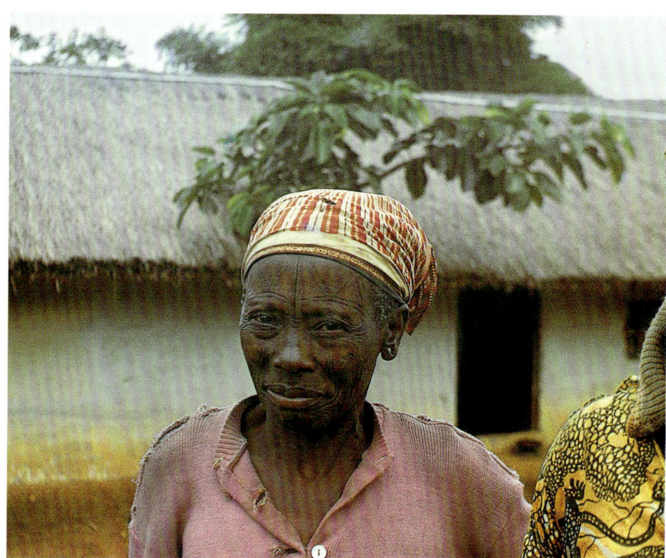

SCARIFICATION

In the past, Lega men and women wore scarification marks on their faces. These can still be seen on some older people (fig. 8.107). On both figures and masks (figs. 8.108, 8.109), the artist often represents the marks with dots or lines.

COWRIE SHELLS

Cowrie shells, traded into the area from the Indian Ocean, serve as forms of currency among the Lega and their neighbors (figs. 8.110–8.115). Cowries also have meaning in Bwami. The first emblem of Bwami membership for a man is a small cap with four cowrie shells attached (see Cameron 1995, fig. 8.1a,b); Biebuyck 1973, 160). Figures and busts often have cowries or representations of cowries on top of the head to signify this hat and to indicate that the figure represents a Bwami member. Other artists have attached cowries to figures to represent eyes, and still others have carefully carved the eyes to look like real cowrie shells. Occasionally an artist might represent a field of cowrie shells to give texture to an animal figure or an insignia.

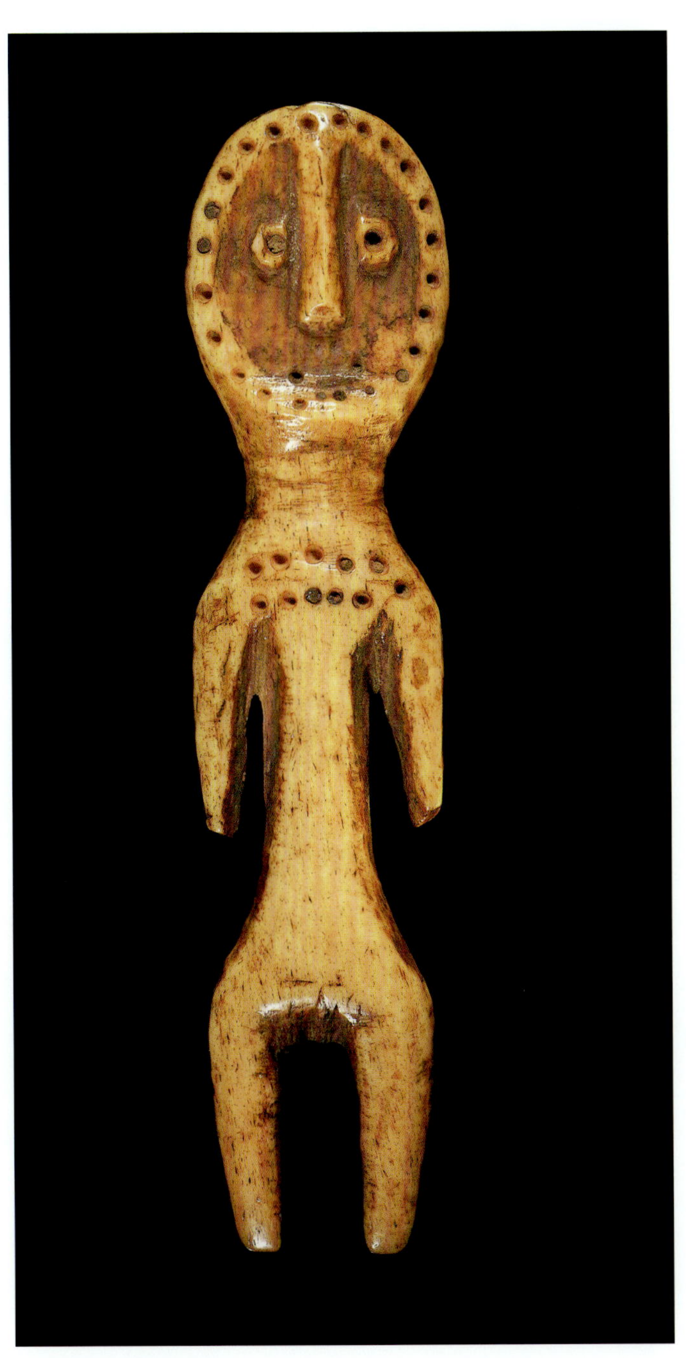

8.108 Human figure.
Ivory. H: 16.3 cm (6⅜ in.).

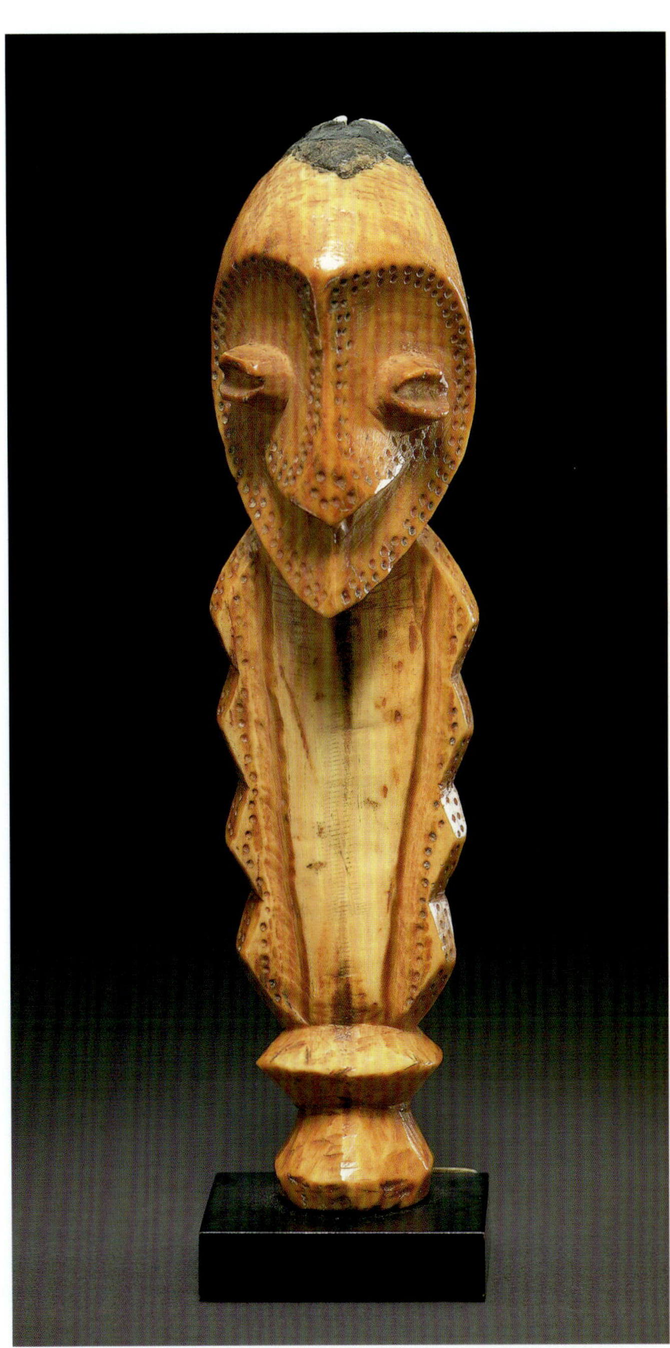

8.109 Human figure. Ivory and
cowrie shells. H: 15.6 cm (6⅛ in.).

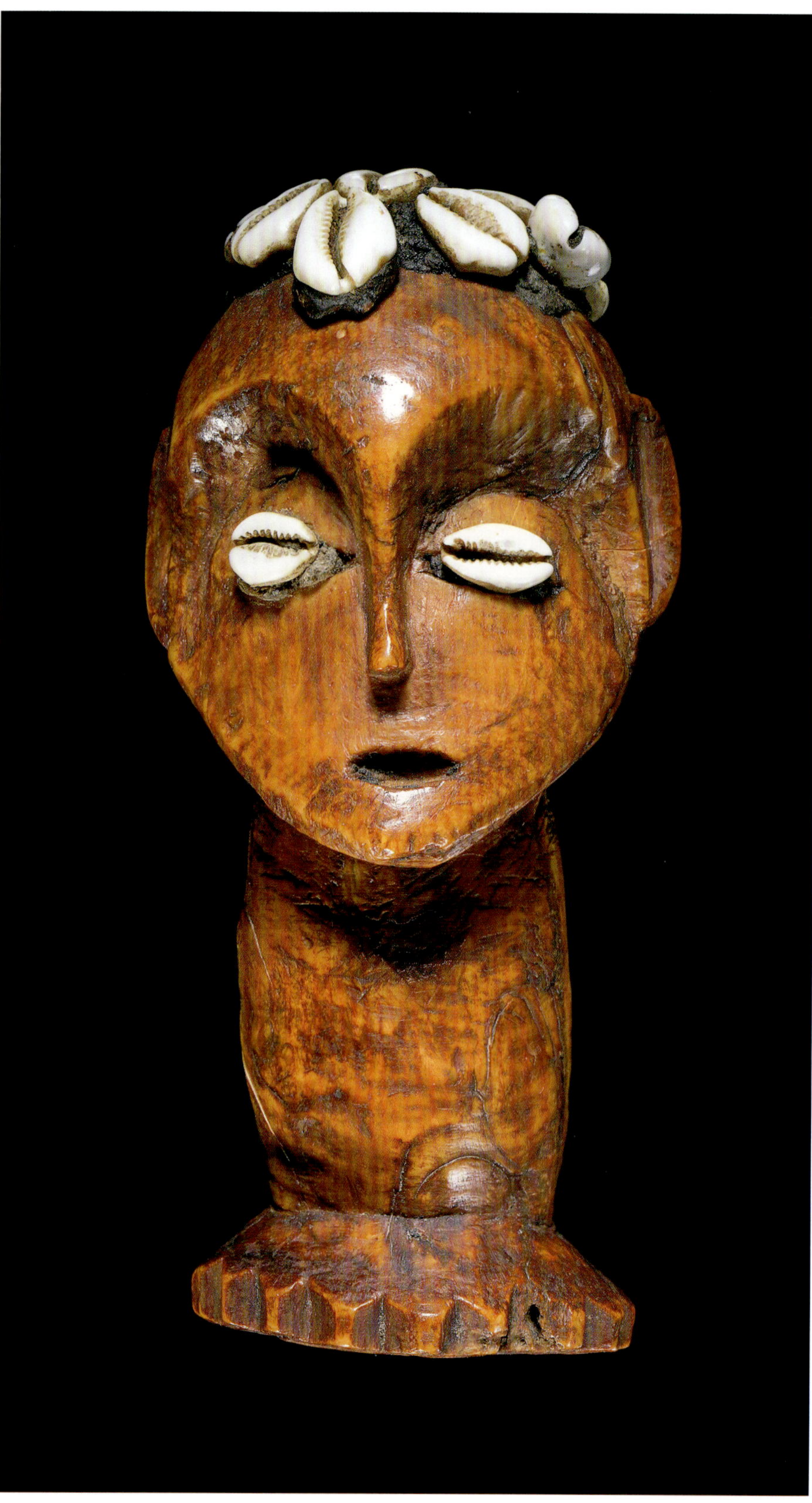

8.110 Human bust. Ivory and cowrie shells. H: 17.7 cm (7 in.).

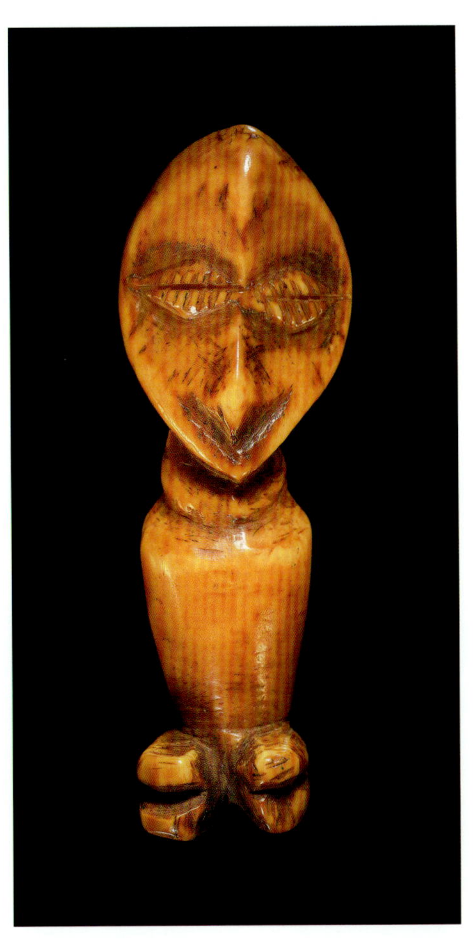

8.111 Human figure.
Ivory. H: 9.7 cm (3¾ in.).

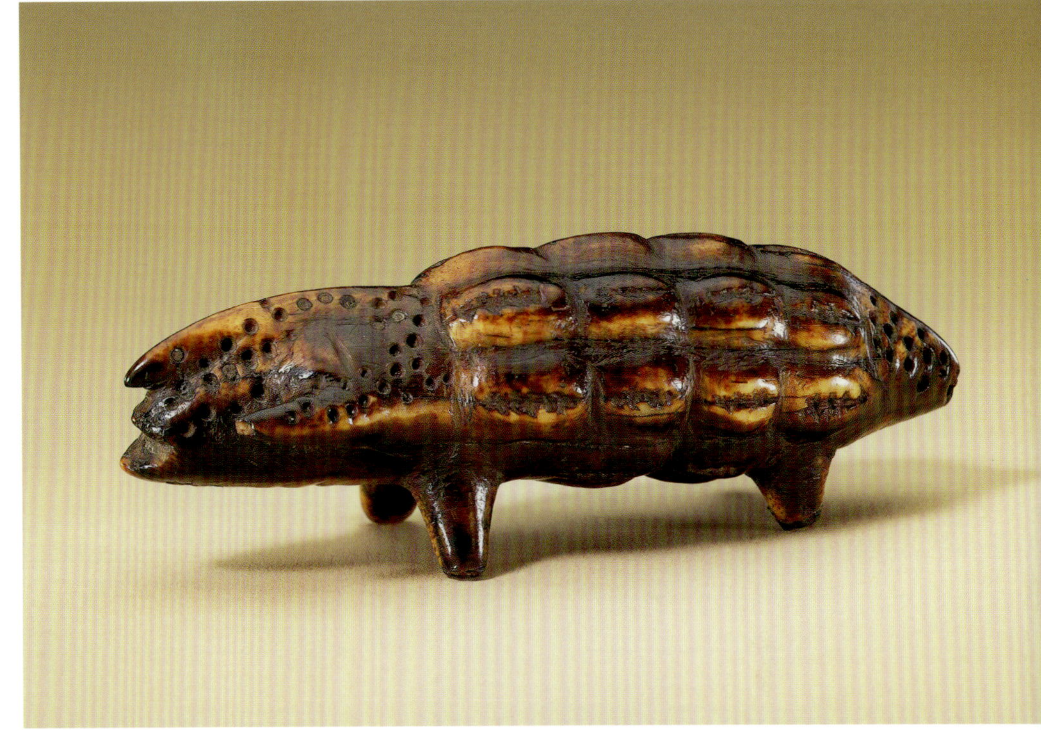

8.112 Animal figure.
Ivory. L: 11.7 cm (4⅝ in.).

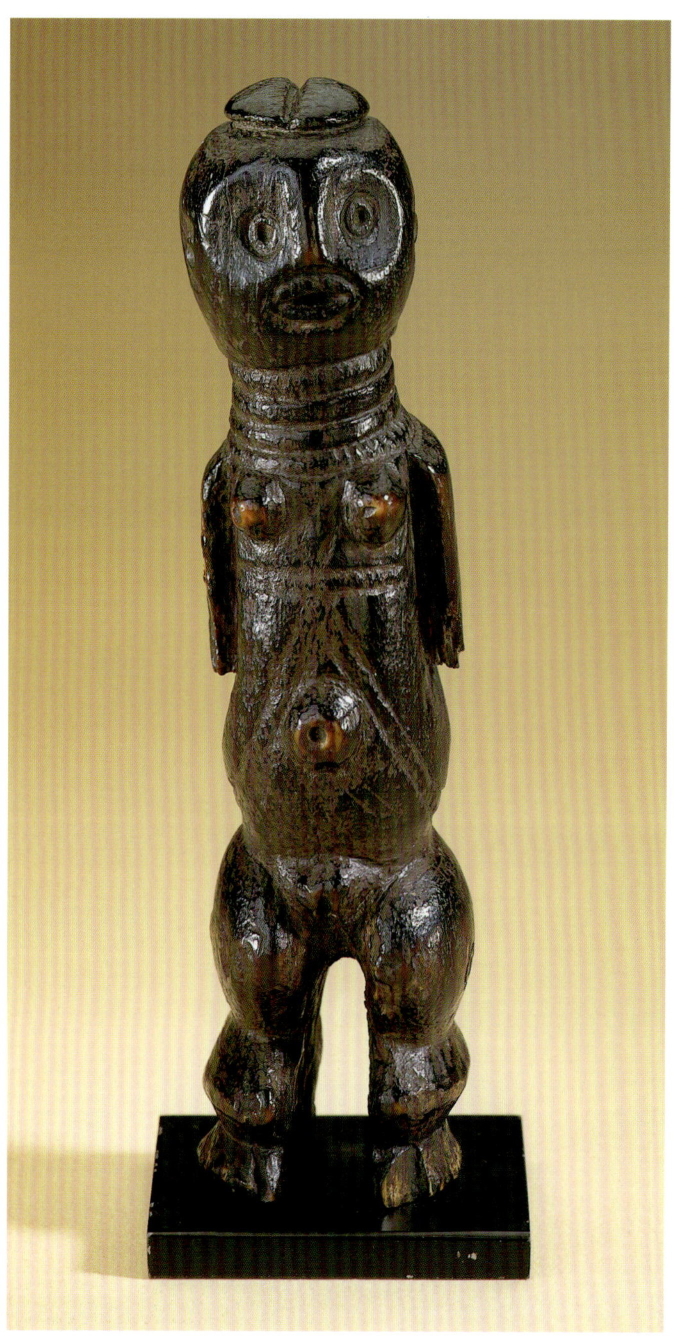

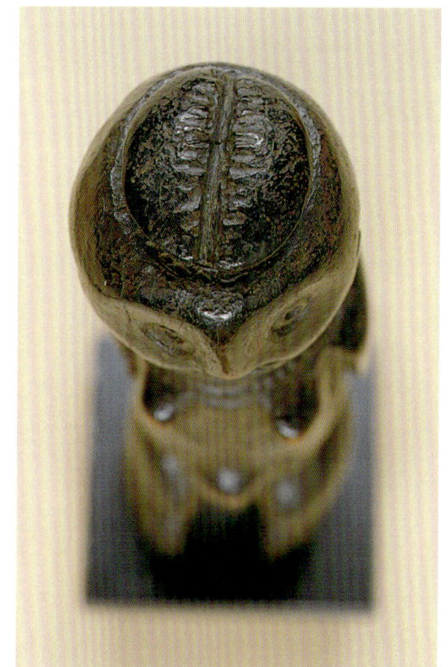

8.113A, B Front view and view of the top of the head of a human figure. Ivory. H: 15 cm (5⅞ in.).

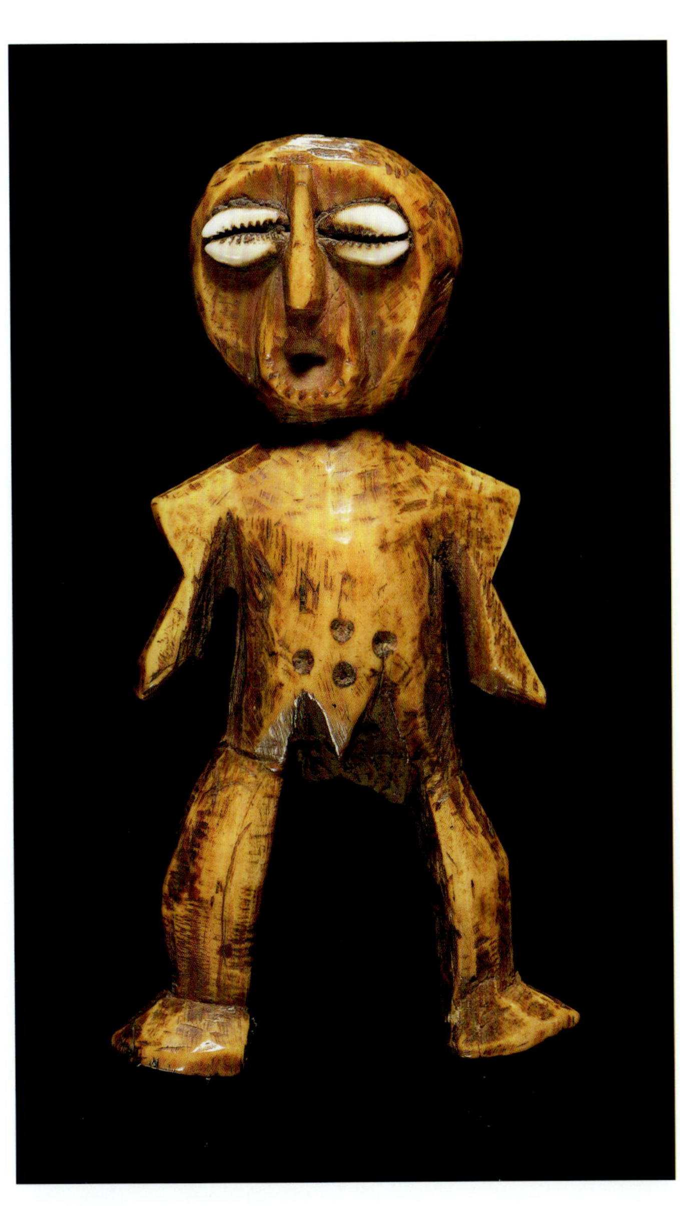

8.114 Human figure. Ivory and cowrie shells. H: 13 cm (5⅛ in.).

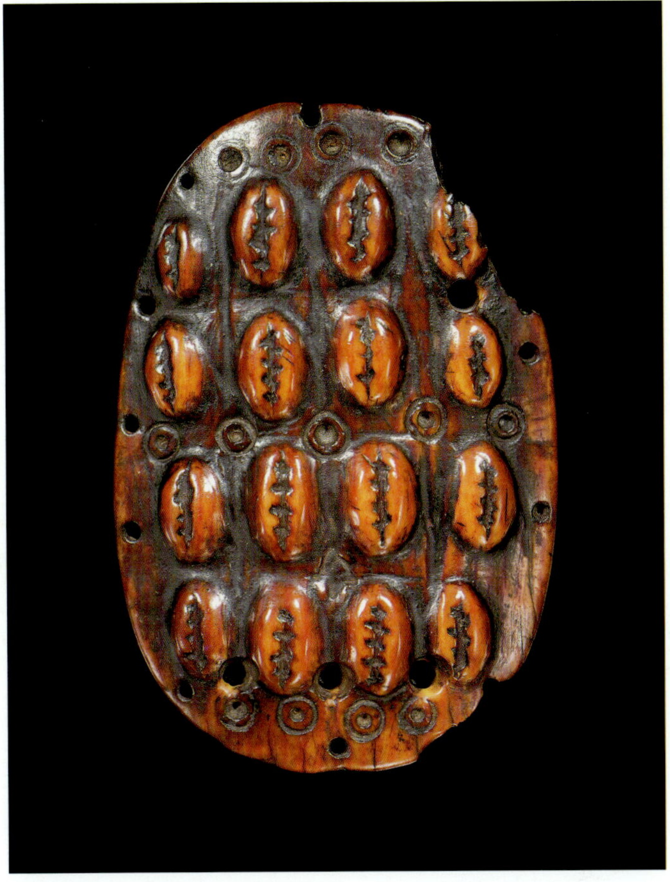

8.115 Pendant or insignia. Ivory. H: 9 cm (3½ in.).

9 Lega Masks

Lega "masks" fall into the category of Bwami initiation objects. The Lega further divide them into five types according to material, size, and form: *lukwakongo*, *kayamba*, *idimu*, *muminia*, and *lukungu* (Biebuyck 1973, 164). They serve as an important mark of rank, identifying the owners as members of specific Bwami levels (Biebuyck 1986, 125–26).

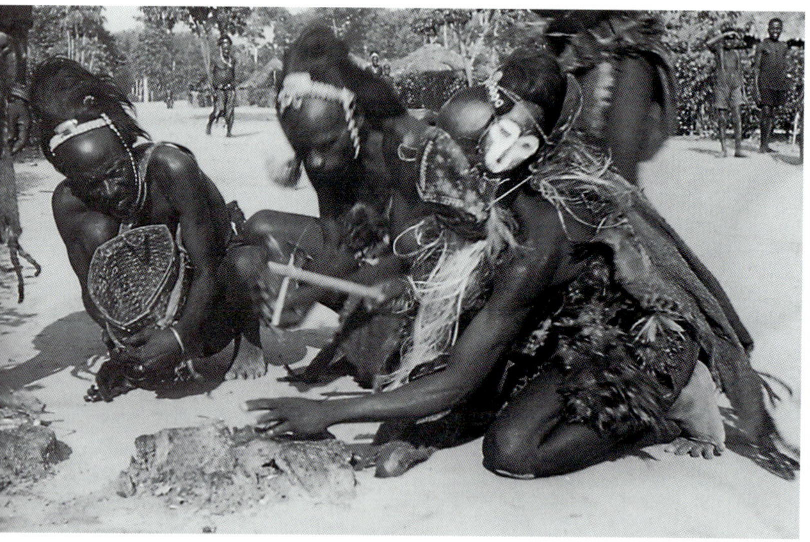

9.1

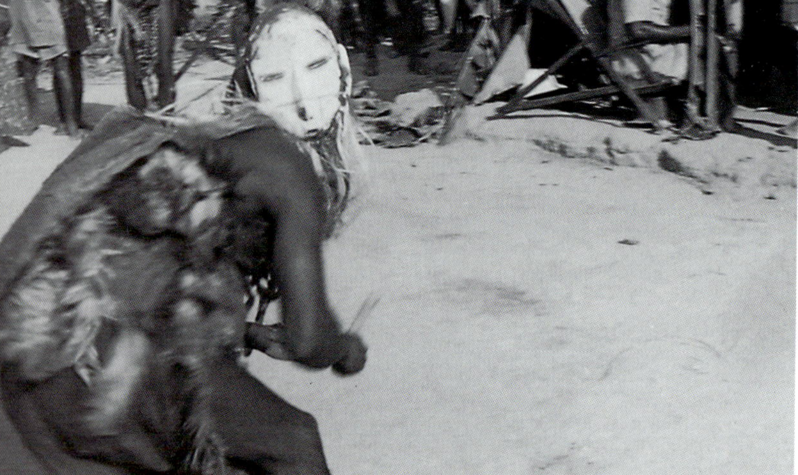

9.2

Contrary to the Lega mask categories based on form and material, most Western definitions of masks are based on function. "Mask" describes an object that covers the face and transforms the wearer.[1] Using this definition, the Lega have very few, if any, true masks.[2] Most of what we know as Lega "masks" are sculptures of a human face that are rarely worn over the face and never for purposes of true transformation (Biebuyck 1993, 190).[3]

Like many initiation objects, the Lega mask can be assigned different uses and meanings depending on the context of the performance (Biebuyck 1954, 113). In Bwami ceremonies, masks are attached to different parts of the body, piled in stacks, hung on fences, displayed, dragged on the ground, and occasionally worn on the forehead with the beard draping over the face of the wearer (figs. 9.1–9.5; Biebuyck 1973, 167–68; 1994, 42). The small wooden *lukwakongo* masks, for example, are rarely worn on the face. Instead Bwami members attach them to their arms, the sides of their heads, or their foreheads; they hang them on fences, as noted above; or they hold them in their hands. To facilitate presenting the handheld masks, artists carve handles on their backs (figs. 9.6–9.12).

The sculpture, or "mask," manipulated by a senior Bwami member can assume the roles of many different characters during performances. The Bwami member can be compared to a puppeteer and the mask to a puppet. Characterization occurs around the mask, but the puppeteer is not transformed. For lack of a better term, however, I will continue the established tradition and use "mask" to refer to these masklike sculptures.

Interestingly, Lega masks differ from Western definitions as well as from masks used in many other African masquerade traditions in that while women do not own them, both men and women handle and present them in very similar performances. Biebuyck gives several descriptions of women using different masks, including *idimu* and *lukwakongo* (1986, 133, 145, 149, 175). He stresses that the only mask a woman uses is the one belonging to her high-ranking husband (Biebuyck 1994, 50). One account describes women with masks over their faces:

9.1 The Bwami member at the right wears four masks (two of which are visible) in a performance symbolizing the search of a teacher for a receptive student, circa 1952–1954. Photograph courtesy of Daniel P. Biebuyck.

9.2 A Bwami member wears a mask on the side of his head during a performance, circa 1952–1954. Photograph courtesy of Daniel P. Biebuyck.

9.3 Ivory and wood masks displayed on a specially constructed fence. Note the ropes made of feathers that hold the display together, circa 1952–1954. Photograph courtesy of Daniel P. Biebuyck.

9.4 Ivory and wood masks displayed on a specially constructed fence. Note the ropes made of feathers that hold the display together, circa 1952–1954. Photograph courtesy of Daniel P. Biebuyck.

9.5 A display of *lukwakongo* masks, circa 1952–1954. Photograph courtesy of Daniel P. Biebuyck.

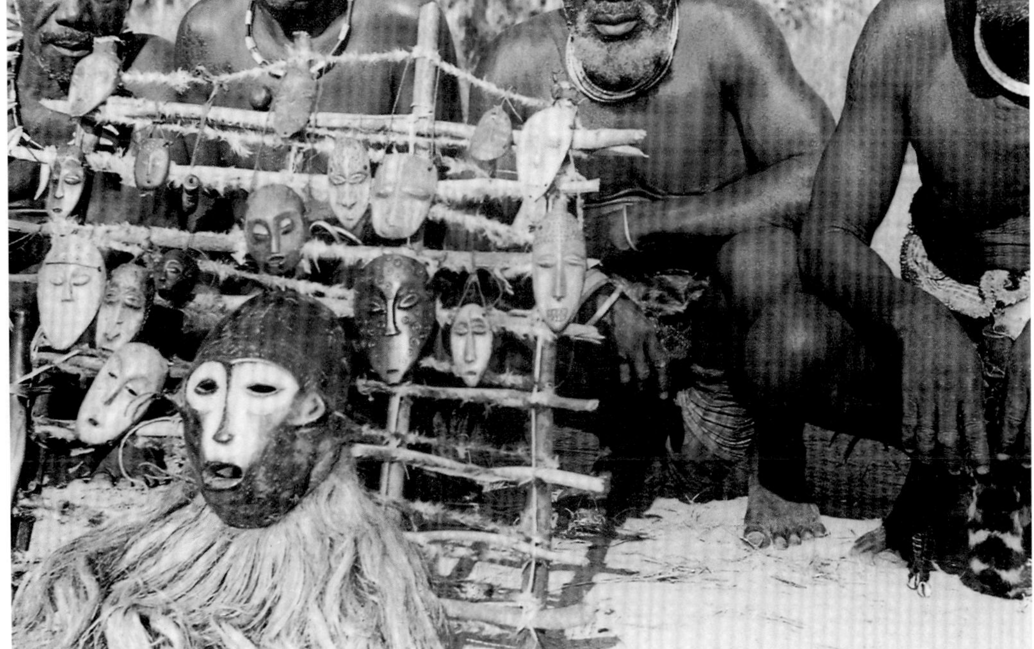

9.3

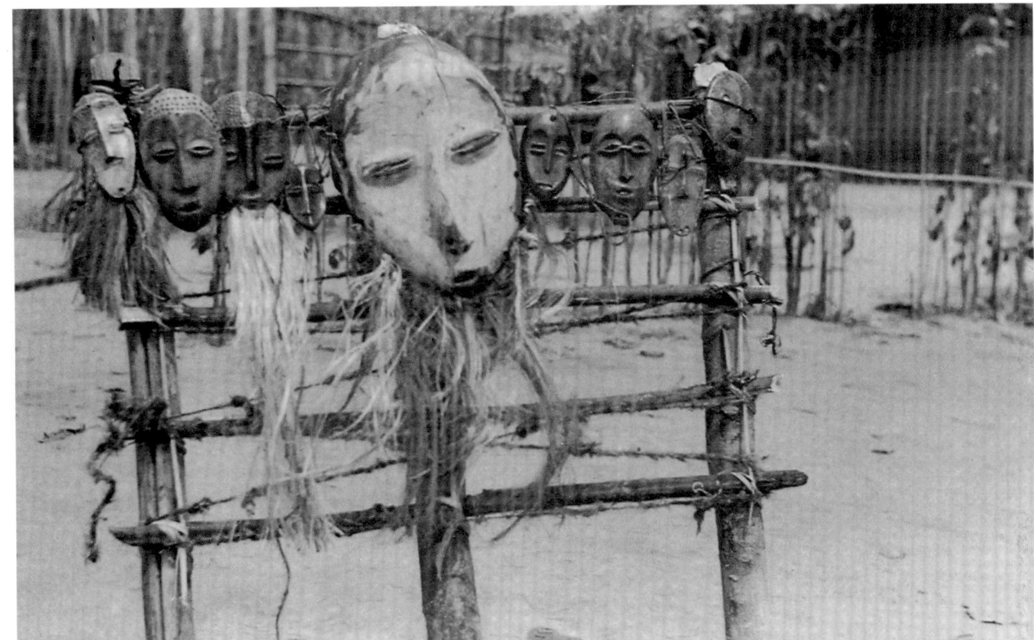

9.4

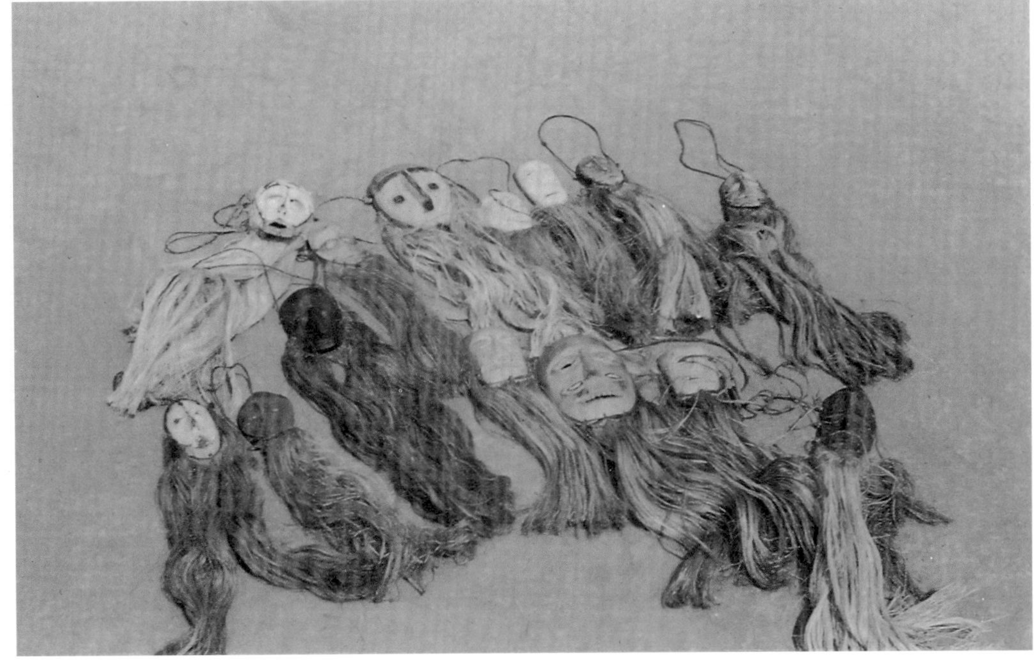

9.5

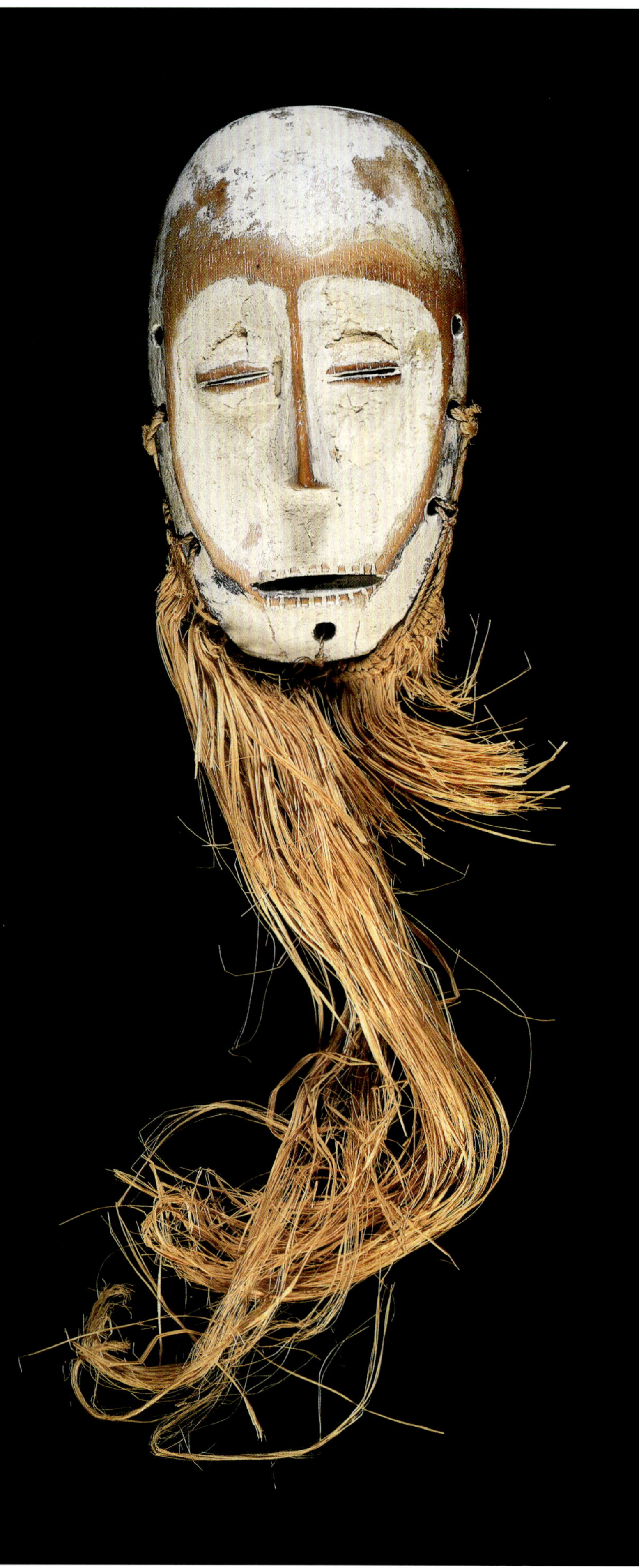

9.6 Mask (*lukwakongo*). Wood, pigment, and plant fiber. H: 34.5 cm (13¾ in.).

9.7A, B Front and back views of a mask (*idimu*). Wood and pigment. H: 26.4 cm (10⅜ in.).

9.8 Mask (*lukwakongo*). Wood, pigment, and plant fiber. H: 38.3 cm (15⅛ in.).

> The masks appeared about five o'clock the next morning. A row of kalonda women emerged from behind the houses. Each woman, cloaked in white bark cloth (hung over the head like a hood but leaving the face visible), wore a small mask affixed to her cap high against the forehead, the beard falling to the lower part of the face. Moving silently and slowly, in bent or crouched position, the women reached the dance ground and sat down on stools in a line, facing a feather rope tied between two poles. Only the most senior initiated wife of each yananio present wore her husband's mask. The women were alternately identified as the Big-Ones-Who-Are-In-(the village called) Harmony, Big-Ones-Who-Are-Nice, and Big-Ones-Who-Are-Well-Prepared (for the ceremonies). They are also referred to as the "row of Nyakamuno," which in this context meant women called together for serious business. [Biebuyck 1986, 133]

Even though the women wear the masks with a costume and the beard draped over their faces, no transformation occurs, and they act out characters as women and men regularly do in Bwami performances.

A concept that unites many of these masklike sculptures is the portrayal and importance of ancestors. The names of several of the mask forms refer to death: "lukungu, skull; lukwakongo, death gathers in; idimu, ancestor" (Biebuyck 1954, 113). Masks are among the initiation objects displayed on the grave before being passed to new owners. When the next member of the owner's lineage reaches the appropriate level, he is given the mask (Biebuyck 1953c, 1078–79; 1986, 131; 1954, 111–13; 1973, 211–13). Thus Bwami members pass masks down through many generations, and the history of each piece is carefully remembered. With objects that specifically represent Kindi, such as the ivory *lukungu* mask, the genealogy is especially strong. The proverb "On ivory, mushrooms do not grow" compares ivory to a man's skeleton, suggesting the former's ability to serve as a permanent, durable memory of previous owners (Biebuyck 1973, 174). The reference to the mask as a skull, the association of ivory with human remains, and the connection of the mask and the grave all stress continuity. These masks connect the past and the present, creating an un-broken chain of ancestors (Biebuyck 1973, 104–5; 1976, 339).

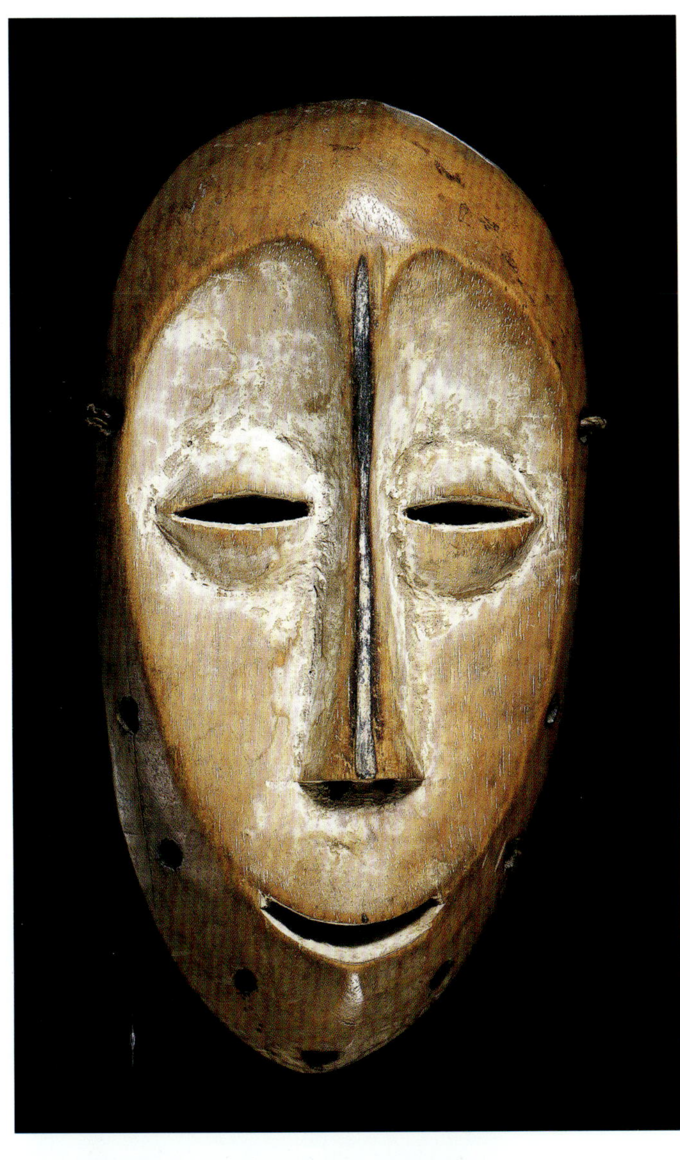

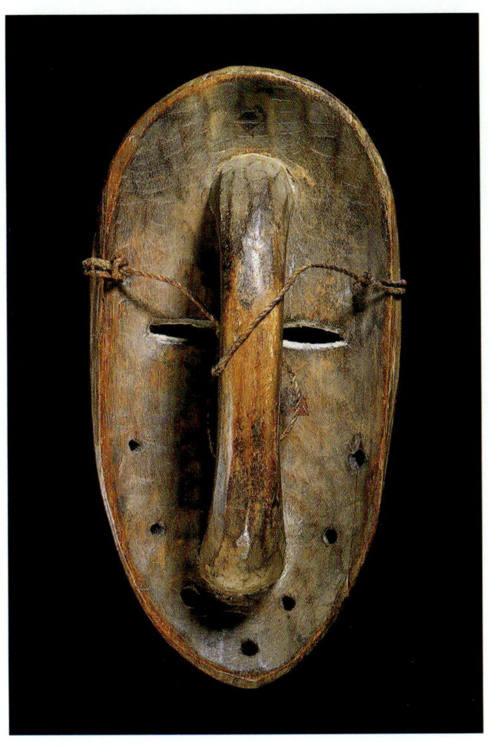

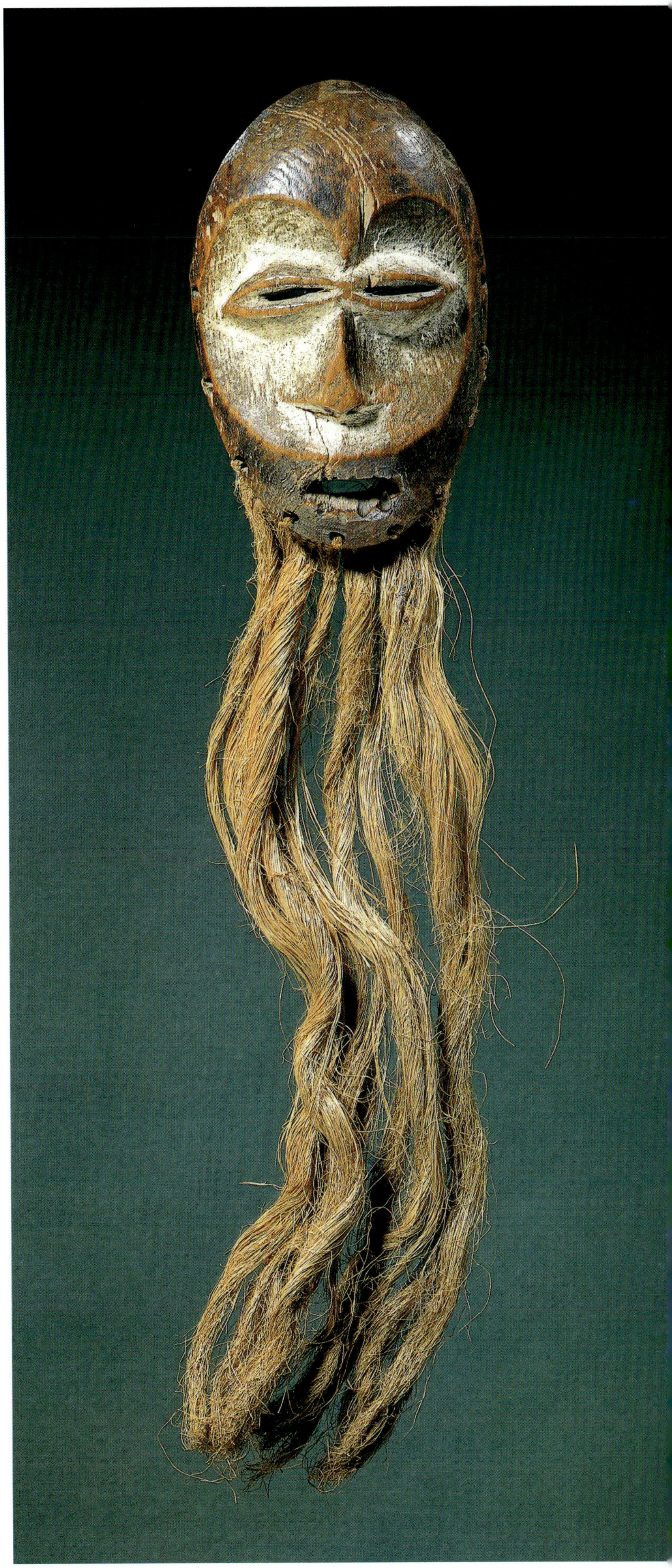

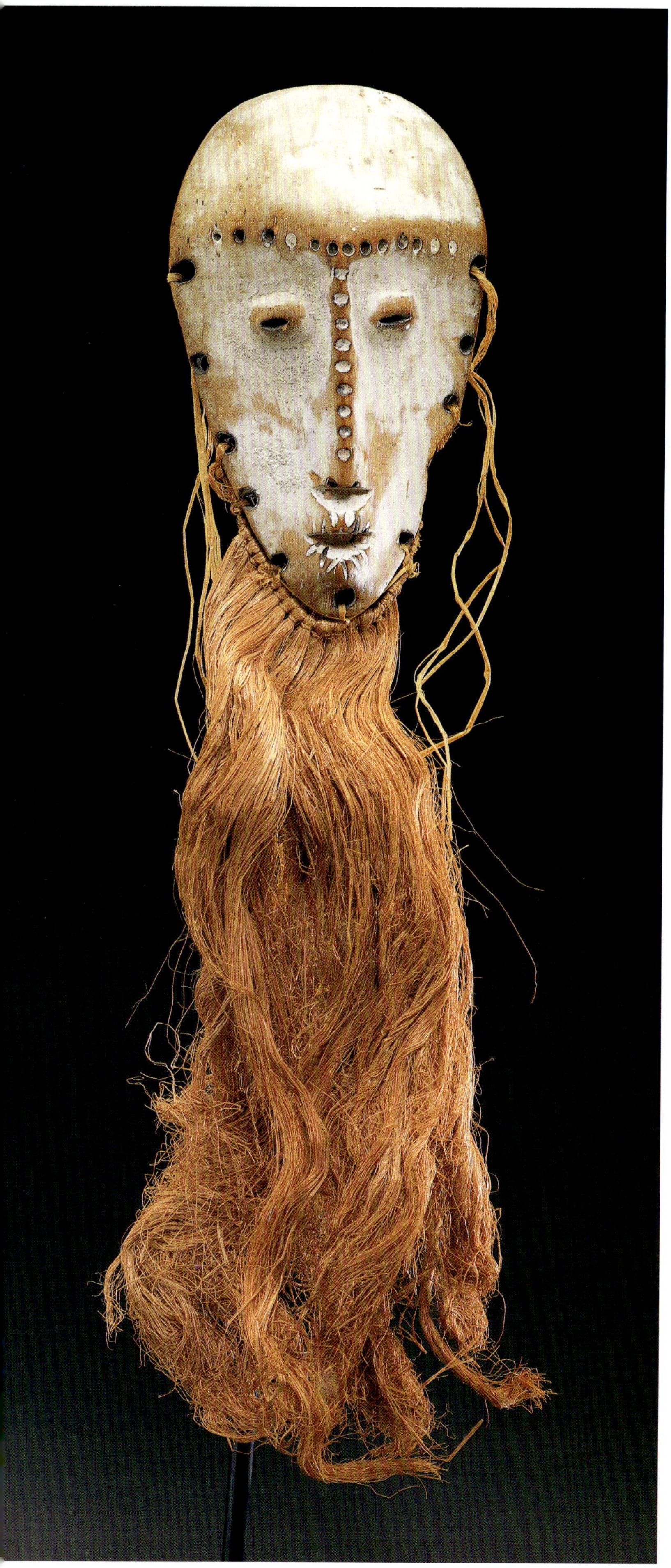

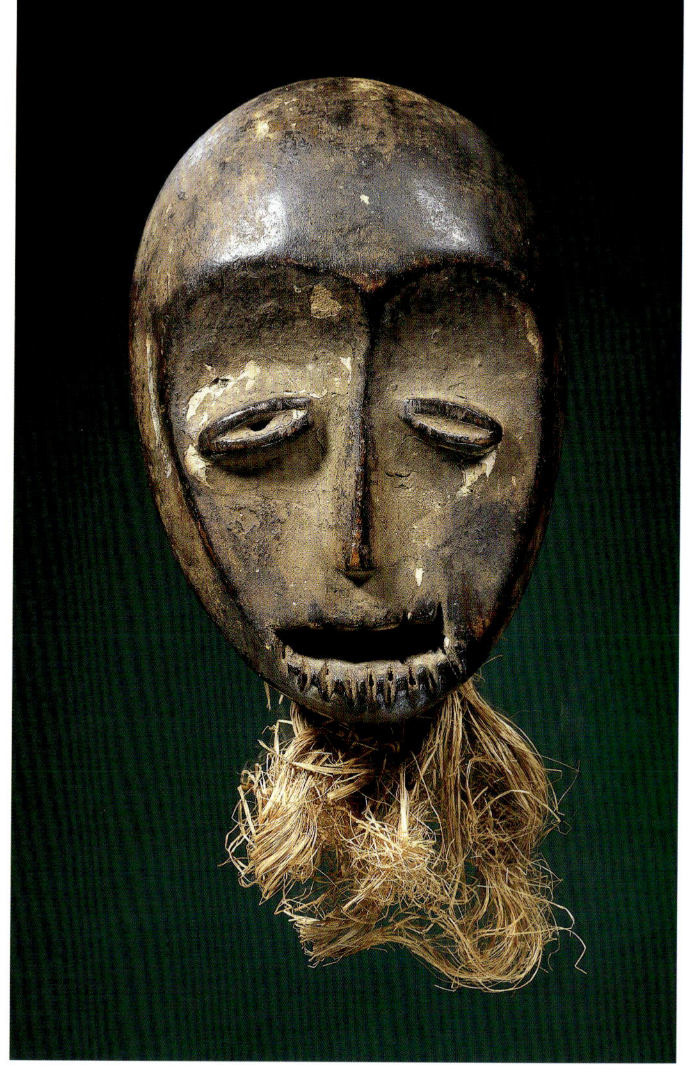

9.9 Mask (*lukwakongo* or *idimu*). Wood, pigment, and plant fiber. H: 44.5 cm (17½ in.).

9.10 Mask (*idimu*). Wood, pigment, and plant fiber. H: 27.3 cm (10¾ in.).

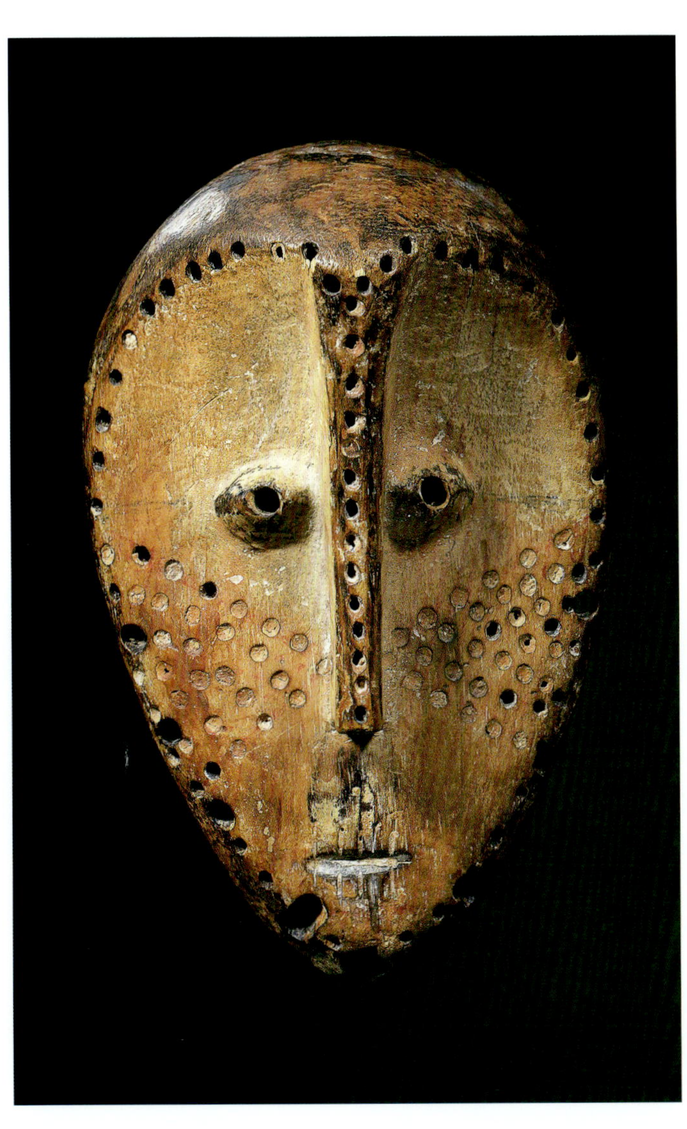

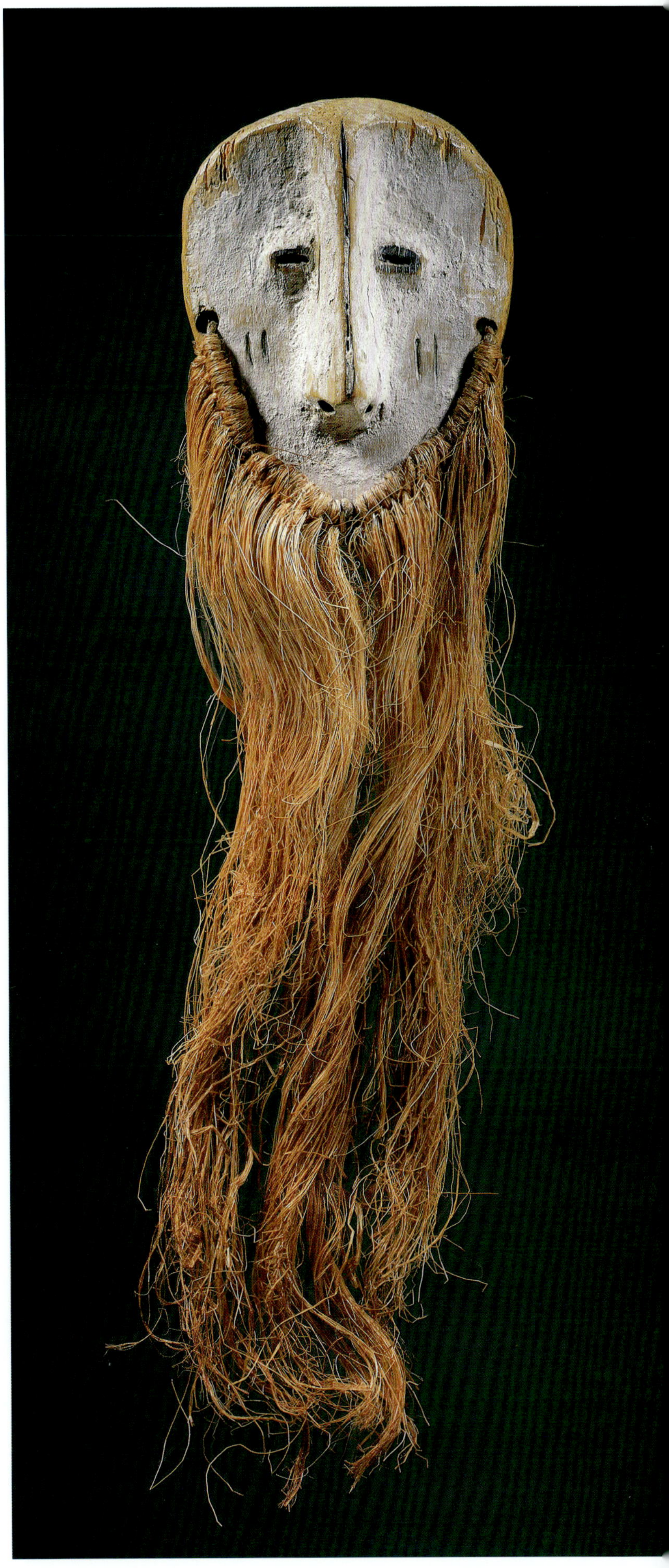

9.11 Mask (*lukwakongo*). Wood and pigment. H: 16.5 cm (6½ in.).

9.12 Mask (*lukwakongo*). Wood, pigment, and plant fiber. H: 32.5 cm (12¾ in.).

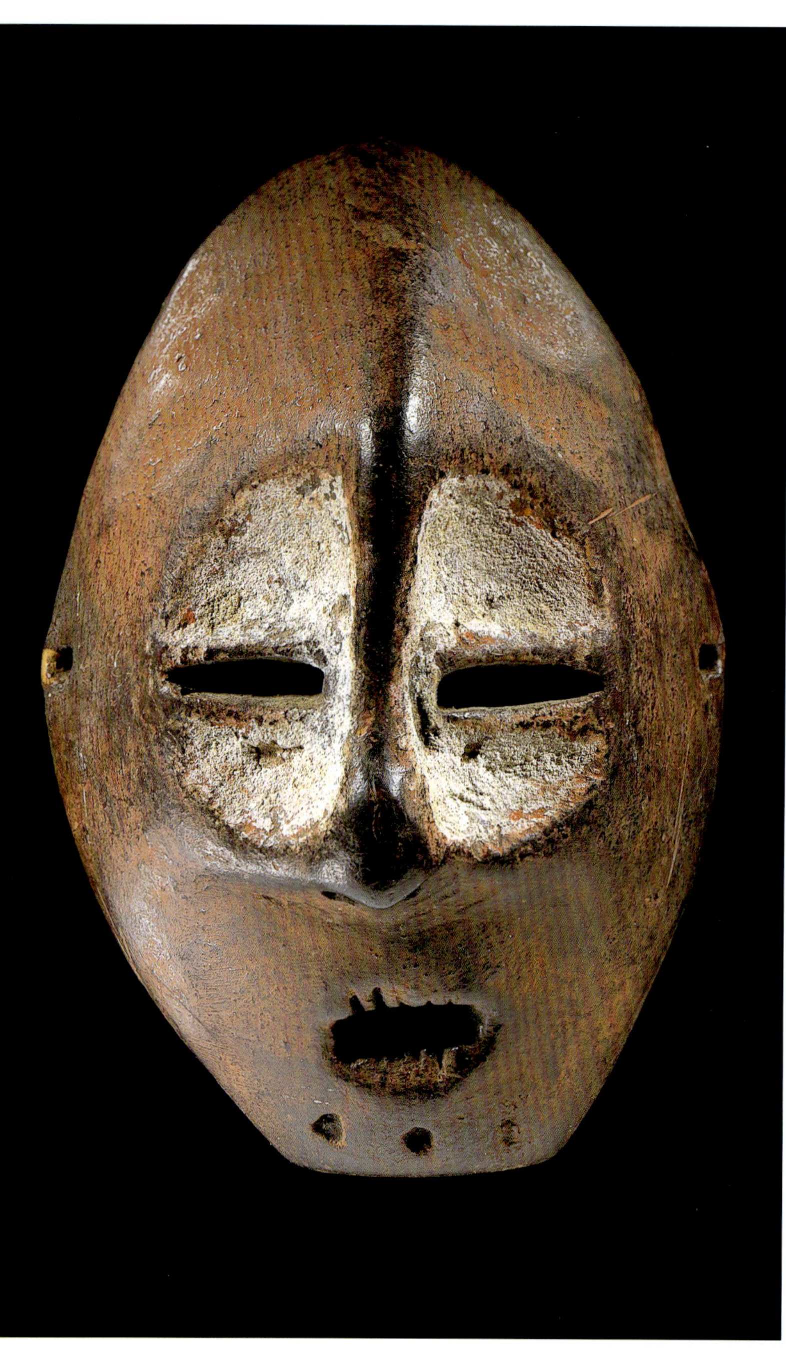

9.13 Mask (*lukwakongo*). Wood and pigment. H: 14 cm (5½ in.). FMCH 378.123; Museum Purchase.

It should be noted that in spite of its focus on continuation of the clan and on ancestors, Bwami is not, strictly speaking, an ancestor cult (Biebuyck 1954, 113). The very existence of Bwami, its age, and the unbroken line of high-level Bwami members serve to legitimize current political and social structures rather than offer supernatural help. Nevertheless, it is impossible not to see some connections between the Bwami and the Lega belief in ancestors.[4] When individuals die, the Lega say that they live as disembodied ancestors in a situation that reflects the status and relationships they had when alive. The ancestors are able to communicate with the living through apparitions and mediums, and to affect the lives of those on earth in both positive and negative ways. Therefore, a good relationship with the ancestors is an important consideration in Lega life and institutions.

In order to facilitate this communication and to appease the ancestors, official ancestor cults exist on both a domestic and public level. Although Bwami is not one of the official cults, the only dead able to return to, communicate with, and affect the living are those who in life had Bwami rank. Ceremonies to honor specific ancestors use Bwami rituals, songs, and sayings that reflect the rank of the deceased. Bwami exists in the worlds of the living and the dead, acting as a bridge between them. Thus, Bwami is important in both realms and is essential to the cult of the ancestors.

LUKWAKONGO

Lukwakongo masks are wooden and fairly small (figs. 9.13–9.30); they usually incorporate white powder covering a bearded face. They portray in a stylized manner an idealized Lega man (Biebuyck 1986, 128–29). The teacher gives the Lutumbo lwa Yananio initiate a *lukwakongo* mask in a ceremony during which all members of this Yananio sublevel display their masks (Biebuyck 1994, 50). When the

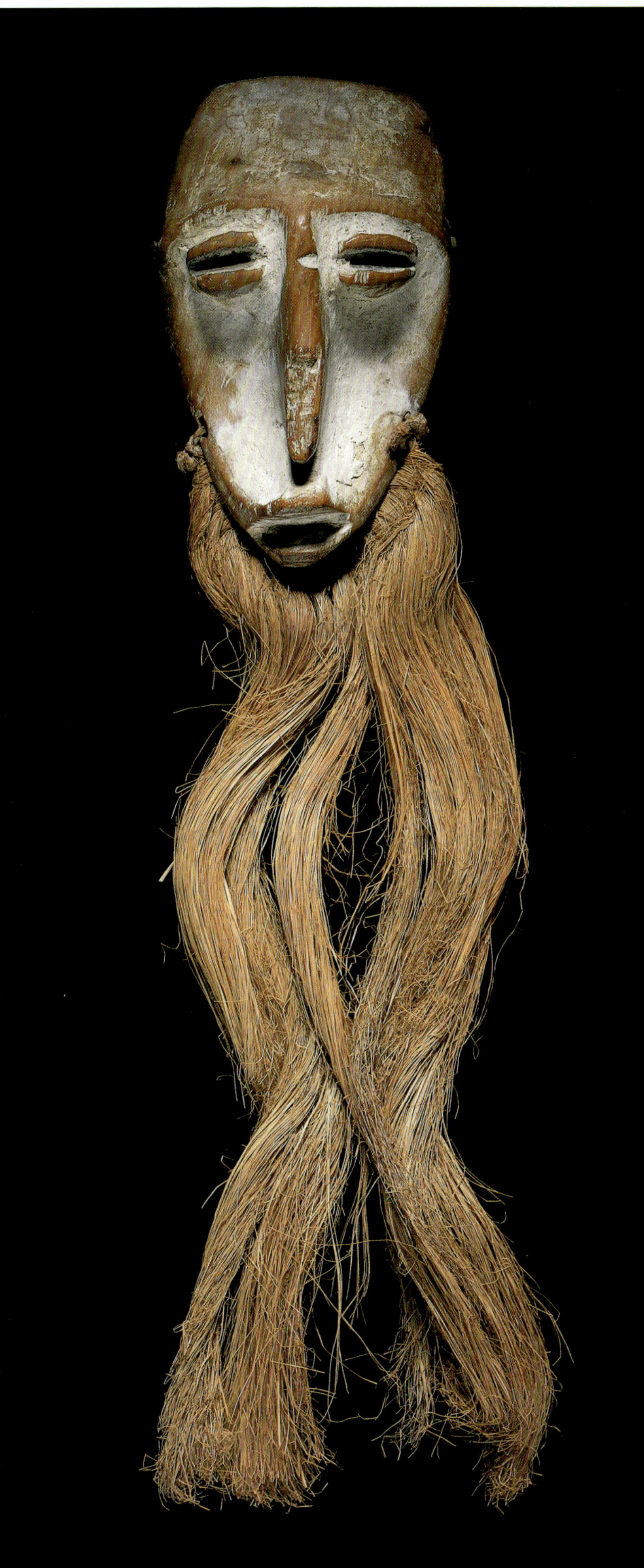

owner of the mask dies, it is displayed on his grave and then given to the teacher of the Bwami member who will inherit it (usually the nephew of the deceased) to safeguard until the appropriate time (Biebuyck 1986, 131).

Once received, the *lukwakongo* mask is the most important insignia of rank until the owner moves to Kindi and trades his wooden mask for an ivory one. His wife keeps the mask in her husband's Bwami basket, which is hidden in her house. She is responsible for carrying it to any initiations they attend (Biebuyck 1986, 131). As an initiation object the *lukwakongo* mask is combined with other items, sayings, drama, and music to create layered metaphors. Masks as a group have a narrow range of meaning that usually focuses on continuity and the permanence of Bwami (Biebuyck 1986, 132).[5] Although mainly used in Yananio rites, *lukwakongo* can appear in ceremonies of other levels including women's initiations (Biebuyck 1986, 148).

The features of the mask carry meaning that is shaped and intensified by action (Biebuyck 1986, 126). The unspeaking carved mouth refers to the pursed lips of the displeased teacher. The masks with no eyes represent the old, blind, high-level member of Bwami who is the best advisor. The fact that the masks are hatless calls to mind the candidate who was unsuccessful because he or she lacked a sponsor or teacher. The dotted designs found on some masks, especially in the *muminia* category, are representations of facial scarifications and remind the viewer of the fleeting nature of youth (see fig. 8.107; Biebuyck 1994, 52). As a person ages, the marks fade and grow soft.

Members of Yananio and Kindi individually own the wooden *lukwakongo* masks and the ivory *lukungu*, respectively. The masks, especially the smallest ones, are compared to the blacksmith's hammers. Just as one knows what is happening upon hearing the hammers, so the mask owners should be constantly reminded of their duties in Bwami (Biebuyck 1986, 126; 1994, 46).

9.14 Mask (*lukwakongo*). Wood, plant fiber, and pigment. H: 37.9 cm (15 in.).

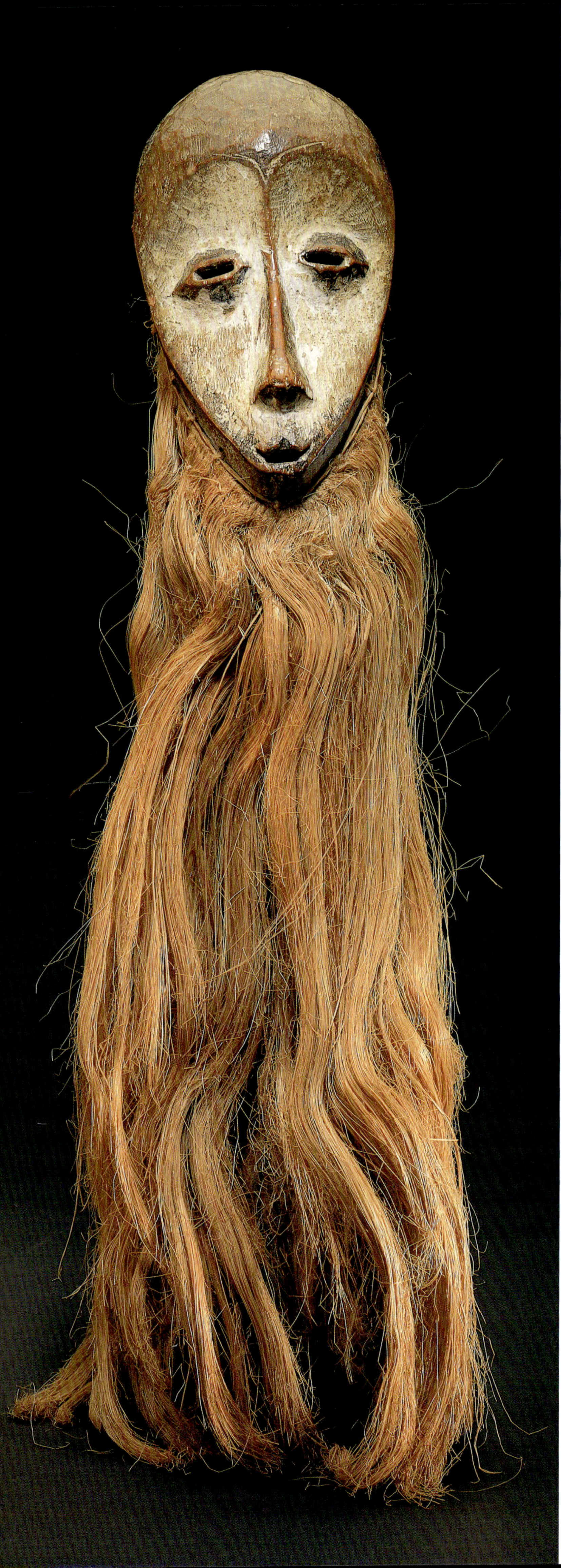

9.15 Mask (*lukwakongo*).
Wood, plant fiber, and pigment.
H: 57.5 cm (22¾ in.).

9.16 Mask (*lukwakongo*).
Wood, pigment, and plant fiber.
H: 25.5 cm (10 in.).

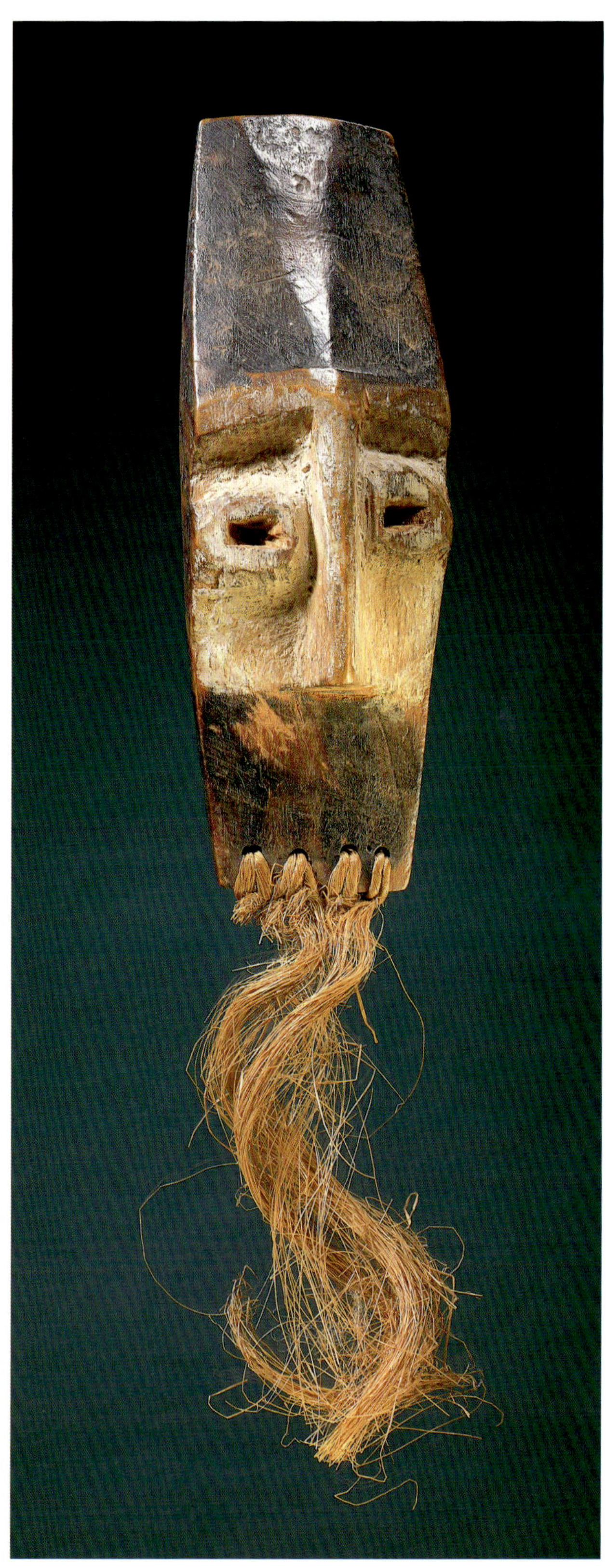

9.17 Mask (*lukwakongo*).
Wood. H: 20.1 cm (8 in.).

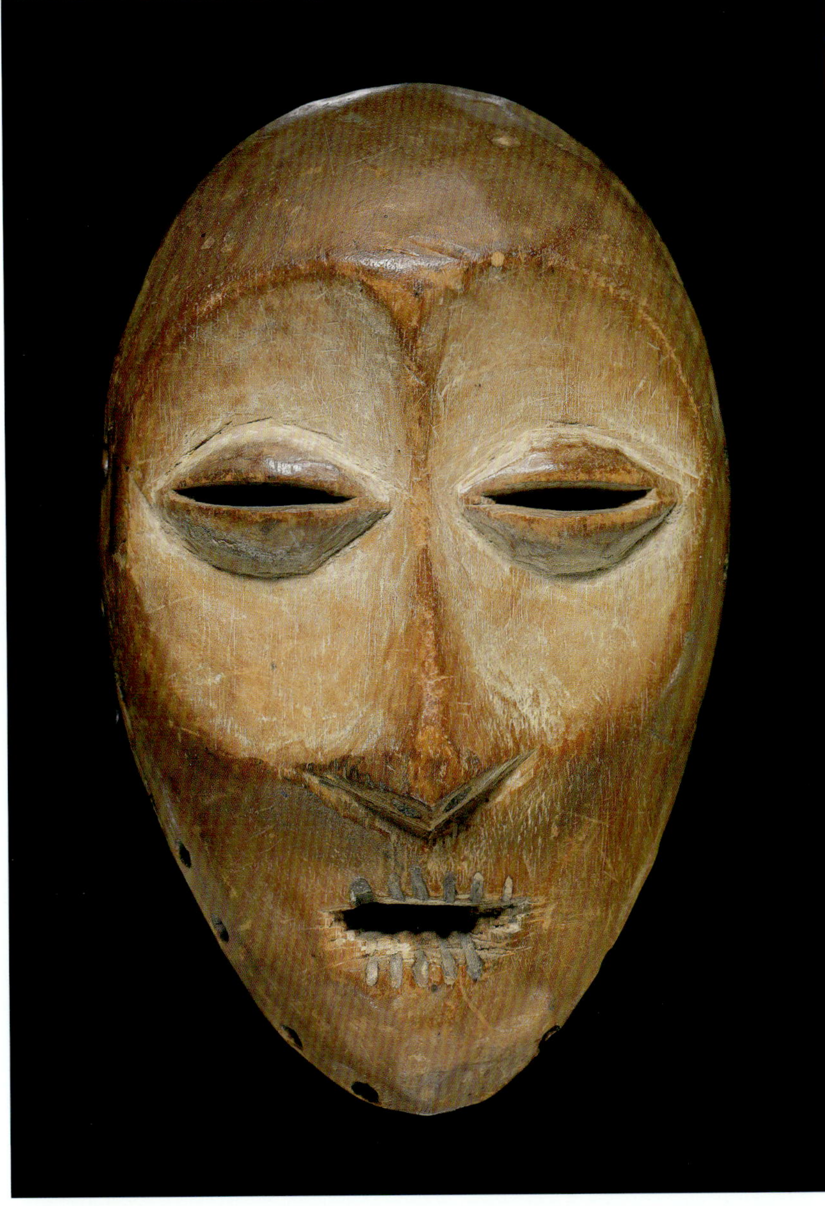

9.18 Mask (*lukwakongo*).
Wood. H: 12.6 cm (5 in.).

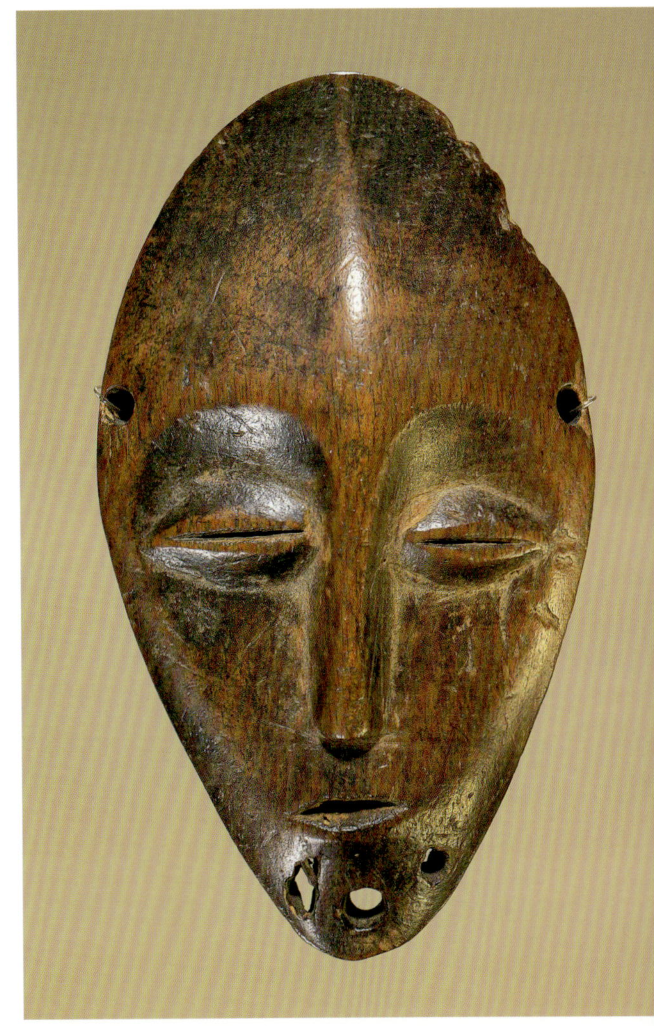

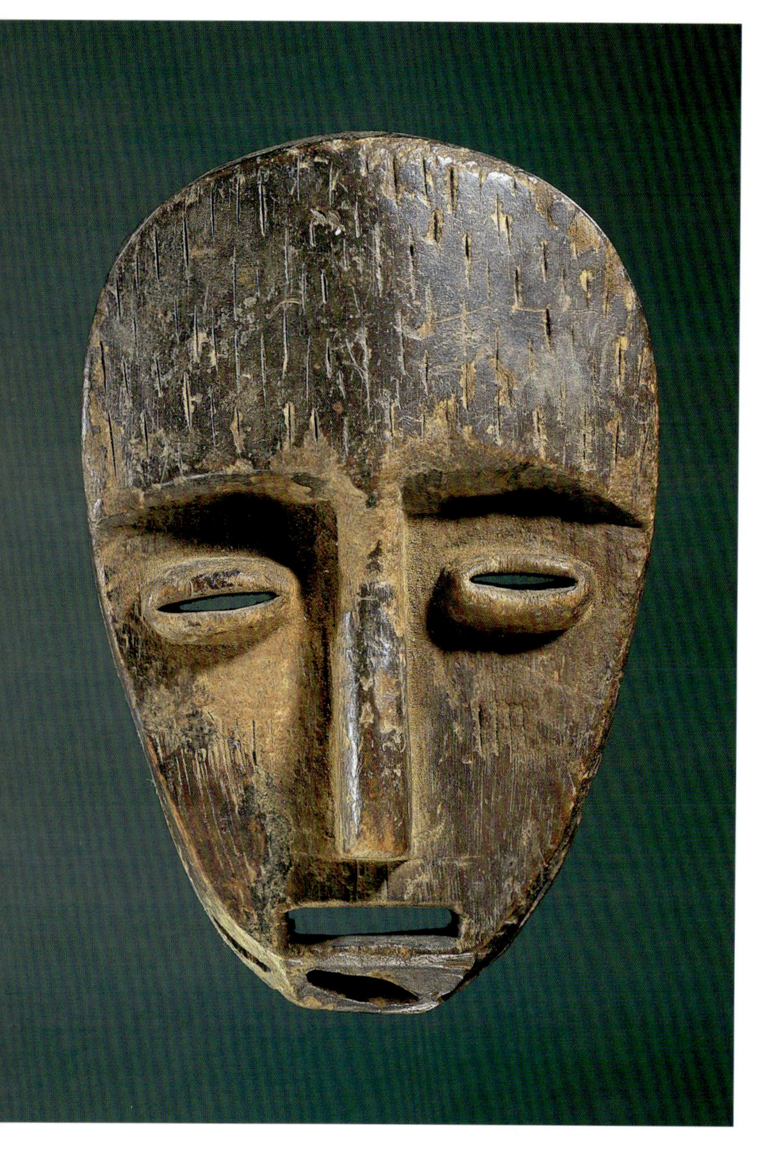

9.19 Mask (*lukwakongo*). Wood. H: 17.2 cm (6¾ in.).

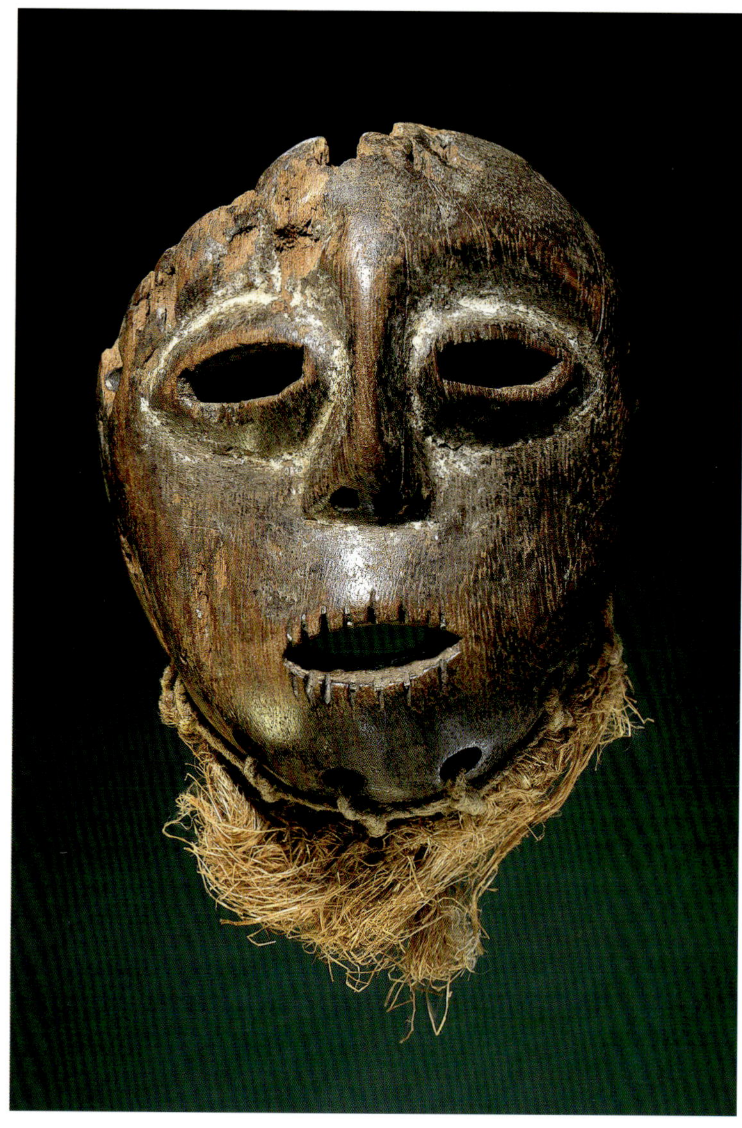

9.20 Mask (*lukwakongo*). Wood, plant fiber, and pigment. H: 14.5 cm (5¾ in.).

9.21 Mask (*lukwakongo*). Wood, pigment, and plant fiber. H: 32.2 cm (12¾ in.).

9.22 Mask (*lukwakongo*). Wood and plant fiber. H: 41.3 cm (16¼ in.).

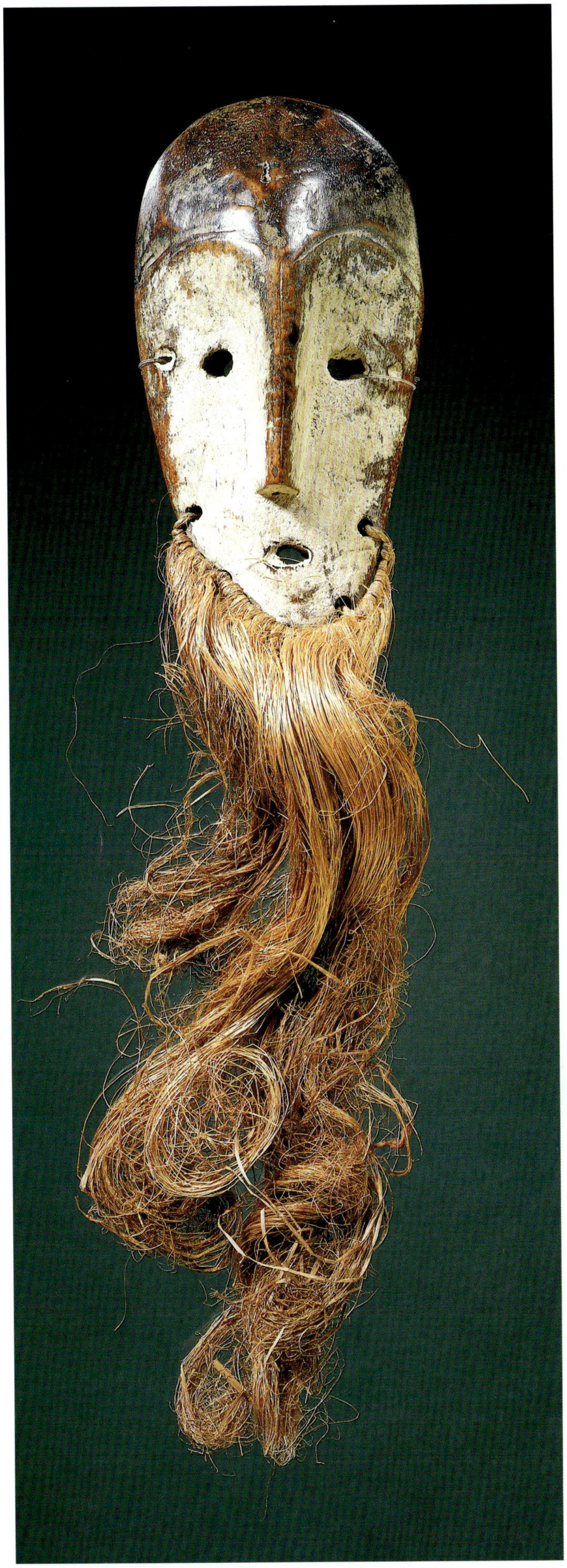

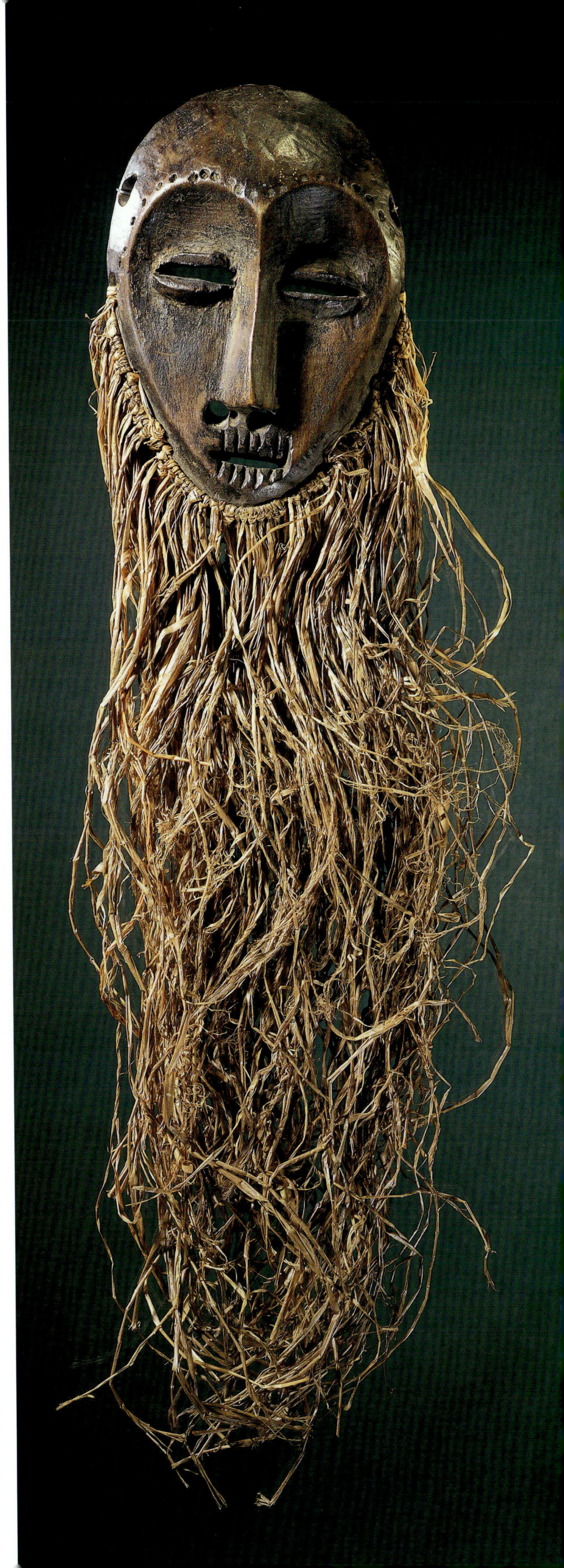

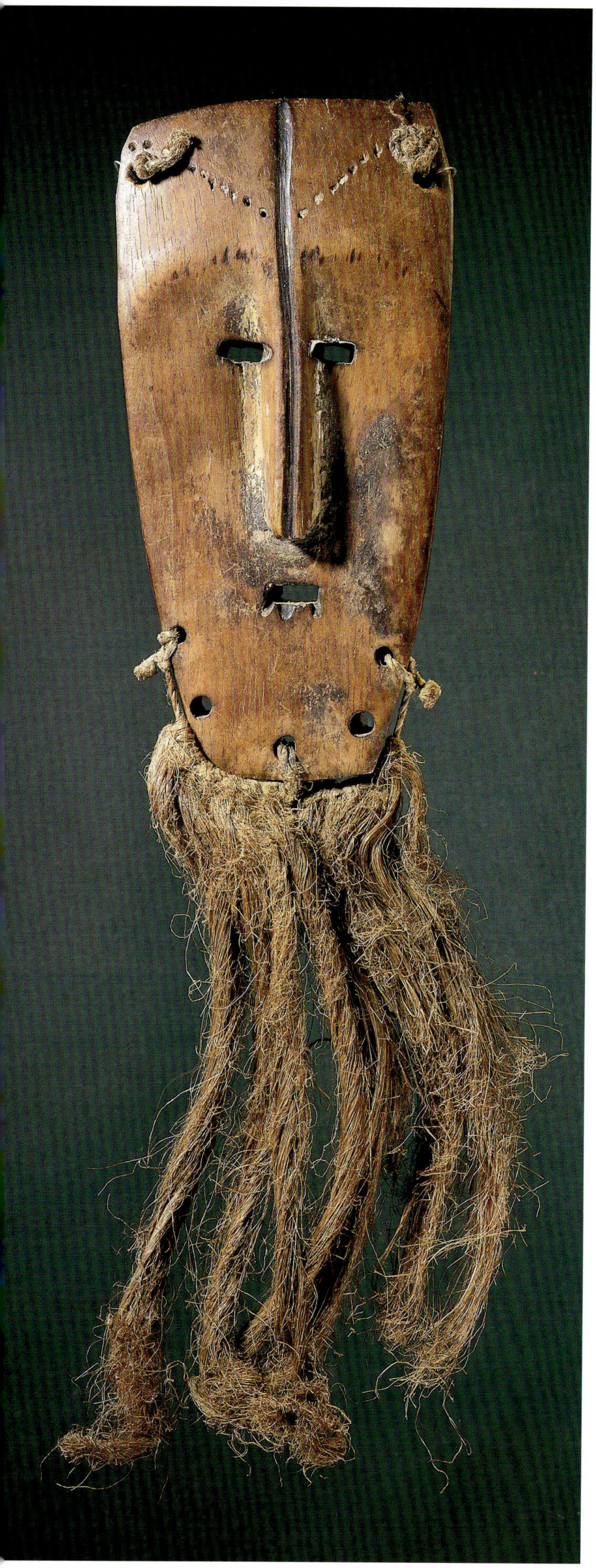

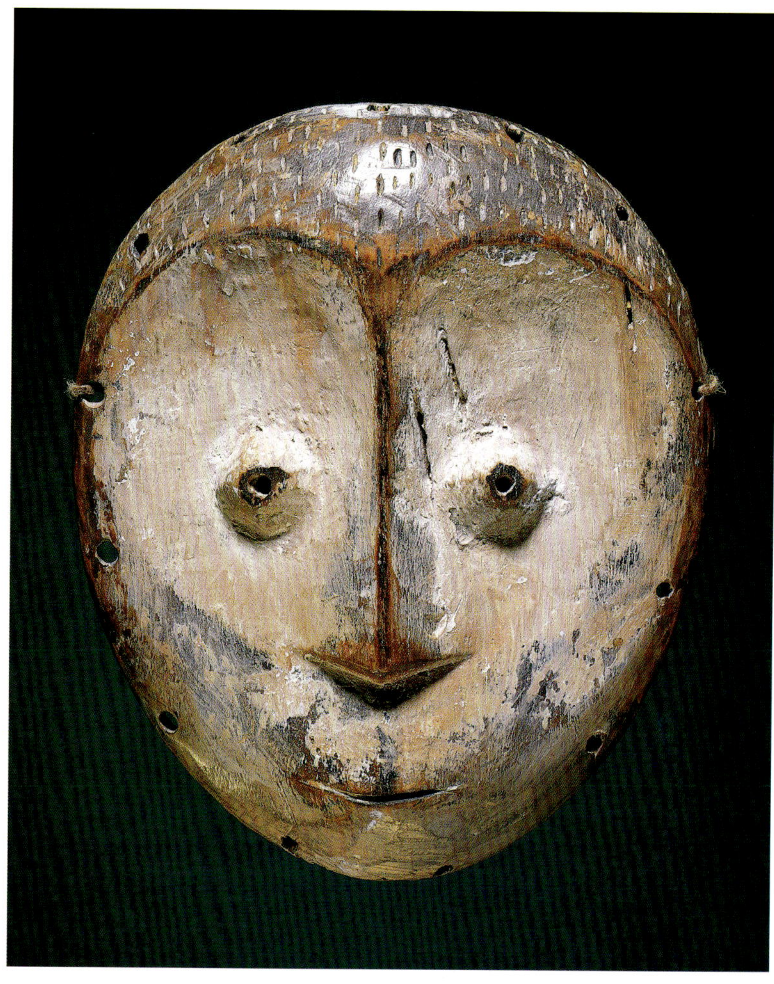

9.24 Mask (*lukwakongo*). Wood and pigment. H: 16.2 cm (6⅜ in.).

9.23 Mask (*lukwakongo*). Wood, plant fiber, and pigment. H: 35 cm (13¾ in.).

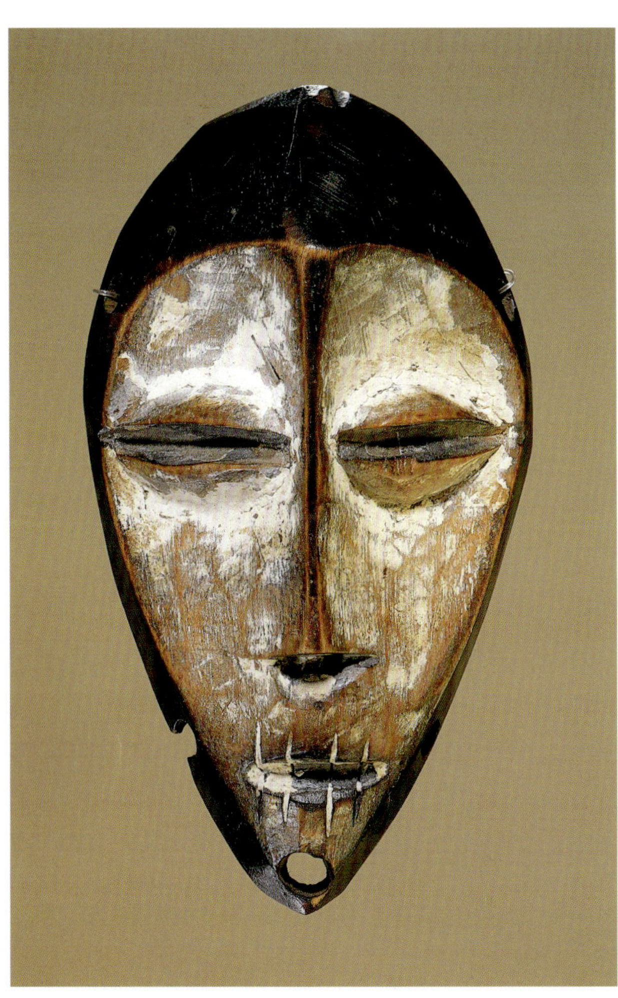

9.25 Mask (*lukwakongo*). Wood and pigment. H: 11.5 cm (4½ in.).

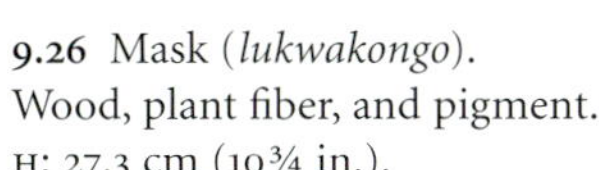

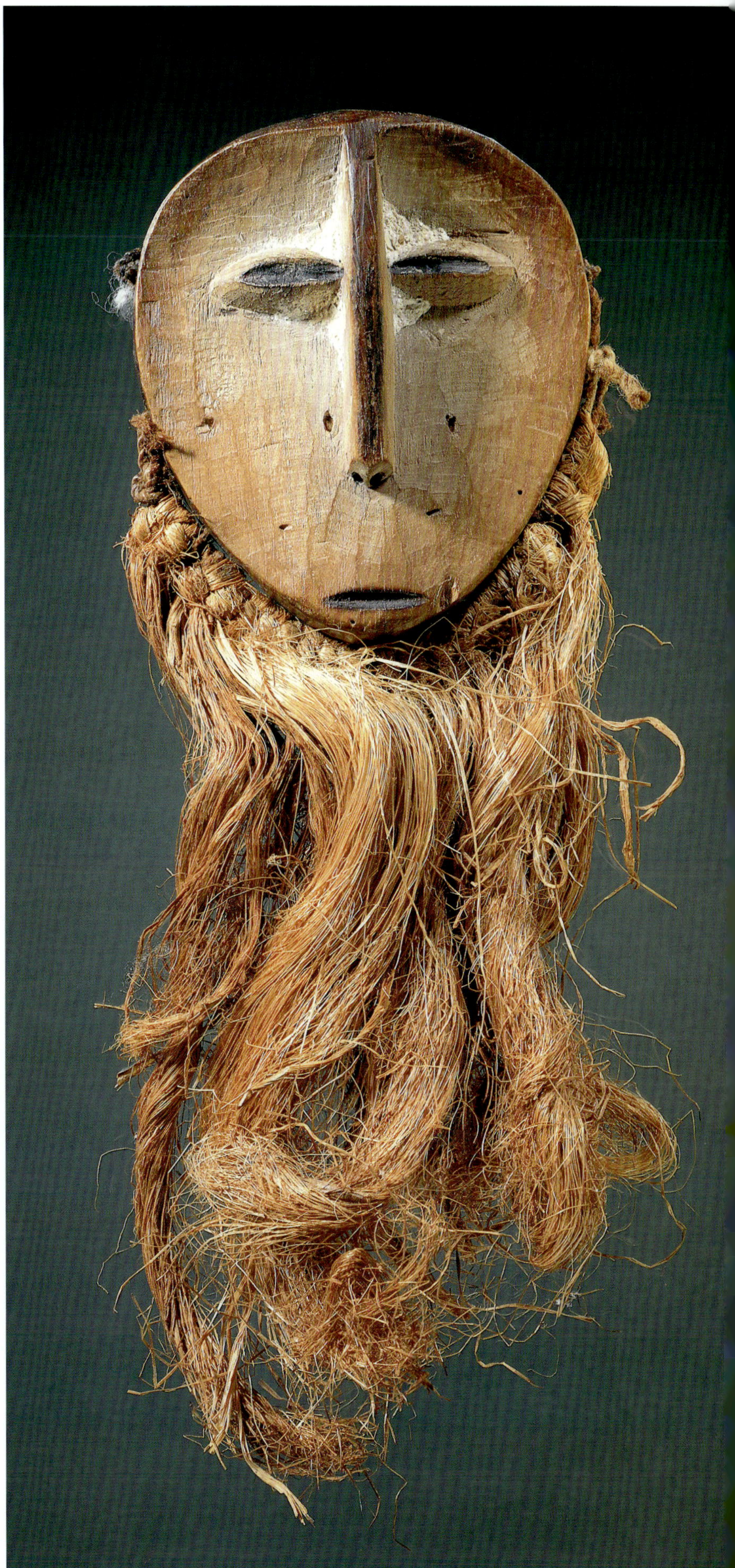

9.26 Mask (*lukwakongo*). Wood, plant fiber, and pigment. H: 27.3 cm (10¾ in.).

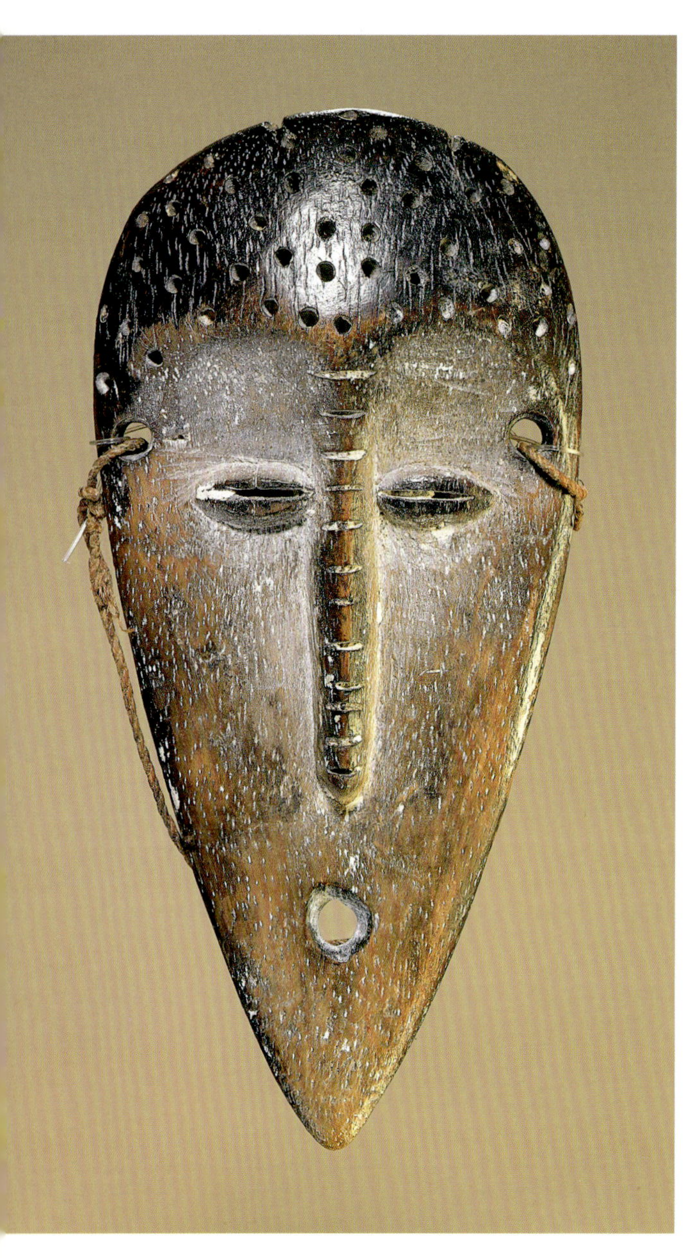

9.27 Mask (*lukwakongo*). Wood, pigment, and string. H: 14.2 cm (5½ in.).

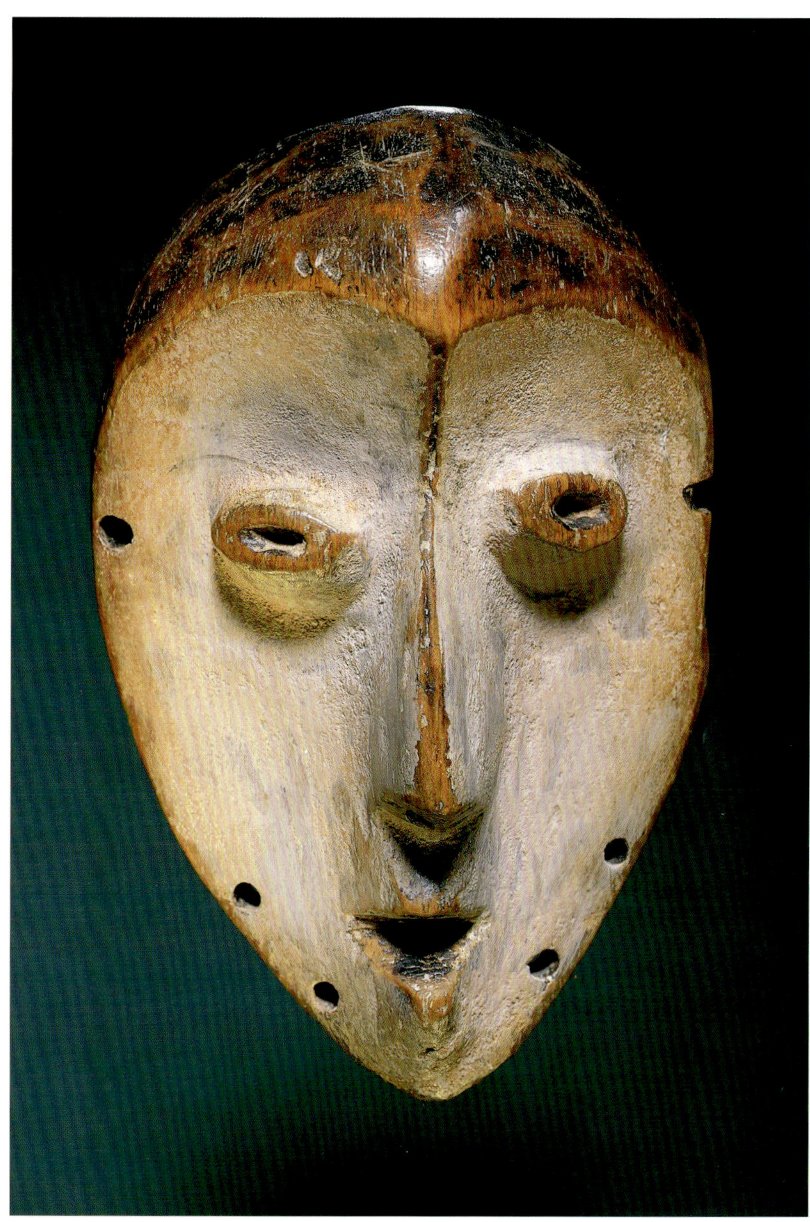

9.28 Mask (*lukwakongo*). Wood and pigment. H: 13 cm (5⅛ in.).

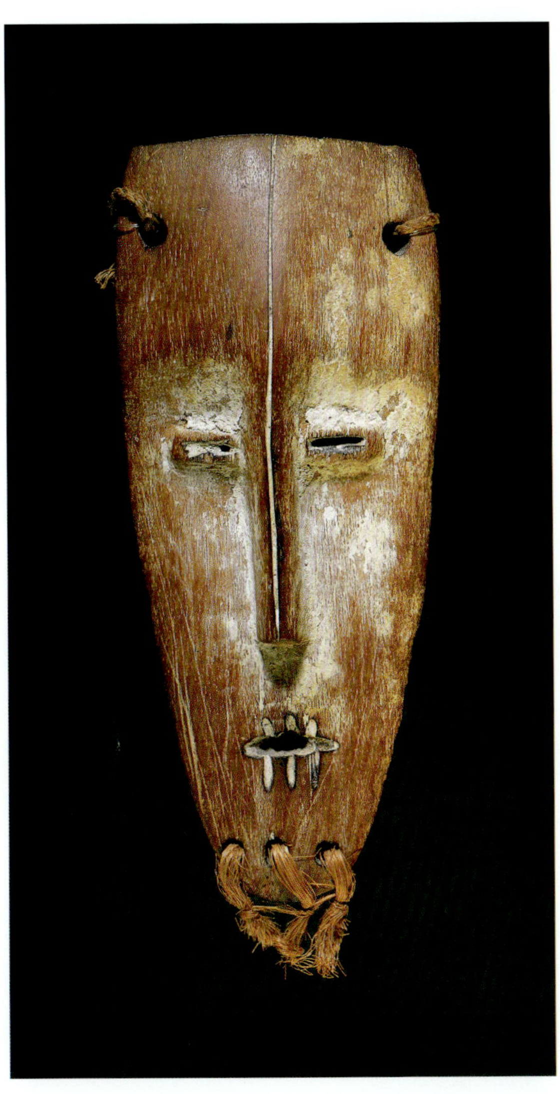

9.29 Mask (*lukwakongo*).
Wood. H: 6 cm (2⅜ in.).

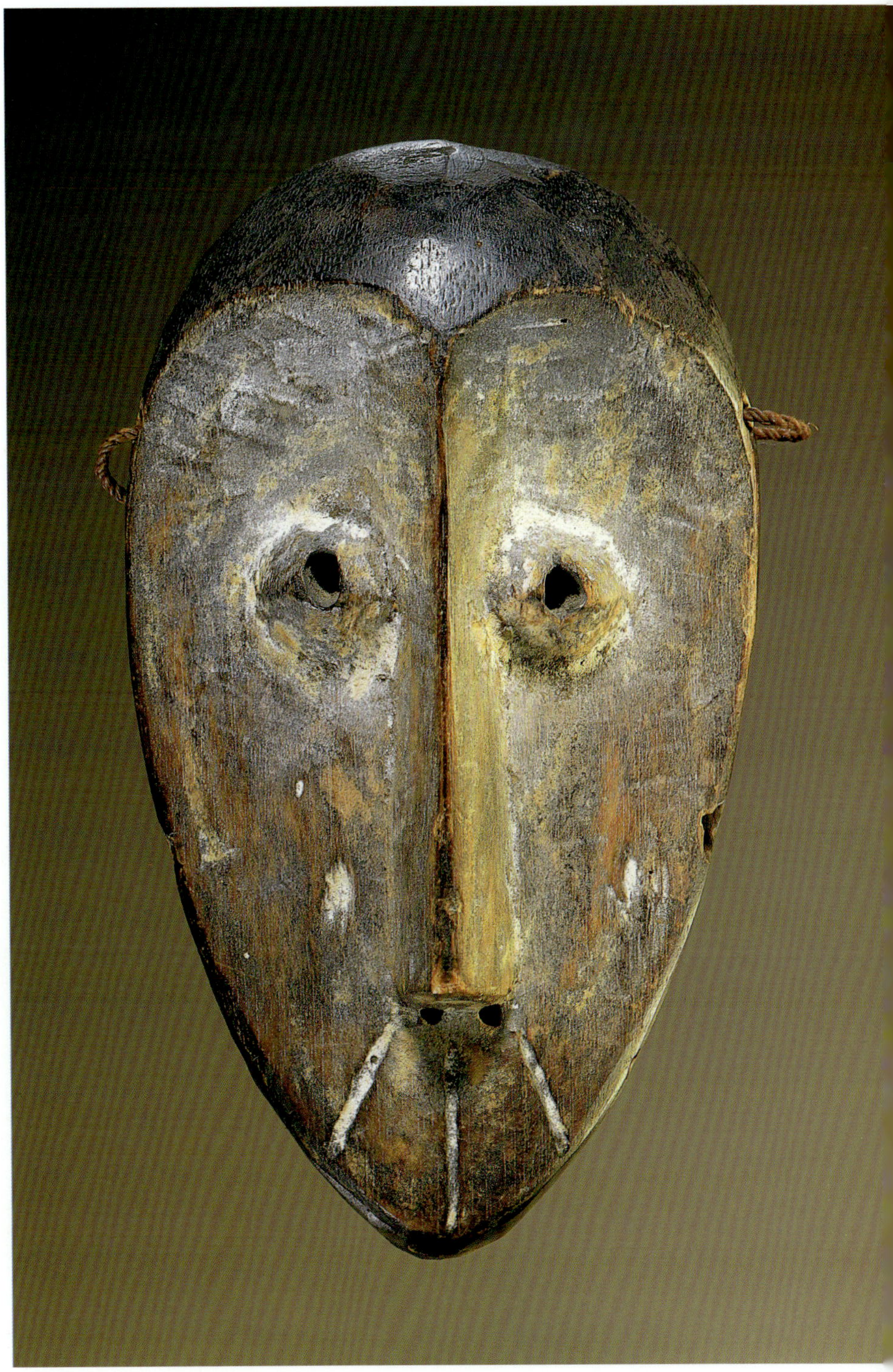

9.30 Mask (*lukwakongo*).
Wood, pigment, and string. H: 17.7 cm (7 in.).

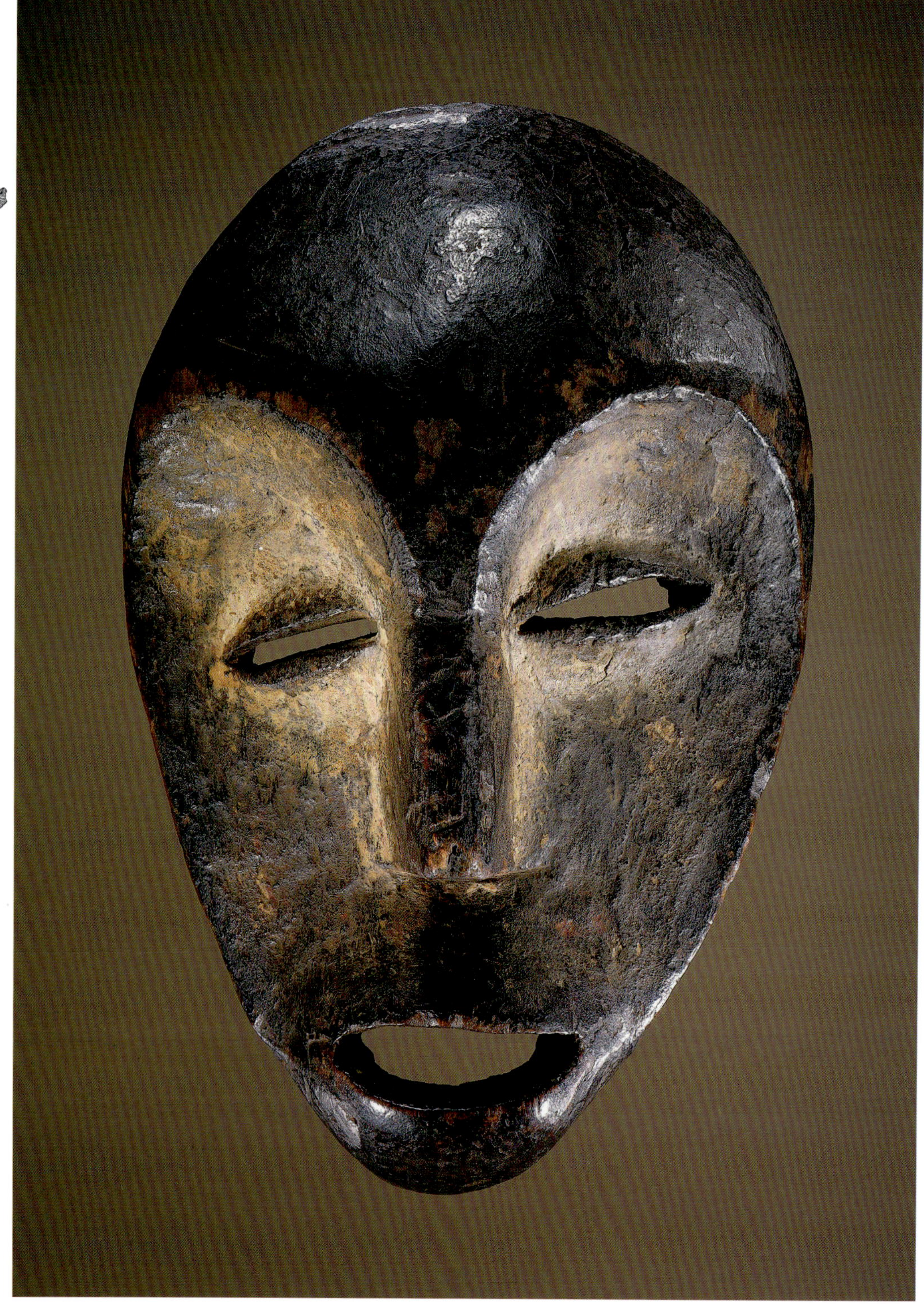

9.31 Mask (*idimu*). Wood and pigment. H: 24.7 cm (9¾ in.).

9.32 Mask (*idimu*). Wood, pigment, and plant fiber. H: 31.2 cm (12¼ in.).

IDIMU

An *idimu* mask resembles the *lukwakongo* but is large, bearded, and always white (figs. 9.31–9.49; Biebuyck 1994, 54). This mask is usually wood but can occasionally be made of ivory (Biebuyck 1986, 174). In contrast to the *lukwakongo*, the *idimu* mask is owned collectively and is kept by an appropriate member of Yananio or Kindi (usually the newest or oldest). It is occasionally safeguarded by a member of a comparable level in another ritual community (Biebuyck 1986, 174), creating links between the two bodies. It appears in both Yananio and Kindi initiations (Biebuyck 1994, 54).

In a major performance, the *idimu* mask is hung from a fence surrounded by all the smaller, individually owned *lukwakongo* masks that belong to those in attendance. The mask represents the source or man who brought the higher Bwami levels to a community and gave them to all the members present who are represented by their individual masks (Biebuyck 1994, 54).

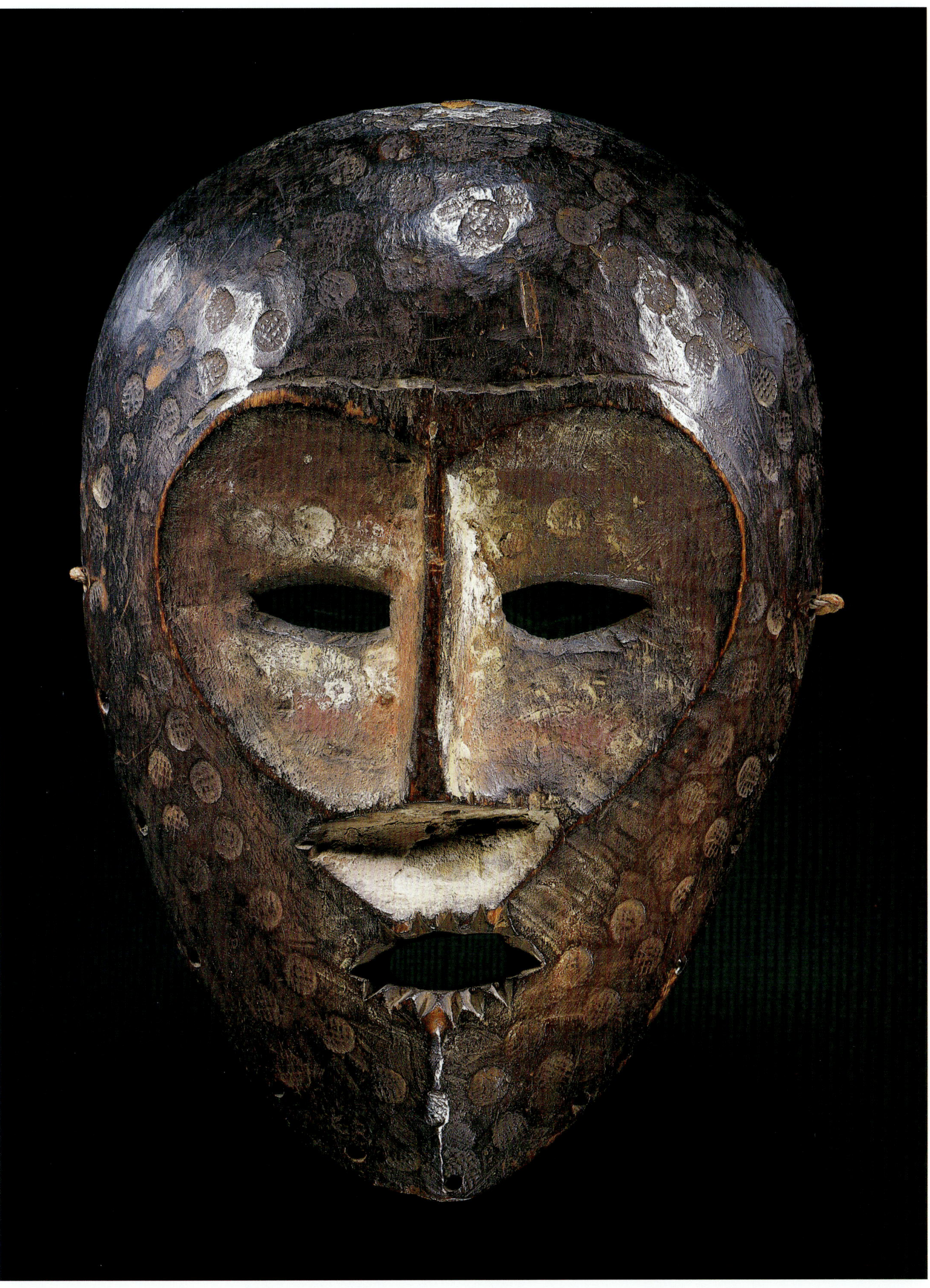

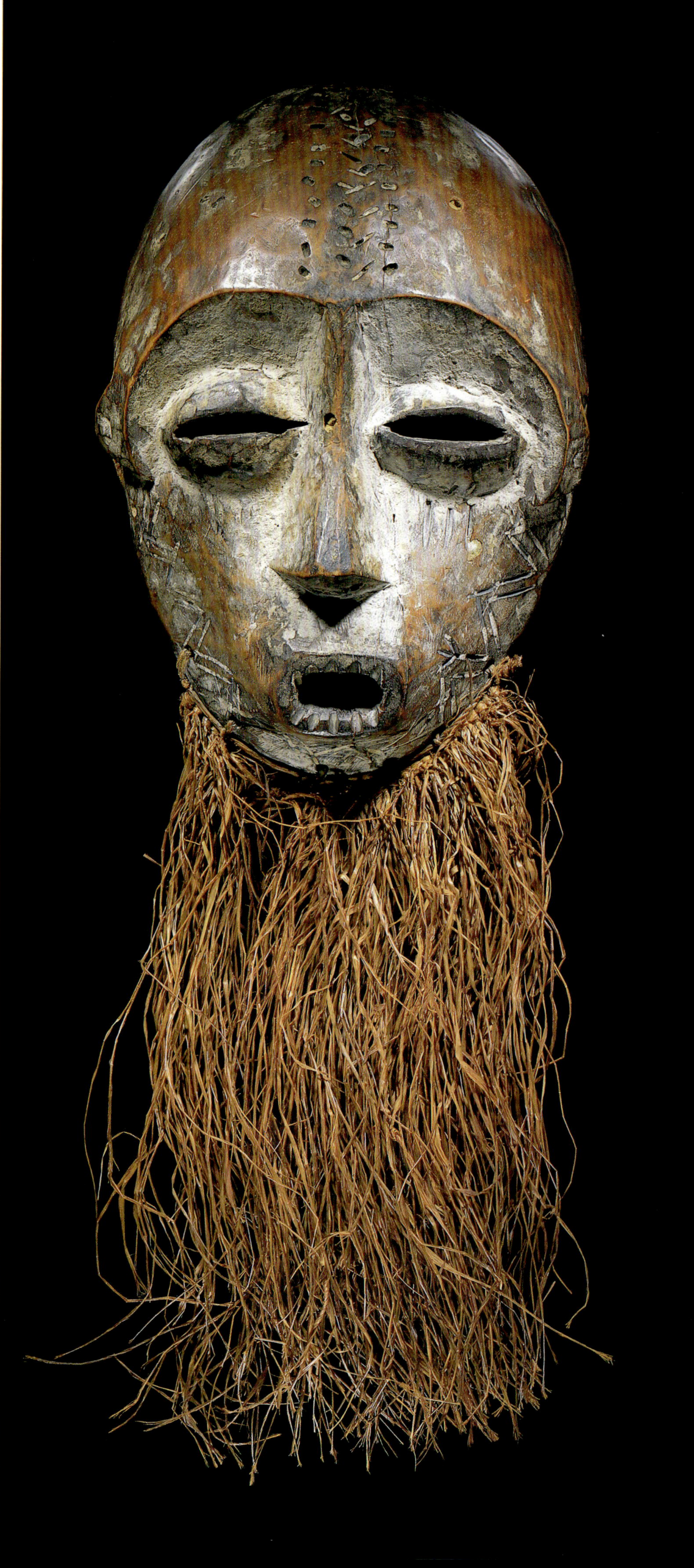

9.33 Mask (*idimu*). Wood, pigment, and plant fiber. H: 59.5 cm (23½ in.).

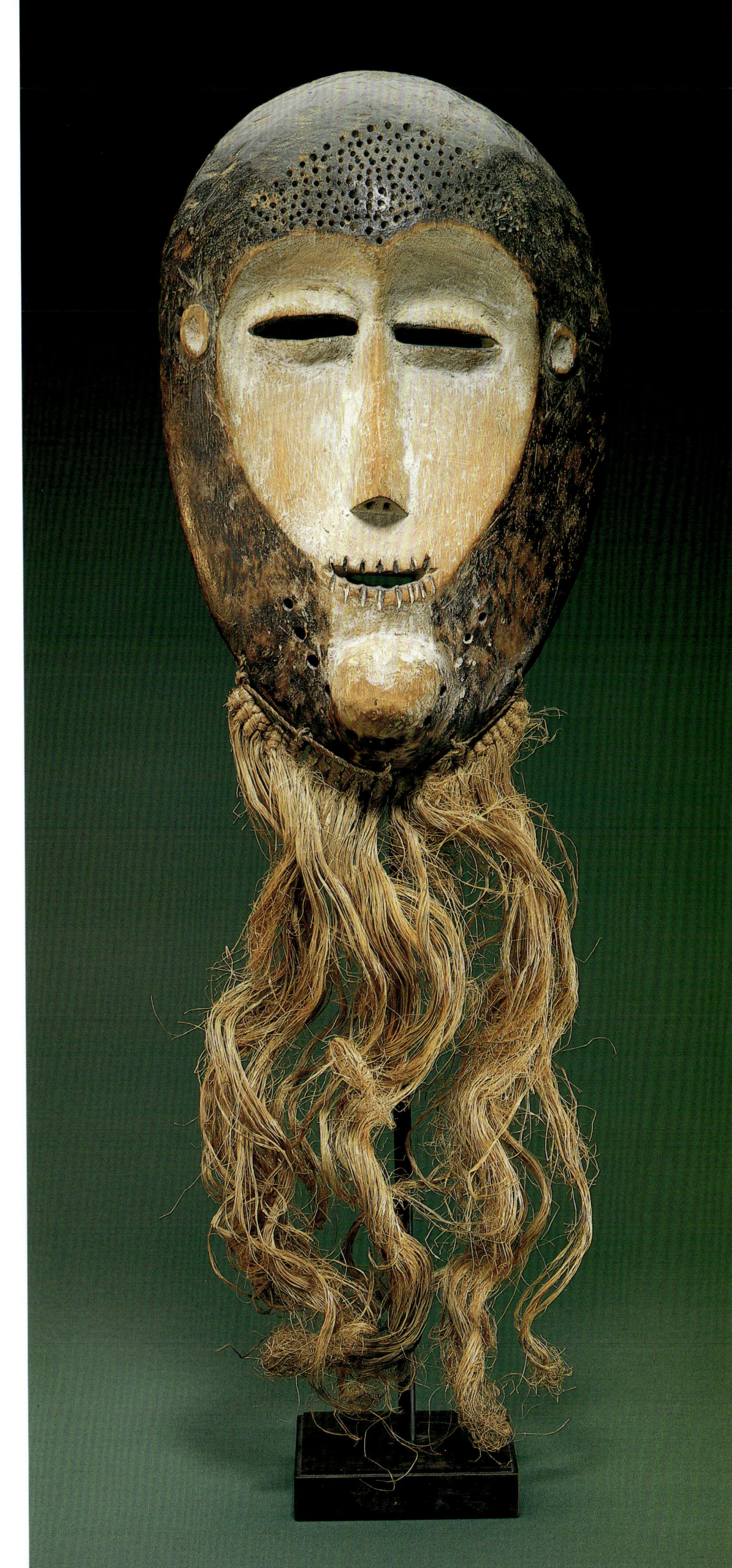

9.34 Mask (*idimu*). Wood, plant fiber, and pigment. H: 60 cm (23¾ in.).

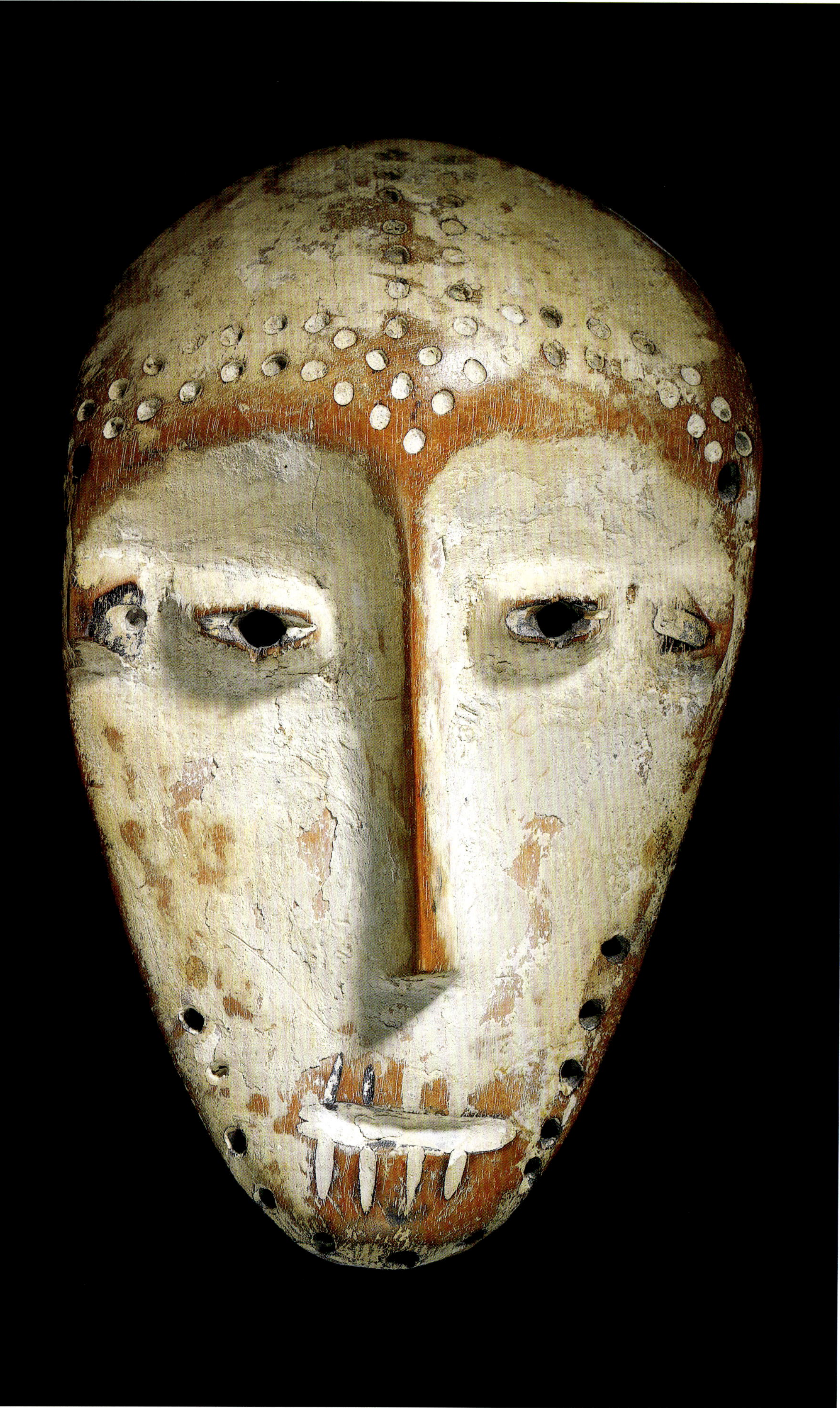

9.35 Mask (*idimu*). Wood and pigment. H: 26 cm (10¼ in.).

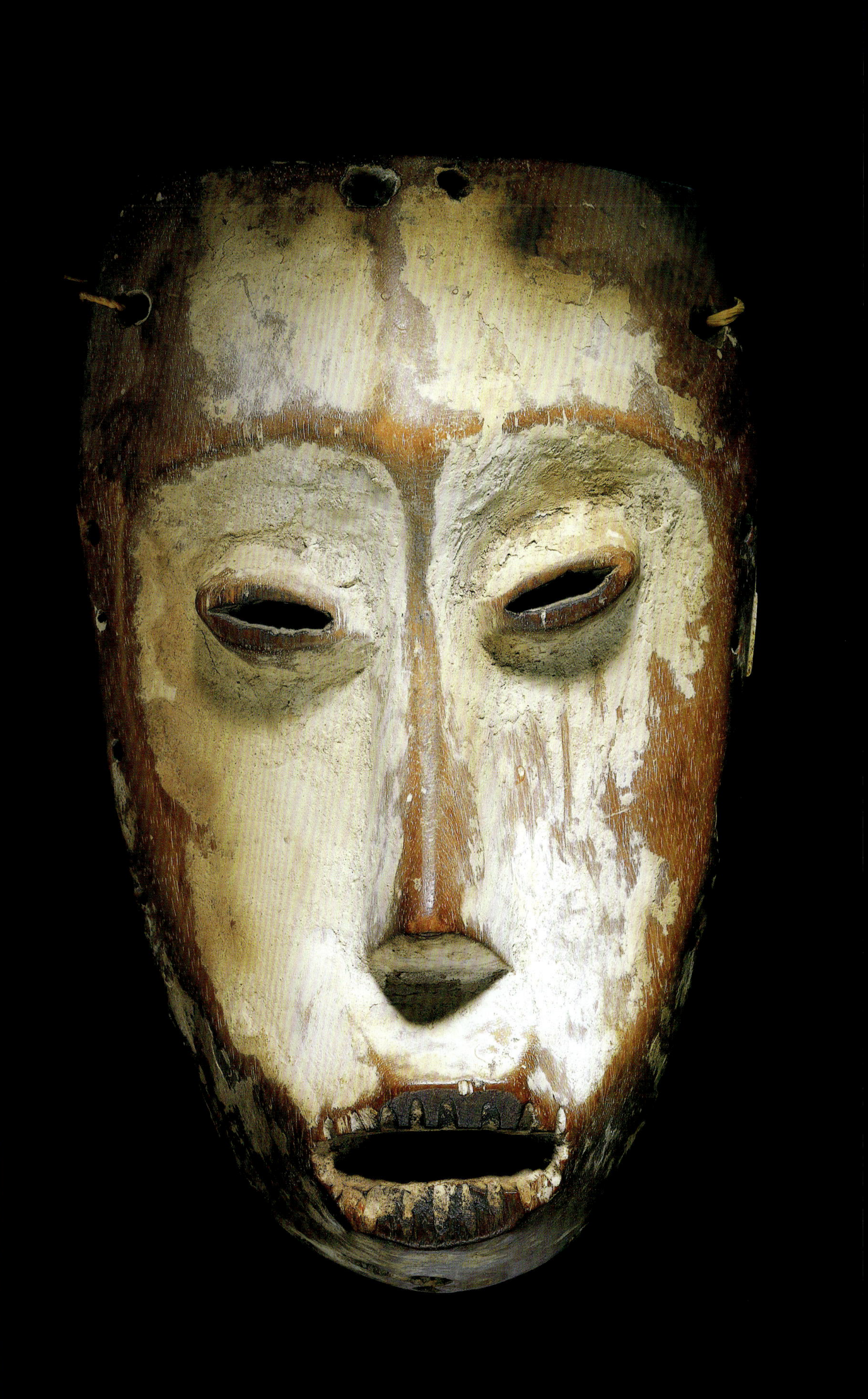

9.36 Mask (*idimu*). Wood and pigment. H: 26.7 cm (10½ in.).

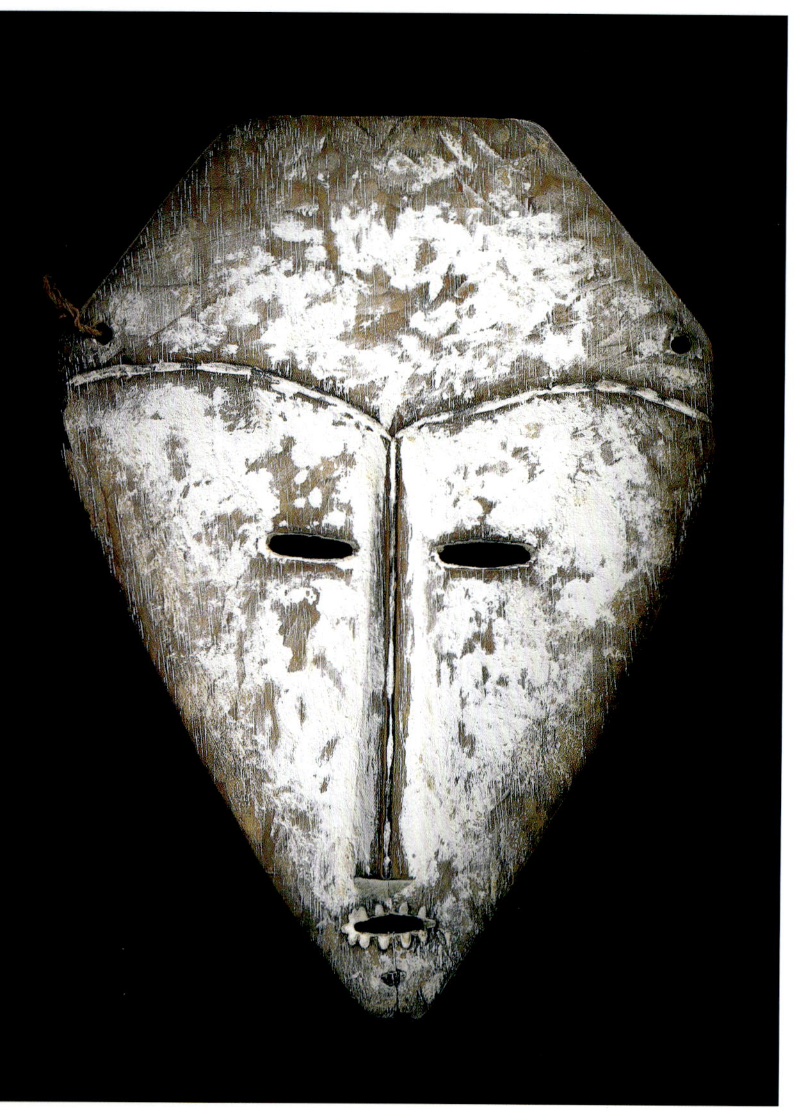

9.37 Mask (*idimu*). Wood, pigment, and plant fiber. H: 29.6 cm (11¾ in.).

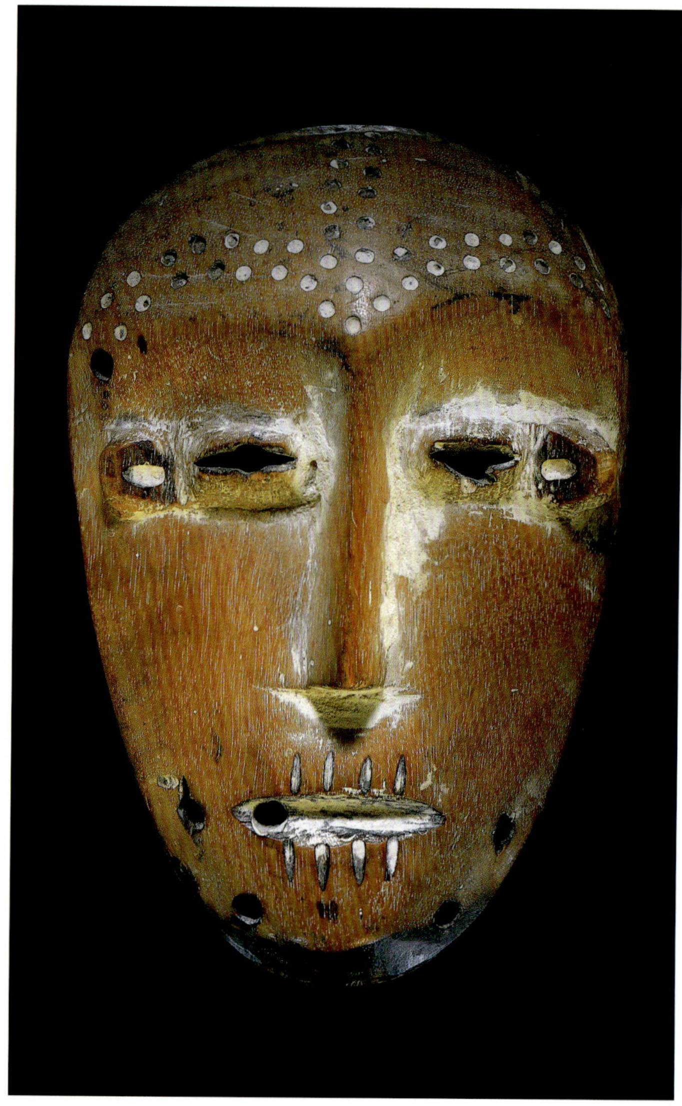

9.38 Mask (*idimu*). Wood and pigment. H: 26.7 cm (10½ in.).

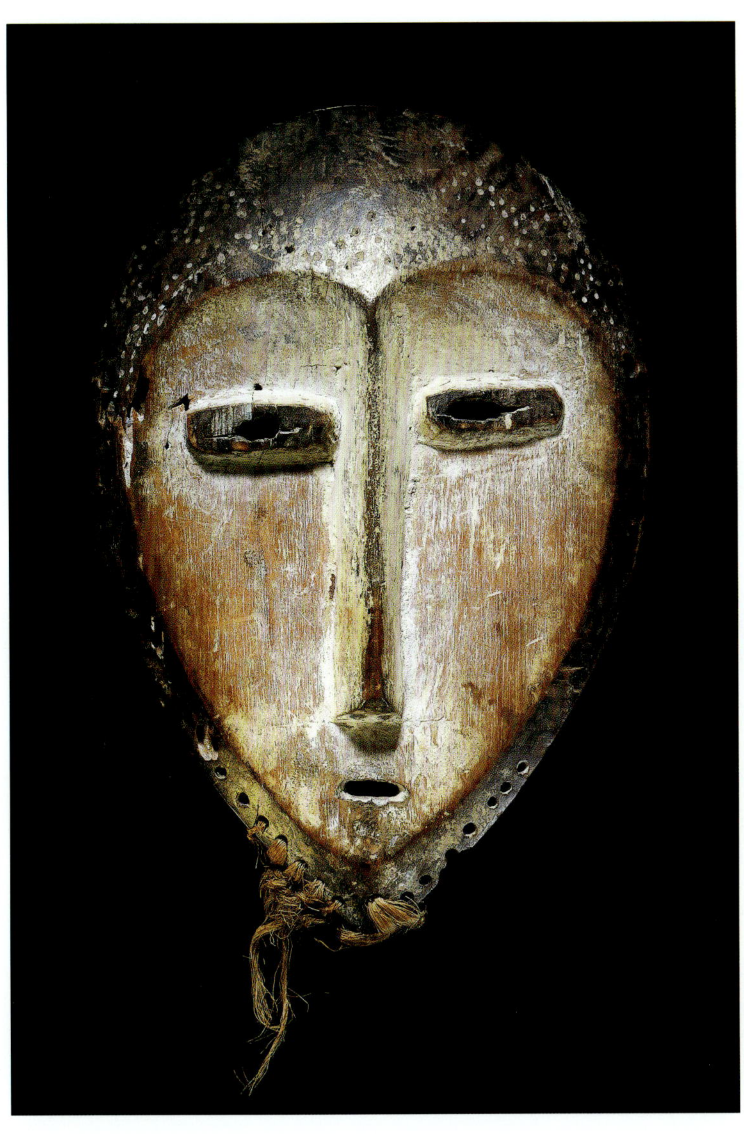

9.39 Mask (*idimu*). Wood, pigment, and plant fiber. H: 27.8 cm (11 in.).

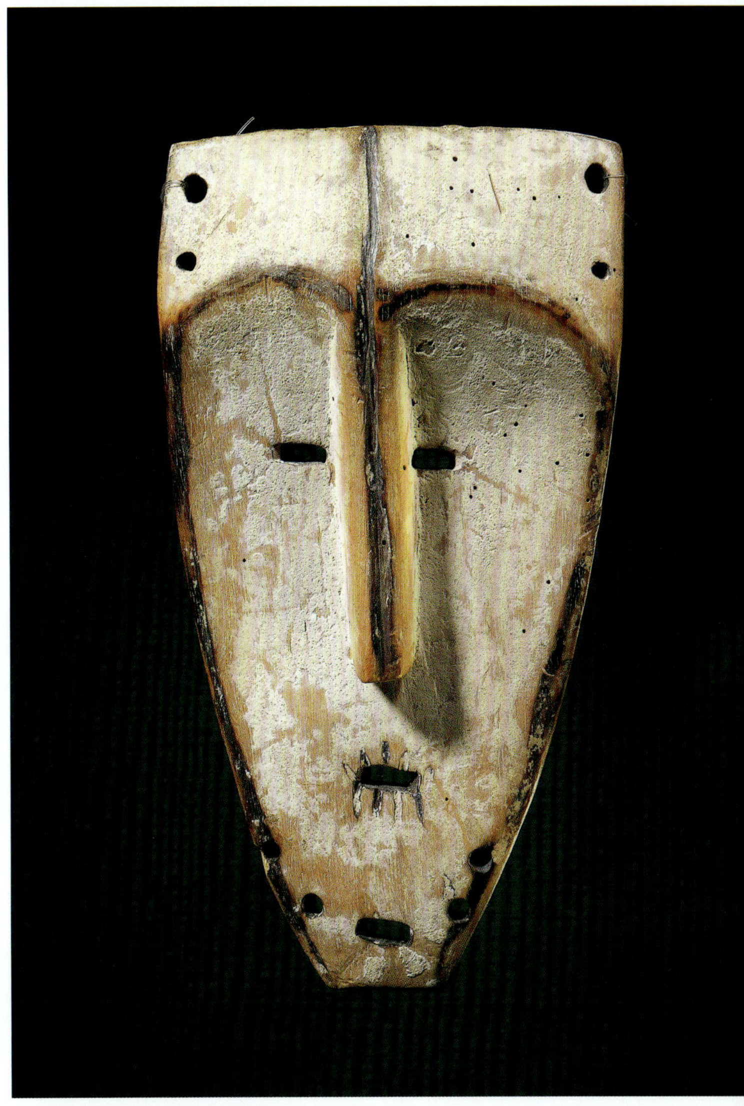

9.40 Mask (*idimu*). Wood and pigment. H: 21 cm (8¼ in.).

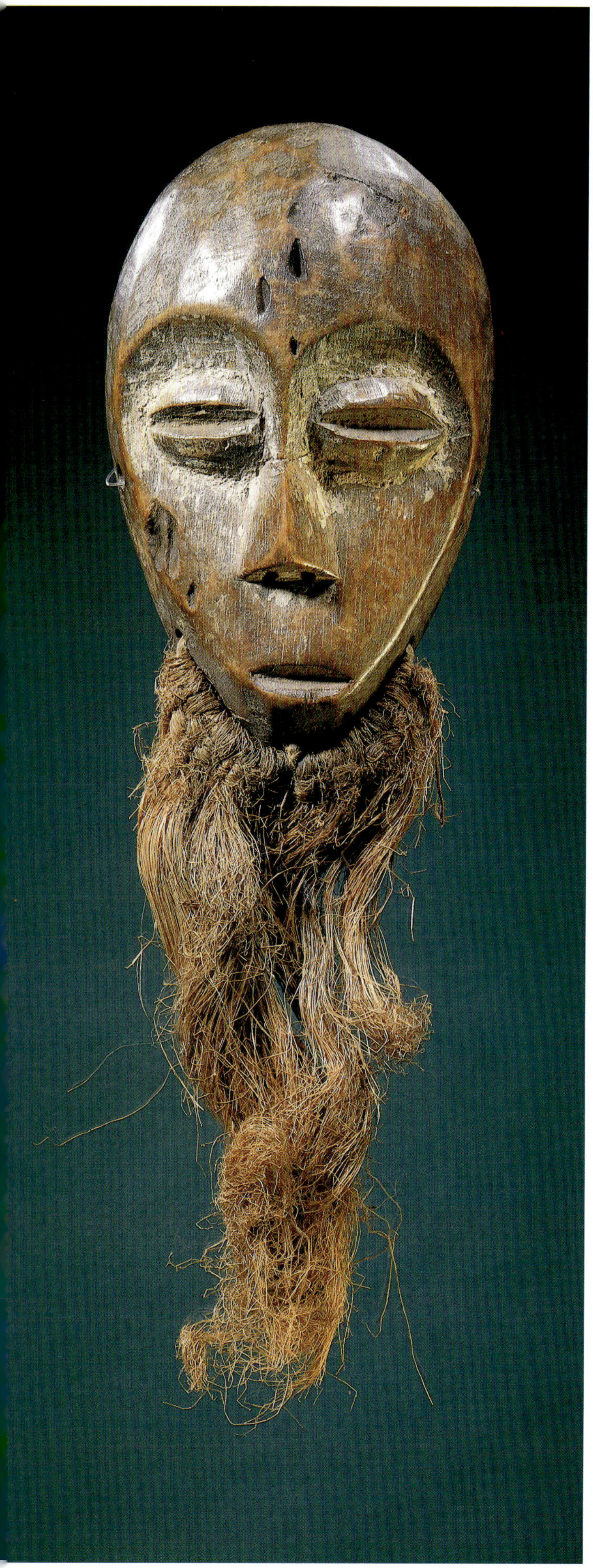

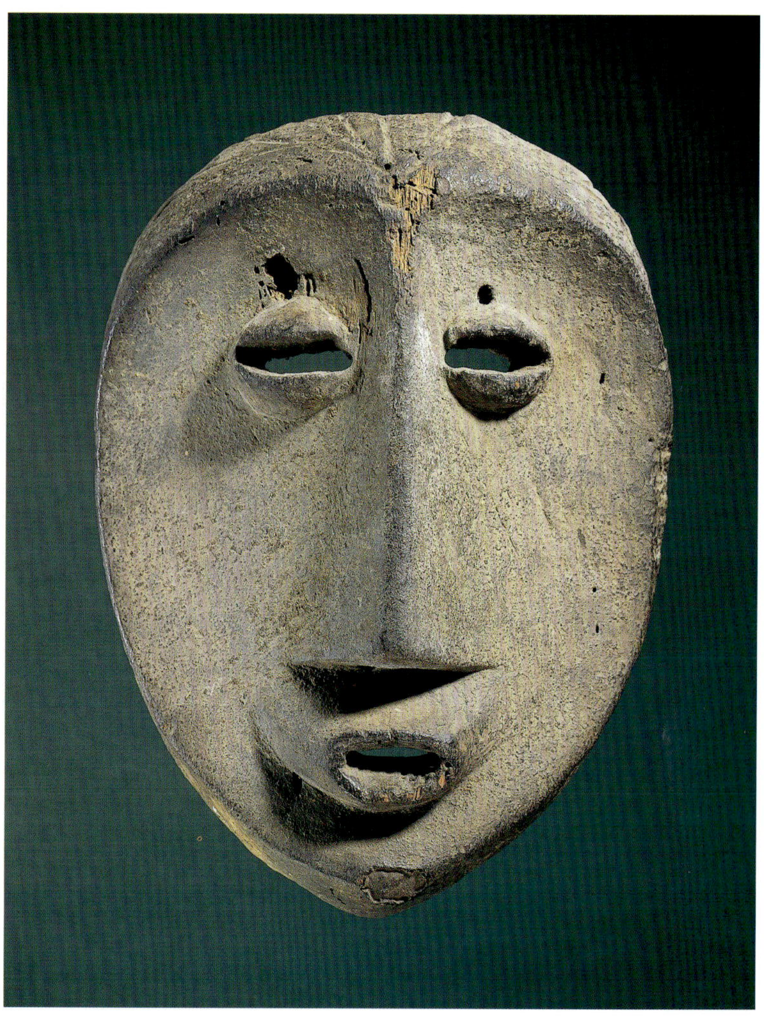

9.42 Mask (*idimu*).
Wood. H: 20.5 (8 in.).

9.41 Mask (*idimu*). Wood, plant fiber, and pigment.
H: 26.7 cm (10½ in.).

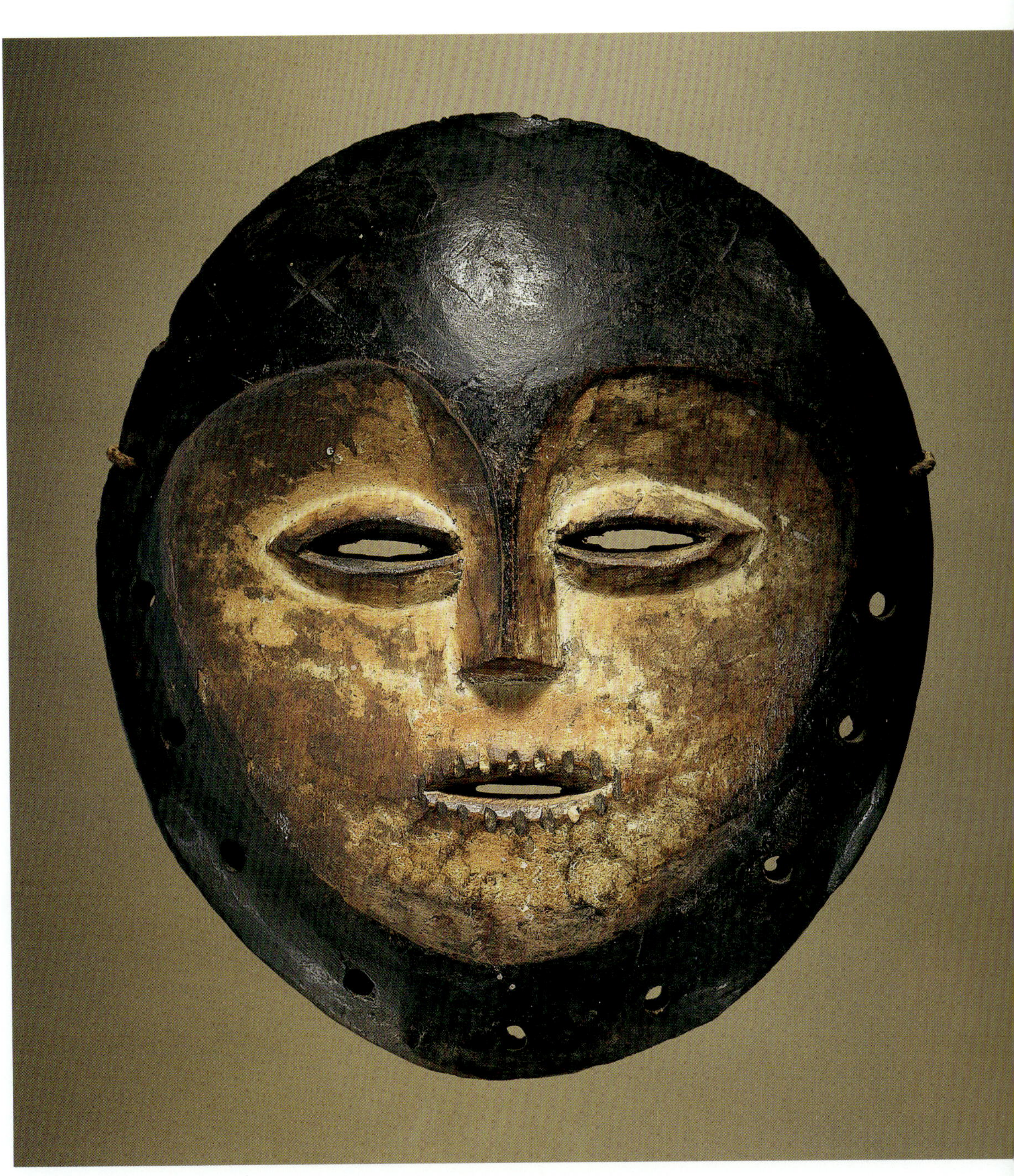

9.43 Mask (*idimu*). Wood, pigment, and plant fiber. H: 23.4 cm (9¼ in.).

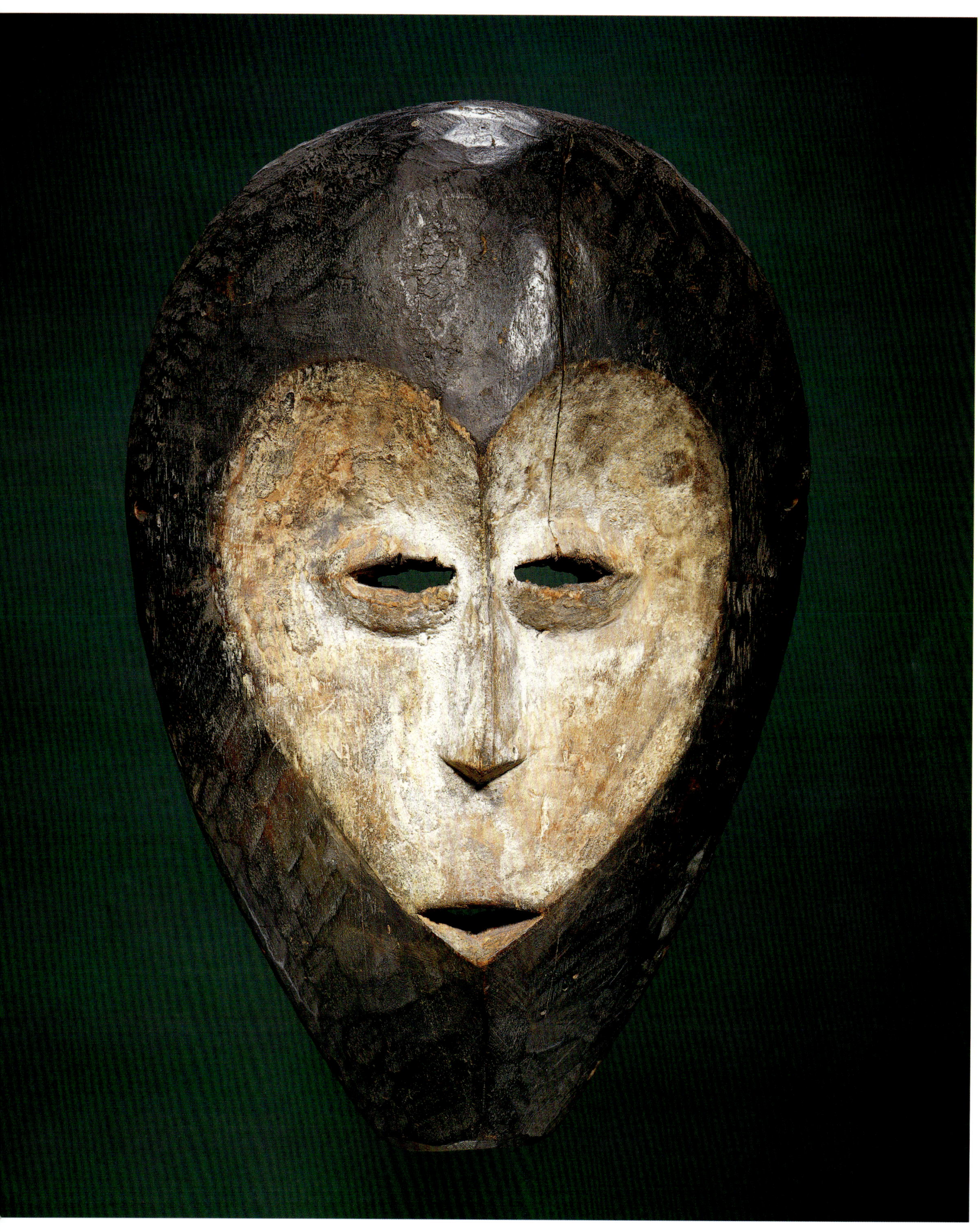

9.44 Mask (*idimu*). Wood and pigment. H: 34 cm (13⅜ in.).

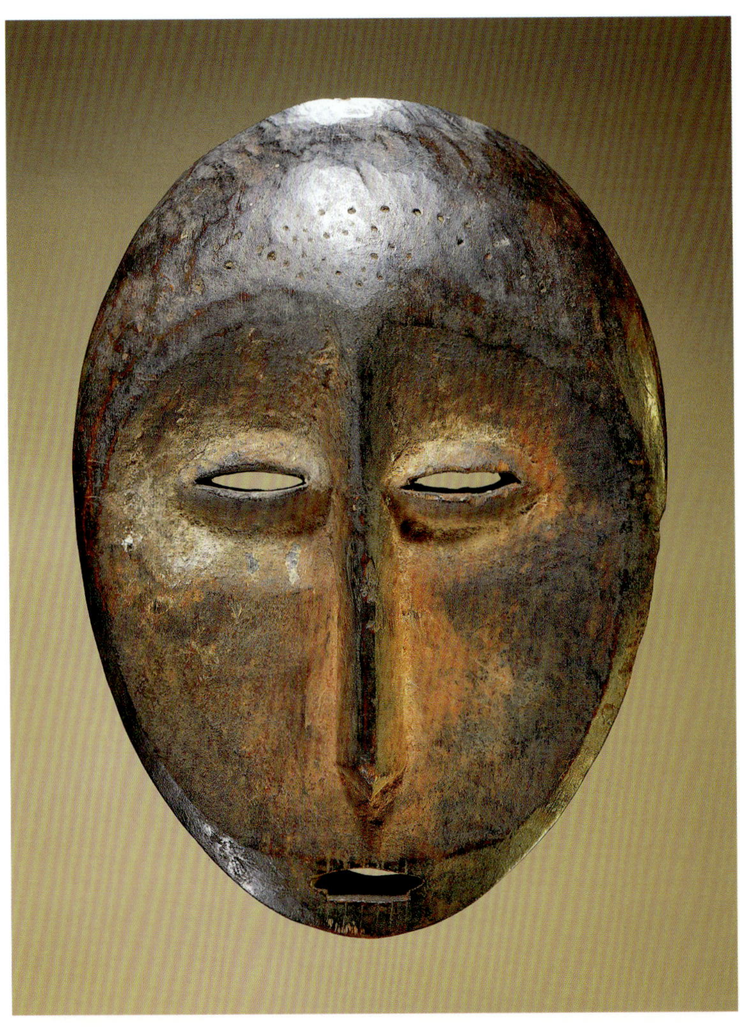

9.45 Mask (*idimu*). Wood and pigment. H: 23.3 cm (9⅛ in.).

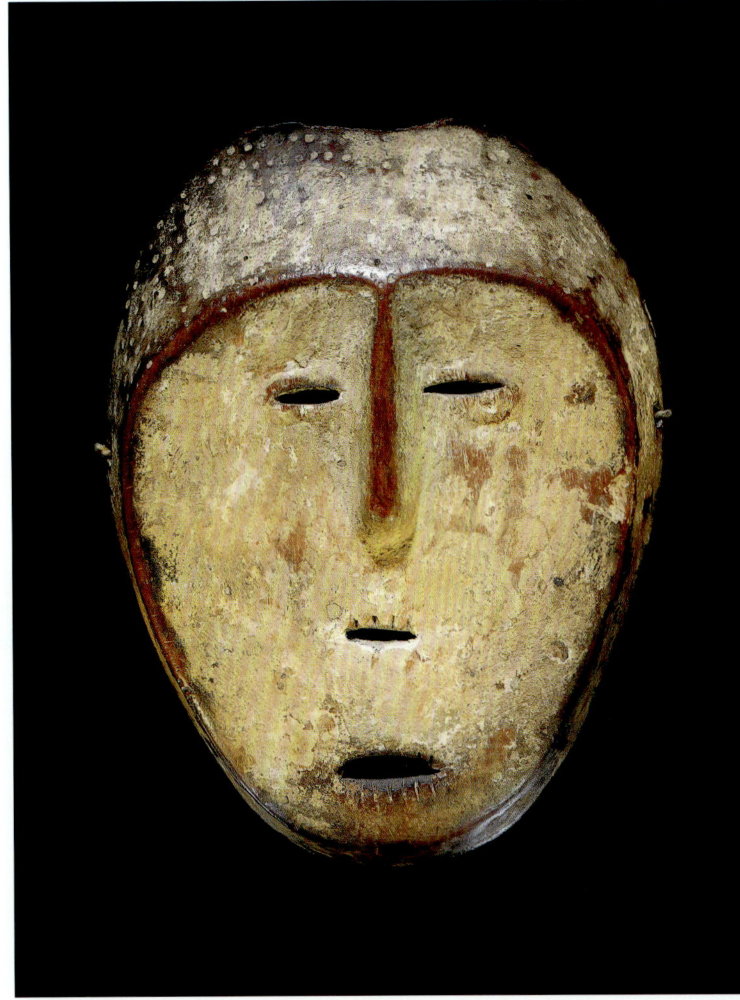

9.46 Mask (*idimu*). Wood, pigment, and string. H: 23 cm (9 in.).

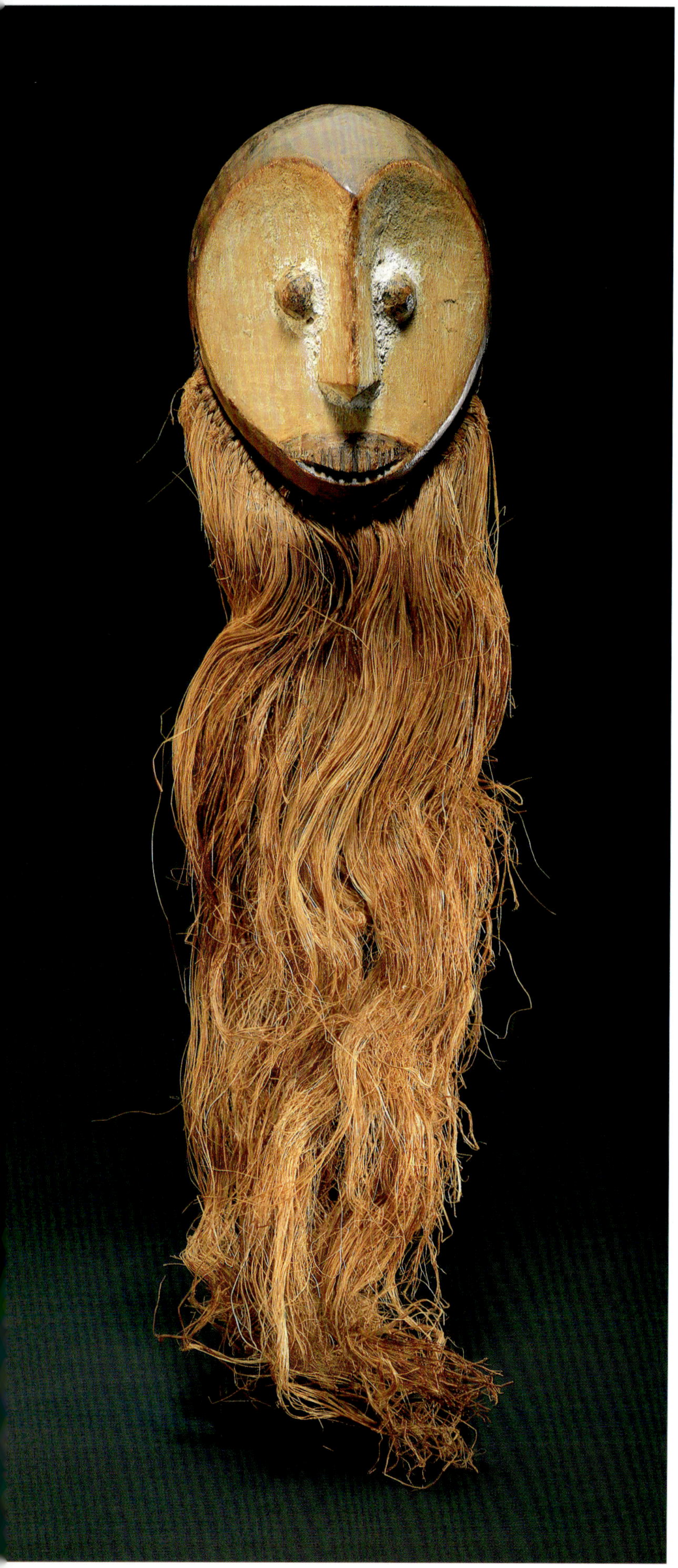

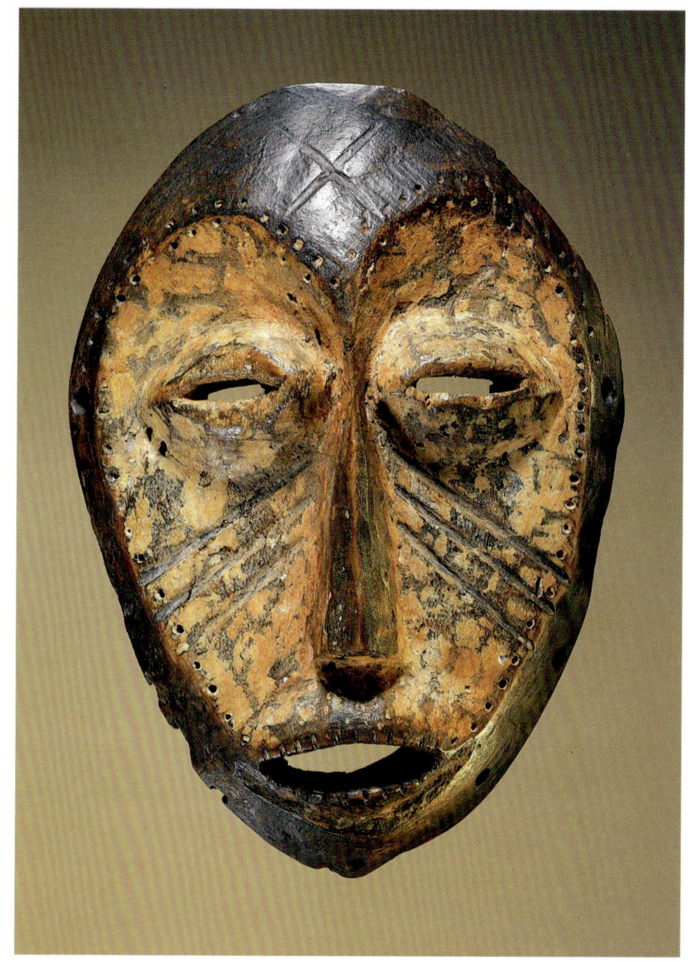

9.48 Mask (*idimu*). Wood and pigment. H: 22.3 cm (8¾ in.).

9.47 Mask (*idimu*). Wood, plant fiber, and pigment. H: 57.5 cm (22⅝ in.).

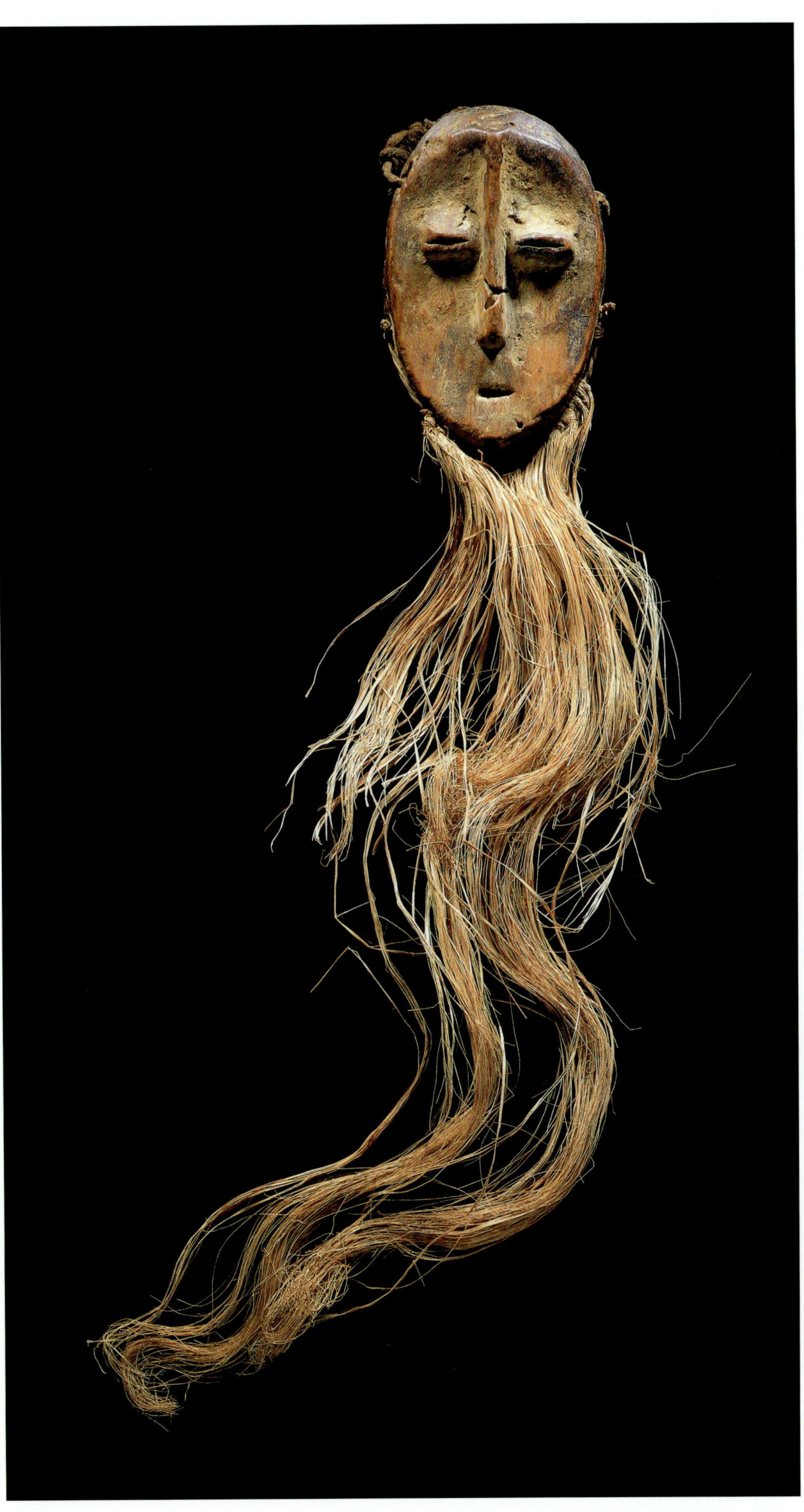

9.49 Mask (*lukwakongo* or *idimu*). Wood, plant fiber, and pigment. H: 51 cm (20 in.).

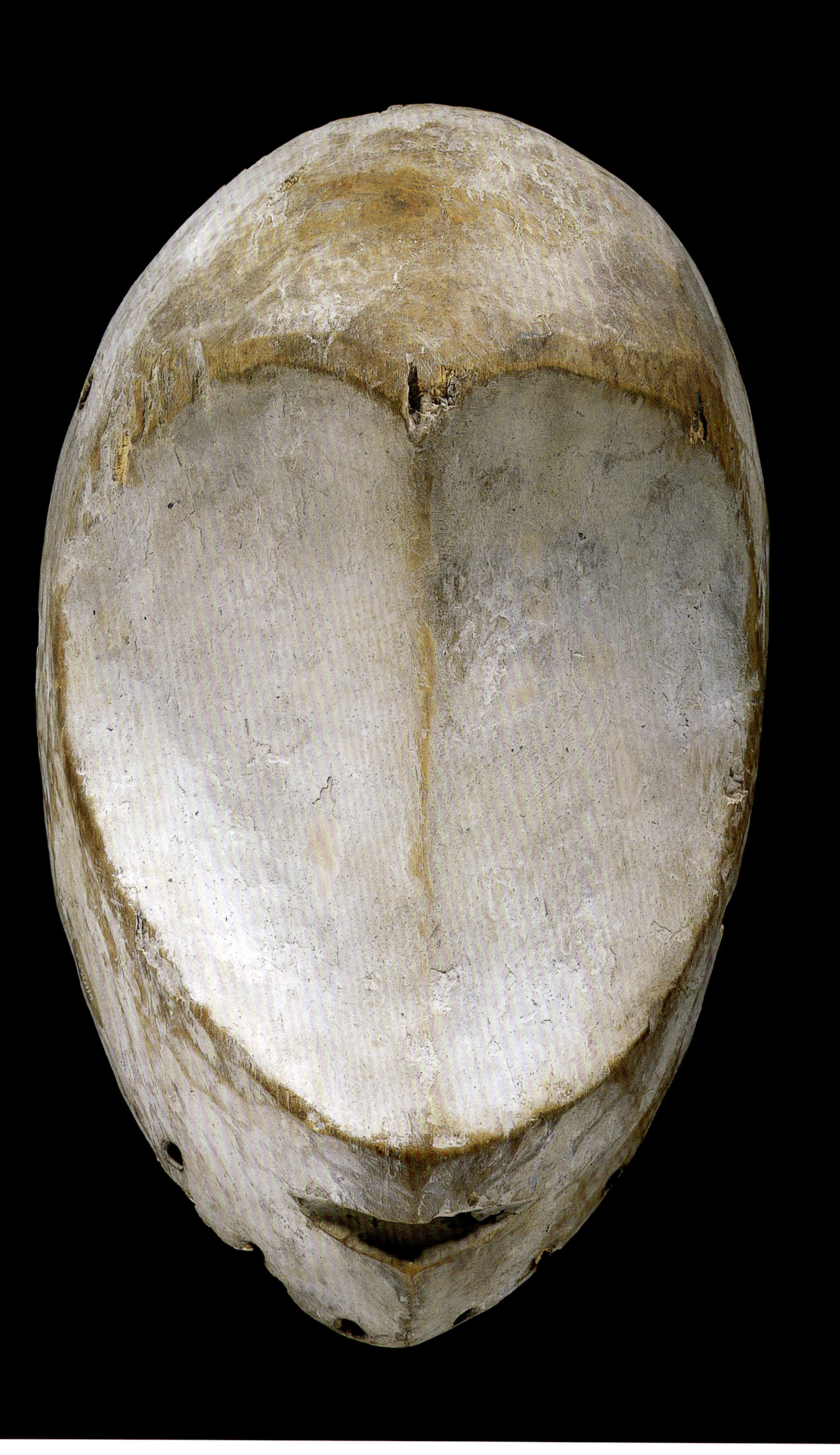

9.50 Mask (*idimu*). Wood and pigment. H: 26.4 cm (10⅜ in.).

9.51 Mask (*idimu*). Wood and pigment. H: 22.3 cm (9¼ in.).

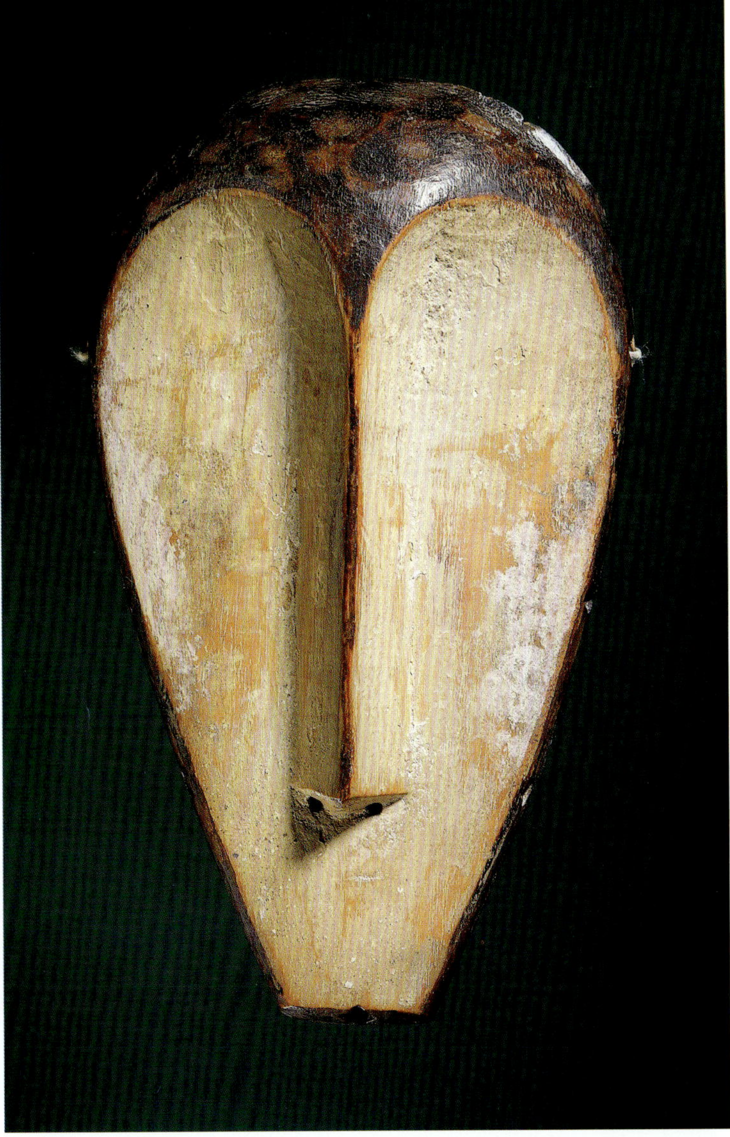

9.52 Mask (*idimu*). Wood and pigment. H: 21.2 cm (8⅜ in.).

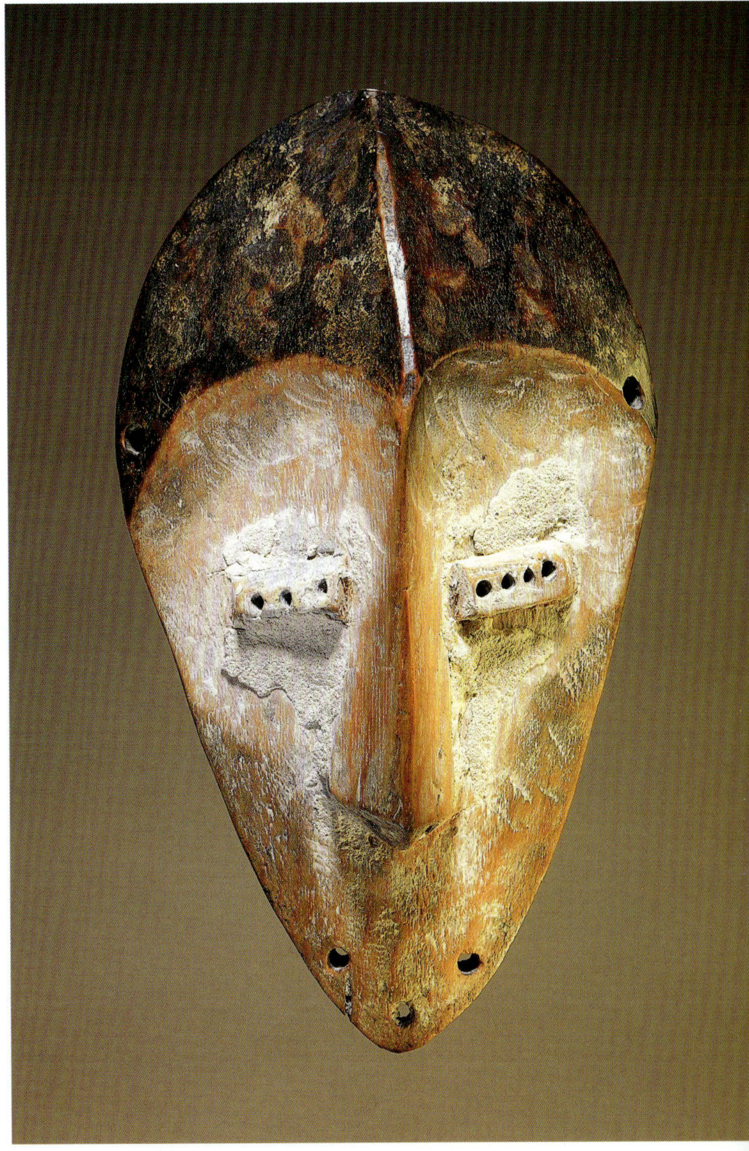

MASKS WITH NO EYES

Some *idimu* masks have no eyes (figs. 9.50–9.52). It has been suggested that Bwami members attached cowrie shells to serve as eyes, but this seems unlikely since the kaolin on these examples is even, showing no scars to indicate missing elements. Perhaps, instead, the masks illustrate the saying "Big-One of the men's house, the guardian, has no eyes" (Biebuyck 1986, 77). Although this important high-level Bwami member does not see with his eyes, he sees with his heart and guards the affairs of the community.

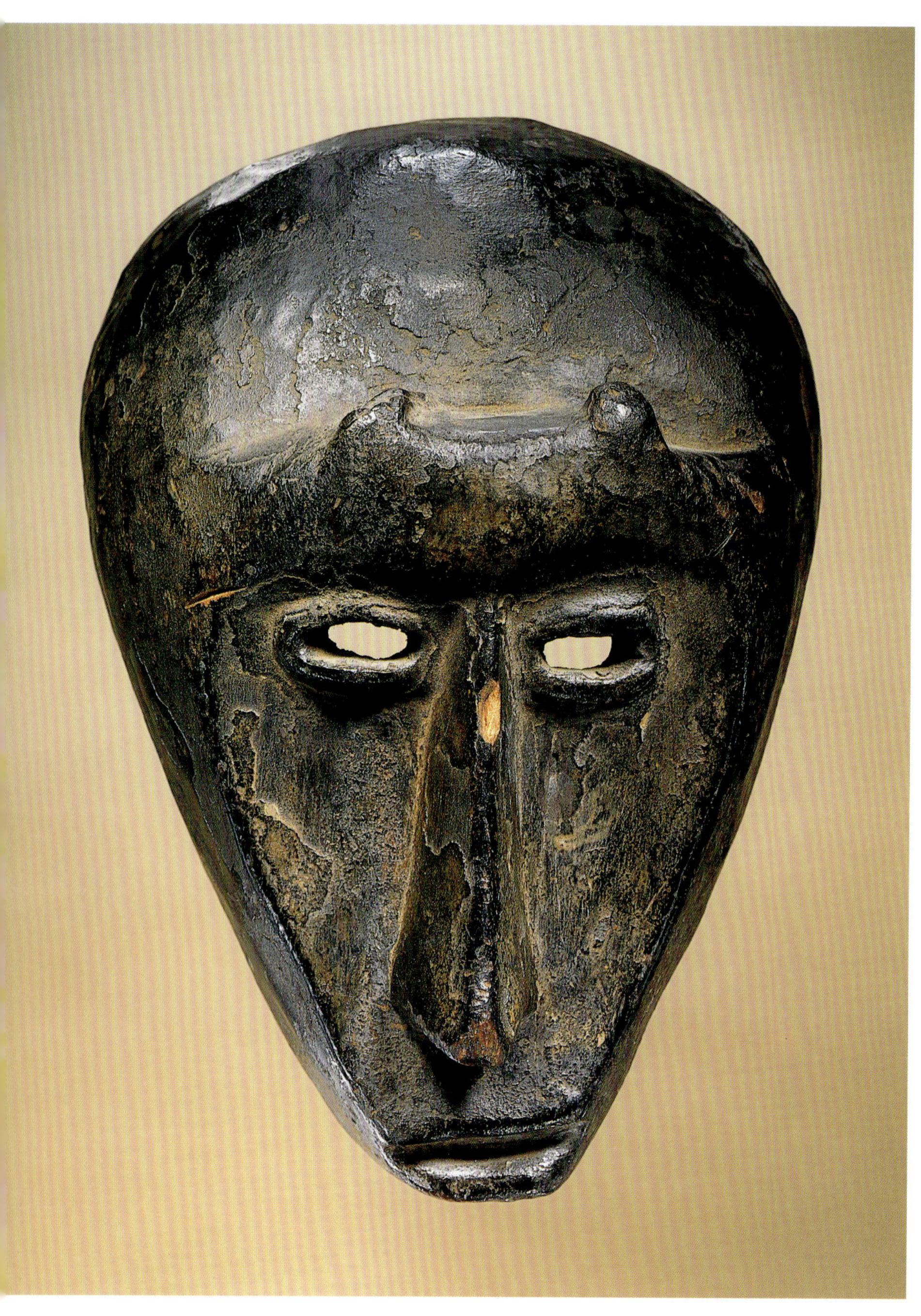

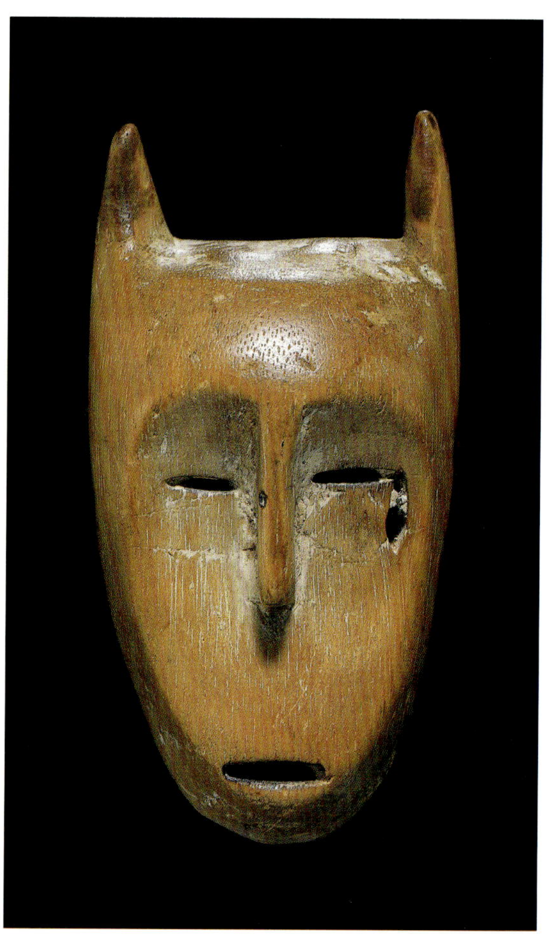

9.54 Mask (*kayamba*). Wood, pigment, and plant fiber. H: 12 cm (4¾ in.).

9.53 Mask (*kayamba*). Wood. H: 26.5 cm (10½ in.).

KAYAMBA

Horned masks called *kayamba* are rare because they are only found in a few areas (figs. 9.53–9.61). Accomplished teachers own them, although they are occasionally found in a communally owned basket. Like all other masks, they are combined with sayings, drama, music, and so forth in performances by men and women (Biebuyck 1986, 159–60; see Biebuyck 1973, pl. 37, for a photograph of masks in performance).

MUMINIA

Descendants of those who brought Kindi into a given area own the *muminia* mask (fig. 9.62, and see figs. J and 3.12; Biebuyck 1994, 176). Each community has only one mask of this type; it must be present for initiations into all levels to occur (Biebuyck 1986, 161). It is the only mask to appear in the first initiation into Bwami and takes on both a positive and negative persona. It represents a powerful high-level member of Bwami and a troublemaker (Biebuyck 1986, 161–65).

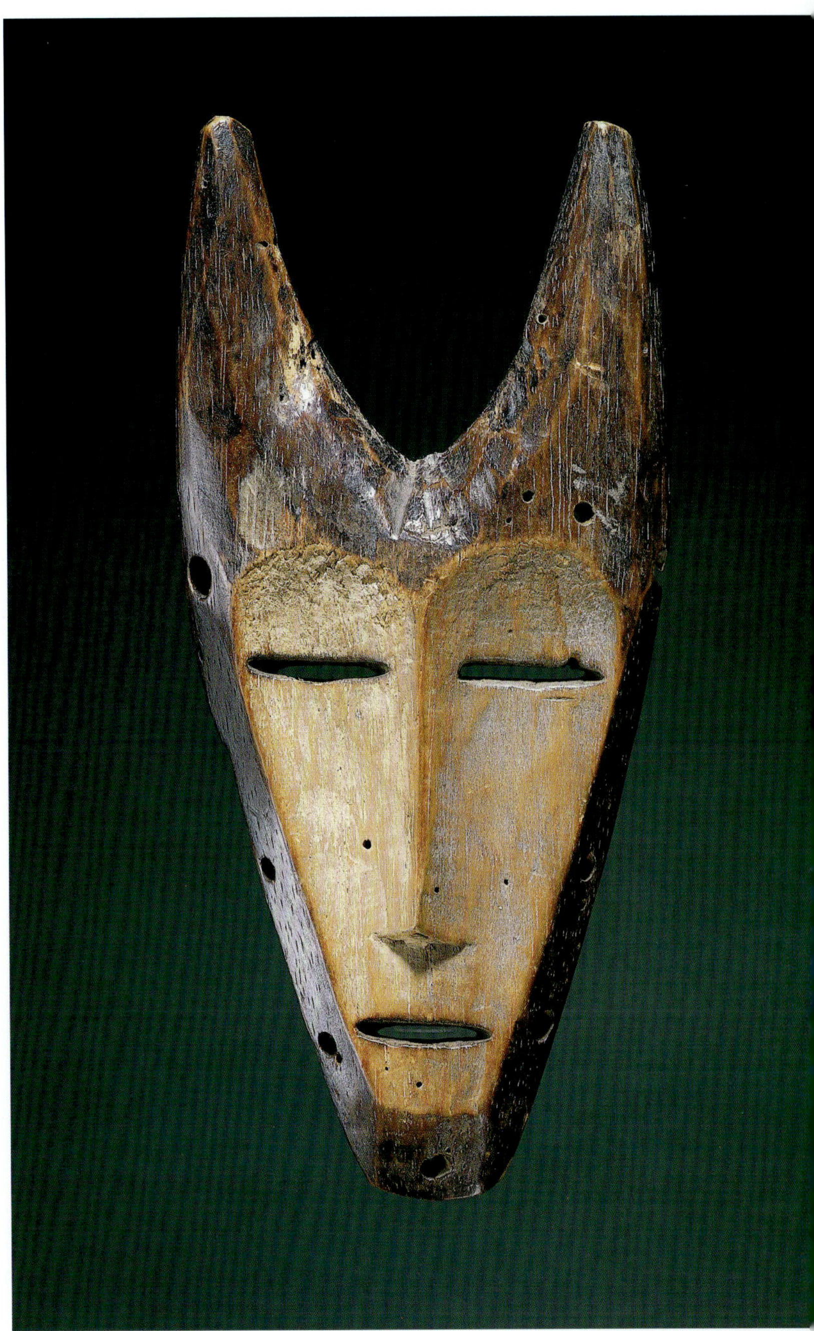

9.55 Mask (*kayamba*). Wood and pigment. H: 23.5 cm (9¼ in.).

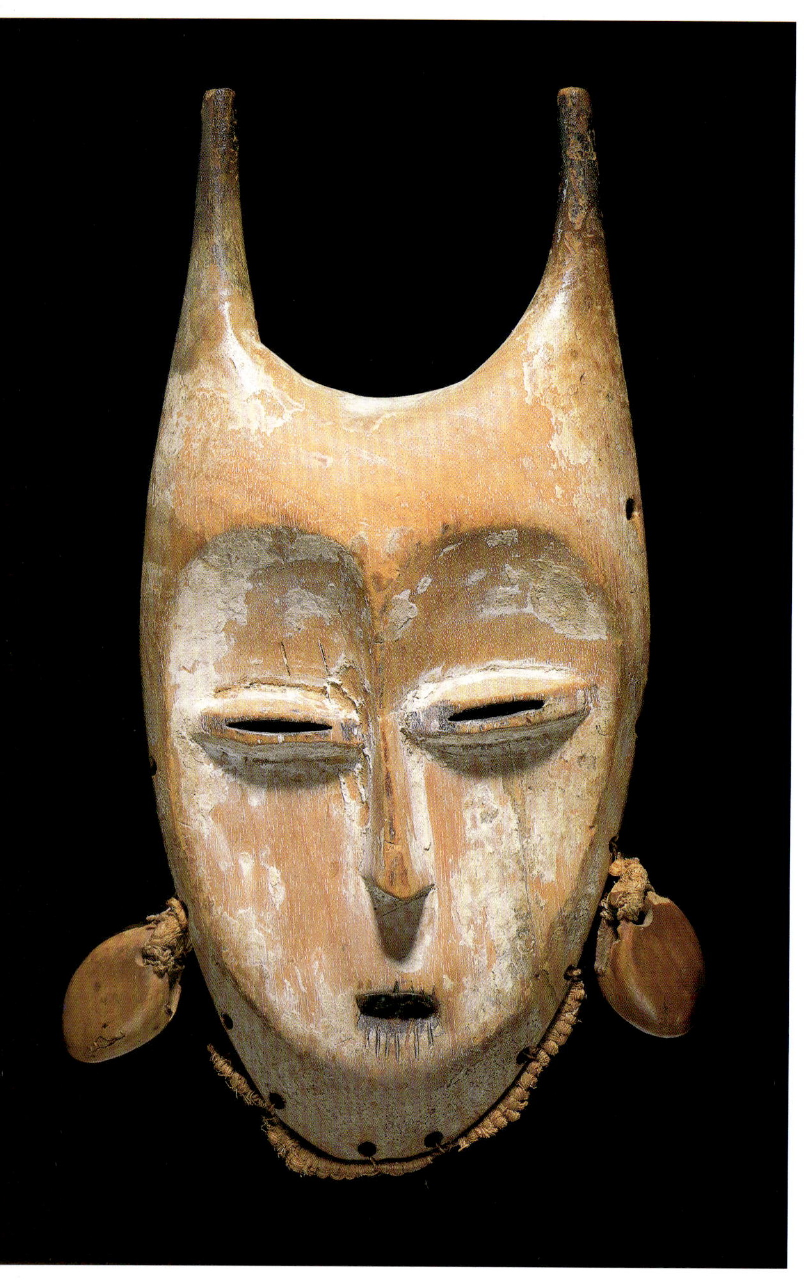

9.56 Mask (*kayamba*). Wood, pigment, plant fiber, and seedpods. H: 36.2 cm (14¼ in.).

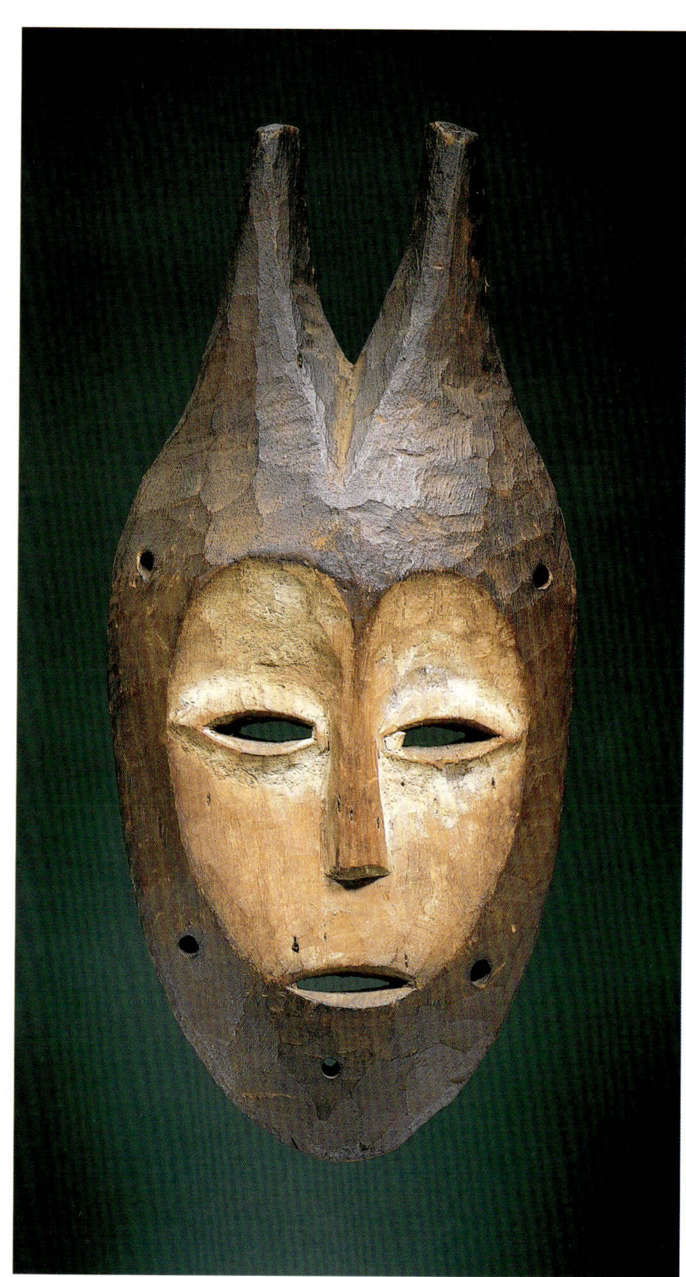

9.57 Mask (*kayamba*). Wood and pigment. H: 34.5 cm (13½ in.).

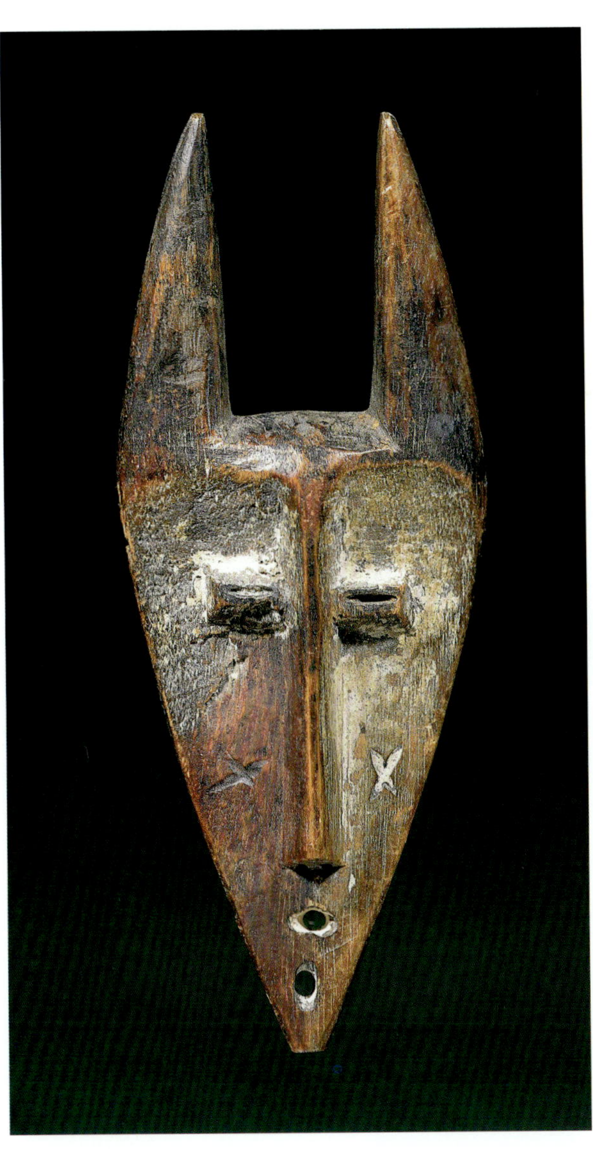

9.58 Mask (*kayamba*). Wood and pigment. H: 19 cm (7½ in.).

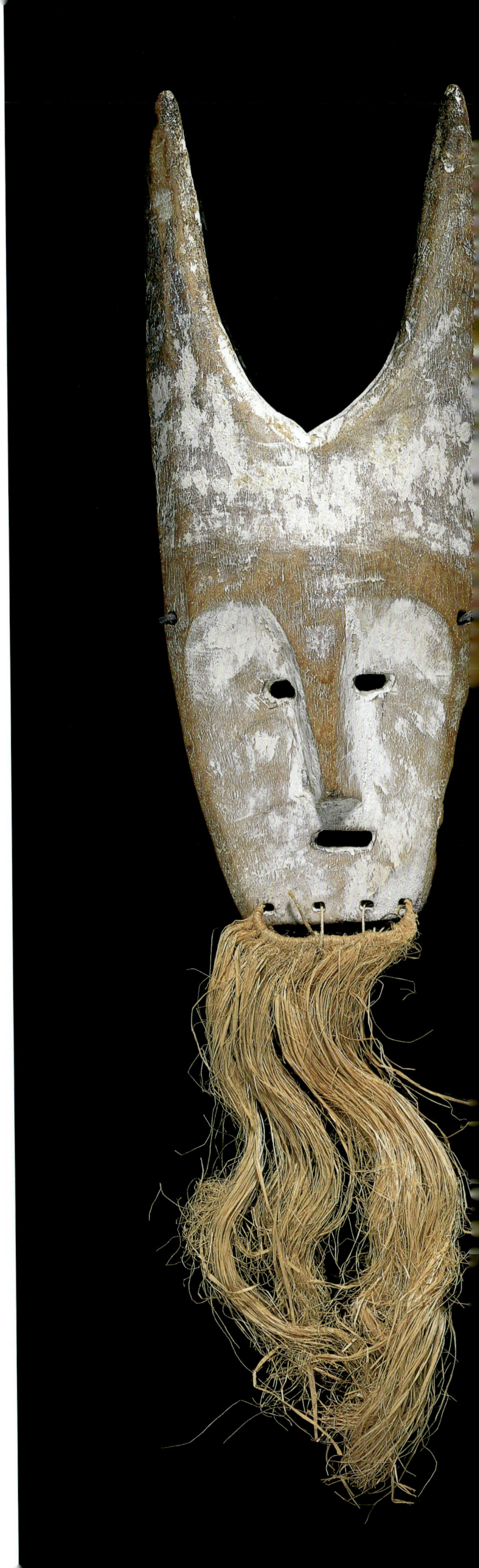

9.59 Mask (*kayamba*). Wood, pigment, and plant fiber. H: 56.5 cm (22¼ in.).

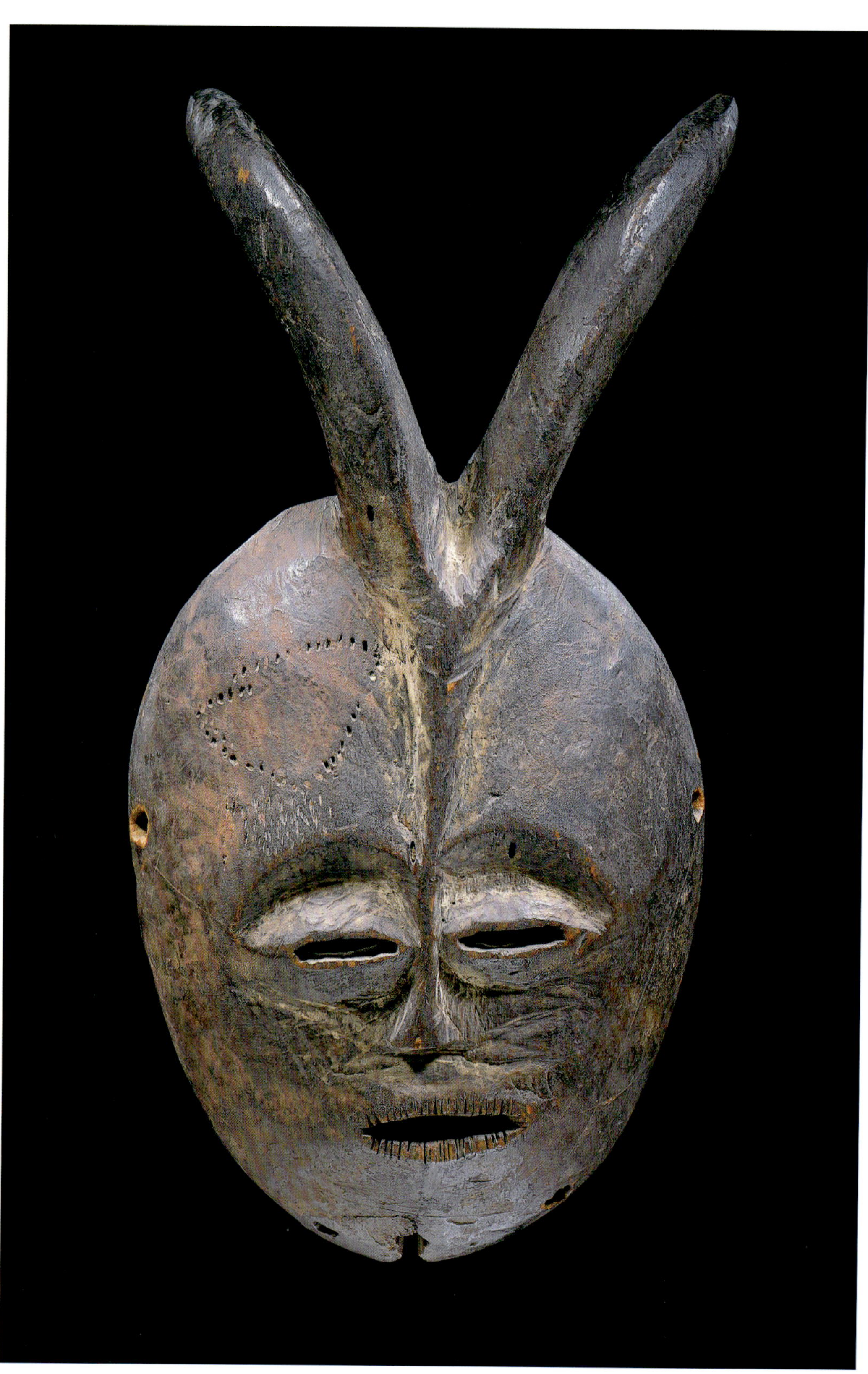

9.60 Mask (*kayamba*). Wood and pigment. H: 43.2 cm (17 in.).

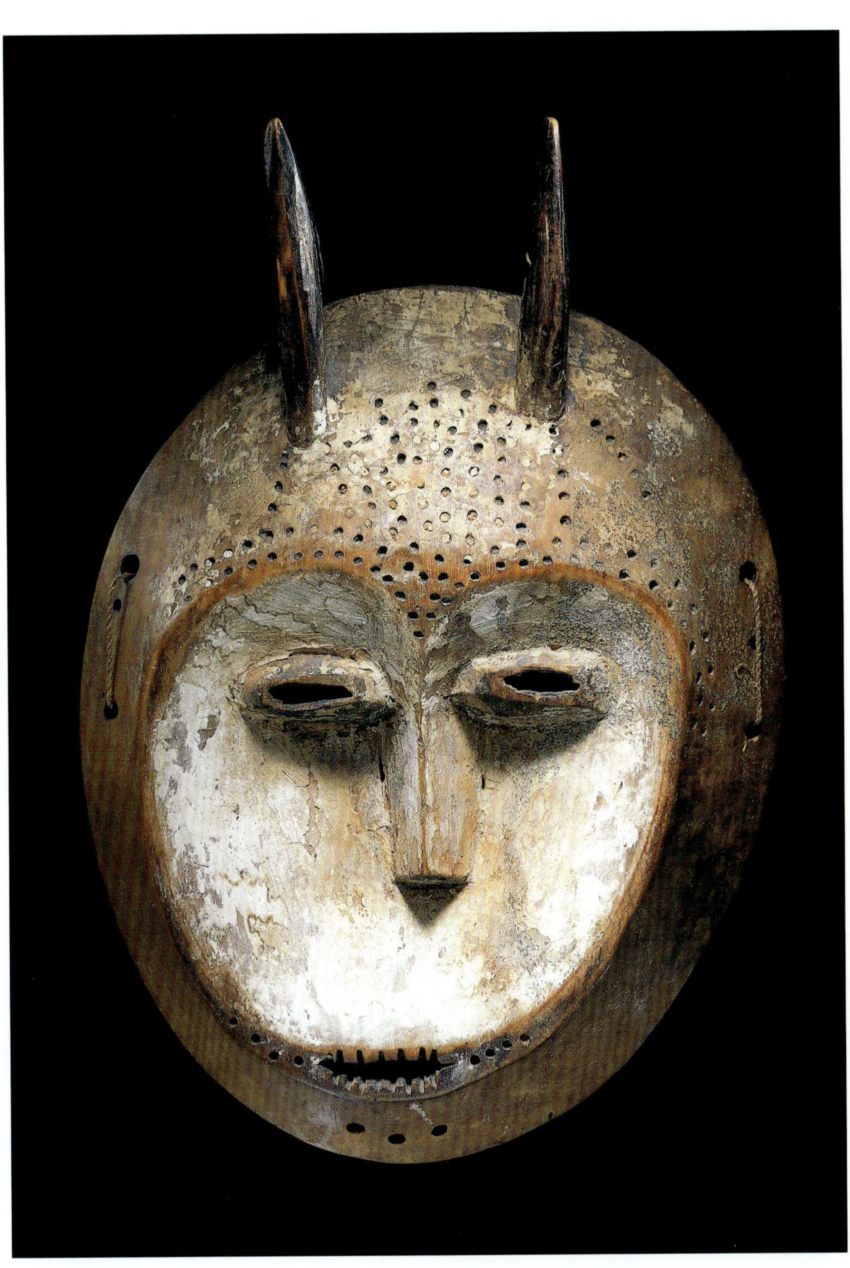

9.61 Mask (*kayamba*). Wood, pigment, and fiber. H: 36.5 cm (14⅜ in.).

9.62 Mask (*muminia*). Wood and pigment. H: 25.2 cm (10 in.).

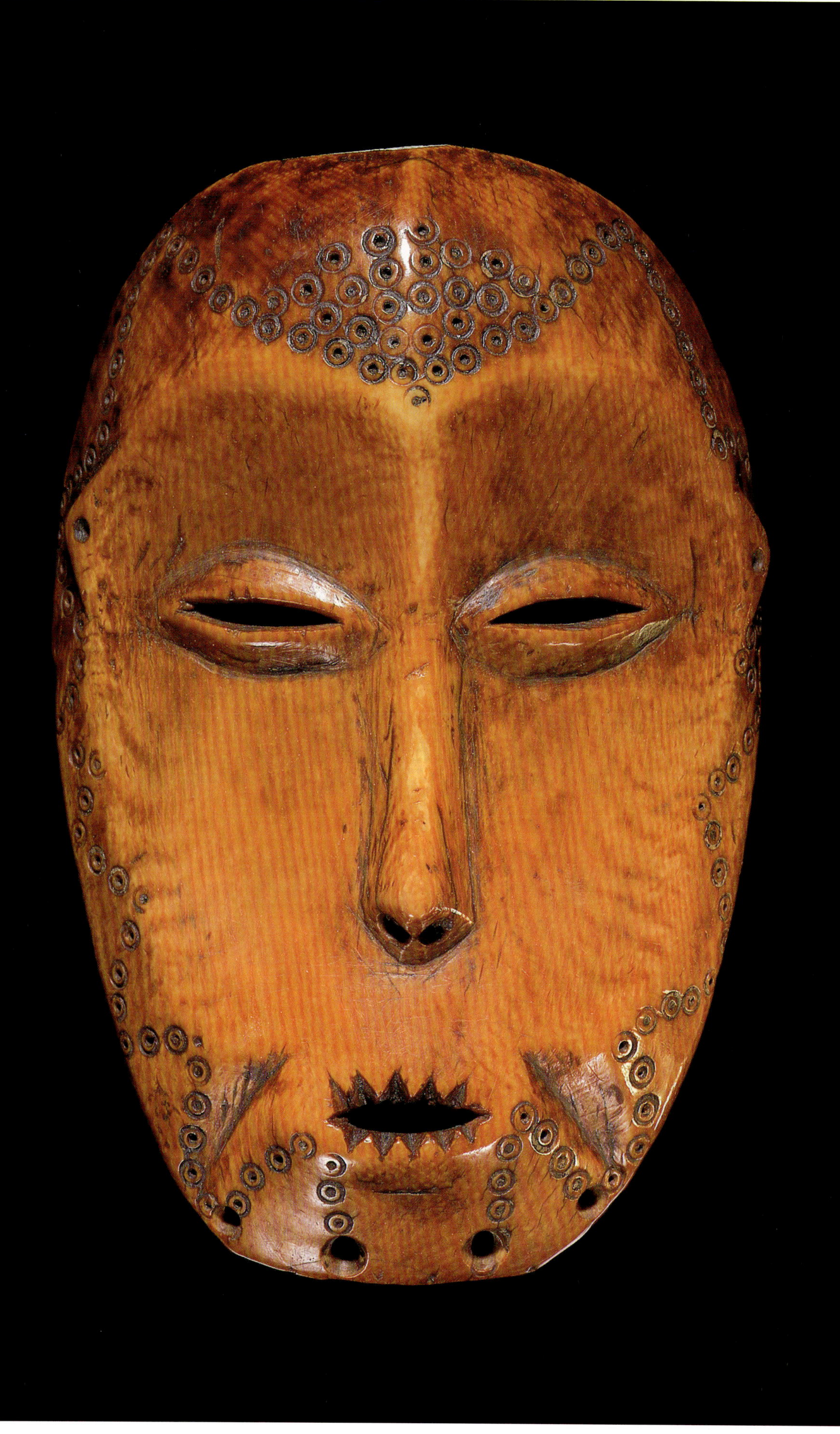

9.63 Mask (*lukungu*).
Ivory. H: 20 cm ($7\frac{7}{8}$ in.).

LUKUNGU

Lukungu is the final category of all initiation objects (figs. 9.63–9.70). It is a small, individually owned ivory or bone mask that marks the rank of Lutumbo lwa Kindi (Biebuyck 1953c 1078–79; 1994, 38). The use and meaning of *lukungu* masks are more restricted than those of other masks; the *lukungu* is never worn on the face or body of the owner or any other member of Kindi (Biebuyck 1973, 213–14). It is only brought out during Kindi initiations (Biebuyck 1953c, 1078). At death, it is placed on the grave, after which it is inherited by a nephew who has the right to own it (Biebuyck 1954, 11). When *lukungu* masks are brought out, they are oiled and then displayed on a fence or in front of their seated owners (Biebuyck 1973, 213–14). They sometimes form the face of a larger figure created by an assemblage of other initiation objects (Biebuyck 1994, 50).

While women can use other masks in performances, they do not handle their husband's *lukungu* masks (Biebuyck 1994, 52). In an interesting ceremony that seems to equate the wife, who is also a member of Bwami (symbolized by her hat), with the mask in communities that do not use *lukungu*, the wives of Lutumbo lwa Kindi members stand behind the fence wearing their husbands' hats and placing their own hats on the ground before the fence in the position where the *lukungu* would be placed in communities that make use of it (Biebuyck 1986, 156).

The ivory *lukungu* masks call to mind death and the skulls of war victims (Biebuyck 1973, 213–24). Lesser initiation objects encountered at lower Bwami levels are presented in conjunction with multiple explanations. When an initiate reaches the final Kindi initiation, however, he is presented with a group of objects and given no explanations: "By completing all the grades, they have gained information and understanding" (Biebuyck 1986, 151) and do not require definitions or interpretations.

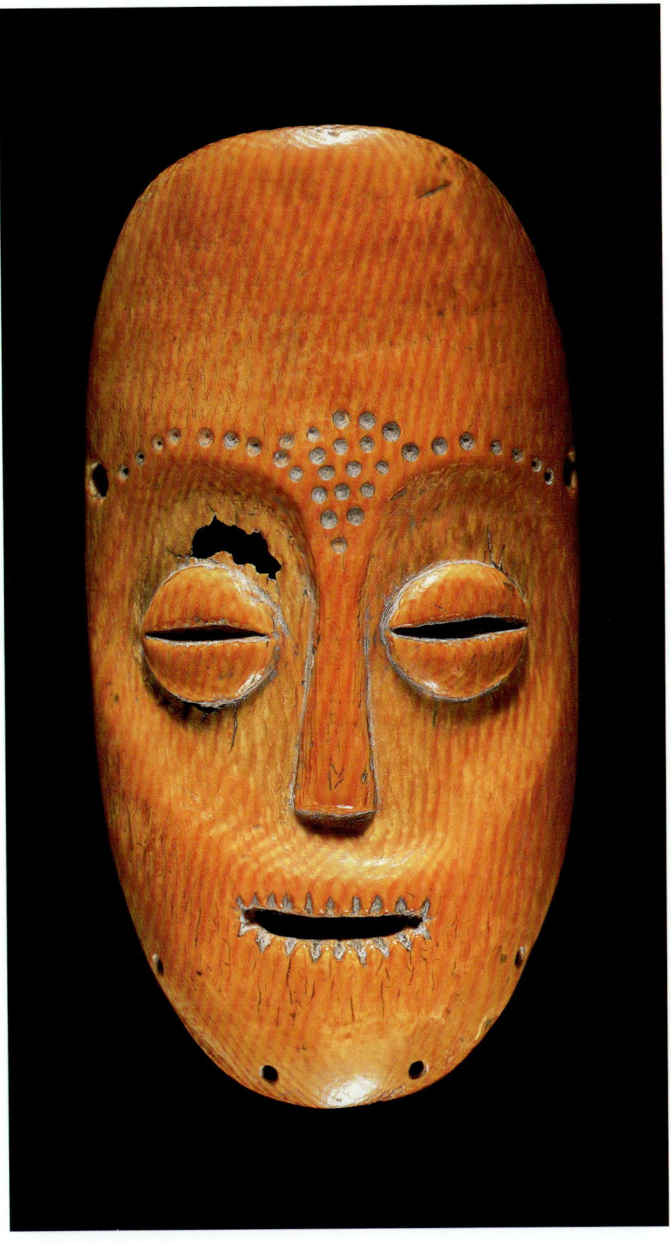

9.64 Mask (*lukungu*).
Ivory. H: 14.5 cm (5¾ in.).

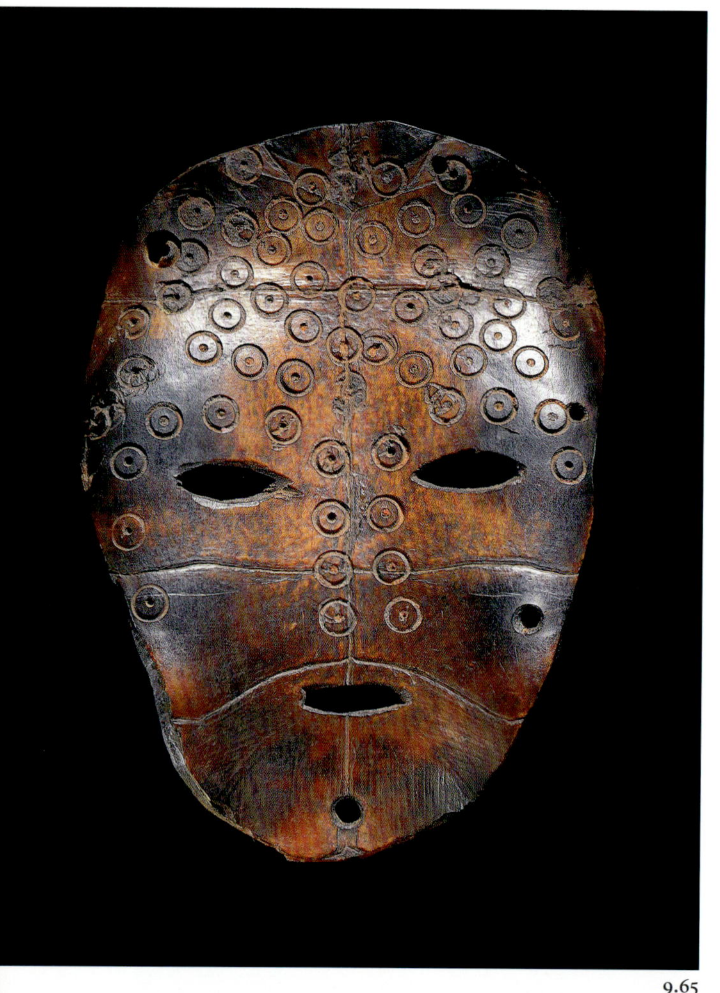

9.65

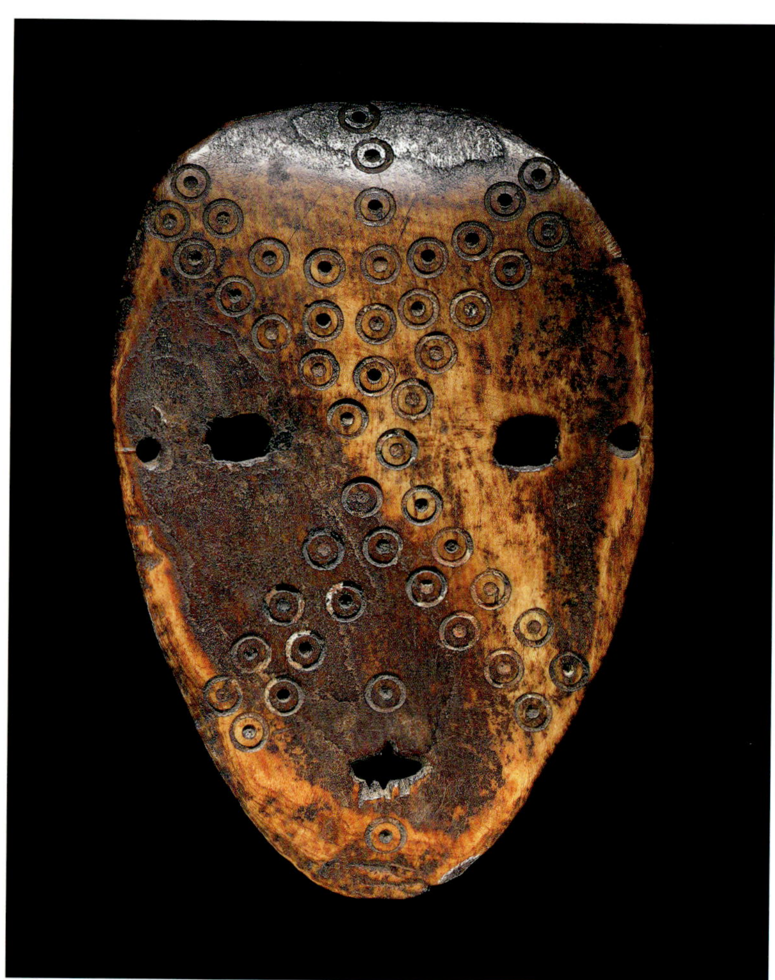

9.66

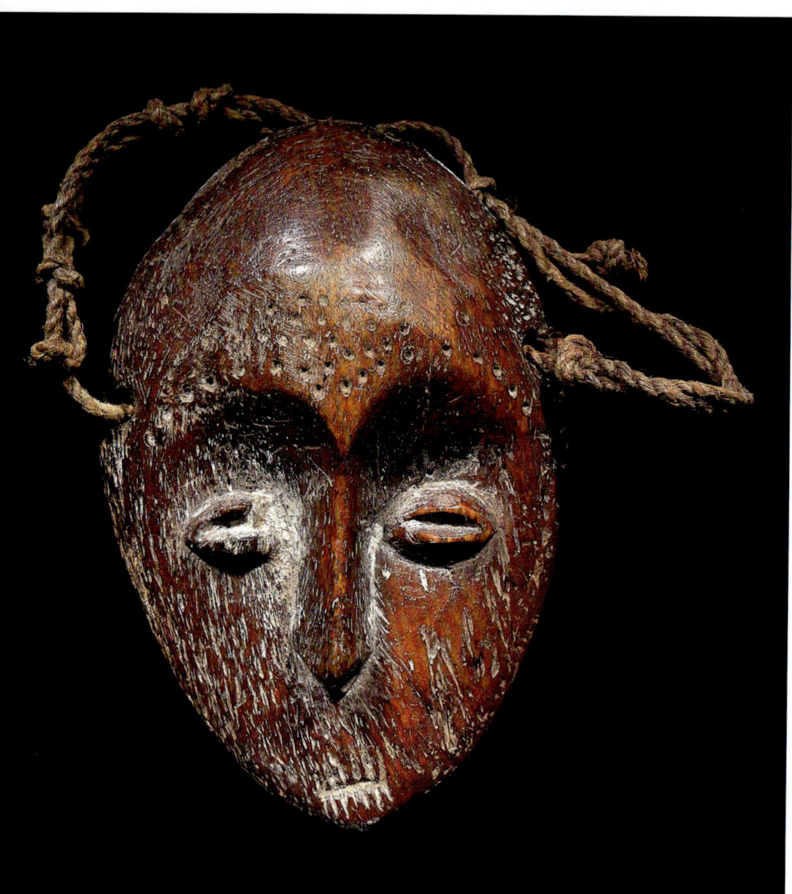

9.67

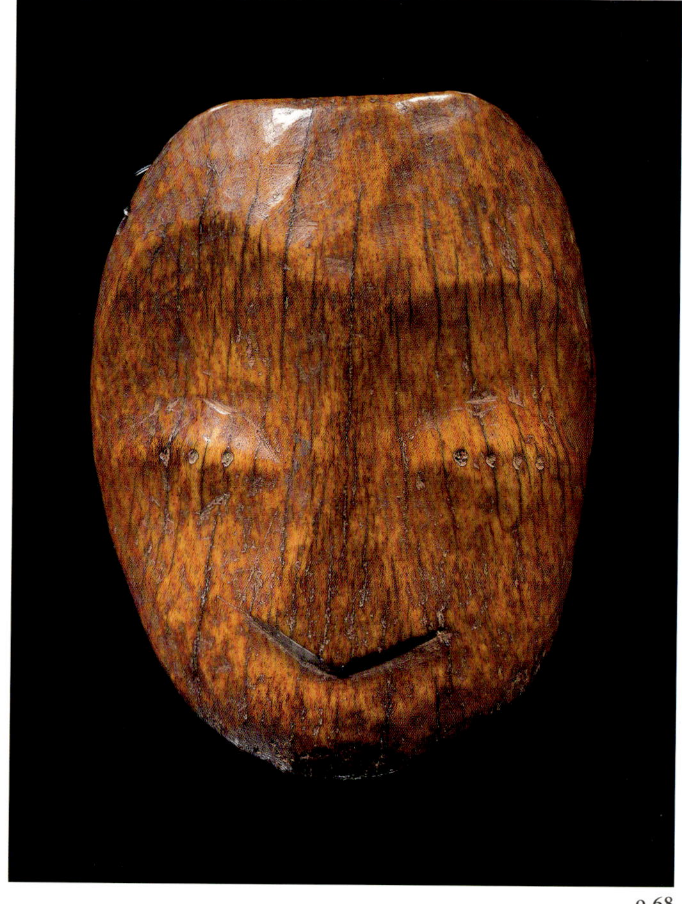

9.68

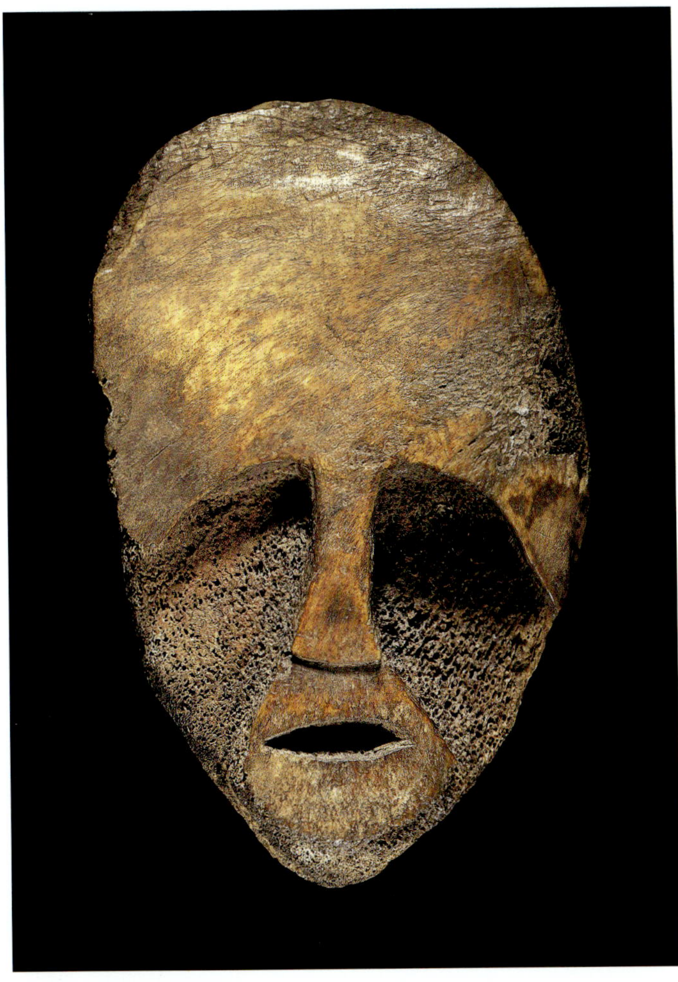

9.69 Mask (*lukungu*).
Bone. H: 12.1 cm (4¾ in.).

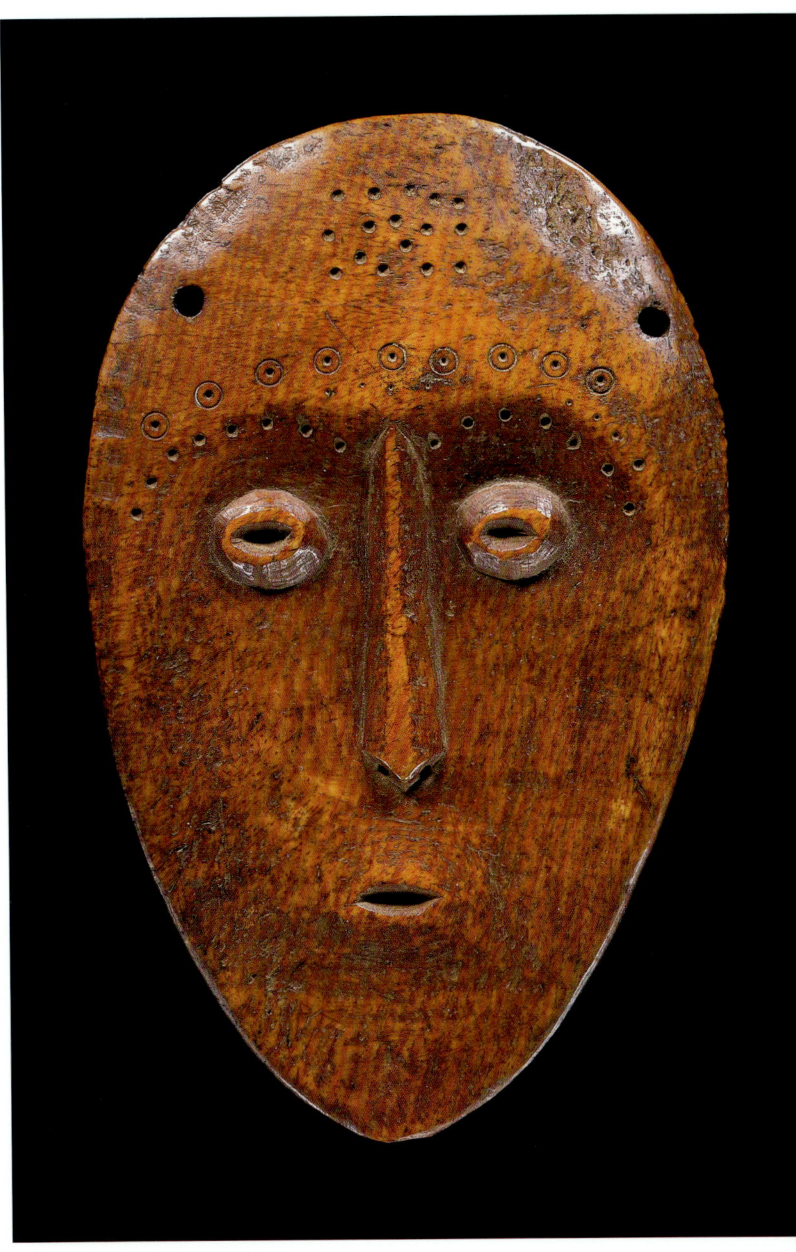

9.65 Mask (*lukungu*).
Bone. H: 15.5 cm (6⅛ in.).

9.66 Mask (*lukungu*).
Bone. H: 17.6 cm (7 in.).

9.67 Mask (*lukungu*).
Ivory (?), bone (?), and fiber.
H: 12.2 cm (4¾ in.).

9.68 Mask (*lukungu*).
Ivory. H: 14.1 cm (5½ in.).

9.70 Mask (*lukungu*). Ivory.
H: 17.9 cm (7 in.). FMCH X73.584;
Gift of Jay T. Last.

Conclusion: The Mythical versus the Real

> There alone is the land prosperous [in good health] where the bwami initiates dance with dried banana leaves.[1]
>
> Lega Proverb (Biebuyck 1976)

The Bwami Society and its use of art forms as described in this book is something of an ideal reconstruction. As indicated previously, my discussion relies heavily upon Daniel Biebuyck's published accounts of Lega society, Bwami, and art, which are based on his field research of 1952–1954. The century before that, however, had been traumatic for Lega culture and politics, and many institutions were greatly altered during this period.

Many scholars have tried to untangle the evidence and to suggest a history for the Lega area. As early as 1936, A. Moeller wrote a volume entitled *Les grandes lignes des migrations des Bantu de la province orientale du Congo Belge* in which he outlined a migration theory. More recent authors include Raymond E. Mutuza (1972), Muyololo (1974), Yogolelo (1975), Felix (1989), and Jan Vansina (1990). All agree that the Lega moved into their current home from the north and that all the Lega social structures were in flux for great lengths of time. Muyololo suggests that there was a short stable period during the beginning of the nineteenth century (1974, 9).

If there was peace in the Lega area during that time, it ended quickly with the arrival of the Tarab caravans in the 1860s.[2] The Tarab were Tanzanian Arabs who were involved in a long-distance trade network throughout East Africa from the interior to the port cities on the Indian Ocean. They sought ivory and slaves, which the Lega could provide in abundance. The Tarab were not interested in controlling territory; they were solely desirous of profit. They settled on the shores of Lake Tanganyika, establishing trading outposts for caravans that traveled into the hinterlands. The Tarab raided throughout this area for almost fifty years, leaving their imprint on all the peoples of the region.

The Lega, even with the Bwami focus on peace making, learned to fight off the slave caravans and obtained a fierce and negative reputation in the process of doing so. Descriptions from that time do not seem appropriate to a people following the Bwami ethic. David Livingstone, who traveled through the area between 1865 and 1873, states that the people of Maniema were "generally thieves, and otherwise bad characters" (Wheeler 1874, 2: 28). Verney Lovett Cameron visited the Tarab settlement on the shores of Lake Tanganyika in August 1874. Based on information he received from the Tarab who had traveled in the Lega area, he wrote that the Lega were "fierce and warlike and using poisoned arrows, a mere scratch from which proved fatal in four or five minutes unless an antidote, known only to the natives, was immediately applied" (1971, 1: 9).

Some Tarab settled among the Lega and were influential in those communities. In some towns, the Tarab replaced clan and community leaders who were high-level Bwami members with Lega men who were willing to cooperate with them (Corbisier 1968, 7). In the 1950s the Lega complained to Biebuyck about the many ivory masks and figures that were lost during the period of Tarab control (1976, 343). There are also documented cases of Lega ivories being sold at the slave markets of Nyangwe in 1898 (Biebuyck 1976, 343), these presumably coming from Tarab sources.

Ernesto Cordella has described the result of Tarab pressure on the Bembe, southern neighbors of the Lega (1906, 869). The Tarab, who were of Arab descent, had light skin. The Bembe thus assumed that all light-skinned people were Tarab, and the Bembe leaders thought that all Whites were involved in the slave trade. Cordella reports that women, in particular, felt that any man who looked at a White person would die.

In 1885, the Congo Free State was formed and Belgians began to move into the area. The first governor of the region was appointed in 1889, and the "Arab wars," military antislavery campaigns designed to rid the area of Tarab presence, began in 1891. With the appointment of Delhaise as administrator in 1905, the Lega rejoiced and celebrated the departure of the Arabs. Irreparable and long-term damage to the Lega as a whole and to Bwami had, however, occurred. The Tarab had persecuted Bwami and put either low-level or nonmembers into important political positions similar to clan heads. When the Belgians began to appoint chiefs, they appointed these non-Bwami individuals because they were accommodating (Corbisier 1968, 7). Antagonism began to develop between Bwami and those who had functioned as clan heads under the Tarab.

Bwami was officially outlawed in 1933 and then abolished in 1948. Between these two dates, the society was alternately tolerated and persecuted. The Belgians understood that Bwami was an influential group that controlled the political workings of the Lega in many ways. Most of the Belgian administrators and missionaries, however, did not understand the intricate nature of Bwami or its essentially nonreligious code of ethics. Constantin Lanaers wrote about Bwami in 1946:

> The influence of muami is very great. Nothing public or family oriented can happen without them. They are the guardians of the customary and form by consequence a secret opposition to all that might be obtained. European influence, civilization, and religion cannot diminish their authority and drain their source of revenue.... Their reputation is based on fear. They are supposed to hold back the occult powers in the bag containing the instruments in the form of stones, shells, etc. To disobey them brings diverse punishment: fines and even occasionally death. In connivance with sorcerers, they always find occasion to take vengeance. [Laneers 1946, 65–66]

The presence of mines and Belgian recruitment for the Force Publique—the colonial army made up of Congolese men—also caused great disruption within Lega communities. The first mining company, Compagnie Minière des Grands Lacs (MGL), arrived in 1923. By 1932, there were three major mining groups in the Maniema area (Muyololo 1974, 8). Men left their homes, usually involuntarily, to work in the mines and were also forced to bring their own foodstuffs (Biebuyck 1973, 11–14). Often the men would earn enough money for an initiation and then return to their homes; others never returned. Men drafted into the Force Publique traveled away from their birthplaces (Corbisier 1968, 20), and when they returned, they brought with them new ideas and influences.

Through all this upheaval, Bwami continued to exist—hidden and in perhaps altered forms—and to produce initiation objects. When Biebuyck worked among the Lega in the early 1950s, Bwami had been legally abolished (for the second time) for only five years. The Lega were suspicious of Biebuyck, thinking that this Belgian might be gathering information to trap them. In the introduction to *Lega Culture* (1973), Biebuyck describes how he gained the trust of members of Bwami. Even with their trust, however, Muyololo suggests that the Lega presented Biebuyck with a sanitized version of Bwami (1974, 35).

During the times of Tarab and Belgian control, Bwami members lost vast numbers of artworks. Some had been confiscated and destroyed. Many had been lost, and yet others had been sold and continue to appear on the art market. Evidence seems to indicate that the decline began under Tarab influence. In 1909, before the Belgians began their persecution of Bwami, Delhaise commented on the scarcity of Lega artists. Corbisier proclaimed that the last Lega sculptor died in 1930 (1968, 20).

If Bwami still existed and if there was a growing need for masks and figures for new members and to replace those lost to the outside world, why did artists not proliferate? The answer may be twofold: first, being an artist among the Lega was not a particularly prestigious or profitable vocation; second, the Tarab or Belgians knew that the artworks were used in Bwami and perhaps targeted the artists. With little profit or prestige to gain, artists perhaps chose to forgo Bwami commissions.

Rather than creating new artworks, members of Bwami began to compensate for their losses by embracing a number of different strategies. Artists created cruder artworks that would not attract attention and whose styles had been corrupted by outside influences. They adopted new art forms, such as figures carved by neighboring groups, which would not draw the attention of colonial officials. Finally, Western-made objects, such as light bulbs and lead soldiers, and foreign materials (processed rubber, porcelain, and such) began to appear. These objects might be given the names of known initiation objects (de Kun 1966, 78). In one interesting case, a Madonna figure was adopted and new sayings were created to tie it to Bwami contexts: "We come to pray to Jesus son of God" (Muyololo 1974, 61). New materials were often given double meanings. Biebuyck records a light bulb being used with the saying "He who seduces the wife of a great-one, eats an egg with rotten odor" (1976, 345). On the surface, like many other sayings, this seems to warn against adultery with high-level female Bwami members. Biebuyck explains, however, that it addresses the disruption caused by Belgian courts

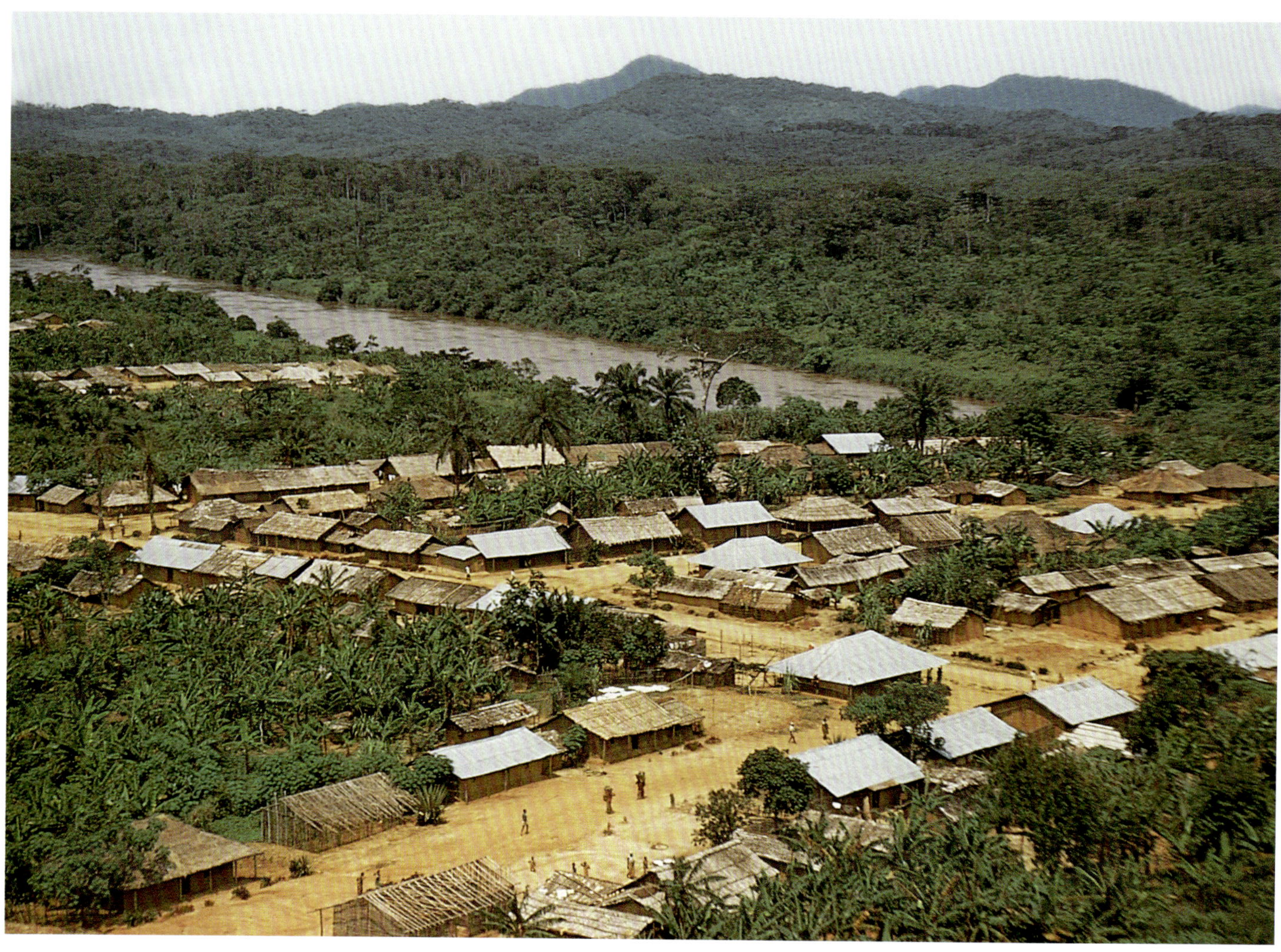

10.1 Aerial view of Shabunda. Photograph by Eliot Elisofon, 1967. Eliot Elisofon Photographic Archives, National Museum of African Art, Smithsonian Institution, no. T 3 LGA 1.2 EE 67.

when they allowed a member of Kindi and his high-level wife to divorce (1976, 345).

Neither Bwami nor the Lega clan system has weathered the nineteenth and twentieth centuries well, but they have survived and the struggle continues. With the independence of the Congo in 1960, Bwami was made legal again. During the early 1960s, with the political turmoil that followed independence, Bwami members, like the rest of the Lega community, found themselves impoverished, and they used their status—and implied threats against an uninformed Lega public—to obtain food (Muyololo 1974, 13). These actions reinforced negative stereotypes surrounding Bwami.

As I write, the Lega are again suffering because of external politics. Over two million refugees from the Hutu and Tutsi massacres flooded into the Kivu area in 1994 and exhausted the land. Then this same region became the stronghold of a rebel force that overthrew President Mobutu's government in 1997 and put Laurent Kabila in power. Soon afterward, a new rebel force, which had as its goal the overthrow of Kabila, took control of Kivu.

In checking the news daily, I have discovered BBC correspondent Andrew Harding's firsthand reports from the Lega town of Shabunda (fig. 10.1). In a broadcast of Wednesday, September 13, 2000, he reported that over ten thousand people were trapped in the small town, unable to go to their fields or hunt for fear of being kidnapped or killed by the Mai Mai, a Congolese militia group. This is typical of the current events in the Lega area even under the new president, Joseph Kabila (Laurent Kabila's son who inherited the presidency after his father's assassination). Until the political situation is resolved and the outside world can safely make contact with the Lega, the West will not know the ways in which Bwami is surviving.

Corbisier concluded his monograph concerning the Lega with the statement "perhaps, one day, we will see a resurrection of Lega artistic sense" (1968, 9). Artists might never again work in the "classic" style of figures and masks, but I choose to believe that the Lega artistic sense has never died. Because of the persecution of Bwami, the Society has gone into hiding and found new forms of expression. While we have only glimpses of what Lega artists are now creating, my hope is that a new Lega art will soon come to light and flourish.

Appendix

As African art moves into the collections of museums and private individuals, much information about its place of origin and the hands it has passed through is lost. Because Lega artworks do not always offer clues as to the region where they were created, the lack of collection information makes a more detailed knowledge of the individual pieces almost impossible. In the process of assembling his collection, Jay Last attempted to gather as much information as he could about individual pieces. Despite Jay's diligence, there was often precious little information that could be retrieved. What does exist gives some feel for the sources and histories of the pieces. Where available, this appendix presents provenance, and exhibition and publication histories.

FIGURE A (PREFACE)—HUMAN FIGURE
EXHIBITION: *African Arts,* Robert H. Lowie Museum of Anthropology, University of California, Berkeley, 1967.
BIBLIOGRAPHY: Robert H. Lowie Museum of Anthropology, *African Arts* (Berkeley: Robert H. Lowie Museum of Anthropology), pl. 183.

FIGURE B (PREFACE)—BUST WITH MULTIPLE HEADS
PROVENANCE: Charles Ratton.
BIBLIOGRAPHY: Eliot Elisofon and William Fagg, *The Sculpture of Africa* (London: Thames and Hudson, 1958).

FIGURE C (PREFACE)—MULTIHEADED HUMAN FIGURE
EXHIBITION: *African Arts,* Robert H. Lowie Museum of Anthropology, University of California, Berkeley, 1967.

FIGURE E (PREFACE)—MASK
EXHIBITION: *African Negro Art,* Museum of Modern Art, New York 1935.
BIBLIOGRAPHY: James Johnson Sweeney, ed, *African Negro Art* (New York: Museum of Modern Art, 1935). Photographed by Walker Evans.

FIGURE I (PREFACE)—MASK (*IDIMU*)
PROVENANCE: Field collected by Nicolas de Kun, 1950s.

FIGURE Q (PREFACE)—HUMAN FIGURE (*NKUMBA* OR *MULIMA*)
PROVENANCE: Field collected by Nicolas de Kun, 1950s.
EXHIBITION: *African Arts,* Robert H. Lowie Museum of Anthropology, University of California, Berkeley, 1967.
BIBLIOGRAPHY: Robert H. Lowie Museum of Anthropology, *African Arts* (Berkeley: Robert H. Lowie Museum of Anthropology).

FIGURE 2.2—HAT (*SAWAMAZEMBE*)
EXHIBITION: *Crowning Achievements: African Arts of Dressing the Head,* Fowler Museum of Cultural History, University of California, Los Angeles, 1995.
BIBLIOGRAPHY: Mary Jo Arnoldi and Christine Mullen Kreamer, eds., *Crowning Achievements: African Arts of Dressing the Head* (Los Angeles: Fowler Museum of Cultural History, University of California, Los Angeles, 1995), fig. 8.12.

FIGURE 3.7—HUMAN FIGURE (*KALIMBANGOMA*)
PROVENANCE: Jean Willy Mestach.

FIGURE 5.9—HAT
EXHIBITION: *Crowning Achievements: African Arts of Dressing the Head,* Fowler Museum of Cultural History, University of California, Los Angeles, 1995.
BIBLIOGRAPHY: Mary Jo Arnoldi and Christine Mullen Kreamer, eds., *Crowning Achievements: African Arts of Dressing the Head* (Los Angeles: Fowler Museum of Cultural History, University of California, Los Angeles, 1995), fig. 8.5.

FIGURE 5.13—HAT (*LUKUNIA*)
EXHIBITION: *Crowning Achievements: African Arts of Dressing the Head,* Fowler Museum of Cultural History, University of California, Los Angeles, 1995.
BIBLIOGRAPHY: Mary Jo Arnoldi and Christine Mullen Kreamer, eds., *Crowning Achievements: African Arts of Dressing the Head* (Los Angeles: Fowler Museum of Cultural History, University of California, Los Angeles, 1995), fig. 8.4.

FIGURE 5.14—HAT (*LUKUNIA*)
EXHIBITION: *Crowning Achievements: African Arts of Dressing the Head,* Fowler Museum of Cultural History, University of California, Los Angeles, 1995.
BIBLIOGRAPHY: Mary Jo Arnoldi and Christine Mullen Kreamer, eds., *Crowning Achievements: African Arts of Dressing the Head* (Los Angeles: Fowler Museum of Cultural History, University of California, Los Angeles, 1995), fig. 8.3.

FIGURE 5.18—HAT (*MUZOMBOLO*)
EXHIBITION: *Crowning Achievements: African Arts of Dressing the Head,* Fowler Museum of Cultural History, University of California, Los Angeles, 1995.
BIBLIOGRAPHY: Mary Jo Arnoldi and Christine Mullen Kreamer, eds., *Crowning Achievements: African Arts of Dressing the Head* (Los Angeles: Fowler Museum of Cultural History, University of California, Los Angeles, 1995), fig. 8.14.

FIGURE 5.27—HAT
EXHIBITION: *Crowning Achievements: African Arts of Dressing the Head,* Fowler Museum of Cultural History, University of California, Los Angeles, 1995.
BIBLIOGRAPHY: Mary Jo Arnoldi and Christine Mullen Kreamer, eds., *Crowning Achievements: African Arts of Dressing the Head* (Los Angeles: Fowler Museum of Cultural History, University of California, Los Angeles, 1995), fig. 8.21.

FIGURE 6.18—SPOON
PROVENANCE: Jos Walsharts, Antwerp.

FIGURE 6.19 — SPOON
PROVENANCE: Jos Walsharts, Antwerp.
EXHIBITION: *Elephant: The Animal and Its Ivory in African Culture,* Fowler Museum of Cultural History, University of California, Los Angeles, 1992.
BIBLIOGRAPHY: Doran Ross, ed., *Elephant: The Animal and Its Ivory in African Culture* (Los Angeles: Fowler Museum of Cultural History, University of California, Los Angeles, 1995), fig. 14-6, second from left.

FIGURE 8.34 — HUMAN FIGURE
PROVENANCE: Jef Vander Straete, Lasne, Belgium.

FIGURE 8.45 — HUMAN FIGURE
PROVENANCE: New York Museum of Primitive Art, accession number 63.102, written on left foot.
EXHIBITION: *Elephant: The Animal and Its Ivory in African Culture,* Fowler Museum of Cultural History, University of California, Los Angeles, 1992.
BIBLIOGRAPHY: Doran Ross, ed., *Elephant: The Animal and Its Ivory in African Culture* (Los Angeles: Fowler Museum of Cultural History, University of California, Los Angeles, 1995), fig. 14-4, right.

FIGURE 8.47 — HUMAN FIGURE
PROVENANCE: Field collected by Nicholas de Kun, 1950s.

FIGURE 8.48 — HUMAN FIGURE
PROVENANCE: New York Museum of Primitive Art, accession number 57.250, written on left foot.

FIGURE 8.60 — HUMAN FIGURE
PROVENANCE: Field collected by Nicholas de Kun, 1950s.

FIGURE 8.63 — HUMAN FIGURE
PROVENANCE: Professor van Hove, served in the Belgian Congo in the 1920s, remained in his collection until his death in mid-1970s.

FIGURE 8.71 — HUMAN BUST WITH MULTIPLE HEADS
PROVENANCE: Field collected by Nicolas De Kun, possibly in Penelusenge.
EXHIBITION: *African Arts,* Robert H. Lowie Museum of Anthropology, University of California, Berkeley, 1967.
BIBLIOGRAPHY: Robert H. Lowie Museum of Anthropology, *African Arts* (Berkeley: Robert H. Lowie Museum of Anthropology), pl. 182.

FIGURE 8.82 — FIGURE (*WAYINDA*)
PROVENANCE: Field collected by Nicolas de Kun in the village of Kangumu, Pangi, 1950s; acquired by Jay Last from de Kun, 1971

FIGURE 8.93 — HUMAN FIGURE
PROVENANCE: Sacré, Brussels.

FIGURE 8.105 — HUMAN FIGURE
PROVENANCE: Sacré, Brussels.

FIGURE 8.108 — HUMAN FIGURE
PROVENANCE: Field collected by Nicolas de Kun, 1950s.

FIGURE 9.49 — MASK (*LUKWAKONGO* OR *IDIMU*)
PROVENANCE: Field collected by Nicholas de Kun, 1950s.

FIGURE 9.52 — MASK (*IDIMU*)
PROVENANCE: Field collected by Nicolas de Kun, 1950s.

Endnotes

INTRODUCTION

1. The emphasis in the field of African art on the arts of chiefdoms and kingdoms recalls the pressure put on colonial officials by their European governments to find or manufacture centralized political structures. Management of any group was easier if the colonial government could control its paramount leader. This situation resulted in many noncentralized societies being forced to adopt foreign political structures. As Arnold Rubin has pointed out (1981, 9), working with the arts of a kingdom often simplified a scholar's research: "Research in centralized societies is usually easier, insofar as essential decisions about access and co-operation are usually made by a single person or a small number of people, and questions about particular subjects can be referred to authorities—musicians or brasscasters, tax-collectors or priests, including, in non-literate societies, the professional rememberers who are the custodians of the mandates of privilege and prerogative." Rubin also cites other aspects of the arts of centralized societies that have attracted American and European researchers: the urban nature of many, the supposed antiquity of their art forms, and the use of prestige materials and relatively complex technologies. Although Rubin meant his laundry list to remind us that centralized societies are not necessarily the best and that these networks "increase[ed] alienation of individuals from each other and from the community to which they belong" (1981, 8), Suzanne Blier (1998) gives a similar laundry list as a reason to study royal arts. Whether these characteristics are seen as positive or negative, arts of centralized peoples are in many ways comparable to the political arts of Western societies, which have advanced centralization—even in democratic settings—to perhaps the highest levels possible. These similarities may make such art forms more comfortable and attractive to Western scholars. By contrast, the arts of noncentralized peoples become more difficult to decipher from aesthetic and contextual bases.

2. *Warega* is the Swahilized form of *Balega* or *Lega,* the name we consider correct today. The Arabs who were present in the area during the nineteenth century used the form *Warega,* and that name has continued in popular use in many areas even to the present.

3. Biebuyck gives a methodological account of his fieldwork as well as presenting the challenges attendant on researching a "secret" society in the introduction to his *Lega Culture* (1973, xv–xxii).

4. The objective is to give sufficient background on Bwami for the reader to appreciate the Society, which one scholar has referred to as a socio-artistic organization that produces, uses, and safeguards the artwork (Muyololo 1974, 53). I refer those who would like more detailed information on Bwami to the writings of Daniel Biebuyck, the leading authority on the Society. He provides in-depth descriptions and analyses of Bwami in *Lega Culture* (1973), *The Arts of Zaire: Volume II, Eastern Zaire* (1986), and numerous articles that are listed in the References Cited section of this volume.

CHAPTER 1

1. Starting with the establishment of the Congo Free State in 1884–1885, the country has undergone various name changes. After its annexation to Belgium in 1908, it became the Belgian Congo. The name changed again to the Republic of Congo after it gained independence in 1960; this was swiftly followed by the Democratic Republic of the Congo. Since Kongo is the name of a single ethnic group who live at the mouth of the Congo River, President Mobutu Sese Seko's government changed the name to the Republic of Zaire in 1971, striving for a name that could represent the entire nation. The government of President Laurent Kabila, in an attempt to rid the country of anything associated with Mobutu, again changed the name to the Democratic Republic of the Congo in 1997.

2. With the changes in government during the last five years, complicated by the rebel forces that currently hold the area, the exact number and the names of the provinces at the present time are unclear. The map in figure 1.2 represents my best understanding of the current official administrative divisions.

3. If a divorce occurs, the dowry must be returned to the woman's family, a definite incentive for long marriages (Biebuyck 1973, 42–44; Liétard 1924).

CHAPTER 2

1. *Mwami* is the singular form of *bwami.* When a man is a member of Bwami, he takes the title of *mwami.* In areas where Bwami is more centralized, *mwami* is the title reserved for the king.

2. In some areas there is a beginning level for women called Kyogo that is analogous to the men's Kongabulumbu level (Biebuyck 1994, 62).

3. For more on the intricacies of Bwami grades, see Delhaise 1909, 337; de Kun 1966, 74; Corbisier 1968, 11; Biebuyck 1973, 72; 1986, 12–13; Mulyumba wa Mamba 1978, 23–25.

4. See the section on masks (p. 180) for an example of this requirement.

5. Muyololo also adds that the incorporation of women into Bwami has driven away the best artists and intellects (1974, 58). He does not elaborate or offer any supporting information to confirm this cryptic and rather alarming statement.

6. Translation mine.

CHAPTER 3

1. S. H. Butcher, *Aristotle's Theory of Poetry and Fine Art with a Critical Text and Translation of the Poetics* (London: Macmillan and Co., Ltd., 1927), ch. 22, 1459a5–8.

2. There are many different theoretical approaches or frameworks that can be marshaled to analyze the performances in Bwami initiations. In referring to metaphor, I have chosen a literary approach. My use of metaphor owes much to I. A. Richards (1965). Richards argues that a word's meaning is not fixed but is defined by use. Within such a system, all language has a built-in ambiguity that can be employed to extend meaning.

Total theater is another framework that can be used to describe the Lega performances. In total theater, all arts work together to produce a *gesamtkunstwerk,* or total artwork (Kirby 1969, xiii). The most important dynamic of total theater is the interaction between the parts. One interesting outcome of the search for total theater was the name "Surrealism." Guillaume Apollinaire, in a program note for the ballet *Parade*—a production that combined a script by Jean Cocteau, music by Erik Satie, choreography by Léonide Massine, and designs by Pablo Picasso—wrote "there has resulted in *Parade* a kind of sur-réalism" (as quoted by Kirby 1969, xxiv). Perhaps there is a similarity between Surrealism, where layers of reality are placed on a canvas, stage, and/or performance, and the Bwami performance.

3. *As You Like It,* Act II, Scene 7.

4. Biebuyck also refers to this as metaphor (1982, 65).

5. Burk records seeing houses in the bush where an older man was quizzing a group of boys about an object strung between two posts (1956).

6. A complete analysis of the metaphorical complex of meaning found in Bwami ceremonies may not be recoverable in the twenty-first century. Because of the political unrest in the Congo, it is impossible to know the current status of Bwami and its viability in the future. Past scholars have carefully studied the objects and the sayings. On September 12, 1906, the Belgian commandant Delhaise witnessed a high-level initiation ceremony with fourteen "dances" and gave brief descriptions that sometimes include mention of the involved objects and sayings, as well as the dances (1909, 231–39). His account, however, reflects his limited ability to decipher the wisdom contained in the performances. Because he did not speak the language or have an intimate familiarity with the elements of Lega life that underlie the performative elements, he was forced to depend on the translations and explanations of others. Only Daniel Biebuyck gives us multiple accounts that combine all three layers of meaning, but he focuses on the sayings and objects, giving only simple descriptions of the dramatic action and no description of the music.

7. Leuzinger, citing no sources, discusses a Lega figure with both arms raised and states: "The imploring gesture with arms raised up above a slender body, eloquently expresses an appeal for and to the celestial power" (1967, 192). This is either a source of this misunderstanding or shows what a common mistake it can be when one culture places its own cultural explanation on the art of another.

8. Muyololo suggests that the punishment can require the death of up to ten family members (1974, 56). This level of punishment may be in fact a threat told to non-Bwami members that is rarely, if ever, carried out.

9. Among the Sile-Lega most sculpture is held by members of Ngandu, the highest level of Bwami in that area (Mulyumba wa Mamba 1977, 328).

CHAPTER 4

1. *Wa,* in most Bantu languages, means *of,* that is, originating from something or somewhere. Examples of use might be a person who is from or "of" a town, or a child who is "of" a family. In this context, the artist does not just use an adze, he is "of" the adze.

2. See Vogel 1986, xi-xvii; Hallen 1998, 1: 37–42.

CHAPTER 5

1. Biebuyck 1986, 31. The bracketed interpolations are Biebuyck's.

2. Currently due to persecution of Bwami members, many initiates wear the skullcap and other special hats only during Bwami initiations and special ceremonies (Biebuyck, personal communication, 1994).

CHAPTER 6

1. This Discussion of stools summarizes Biebuyck's "Symbolism of a Lega Stool" (1977).

CHAPTER 7

1. See Cameron 1992 for a summary of the relationship of the elephant and Kindi.

2. See Biebuyck 1973, pl. 25, for a photograph of animal figures grouped in use.

CHAPTER 8

1. He gifted a group of these figures to the Musée Royal de l'Afrique Centrale, Tervuren, Belgium.

2. Whether the artist is given more direction for masks and other objects that display a greater uniformity of style is unclear.

3. It is unclear in the literature whether *maginga* and *kalimbangoma* are mutually exclusive categories or perhaps overlapping. De Kun seems to say that all anthropomorphic figures in ivory are *maginga* (1966, 87). Biebuyck, in an earlier work, states that "any stylized human figurine may be referred to as *iginga*" (1973, 161). In his later writings, the definition seems to have become more restricted.

4. Jay Last first drew my attention to these scratches. Since then I have confirmed the scratches on all of the figures of this type that I have seen.

CHAPTER 9

1. See Nunley and McCarty 1999, 15: "In using this term we are referring to an object placed over the face or covering the entire head so that the face is more or less concealed." See also Kasfir 1988, 5: "A mask... [is] something which nonetheless both covers and transforms."

2. De Kun calls many Lega masks "hand-masks" or "pseudo-masks" (1966, 84).

3. For discussions of how Western definitions of masks do not fit many African forms of masquerading, see Kubik 1993 and Cameron 1995.

4. This discussion is based on Mulyumba 1968.

5. Muyololo (1974, 46) claims that the true purpose of *lukwakongo* is to warn Bwami members of the horrible death that will befall them if they disclose Bwami's secrets to an outsider. He says that the ceremony that reveals this meaning, held late at night in the presence of powerful women responsible for carrying out punishments through sorcery, was hidden from Biebuyck because he would have been displeased by the violent implications.

CHAPTER 10

1. Biebuyck 1976, 343

2. This sketch of the Tarab presence is based on Felix 1989, 22–27.

References Cited

Altman, Ralph C.

1963 *Balega and Other Tribal Arts from the Congo.* Los Angeles: Dickson Art Center, University of California.

Biebuyck, Daniel P.

1953a "La monnaie musanga des Balega." *Zaïre* 7, no. 7: 675–86.

1953b "Répartition de droits du pangolin chez les Balega." *Zaïre* 7, no. 8: 899–934.

1953c "Some Remarks on Segy's 'Warega Ivories.'" *Zaïre* 7, no. 10: 1076–82.

1954 "The Function of a Lega mask." *Archives internationales d'ethnographie* 47: 108–20.

1966 "On the Concept of Tribe." *Civilisations* 16, no. 4: 500–15.

1967 "Effects on Lega Art of the Outlawing of the Bwami Association." *Journal of the New African Literature and the Arts* 1, no. 3: 87–94.

1969 "Introduction." In *Tradition and Creativity in Tribal Art*, 1–23. Berkeley: The University of California Press.

1973 *Lega Culture: Art, Initiation, and Moral Philosophy among a Central African People.* Berkeley: University of California Press.

1976 "The Decline of Lega Sculptural Art." In *Ethnic and Tourist Arts: Cultural Expressions from the Fourth World*, edited by Nelson H. Graburn, 334–49. Berkeley: University of California Press.

1977a "Schemata in Lega Art." In *Form in Indigenous Art: Schematisation in the Art of Aboriginal Australia and Prehistoric Europe*, edited by Pete Ucko, 59–65. Canberra: Australian Institute of Aboriginal Studies.

1977b *Symbolism of the Lega Stool.* Philadelphia: ISHI Publications.

1979 "The Frog and Other Animals in Lega Art and Initiation." *Africa-Tervuren* 25, no. 3: 76–84.

1981 "Plurifrontal Figurines in Lega Art in Zaire." In *Shape of the Past: Studies in Honor of Franklin D. Murphy*, edited by Giorgio Buccellati and Charles Speroni, 115–27. Los Angeles: Institute of Archaeology and Office of the Chancellor, University of California.

1982 "Lega Dress as Cultural Artifact." *African Arts* 15, no. 3: 59–65, 92.

1983 "Lega Spoons." In *Liber Memorialis Prof. Dr. P. J. Vandenhoute, 1913–1978*, 51–66. Ghent, Belgium: Seminarie voor Etnische Kunst, Sint-Hubertusstraat.

1986 *Eastern Zaire.* Vol. 2 of *The Arts of Zaire.* Berkeley: University of California Press.

1993 *Face of the Spirits: Masks from the Zaire Basin.* Antwerp: Snoeck-Ducaju & Zoon.

1994 *La sculpture des Lega.* Paris: Galerie Hélène & Philippe Leloup.

Biebuyck, Daniel P., and Nelly Van den Abbeele.

1984 *The Power of Headdresses: A Cross-Cultural Study of Forms and Functions.* Brussels: Tendi S. A.

Bishikwabo, Chubaka

1979 "Notes sur l'origine de l'institution du 'bwami' et fondements du pouvoir politique au Kivu Oriental." *Les Cahiers du* CEDAF, series 1, no. 8.

Blier, Suzanne Preston

1998 *Royal Arts of Africa: The Majesty of Form.* London: Calmann and King Ltd.

Burk, Ellen I.

1956 "The Lega School of Circumcision." *Zaïre* 10, no. 4: 375–77.

Burk, Ellen I., David Byakilema, Paul Ardoise, Paul Kisubi, and André Mbmbalwa

1956 Proverbes Lega." *Zaïre* 10, no. 7: 711–15.

Butcher, S. H.

1895 *Aristotle's Theory of Poetry and Fine Art with a Critical Text and a Translation of the Poetics.* London: Macmillan and Co.

Cameron, Elisabeth L.

1988 "Sala Mpasu Masks." *African Arts* 22, no. 1: 34–43.

1991 *Reclusive Rebels: An Approach to the Sala Mpasu and Their Neighbors.* San Diego: San Diego Mesa College.

1992 "The Stampeding of Elephants: Elephant Imprints on Lega Thought." In *Elephant: The Animal and Its Ivory in African Culture*, edited by Doran H. Ross, 295–308. Los Angeles: Fowler Museum of Cultural History, University of California, Los Angeles.

1995 "Lega Hats: Hierarchy and Status." In *Crowning Achievements: African Arts of Dressing the Head*, edited by Mary Jo Arnoldi and Christine Mullen Kreamer, 147–58. Los Angeles: Fowler Museum of Cultural History, University of California, Los Angeles.

Cameron, Verney Lovett

1971 *Across Africa.* 2d ed. 2 vols. New York; London: Johnson Reprint Corporation.

Corbisier, François

1968 *La sculpture du Moami: Lega et Bembe.* Unpublished manuscript.

Cordella, Ernesto

1906 "Recognizione nel Bacino dell'Elila (Stato indipendente del Congo)." *Bulletino della società geographica italiana* 7: 864–78, 963–78.

Cornet, Joseph

1971 *Art of Africa: Treasures from the Congo.* Translated by Barbara Thompson. London: Phaidon.

1975 *Art from Zaire: 100 Masterworks from the National Collection.* New York: African-American Institute.

Coyne, Richard

1995 *Designing Information Technology in the Postmodern Age: From Method to Metaphor.* Cambridge, Mass.: MIT Press.

Defour, Georges

n.d. *La corde de la sagesse Lega.* Bukavu, Zaire: Editions Bandari.

De Kun, Nicolas

1966 "L'art Lega." *Africa-Tervuren* 12: 69–99.

Delhaise, Le Commandant

1909 *Les Warega.* Brussels: Albert de Wit.

De Man, Paul

1996 *Aesthetic Ideology.* Edited and with an introduction by Andrzej Warminski. Minneapolis: University of Minnesota Press.

Engels, J.

1939 "Enquête sur le droit coutumier des Benia Beia, territoire Kihembwe." Pangi: Documents A.I.M.O.

Fagg, William

1965 *Tribes and Forms in African Art.* New York: Tudor Publishing Co.

Felix, Marc L.

1989 *Maniema: An Essay on the Distribution of the Symbols and Myths as Depicted in the Masks of Greater Maniema.* Munich: Fred Jahn.

Hallen, Barry

1998 "African Aesthetics." In *Encyclopedia of Aesthetics,* edited by Michael Kelly, vol. 4, 37–42. New York: Oxford University Press.

Hawkes, Terence

1972 *Metaphor.* London: Methuen.

Kasfir, Sidney

1988 *West African Masks and Cultural Systems.* Tervuren: Musée Royal de l'Afrique Centrale.

Kirby, E. T.

1969 "Introduction." In *Total Theatre: A Critical Anthology,* edited by E. T. Kirby. New York: E. P. Dutton and Co., Inc.

Kjersmeier, Carl

1967 *Centres de style de la sculpture nègre africaine.* 2d ed. 4 vols. New York: Hacker Art Books.

Kubik, Gerhard

1993 *Makisi, Nyau, Mapiko: Maskentraditionen im Bantu-sprachigen Afrika.* Munich: Trickster Verlag.

Lenaers, Constantin

1946 "Chez les Warega." *Grands lacs,* nos. 82–84: 65–69.

Leuzinger, Elsy

1967 *Africa: The Art of the Negro Peoples.* 2d ed. New York: Crown Publishers, Inc.

Liétard, L.

1924 "Les Waregas." *Bulletin de la société royale belge de géographie* 3: 133–45.

Moeller, A.

1936 *Les grandes lignes des migrations des Bantu de la Province Orientale du Congo Belge.* Brussels: Institut royal colonial belge.

Mulyumba, B. [Mulyumba wa Mamba, Itongwa]

1968 "La croyance religieuse des Lega traditionnels." *Etudes congolaises* 11, no. 3: 1–14; 11, no. 4: 3–19.

Mulyumba wa Mamba, Itongwa

1973 "Les proverbes, un langage didactique dans les sociétés africaines traditionnelles: Le cas des Balega-Bashile." *Les Cahiers du* CEDAF, series 4, no. 8: 2–50.

1977 "La structure sociale des Balega-Basile." Ph.D. diss., Université Libre de Bruxelles.

1978 "Aperçu sur la structure politique des Balega-Basile." *Les cahiers du cedaf,* series 1, no. 1: 2–57.

Nunley, John W., and Cara McCarty

1999 *Masks: Faces of Culture.* New York: Harry N. Abrams, Inc., in association with the Saint Louis Art Museum.

Mutuza, Raymond E.

1972 *Equisse d'une problématique sur l'origine les migrations et l'unité culturelle des lega.*" Ph.D. diss., Université de Paris.

Muyololo, Lutala Amuri

1974 *Problématiques des arts Lega.* Ph. D. diss., Université Nationale du Zaïre.

Olbrechts, Frans M.

1982 *Congolese Sculpture.* 2d ed. Translated by Daniel J. Crowley and Pearl Ramcharan-Crowley. New Haven, Conn.: Human Relations Area Files, Inc.

Paivio, Allan

1971 *Imagery and Verbal Processes.* London: Holt, Rinehart and Winston.

Richards, I. A.

1965 *The Philosophy of Rhetoric.* New York: Oxford University Press.

Rubin, Arnold

1981 "Metropolitan Myopia and the Myth of Antiquity in Nigerian Art Studies." In *Observations and Interpretations: 2000 Years of Nigerian Art,* edited by John Povey and Arnold Rubin, 5–11. Los Angeles: African Studies Center, University of California.

Segy, Ladislas

1952 *African Sculpture Speaks.* New York: Lawrence Hill and Co.

Shakespeare, William

2000 As Yo*u Like It.* Edited by Frances E. Dolan. New York: Penguin Books.

Vansina, Jan

1990 *Paths in the Rainforests: Toward a History of Political Tradition in Equatorial Africa.* Madison: The University of Wisconsin Press.

Vogel, Susan Mullin

1986 *African Aesthetics: The Carlo Monzino Collection.* New York: Center for African Art.

Waller, H., ed.

1874 [1970] *The Last Journals of David Livingstone in Central Africa, from 1865 to His Death: Contained by a Narrative of His Last Moments and Sufferings, Obtained from His Faithful Servants, Chuma and Susi.* London: J. Murray.

Yogolelo, Tambwe ya Kasimba

1975 "Introduction à l'histoire des Lega: Problèmes et méthodes." *Les Cahiers du* CEDAF, series 2, no. 5: 3–27.

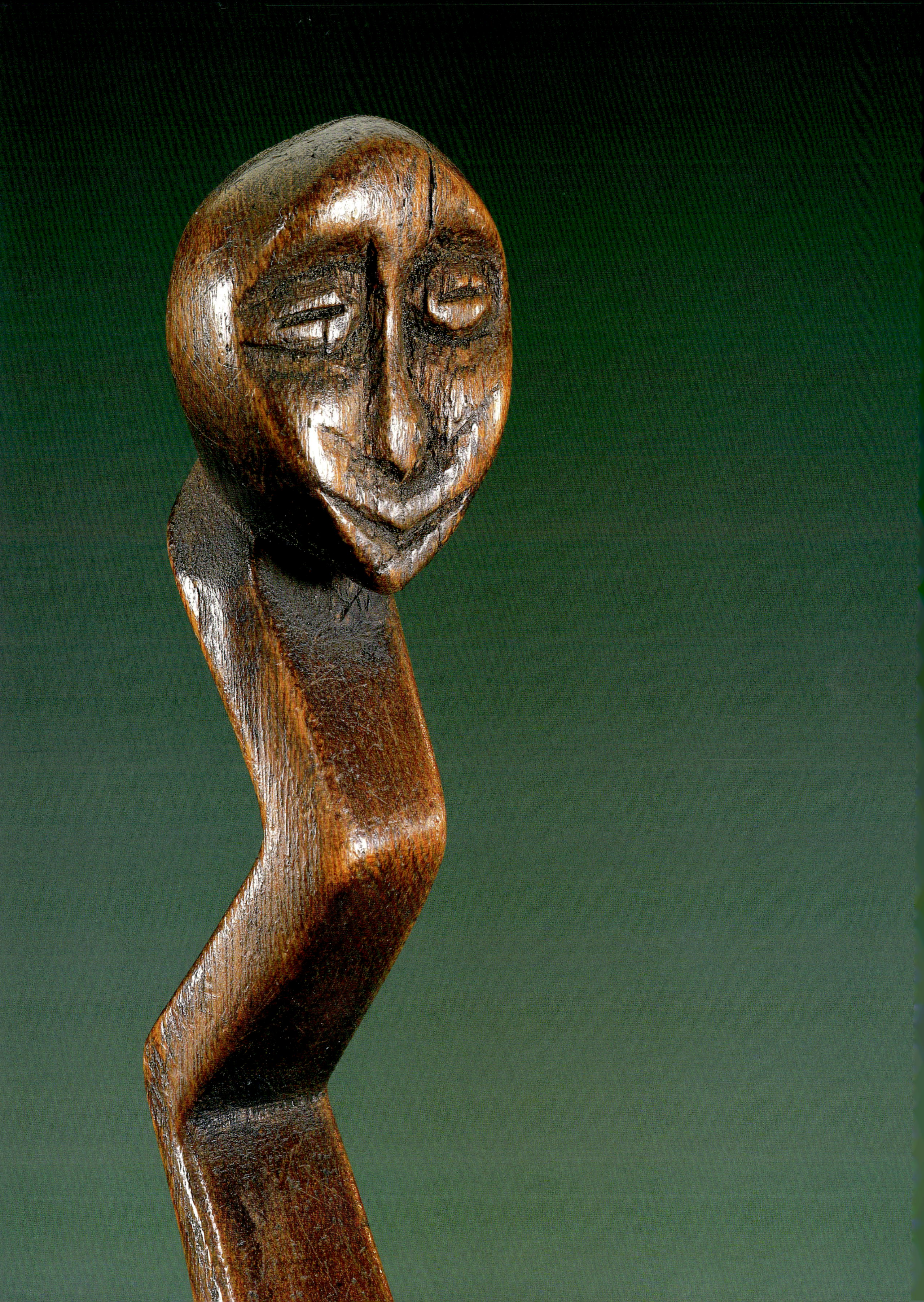

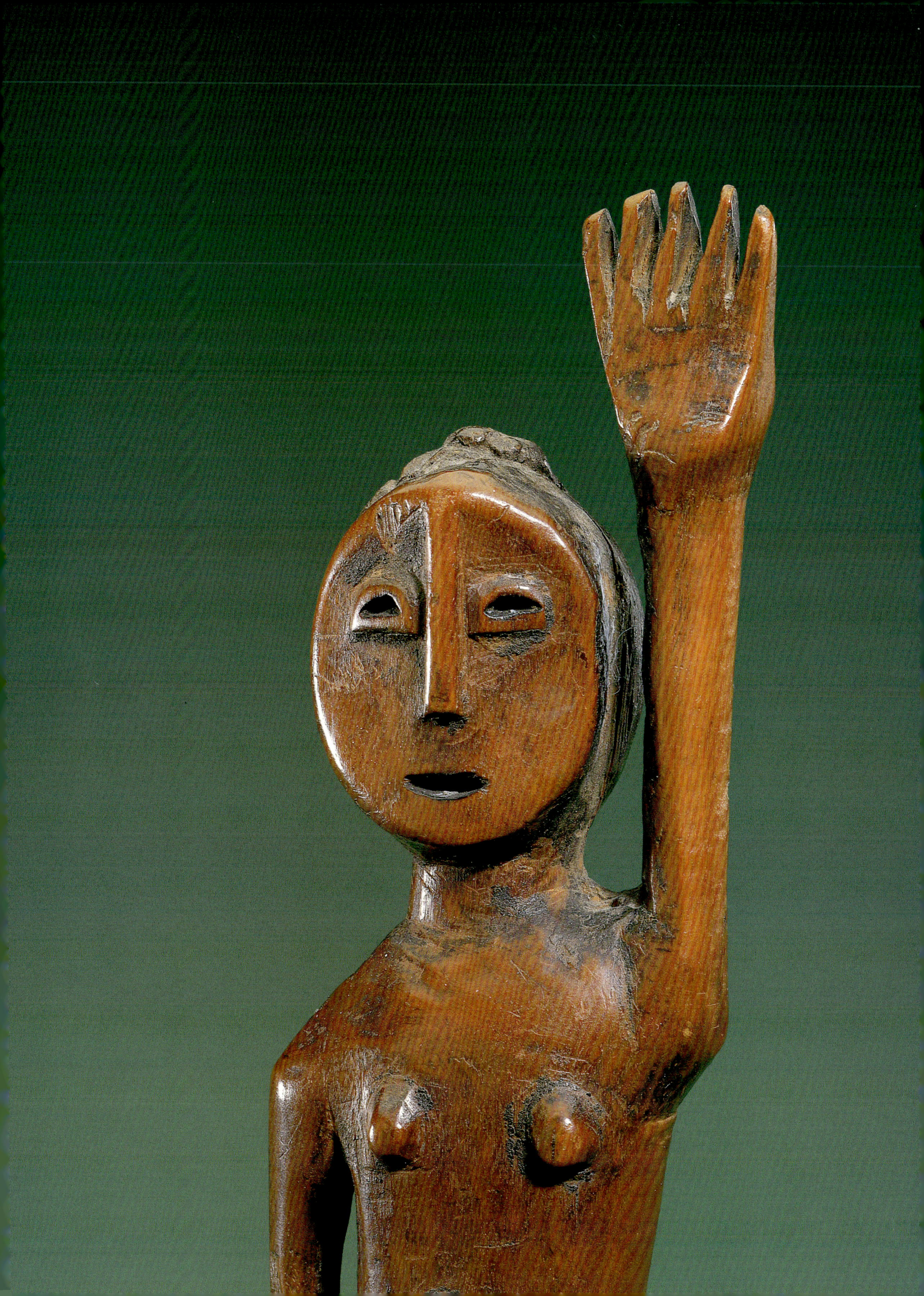

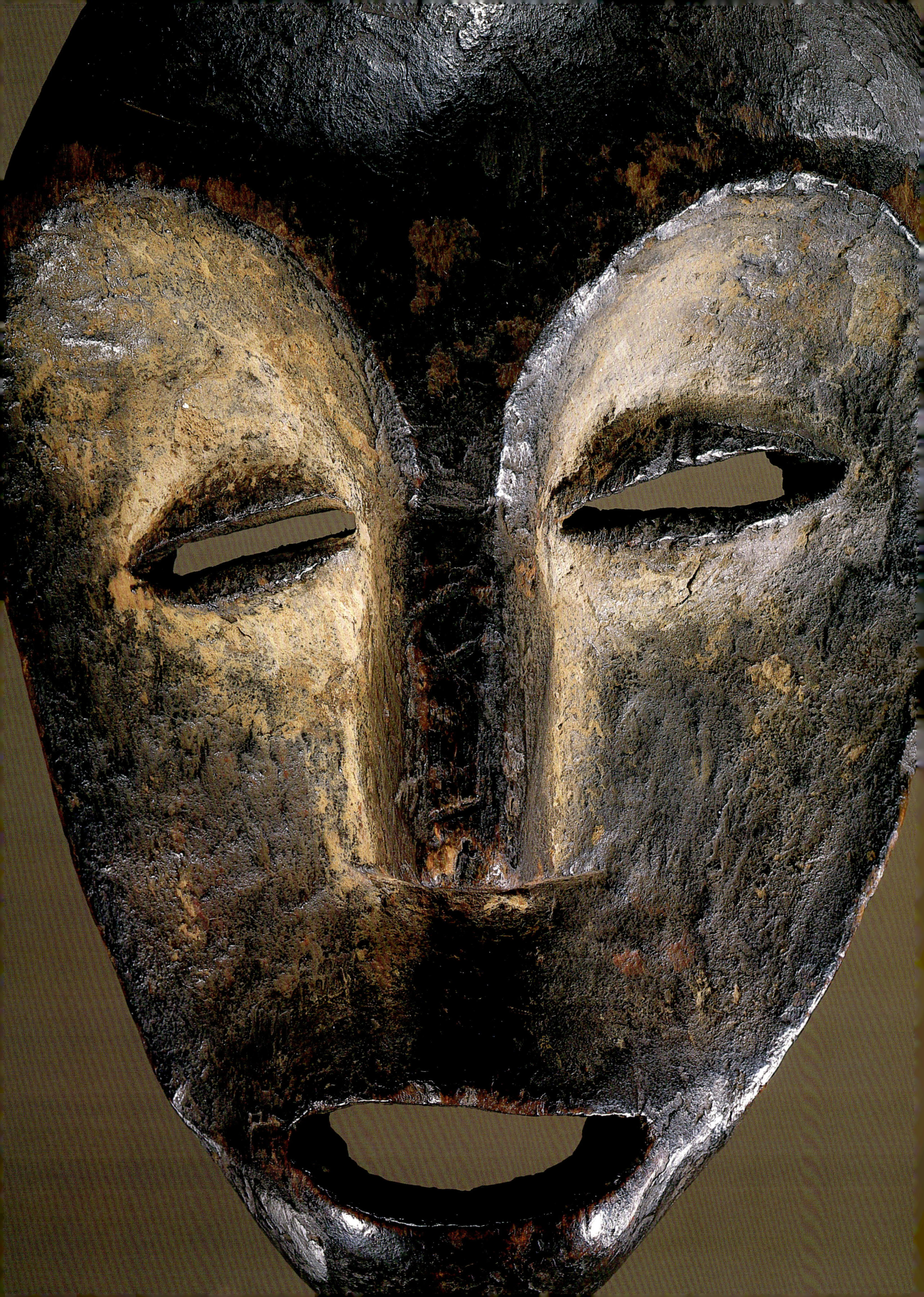

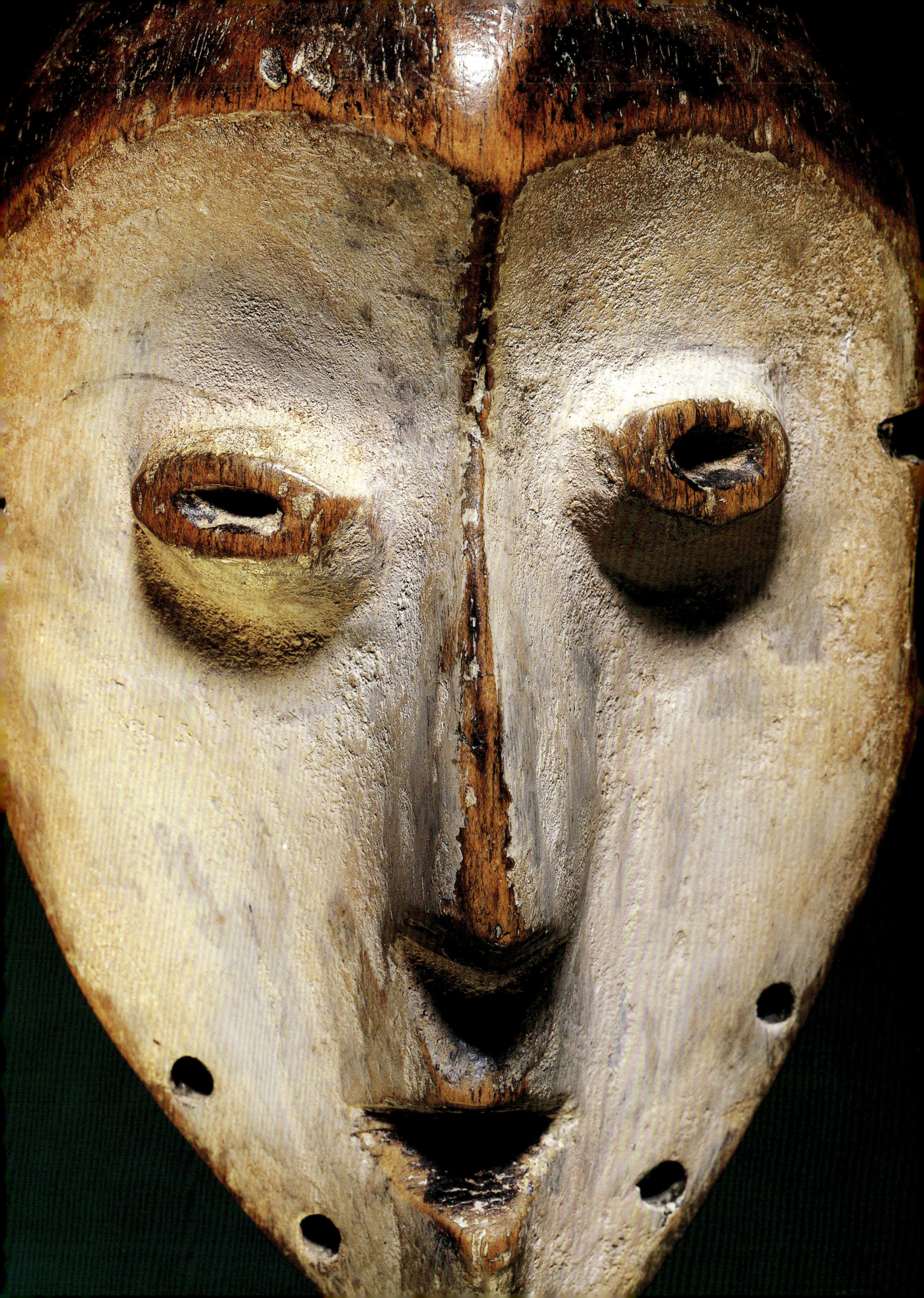

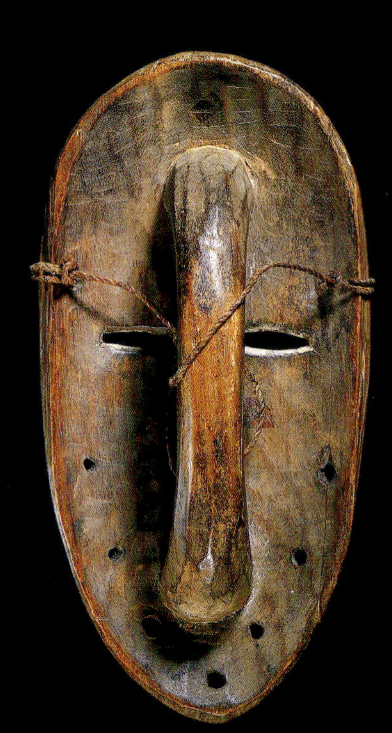